ANÍBAL QUIJANO

ON DECOLONIALITY

A series edited by Walter D. Mignolo and Catherine E. Walsh

On Decoloniality interconnects a diverse array of perspectives from the lived experiences of coloniality and decolonial thought/praxis in different local histories from across the globe. The series is concerned with coloniality's global logic and scope and with the myriad of decolonial responses and engagements that contest coloniality/modernity's totalizing violences, claims, and frame, opening toward an otherwise of being, thinking, sensing, knowing, and living, that is, of reexistences and worlds making. Aimed at a broad audience, from scholars, students, and artists to journalists, activists, and socially engaged intellectuals, On Decoloniality invites a wide range of participants to join one of the fastest-growing debates in the humanities and social sciences that attends to the lived concerns of dignity, life, and the survival of the planet.

FOUNDATIONAL ESSAYS

ANÍBAL QUIJANO

ON THE COLONIALITY OF POWER

Edited by

**WALTER D. MIGNOLO,
RITA SEGATO, AND
CATHERINE E. WALSH**

DUKE UNIVERSITY PRESS   DURHAM AND LONDON   2024

i

Project Editor: Brian Ostrander
Designed by Matthew Tauch
Typeset in Alegreya and Anybody
by Westchester Publishing Services

Library of Congress Cataloging-in-Publication Data
Names: Quijano, Aníbal, author. | Mignolo, Walter, editor. |
Segato, Rita Laura, editor. | Walsh, Catherine E., editor.
Title: Aníbal Quijano : foundational essays on the coloniality of
power / edited by Walter D. Mignolo, Rita Segato and Catherine
E. Walsh.
Other titles: Foundational essays on the coloniality of power |
On decoloniality.
Description: Durham : Duke University Press, 2024. | Series: On
decoloniality | Includes bibliographical references and index.
Identifiers: LCCN 2023037599 (print)
LCCN 2023037600 (ebook)
ISBN 9781478030324 (paperback)
ISBN 9781478026099 (hardcover)
ISBN 9781478059356 (ebook)
Subjects: LCSH: Postcolonialism—Latin America. | Decolonization—
Latin America. | Power (Social sciences)—Latin America. | Race
relations. | Eurocentrism. | Economic development—Social
aspects—Latin America. | Latin America—Social conditions. |
Latin America—Relations. | BISAC: SOCIAL SCIENCE / Ethnic
Studies / Caribbean & Latin American Studies | SOCIAL SCIENCE /
Sociology / Social Theory
Classification: LCC F1410 .Q486 2024 (print) | LCC F1410 (ebook) |
DDC 305.868/72—dc23/eng/20231025
LC record available at https://lccn.loc.gov/2023037599
LC ebook record available at https://lccn.loc.gov/2023037600

Cover art: Aníbal Quijano at a political rally in Villa
El Salvador, December 1979.

CONTENTS

1   Introduction
    Catherine E. Walsh, Walter D. Mignolo, and Rita Segato

32   **1**   Paradoxes of Modernity in Latin America

64   **2**   The Aesthetic of Utopia

73   **3**   Coloniality and Modernity/Rationality

85   **4**   Questioning "Race"

95   **5**   Coloniality of Power and Social Classification

132   **6**   The Return of the Future and Questions
            about Knowledge

146   **7**   Coloniality of Power, Globalization,
            and Democracy

188   **8**   The New Anticapitalist Imaginary

204   **9**   Don Quixote and the Windmills in
            Latin America

229   **10**   The "Indigenous Movement" and Unresolved
             Questions in Latin America

256   **11**   Coloniality of Power, Eurocentrism, and Latin America

303   **12**   Coloniality of Power and De/Coloniality of Power

317   **13**   Thirty Years Later: Another Reunion: Notes for Another Debate

331   **14**   The Crisis of the Colonial/Modern/Eurocentered Horizon of Meaning

347   **15**   Latin America: Toward a New Historical Meaning

361   **16**   Coloniality of Power and Subjectivity in Latin America

379   **17**   "Bien Vivir": Between "Development" and the De/Coloniality of Power

392   **18**   Labor

411   **19**   Notes on the Decoloniality of Power

418   **20**   Modernity, Capital, and Latin America Were Born the Same Day: Interview by Nora Velarde

443   BIBLIOGRAPHY
457   INDEX

INTRODUCTION

Catherine E. Walsh, Walter D. Mignolo, and Rita Segato

Aníbal Quijano: Foundational Essays on the Coloniality of Power is the first collection in English of selected essays of this influential Latin American thinker.[1] Yet, as we argue here, this volume not only introduces English-language readers to Aníbal Quijano's thought but also provides a fundamentally distinct lens for reading today's modern-colonial world-system from its origins in the so-called periphery, that is, from South America and the Global South.

For some time now, Aníbal Quijano's proposition to see history and society from what he has called the "perspective of the coloniality of power" has crossed the North-South geopolitical border in the opposite direction—from South to North—when this border normally regulates the traffic of theoretical models and other "patents" in only one direction. Some of what Quijano has said, specifically his vocabulary and his approach, have traveled. The terms he used can be heard at conferences and in seminars and classrooms. However, as he himself pointed out in frustration, often these terms have circulated like coins of an academic market or even as clichés of an intellectual fashion. By presenting this collection, we encourage the fuller understanding and broader implementation of Quijano's astute analyses and concepts, developed over the course of his long career as an activist, a militant, and a scholar.

I. The World Relevance of Quijano's Work

The fact that Quijano thought in and from Latin America and toward the globe may be motive enough for some to question what this collection of his essays might offer to English-language readers in the Global North and other regions of the world. Here we outline four of Quijano's key interventions crucial for understanding the planetary relevance of his thought and work.

The first intervention is the intimate relation that the coloniality of power constructs among race, global capitalism, and Eurocentered modernity and knowledge. For Quijano, an understanding of today's globally hegemonic matrix of power requires a consideration of its historical foundations and processes. It was in sixteenth-century "America" that this model of power took form and established its global vocation. According to Quijano, in America two historical processes converged. One was the codification of the differences between conquerors and conquered in the idea of "race," a supposedly different biological structure that placed some in a natural situation of inferiority to the others. The conquistadors assumed this idea as the constitutive, founding element of the relations of domination that the conquest imposed. On this basis, the population of America and later the world was classified within the new model of power.[2]

The second historical process was "the constitution of a new structure of controlling labor and its resources and products. This new structure was an articulation of all historically known previous structures of controlling labor including slavery, serfdom, small independent commodity production and reciprocity, which wove them together and placed them upon the basis of capital and the world market."[3] As Quijano further explained, "the new historical identities produced on the foundation of the idea of race in the new global structure of the control of labor were associated with social roles and geohistorical places." Both race and the division of labor remained structurally linked and mutually reinforcing. In this way, a systematic racial division of labor was imposed in which Western Europe became the central site for the control of the world market, the commodification of the labor force, and the establishment of raced assignments and relations of waged and nonwaged labor.

It is in this context, argued Quijano, that modernity took form and took hold. "Starting with America, a new space/time was constituted materially and subjectively: this is what the concept of modernity names," a concept that localized the hegemonic center of the world—and, relatedly, of knowledge—in the north-central zones of Western Europe.[4] Moreover and as Quijano explained, "the intellectual conceptualization of the process of modernity produced a perspective of knowledge and a mode of producing knowledge that gives a very tight account of the character of the global model of power: colonial/modern, capitalist, and Eurocentered." This perspective of knowledge "was made globally hegemonic, colonizing and overcoming other previous or different conceptual formations and their respective concrete knowledges, as much in Europe as in the rest of the world."[5]

For Quijano, the necessities and interest of capital alone are not sufficient for explaining the character and trajectory of this perspective of knowledge. Thus, he gave importance to the intimate ties of race, global capitalism, and Eurocentered modernity, which formed the foundation and reason of the coloniality of power. That these ties first took shape in the Americas is important for not only understanding the foundational relation today of "Latin" America in the globe but also comprehending the significance of colonialism and coloniality in the organization, establishment, and continuance of hegemonic global power. This relation and significance are, without a doubt, crucial today for all who struggle against this power and for building an otherwise of knowledge, existence, and life.

The second major intervention Quijano offers is related to the first and is based on the lived weight of coloniality particularly for Native peoples.

In his analysis of the idea of "race" as the basis of social classification, social domination, colonial relations, and new historical social identities in America, Quijano evidences the invention of the term *indio*, meaning "Indian," as a racialized, homogenous categorization. With the imposition of "Indian" as a new identity, the colonial power aimed to erase millennial cultures, languages, cosmologies, and knowledges as well as forms of collective organization, governance, and existence tied to the land. "Indian" racialized, inferiorized, objectified, negated, grouped, dispossessed, and controlled Native peoples, marking the colonial difference in "Latin" America, in settler-colonial nations such as Canada and the United States, and later in other parts of the world. Christianity, civilization, and modernity were tools to counter a supposedly savage and barbarian precolonial past. While the processes and practices that have maintained the colonial difference vary in different regions of the globe—including with respect to the contexts of invader, settler, and internal colonialisms—the project remains much the same: to sustain the colonial matrix of power and its idea of "inferior races." As Quijano made clear, this power matrix, which originated five centuries ago, has been hegemonic worldwide since the eighteenth century, enabled and further consolidated by the nation-state system, "a *private* system of control over collective authority, as an exclusive attribute of the colonizers, and thus of 'Europeans' or 'whites.'"[6] Indigenous peoples continue to make evident today the problem of nonnational and nondemo-cratic nation-state systems; their demands, as Quijano wrote, are not for more nationalism or increased state power but rather "for an 'other' state, that is, to decolonize the state which is the only way to democratize it."[7]

As Native peoples know all too well, dispossession and genocide, along with capture, cooptation, and individuation (including through inclusion-based policies) continue to characterize the present. "In much of today's former colonial world, especially the Americas and Oceania, the 'whites' and 'Europeans' have managed to keep local control of power in all its basic dimensions. In the Americas, therefore, the issues surrounding the debate on 'the Indigenous' can only be investigated and discussed in relation to and from the perspective of the coloniality of the power matrix that haunts us, because outside of that perspective, such issues make no sense."[8]

Despite being up against coloniality's lived weight, Indigenous peoples have always engaged in collective resistance and affirmative refusal, con-structing and maintaining decolonial/decolonizing otherwises.[9] While co-loniality/decoloniality may not be the referenced terms, with colonization/decolonization the more usual ones, the relation is clear: subversions, resur-gences, and dignification of existence, knowledge, and life.[10] This is some-thing Quijano understood well. It is present in his analysis of the coloniality of power and the intimate relation it constructs between race, global capitalism, Eurocentered modernity, and knowledge. And it is present in his critique of state hegemony, his notes on decoloniality, his reflections on Indigenous movements, and his thinking with the decolonial Indig-enous concept of "life in plentitude," or *bien vivir*. In all of this, Quijano opens paths of rumination that move from Latin America to elsewhere in the world, encouraging interconnections.

A third major intervention Quijano offers is his argument that the struc-ture of coloniality is an open rather than a closed totality.[11] As he maintained, the coloniality of power is not a homogeneous historic whole. If this were the case, change would imply the complete departure from one historic to-tality with all its components so that another derived from it could take its place. Change happens in a heterogeneous and discontinuous way, within a historical field of social relations that is open and moves with time and space and whose matrices of power are also discontinuous and heterogeneous.[12] As such, the coloniality of power does not profess to depict all forms of colonial/modern power and structural domination over existence. Rather, it is an analytical and conceptual framework that invites use, provoking reflections on and expansions of its operation, domains, and configurations.

This, in part, was María Lugones's project in identifying the coloniality of gender. Lugones used and expanded Quijano's lens, recognizing its heteronormative and male-centered perspective and broadening and complicating coloniality's matrix of power. Despite the limitations she saw in Quijano's framework, Lugones also saw its value and possibility. "I mean to begin a conversation and project," said Lugones, "to begin to see in its details the long sense of the process of the colonial/gender system enmeshed in the coloniality of power into the present, to uncover collaboration, and to call each other to reject it in its various guises."[13] In this crucial work—reflected in the growth of decolonial feminisms throughout the globe—Lugones clearly evidences coloniality's open framework and invitational character.

As Quijano argued in his later texts, the matrices of global power today are never static but instead are in constant mutation and configuration, with direct effects on our daily lives, behavior, and social relations.[14] The insurgencies against this power are also in constant flux and creation, as are the decolonial constructions, subversions, and affirmations. By inviting thought, analysis, and reflection on both the colonial matrix of power and decoloniality's lived practice, Quijano calls forth the presence and possibility of radically different worlds.

Hope is the fourth major intervention, that is, Quijano's hopeful and forward-looking vision of the possibility of radically different worlds.

In a 1988 text that critiques neoliberalism in its public (i.e., state) and private capitalist manifestations, both part of the same instrumental rationality according to Quijano, he closes with this line: "The ship of liberating rationality travels today with a new hope."[15] This opinion and conviction, further elaborated in his later texts, was that a liberating and liberation-based rationality was and is in process. The concept and practice of decoloniality embodies this hope.[16]

As two of us have pointed out elsewhere, "decoloniality was born in response to the promises of modernity and the realities of coloniality, in the sense that Quijano introduced it. The conceptualizations and actionings of decoloniality are therefore multiple, contextual, and relational; they are not only the purview of people who have lived the colonial difference but, more broadly, of all of us who struggle from within modernity/coloniality's borders and cracks, to build a radically distinct world."[17]

While the historical relation of coloniality/decoloniality is certainly key in many of Quijano's texts, his frequent reference to the "new" encourages considerations of the multiple ways that the coloniality of power is actually being contested and subverted. In "Latin America: Toward a New Historical Meaning," for instance, he argued that the contemporary acceleration, polarization, and deepening of the control over labor "has produced not only a lot of polarization but also two irreversible limits." Moreover, "new approaches take into consideration the limits relating to the living conditions on the planet . . . and address the limits on relations regarding social existence based on the perverse combination of two mental constructs, race and gender. The thing called race is being subverted. The victims of the coloniality of power are creating true subversion."[18] Even more, these victims are also producing radical critiques of Eurocentrism and with it a subversion of authority, Quijano contends. While subversion has certainly been present since colonial times, Quijano's words offer hope in and for these times, new rationalities of and for the present.

Still, the "new" for Quijano does not pretend to discard the old. "What is going on is that new rationalities are reappearing out of those that were colonized; they are even producing other new ones. What we will probably have in the future," he maintains, "is not so much a rationality shared by all, decreed by some God, but rather several rationalities—that is, several means of producing meaning and explanations—that nevertheless must have common ground so as to be able to communicate. We are speaking of something new where people can communicate, learn from each other, and even choose to leave one identity for another or have many diverse identities."[19]

While Quijano's reflections here are from his native Latin America, they open dialogue on what is occurring in other regions of the world. To use another of Quijano's phrases, a "new alternative horizon of historical sense" is emerging.[20] Herein lies Quijano's hope and forward-looking vision: a proposition and guide for decolonial thinking and doing across the globe today.

II. Quijano's Conceptual Framework

> . . . another distinctive episteme is emerging. There's an epistemic subversion, and it not only has an important field of activity in Latin America, it also forms part of the ideas that are up for debate around the world at this moment, ideas that originated in

Latin America. The very notion of the coloniality of power and its epistemic foundations, the idea of decoloniality of power, are of Latin America in origin. It is no historical accident, of course; quite the contrary.

This is why the coloniality of power must be called into question, its bases called into question, the very idea of race called into question, the idea of gender and of ethnicity as well. It isn't an idle question. *The answer to it isn't just academic; it is political and vital.* That is, it doesn't refer to official politics via the state but to the politics of daily life.

—"Notes on the Decoloniality of Power" (emphasis added)

The impact of Aníbal Quijano's work has been felt since the 1990s and has grown consistently since then even though he left no major books in either Spanish or English. His talks, workshops, teaching, activism (e.g., the World Social Forum), and articles were all conducted in Spanish. A few of the resulting works have been translated into English through the years and dispersed in unrelated publications.

Quijano was trained as a sociologist, and his life and work were not those of an academic, although he was one.[21] He was mainly an intellectual activist, thinking on his feet and delivering his thinking orally. His intellectual work and activism go back to the late 1960s and the 1970s when the debate on economic and political dependency in Latin America was extensive, involving scholars from Brazil, Chile, Peru, and Argentina. From these years came his friendship and professional relationship with Immanuel Wallerstein as well as the Fernand Braudel Center that Wallerstein founded at Binghamton University in 1976.

There are four theories that originated in Latin American during the 1960s that have had a global impact: the theology of liberation, the pedagogy of the oppressed, dependency theory, and, more recently, the coloniality of power. The latter introduced a discontinuity in the social sciences that must be understood in the context of the change of era unlocked by the fall of the Berlin Wall and the end of the Cold War.[22] Such observation is helpful to distinguish Quijano's coloniality of power from Wallerstein's modern world-system. Wallerstein devised the modern world-system based on his lived experience and intellectual formation in the North Atlantic. Quijano devised coloniality and the modern/colonial world-system ground on his lived experience in the South American Andes and his intellectual immersion in the debates of his time, mentioned above. While the relationship between Quijano and Wallerstein was friendly, solidary, and intellectually connected, a closer look reveals their divergent paths.

Quijano added "coloniality" to Wallerstein's modern world-system. The North Atlantic modern world-system became the modern/colonial world-system, sensed and perceived in and from the South American Andes. The content may be similar, but the lived experience that sustains the content is engrained in the partition and ranking of planetary regions. Because this distinction is overlooked, however, the groundings in which Quijano and Wallerstein enunciate had already been shaped by coloniality of power. Wallerstein sensed and perceived modernity and the First World. For Quijano, it was coloniality that permeated life and memory of the Third World. The fracture, the slash (/), that divides and unites modernity/coloniality had been earlier perceived by Raúl Prebisch's distinction between center and periphery. Prebisch (1901–1966) was an Argentine liberal economist and executive secretary of the United Nations Economic Commission for Latin America and the Caribbean who called into question the idea of developing the underdeveloped. Wallerstein added "semiperiphery" to Prebisch's compound center/periphery, First World/Third World.

Eastern Europe was Wallerstein's semiperiphery. Two other Wallerstein sources, beyond his debt to Prebisch, were Frantz Fanon's Africa and Fernand Braudel's historical capitalism. The latter overruled the former in Wallerstein analytics. Of the three sources (Prebisch, Fanon, and Braudel), Wallerstein named the research center he created in Binghamton after the latter. The point I am stressing with these tidbits is the geopolitics of knowing, sensing, and believing, upon which conceptual structures are displayed, that relates and at the same time differentiates Quijano from Wallerstein. In a nutshell, while Braudel was an anchor for Wallerstein, the intellectual, activist, and dissident Marxist José Carlos Mariátegui (1894–1930) was the equivalent for Quijano. Consequently, the modern world-system is a North Atlantic (critical) perspective, while the modern/colonial world system and the coloniality of power are a South American (decolonial) perspective.[23]

It was Prebisch also who introduced the concepts "economic dependency" and "unequal development" in the 1950s, which opened up the debate known today as "dependency theory" during the 1960s in which Quijano was involved.[24] A frequently cited Quijano essay is "Coloniality of Power, Eurocentrism, and Latin America."[25] This essay is revealing of what Prebisch meant to Quijano and to Wallerstein. Quijano perceived and sensed the power differential while dwelling in the periphery like Prebisch, while Wallerstein sensed and perceived the weight of the center. Decolonially speaking, knowing and understanding are sensorial before being rational. Quijano wrote:

> When Raúl Prebisch coined the celebrated image of center and periphery to describe the configuration of global capitalism since the end of World War II, he underscored, with or without being aware of it, *the nucleus of the historical model for the control of labor*, resources, and products that shaped the central part of the new global model of power, starting with America as a player in the new world economy. Global capitalism was from then on colonial/modern and Eurocentered. Without a clear understanding of those specific historical characteristics of capitalism, the *concept of a "modern world-system," developed principally by Wallerstein but based on Prebisch and the Marxian concept of world capitalism*, cannot be properly understood.[26]

Quijano did not mention the concept of race in this specific paragraph, although it is explicit in the essay from which this quotation is extracted. Race was for Quijano what class was for Prebisch and Wallerstein. Quijano, following up on Mariátegui instead of Braudel, reformulated center/periphery by following the path of his Peruvian intellectual predecessor, Mariátegui, who was a self-taught intellectual, journalist, and philosopher. Mariátegui and Quijano distinguished themselves for their essayistic writing and wide thinking beyond academic and disciplinary regulations, while Wallerstein respected the formality of the social science's disciplinarity.

Quijano's extensive reflection on Mariátegui could be found in his foreword in the 2007 reprint of *7 ensayos de interpretación de la realidad peruana*.[27] Here, Quijano outlined the political, economic, and subjective transformation of Peruvian society, connected to the mutation of international political economy and the conflicts between the ascending Peruvian bourgeoisie, in connivance with the elite landowners of Peru, pertaining to the disputes between the United States and Britain in Latin America. It was at this juncture that the question of land and the "the problem of the Indian" were made evident, first denounced by Peruvian liberal thinkers (e.g., González Prada), and later followed by Mariátegui from a dissident Marxist perspective: race and racism were outside orthodox Marxism, but it was central for Mariátegui and later on for Quijano.

Mariátegui's own Marxism placed the question of the land, the question of the Indian, and the question of race in the front row. In so doing he was quickly excluded from Eurocentric Marxist orthodoxy. Quijano's essay on Mariátegui did not miss this point, as Quijano distanced himself from Marxist materialist orthodoxy. Quijano's path paralleled similar reactions in the 1960s among a new generation of Marxist followers of Antonio Gramsci to reject Marxist orthodoxy.[28] However, the concept of race and land were absent in Gramsci and in many of his Latin American followers who held onto the Eurocentered concept of class. For Mariátegui, race and land took over class, and for Quijano, race became the anchor to justify the exploitation of labor and the expropriation of land.

All of these take us to the crucial decolonial shifting from Eurocentric epistemology. This shift appears in Quijano's foundational article on coloniality and modernity/rationality (in this volume). Here Quijano's emphasis on the question of knowledge (rather than the economy) is of note. The radical epistemic shift was to place the control of knowledge over the control of the economy. Quijano certainly understood the role of the economy in the colonial matrix of power. After all, he was deeply familiar with Marxism. But he believed that the economy known today as "capitalism" was not limited to the expropriation of land and the exploitation of labor. In order to make that possible, the control of knowledge and consequently of intersubjective relations is necessary. There is a deviation, if not a reversal, here from the canonical infrastructure/superstructure. The colonial will to power, mediated by knowledge, becomes the infrastructure, while the economy becomes the instrumental superstructure to implement the colonial will.

Quijano realized that what there is (the ontic dimension of living) and what we do are always regulated by the knowledge and understanding (the ontological) we have about what there is, what we do, and what is done by others. Hence, although he kept employing the word "capitalism" in reference to economic coloniality, the decolonial meaning of the word was distinct from Wallerstein's modern notion of "historical capitalism." In one of Quijano's last essays, "Notes on Decoloniality of Power" (written in 2015 and included in this volume), he argues that "there is a bigger issue that is in crisis, which is this power structure, whose legitimacy is in crisis, whose foundations no longer have legitimacy." He motioned us to look beyond the surface of capital and capitalism, to focus on the colonial matrix of power.

Quijano confronted not only "the question of knowledge" but mainly the question of the "totality of knowledge" head-on. At this point it is crucial to delink from the canonical Western distinction between epistemology and ontology. They are two related philosophical concepts. The first frames the regulation of scholarly knowledge, while the second refers to what there is (*onto*) that appears to the discursive (*logos*) gazes according to certain regulations of scholarly knowing. The ontic is meaningless without the ontological. Hence, ontology is a philosophical concept mediated by epistemology. Economy and capitalism are two ontological entities that cannot be changed without chafing the epistemology that supports the concepts of economy and capitalism. For that reason, Quijano proposed in his foundational article "Coloniality and Modernity/Rationality" that "decolonization" requires "epistemological reconstitution." Now, epistemological reconstitution cannot be a universal model but instead must come from the local histories disrupted by the coloniality of power. The "bigger issue that is in crisis" is the colonial matrix of power of which economic coloniality (capitalism for liberals, neoliberals, and Marxists) is one of the four domains outlined by Quijano.[29]

As said earlier, the meaning of "capitalism" differs in Wallerstein's historical capitalism and Quijano's colonial matrix of power. Here, the economy is one of the four domains articulated by the modern/colonial structure of knowledge. Thus, decolonization, particularly the decolonization advanced in specific local histories, must be connected to the coloniality of power that requires the task of epistemological decolonization. Without this specification, any invocation of decolonization and decoloniality would be floating invocations lacking the specifics of what is being claimed to be decolonized. For these reasons, decoloniality after Quijano is not an abstract universal but rather the connector among diverse and specific localities that have been disrupted by coloniality, both as will to colonial power and the implementation of the instrument, the colonial matrix of power. In this regard, decoloniality is the general grammar that connects specific local works of decolonization that presuppose gnoseological reconstitution of epistemology, or epistemological reconstitution in Quijano's own vocabulary.

Through Mariátegui, Quijano focused on the modern/colonial concept of race. Although race accounts for the power differentials and inequalities undergirding the formula center/peripheries, the experience, and debates, treatment of racism acquires its specificities in particular local histories and historical periods. Racism in the United States is not experienced, conceived, debated, or treated as it is in China, South Africa, and the South American Andes. However, the concept of race is the colonial connector among diverse planetary localities disrupted by coloniality. In his celebrated work *7 Interpretive Essays on Peruvian Reality* (1928), Mariátegui framed the racial question in the South American Andes:

La suposición de que el problema indígena es un problema étnico se nutre del más envejecido repertorio de ideas imperialistas. El concepto de las razas inferiores sirvió al Occidente blanco para su obra de expansión y conquista. Esperar la emancipación indígena de un activo cruzamiento de la raza aborigen con inmigrantes blancos es una ingenuidad anti-sociológica, concebible solo en la mente rudimentaria de un importador de carneros merinos. La degradación del indio peruanos es una barata invención de los leguleyos de la mesa feudal.

The belief that the Indian problem is ethnic is sustained by the most outmoded repertory of imperialist ideas. The concept of inferior races was useful to the white man's West for purposes of expansion and conquest. To expect that the Indian will be emancipated through a steady crossing of the aboriginal race with white immigrants is an antisociological naivete that could only occur to the primitive mentality of an importer of merino sheep. The people of Asia, who are in no way superior to the Indians, have not needed any transfusion of European blood in order to assimilate the most dynamic and creative aspects of Western culture. The degeneration of the Peruvian Indian is a cheap invention of sophists who serve feudal interests.[30]

Quijano identified the concept of race as a mental category of modernity and by so doing was able to translate Mariátegui's insight into the larger picture of global coloniality. That is, race/racism was not a specific problem in the Andes. What Mariátegui perceived in Quijano's reading was the local manifestation of the crucial issue of global coloniality and in the constitution of the colonial matrix of power. But that was not all. It was a mental category of knowledge that fulfilled the ideal of the human/humanity modeled on males' experience during the European renaissance. Consequently, the concept of race anchored and implied, outside of the Christian European experience, the sexual aspects in defining and ranking Western concepts of the human/humanity. Furthermore, the concept of race was instrumental in separating the human/humanity from all the living energies on Earth, immobilized and objectified by the Western concept of nature. Nature, or what is not made by humans, was imagined as distinct from culture, which is everything made by humans.[31] As Quijano stated,

The idea of race, in its modern meaning, does not have a known history before the colonization of America. Perhaps it originated in reference to the phenotypic differences between conqueror and conquered. However, what matters is that soon it was constructed to refer to the supposed differential biological structure of those groups.

Social relations founded on the category of race produce new historical social identities in America—Indians, Blacks and mestizos—and redefined others. Terms such as "Spanish" and "Portuguese" and, much later, "European," which had until then indicated only geographic origin or country of origin, acquired from then on a racial connotation in reference to the new identities. Insofar as the social relations that were being configured were relations of domination, such identities were considered constitutive of hierarchies, places, and corresponding social roles.[32]

Quijano's argument demonstrates that racialization goes beyond skin color and what was called the "ethnoracial pentagon" in the United States during the 1970s.[33] The ethnoracial pentagon of white, Asian American, African American, Native American, and Hispanic/Latino is the current and local manifestation in the United States of a larger phenomenon: the classification and ranking of people, continents, nations, and regions of the world. Quijano's groundbreaking argumentation brought to light that the colonial differential, that which holds together the modern/colonial world-system, was built and maintained on the concept of race. In that sense, the above quotation elucidates the distinction between Wallerstein's modern world-system and Quijano's coloniality of power (or modern/colonial world-system).

Distinctions such as barbarian and civilized, developed and underdeveloped, and First World and Third World are all Western conceptualizations that create two opposing poles. What are seen as oppositions in the rhetoric of modernity are invented entities, which are entangled with the colonial difference. Barbarians are not ontically inferior or anterior to the civilized. The constitution of ideas of the civilized and of civilization needed to invent the idea of the barbarian in space and the primitive in time. They needed these ideas to trace their frontiers. The logic of either/or is the logic of Western modernity enacting coloniality. It was a convenient opposition and ranking, since it justified the claims to civilize the barbarians, develop the underdeveloped, democratize the undemocratic, and contain any invented threat to the modern/colonial world's order. Mariátegui was already intuiting the large problem when he said that "the belief that the Indian problem is ethnic is sustained by the most outmoded repertory of imperialist ideas."

The concept of race fuels and holds together the colonial matrix of power.[34] Projected over people and regions of the planet, race served to constitute the idea of the civilized human and the lesser human: barbarians, primitives, and underdeveloped.[35] This illuminates our understanding of the past and current international world order as well as the emotional impact on people with the privilege to classify, the people who are being classified, and the people who occupy the gray zone between these groups. The process of colonizing the land called America in the sixteenth and seventeenth centuries, conquering the people of the continent, and capturing and transporting enslaved Africans was the foundation of a pattern of intersubjective relations. These processes entangled the European population with Native peoples and enslaved Africans.[36] No one escaped from the emerging hierarchical relations being established, which were transformed and have persisted until today. The arrogance of power settles in the subjectivity of the conquering (and classifier) population in the same way that the sense of inadequacy and inferiority is implanted in the subjectivity of the classified population.

The established power differential, however, is not static. The dominated, Quijano suggested, "learned, first, to give new sense and meaning to the outsiders' symbols and images and then to transform and subvert them by including their own in regard to images, rites, or expressive matrices of outsider origin."[37] It was impossible for the invaded and disrupted Native population to continue living as they did, and it was impossible to dwell in the shoes of a language, memory, culture, and praxis of living that was alien to them. The burden was passed to future generations who would adapt themselves to the imposed foreign culture or reoriginate their own, no longer as it was but enriched with the Native appropriations of the invading culture.

Once the logic of coloniality enters like a virus in the subjectivity of all parties involved, it invades all areas of experience from everyday life to institutional political and economic governance. For the Native population (in the Americas, Asia, and Africa), there is no possibility of returning to the past or belonging to the subjectivity of the settlers or invaders. Adaptation always leaves a residue in the population of the origin country and the population that migrated to the North Atlantic region. For the invading population, a new dimension disrupts their historical continuity until that moment. Once the colonial matrix of power is established, no one is outside of it. The current rise of the "white replacement theory" in words and deeds in the United States and in the European Union bears witness. But now, the directionality of the power differential has paradoxically changed direction: the intruders are Blacks, Muslims, Jews, immigrants, and refugees, while the intruded upon are white and Western Christians. Although this is obvious, it poses a reversal of fortune from the previous 450 years, when the intruders were Western Christians and secular whites and the intruded upon were everyone else. But it is also a powerful sign of the discredit and disbelief in the reality of classifications and in the reliability of the classifiers.

Recent shootings in the United States, the European Union, and New Zealand are all domestic cases of increasing national racial conflicts. Less discussed but there for everyone to see are the racial conflicts in the global interstate order, also known as international order. The officers of the state, of any state, national or monarchic, are human beings also embedded in the racial matrix. Diplomacy, of course, is there precisely to keep interstate relations as detached as possible from personal emotions, but these emotions have not yet been eliminated. Race/racism connects the emotions (pro and cons) of the public sphere with the state.

Quijano's conceptualization of race as an epistemological issue has enormous consequences. Race is generally not discussed, for instance, in interstate relations. It seems obvious from the history of the colonial matrix of power that the racial component is present in the current international conflicts between the United States, the North Atlantic Treaty Organization, and the European Union on the one hand and China, Russia, and Iran on the other. While the economy and historical-political power differentials exist between the states and regions, something more moves the emotions that can be observed in the discourse of politicians and the anchors of mainstream media. That the Chinese are "yellow" is a European myth invented by the scientific classification of Carl Linnaeus (1707–1778) and the ideological rendering of Immanuel Kant (1724–1804).[38] The European image of Africans, the people and the state, has been shaped by the long history of the European mentality. Russians are Slavics and Christian Orthodox. The expression "white superiority" obtains at all levels of experience, from the public sphere to interstate relations, but is not restricted to skin color. A large part of the Russian and Iranian population is white-skinned.

"Globalization" was not alien to Quijano. However, he departed from mainstream debates on globalization mainly because he injected race into the equation and revealed that globalization is not just something that happened in history but instead is the outcome of globalism: the five hundred years of Western global designs and racial classifications, since the sixteenth century, managed through the colonial matrix of power. Quijano introduced the decolonial perspective on globalization through the concept of race. In the last decades of the twentieth century and the beginning of the twenty-first century, he routinely observed, "What is termed 'globalization' is the culmination of a process that began with the constitution of America and colonial/modern Eurocentered capitalism as a new global power. One of the fundamental axes of this model of power is *the social classification of the world's population around the idea of race*, a mental construction that expresses the experience of colonial domination *and pervades the more important dimension of global power*, including its specific rationality: Eurocentrism."[39]

"Notes on the Decoloniality of Power" (2015), presented in this volume, is a short although overwhelming statement of the formation and consequences of coloniality and of the decoloniality of power. There, Quijano explicitly connects race with gender and ethnicity. Together, they form the three energies that govern the coloniality of power and the colonial matrix of power.[40] But what does he understand by power structure, on the one hand, and the colonial matrix of power, on the other? For him "power" is a mesh of relations of three forces: domination, exploitation, and conflict. This model of power could be found in many geohistorical civilizations before 1500. What distinguished the mesh of relations that Quijano called the "matrix of power" from the colonial matrix of power? To understand this distinction means to understand his radical departure from Western political theory and ways of thinking.

As we mentioned before, Quijano posited coloniality as the main feature of the colonial matrix of power. It consists in the classification of the global population anchored on the idea of race.[41] Hence, classification is not a manual operation. Sure, it can be done in images, but arguments would be necessary to make sense of the images. If race/racism is a mental category that shapes people's sensorium, it is because it is the outcome of thoughts manifested in oral and written expressions. Classifications are neither given nor inscribed on the bodies and the regions classified. Classifications are signs projected onto what is classified. To do so requires actors, institutions in positions of power, and a sign system to materialize the destitution of alien sign systems.

For example, "America" was a name invented and imposed on existing sign systems of the territories theretofore known as Anahuac, Tawantin-suyu, Mapu, Abya Yala, and Turtle Island. Asians did not know they lived in Asia until Christian missionaries landed in Japan and China toward the end of the sixteenth century with the Western world map dividing the planet into four continents. The idea of race restructured ethnic relations. Ethnically speaking, "European" was not only the descriptor of a given ethnicity, coexisting with others such as "Chinese," "African," "American," and

"Asian." It was also the marker of a superior ethnic rank and the generation of the classification. In its turn, gender relations were also remodeled by the idea of race: Spanish women in the colonies and British women in the plantations were in a dominating position vis-à-vis Indian and African men. The classificatory logic of coloniality remains active today, although it is increasingly contested in the interstate system and within nation-states.

Quijano's demand in the epigraph at the start of section II that "the coloniality of power must be called into question in all its domains" is not an academic but rather an existential call, Quijano insisted. It is a political and vital one. He insisted on bringing back together the tree of life with the tree of knowledge that were separated in Western modernity. How should this call be pursued? In "Coloniality and Modernity/Rationality" (1992), Quijano's foundational article on the coloniality of power, he called for "decolonization as epistemic reconstitutions" in the following terms:

> The critique of the European paradigm of rationality/modernity is indispensable; even more, it is urgent. But it is doubtful if the criticism consists of a simple negation of all its categories, of the dissolution of reality in discourse, of the pure negation of the idea and the perspective of totality in cognition. *It is necessary to extricate oneself from the linkages between rationality/modernity and coloniality.* . . . It is the instrumentalization of the reasons for power, of colonial power in the first place, that produced distorted paradigms of knowledge and spoiled the liberating promises of modernity.[42]

The urgency of Quijano's call can be understood through Albert Einstein's well-known dictum that problems cannot be solved within the same frame of mind that created the problems. Einstein was alluding to the physical sciences, but his notion could be extended to the colonial matrix of power. One of the failures of decolonization during the Cold War was to leave the colonial matrix of power untouched. The colonial matrix of power was also unseen because it was covered by the rhetoric of modernity. How should it be pursued? First, we must extricate and delink ourselves from the linkages between modernity/rationality and coloniality. Second, we must engage in epistemological and subjective reconstitution. This means delinking in order to relink with something else. For this second step, there cannot be one global or universal model. The entire planet, local histories and selves, have been subjected through the years to the promises and demands of modernity. Therefore, the path of reconstructing epistemology will depend on whoever, communally, needs to engage with it. If there is no one model, it is indispensable to start from someplace else. It must begin from the exteriorities of what modernity destituted and what is relevant for any decolonial project whose basic premise is epistemological and subjective reconstitutions.[43] How did Quijano do it? He shifted the geography of knowing, and instead of starting from modernity and moving toward coloniality, his experiences, emotions, and reasoning began from coloniality. From there he unveiled the fictional promises of modernity.[44]

The promises of modernity never went without being contested. The reason is simple: there is no promise of modernity without implementing coloniality. And that creates conflicts. Quijano's latest essays explored the growing and creative thinking and doing of the Pueblos Originarios/ First Nations in reconstituting their knowledges and paths of knowing (gnoseology), reducing Western knowledges and paths of knowing (epistemology) to their own limited dimensions. One of these essays was titled "'Bien Vivir': Between 'Development' and the De/Coloniality of Power" (in this volume). The quotation marks around "Bien Vivir" and "Development" indicate that the political horizon of *bien vivir* cannot be achieved by developmental projects. Development promises and provides better life (*vivir mejor*) for a minority and worse living conditions (*vivir peor*) for the vast majority. Here you have in a nutshell why there cannot be modernity without coloniality.

Raúl Prebisch earlier realized the trap in the rhetoric of development and modernization announced in 1949 by US president Harry Truman (1884–1972).[45] Given the power relations between industrial centers and peripheries, which have provided raw materials and labor to the benefit of the industrial center, development was a dead-end road. The horizon of *bien vivir* originated someplace else: in the praxis of the living and thinking of Pueblos Originarios/First Nations. The horizon has been stamped in the constitutions of Bolivia and Ecuador. Doing and thinking in the horizon of *bien vivir* has different meanings for Indigenous and non-Indigenous people. The horizon is the same, but the roads leading toward it are parallel and cannot be fused or absorbed. Hence, delinking from Western universality brings to the fore decolonial pluriversality that emerges, precisely, from people working and following the common path of their destituted local histories and praxis of living and thinking.

Quijano sensed the global momentum of the double processes of delinking/relinking and constitution/reconstitution (learning to unlearn). He perceived the momentum not as a universal model but instead as the plurality of decolonial epistemological and subjective reconstitutions of what has been destituted:

There's a process of decoloniality of power, an indigenized population around the world that's starting to emerge. Therefore, *another distinctive episteme is emerging. There's an epistemic subversion, and it not only has an important field of activity in Latin America, it also forms part of the ideas that are up for debate around the world at this moment, ideas that originated in Latin America.* The very notion of the coloniality of power and its epistemic foundations and the idea of decoloniality of power are of Latin America in origin. This is no historical accident, of course; quite the contrary.[46]

What is emerging is not a new universal within the universal frame of Western epistemology. In "Notes on the Decoloniality of Power," Quijano argues that while coloniality of power remains active, the idea of race lost much of the legitimacy that it had up to World War II, although it remains active in everyday life and on people/our subjectivities. And he adds, *"This is why the coloniality of power must be called into question, its bases called into question, the very idea of race called into question, the idea of gender and of ethnicity. It isn't an idle* question. The answer to it isn't just academic; it is political and vital. *That is, it doesn't refer to official politics via the state but instead to the politics of daily life."*[47]

III. The Need of Quijano's Coloniality of Power in English

As mentioned above, Aníbal Quijano's proposition to see history and society from what he has called the "perspective of the coloniality of power" has crossed the North-South geopolitical border in the opposite direction—from South to North—when this border normally regulates the traffic of theoretical models and other "patents" in only one direction. Quijano's vocabulary and his approach have traveled. The terms he used can be heard at conferences and in seminars and classrooms. However, as he often pointed out with righteous anger, more often than not they have circulated like coins of an academic market or even as clichés of an intellectual fashion. Quijano became upset with this for two reasons: his vocabulary had been used in a superficial manner, and he knew that such use would inevitably lead to obsolescence.

One might assert that the reason for this triviality is related to the disrespect for the "parenthood" that gave rise to it. After all, the role of people who work in the humanities and the social sciences is to donate names that will turn evident in a reflexive way what had remained until the moment of nomination as a blind spot in the visual field of an era. Those names that emerge and transform the consciousness of an era do not have owners, but they do certainly claim some parentage. Authors, in the most radical sense of the word, are name givers. And the names they donate to the world do not belong to them as possessions or property. Nevertheless, they do have with them a filial relationship. This filial relationship is important because it allows for the coordinated use of a composed universe of ideas whereby every category at stake needs to be understood in context and relation to the group to which it belongs. Unfortunately, this has not been the case for Quijano's ideas, despite the extensive circulation of his vocabulary.

Quijano's words instead have been circulating scattered, orphaned, and therefore unconnected. That is what makes this English-language anthology so important. His words have migrated to the epistemic North separated from the original matrix that gave cohesion to their meaning and have lost the deep interconnections they had at their birth. We can recount some examples of this problem. On countless occasions, authors have placed faith in the possibility that changes in state policy could solve the problems pointed to by decolonial critique. Others have mistaken decolonial perspective with postcolonial theory. Quijano rebuffed them, saying "it is impossible, since, as far as I am concerned, the postcolonial does not exist."[48] Finally, thinkers have pretended to use the decolonial perspective by applying the category "subalterns" to describe the inhabitants of the colonized world, a category that Quijano never used. These recurring examples show how the perspective of the coloniality of power is often detached from its original meaning precisely because an adequate representation of Quijano's works has not been available in English.

Anglophone readers will find it useful to hear the way Quijano himself talked about his body of work and ideas. He never referred to his repertoire of categories as a "theory" but instead described it as a "perspective," a way of looking at the world. A theory would be a closed and finished model. Instead, a perspective is given by a set of donated terms, which create a vision that organizes the world differently, reshaping it and making this reorganization of its entities a constant and open work without limits or constraints. The density and imbrication of elements within the perspective of the coloniality of power is conveyed by the image of a labyrinth. In his last years, Quijano described himself as "lost in his labyrinth" of interwoven ideas and lost in a continuous two-way flow of interconnection and constant expansion.

Quijano's theoretical universe should be considered as "organic" rather than "systemic," as it is not a closed and complete system of ideas but instead is a living and constantly moving organism. It heads toward an open "horizon" rather than a preconceived and previously designed "utopia." Quijano's vocabulary stands out for its surgical precision at naming the elements of his perspective. Many authors have elaborated the critique of colonial history and racism and its impacts up to the present, but the tool kit provided by Quijano's vocabulary impresses his crystal clear accuracy for the approach of those topics. Some of these terms and their idiosyncratic definitions, which can be traced back in the texts included in this anthology, are mentioned below.

Quijano's formulation of the perspective of the coloniality of power was gradually developed from the second half of the 1980s onward and followed the end of the Cold War and the fall of the Berlin Wall. The end of this era caused a break in the compulsory ideological loyalties of the bipolar world of capitalism or socialism. It then became possible to imagine and speak of a new critical perspective. While keeping some precepts from Marxism, that perspective took flight in a broader and more inventive way, featuring a worldview based on the Latin American experience. Yet as Quijano emphasized, that view affects and modifies the interpretation and understanding of all reality on a global scale.[49]

The collapse of this bipartite world, with its compulsory adhesions, is the emergence of what Quijano describes as an equally Eurocentric project on both sides of the global political spectrum. The author's courage is striking when, revealing his Mariáteguian lineage, he fearlessly declares that when viewed from the perspective of the peoples, both sides are guilty of the same Eurocentrism because of the technocratic character of their projects and their adherence to the raison d'état.

Another break of Quijano's perspective with the orthodox Left lies in the fact that the core of the coloniality of power dwells on the invention of race, which is considered strictly colonial since conquest and colonization have been ideologically based on the racialization of the bodies, products, and knowledge of the "defeated" peoples. This is how Eurocentrism emerges as the ideological basis of the "coloniality of knowledge." Therefore, despite being a critical and antisystemic perspective, it focuses not on class struggle but rather on denouncing the racialization of bodies, landscapes, knowledge, and products resulting from conquest and colonization.

Quijano's enunciation of the permanence of a coloniality of power, that is, of a colonial structure that continues to shape the world order and also human subjectivity despite the end of the historical stage governed by a colonial and slave-owning legal order, produces an epistemic subversion; that is, it inflects the view of the world and gives it a twist, a shift in perspective, a decolonial turn.

This shift in perspective reveals that the colonial event reoriginated the world by creating categories that did not exist before. "Indian," "Black," and "white" now classify human beings in a new way that serves as a basis for the exploitation of the modern world-system. National independences never dissolved that classification. Therefore, coloniality has remained, and it proliferates as a pattern for work exploitation, social hierarchies, political administration, and even subjectivity itself. Before the Iberian ships had arrived on the shores of the Caribbean and Abya Yala, there was no Europe, no Spain or Portugal, not even America. Let us not forget the revealing year in which the unification of the Iberian Peninsula took place upon the conquest of the Emirate of Granada: 1492. The "Indian," "Black," and "white" categories for the classification of peoples did not exist either, and once created, they brought together very diverse civilizations: those of large populations with a centralized organization and technological development and those of nonstate populations with rudimentary technology.

The first scene of this epistemic turn was, according to Quijano, later accompanied in his proposal by Immanuel Wallerstein (1992), the reordering of history, since it inverts the order of precedence established in the Western historiographical imagination to state that America precedes and invents Europe. This is so because the "New World" emerges as a new space; the American novelty displaces the European tradition and establishes the spirit of modernity as an orientation to the future. Upon the emergence of "America," the golden age runs from the past to the future. The source of legitimation moves from the past—the "sacred history" that, being interpreted by priests, validated and admitted (or not) scientific breakthroughs and technological inventions—to the future as the source of value. Since then, novelty turns out to be good, and what defines the spirit of modernity appears on the horizon: the act of discovering is discovered as a historical project. That is why in Quijano's discourse "colonial" comes before "modernity." The expression "colonial/modernity" indicates that the colonial process was the indispensable condition and kickoff for modernity. This is so just as conquest and colonization were the precondition for capitalism, since only the minerals of the New World would allow the primitive accumulation of the initial phase of capital: without Potosí, there would be no capitalism.

The emergence of America, its foundation as a continent and a category, reconfigures the world and originates the only vocabulary we have today to narrate such a story. The entire narrative of this process, then, needs a new lexicon to describe its events, consequently giving rise to a new era with a new repertoire of categories and a new epistemic framework to grasp the world. America becomes the New World in the strictest sense, as it reestablishes or—in Quijano's words—reoriginates the world. America is the epiphany of a new time, and therefore Quijano accepts the position not of "subalternity" but rather that of protagonism.

History is "reoriginated" (a category essential in Quijano's thinking) and will welcome "the return of the future" by freeing itself from its right- and left-wing enclosures and heading to the ancestral paths of the peoples and their own historical, communal, and cosmology-centered projects. To understand the possibility of this process, it is necessary to perceive the historical/structural heterogeneity of America's social existence. Such heterogeneity is irreducible and permanent. It represents what Quijano called the "Arguedian knot," evoking the novel *Todas las sangres* (All the Bloodlines) by José María Arguedas. In other words, it is an articulation or an interweaving of multiple stories and projects that will have to combine themselves in the production of a new time. For Quijano, capital takes over the heterogeneous forms of work and exploitation. Along with salaries, servile and slave labor relations have not disappeared and are expanding today because of the structural exclusion and permanent marginality resulting from the labor market. At the same time, productive forms based on communal solidarity and reciprocity have not only persisted in Indigenous, rural, traditional, and Black communities but have also been reinvented in forms of popular and solidarity economies. Latin America is heterogeneous not only because it embraces diverse production relations but also because diverse temporalities, histories, and cosmologies coexist there. It is heterogeneous because of the diverse peoples who inhabit it.[50]

The ideological and immediate material efficacy of this perspective is made up of what Quijano calls "the movement of society." Whereas social movements are subject to capture by vanguards that inevitably distance themselves from the people because of their power and control projects, Quijano argued that the movement of society has two fronts that emerge from contemporary politics. The first one involves popular economy with a communal structure, which especially comes up in times of economic catastrophe on a local or national scale and typically arises from unemployed groups or those who were expelled from their territories. The second includes the movements of Indigenous people, Indigenous-peasant organizations, and Black communities. Quijano calls this flow of great political force that bursts onto the present "the return of the future."

To properly understand the perspective of the coloniality of power, it is essential to consider three representations of time in Quijano's work: "re-origination," "open horizon as destiny," and "the return of the future." The last one is an original and sophisticated concept with Andean roots, which Quijano uses to introduce another form of temporality that affects political conception.

The historiographical perspective and the construction of temporality that Quijano proposes firmly differ from dogmatic historicism in order to support the idea of a time that remains behind a series of "historical events" that are typical of linear time. Coloniality is nothing more than a time that remains. It is a line of force that is in the background and remains there despite particular events. This is a broader perspective that defies the linearity of historical exceptionalism and dogmatic historicism and considers the existence of long periods. And it does so by identifying foundational events, which bring about enduring structures and mentalities that cross over the historical time of such events. Ideas such as the coloniality of power exactly highlight the permanence and long duration of subjectivities. In contrast, historicism severs the necessary connection between events by focusing on unconnected historical episodes. The option for partial unrepeatable events not only blocks the perception and understanding of continuities but also presupposes an empty and free time that is not affected by often hidden and unnamed lines of force that cross it.[51]

In this perspective, the reorigination or epistemic shift is essential because it indicates the mutation of subjectivity since the event of conquest and colonization. The decolonial shift takes place when we realize that it is impossible to narrate the process of conquest and colonization without using a vocabulary following the event. When we narrate this process, we are already located in a reoriginated world, a new world in which we can only speak the categories that did not exist before. For example, we say that "Spain discovered America," but this is an untenable statement, since "Spain" did not exist before "America." If we analyze the chronology of events, we will be shocked to see that the Kingdom of Castile reaches the southern tip of the Iberian Peninsula to finish the conquest and begins the unification of what will become the Spanish nation precisely in 1492. This means that the process of annexation reaches the southern coast of the Iberian Peninsula and goes on overseas without breaking its continuity. It is therefore the same historical process: the conquest and colonization on both coasts are part of a continuous, uninterrupted process. However, the reorigination of the world based on a new lexical or categorical framework, through which we see and classify the entities of our planet and narrate past events, prevents us from envisaging the ongoing conformation of Spain. Similarly, we often and inevitably repeat the word "discovery," even though we know very well that the continent was already inhabited. This slip reveals that we are naming something else: the novelty of discovering as a value.

The second concept is that of the open horizon as destiny. Quijano had written about utopia in different essays, but more recently he took on the image of "horizon": a horizon of destiny, that is, an open path led by some ideas and aspirations but neither predefined nor fenced in by preconception. The idea of horizon is that of life and history in motion, not governed by the ideal of a compulsory future, of an imperative future, a motion that is not seized by its end. It is like the winds of history passing through the scene in an always uncertain way. Uncertainty is utopia itself, as with the instability of tectonic plates. History is motion. Life is motion: true and mere "historical faith" about an always uncertain future that cannot be imprisoned. This is the notion of horizon that Quijano sets out and that little by little modifies and replaces the usual notion of utopia as a must-be of the future. We only know about the present, and we can act in the present. The future is open.

The third central idea in this perspective is the "return of the future," meaning a horizon that reopens to the path of peoples' history after the defeat by the capitalist liberal state and the bureaucratic despotism of "real socialism" as well. The hegemony of Eurocentrism has governed both projects. The collapse of the strict loyalties, either to the Left or to the Right, prevented us from thinking freely. It has permitted the reemergence of peoples holding communal structures—such as Indigenous peoples, Indigenous-peasant groups, and Black communities—in politics, that is, in another kind of politics. In the post–Cold War period, encouraged by the apparent benevolence of the multicultural era, diverse peoples who were thought to be extinct reappeared on the scene, showing themselves still alive. The contemporary reemergence of an Indigenous historical subject or the acknowledgment in Latin America that some peasant communities were in fact Indigenous peoples as well as the deconstruction of *mestizaje* indicate that the matrix (*patrón*) of coloniality is coming apart. There is an ongoing reidentification of peasants as Indigenous peoples, of mestizos as Indigenous and Black people, and more people are retracing their nonwhite ancestry.[52]

That is why the category of the return of the future is so important. In the Quechua and Aymara understanding of time, the past is in the future, and Quijano's essay title "The Return of the Future" is a clear reference to this Andean construction of time.[53] We could say, then, from the point of view of the critique of coloniality that only in the future will we be able to find the path and flux of a lost, interdicted past. It is thus clear that the continuity of community solutions for everyday life, which has been interrupted and blocked, is making its own way in the present after the crisis of the political paradigms of the 1970s. This makes possible a connection between archaic forms of life and current historical projects that find their roots in the former. Yet, we are speaking of not a restoration or of nostalgia but rather the liberation of diverse peoples' historical projects that had been interfered with and withheld by the matrix of coloniality. The return of the future becomes possible, a future that could not have been possible but now is. We are not speaking of the nostalgia for a static golden age that is stuck in a remote past or of a loss, much less the confinement of traditions. It is not about the "noble savage" of a pristine origin or about culturalism (a variant of fundamentalism) but instead is about a reclaimed historical path that now has the floodgates open to smooth its continuity in the present. It is the recovery of a historical flow that has been blocked by conquest, colonization, and coloniality and is now reinstalled as the historical project of peoples' continuity. That is why Aníbal Quijano rarely speaks in terms of "decolonizing" in order to avoid an idea of recoverable origin. Time was always in motion for all peoples. All peoples are in history all the time. This is the point in which the perspective of the coloniality of power approximates poststructuralism, since it designs a struggle for a horizon Other by tearing apart the fabrics of discourse and, through its ruptures, making way for the histories withheld by the warlike and ideological intervention of conquest and colonization.

Notes

Each of the three sections of this introduction was written by one of us, respecting the personal relation and intellectual debts that we individually and collectively owe to Aníbal Quijano.

1   Aníbal Quijano was born in Yanama, Peru, in 1928. At a young age he became involved in Marxist-socialist revolutionary politics. He was incarcerated several times for his political thought, and on numerous occasions his writings were confiscated. Quijano was an active part in the 1960s and 1970s of the conceptualization of dependence theory—introducing his concept of structural heterogeneity—and of the shaping of Latin American critical thought. His intellectual militancy of these years is documented in the well-known Latin American journal

Sociedad y política. Trained as a sociologist and being an invited professor in many universities in the Americas and throughout the globe, Quijano refused the identification of full-time academic. His intellectual interest, energy, and contribution were, until his passing in 2018, always militant in scope: a perspective for analyzing and rereading the world from Latin America, from the complex weave of race and capital that is the coloniality of power, the focus of this book.

2   Quijano, "Coloniality of Power, Eurocentrism, and Latin America," *Nepantla: Views from the South* 1, no. 3 (2000): 533, in this volume.

3   Quijano, "Coloniality of Power, Eurocentrism, and Latin America," 534.

4   Quijano, "Coloniality of Power, Eurocentrism, and Latin America," 548.

5   Quijano, "Coloniality of Power, Eurocentrism, and Latin America," 550.

6   Quijano, "The 'Indigenous Movement' and Unresolved Questions in Latin America," in this volume.

7   Quijano, "Estado-Nación y 'movimientos indígenas' en la región andina: Cuestiones abiertas," *Observatorio Social de América Latina* (Buenos Aires) 7, no. 19 (2006): 3. See also Catherine E. Walsh, "Undoing Nation-State," in *Rising Up, Living On: Re-existences, Sowings, and Decolonial Cracks*, 180–229 (Durham, NC: Duke University Press, 2023).

8   Quijano, "The 'Indigenous Movement.'"

9   For a discussion of affirmative refusal, see Leanne Betasamosake Simpson, *As We Have Always Done: Indigenous Freedom through Radical Resistance* (Minneapolis: University of Minnesota, 2017). Recalled as well are the practices of marronage among Black ancestral communities.

10 One example is the reframing of indigeneity as a historical and transhemispheric category and collective Indigenous proposal that originates from the experiences that unite Native peoples and that "interpellate a collectivity of Indigenous nations, as well as non-Indigenous allies that struggle to transcend the conditions of internal/external colonialisms and their logics of elimination." See Emil Keme, "For Abiayala to Live, the Americas Must Die: Toward a Transhemispheric Indigeneity," *Native American and Indigenous Studies* 5, no. 1 (Spring 2018): 46.

11 See Quijano, "Coloniality of Power and Social Classification," in this volume.

12 Quijano, "Coloniality of Power and Social Classification."

13 María Lugones, "The Coloniality of Gender," *Worlds and Knowledges Otherwise* 2 (Spring 2008): 4, https://globalstudies.trinity.duke.edu /sites/globalstudies.trinity.duke.edu/files/file-attachments/v2d2 _Lugones.pdf.

14 See, for example, in this volume, "Coloniality of Power and De/Coloniality of Power," "Notes on the Decoloniality of Power," and "Latin America: Toward a New Historical Meaning."

15   Aníbal Quijano, "Lo público y lo privado: Un enfoque latinoameri-
      cano," in *Por la Imaginación Política: De la socialización a la descolonialidad
      del poder*, comp. Danilo Assis Clímaco (Lima: Red de Descolonialidad y
      Autogobierno Social/Programa Democracia y Transformación Social,
      2000), 236. Translation by Catherine Walsh. Both public and private
      neoliberalism were, in Quijano's mind, part of the same instrumental
      rationality.

16   Here it seems relevant to note that "decoloniality" was not a central
      component of Quijano's early work on the coloniality of power. This
      only began to emerge after the first half of 2000, largely the result
      of collective discussions and reflections of what has been referred to
      as the modernity/(de)coloniality group, organized around Quijano's
      thought and in which he played a central part.

17   Walter D. Mignolo and Catherine E. Walsh, *On Decoloniality: Concepts,
      Analytics, Praxis* (Durham, NC: Duke University Press, 2018), 4–5.

18   See Quijano, "Latin America: Toward a New Historical Meaning," in
      this volume.

19   See Quijano, "Latin America."

20   See Aníbal Quijano, "Otro horizonte de sentido," *América Latina en Mov-
      imiento*, 441 (July 2, 2014): 2–5.

21   Quijano was a faculty member of the Universidad de San Marcos
      in Lima; a visiting professor at the State University of New York at
      Binghamton; a scholar of the Fernand Braudel Center for the Study of
      Economies, Historical Systems, and Civilizations; and an invited profes-
      sor and speaker at various universities throughout the Latin American
      region and Europe.

22   Rita Segato, *The Critique of Coloniality: Eight Essays* (London: Routledge,
      2022).

23   For more details, see Walter D. Mignolo, "Colonialidad Global, Capi-
      talismo y Hegemonía Epistémica," in *Indisciplinar las Ciencias Socia-
      les: Geopoliticas del conocimiento y colonialidad del poder; Perspectivas desde
      lo Andino*, ed. Catherine Walsh, Freya Schiwy, and Santiago Castro-
      Gomez, 215–44 (Quito: Abya Yala, 2002).

24   Vincent Ferraro, "Dependency Theory: An Introduction," in *The Develop-
      ment Economics Reader*, ed. Giorgio Secondi, 58–64 (London: Routledge,
      2008).

25   Quijano's original text was published with the title "Colonialidad del
      poder, eurocentrismo y América Latina" in *La colonialidad del saber:
      Eurocentrismo y ciencias sociales: Perspectivas latinoamericanas*, ed. Edgardo
      Lander (Buenos Aires: CLACSO, 2000), and reprinted as "Coloniality of
      Power, Eurocentrism, and Latin America" in *Coloniality at Large: Latin
      America and the Postcolonial Debate*, ed. Mabel Moraña, Enrique Dussel,

and Carlos A. Jáuregui (Durham, NC: Duke University Press, 2008), included in this volume.

26   Quijano, "Coloniality of Power, Eurocentrism, and Latin America," in this volume (emphasis added). See also his distinction between "capital" and "capitalism" in "Notes on the Decoloniality of Power," in this volume.

27   See Quijano, "Prólogo: José Carlos Mariátegui."

28   Aníbal Quijano, "José Carlos Mariátegui: Encuentros y debates," in José Carlos Mariátegui, *7 ensayos de interpretación de la realidad peruana* (1928) (Caracas, Venezuela: Biblioteca Ayacucho, 1979), ix–xc. The year before, the Argentina intellectual José María Aricó, one of the leaders of the Gramscian Left in Argentina and Brazil in the 1960s, published the booklet *Mariategui y los origenes del Marxismo Latinoamericano* (Buenos Aires: Cuadernos de Pasado y Presente, 1978). The two texts, read side by side, illustrate the two readings of Mariategui's work: the foundation of decolonial thinking, in Quijano, and the origin of Latin American Marxism. See, in addition, Walter D. Mignolo, "Mariategui and Gramsci in 'Latin' America," *The Politics of Decolonial Investigations*, 387–420 (Durham, NC: Duke University Press, 2021); and Catherine E. Walsh, "Thinking Andean Abya Yala with and against Gramsci: Notes on State, Nature, and *Buen Vivir*," in *Gramsci in the World*, ed. Roberto M. Dainotto and Fredric Jameson, 190–203 (Durham, NC: Duke University Press, 2020).

29   Lugones, "The Coloniality of Gender."

30   Translated by Marjori Urquidi. Jose Carlos Mariategui, "The Problem of the Indian," in *Seven Interpretative Essays on Peruvian Reality* (Austin: University of Texas Press, 1971), https://www.marxists.org/archive/mariateg/works/7-interpretive-essays/essay02.htm.

31   An annual workshop was held at Binghamton in the late 1990s and was organized by the Puerto Rican sociologist Kelvin A. Santiago, with the presence of Aníbal Quijano. In one of those meetings, Sylvia Wynter was a special participant. She later published an extensive essay connecting her own Caribbean and Fanonian perspective with Quijano's coloniality of power. See Wynter, "Unsettling the Coloniality of Being/Power/Truth/Freedom."

32   Quijano, "Coloniality of Power, Eurocentrism, and Latin America," 182. See also in this line of thought Walter D. Mignolo, "Racism as We Sense It Today," in *The Politics of Decolonial Investigations*, 85–99.

33   Historian David A. Hollinger has been credited for coining the felicitous term "ethnoracial pentagon." See Jill Goetz, "UC–Berkeley Historian David Hollinger to Discuss Racial, Ethnic Classifications and Their Relation to Culture in Cornell Lecture April 28," Cornell University, April 21, 1997, https://news.cornell.edu/stories/1997

/04/uc-berkeley-historian-david-hollinger-discuss-racial-ethnic
-classifications-and.

34 María Lugones and Rita Segato have made substantial contributions to
the intersections of sex/gender/race, grounding their argument in Quijano's coloniality of power. See, for example, Lugones, "The Coloniality of
Gender"; and Rita Segato, "A Manifesto in Four Themes," *Critical Times. Interventions in Global Theory* 1, no. 1 (2018): 198–211, https://read.dukepress
.edu/critical-times/article/1/1/198/139314/A-Manifesto-in-Four-Themes.
The spread of Quijano's conceptual framework should be noticed in that
while Lugones's work operates in the context of US "women of color,"
Segato's work is grounded in the history and culture of Latin America.

35 Wynter, "Unsettling the Coloniality of Being/Power/Truth/Freedom."

36 The vocabulary to name actors and social roles was Spanish, from neither Pueblos Originarios' own languages nor the diversity of African
languages spoken by the enslaved population. Coloniality of knowing
and sensing is a semiotic phenomenon; it operates through the sign
system spectrum (orality and literacy, images, sounds, and tastes in
foods and cultural expressions).

37 Quijano, "Coloniality of Power and Subjectivity in Latin America," in
this volume.

38 Emmanuel Chukwudi Eze, "The Color of Reason: The Idea of 'Race' in
Kant's Anthropology," in *Postcolonial African Philosophy: A Critical. Reader*,
ed. Emmanuel Chukwudi Eze, 103–40 (London: Blackwell, 1997).

39 Quijano, "Coloniality of Power, Eurocentrism and Latin America," in
this volume (emphasis added).

40 On the word "patron" in Spanish and its English translation into "matrix," see Quijano, "The 'Indigenous Movement' and Unresolved Questions in Latin America," in this volume.

41 "Estado-Nación, ciudadanía y democracia" [1997], in Aníbal Quijano,
*Cuestiones y horizontes: De la dependencia histórico-estructural a la colo-
nialidad/descolonialidad del poder*," ed. Danilo Assis Clímaco (Buenos
Aires: CLACSO, 2014), 611.

42 Quijano, "Coloniality and Modernity/Rationality," in this volume (emphasis added).

43 For an expansion on this idea, see Walter D. Mignolo, "Introduction,"
in *The Politics of Decolonial Investigations*, 1–84 (Durham, NC: Duke University Press, 2021).

44 Michel-Rolph Trouillot, "North Atlantic Universals: Analytical Fictions,
2492–1945," *South Atlantic Quarterly* 101, no. 4 (2002): 839–58. Trouillot's felicitous expression reinforces his shifting and unveiling of the
abstract universal of Western modernity.

45 "The old imperialism—exploitation for foreign profit—has no place in
our plans. What we envisage is a program of development based on the

concepts of democratic fair-dealing." Harry S. Truman's, "Inaugural Address," Harry S. Truman Library & Museum, January 20, 1949, https://www.trumanlibrary.gov/library/public-papers/19/inaugural-address.

46 Quijano, "Notes on the Decoloniality of Power," in this volume (emphasis added).

47 Quijano, "Notes on the Decoloniality of Power" (emphasis added).

48 Aníbal Quijano, personal communication to the author.

49 See Segato, "Aníbal Quijano and the Coloniality of Power."

50 See Segato, "Aníbal Quijano and the Coloniality of Power."

51 See Mario Rufer, "El perpetuo conjuro: tiempo, soberanía y una mirada poscolonial sobre la escritura de la historia," *Revista Historia y Memoria*, Dossier Miradas de la Historia, Bogotá, 2020.

52 See Rita Segato, "The Deep Rivers of the Latin American Race: A Rereading of Mestizaje," in *The Critique of Coloniality: Eight Essays*, 159–84 (London: Routledge, 2022).

53 The expression of "the return of the future" as a past in motion is rooted in Aymara thought and language: *qhip nayra uñtasis sarnaqapxañani* means "the past lies ahead, the future lies behind." In Quechua as well, there is the same relational cyclic structure. Hurtado de Mendoza states that it is "natural for Quechua speakers to state that the past lies ahead and the future lies behind. Also, "*pachakuti* are not a return to previous stages, instances or states just to repeat them, but to reorder, reform or transform them upon new principles, following new paradigms." William Hurtado de Mendoza Santander, *Pragmática de la cultura y lengua Quecha* (Cusco: Centro de Estudios Regionales Andinos Bartolomé de las Casas, 2001), 77–78 and 73. From a different interpretive model, Martina Faller and Mario Cuéllar explain that in Quechua, "returning from a temporal unit does not mean that we are returning to the same point in time. Instead, we suppose that these units are conceptualized as abstract containers that are filled with different events in every return." Martina Faller y Mario Cuéllar, "Metáforas del tiempo en el quechua," University of Manchester, 2003, https://personalpages.manchester.ac.uk/staff/martina.t.faller/documents/Faller-Cuellar.pdf.

1

PARADOXES OF MODERNITY IN LATIN AMERICA

The world crisis of capital has intensified the debate over contemporary society and culture. It is not only the economy that has been called into question; indeed, the entire framework of knowledge, the presuppositions of rationality in the relationships between peoples themselves and with the world around them, the projects of historical meaning, the balance of fundamental human experiences, such as capitalism and socialism as it actually exists—all perspectives and all alternatives are open to critical appraisal once more.

The position and significance of Latin America in this debate are fundamental. This is the case not only because Latin America has been a victim of the most perverse effects of the crisis, but, more significantly, because of the weight of its historical presence in the construction of the culture of our time, because of the fecundity it possesses for the reconstitution of that culture.

This surely explains the intensification of the Latin American debate itself, although this may be denied by certain groups in certain places whose exclusive concern is that of access to one or another rungs of presently established power. Behind this facade, nevertheless, genuine and critical questions are being posed whose intellectual or pragmatic exploration surely will affect not only Latin America. One of these questions—in one sense the most decisive and central one—is the relationship between the private and the public, because within this relationship virtually every area of contemporary social existence is implicated. Beyond the circumstantial disputes on the Peruvian scene, the debate in question does in fact encompass all the meaning and all the legitimacy of the principal historical projects now available.

Modernity and "Modernization" in Latin America

The pressure to "modernize" has been exerted on Latin America during the greater part of this century, but especially, and in a very distinctive manner, since the end of World War II. In the first place, this pressure was exerted to a large degree by the actions and interests of agencies who were not Latin American, who were, as it were, external. In the second place, such pressure appeared formally as an invitation to accept fully the methods of production, the styles of consumption, and the culture and social and political organization of developed capitalist countries, considered as paradigms of a successful "modernization." In practice, this amounted to the requirement of changes and adaptations in the region to the needs of capital in its phase of inter- or transnational maturity.

By the end of the war the nucleus of historical rationality of modernity had been weakened, and modernity itself had entered into a period of crisis in the face of violent attacks by dark political forces that appealed to the irrationalities of the species, to prejudice and to the myths founded upon it, in opposition to the initial achievements of modernity, seeking to convert the people to the cult of violence and offering naked power as its most attractive legitimating principle. Of course, such forces, like Nazism, had been defeated in the war. However, after this experience, after Auschwitz, the promises of modernity would not again be "vivified with the enthusiasm and hopes of yesteryear," as Jose Medina Echevarria pointed out at the beginning of the Latin American debates of the 1960s. Even worse, there is no doubt that it was in this context that the dark reign of instrumental reason was consolidated, claiming for itself alone, and against historical reason, the prestige and luster of the name of modernity. It is still worth noting that it was not clear to many—and was not admitted by others—that this reign not only blanketed the Western world but also consolidated itself under Stalinism.

It seems necessary at this point to raise questions concerning two of the consequences of this process in respect to Latin America. First, since "modernization" arrived late in these lands, from the outside, already constituted and already in practice, an idea took shape to which many are still prisoners: the idea that Latin America has always been only a passive and late recipient of modernity. Second, and by implication, there is the question of the confusion between modernity and "modernization." Because of this confusion (although intellectual snobbery plays an important role here), today it is not difficult to find in Latin America political and intellectual groups who once again enter the temples of the same gods who rely on the irrationalities of the species to win converts to the cult of naked power.

Modernity as a category was certainly molded in Europe, particularly from the eighteenth century onward. It was, however, a result of a complex of changes that occurred throughout the totality of the world that was subjected to European domination beginning at the end of the fifteenth century. If the intellectual elaboration of these changes had Europe as its principle center, this corresponded to the centrality of Europe's position in this totality, to its position of dominance.

This new historical totality, in whose context modernity was produced, was constituted at the beginning of the conquest and was the incorporation of what was to become Latin America into the world of Europe. The process of production of modernity had a direct and inextricable relationship to the historical creation of Latin America. In respect to this relationship, I not only refer to the well-known fact that Latin American production, primarily of precious metals, was at the base of the original accumulation of capital. Nor do I refer only to the fact that the conquest of America was the first moment of the formation of the world market as the real context within which capitalism and its world-logic could emerge as the material foundation of the production of European modernity.

For Europe, the conquest of America was also a discovery. It was a discovery in the plain geographical sense but most of all a discovery of experiences and of original and different historical meanings that revealed, to the astonishment of Europe (well beyond the appeal of exoticism), distinct historical crystallizations of certain ancient aspirations that until then had no existence other than in myths attributed to an unknown past. It is of no importance that this European vision of the American experience exaggerated reality, exalted by an imagination whose boundaries had been dissolved by the wonder of discovery. It is not important, because this stretching of the frontiers of the European imagination was precisely the consequence of America. And from our perspective, we cannot overlook the fact that exaggerated or not, many of the forms of social existence that the Europeans sought were in fact indigenous to the reality of the American experience, especially the Andean experience: the joy of a social solidarity devoid of violent injustice, the legitimacy of a diversity of solidarities, and reciprocity in the relationship to property and the surrounding world, so completely different from the conditions of European society at that time.

I suggest therefore that this discovery of America produced a profound revolution in the European imagination and, consequently, in the imagination of the Europeanized world of domination: *it produced a replacement of the past as the site of a forever-lost golden age with the future as a golden age to achieve or to construct.*

Without America, how could we imagine the emergence of the peculiar European utopia of the sixteenth and seventeenth centuries, a utopia in which the first signs of a new rationality are already discernible, a rationality that installed the future as the realm of hope and of rationalization in place of the omnipresent past that until then had been the exclusive reference point for all legitimacies, for all explanations, for all the dreams and nostalgias of humanity?

This seems to me to be the central meaning of the utopias that were created in Europe after the discovery of America. And the rise of these specific utopias should be recognized as the first moment of the process of the creation of modernity. Without the new place of the future in the imagination of humanity, the very idea of modernity would be unthinkable.

For Europe at that time, still not having overcome the crisis of feudal society, the utopia of a society without ominous hierarchies, injustice, or obscurantism was the ideology for a long struggle against feudalism, the despotism of absolute monarchies, the power of a church that controlled and blocked the development of knowledge, the supremacy of private interest that grew with mercantilism. In other words, the promise of modernity originated from the struggle for a rational society. At this first moment of the process of the creation of modernity, America occupied a fundamental place.

I would also suggest that there was a close association between America during the crystallization stage of modernity, the seventeenth century, and the movement called the Enlightenment, or Illuminism. During that period, America was not only a recipient but also a part of the universe in which that movement was created and in which it developed, because it developed simultaneously in Europe and in colonial Latin America.

That the Enlightenment movement occurred simultaneously in Europe and America throughout the seventeenth century can be seen first of all by the fact that the institutions, research, concepts, and knowledge that emerged as the Enlightenment were simultaneously formed and diffused in both Europe and America. The Societies of the Friends of the Country (Las Sociedades de Amigos del País) were formed in both places and also at the same time. The same questions for research and the same topics of discussion and investigation were circulated. The same spirit of interest in the exploration of nature using the same instruments of knowledge were disseminated. And everywhere the urge to reform society and its institutions was affirmed to clear the path for political liberty and freedom of conscience and the critique of inequalities and abuses in the relationships between peoples.

When Humboldt came to America, he could not restrain his surprise that the circles of American intellectuals and scholars in each of the principal centers he visited knew the same things and studied the same things as their European counterparts, not only because they read the same materials but most of all because they posed the same questions and attempted to explore these questions with the same passionate eagerness, even if under less propitious conditions. Thus, the spirit of modernity and its promises and demands began to develop with equal intensity in Europe and America.

Many Latin American intellectuals and politicians were direct participants in the debates and the political experiences of the European Enlightenment. For instance, it should not be considered a mere anecdotal fact that the Peruvian Pablo de Olavide was celebrated in the Enlightenment circles of Europe, that he was a friend of Voltaire, and that he participated in the inner circles of the French Encyclopedists and in the political experiences of the Spanish Enlightenment. When de Olavide became a victim of persecution by the Inquisition, his first bio-bibliography was published by Diderot himself, initiating a vast movement in solidarity with the Peruvian in all the circles of European Enlightenment. It is not surprising, then, that at the beginning of the following century, when the Cadiz parliament (Cortes de Cadiz) met in 1810, the Latin American deputies were among the most coherent bearers of the spirit of modernity, the most advanced defenders of radical liberalism. As such, they played an outstanding role in the writing of the liberal constitution in a commission presided over by one of their own, the Peruvian Morales Duárez, who was later elevated to the presidency of parliament.

The Paradox of Modernity in Latin America

It is clear, then, that the movement for modernity occurred in the seventeenth century in Latin America at the same time as in Europe. Here, nevertheless, we discover a surprising and paradoxical fact.

While in Europe modernity spread and flourished—nourished by the development of capitalism with all that it implied for the production of material goods and the relationships between peoples—in Latin America, especially from the last third of the eighteenth century onward, a noticeable contradiction developed between, on the one hand, the ideological and social requirements of modernity and, on the other, the stagnation and disarticulation of the mercantile economy and even its retrogression in certain areas of the Andes. As a consequence, those who rose to the top of society and power were those most allied with inequality and injustice, with despotism and obscurantism. With the well-known exceptions of those areas most immediately linked to European capitalist development, most of what emerged as Latin American was characterized by this contradiction.

In Europe, modernity took shape along definite lines as part of daily experience as well as social practice and legitimating ideology. In Latin America, on the contrary, until well into the twentieth century, a profound and extended breach persisted between the ideology of modernity and social practice, not infrequently within the same social and political institutions. In particular, modernity became a form of legitimating ideology for political practices that clearly were in opposition to its discourse, while modern social practices were repressed because they could not be legitimated by any application of the dominant ideologies.

The use of modernity as a "legitimating" ideology of antagonistic social practices allows us to appreciate the ideological weight of modernity in Latin America, in spite of its imprisonment in a social universe of the opposite sign. Modernity allows us to explain, for example, the curious relationship between nominally liberal institutions and the conservative power that was established with independence. This cannot be explained in turn without recalling that modernity, as a movement of consciousness, was not simply an imported foreign product but a product of Latin American soil itself, when that soil was still a fertile and rich territory for mercantilism even though under colonial domination.

In sum, modernity in Latin America, especially since the nineteenth century, learned how to live as intellectual consciousness but not as daily social experience. Perhaps this explains the trap fallen into by Latin American liberalism in this century: being compelled to cultivate the chimera of modernity without revolution. It has still not worked its way free from this trap.

Power and Modernity in Europe

At the same time, while the Latin American history of modernity is certainly paradoxical, its European avatar not only did not itself form modernity from contradiction but rendered it a victim of the Procrustean demands of the very power to which it owed its existence: bourgeois reason.

During the process of the creation of modernity, the idea of rationality inherent within it did not mean the same thing in each of the centers that created it and disseminated it in Europe. In simplistic terms, within the limits of the present discussion, it should be noted that in the northern or Saxon countries, the predominant idea of rationality was, from the beginning, fundamentally linked to what, since Horkheimer, has been known as "instrumental reason." Above all, this is a relationship between ends and means. The rational is the useful. And utility acquires its meaning from the dominant perspective (i.e., that of power).

On the other hand, in the countries of the South, the predominant idea of rationality was formed, especially in the debate concerning society, primarily in relation to the definition of ends. These ends were those of the liberation of society from all inequality, injustice, despotism, and obscurantism. In other words, these ends were defined against the existing arrangements of power. There, modernity was conceived as a promise of rational social existence as well as a promise of freedom, of equity, of solidarity, of the continuous improvement of the material conditions of *these* forms of social existence, not of any other. This is what came to be recognized from that time forward as "historical reason."

I stress the fact that I am engaging in deliberate oversimplification, given the limits of space, in drawing this distinction between northern and southern Europe in respect to conceptions of rationality and modernity. Nevertheless, this does not imply arbitrariness on my part. It is no happenstance that the leaders of the antimodernist movement of the North American neoconservatives, such as Irving Kristol, for example, insist on their rejection of "French-Continental Enlightenment" and their adherence to the "Anglo-Scottish Enlightenment"—that of Locke, Hume, Smith—in order to justify the privileges of some in respect to others in society. Nor is it coincidental that one of the most strident spokespersons of the neoconservatism addicted to Reaganism, Jeanne Kirkpatrick, does not hesitate to affirm that without the defense of authority and order—including inequality, despotism, and injustice—modernism is but a mere utopia in the pejorative sense of the word.

This difference became a crucial question for the fate of modernity and its promises as hegemony in the power of capital and the relationships of power between the bourgeoisies of Europe moved, at the beginning of the eighteenth century and especially throughout the century, under the control of the British bourgeoisie. In this way, the "Anglo-Scottish" wing of the Enlightenment and of modernity imposed itself on the entirety of bourgeois reason, not only in Europe but also on a world scale because of the imperial power achieved by the British bourgeoisie. Instrumental reason imposed itself upon historical reason.

The world dominance of the "Anglo-Scottish" version of modernity, that of instrumental reason, was strengthened and extended when British imperial hegemony gave way to North American hegemony at the end of World War II. The Pax Americana established after the defeat of Nazism and the further weakening of historical reason during that period exacerbated both the characteristics and the consequences of the domination of instrumental reason.

It is under the domination of the Pax Americana and its extreme version of instrumental reason that after World War II, pressure was exerted on Latin America to "modernize" (i.e., to accept a rationality shorn of all connections with the original promises of modernity, a rationality now totally and solely possessed by the demands of capital and productivity, by the efficiency of the means to secure the ends imposed by capital, and by empire, in the last analysis, reason as the mere instrument of power). This reinforced in wide sectors of Latin America the delusive chimera of modernity without revolution. The consequences are still with us. We have not yet escaped the dark tunnel of militarism and authoritarianism.

Perhaps the most complete example of what is implied by successful "modernization" in Latin America is provided by the transition from the oligarchic state to the modernized state. In all these countries, states have "modernized"; their institutional apparatuses have grown and have even become professionalized to a certain degree, most of all their institutions of repression. The state is less of a prisoner of society and is in a certain sense (i.e., in respect to the scope of its activities) more national. None of this, however, has made it more democratic, more equipped to satisfy the needs of its population, or more legitimately representative or even, it would seem, more stable.

The present hegemony has, however, affected more than bourgeois reason. For even that which originated as an alternative to bourgeois reason, the most direct and legitimate bearer of the liberationist promises of modernity over a long period of time yielded to the seductions of instrumental reason. Socialism could not establish itself except as "socialism as it actually exists," as Stalinism.

This is the modernity that has burst into a crisis proclaimed by new prophets, almost all of them apostates of their previous faith—socialism—or, at the very least, of radical liberalism. However, these prophets of "postmodernity"—on both sides of the Atlantic—also want to persuade us that the liberationist promises of modernity not only are now but have always been impossible, that no one can still believe in them after Nazism and Stalinism, and that the only thing real is power, its technology, its discourse.

The crisis of modernity as redefined by the complete dominance of instrumental reason follows the same course as the crisis of capitalist society, particularly as each of these crises has developed since the end of the 1960s. This form of modernity, of course, deserves no defense, nor should it be the object of any form of nostalgia, especially in Latin America. It was under its dominion that the task of satisfying the worst imperatives of capital were imposed upon us for the benefit of the bourgeoisie of Europe and the United States, beginning at the very moment in independence when the hegemony of historical reason over the consciousness of the Latin Americans was displaced, although without any loss of the prestige of the label of modernity.

The problem, moreover, is that the prophets of postmodernity and of antimodernity not only invite us to celebrate the funeral of the liberationist promises of historical reason and its specific form of modernity but, even more importantly, never again to pose the questions implied by that modernity, never again to struggle against existing power for the liberation of society, to accept from now on only the logic of technology and the discourse of power. Behind the smoke screen of this debate, it is impossible not to perceive the familiar spirit of those same forces that, after the crisis that led to World War I, organized themselves to attack and to attempt to destroy the very seeds of all utopias of equality, solidarity, and liberty. They were, of course, not totally successful. But historical reason was debilitated in the face of their onslaught. Today, these same forces seem to be emerging once again in search of final victory. On the other hand, the conjunction of both crises has had the effect that certain crossroads of debate concerning society have been turned into what appear to be genuine cul-de-sacs. This is particularly serious in respect to the debate concerning the problems of the dependent societies, societies constructed on the basis of extreme inequalities, societies that in no sense have succeeded in achieving a definitive eradication of the arbitrary and despotic exercise of power, not even in the limited sense that this has taken place in the advanced capitalist societies. Upon the dependent societies, such as those of Latin America, descends the weight of all the problems of the extreme concentration of power and, at the same time, those generated by the styles and levels of life characteristic of the capitalist development of Europe and the United States.

In Latin America, however, modernity has a more complex history than that which characterizes it as linked to the history of Euro–North America. Within this history there not only remain the elements of a proposal for an alternative rationality, but, even more importantly, these elements are again beginning to reconstitute themselves. This is true, among other reasons, because the logics of capital and instrumental reason have not been able, precisely because of the weakness of their development, to extinguish or to negate definitively those same historical meanings that, when revealed to the wonder of Europe at the beginning of the fifteenth century, engendered the onset of a new rationality. These meanings have been bruised and wounded but are by no means buried.

The Tension of Subjectivity in Latin America

In the 1960s, we Latin Americans discussed the problems of social reality and change in this reality. Now, however, we are desperate to establish our identity. What is behind this search for identity is that the formative elements of our reality have not abandoned their strained relationships among themselves: they are slowing down and rendering more difficult the historical sedimentation that could have compacted and made firm the foundation of our social existence and made less urgent, and perhaps less recurrent, the necessity of journeying, always, in pursuit of identity.

The present intersubjective universe of Latin America could hardly be presented as a culture constructed around defined nuclei of articulation or one composed out of materials that have completely fused. But this is due only in part to its past; in larger part it is due to the uninterrupted reproduction of its dependency, its position under Euro–North American domination. This is not only a question of subordination but, above all, a recognition that the very construction of this universe takes place as a function of this dependency.

One of the most insistent expressions of the internal tensions of Latin American intersubjectivity is the permanent note of duality in intellectual style, in sensibility, in imagination. This duality cannot be attributed simplistically to the opposition between the modern and the nonmodern, as the apologists of "modernization" have continually claimed. Rather, it relates to the rich, varied, and dense condition of the elements that nurture this culture but whose oppositions have not been completely fused into new meanings and consistencies that can be articulated autonomously within a new and distinctive structure of intersubjective relationships.

The plentitude and perhaps the precariousness of this process of the production of a new and autonomous cultural universe are related to the same factors that reproduce imperial domination and the hegemony of instrumental reason, factors that have been strengthened under the forces of "modernization."

Perhaps the best exemplar of the presence of this tension and this note of duality in the Latin American intelligentsia is Mariátegui.[1] A Marxist, today considered the greatest of Latin American Marxists, Mariátegui was also not a Marxist. He believed in God, explicitly. He proclaimed that it is not possible to live without a metaphysical conception of existence. And he always felt himself close to Nietzsche. Mariátegui's discoveries concerning the specificity of the social reality of Latin America cannot be understood outside of this tension in his thought and his entire orientation toward life, because outside of this tension these discoveries would perhaps never have been made. At the very least, all those who at the same time analyzed the same reality but whose sole attachment was to European rationalism accomplished nothing more than the search of our land for the reproduction of Europe.

The same tension permeates everything and everyone—or almost everyone—in Latin America. But this is not only a result of our reading European books while living in a completely different world. If it were only this, we would only be "Europeans exiled in these savage pampas"—as many have urged—or we could have as our only aspiration to be accepted as Europeans or, better yet, Yankees, as undoubtedly is the dream of many. We could not, consequently, cease to be all that we have never been and never will be.

It is a matter of the specificity or, if you wish, one of the meanings that are forming the Latin American identity: the relationship between history and time is here completely different than that which appears in Europe and the United States. In Latin America, what in these other histories is sequence is a simultaneity. It does not cease being a sequence. But it is pre-eminently a simultaneity. Thus, for example, what in Europe were stages of the history of capital, here form the layers of capital. In Latin America, the stages of capital coexist as layers: operative here is "original accumulation," competitive accumulation, monopolistic inter- and transnational accumulation. We cannot say that they are only stages in a sequence, for they function within a pyramidal structure of layers of domination. But neither can we completely deny them their condition as stages. Time in this history is simultaneity and sequence, simultaneously.

We have to deal with a different history of time and a different time of history. This is what a lineal or, even worse, unilineal perception of time, a unidirectional perception of history—such as that which characterizes the dominant version of Euro–North American rationalism under the hegemony of instrumental reason—cannot, in its own cognitive matrix, incorporate into its own modes of producing or rendering rationally meaningful its own perspectives. And it is also this which we ourselves, although forever anguished by the intimation of its presence, have also not been able fully to identify or to appropriate as our own historical meaning, our identity, as a cognitive matrix, because we were not able to free ourselves in time from that same rationalism.

Nevertheless, at least for many of us, this was the most genuine meaning of our searchings and perplexities during the period of the agitated debates over dependency. However, it is undoubtedly true that we were only able to glimpse it here and there. It is not therefore by any means accidental that it was not a sociologist but rather a novelist such as Gabriel García Márquez who, by good fortune or through awareness, discovered the path to this revelation, because of which, indeed, he merited the Nobel Prize. Thus, in what other way than the mythical-aesthetic could we become aware of this simultaneity of every historical time in the same Time? What other way than by converting all times into one Time? And what, other than mythical, could this Time of all times be? Paradoxically, this strange manner of revealing the nontransferable identity of a history turns out to be a rationality, for it renders the universe intelligible and renders intelligible the specificity of that universe. This, in my judgment, is what García Márquez essentially did or achieved in *One Hundred Years of Solitude*.

This relationship between history and time in Latin America exercises itself in other dimensions. The past runs through the present in a manner distinct from the way it existed in the European imagination before modernity. It is not the nostalgia of a golden age because of being, or having been, the continent of innocence. Among us, the past is or can be an experience of the present, not its nostalgia. It is not lost innocence but rather integrated wisdom, the union of the tree of knowledge with the tree of life that the past defends within us against instrumental rationalism as the form of an alternative proposal of rationality. Reality is seen, makes itself seen, as a totality, with all its magic. Rationality here is not a disenchantment of the world but rather the intelligibility of its totality. The real is not the rational except insofar as it does not exclude its magic. Juan Rulfo and José María Arguedas narrated this rationality from the privileged seats of our inheritance of the original rationality in Latin America.[2] But the title that gave it a name for universal communication, "magical realism"—entirely a *contradictio in termini* for European rationalism, the disenchanter of the world—came, perhaps not totally by chance, from Alejo Carpentier,[3] the most intellectual or, if you prefer, the most "European" of the Latin American narrators who had the audacity and the good fortune to make the "journey to the seed." Perhaps this is because there were few such as he in whom European intellectual formation could be carried to the boundary of all its tensions and reconstituted by the recognition of a "real miracle."

This relationship of tension between the past and the present, the simultaneity and the sequence of the Time of history, the note of duality in our sensibility, cannot be explained outside of the relations of domination between Europe and Latin America, the copresence of Latin America in the production of the original modernity, the excision of rationality and the hegemony of instrumental reason, in short, the stamping feet of modernization in Latin America.

It is because of this specific history, because of the noninterrupted production of our dependency in this history, that each time there is a crisis in European rationality and, consequently, in the intersubjective relations between the European and the Latin American, the process of sedimentation of our very subjectivity also enters into crisis, and we once again set forth in pursuit of our elusive identity. Today the reason that this quest is more urgent than at other times is surely that the criollo—the oligarchic culture that arose after the metamorphosis of modernity in Latin America—has lost, irrevocably, the social bases for its reproduction and is in advanced bankruptcy without it yet being clear what will replace its hegemony. For this reason, there is no doubt that this anguished demand for identity is stronger in all those countries and among those groups where the pressures of the transnational to form a new "criollo-oligarchic" culture, a new colonialism, have not succeeded in vanquishing what was created from the Indian and the Black, from all that is natively constituted in our intersubjective relations: have not yet succeeded in subordinating these cultural creations and leaving them once again chained in the shadows of domination.

That which is native in our culture is an unfinished product of the way in which the elements that emerge from the relationship of domination and conflict have been reorganized and rechanneled when the bases and the institutions of power were eaten away and partially demolished by the eruption of the dominated toward the front stage of history, in other words, when the basic elements of our subjective universe once again became original. With these elements a new utopia is being constituted, a new historical meaning, a proposal for an alternative rationality.

THE BASIS OF ANOTHER MODERNITY: THE OTHER PRIVATE AND THE OTHER PUBLIC

Undoubtedly, the most notable of the cul-de-sacs that have been made apparent by the current crises of instrumental reason and capitalist society is that which encloses the conflict between private property and state property in the means of production to such an extent that even the most general discussion of the relationships between state and society eventually comes to be structured around this dispute.

Of course, posed in these terms, the debate between the public and the private in the economy and the society cannot escape from its current entrapment. Both sides of the debate and of the conflict display, fundamentally, the same assumptions and categories of thought. The private is seen as the private sphere molded by capitalistic interest. That which is the state or the public is the state-public of the private sphere viewed in this manner, its rival perhaps but not its antagonist. In both perspectives, it is the same instrumental reason that bites its own tail. Although this cul-de-sac in the current debates is not confined to Latin America or even to the totality of the so-called Third World, we will here restrict our discussion to Latin America.

Two extreme positions compete for dominance in the economic orientation of present-day society. One is "really existing socialism," which we now know as that which was organized under Stalinism and for which the proposed total nationalization of the means of production, the mechanisms of distribution, and the decisions concerning the direction of the total operations of the economy are at its center. As received in Latin America, this idea has been influential not only in those proposals defined as socialist but also in the various shades of populism-nationalism-developmentalism. Seventy years later, we can be reasonably assured that we can proceed no further along this path as an attempt to attain a rational society from the point of view of the promises of socialism. The economy can only be developed until it reaches the limit where bureaucratic asphyxia becomes extreme. Neither equity, social solidarity, freedom, nor a producer's democracy can take root or be developed along this path.

The other extreme is the proposal of "neoliberalism," for which private capitalist property in the means of production and the "invisible hand" of the market—ideally free from any limitations, control, or orientation on the part of the state—are the sine qua non for the creation and generalized distribution of wealth and full political democracy. But this proposal—and certainly for a longer time than the seventy years of "actually existing socialism"—has proven, beyond any doubt and particularly in the experience of the immense majority of Latin Americans, that it also does not lead to equality, social solidarity, or political democracy.

In the historical experience that we currently live in and observe, this form of the private leads to the verticalism of the big business corporations, a likely equivalent of the "modernized" verticalism, of the bureaucracies of "really existent socialism" (i.e., liberalized through the reintroduction of greater market relations). And it is in the name of these proposals and of these interests that the freedom and democracy of society and of the state fail to be consolidated in Latin America, and their limited existence in the developed capitalist countries are once again threatened.

The current liberalization of the economy and of the state in the major countries of "really existing socialism" appears in the mass media not as what it actually is, the unveiling of the specific historical character of that experience, but rather as the definitive eclipse of the very idea of socialism. "Neoliberalism" can thus present itself as the only option effectively equipped to establish or to continue the course toward the development of wealth and democracy in contemporary society.

In Latin America today, few besides the immediate defenders of the domination of capital and its empires can with confidence believe in the songs of the siren of "neoliberalism." But at the same time, after the recent experiences of "really existing socialism," it is unlikely that the partisans of the nationalization of the economy by the state can be as numerous as they once were. Perhaps it is this and no other thing that is being expressed in the virtual paralysis of economic activity in our countries. All of them without exception are marking time, frequently for the short term, without the advancement of long-range projects or even many proposals in that direction. In fact, the debate between neoliberalism and the type of "neodevelopmentalism" that it opposes ("neo" because its themes and proposals, although the same as the old developmentalism, are now weak and barely audible) has been turned into a trap, a dead end from which there appears to be no exit.

It does not seem to me difficult to discover the source of entrapment of this debate, the fact that in opposition are the private capitalist sphere and the state capitalist sphere (i.e., two faces of the same instrumental reason), each masking its social agents that now compete for the center of control of capital and power: the private bourgeoisie and the bureaucracy (for some, the state bureaucracy). In the last analysis, in neither of them resides a solution to the urgent problems of our societies, much less the liberationist promises of historical reason.

Private capitalism or, more generally, private mercantilism implies an interest opposed to society as a whole; hence, it cannot be compatible with equity, with solidarity, with freedom, or with a democracy that is constituted by these factors except within the limits set by private interest. That which is the state or that which is the public of this private sphere is the exact expression of this limited compatibility: this accommodation emerges and imposes itself precisely when the ultimate logic of domination is in danger. And it only expresses itself in its limited forms under the pressure of the dominated. State capitalism, "really existing socialism," and the "welfare state" belong to the same family but perform within different contexts and fulfill different needs. Although the complete nationalization of the economy and the dominance of the state over society are presented as instruments of the global interest against the private, since domination and inequality are not extinguished or even approach extinction, the private is in fact being reestablished in these economies. Thus, the private bears the advantage of appearing as the necessary option when the bureaucratic asphyxia caused by the advance of the state smothers the dynamisms of production.

The private sphere seems, then, to be working. But the historical experience of Latin America permits the suggestion that the capitalist or mercantilist form of the private is not the only form possible, nor is the public, in the specific form of the state, the only other face for the private or for everything private. In fact, although this point is not usually formally made in the debate over these questions, there is another private and another public that not only formed a part of the previous history of Latin America but also continue to be active and are beginning to emerge within larger and more complex spheres of action.

By way of making this point more graphic, and not because I propose it as a desirable or effective option, I would offer at this point the example of the ancient Andean community and broach the question of its characteristics: Is it private or state-public? The answer is private. It functioned and continues to function. It functioned before imperial and colonial domination, and it functioned during the colony as the only sphere of reciprocity, solidarity, democracy, and freedom, as a refuge for the joy of solidarity under domination. It functioned later in the face of the onslaught of a liberalism already won over to instrumental reason, in the face of *gamonalismo*.[4] And it still functions in the face of capital. And it is private.

What I mean to suggest with this example is that there is another private, a private that is not capitalist, not mercantile. There is not only one sphere of the private. And this private functions effectively. How are we to name this sphere of the private? For the moment, conscious of the provisionality of the term, I propose naming it the "social-private" to differentiate it from the "egoist private."

I must reaffirm, however, that I am not in any manner proposing a return to an agrarian communitarianism such as that present in precolonial Andean history or even that existing today. Today's society, its needs and possibilities, are undoubtedly too complex to be enclosed and fulfilled within an institution such as this. At the same time, neither does this imply that such an institution can or cannot be a base, or one of the bases, for the construction of another rationality. After all, was it not under its impact on the European imagination that the history of European modernity and the powerful utopia of a rational society began?

By the same token, it should be clear that if I allude to the reconstitution of a private equivalent to Andean social community in Latin America, it is because in its present historical experience in the context of a complex and tremendously diversified society, it is possible to discern and observe this private sphere's mode of operation: communitarian and collective organization, democratically constituted and relying on reciprocity as the foundation of solidarity and democracy. Today it in fact constitutes one of the most widespread forms of organizing the daily life and experience of vast populations of Latin America in their dramatic search to organize themselves for survival and to resist the crisis and the logic of underdeveloped capitalism.

These forms of social experience cannot in any way be considered as simply conjunctural or transitory. Their institutionalization has already taken on sufficient weight that it can be recognized as consolidated social practice for a great many sectors of the population, especially those who inhabit the universe of the poor of the cities. And these are in many cases the large majority of the population. For example, in Peru, what is known as the *barriada*,[5] slums and shanty towns, constitutes about 70 percent of the urban population, which in turn is 70 percent of the national population. Not only because of the social existence of this majority but also because of its preponderance in the nation's populace as a whole, it would be no exaggeration to affirm that the *barriada* is today, particularly in respect to the constitution of a new intersubjectivity, the fundamental social and cultural experience of Peru in the last thirty years. And the new forms of the social-private are a central aspect of this experience.

Andean reciprocity has, then, given rise to present-day reciprocity among the most oppressed layers of the urban "modernized" society of dependent capitalism and underdevelopment in Latin America. And on its soil a new social-private has been constructed, an alternative to the dominant capitalist sphere of the private.

Two issues must be clarified at this point. First, there is no doubt that the capitalist sphere of the private is widely dominant in the country as a whole as well as in the overall urban population of the *barriada* and the layers of the poor among this population. Its logic, moreover, not only coexists but also undoubtedly penetrates and modifies the reality that emerges from solidarity and democracy. The institutions that have been formed on the basis of reciprocity, equality, and solidarity are islands in a sea dominated by capital in the urban world. They are part of this sea, and in turn they modify and exercise some control over the logic of capital. Second, these institutions do not exist dispersed and unconnected with one another. On the contrary, especially in recent decades, they have tended to articulate with one another to form vast networks that frequently cover the entire space of the nation. These institutions, in other words, are coming together to form—as did (or still do) traditional labor unions—specific sectors or national organizations. But in the case of the new organizations of the social-private, the linkages among sectors and the totality of sectors form an urban chain in a manner that does not necessarily imply a separate organization. In other words, the institutionalized sphere of the social-private tends to generate its own institutionalized public sphere that, nevertheless, does not necessarily have the character of a state. It does not convert itself into an institutional apparatus that is separate from the social practices and institutions of everyday life or society as a whole but instead is superimposed on top of these practices and institutions. The institutional sphere that articulates globally or sectorally the social-private has a public character, but it is not constituted by state power. Instead, it is constituted as a power in society.

Once these social-private institutions and their public sphere are established within the dominant context of the individual—private and its state—they cannot help but be affected by the latter or by the dominant logic of capital. Manipulation, bureaucratization, and the exploitation of power are evidence of the penetration and the performance of the individual-private, the logics of capital and its state. In spite of this, reciprocity, solidarity, and democracy resist. Nevertheless, they may be defeated and change their essence or disintegrate. This does happen and not infrequently. What is surprising, however, is that even under these conditions, the practices and institutions of the new private-social and the practices of its nonstate public institutions continue to persist, to reproduce themselves, to expand in number and kind, and to convert themselves into a new and vast network of organization of a new "civil society."

The fact that this process has spread and tends to reproduce itself in Peru is no doubt due to the violence of the crisis of that society, and, obviously, it is part of the crisis itself. An important part of the population has been driven by necessity in the face of the economic hardship to rediscover and reconstruct in a new and more complex historical context one of the deepest and most characteristic heritages of the rich and extensive Andean cultural experience.

This new social-private and its nonstate public articulation are viable. They are so viable and possess such a capacity for survival that they function under the most adverse and extreme conditions. It is of supreme importance to point out that it is precisely against these very conditions that the organizations of the social-private and the nonstate public allow for the satisfaction of the necessities of human survival. In other words, insofar as a social practice is based on solidarity, equality, freedom, and democracy, it is capable of allowing its bearers to survive in spite of and in resistance to the logics of the present power of capital and of instrumental reason. It is therefore neither arbitrary nor adventuresome to suggest that under favorable conditions, if they were not as today under the constant assault of an enemy who is the owner of power, these new social practices and their attendant public institutional networks would be able to not only allow for survival but also serve as a framework and a foundation of a truly democratic integration of society and, at the same time, open the possibility to achieve a full and differentiated realization of individual potentials (i.e., to realize the liberationist promises of a rational, modern society in the genuine meaning of these terms).

Latin America: An Option for Another Rationality

What is today spreading through and dominating the crisis of modernity in Latin America is not only the final dislodgement of historical reason, to the advantage of instrumental reason, but is also a species of culturalism whose central claim is the rejection of all modernity, including, of course, liberationist rationality itself, and the return to the particular characteristics of specific cultures as the sole legitimating criteria of social practices and their institutions.

Both of these sources of pressure on contemporary society converge in their interests. Together, in fact, they are the foundation of all the fundamentalisms that currently prosper in every latitude and in every doctrine. Both seek the sovereignty of prejudice and myth as principles of orientation for social practice, because it is only upon these that a defense can be made of all inequalities and all hierarchies, of all racisms, all chauvinisms, all xenophobia. In this respect, there are no major differences between North American fundamentalism and that of Le Pen in France, the racists of South Africa, the followers of Sun Yung Moon, the Islamic fundamentalists, and the Stalinists. This is because there exists no real incompatibility between the ideological hegemony of fundamentalism in the orientation of social practice and that of instrumental reason as a basis of domination. If this were not the case, one could not, for example, understand the peculiar doctrine of Jeanne Kirkpatrick concerning "traditional" autocracies.

Since Euro–North American rationality—one has to insist on its instrumental rationality—has been a part of colonialism and imperialism, which have not only exploited the labor of the world's peoples but also despised and destroyed, when they were able to, their cultures, the idea of a simplistic rejection of all modernity and rationality that has its attractions in many quarters. This is understandable, but we must not blind ourselves to the potential and actual contraband that under this attractive mantle dominant groups everywhere attempt to smuggle in to preserve their power against the growing pressures for the liberation of society.

It is necessary to point out that as the current crisis of capitalist society has become more visible and prolonged, faith in instrumental reason has been deteriorating in widening sectors of our societies, and correspondingly, the need for a different sense of historical meaning has been gaining in intensity and urgency; this is taking place on a universal scale. Paradoxically, particularly among the dominated peoples in our societies, this is what has engendered the demand for a break with European modernity, with Euro–North American rationality, and has resulted in a turn toward a purely culturalist particularism. But it has engendered equally the search for new foundations for a liberationist rationality in the heritages of those very cultures that Eurocentrism, once all-powerful, attempted to convince itself and others were alien to all rationality or had been totally sterilized by domination.

In the case of Latin America, it is a well-known fact that the rediscovery of the specific rationality of the dominated cultures has also involved the rediscovery of the same principles that were revealed to the European imagination at the end of the fifteenth century and that gave rise to the utopia of a liberationist modernity. The documentation of this fact is both vast and convincing.

It is not, then, as part of an artificial culturalism that the debate concerning the relationships between its own cultural heritage and the need for a new historical rationality has returned to front stage in Latin America. Most of all, I would suggest, it is because of the social experiences of vast collectivities that the principles of this cultural heritage can be recognized as bearers of a historical meaning opposed equally to the empire of instrumental reason and to an obscurantist culturalism. The social practices constructed from the warp and woof of reciprocity, equity, solidarity, individual freedom, and everyday democracy have proven their capacity in extremely adverse circumstances to be part of the new fabric of a liberationist ideology.

Here, it is necessary to add some precision to our argument. In the first place, it must be remembered that at the moment in which America created modernity simultaneously with Europe, its protagonists were those who wielded domination, the descendants of Europe. Their very condition as rulers prevented them from seeing that in the culture of the dominated, the "Indians," were to be found many of the elements from which European rationality had from the beginning been fashioned. When this relationship was obscured and banished by the ascendancy of the relationship between

domination and instrumental reason, the obstructed vision of the dominators became even more acute.

The oligarchic-criollo culture that was the privileged product of this
encounter is today in Latin America ending its time of domination. Un-
dermined and—in the majority of countries—its social foundations and
its sources of sustaining power in disintegration, this culture has ceased
to reproduce itself. Its passage left the imminent threat open to the final
enthronement of "modernization" within culture (i.e., the reign of instrumental reason). This might perhaps have happened if the period of the expansion of international capital that impelled "modernization" had not met
with its present limits and entered into a deep and prolonged crisis along
with the entire apparatus of power in these countries. Nevertheless, it is
in this context of crisis that social, ethnic, and cultural diversity has been
strengthened. Consequently, we are not living through a unilineal and unidirectional transition between "tradition" and "modernization," as so many
ideologues of "modernization" insist. On the contrary, it is a time of conflict and of crisis in society and in culture. The more underdeveloped the
regime of capital, the wider the cracks through which the global cultural
heritage that is foreign to capitalism reemerges. And to be sure, all this
has occurred with the emergence of the dominated to the front stage of
this conflict.

We do not have to infer from all this that the global, cultural heritage of
Latin America, or the culture that is being produced and inhabited by the
dominated, comes only from precolonial ancestral sources. Nothing of
the kind. It is fed from the wellsprings of ancient achievements of rationality in these lands, achievements that produced reciprocity, solidarity, and
the joy of collective labor. These sources conjoin with those that emanate
from the African experience, and together they preserve the integrity of
the tree of life—split, in other cultures, into the tree of life and the tree of
knowledge—preventing rationality from being distorted into a thin and
superficial rationalism. The flows from these sources merge with the currents of European and Euro–North American culture that do not cease
to influence us but that our previous heritage seeks constantly to separate
from, indeed to liberate from, the clogging sands of the "mere reason" of
power. More recently, cultural sources from Asia continue to contribute to
the enrichment of our multiple heritage, making it more complex, diverse,
heterogeneous, and abundant. This heritage, then, is neither debilitated
nor susceptible to being entirely absorbed by instrumental reason. The

peculiar tension of Latin American thought is constructed from the totality of this complex heritage.

There is no need therefore to confuse the rejection of Eurocentrism in the culture and instrumental logic of capital and North American and other imperialisms with some obscurantist demand to reject or abandon the original liberationist promises of modernity: most of all, *the desacralization of authority in thought and in society; liberation from social hierarchy, prejudice, and the myths founded upon prejudice; the freedom to think and to know; to doubt and to question; to express and to communicate; individual liberty freed from individualism; the idea of the equality and fraternity of all humanity and the dignity of every person.* Not all this originated in Europe. Neither was all of it fulfilled or even respected there. But it was with Europe that all this sailed to America.

Hence, the proposal of the social-private and its institutions of articulation in the nonstate public, as an alternative to the cul-de-sac into which we have been carried by the statists and privatists of capital and its power, is a Latin American proposal rooted in the perspective that Latin America is, as is no other existing historical territory, the most ancient and consistent provider of a historical rationality constituted by the confluence of the rational achievements of every culture. The utopia of a liberationist rationality of society in Latin America is not today only an illuminationist vision. Part of our daily life has become intertwined with it. It can be repressed, perhaps defeated. What it cannot be is ignored.

The Issues and the Risks

The issues that open at this point are large and many. I cannot attempt to approach or pose even the most important ones, much less discuss them in depth, within the limits of this discussion. But some of them must be stated.

In the first place, we are in the presence of a clear necessity to reformulate the problematic of the public and the private and not only within the debate in Latin America. Inasmuch as it seems to me somewhat easier to grasp the idea and the image of another sphere of the private, distinct from and ultimately opposed to the sphere of that private derived from and linked to private property and the apparatus of power that accompanies it, I believe that it is necessary to explore further the problem of the nonstate public (i.e., that public distinct from and also opposed to the state and to the public linked to it).

A primary aspect of this question of the public and the private is that in the relationship that is established between both these terms within capital and generally within every power that includes the state, the private appears as an autonomous sphere of practices and institutions that are defended and, at the same time, are articulated and expressed by the state. The dominant problem is that of the autonomy of the private sphere in relation to the state as well as the autonomy of the state to impose itself on society. It is probably because of this that in this contradictory relationship, the public institutions that link together diverse practices of civil society are not as visible as are the public institutions of the state. This is especially the case because the state is, by its very nature, a sphere of practice and institutions placed on top of and outside of the everyday life of civil society. On the other hand, in the emergent relationship between the social-private and the nonstate public, there does not exist—and there is no need to raise the question of—opposition and conflict, since here the public only exists as an aspect of the articulation of the prevailing social-private and could not exist in any other way except by altering its very nature and changing itself into a state. In contrast, every state can exist and generate and reproduce its specific institutions not only outside of but often in opposition to the characteristic institutions of civil society. Latin America has displayed throughout its entire history this peculiar disjuncture. And there is no doubt that in the debate over the state and civil society in Latin America, this is the question that poses the greatest confusion precisely because the conventional analysis begins with the presupposition of the correspondence between the institutions of the state and the character of civil society. As such, the conventional analysis precludes the questioning of the representativeness of the state even though all our historical experience weighs against this presupposition. And now under the crisis, this disjunction between society and the state reveals that representation has been for a long time in question.

This problematic raises the issue of freedom and democracy in relation to the public and the private that is critical in the current debate inside and outside of Latin America. As everyone knows, a school of thought of "Scottish–Anglo–North American" origins, dominant today in political theory, deals with the problem of individual freedoms as if they were the domain of the private and in need of defense against the penetration of the state-public. On the other hand, this affirms the necessity of order and authority whose exercise and defense requires the action of the state. Thus, a contradictory relationship is affirmed between freedom and order and authority, which in the last analysis is the same relationship that exists between the state and civil society.

From this perspective, the problem has no basis for a solution other than an empirical one. This is evident in the less than enviable history of the relationships between order and freedom, especially in Latin America. But our experience in this regard is hardly less propitious than some of the historical experiences of Europe.

I would suggest therefore that it is no surprise that it is not historical reason, liberationist reason, that governs practice as well as theory in the relations between freedom and order but that other reason, instrumental reason, even though the idea of political freedom itself was one of the achievements of modernity. This allows us to underscore the fact that the relationships between personal freedom and the needs of the global society or "order" appear in a radically different way in the context of the relationships between the social-private and the nonstate public, to the precise degree that the needs of the global society that the nonstate public expresses are not and cannot be anything other than the articulation of the needs of collective solidarity, of reciprocity, and of democracy with differentiated individual fulfillment. At the very least, this potentiality is constitutive of this relationship, in contrast to that which is contained in the relationship of mutual exteriority that obtains between the state and society and their respective public and private.

The defense of personal freedom and even of equality, given certain conditions, may not be all that difficult to achieve in the area of the private. The historical problematic has always been to constitute and assert them in the sphere of the public, for it is there that they are at risk. To assert personal freedom in the experience of the relationships between the private and the state has until now ultimately only been possible for some at the cost of others. There have always been not only those "more equal" than others but also those more free. In the alternate context, "order" could only be the realization of the personal freedom of everyone. But this is exactly what order does not achieve and cannot achieve in the relations between state and society. Order always serves the freedom of some over that of others. One can see that this relationship between the social-private and the nonstate public that is emerging in Latin America forces us to reformulate the problem of human freedom and democracy in a different light and from a different perspective. But let us return for a moment to the social-private as such, because this allows us to look in the direction of the problem of production and distribution and to consider their ramifications and bases in this new context. In particular, it is necessary to pose the problem of reciprocity, which I previously introduced as the basic principal sine qua non of the other private. Although the breaking down of reciprocity and its replacement by the market is fundamental to the mercantile or capitalist sphere of the private, in the social-private the market cannot occupy the same position and cannot have the same character.

Although the concept of the market in the current debate has been almost transformed into a mystical category, it is surely obvious to everyone that it represents a correlation of forces and nothing else. That is to say, it implies a relationship of power, a structure of power or a phase or moment of power. The rationality of the market therefore does not have to admit of any content, save that of the most instrumental reason. By its very nature, the market excludes reciprocity or can only accept it under exceptional circumstances as one of its means to achieve its own ends. Why? Because reciprocity is a special type of exchange: it is not necessarily based on exchange value and usually tends to be based on use value. It is not abstract equivalence, what things have in common, that counts, but precisely their diversity. In one sense it is an exchange of services that may assume the form of an exchange of objects, but not always and never necessarily. We find therefore that it is extremely viable to articulate reciprocity with equality and solidarity, an articulation that is the basis of the social practices that are now our object of exploration. Reciprocity is not a univocal category, nor is it a single form of practice, at least as it appears in the anthropological literature. Nevertheless, while the market implies fragmentation and a differentiation of interests in society and is attached to an atomistic vision of the world, reciprocity implies the articulation of the interests of society; it is part of a globalizing concept of the world.

For example, in Andean history reciprocity did not prevent the existence of either power or domination. It operated at two levels. It functioned at the base and at the apex of the structure of domination as a mechanism of solidarity, an exchange among equals. At the same time, it operated between the rulers and the dominated as a mechanism of articulation and solidarity among unequals. This indicates that reciprocity does not necessarily require equality. But in contrast to the market, it requires solidarity. In the market, persons function as exchanges of equivalent objects. In reciprocity, objects are all but symbols of the persons themselves. The market is impersonal, by nature. Reciprocity is personal.

In the current process of the constitution of the social practices we are discussing, reciprocity appears as linked to equality, to freedom and to democracy, not only to solidarity. This makes us visibly aware of the conflu-ence between the rationality of Andean origins and that which came from modern European modernity. If it is not for this fact completely free of the grip of domination, it still deserves to be studied in this new context as a principle of a new rationality, a product, in fact, of a history nourished by multiple and diverse histories. But it requires also to be perceived as part of a structure of power, not as a form of dissolution of all power. The ar-ticulated diversity involved in reciprocity—the social solidarity, the social equality, the personal liberty, as constituent elements of a new structure of democracy—does not imply the dissolution of all power. However *demos* it may be, it does not cease also to be *kratos*. This, furthermore, is what is in-volved in the formation of a public sphere for this new private. But it also implies a structure of power of a different nature than that in which the capitalist sphere of the private and the state are articulated: it is a power returned to the social. This surely must be what is being sought in the enor-mous pressure that can be observed being exerted everywhere today, the demand of the social to be politically expressed in a direct fashion but not necessarily in the state.

This is an issue too important to be omitted from the problematic under discussion. It is utterly necessary to make it clear that this new sphere of the private and new sphere of the public cannot achieve hegemony within social practice except to the degree that they are able to emerge as an al-ternative power to that which currently is in place. The present sphere of the private and its state will not fail to attempt to block, fragment, distort it or liquidate this emergence. There is no way that these new institutions can develop and consolidate except as a power capable of defending itself against the present power by ultimately triumphing over that power. But in contrast to other alternatives, this alternative of power is not only a goal but a path. And the path is being traveled.

It would not be appropriate to attempt to go beyond the limits of this discussion to open questions whose exploration would take us even fur-ther afield. The issues I have raised, I believe, are sufficiently important to initiate the debate. It is still necessary, however, to note certain qualifi-cations and a few clarifications.

Some may ask if the institutions of the social-private and the nonstate public—given that they are based on reciprocity and solidarity, although they now also incorporate equality, freedom, and democracy—are re-stricted to certain cultural areas, perhaps even ethnic areas where reci-procity is a central part of cultural history (as, for example, the case of

Andean culture), for it is not surprising that such practices and social institutions are present in Peru and other countries of the Andean world. But what have these practices to do with other areas of Latin America and especially with those of the Southern Cone?

There is no doubt that the new social practices that are establishing themselves as possible carriers of a new historical rationality find a more receptive and fertile soil where they intertwine their roots with previous historical heritages. This is surely the case with the populations of Andean origin. Nevertheless, abundant evidence exists of the presence of similar practices in virtually every sector of impoverished urban populations living under the prolonged crisis now in course in every, or almost every, Latin American country. As testimony to this, we need only to allude to the history of urban land invasions for the establishment of settlements, to their forms of organization, mobilization, and support. We are not that far distant, for instance, from the unfolding of that history in Chile as well as its subsequent repression there. On the other hand, while on the subject of Chile, recent investigations on the effects of the agrarian counterreform since 1973 have pointed out the formation of peasant communities in areas where before there only existed sharecroppers or tenants: groups of peasants have discovered that by joining their smallholdings and their scant resources, they could survive; individually, they could not. This discovery of reciprocity and of solidarity among equals as the very condition of survival is not, then, necessarily occurring only as a prolongation of particular ancient cultures, although in Latin America it would be difficult to deny the force of strong cultural contradiction. Equivalent social practices are in fact documented in almost all these countries. And this is not always a result produced by a limited need, such as survival, but rather of the need to find a collective historical meaning to persevere in the face of the collapse of those meanings that until now were dominant or effectively stable. The wide network of organizations in which the Christians of liberation theology, the poor, the persecuted, and nuclei of intellectuals and professionals have joined together in resistance in all of our countries is ample demonstration of this possibility.

In the recent experience of some countries, Peru, for example, certain names such as "self-management" (*autogestión*), "associative enterprises" (*empresas asociativas*, etc.) have been used as denominations of institutions, whose character has always been essentially bureaucratic, in order to present those institutions—indeed with much propagandistic success, especially outside Peru—as vehicles of direct democracy. What is most notable about this is that these were the work of political regimes, undoubtedly reformist, who sought to construct an institutional structure to affirm what in their view was a community of interests between entrepreneurs and workers or in general between all the social interests of the nation itself, while at the same time being clearly involved in the "modernization" of the apparatus of the state, especially its military and police sectors. This "modernization" of the state was almost solely responsible, according to all available information, for the raising of the foreign debt of Peru from some $800 million to about $10 billion in twelve years. This "modernization" of the state apparatus included the assemblage of a large sector of state capital whose management enormously increased the technobureaucratic stratum of society that, in turn, sought an alliance with international financial capital. The social groups linked to the entities called "self-managing" were viewed as a basis of the corporatist reorganization of the state, as a means of overcoming an extremely prolonged crisis of representation. The regime fell apart, principally a victim of its own contradictions, without achieving any of its objectives. And the crisis has reinforced for many the recurrent stereotype that any time in the past was better. In Latin America in recent decades, the experience of so many people has been so disastrous that they have come to believe that there will always be something worse waiting for them in the future. This may be the reason there has arisen the suspicion that the new social practices that characterize the social-private and the nonstate public will always be at risk of being co-opted, of being redefined or distorted for the social purposes as under Velasquismo.[6] Without doubt this risk is real, as is that of more open repression directed at the destruction of these practices and not only at their distortion. But what is of most concern in the present discussion is the insistence on the different nature and the different historical meaning of these current practices of the new private and the nonstate public compared to those of Velasquismo. I think that these, after all is said and done, are not difficult to discern.

It may be necessary to make a similar clarification in respect to all the political and ideological derivations associated with the category of "informality" that is put to so many uses today in Latin America. Here, it will be sufficient to underscore something that I have already touched on. In the world of the Latin American *barriada* (or *callamperias*), or of *favelas* (or *ciudades perdidas, rancherios,* etc.), the normative structures of the capitalist market and those of reciprocity and solidarity exist side by side, oppose one another, and make use of one another. A good part of the population moves flexibly between both normative universes according to their needs, an indication that their total adhesion and definitive loyalty to either universe does not yet exist. In this sense, not only social-psychologically but also structurally, this population continues to be marginal and forms a part of the great social diversity that today characterizes the structure of Latin American society. The "informal" economy is inhabited, in large measure, by this population, although another part of it corresponds to persons definitely won over by the logic and norms of capital and its interests. Indeed, it is this conflict between the perspectives belonging to the logic and the interests of capital and those belonging to reciprocity and solidarity that certain political initiatives seek to resolve in favor of the former.

Obviously, for neoliberalism, nothing could be more plausible than the economy called "informal." In that world, the roles of the market can operate with the maximum of possible freedom; the quality and price of what is produced (goods or services) are not subject to any controls; wages are not regulated by any legal structure; there is no social security, there are no vacations, compensations, or rights to unionize. No one pays any direct taxes, although everyone demands services from the state. No organization of the exploited will be tolerated. All of this allows for a complicated meshing of articulation between the large "formal" enterprise and the "informal" market and "informal" labor, the beneficiaries of which are obvious since no "informal" economy is in reality outside the global financial apparatus of capitalism of its respective country. And no one has demonstrated that the channels for the transfer of value and benefits between the "informal" and the "formal" economy have been closed. None of this should inhibit anyone from pointing out the exceptional energy and capacity of initiative that the "informals" put into motion every day in order to be able to not only survive in the severe circumstances of this crisis but also produce, earn, and obtain employment, income, housing, etc. at the margin and at times in resistance to the state. All of this undoubtedly can and must be further stimulated and developed. But can it also be oriented and channeled? And there is the problem. Will it be developed toward the full development of capital or toward solidarity, reciprocity, the direct democracy of producers?

We must be cautious. The choice is not drawn only between statism and controlism on the one side and freedom of the market and profit earnings on the other. The defenders of the latter present such freedom as the only real guarantor of democracy against the threat of statist totalitarianism from the first alternative of this choice. This dilemma is false. Each of these paths assuredly leads to the same place: to the verticalism of corporations that can and do compete with the state but are always profoundly articulated with the state. The split between the private sphere and the state is nothing other than a difference within the same instrumental rationality whose dominion has resulted in the present secular crisis and disorder.

Statism and capitalist privatism are actually nothing other than the Scylla and Charybdis of the navigators of our present history. We neither have to chose between them or fear them. The ship of the new liberationist rationality sails today with a new hope.

Translated from the Spanish and edited by Larry Carney

Notes

First published in the *International Journal of Politics, Culture, and Society* 3, no. 2 (Winter 1989).

Translator's Note: The "public" and the "private" of the title and text of this essay generally correspond to the Spanish neuter substantival forms "lo publico" and "lo privado" as used by the author. They are accurately translatable as "the public" and "the private" in the sense of "that which is public" and "that which is private." I have in places used this translation and at other places varied it with the terms "the public (private) sphere" or the "sphere of . . ." in deference to more familiar and less awkward English usage. As specific contexts within the text make clear, these latter terms are not to be understood as confined to the conceptual apparatus of the "public/private split" that informs most conventional political discussions in contemporary capitalist societies. As will be made plain in his subsequent argument, it is this very conceptual apparatus that, among other issues, the author wishes to call into question.

1   José Carlos Mariátegui (1895–1930), Peruvian writer and political activist, is generally regarded as the most original of the first group of Latin Americans to apply historical materialist analysis to the economic, social, and cultural problems of the region. His best-known and most characteristic work is the collection of essays *Seven Interpretive Essays on Peruvian Reality*.

2   Juan Rulfo (1918–1986) pioneered many of the literary techniques of the "magic realism" school of fiction in Latin America. These techniques are most clearly on display in the collection of his short stories of his native Mexico titled *The Burning Plain*. Peruvian writer José María

Arguedas (1911–1969) was a student of Quechua culture and wrote passionately of the tensions of Peruvian society revolving around the domination of the Indians by the Spanish-speaking minority.

3 Cuban writer Alejo Carpentier (1904–1980) dealt with the "tensions" of Latin American culture and social existence most trenchantly in his masterpiece, the novel *The Last Steps*.

4 *Gamonalismo* refers to the power structure based on the domination of the landlords over the Indian serfdom in the Andean countries of Latin America.

5 Although *barriadas* and other similar "marginal" urban settlements surrounding Latin American cities are often described as "slums" and "shantytowns," they typically display a highly heterogeneous assemblage of housing types, levels of living, and lifestyles. They are, however, largely outside the "regulated" or "formal" zones of settlement and provide both opportunity and refuge for masses of the urban poor and the economically straitened working classes.

6 Velasquismo was the ideology and practices of the reformist, corporatist military juntas that ruled Peru from 1968 to 1980. Juan Velasco Alvarado headed the first of these juntas (1968–1975).

2

THE AESTHETIC OF UTOPIA

It is a consistently demonstrated fact that the transformation of the world takes place first as an aesthetic transfiguration.[1] We must therefore admit that there is a fundamental relationship between utopia and aesthetics.

Why is utopia established and housed first in the realm of aesthetics? The question opens up a vast territory, the exploration of which will probably help us greatly to decipher some of the more obscure signs of contemporary passions, especially in a world such as Latin America, one constituted on the conflict over colonial domination. In particular is the knot that imprisons our current debate: the one formed on one side by the question of social liberation and on the other by that of identity (identities?).

Life Is Carved from the Same Wood as Dreams

We must inevitably begin on the path set by the question itself: in some strange way, utopia seems to be built of and to consist of the same material as aesthetics. It doesn't just reside there, like a human embryo in a test tube. There must therefore be a natural relationship between the two, not merely an external or contingent one. In this specific sense, we have to accept utopia as a phenomenon that is aesthetic in nature. That is not the same thing, however, as saying that utopia is nothing more than an aesthetic phenomenon.

If we accept that utopia is not a mere fantasy or arbitrary construct and thus is easily dispensable and even contemptible but instead is a project of reestablishing the historical meaning of a society,[2] the result is not simply that utopia fills the peculiar territory of the intersubjective relationships that we recognize as society's imaginary, where the realm of aesthetics lies. That in itself would be very important. But what's at stake, above all, is that there's an aesthetic sense in every utopia without which the antennas of the social imaginary wouldn't home in on a new historical meaning.

To put it in colloquial terms, we could say that one goes off in search of a new society, a new history, a new meaning (that is, a new rationality), not solely because the ruling order is suffering materially but most of all because it upsets us. Every utopia that subverts power also thereby implies a subversion of aesthetics. It is aesthetic in nature. This fact establishes a radical departure from the expectations of all those who accept or support the full legitimacy of the ruling order, of its particular rationality, even if they are its material victims and their struggle neither entails nor leads to any goal other than that of switching places and roles within the same order. In this sense, it isn't enough to fight the exploiters. Utopia cannot necessarily be located within this framework. For utopia to be present requires a constant struggle against exploitation, against every form of exploitation. The presence of utopia requires a struggle against domination, against every form of domination.

Along this same path, two questions come out to meet us. First, if utopia and aesthetics are made from the same material, shouldn't it also be the case that aesthetics is utopian in nature? Second, what does the material they have in common consist of, and where does it come from?

Both questions lead, or seem to lead, to the same answer. Utopia, any utopia, is born as a search for liberating a society from the present order and its specific perspective on rationality. Utopia projects an alternative for liberation in both dimensions and thus entails a subversion of the world in its materiality as well as in its subjectivity. Any aesthetic rebellion, for its part, likewise entails a subversion of the imaginary of the world, a liberation of that imaginary from the matrices that structure it and at the same time imprison it. Any new aesthetic is consequently utopian in character.

However, while every utopia is aesthetic in character, not all aesthetics are utopian in character. That trait is found only in a subversive aesthetic. Thus, though every utopia is indeed made of aesthetic material and appears first in the realm of aesthetics, not all aesthetics appear first in the realm of utopia. The relationship between the two is fundamental, no doubt, but this isn't a reciprocal symmetry. Utopia, any utopia, projects the dreams and hopes of the dominated but also of those who are not themselves dominated but figure among the "humiliated and outraged" of this world, in other words, those who find exploitation and domination, whatever form they take, offensive and humiliating for all men and women on Earth. That is why utopia couldn't exist without an aesthetic component. The realm of aesthetics, on the other hand, is a field disputed between a dominant matrix and an alternative of subversion and liberation. Aesthetics forms part of the structure of intersubjective relationships of power. But no subjective aesthetic alternative could help but have a utopian component. Power is, after all, the common enemy. The material that utopia and aesthetics share is rebellion against power, against any sort of power.

In this sense, any aesthetic approach that isn't resigned to commenting on what already exists, that aims to free the creative imagination—that is, the real imaginary, its ways of establishing itself, its forms of expression, and its ways of producing them—subverts the intersubjective universe of power. This is a moment and a part of establishing a new rationality, a new historical meaning for social existence, whether at the individual or the collective level, because it is only within, or in reference to, this process that the liberation of the imaginary really come about. It is precisely in this way that utopia emerges and takes up residence, first, in the realm of aesthetics.

By the same token, a critique of power relations, whether the existing ones or those presented as alternatives, that doesn't restrict itself to denouncing them but instead also tends toward arguing for an alternative rationality will not aim only at the materiality of social relations but also at the intersubjective relations that are interwoven with them. It will depart from and entail an aesthetic. Otherwise, it will expose its technocratic and reductionist character, whatever its name or formal claim on identity might be, its instrumentalism, its essential relationship with power, not with liberation.

It would perhaps not be very hard to accept that in the current historical crisis, this is one of the questions at issue. After all, the idea that "actually existing socialism" was the product of such technocratic reductionism is nothing new, in particular the theory imposed since Stalin of the "super-structure" as a "reflection" of the "base."

What Is New in the World

New utopias and aesthetics don't make their entrance on the world's stage every day, nor are they produced solely through the vision of intellectuals and artists. They emerge in the twilight of a historical period when, as is historically verifiable, the arriving world is again open to options for meaning, for alternative rationalities.

I suggest that this is what's happening today, though the dominant opinion is almost radically hostile. Indeed, we are faced with a peculiar paradox. Most people would agree that a period in history has come to an end. But the overwhelming majority would also agree that any utopia, any possibility for a utopia, has thereby been swept away from history. If that is indeed the case, the end of this period is neither more nor less than the end of history. The historical world will never open up any new options; it cannot become in any way new in the future.

With the fall of the Berlin Wall, the twentieth century can be said to have come to an end historically, even if its chronology still had another decade to run. Everything that was built as a real project of antibourgeois utopias in this period, culturally and politically, lies in ruins.

A historical period is more than a mere chronology. It is, first and foremost, a particular structure of meanings, that is, of rationality, a setting for conflicts among notions of rationality and for the hegemony of some of them. It is the exhaustion of the latter that brings the period to a close. Then, another conflict outlines the horizon of the period that is being established between the discourse of the triumphant order and the new utopia. This century has been the setting for the conflict between two forms of the same rationality, both heirs to the same instrumental version of European modernity: private capitalism and (the capitalism of?) "actually existing socialism." The curtain is going down with the triumph of the former.

Since "actually existing socialism" hid behind its name to take the place of socialist democracy in the imaginary of those facing social alienation, the winners pretend to see in their rivals' collapse nothing less than the death of the hope whose name had been usurped in the recently concluded contest.

Their powerful mass media seek to overwhelm us with the final victory of capital, its power, its technology, its discourse. They have, they tell us, forever dashed the dreams of liberation, of solidarity, of direct control over authority. Those were just tall tales, contemptible fantasies. An unmitigated pragmatism spreads like a steamrolling ideology, proclaiming the end of every (other) ideology in order to sing the funeral dirge for all hope of subverting this order. In fact, some fools even believe that it isn't just this period but all of History that is coming to an end, as in Fukuyama's *The End of History*,[3] and that the eternal kingdom of capital and the liberal order is beginning. All utopia seems indeed to have died, buried under the rubble of all the walls of "actually existing socialism" or locked inside the Weberian iron cage of instrumental reason.

E pur si muove. The world is already new again, in many senses. And above all, it already contains visible, active options for historical meaning. In other words, the time to come will not just be a prolongation of the past, as capitalist millenarianism now dreams, but rather a historically new time.

Let me point out some of the defining traits of what's new here. To begin with, we are living for the first time in a global world, literally: one that covers the entire globe. The consequences and implications of this on all sorts of phenomena and on all the categories concerning them (nations, states, ethnic groups, races, castes, genders, and so on) that form the vast family of power can barely be glimpsed today, and this is not the place to discuss them. But few, I am sure, would dare expect that the ruling power, that of capital, will manage to make its way unscathed through the time to come.

In the current debate on the crisis of modernity, it isn't just the rationality of the opposing notions of power that's at issue, as most critics of modernity maintain, nor is it certain that the latter can be definitively pushed aside in benefit of the eternal dominance of the elements of modern rationality that can be instrumentalized for the ends of power. More profoundly, the very foundations of the cognitive paradigm that allows for such instrumentalization are at stake. The dichotomous separation of subject and object, the sequential linearity between cause and effect, the exteriority and lack of communication between objects, and the ontological identity of objects—in other words, all that's contained in the image of the separation between the tree of life and the tree of knowledge, where the process of the disenchantment of the world begins—point to some of the central dimensions of the problem. The structures of the intersubjective universe that uphold the Eurocentrist domination in the intellect and in the material relations of power are at issue. This fact certainly raises the risk of a return of every sort of culturalist fundamentalism, even the imposition of the most malicious forms of Eurocentrism. But the doors to (re?) establishing a relationship of communication between society and the universe have also been opened.

We are still in the early days of the "technological revolution." So far it has made possible the globalization of the world and the spread of the dominion of capital over all peoples and the dominion of its beneficiaries, mainly Euro–North Americans, over all other groups in the world. But the technological revolution has also made it possible to question its epistemology, its worldview, its rationality. And we are barely at the threshold of the implications of this for the technological creations of the future, for the potential of technological reappropriation through other rationalities, for reoriginalizing other cultures, and, in the immediate future, for the possibilities of new aesthetic creations that all this opens up by producing new sounds, colors, new images and forms, and new realities.

The globalization of the world perhaps exacerbates the dominators' old fantasy: homogenizing the world. The world has certainly become more interconnected, and this points to a common pool of meanings. But it is, at the same time, more diverse, more heterogeneous. The "West" penetrates, disarticulates, other worlds. But in exchange it produces vast multitudes of migrating people. Migration has almost become a contemporary human condition. And the migrations aren't just of workers but are also cultural universes that penetrate and remake the "centers" of global power. What in Africa is still eroding and disarticulating a mode of social existence (Chinua Achebe, *Things Fall Apart*) turns into a genuine metamorphosis among migrants, producing in England a not-so-underground remaking of everyday life (Salman Rushdie, *The Satanic Verses*). And in Latin America, as in the Black United States, probably because these are the two oldest territories for colonial domination and migration, it sparks a process of cultural reoriginalization, that is, of producing original meanings, not merely subaltern versions of Euro–North American culture (José María Arguedas, *El zorro de arriba y el zorro de abajo*; Toni Morrison, *Song of Solomon*). The "Arguedian knot," that peculiar interweaving of utopia with social liberation and the liberation of identity, turns out to be not exclusive to the Andean world or to Latin America but rather to the whole historical world established by colonial domination. But perhaps it will also end up squeezing the dominators themselves in their own home countries.

Observing the trends through which the next worldwide accumulation arises, not only can we see the productive sectors, the technology, and the possible spatial distribution of control over this structure. The question can also be raised about the limits of commercialization of the labor force, beyond the problem of employment-unemployment-underemployment within capital. And one of the possible options for labor and for workers in view of these limits is the spread of reciprocal relationships in control over resources, production, and distribution, as is already happening and not just in Latin America. The conflicts within power and against it going forward cannot remain solely within wage-capital relations.

Utopia Time

Given these issues, it isn't too much to suggest that we are also involved in a process of reconstituting the imaginary from new facts that vie to appear, to escape their former prisons, to take shape and become images and systems of images. But all this can only be fully constituted to the degree that social existence as a whole may process, in the same movement, the need, as sentiment and as interest, to search and to struggle for alternative rationalities instead of those of the currently ruling power, its order, and its world. This potential aesthetic can only be established as an aesthetic of utopia.

And that's what it's all about. Though we can't see it through the dust cloud raised by falling walls or hear it through the blaring fanfare of capitalism, a new moment is now upon us in the never-ending struggle and the ever death-defying hope that authority can be replaced by freedom, and the ethics of interest can be replaced by the ethics of solidarity.

This hope is very ancient yet new. At the threshold of the new period, it was remade in the vast revolutionary wave that swept the planet of capital in the 1960s, the epicenter of which was Paris, May 1968. The idea of direct democracy—direct control over authority, solidarity, and individual freedom—could be rediscovered and restored based on that. That was the precise sign that the whole historical period just finished had been exhausted and that a new utopia of struggle against alienation had arrived.

The utopia of the time to come is now among us. The more polished and precise, the more completely the edifice of "actually existing socialism" has collapsed. The more urgent, the more completely private capitalism has won and the more global its dominion has become.

Latin America: Celebrating the Origin

Latin America enters this horizon as the region best suited for the history of the time to come. Perhaps it is no mere coincidence, after all, that the debate over aesthetics and society has now become not just more intense here but, above all, deeper and richer (Juan Acha, Mirko Lauer, and Néstor

García Canclini, among others) than anywhere else. Because the utopia of social liberation and the utopia of identity can only be resolved together in Latin America, not one without the other, an aesthetic of utopia will be required here more than anywhere else in this world.

What the culture of the dominators dishonors, precludes, or hides, especially in cultures of colonial origin, stuck in the labyrinth of an uncertain identity, is almost always what the dominated speak, dream, or love: the ways they relate to forms, to color, to sound, to their bodies, and to the world; everything they do or avoid doing to satisfy themselves or fulfill themselves without appealing to the dominators or asking for permission; the ways they free themselves from the matrices of forgetting or memory, which are imposed on them like a lock on the cage of domination; and, above all, the glory of the celebration against instrumental reason.

Domination imposes imitation on its victims, then shame. Domination pushes them to simulate, then condemns them, and produces hybridity and disgrace. Criollo oligarchy culture was the long-term form that this imposition took in the period preceding capitalist globalism. But the hegemony of that culture lies in ruin. Its final images and its aesthetic of imitation, limitation, simulation, and hybridity are dissipating, while the presence of the dominated grows stronger and more vivid in the remaking of the intersubjective universe in Latin America. The Indian and Black worlds are leading to the re-creation of all the rhythms, all the threads of relationship to the universe, to their own reception of what is coming from globalization and all that's new in the world. There is an effective process of reorginalizing culture in Latin America, because each of the elements that are remaking it is new: Indianness, Blackness, and all the rest in the framework of today's new world. The dominators, however, are new as well. And the birth of this new history, which may bring about the liberation of the imaginary of the dominated and the subversion of the world, is not only unknown to them but in fact makes them actively hostile. Now, they are bent on replacing criollo-oligarchic culture with its colonial-transcolonial equivalent. To modernize is to Europeanize, the non-European is exotic, and we can't go on being exotic, as one of their most famous actors has now proclaimed (Vargas Llosa, *Le Nouvel Observateur*, 1966). But even scraping themselves raw against the jagged edges of Europeanization would only get them as far as a new simulation. Haven't they spent their entire history pretending to be what they never were? And isn't that exactly what engineered the dark labyrinth that forms our identity issue?

In Latin America, the struggle against class domination, against color discrimination, against cultural domination also runs through the road of returning honor to everything that culture dishonors; of granting freedom to that which forces us to hide in the labyrinths of subjectivity; of ceasing to be what we've never been, what we'll never be, what we don't have to be. In order to begin, in short, the process requires reorginalizing culture and employing with it the materials that will return to this celebration its privileged space in existence.

Lima, Summer 1990

Notes

First published in *Hueso Húmero* (Lima), no. 27 (December 1990): 32–42.

1   See, for example, Lunn, *Marxism and Modernism*.
2   Quijano, *Modernidad, identidad y utopía en América Latina*.
3   Fukuyama's book is actually a crude and simplistic version of Alexandre Kojève's thesis. See Auffret, *Alexandre Kojève*.

3

COLONIALITY AND MODERNITY/RATIONALITY

The conquest of the societies and the cultures that inhabit what today is called Latin America began the constitution of a new world order, culminating five hundred years later in a global power covering the whole planet. This process implied a violent concentration of the world's resources under the control and for the benefit of a small European minority and above all of its ruling classes. Although occasionally moderated when faced with the revolt of the dominated, this process has continued ever since. But now during the current crisis, such concentration is being realized with a new impetus in a way perhaps even more violent and on a much larger global scale. The "Western" European dominators and their Euro–North American descendants are still the principal beneficiaries, together with the non-European part of the world that is not quite former European colonies, Japan mainly, and mainly their ruling classes. The exploited and the dominated of Latin America and Africa are the main victims.

A relation of direct, political, social, and cultural domination was established by the Europeans over the conquered of all continents. This domination is known as a specific Eurocentered colonialism. In its political, above all formal and explicit, aspect, this colonial domination has been defeated in the large majority of the cases. America was the first stage of that defeat and afterward, since World War II, Asia and Africa. Thus, the Eurocentered colonialism, in the sense of a formal system of political domination by Western European societies over others, seems a question of the past.

Its successor, Western imperialism, is an association of social interests between the dominant groups (social classes and *ethnies*) of countries with unequally articulated power rather than an imposition from the outside.

However, that specific colonial structure of power produced the specific social discriminations that later were codified as "racial," "ethnic," "anthropological," or "national" according to the times, agents, and populations involved. These intersubjective constructions, products of Eurocentered colonial domination, were even assumed to be "objective," "scientific," categories, thus of a historical significance, that is, as natural phenomena not referring to the history of power. This power structure was and still is the framework within which operate the other social relations of classes or estates.

In fact, if we observe the main lines of exploitation and social domination on a global scale, the main lines of world power today, and the distribution of resources and work among the world population, it is very clear that the large majority of the exploited, the dominated, and the discriminated against are precisely the members of the "races," "ethnies," or "nations" into which the colonized populations were categorized in the formative process of that world power, from the conquest of America and onward.

In the same way, in spite of the fact that political colonialism has been eliminated, the relationship between the European—also called "Western"—culture and the others continues to be one of colonial domination. It is not only a matter of the subordination of the other cultures to the European in an external relation; we have also to do with a colonization of the other cultures, albeit in differing intensities and depths. This relationship consists, in the first place, of a colonization of the imagination of the dominated; that is, the relationship acts in the interior of that imagination and, in a sense, is a part of it.

In the beginning colonialism was a product of a systematic repression, not only of the specific beliefs, ideas, images, symbols, or knowledge that were not useful to global colonial domination, while at the same time the colonizers were expropriating from the colonized their knowledge, especially in mining, agriculture, and engineering, as well as their products and work. The repression fell, above all, over the modes of knowing, of producing knowledge, of producing perspectives, images and systems of images, symbols, and modes of signification over the resources, patterns, and instruments of formalized and objectivized expression, intellectual or visual. This was followed by the imposition of the use of the rulers' own patterns of expression and of their beliefs and images with reference to the supernatural. These beliefs and images served not only to impede the cultural production of the dominated but also as a very efficient means of social and cultural control when the immediate repression ceased to be constant and systematic.

The colonizers also imposed a mystified image of their own patterns of producing knowledge and meaning. At first, they placed these patterns far out of reach of the dominated. Later, they taught them in a partial and selective way in order to co-opt some of the dominated into their own power institutions. Then, European culture was made seductive: it gave access to power. After all, beyond repression, the main instrument of all power is its seduction. Cultural Europeanization was transformed into an aspiration. It was a way of participating and later to reach the same material benefits and the same power as the Europeans: namely, to conquer nature, in short for "development." European culture became a universal cultural model. The imaginary in the non-European cultures could hardly exist today and, above all, reproduce itself outside of these relations.

The forms and the effects of that cultural coloniality have been different as regards times and cases. In Latin America, the cultural repression and the colonization of the imaginary were accompanied by a massive and gigantic extermination of the Natives, mainly by their use as an expendable labor force, in addition to the violence of the conquest and the diseases brought by Europeans. Between the Aztec-Maya-Caribbean and the Tawantinsuyan (or Inca) areas, about sixty-five million inhabitants were exterminated in a period of less than fifty years. The scale of this extermination was so huge that it involved not only a demographic catastrophe but also the destruction of societies and cultures. The cultural repression and the massive genocide together turned the previous high cultures of America into illiterate peasant subcultures condemned to orality, that is, deprived of their own patterns of formalized, objectivized, intellectual, and artistic or visual expression. Henceforth, the survivors would have no other modes of intellectual and artistic or visual formalized and objectivized expressions except through the cultural patterns of the rulers, even if subverting them in certain cases to transmit other needs of expression. Latin America is, without doubt, the most extreme case of cultural colonization by Europe.

In Asia and in the Middle East, the high cultures could never be destroyed with such intensity and profundity. But they were nevertheless placed in a subordinate relation not only in the European view but also in the eyes of their own bearers. Through the political, military, and technological power of its foremost societies, European or Western culture imposed its paradigmatic image and its principal cognitive elements as the norm of orientation on all cultural development, particularly the intellectual and the artistic. That relationship consequently became a constitutive part of the conditions of reproduction of those societies and cultures that were pushed into Europeanization of everything or in part.

In Africa, cultural destruction was certainly much more intensive than in Asia but less than in America. Nor did the Europeans there succeed in the complete destruction of the patterns of expression, in particular of objectification and visual formalization. What the Europeans did was to deprive Africans of legitimacy and recognition in the global cultural order dominated by European patterns. The former was confined to the category of the "exotic," that is, doubtless what is manifested, for example, in the utilization of the products of African artistic expression as motive, starting point, and source of inspiration for the art of Western or Europeanized African artists but not as a mode of artistic expression of its own, of a rank equivalent to the European norm. And that exactly identifies a colonial view.

Coloniality, then, is still the most general form of domination in the world today, once colonialism as an explicit political order was destroyed. Coloniality doesn't exhaust, obviously, the conditions or the modes of exploitation and domination between peoples. But coloniality hasn't ceased to be, for five hundred years, their main framework. The colonial relations of previous periods probably did not produce the same consequences, and above all, they were not the cornerstone of any global power.

"Race" and Coloniality of Power

Coloniality of power was conceived together with America and Western Europe and with the social category of "race" as the key element of the social classification of colonized and colonizers. Unlike in any other previous experience of colonialism, the old ideas of superiority of the dominant and the inferiority of the dominated under European colonialism were mutated in a relationship of biologically and structurally superior and inferior.[1]

The process of Eurocentrification of the new world power in the following centuries gave way to the imposition of such a "racial" criteria to the new social classification of the world population on a global scale. So, in the first place, new social identities were produced all over the world: "whites," "Indians," "Negroes," "yellows," and "olives," using physiognomic traits of the peoples as external manifestations of their "racial" nature. Then, on that basis the new geocultural identities were produced: European, American, Asiatic,

African, and, much later, Oceania. During European colonial world domination, the distribution of work of the entire world capitalist system between salaried, independent peasants, independent merchants, and slaves and serfs was organized basically following the same "racial" lines of global social classification, with all the implications for the processes of nationalization of societies and states, and for the formation of nation-states, citizenship, democracy, and so on around the world. Such distribution of work in the world capitalist system began to change slowly with the struggles against European colonialism, especially after World War I, and with the changing requirements of capitalism itself. But distribution of labor is by no means finished, since Eurocentered coloniality of power has proved to be longer lasting than Eurocentered colonialism. Without distribution of labor, the history of capitalism in Latin America and other related places in the world can hardly be explained.[2]

So, coloniality of power is based upon "racial" social classification of the world population under Eurocentered world power. But coloniality of power is not exhausted in the problem of "racist" social relations. The coloniality of power pervaded and modulated the basic instances of the Eurocentered capitalist colonial/modern world power to become the cornerstone of this coloniality of power.

Eurocentrism, Cultural Coloniality, and Modernity/Rationality

During the same period as European colonial domination was consolidating itself, the cultural complex known as European modernity/rationality was being constituted. The intersubjective universe produced by the entire Eurocentered capitalist colonial power was elaborated and formalized by the Europeans and established in the world as an exclusively European product and as a universal paradigm of knowledge and of the relation between humanity and the rest of the world. Such confluence between coloniality and the elaboration of rationality/modernity was not in any way accidental, as is shown by the very manner in which the European paradigm of rational knowledge was elaborated. In fact, the coloniality of power had decisive implications in the constitution of the paradigm, associated with the emergence of urban and capitalist social relations, which in their turn could not be fully explained outside colonialism and coloniality, particularly not as far as Latin America is concerned. The decisive weight of coloniality in the constitution of the European paradigm of modernity/rationality is clearly revealed in the actual crisis of that cultural complex. Examining some of the basic questions of that crisis will help to illuminate the problem.

The Question of the Production of Knowledge

For a start, in the current crisis of the European paradigm of rational knowledge, the latter's fundamental presupposition is questioned: namely knowledge as a product of a subject-object relation. Apart from the problems of validation of knowledge implied, that presupposition raises other problems worthy of a brief presentation here.

First, in that presupposition, the "subject" is a category referring to the isolated individual because it constitutes itself in itself and for itself, in its discourse and in its capacity of reflection. The Cartesian "cogito, ergo sum" means exactly that. Second, the "object" is a category referring to an entity not only different from the "subject" individual but also external to the latter by its nature. Third, the "object" is also identical to itself because it is constituted by "properties" that give it its identity and define it; that is, the properties demarcate the "object" and at the same time position it in relation to the other "objects."

What is in question in this paradigm is, first, the individual and individualist character of the "subject," which like every half-truth falsifies the problem by denying intersubjectivity and social totality as the production sites of all knowledge. Second, the idea of "object" is incompatible with the results of current scientific research, according to which the "properties" are modes and times of a given field of relations. Therefore, there is not much room for an idea of identity as ontologically irreducible originality outside the field of relations. Third, the externality of the relations between the "subject" and the "object," founded on differences of nature, is not only an arbitrary exaggeration of the differences, since current research rather leads to the discovery that there exists a deeper communication structure in the universe. Much more important and decisive is that in such a cognitive perspective, there is implied a new radical dualism: divine reason and nature. The "subject" is bearer of "reason," while the "object," is not only external to it but also different in nature. In fact, it is "nature."

One can, of course, recognize in the idea of "subject" as an isolated individual an element and an instance of the process of liberation of the individual with respect to the ascriptive social structures that imprisoned it in Europe. The latter condemned the individual to one single place and social role during its entire life, as happens in all societies with rigidly fixed hierarchies sustained by violence and by ideologies and corresponding imagery. This was the case of the premodern European cultures/societies. That liberation was a social and cultural struggle associated with the emergence of social relations of capital and of urban life. But, on the other hand, that proposal is today inadmissible in the current field of knowledge. The differentiated individual subjectivity is "real," but it is not an entity, so it doesn't exist only vis-à-vis itself or by itself. It exists as a differentiated part of, but not separated from, an intersubjectivity or intersubjective dimension of social relationship. Every individual discourse, or reflection, remits to a structure of intersubjectivity. The former is constituted in and vis-à-vis the latter. Knowledge in this perspective is an intersubjective relation for the purpose of something, not a relation between an isolated subjectivity and that something.

Probably it is not accidental that knowledge was considered then in the same way as property, as a relation between one individual and something else. The same mental mechanism underlies both ideas at the point when modern society was emerging. Nevertheless, property, like knowledge, is a relation between people for the purpose of something, not a relation between an individual and something. These phenomena differ in that the property relation exists in a material as well as an intersubjective manner; knowledge, on the other hand, exists only as an intersubjective relationship.

It seems, then, that one can demonstrate the association between individualism/dualism and the European social and cultural conflicts at the time when the main European paradigm of rationality was elaborated. But in that individualism/dualism there is another component, the explanation of which is not exhausted in the internal context of Europe: the "Other" is totally absent or is present, can be present, only in an "objectivized" mode.

The radical absence of the "Other" not only postulates an atomistic image of social existence in general; that is, it denies the idea of the social totality. As European colonial practice was to show, the paradigm also made it possible to omit every reference to any other "subject" outside the European context, that is, to make invisible the colonial order as totality, at the same moment as the very idea of Europe was establishing itself precisely in relation to the rest of the world being colonized. The emergence of the idea of the "West" or of "Europe" is an admission of identity, that is, of relations with other cultural experiences, of differences with other cultures. But, to that "European" or "Western" perception in full formation, those differences were admitted primarily above all as inequalities in the hierarchical sense. And such inequalities are perceived as being of nature: only European culture is rational, as it can contain "subjects"; the rest are not rational, as they cannot be or harbor "subjects." As a consequence, the other cultures are different in the sense that they are unequal, in fact inferior, by nature. They only can be "objects" of knowledge, domination practices, or both. From that perspective, the relation between European culture and the other cultures was established and has been maintained as a relation between "subject" and "object." It blocked, therefore, every relation of communication, of interchange of knowledge and of modes of producing knowledge between the cultures, since the paradigm implies that between "subject" and "object" there can be but a relation of externality. Such a mental perspective, enduring as practice for five hundred years, could only have been the product of a relation of coloniality between Europe and the rest of the world. In other terms, the European paradigm of rational knowledge was elaborated not only in the context of but also as part of a power structure that involved the European colonial domination over the rest of the world. This paradigm expressed, in a demonstrable sense, the coloniality of that power structure.

As has been widely discussed especially since World War II, the formation and the development of certain disciplines, such as ethnology and anthropology, have always shown that kind of "subject-object" relations between the "Western" culture and the rest. By definition, the other cultures are the "object" of study. Such studies about the Western cultures and societies are virtually nonexistent except as ironical parodies ("The ritual among the Nacirema"—an anagram of "American"—is a typical example).

The Question of Totality in Knowledge

In spite of its absence in the Cartesian paradigm, the intellectual necessity of the idea of totality, especially in relation to social reality, was present in the European debate, early on in the Iberian countries (Victoria, Suárez) and in the preservation of power defended by the Catholic Church and the Crown, and in France somewhat later (eighteenth century) and then already as a key element of social criticism and of alternative social proposals. Above all, from Saint-Simon, the idea of social totality was spread together with proposals of revolutionary social change, in confrontation with the atomistic perspective of social existence then predominant among the empiricists and among the adherents of the existing social and political order. In the twentieth century, totality became a perspective and a category generally admitted in scientific investigations, especially those about society.

European-Western rationality/modernity is constituted not only in a disputatious dialogue with the church and with religion but also in the very process of restructuration of power, on the one hand, in capitalist and urban social relations and nation-states and, on the other, in the colonization of the rest of the world. This was probably not divorced from the circumstance that the idea of social totality was developed according to an organicist image, which led to adopting a reductionist vision of reality.

In fact, that perspective was certainly useful to introduce and to fix the idea of social totality, that is, society. But it was also instrumental in making the same with two other ideas, the first of which is society as a structure of functional relations among each and every one of the parts and therefore linked to the action of one sole logic and thus a closed totality. This led later to a systemic idea of totality in structural-functionalism. The other idea was society as an organic structure, where the parts are related according to the same rules of hierarchy between the organs as the image we have of every organism and in particular the human one. Where there exists a part ruling the rest (the brain)—though it cannot expunge them in order to exist—the rest (in particular the extremities) cannot exist without being subordinately related to the ruling part of the organism.

It is an image diffused with the enterprise and the relations between entrepreneurs and workers, prolonging the legend of Menenius Agrippa's ingenious discourse in the beginning of the Roman Republic, which was to dissuade the first strikers in history: the owners are the brain, and the workers are the arms that form society together with the rest of the body. Without the brain, the arms would be meaningless, and without the latter, the brain could not exist. Both are necessary in order to keep the rest of the body alive and healthy, without which neither the brain nor the arms could exist. Kautsky's proposal, adopted by Lenin, is a variant of this image, where the proletarians are unable by themselves to elaborate their class-consciousness, and the bourgeois intelligentsia, the petite bourgeoisie, or both are the ones who have to teach it to them. Not by accident, Lenin explicitly argued already in his polemic with the Russian Populists ("Who are the Friends of the People") that society is an organic totality. In Latin America, the image has been used repeatedly, recently, for instance, by Jaime Paz Zamora,[3] in a journalist interview, referring to the relation between the political parties and the trade unions, between the intellectuals and the workers in Bolivia: the parties are the head, the unions are the feet. This idea frequently impregnates the practices of most of the political parties and their popular "bases."

This organicist concept of social totality, of society, is not incompatible with the general paradigm of knowledge as a subject-object relation or its systemic variant. They are an alternative option in the atomistic perspective of reality, but they sustain themselves in the same paradigm. However, during the nineteenth century and a great part of the twentieth, social criticism and the proposals of social change could be propped up by the organic view, because the latter made manifest the existence of power as articulator of society. It thus contributed to establishing and debating the question of power in society.

On the other hand, those organicist ideas imply the presupposition of an historically homogenous totality, in spite of the fact that the order articulated by colonialism was not homogenous. Hence, the colonized part was not, at bottom, included in that totality. As is well known, in the Europe of the Enlightenment the categories of "humanity" and "society" did not extend to the non-Western peoples, or only did so in a formal way, in the sense that such recognition had no practical effects. In any case, in accord with the organic image of reality, the ruling part, the brain of the total organism, was Europe and, in every colonized part of the world, the Europeans. The well-known claptrap that the colonized peoples were the "white man's burden" (Kipling) is directly associated with that image.

In this way, finally, the ideas of totality, which elaborated an image of society as a closed structure articulated in a hierarchic order with functional relations between its parts, presupposed a unique historical logic to the historical totality, and a rationality consisting in the subjection of every part to that unique total logic. This leads to conceiving society as a macro-historical subject endowed with a historical rationality, with a lawfulness that permits predictions of the behavior of the whole and of all its part as well as the direction and the finality of its development in time. The ruling part of the totality incarnated, in some way, that historical logic with respect to the colonial world, that is, Europe. Not surprisingly then, history was conceived as an evolutionary continuum from the primitive to the civilized, from the traditional to the modern, from the savage to the rational, from precapitalism to capitalism, etc. And Europe thought of itself as the mirror of the future of all the other societies and cultures, as the advanced form of the history of the entire species. What does not cease to surprise, however, is that Europe succeeded in imposing that "mirage" on the practical totality of the cultures that it colonized and, much more, that this chimera is still so attractive to so many.

The Epistemological Reconstitution: De-Colonization

The idea of totality in general is today questioned and denied in Europe by not only the perennial empiricists but also an entire intellectual community that calls itself postmodernist. In fact, in Europe the idea of totality is a product of colonial/modernity. And it is demonstrable, as we have seen above, that the European ideas of totality led to theoretical reductionism and to the metaphysics of a macrohistorical subject. Moreover, such ideas have been associated with undesirable political practices behind a dream of the total rationalization of society.

It is not necessary, however, to reject the whole idea of totality in order to divest oneself of the ideas and images with which it was elaborated within European colonial/modernity. What is to be done is something very different: to liberate the production of knowledge, reflection, and communication from the pitfalls of European rationality/modernity.

Outside the "West," virtually in all known cultures, every cosmic vision, every image, in other words, all systematic production of knowledge is associated with a perspective of totality. But in those cultures, the perspective of totality in knowledge includes the acknowledgment of the heterogeneity of all reality; of the irreducible, contradictory character of the latter; of the legitimacy, that is, the desirability, of the diverse character of the components of all reality and therefore of the social. The idea of social totality, then, not only does not deny but also depends on the historical diversity and heterogeneity of society, of every society. In other words, social totality not only does not deny but also requires the idea of an "Other" that is diverse, different. That difference does not necessarily imply the unequal nature of the "Other" and therefore the absolute externality of relations, the hierarchical inequality, or the social inferiority of the Other. The differences are not necessarily the basis of domination. At the same time—and because of that—historical-cultural heterogeneity implies the copresence and the articulation of diverse historical "logic" around one of them, which is hegemonic but in no way unique. In this way, the road is closed to all reductionism as well as to the metaphysics of a historical macrosubject capable of its own rationality and of historical teleology, of which individuals and specific groups—classes, for instance—would hardly be carriers or missionaries.

The critique of the European paradigm of rationality/modernity is indispensable; even more, it is urgent. But it is doubtful if the criticism consists of a simple negation of all its categories, of the dissolution of reality in discourse, of the pure negation of the idea and the perspective of totality in cognition. It is necessary to extricate oneself from the linkages between rationality/modernity and coloniality, first of all, and definitely from all power that is not constituted by free decisions made by free people. It is the instrumentalization of the reasons for power, of colonial power in the first place, that produced distorted paradigms of knowledge and spoiled the liberating promises of modernity. The alternative, then, is clear: the destruction of the coloniality of world power. First of all, epistemological decolonization, as decoloniality, is needed to clear the way for new intercultural communication, for an interchange of experiences and meanings, as the basis of another rationality that may legitimately pretend to some universality. Nothing is less rational, finally, than the pretension that the specific cosmic vision of a particular *ethnie* should be taken as universal rationality even if such an *ethnie* is called Western Europe, because this is actually intended to impose a provincialism as universalism.

The liberation of intercultural relations from the prison of coloniality also implies the freedom of all peoples to choose, individually or collectively, such relations: a freedom to choose between various cultural orientations and, above all, the freedom to produce, criticize, change, and exchange culture and society. This liberation is part of the process of social liberation from all power organized as inequality, discrimination, exploitation, and domination.

Notes

First published in Spanish in *Perú Indígena* 13, no. 29 (1992): 11–20. English translation by Sonia Therborn, in *Globalizations and Modernities: Experiences, Perspectives and Latin America*, Stockholm, FRN-Report, 1999: 5, 1. Reprinted in *Cultural Studies* 21, nos. 2–3 (March/May 2007): 168–78.

1 Here is not the place for a more detailed discussion on the origins of the idea of "race." See Quijano, "Raza, etnia y nación en José Carlos Mariátegui."

2 As for Latin America, see Quijano, "America Latina en Ia Economia Mundial."

3 A former Bolivian politician who served as the sixtieth president of Bolivia from 1989 to 1993.

4

QUESTIONING "RACE"

The idea of "race" is surely the most efficient instrument of social domination produced in the last five hundred years. Dating from the very beginning of the formation of the Americas and of capitalism (at the turn of the sixteenth century), in the ensuing centuries it was imposed on the population of the whole planet as an aspect of European colonial domination.[1]

Imposed as the basic criterion for social classification of the entire world's population, "race" was taken as the principal determinant of the world's new social and geocultural identities: on the one hand, "Indian," "Black," "Asiatic" (earlier "yellow" and "olive-skinned"), "white," and "mestizo," and, on the other hand, "America," "Europe," "Africa," "Asia," and "Oceania." On its basis was constituted the Eurocentering of capitalist world power and the consequent global distribution of labor and trade. Also on its basis arose the various specific configurations of power, with their crucial implications for democratization and for the formation of modern nation-states.

In this way, "race," a phenomenon and an outcome of modern colonial domination, came to pervade every sphere of global capitalist power. Coloniality thus became the cornerstone of a Eurocentered world.[2] This coloniality of power has proved to be more profound and more lasting than the colonialism in which it was engendered and that it helped to impose globally.[3]

"Racism" and "Race"

"Racism" in daily social relations is not, to be sure, the only manifestation of the coloniality of power, but it is certainly the most obvious and the most omnipresent. For this reason, it has remained the principal arena of conflict. As an ideology, "race" even prompted attempts in the mid-nineteenth century to build on its basis a whole scientific theory.[4] This in turn provided the rationale almost a century later for the National Socialist (Nazi) project of German world domination.

The defeat of this project in World War II contributed to the delegitimation of racism—at least as a formal and explicit ideology—for a large part of the world's population. But the social practice of racism nonetheless remained globally pervasive, and in some countries, such as South Africa, the ideology and practice of social domination became more intensely and explicitly racist. Still, even in these countries racist ideology has had to concede something—mainly because of struggles on the part of its victims but also because of worldwide condemnation—to the point of allowing "Black" elected leaders to take office. And in countries such as Peru, the practice of racial discrimination must now be disguised—often if not always successfully—behind legal formulas referring to differences in education and income that in this country are themselves one of the clearest consequences of racist social relations.[5]

What is really noteworthy, however, is that for the overwhelming majority of the world's population, including opponents and victims of racism, "race" is not just an idea but also exists as part of "nature," that is, as part of the "natural" materiality of individuals (and not only of the materiality of the social relations of power). In this sense, "race" has remained virtually unquestioned since it first appeared.

In societies founded on the basis of colonial power relations, the victims fight for equality between the "races." Societies lacking such origins (at least in any direct form) may assert that relations between the "races" should be democratic, even if they are not exactly relations among equals. But if we examine the way the issue has been posed, including in such countries as the United States and South Africa where the problem has been most intense, only exceptionally and very recently do we find scholars who have questioned not just racism but also the very idea of "race."[6]

There is thus a profound, tenacious, and virtually universal assumption that "race" is a phenomenon of human biology that has necessary implications for the natural history of the species and hence for the history of power relations among people. This is surely what accounts for the exceptional efficiency of this modern instrument of social domination. Nonetheless, what we are dealing with here is a blatantly ideological construct that has nothing to do with anything in the biological structure of the human species and everything to do, by contrast, with the history of the power relations of Eurocentered colonial/modern global capitalism. I want to reflect here on the issues raised by this peculiar connection between real social relations and their intersubjective dimension.

Sex/"Gender" and "Color"/"Race"?

The current crisis of the global power structure—perhaps the most profound that it has faced in its five hundred years—deeply affects the way the world's population is classified socially. This classification has reflected, in various ways, all the forms of social domination and all the forms of exploitation of labor. But on a world scale its central axis has been—and, although in decline, continues to be—the link between the commodification of labor power and the stratification of the world's population on the basis of "race" and "gender."[7]

This pattern of social classification has been quite durable. But the rejection of "racial" hierarchy and the resistance to ranking by "gender" have confronted it with a fundamental challenge. Since the early 1970s, the process of commodification of individual labor power appears to be declining in the technologically upper levels of the capitalist structure of accumulation, while it expands only at the lower levels in unstable and precarious ways.[8] Massive world unemployment and underemployment are the obvious consequences. In this new historical context, nonwage forms of exploitation (slavery, serfdom, reciprocity) are being revived,[9] having never completely died out during the last five centuries of capitalist hegemony. So, the relationships between capital and noncapital and between labor and capital are changing. The social reclassification of the world population is a necessary implication of those tendencies. And "race" and "gender" are in the process of redefining their places and roles in global power relations. The growing resistance to discrimination on the basis of "gender" and "race" is one of the dimensions of the crisis.

The capitalist world is, of course, historically and structurally heterogeneous. This means that the crisis in the capitalist pattern of social classification has distinct rhythms and timetables in each part of that world. Resistance by the victims of racism advances in some regions, while in others it finds not only less space but also, in some cases, open attempts at racism's relegitimation. Such a juxtaposition of resistance to racism with its relegitimation can be seen, for example, in the case of Peru under Fujimorism.[10] But this very juxtaposition at the same time makes the crisis all the more evident. As a result, we finally see called into question not just "racism" but also the very idea of "race." Still, however, even the minority who are moving in this direction find it difficult to shed the old mental chains of the coloniality of power.

Thus, the feminist movement and the debate on the question of "gender" have led increasing numbers of people to admit that "gender" is a mental construct grounded in sexual differences, which expresses patriarchal relations of domination and serves to legitimate them. And some now suggest, analogously, that we should also think of "race" as a mental construct, based in this case on skin color. Thus, "color" would be to "race" as sex is to "gender."

But the two links are not at all equivalent. In the first place, sex and sexual differences are real; they are a subsystem within the overall system known as the human organism, comparable to blood circulation, respiration, digestion, etc. That is, they are part of the biological dimension of the whole person.[11] Moreover, because of this they entail differences in biological behavior between people of different sexes. In addition, this differentiated biological behavior is linked above all to a vital matter: the reproduction of the species. One of the sexes fertilizes, and the other ovulates and can conceive, gestate, give birth, and nurse the newborn.

In sum, sexual difference entails distinct biological roles and behaviors. And although this in no way exhausts—let alone legitimates—the category of "gender," it at least shows that the intersubjective construct of "gender" has a biological point of departure.

No such thing can be said of the link between "color" and "race." First of all, the whole question of using the word "color" to refer to personal traits has to be thrown wide open. The very idea of "color" in this context is a mental construct. If one speaks of political colors ("red," "white," "green"), everyone is presumably disposed to recognize this as a metaphor. But strangely enough, this is not the case when one says that someone is of the "white," "Black," "red," or "yellow" "*race*"! And, more strangely still, few stop to consider that to describe a person's actual skin color by one of these labels requires a total distortion of vision or else a kind of stupidity or, at best, a prejudice.

The history of the "color" construct in social relations has yet to be written. Nonetheless, there are ample historical grounds for affirming that the association of "race" with "color" is belated and tortuous.[12] Color antedates the idea of race; it did not originally have any "racial" connotation. The first "race" was the "Indians," and there is nothing in the historical record to suggest that the category of "Indian" was associated with skin color.

The idea of "race" was born with "America" and originally referred to the differences between "Indians" and their conquerors (principally Castilian).[13] The first conquered peoples to whom future Europeans applied the idea of "color" are not, however, the "Indians." They are the slaves who were kidnapped and sold from the coasts of what is now known as Africa and whom they called "Blacks" ("Negroes"). But, surprising as this may now seem, Africans were not the first peoples to whom the idea of "race" was applied even though the future Europeans were acquainted with them long before they arrived on the coasts of the future America.

During the conquest, the Iberians—Portuguese and Castilian—used the term "Black," a color, as shown in the documents of that period. But the Iberians of that time did not yet identify themselves as "white." This "color" was not constructed until the eighteenth century, when the Anglo-Americans institutionalized the slave status of Africans in North America and the Antilles. Here, obviously, "white" is the constructed identity of the dominators, counterposed to "Black" ("Negro" or "nigger"), the identity of the dominated, as "racial" classification is already clearly consolidated and "naturalized" for all the colonizers and even perhaps among some of the colonized.

Underlying this historical reality is the fact that if "color" were to "race" as sex is to "gender," then "color" would necessarily have something to do with the biology or the biologically differentiated behavior of some part of the organism. However, there is no sign or evidence that any of the subsystems or apparatuses of the human organism (genital or sexual, circulatory, respiratory, glandular, etc.) varies in its nature, configuration, structure, function, or role in accordance with such traits as skin color, shape of eyes, or texture of hair.[14]

To be sure, external bodily traits such as shape, size, skin color, etc. are inscribed in each person's genetic code. In this specific sense we can speak of biological phenomena. But none of this has anything to do with the biological configuration of the organism or with the functions and behaviors or roles of the whole or of any of its parts.

Finally, and in the context of everything we have said, if "color" were to "race" as sex is to "gender," then on what basis could certain "colors" be seen as "superior" to others? In the patriarchal relation between man and woman, "superiority" is attributed to one of the "genders" and not to a particular sex as such or, if so, only by extension from the construction of "gender." Sex is not a construct in the way that gender is.

It is time to recognize that "color" is to "race" only as one construct is to another. In fact, "color" is a belated and euphemistic way of saying "race," a usage that did not become worldwide until the end of the nineteenth century.

The New "Western" Dualism and "Racism"

At the very beginnings of American history, there took root the idea that there are biological differences within the world's population that are decisively linked to the capacity for mental and cultural development. This was the central issue in the famous Valladolid debate over whether or not "Indians" were human. The extreme position, that of Ginés de Sepúlveda, who claimed that they could not be fully human, was rejected in the papal bull of 1513. But the idea of basic biological differences among humans was never questioned. And the prolonged colonial practice of domination/exploitation based on that assumption legitimated the idea permanently. Ever since that time, the old notions of superiority/inferiority implicit in every relationship of domination were considered to be grounded in nature; they were "naturalized" for all subsequent history.

This was certainly the initial moment of what has constituted since the seventeenth century the foundational myth of modernity, namely the idea of an original state of nature and of a process of historical development going from the "primitive" (the closest to "nature," which of course included above all the "Blacks" but also the "Indians") to the most "civilized" (which of course was Europe), with the "Orient" (India, China) in between.[15]

The link between this view of history and the idea of "race" was no doubt obvious at that time from the European perspective. It was implicit in the ideology and practice of colonial domination of the Americas and was reinforced and consolidated through the global expansion of European colonialism. But it was not until the mid-nineteenth century, with Arthur de Gobineau, that this link began to be articulated theoretically.

This time lapse was not accidental, nor was it without consequences in terms of the coloniality of power. On the basis of "America," the Atlantic basin became the new central axis of world trade during the sixteenth century. The peoples and the dominant groups who controlled this axis soon came to comprise a new historical region, and thus "Europe" was constituted as a new geocultural identity and as the hegemonic center of nascent global capitalism. This position made it possible for the Europeans, especially those of Western Europe, to impose the idea of "race" as the basis of the worldwide division of labor and of trade and also in the social and geocultural classification of the world population.

It was in this framework that the pattern of global capitalist power and its corresponding intersubjective experience took shape over the next three centuries. Europe's position as the hegemonic center of the modern capitalist world-system[16] gave it at the same time full hegemony in the intellectual elaboration of that whole vast historical experience—from the mid-seventeenth century on—and gave it the opportunity to mythologize its own supposedly self-made achievement.

Modernity, as a pattern of social, material, and subjective experience, expressed the essential character of this new global power. But its rationality reflected its European roots. That is, it expressed the Eurocentric view of the totality of the colonial/modern capitalist world.

A core aspect of this Eurocentric perspective was the adoption of a new dualism—a new version of the old dualism—as one of the bases of its worldview: the radical separation (not just differentiation) of subject/reason/soul/spirit/mind from object/body, reflecting the final triumph of Cartesianism over alternative approaches (principally that of Baruch Spinoza).[17]

Virtually all known "civilizations" differentiate between "spirit" (soul, mind) and "body." The dualist view of the dimensions of the human organism is thus ancient. But in all earlier cases the two dimensions are always copresent, coacting, never separated. René Descartes is the first to perceive "body" strictly as an "object," radically separated from the activity of "reason," which is the condition of the "subject." According to Descartes, "reason" is divine; "body," although created by God, is not divine but is part of "nature." Within this framework, both categories are mystified. We confront a new and radical dualism. It is a secularization of the long evolving of medieval Christian theology that separated "soul" and "body," precisely in the same terms. And this is what dominates all Eurocentric thought up to our own day.[18]

Without taking into account this new dualism, it is not possible to understand the Eurocentric elaboration of the ideas of "gender" and "race."

Both forms of domination are older than Cartesianism, but the latter is the point of departure for their systematic elaboration. In the cognitive perspective grounded in Cartesian radical dualism, "body" is "nature," ergo "sex." The role of woman, of the "feminine gender," is thus more closely linked to "sex," to "the body." This makes woman an "inferior gender." "Race," for its part, is also a "natural" phenomenon, and some "races" are closer to "nature" than others and are therefore "inferior" to those that have managed to distance themselves as much as possible from the state of nature.

Against this backdrop, we can insist that without rejecting the shackles of the Eurocentric worldview—that is, of the dualism between "body" and non-"body"—we will not get very far in the struggle to free ourselves decisively from the idea of "race" and of "racism" or from that other form of the coloniality of power, the relations of domination between "genders." The decolonization of power, in whatever frame of reference, signifies from the outset the decolonization of all dimensions of consciousness. "Race" and "racism" are situated, more than any other element of modern capitalist power relations, at this decisive juncture.

Translated by Victor Wallis

Notes

Published in *Socialism and Democracy* 21, no. 1 (March 2007): 45–53.

This essay originally appeared as "¡Qué tal raza!" in *Familia, Poder y Cambio Social*, ed. Carmen Pimentel (Lima: CECOSAM, 1999). It was subsequently reprinted in a number of Latin American journals. The present version is slightly expanded and includes updated references.

1   On the invention of the idea of "race" and its background, see Quijano, "Raza, etnia y nación en José Carlos Mariátegui." See also Quijano and Wallerstein, "Americanity as a Concept, or the Americas in the Imaginary of the Modern World-System."

2   On the coloniality of power and on the Eurocentered and colonial/ modern pattern of world capitalism, see my articles "Coloniality of Power, Eurocentrism and Latin America"; "Coloniality and Modernity/ Rationality"; and "Colonialidad del poder y clasificación social."

3   The concept of coloniality of power was introduced in my work "Colonialidad y modernidad/racionalidad," originally published in *Perú Indígena* 13, no. 29 (1992), and later in other Latin American journals (English version in Therborn, *Globalizations and Modernities*). See also

Quijano and Wallerstein, "Americanity as a Concept, or the Americas in the Imaginary of the Modern World-System." On the current debate, see, among many others, Mignolo, "Diferencia colonial y razón postoccidental."

4   Gobineau, *Essais sur l'inegalité des races humaines*.

5   On the widespread incidence of racist attitudes in Peru, see the results of a survey of university students of metropolitan Lima in León, *El país de los extraños*.

6   In Latin America, many prefer to think that there is no racism because we are all "mestizos" or because, as in Brazil, the official ideology is one of "racial democracy." A growing number of Latin Americans who have resided for a time in the United States—including students of the social sciences—return home as converts to the religion of color consciousness, of which they have no doubt been victims. They have become racists in spite of themselves. That is, they are convinced that "race," being defined by "color," is a natural phenomenon and that only "racism"—not race itself—is a question of power. In some cases, this leads to confusion among categories in the debate on cultural conflict and racist ideologies, and they are drawn into making extremely childish arguments. In Peru, a bizarre example is that of de la Cadena, "El racismo silencioso y la superioridad de los intelectuales en el Perú."

7   Relations of domination grounded in sexual differences are older than the current hegemonic colonial/modern pattern of power. But this deepened them by linking them with "race" relations and by viewing both sets of relations in Eurocentric terms. The "racial" classification of the world population redefined the place of "gender" in power relations, placing women of dominant "races" above those of dominated "races" but also above the males of the dominated "races." This led to a strengthening of both forms of domination but above all that based on "race."

8   See my "El trabajo en el umbral del siglo XXI."

9   According to United Nations figures, already before the end of the last century there were more than 200 million workers in slavery worldwide. See the interview of Brazilian anthropologist José de Souza Martins in *Estudos Avançados*, no. 31 (São Paulo: Universidad de São Paulo, Instituto de Estudos Avançados, 1997). This is probably a conservative estimate, as it does not include the recent rapid expansion of slavery in the Amazon basin. In March 2004, President Lula issued a decree prohibiting slavery in the Brazilian *fazendas* (haciendas), but in the conflict between landowners and landless peasants organized in the Movemento dos Sem Terra, hundreds of slave workers are discovered in those *fazendas* almost every day.

10 Shortly before Fujimori fell from power, TV reporters documented open racial/ethnic discrimination in certain nightclubs. At first they were officially penalized, but later the Supreme Court ruled that they had a legal right to discriminate.

11 It is essential to bear in mind that unless one accepts Cartesian radical dualism, the "biological" or "corporal" is just one dimension of the person, who must be viewed as an organism that knows, dreams, thinks, loves, enjoys, suffers, etc. and that all these activities occur with and in the body. So, "body" and "biology," if implying not difference within our organism but instead radical separation from "reason" and "spirit," are only categories of Cartesian radical dualism as one of the founding myths of the Eurocentrist perspective of knowledge.

12 See the references in my "Coloniality of Power, Eurocentrism and Latin America."

13 See Quijano, "Raza, etnia y nación en José Carlos Mariátegui."

14 On these questions, see Marks, *Human Biodiversity.*

15 It is extremely revealing that the only cultural category counterposed to "Occident" was "Orient." "Indians" and especially "Blacks" are thus completely missing from the Eurocentric map of human culture.

16 Wallerstein, *The Modern World-System.*

17 This is clearly the position established in René Descartes, *Discours de la Méthode* (1637) and *Traité des passions de l'âme* (1650). A good discussion of this rupture is Bousquie, *Le corps, cet inconnu.* See also Michel, *Philosophie et phenomenologie.*

18 On these questions, see my article "Coloniality of Power and Its Institutions."

5

COLONIALITY OF POWER AND SOCIAL CLASSIFICATION

Introduction

Coloniality, one of the specific constitutive elements of the world matrix (*patrón*) of capitalist power, is based on the imposition of a racial/ethnic classification of the world's population as the cornerstone of that matrix of power and operates in every level, field, and dimension, both material and subjective, of everyday life and at the social scale.[1] Coloniality originated with the Americas and from there spread around the world. With the establishment of (Latin) America,[2] at the same moment and in the same historical movement, the emerging capitalist power became worldwide, its hegemonic centers located in zones situated on the Atlantic, which would later be identified as Europe, and coloniality and modernity were also established as the central axes of its new domineering matrix. In other words, with (Latin) America, capitalism spread worldwide and became Eurocentered, and coloniality and modernity were set up as and to this day remain the constitutive axes of this specific matrix of power.[3]

Over the course of the deployment of these characteristics of today's power, the new social identities of coloniality (Indian, Black, olive-skinned, yellow, white, mestizo) were being configured, as were the geocultures of colonialism (the Americas, Africa, the Far East, the Near East, the West, and Europe). The corresponding intersubjective relations, in which the experiences of colonialism and coloniality were being fused with the requirements of capitalism, were being configured as a new universe of intersubjective relationships of domination under Eurocentered hegemony. This specific universe is what would afterward be termed "modernity."

Beginning in the seventeenth century in the major hegemonic centers of this world matrix of power—which in that century included, not by chance, Holland (René Descartes, Baruch Spinoza) and England (John Locke, Isaac Newton)—a means of knowledge making was elaborated and formalized in that intersubjective universe to render an account of the cognitive needs of capitalism: measurement, quantification, and the externalization (objectification) of the knowable with respect to the knower in order to control people's relations with nature and among people with respect to nature, especially ownership of the means of labor. Within this same orientation the experiences, identities, and historical relationships of coloniality and the geocultural distribution of world capitalist power were also formally naturalized. This means of knowing was termed "rational," giving to it its character and Eurocentric origins; it was imposed and acknowledged in the whole of the capitalist world as the only valid rationality as well as the emblem of modernity. The major lines of this cognitive perspective remain, despite changes in their specific contents, despite critiques and debates throughout the duration of the world power of colonial and modern capitalism. This is the modernity/rationality that has now at last entered into crisis.[4]

Eurocentrism is therefore not the perspective of Europeans exclusively, or only those who dominate world capitalism, but rather of everyone educated under their hegemony. And though it entails an ethnocentric component, that component does not explain it, nor does it serve as the main source of its meaning. Eurocentrism is a cognitive perspective produced over the long term of the Eurocentered world of colonial/modern capitalism taken as a whole. Eurocentrism naturalizes the experience of people in this matrix of power. That is, Eurocentrism makes it so that this experience is perceived as natural and, consequently, as a given, not subject to being questioned. Since the eighteenth century, especially with the Enlightenment, the mythological idea that Europe preexisted this power patron was established through Eurocentrism: the notion that it had already been a world center of the capitalism that would later colonize the rest of the world, elaborating modernity and rationality on its own and from within.[5] In this order of ideas, Europe and the Europeans stood at the most advanced moment and level on the linear, unidirectional, and continual march of our species. Another of the central cores of Eurocentric coloniality/modernity was similarly consolidated along with this idea: a conception of humanity according to which the world's population is sorted into inferiors and superiors, irrational and rational, primitive and civilized, traditional and modern. Later on, especially since the middle of the nineteenth century and despite the continuing spread of capital around the world, the hegemonic perspective began to give rise to a perception of capitalist power as a worldwide whole and of its long-term reproduction, change, and crisis. The place of world capitalism was filled by the nation-state and relations among nation-states not only as a unit of analysis but also as the one valid approach to understanding capitalism, not only in liberalism but also in so-called historical materialism, the most widespread and Eurocentric approach derived from Marx's heterogeneous legacy.

The intellectual revolt against this perspective and against this Eurocentric mode of knowledge making and regulation of knowing was always present, especially in Latin America.[6] But it did not really take off until after World War II, beginning of course in the areas dominated by and dependent on the capitalist world. As for power, it is always from the margins that intellectual revolt can be seen first and best, because that is where the totality of the field of relationships and meanings that constitute power comes into question. The most influential effort coming out of Latin America to show again the worldwide nature of capitalism was undoubtedly by Raúl Prebisch and those associated with him, who thought of capitalism as a world-system divided into "centers" and "peripheries." This view was taken up and reworked by Immanuel Wallerstein, whose theory of a "modern world-system," from a perspective that combines the Marxian view of capitalism as a world-system with the Braudelian concept of the historical *longue durée*, has been instrumental in reopening and refreshing the debate on the reconstitution of a global perspective in the social science research of the last quarter of the twentieth century.[7] Other components of the Latin American debate are active now in this new context, pointing toward a new idea of social-historical totality, the core of a non-Eurocentric rationality. I refer to proposals about the coloniality of power and about the structural-historical heterogeneity of all the worlds of social existence, which I will discuss forthwith.

The Question of Power in Eurocentrism

Power, as we have known it through history, is a space and a web of social relationships of exploitation/domination/conflict primarily articulated in terms of the struggle for control of the following spheres of social existence: (1) labor and its products; (2) depending on the former, "nature" and its production resources; (3) sex, its products, and the regeneration of the species; (4) subjectivity and its material and intersubjective products, including knowledge; and (5) authority and its tools, especially coercion, for ensuring the reproduction of this matrix of social relations and regulating changes in it. Over the past two centuries, however, up until the questions of subjectivity and gender irrupted into the debate, the Eurocentric gaze has been unable to perceive all of these spheres in the configuration of power, because it has been dominated by the confrontation between two major approaches. One is hegemonic: liberalism. The other is subaltern, though defiant in intent: historical materialism.

Liberalism does not have a univocal perspective on power. Its oldest version (Hobbes) maintains that authority, as agreed upon by previously scattered people, is what places the components of social existence in an order meant for meeting the needs of individual life. Though this view has become current again as an underpinning of neoliberalism, for most of the twentieth century it lost ground to the ascendency of structuralism, structural functionalism, and functionalism, whose common element with regard to this problem is that society is ordered around a limited set of historically invariable patterns so that the components of a society maintain continuous, consistent relationships with each other in terms of their respective functions, which in turn are inherent in the character of each element. Today the old empiricism and new postmodernism coexist and combine with all these variants, for which there is no such thing as a global structure of social relationships, a society as a given totality, distinguishable from others. In this way, they go hand in hand with the old Hobbesian theory.

For historical materialism—the most Eurocentric among the versions in Marx's heterogeneous legacy—social structures are constructed on the basis of relationships established to control labor and its products. These relationships are termed "relations of production." But unlike the variants of liberalism, historical materialism asserts not only that one particular sphere—labor and the relations of production—has primacy over all the rest but also, and just as insistently, that the existing order results from a series of decisions that arise from the primary sphere and permeate the whole. From this point of view, labor control is the base upon which all power relations are articulated and at the same time is the thing that determines each of those relations. Despite their many considerable differences, a set of common assumptions and issues can be discerned in each of these versions, pointing to their common Eurocentric lineage.

There are two questions in particular to highlight here. First, all of these versions presuppose a structure configured by elements that are, despite their diversity in form and character, historically homogeneous and that relate to each other continuously in consistent ways—whether because of their "functions" or the links that determine them—and linearly and unidirectionally in time and space. In this perspective, every social structure is organic or systemic, mechanical. And that exactly is the preferential option of Eurocentrism in the historical production of knowledge. In this option, something called "society," in its capacity as an articulation of multiple existences into a single structure, is either impossible and has no place in reality, as in the old empiricism and the new postmodernism, or, if it does exist, can only do so in a systemic or organic way.

Second, underlying all these versions is the idea that relationships among the components of a social structure are somehow given, ahistorical; that is, they are the product of the action of some agent prior to the history of relations among people. If, as in Hobbes, human actions and decisions are seen as being involved in the origin of authority and order, that is not the case as a matter of historical fact or even a historical myth, properly speaking, but rather as a metaphysical myth that postulates a state of nature, with individual humans who have no relationships with each other apart from continual violence; that is, they have no genuine social relations with one another. If human actions are also seen in Marx as being involved in the origin of "relations of production," for historical materialism this takes place apart from all subjectivity; that is, again, metaphysically, not historically. In much the same way, in functionalism, structuralism, and structural functionalism people are subject ab initio to the rule of certain historically invariable patterns of behavior.

The Eurocentric perspective, in each of its variants, thus entails a historically impossible assumption: that the relations between the elements of a historical matrix of power are already determined prior to any history, that is, as if they were previously defined in an ahistorical or transhistorical ontic sphere. Eurocentric modernity does not appear to have completed the exercise of secularizing the idea of a providential God. Otherwise, conceptualizing the social existence of concrete people as being configured ab initio by historically homogeneous and consistent elements, indefinitely destined to have continual, linear, and unidirectional relations with each other, would be unnecessary and ultimately unthinkable.

The Structural-Historical Heterogeneity of Power

Such a perspective on knowledge would be hard put to account for historical experience. First, there is no known matrix of power whose components relate to each other in this way, especially over the long term. Far from it. What we actually see is always a structural articulation among historically heterogeneous elements, that is, ones that arise from specific histories and distinct timespaces far from one another, which thus have forms and characters that are not only different but also discontinuous, incoherent, and even conflicting with each other at every moment and over the long term. A historically effective demonstration of this, perhaps better than any other experience, is precisely the establishment and historical expansion of the Americas and world capitalism, colonial and modern.

In each of the main spheres of social existence, control of which is disputed by people, whose victories and defeats form the relationships of exploitation/domination/conflict that constitute power, the component elements are always historically heterogeneous. Thus, labor in world capitalism exists today, as it did five hundred years ago, in each and every historically known form (wage labor, enslavement, servitude, small-scale market production, reciprocity), all in the service of capital and articulated around their waged form. But in the same way, in each of the other spheres—authority, sex, subjectivity—each of these historically known forms is present under the general primacy of the forms called "modern": the "nation-state," the "bourgeois family," "modern rationality."

The really remarkable thing about any social structure is that historically discontinuous, distinct, distant, and heterogeneous elements, experiences, and products could be articulated together, regardless of their incongruencies and conflicts, in the common framework that weaves them into a joint structure. The relevant question is to inquire what such a relationship brings forth, allows, or determines and what gives it the character and behavior of a specific, determined historical totality. And as the experience of the Americas and the capitalist world today demonstrates, what first creates the conditions for this articulation in each case is the ability that one group attains or manages for imposing itself on the others and articulating their heterogeneous histories into a new social structure. This is always a history of necessities but also of intentions, desires, knowledge or ignorance, options and preferences, decisions right and wrong, victories, and defeats and thus never of the actions of extrahistorical factors.

The possibilities to act that people have are not endless, not even very numerous or diverse. The available resources are not abundant. Even more significant is the fact that human actions and omissions cannot be separated from what has already been done, what already exists, conditioning the actions (external or not) of subjectivity, knowledge, and desires and intensions. Hence, the options, desired or not, conscious or not, for all or some people cannot be decided or acted out in a historical vacuum. This does not mean, not necessarily at least, that these options come inscribed by extrahistorical, suprahistorical, or transhistorical determinations, like "fate" in the classical Greek tragedies. In short, they are not inevitable. Or was it inevitable that Christopher Columbus would stumble across what he called Hispaniola instead of reaching the place we now call New York? The technical conditions of his venture allowed for one outcome as easily as the other or for the failure of both. Think about the fundamental implications, which are not trivial, of this issue for the history of the capitalist world.

The capacity and strength that allow one group to impose itself on the others is not, however, sufficient for articulating heterogeneous histories into a lasting structural order. They certainly can produce authority, in the form of a capacity for coercion. Strength and coercion—or, in the liberal gaze, consensus—cannot, however, lastingly create or replicate the structural order of a society, that is, the relations among the components of each of the spheres of social existence or the relations among those spheres themselves. Nor can they, in particular, fabricate the meaning of the movement and historical development of the social structure as a whole. The only thing that authority can do is force or persuade people to submit to those relations and to that general meaning of the movement of the society that dwells within them. In this way it contributes to maintaining and reproducing these relations and to controlling its crises and changes.

If, however, liberalism has insisted since Hobbes that authority determines the social order, the structural order of power relations, that is because it also insists that all other spheres of social existence that are articulated into this structure are "natural." But if this nonhistorical character of social existence is rejected as impossible, then the explanation for why social existence consists of specific spheres or fields of social relations and why those fields tend to be articulated in a joint field of relations, the structural configuration of which and whose reproduction or excision over time is known by the concept of society, must be sought in a different historical occurrence. Where can that occurrence be found? The difficulties with structuralist and functionalist theories have already been pointed out not only in accounting for the historical heterogeneity of social structures but also because they imply necessarily consistent relations among their components. We are left, then, with Marx's proposal (one of the sources for historical materialism) regarding labor as the primary sphere in any society and labor control as primary for any social power. This proposal raises two problems that must be discussed.

First, it is true that the experience of Eurocentered, colonial/modern capitalist power shows that labor control is the prime factor in this matrix of power, which is capitalist above all else. In consequence, the control of labor by capital is the central condition of capitalist power. But in Marx this implies, on one hand, that this and all other factors are historically homogeneous and, on the other hand, that labor ever and always determines the character, place, and function of all other spheres in the power structure. Nevertheless, taking a second look at the experience of the global matrix of capitalist power, there is nothing to indicate that its components or even its basics—whether labor, capital, or capitalism—are historically homogeneous. On the contrary, within each of these categories we find every form, stage, and level in their respective histories, not merely coexisting but rather articulating and combining with one another. For example, wage labor exists today, as it did at the dawn of its history, alongside enslavement, servitude, small-scale market production, and reciprocity. And all of these articulate with each other and with capital. Wage labor itself differs with every historical form of accumulation, from so-called original or primitive accumulation, through extensive surplus value, to every gradation of intensity and every level that current technology permits and contains, and up to those forms in which individual labor is virtually insignificant. Capitalism necessarily encompasses this entire complicated and heterogeneous universe under its domination.

Regarding the unidirectional chain of determinations that allow labor to articulate the other spheres and keep them articulated over the long term, the experience of the Eurocentered, colonial/modern capitalist global matrix of power does not in any way demonstrate that its capitalist feature makes any of the other features necessary or inevitable. Moreover, the capitalist character of this matrix of power undoubtedly has decisive implications for the character and meaning of intersubjective relations and authority relations and for relationships surrounding sex and its products. But, first, it is only if we ignore the historical heterogeneity of these relations and the way in which they are ordered within each sphere and with each other that we could possibly think that these implications are unilinear and unidirectional. And second, at this point in the debate it should be obvious that although the current mode of control of labor has implications for social intersubjectivity, for example, we likewise know that opting for a capitalist form of organizing and controlling labor required an intersubjectivity that would make such a thing possible and preferable. Determinations therefore are not and cannot be unilinear or unidirectional. And they are not only reciprocal. They are heterogeneous, discontinuous, inconsistent, and conflict-ridden, as should be expected for relations among elements that each have those same characteristics. The articulation of heterogeneous, discontinuous, and conflict-ridden elements in a common structure, within a given field of relations, thus necessarily entails relations of reciprocal, multiple, and heterogeneous determinations.

Structuralism and functionalism were never able to see these historical necessities. They took a wrong turn, reducing those necessities to the idea of functional relationships among the elements of a social structure. In any case, however, for a structural-historically heterogeneous structure to move, develop, or (if you will) behave like a historical totality, these modes of reciprocal and heterogeneous determination among its components are not enough. It is essential that one (or more) of them have primacy—in the case of capitalism, control over labor and authority, combined—not as a determinant or as the base of determinations in the historical materialism sense but rather strictly as the axis or axes around which the whole complex is structured. In this way, the joint movement of this totality, the meaning of its development, encompasses and transcends each of its component parts. That is, a given field of social relations behaves like a totality. But such a social-historical totality, as an articulation of heterogeneous, discontinuous, and conflict-ridden elements, cannot be closed in any way, nor can it be systemically consistent like a machine, constituting an entity in which the logic of each element fits that of each other component. Its joint movements consequently cannot be unilinear or unidirectional, as would necessarily be the case for organic or systemic or mechanical entities.

Notes on the Question of Totality

Regarding these issues, it is essential to keep researching and debating the implications of the epistemological paradigm putting forward the relationship between the whole and the parts with respect to social-historical existence. Eurocentrism has led virtually everyone to accept that within a totality, the whole has absolute, determinative primacy over each and every one of its parts and therefore that there is one and only one logic governing the behavior of the whole and of each and every one of its parts. The possible variations in the movement of each part are secondary, with no effect on the whole, and are recognized as particularities of a general rule or logic for the whole to which they belong. This is not the proper place, for obvious reasons, to begin a systematic debate on this paradigm, which in Eurocentric modernity has in the end been recognized as one of the keystones of rationality, performed as spontaneously as breathing in concrete knowledge production, treated as beyond question. All I propose to do here is to raise the narrow question of its implications for the specific knowledge of social-historical experience. Under this rubric, it is necessary to recognize that every social-historical phenomenon consists in and expresses a social relationship or a web of social relationships. Therefore, its explanation and meaning can only be found within a field of relations larger than the one to which it belongs. Such a field of relations, with respect to which a given phenomenon may be explained and made sense of, is what here is termed the social-historical totality. The continued presence of this paradigm in social-historical research and debate, particularly since the late eighteenth century, is no accident: it accounts for the recognition of its tremendous importance, especially because it made freedom from empiricist atomism and providentialism possible. Nevertheless, not only has atomistic empiricism remained part of the debate, it has now found new expression in so-called social-philosophical postmodernism.[8] Both of these reject the idea of totality and of its necessity in knowledge making.

The renewal and expansion of the atomistic view of social-historical experience under the full-blown crisis of modernity/rationality is also no accident. This is a complex and contradictory matter. On one hand, it accounts for the fact that it is more evident now that the dominant ideas of totality leave out many, too many, areas of social-historical experience or embrace them only in a distorted way. But on the other hand, the explicit association between denying totality and denying the reality of social power in the new postmodernism is again no accident, just as in the old empiricism.

Indeed, what the totality paradigm allowed us to notice in the history of concrete people's social existence was precisely power as the most persistent form of structural articulation within the social sphere. Ever since, whether to question it or defend it, the starting point has been to recognize its real existence in people's lives. But most of all, it was the critique of power that ended up at the center of social-historical study and debate. By contrast, in the atomistic view, whether in the old empiricism or the new postmodernism, social relationships do not form complex fields of social relations in which all distinguishable spheres of social existence, and therefore of social relations, are articulated together. That is to say, something called "society" would have no place in reality. Therefore, finding an explanation and a meaning for social phenomena would be neither possible nor necessary. Contingent experience, description as representation, would be the only thing that was necessary and legitimate. The idea of totality would be not only unnecessary but, above all, an epistemological distortion. The notion that long-lasting structures of social relationships exist would give way to the idea of unstable, changing flows that never quite solidify as structures.[9]

To deny the reality of social power, empiricism and postmodernism have to deny the idea of social-historical totality and the existence of a primary sphere in the social configuration that acts as the axis for articulating the other spheres. In the old empiricism, power exists only as authority in a single sphere of social relations that themselves are, by definition, discrete. In postmodernism all the way back to its poststructuralist origins, power exists only at the scale of social microrelations and as a discrete, fluid phenomenon. It thus makes no sense for any of these sides in the debate to think of changing something called "society" as a whole and to that end locating its axes of articulation or the determinant facts that need to be changed. Historical change would be strictly an individual matter even if there were many individuals involved in social microrelations.

In this confrontation between the organic, systemic ideas of totality, on one hand, and the denial of any notion of totality, on the other, we would seem to be dealing with completely opposed options, even irreconcilable epistemic perspectives. Both, however, have a Eurocentric lineage in common: for both positions, the only thinkable paradigm of totality is the Eurocentric one. Put differently, both are based on a presupposition that is never discussed or made explicit, which is that any notion of totality implies that the whole and the parts correspond to a single logic of existence. That is, they have a basic homogeneity that maintains the consistency and continuity of their relationships, as in an organism, a machine, or a systemic entity. From this perspective, denying the need for the notion of totality in knowledge production is extreme but not entirely arbitrary. For our current social-historical knowledge needs, today this notion of totality means distorting reality as seriously as the disadvantages of the old atomistic empiricism did.

But what happens when we face totalities that consist of an articulation of historically heterogeneous elements whose relations are discontinuous, inconsistent, and conflict-ridden? The answer is that relations between the whole and the parts in social existence are real but necessarily very different from what Eurocentrism postulates. A social-historical totality is in a relationship field structured by the heterogeneous and discontinuous articulation of diverse spheres of social existence, each of these in turn structured from historically heterogeneous elements that are discontinuous in time and conflict-ridden. This means that the parts in a social power relationship field are more than mere "parts"; they are parts with respect to the entirety of the field, the totality that it constitutes, and consequently they move within the general orientation of that whole, but they are not parts in their separate relationships with each other. Each of them is a complete unity in its own configuration, because they likewise have historically heterogeneous constitutions. Each element in a historical totality is particular and at the same time specific, perhaps even singular. Each of them moves within the general tendency of the group, but they each have or may have relative autonomy, which may be or come to be in conflict with the group. This is also where we find the notion of social-historical change.

Does this mean that the notion of totality has no place or meaning here? Not in the least. What articulates all the heterogeneous and discontinuous spheres in a social-historical structure is a common axis around which the whole tends to move, generally as a group, acting as a totality. But that structure is not and cannot be closed, just as, to the contrary, an organic or systemic structure cannot help but be closed. Therefore, unlike the latter, if such a group tends to move or behave in one singular direction, it cannot do so unilinearly or unidirectionally or unidimensionally, because there are many heterogeneous and even conflicting impulses or logics at work within it, especially considering that there are human needs, desires, intentions, choices, decisions, and actions constantly at play. In other words, historical processes of change are not and cannot be a matter of transforming one historically homogeneous totality into another equivalent one, whether gradually and continuously or in fits and starts. If that were the case, change would entail one totality, with all its components, making a complete exit from the historical stage and then another one derived from it entering to take its place. This is the central, necessary, explicit idea in gradual, unilinear evolutionism, one also implied by the variants of structuralism, functionalism, and also—though it runs counter to its formal discourse—historical materialism. It is not, however, what happens in real experience, least of all with the world matrix of power that was established along with the Americas. Change affects the components of a historical field of social relations in a heterogeneous, discontinuous way. This is probably the concrete historical meaning of what is seen as a contradiction in the historical movement of social existence.

The perception that a field of social relations is made up of homogeneous, continuous elements, even if they are contradictory (in the Hegelian sense), gives rise to a view of history as a series of changes that consist of the transformation of a homogeneous, continuous whole into another equivalent one. The debate about whether this takes place gradually and in a linear fashion or in fits and starts, which can usually be passed off as an epistemological confrontation between "positivism" and "the dialectic," is thus purely formal. It actually entails no epistemological break. This shows that what leads many to set aside any notion of totality is that the systemic or organic ideas surrounding it have come to be seen or sensed as a sort of intellectual straitjacket, since they force us to homogenize actual experience and thus see it in a distorted fashion. This does not mean, of course, that we have to deny the possible or proven existence of organic or systemic totalities. Indeed there are organisms and mechanical objects whose parts relate systemically to one another. But any attempt to view social structures in the same way necessarily distorts them.

From an organic or systemic perspective on social-historical totality, any attempt to manage social-historical totalities, especially when it comes to planning for change, can only lead to experiences that have come to be known, not by chance, as totalitarian. At the same time, however, since it is not inevitable that every idea of social-historical totality has to be systemic, organic, or mechanical, simply denying all notions of totality in social-historical knowledge can only be associated with denying the reality of power at the social scale. In reality, denying all notations of totality reveals the ideological slant linking it to the current established power.

The Question of Social Classification

In the 1980s in the midst of the world crisis of capitalist power, the already foreseeable became undeniable as the bureaucratic despotism regimes—the rivals of private capitalism and the democratizing processes in the capitalist societies and states on the "periphery" and also of the worker movements aimed at destroying capitalism—fell in defeat. This context helped bring flows to light within historical materialism that until then had remained fairly underground, currents that had begun to feel a certain unease with the concept of social classes that they had inherited.[10] But before long the baby was thrown out with the bathwater, as often happens, and social classes were eclipsed on the intellectual and political stage. This result obviously formed part of the worldwide defeat of the regimes and movements that had contested the world hegemony of the hegemonic centers of capitalism or that stood up to capitalism. And it furthered the imposition of the neoliberal discourse of capitalism as a sort of universal common sense, which from that time until quite recently became not only dominant but virtually "the only way to think."[11] It is less obvious, however, whether those who had formerly frequented the fields of historical materialism rid themselves, after the defeat, of one of their weapons of choice only or primarily so they could pass over more easily into the rival camp.

Though that is the most frequently heard explanation, it is probably not the best. It is more likely that what had been happening with the question of social classes among the followers and devotees of historical materialism had been similar to what had gone on with organic or systemic notions about totality: the defeats and, most of all, the disappointments within their own political camp ("actually existing socialism") had made productive use of their version of historical materialism with regard to social classes ever more problematic. That version had managed to turn class from a "dynamic to a static" category, as E. P. Thompson put it, and to a large extent class was, as Parkin described it in the late 1970s, "one of the Marxist products that have been manufactured and marketed in western universities" of Europe and the United States.[12] Given that for a wide majority this was the only version of social classes seen as legitimately correct, treating it too as an intellectual straitjacket came to be seen as common sense. The efforts to make this straitjacket more bearable, though there were not many of them, gained a wide audience in the 1960s. Think, for example, of the response to the works of Nicos Poulantzas, at one end, and of Erik Olin Wright, at the other.[13] Much more fertile efforts, though with smaller audiences at first, such as the work of E. P. Thompson, unfortunately did not lead to a complete alternative proposal.[14]

Where do the difficulties with the theory of social classes in historical materialism come from? The clearest trail leads us to a history with three distinct steps. The first step is the creation of historical materialism in the late nineteenth century as a product of the positivist-Marxist hybridization in late Engels and the European social-democratic theorists, especially those from Germany, with broad long-standing reverberations among socialists from around the world. The second step is the canonization of the version termed "Marxism-Leninism" that was imposed by bureaucratic despotism under Stalin beginning in the 1920s. Finally, the third step is the new hybridization of that historical materialism with French structuralism following World War II.[15] Historical materialism, with respect to the question of social classes, as in other areas with respect to Marx's theoretical legacy, is not so much a rupture as it is a partial, distorted continuation. This intellectual legacy is admittedly heterogeneous and even more so in its last stages, produced precisely when Marx began to question the Eurocentric cores of his own thought, unfortunately without finding an effective resolution to the epistemic and theoretical problems that this entailed. It thus allows for heterogeneous readings. But historical materialism, especially in its Marxist-Leninist version, attempted, not without success, to make Marx's legacy pass for a systematically homogeneous work and to impose its own reading in order to get itself accepted as his only legitimate heir.

As is well known, Marx expressly stated that he was not the discoverer of social classes or of their struggles, since bourgeois historians and economists had done so before him.[16] But although he curiously does not mention it, there is no doubt that it was in the works of Henri de Saint-Simon and the Saint-Simonians that the basic elements of what a century later would be known as the theory of social classes in historical materialism were first formulated, long before Marx.[17] The is true in particular in the famous *Exposition de la Doctrine de Saint-Simon*, first published in 1828 by the so-called Saint-Simonian Left, which had great influence in social and political debates for much of the nineteenth century.

There are yet more remarkable points on which Saint-Simon coincides with historical materialism with respect to the question of social classes. Considering that the *Exposition de la Doctrine* was written after three hundred years of Eurocentered, colonial/modern world capitalist history, it is amazing that the text shows an absolute blindness to the following points: (1) Under capitalism, every form of labor exploitation/domination coexisted and became associated with one another. (2) In the world of capitalism, the social classes did not include only "industrialists" on one side and "workers" or "proletarians" on the other; there were also "slaves," "serfs/servants," "plebeians," and "free peasants." (3) The structure of domination that originated in the colonial experience of "Europeans" or "whites" and "Indians," "Blacks," "Asians," and "mestizos" entailed profound power relations, which in that period were so closely tied to forms of labor exploitation that they seemed to be "naturally" associated with each other. (4) The capital-wage relationship was not the only power axis, not even in the economy; instead, there were other power axes that existed and acted in spheres that were not solely economic, such as "race," gender, and age. (5) In consequence, the distribution of power among a society's population did not derive exclusively from relations surrounding labor control, nor could it be reduced to such relations.

Marx's inquiry into social classes was probably linked to the Saint-Simonian debate. But along with the similarities, there are also noteworthy differences that may be worth pointing out here. In the first place, it is true that Marx maintained the same (Saint-Simonian and Eurocentric) perspective of a unilinear, unidirectional historical sequence of class societies almost to the end of his work. However, it is now well known that as he became familiar with the historical research and political debate of the Russian Narodniks (populists), he realized that this unidirectionality and unilinearity left out other decisive historical experiences. He thus became conscious of the Eurocentrism in his historical perspective, but he did not make the appropriate epistemological leap. Historical materialism subsequently chose to condemn and omit this period of Marx's research, clinging dogmatically to the most Eurocentric aspect of his legacy.

On the other hand, it is true, as everyone knows, that there is a perceptible distinction between the view on class relations that his theory on capital entails and the view that underlies Marx's historical studies. In his theory, capital is a social relationship specific to production, the two fundamental terms of which are "capitalists" and "workers." The former are those who control the relationship, and in that capacity they are the "functionaries" of capital. They dominate the relationship, but they do so to their own private benefit. In that capacity, they are exploiters of the workers. From this point of view, both terms are the basic social classes in *Capital*. On the other hand, however, above all in his analysis of the French conjuncture, particularly in *The Eighteenth Brumaire of Louis Bonaparte*, Marx takes into account various social classes that, depending on the conditions of politico-social conflict, emerge, consolidate, or retire from the scene: commercial bourgeoisie, industrial bourgeoisie, proletariat, large landowners, finance oligarchy, petite bourgeoisie, middle class, lumpenproletariat, big bureaucracy. Likewise, in *Theories of Surplus Value*, he notes that Ricardo neglected to emphasize the constant growth of the middle classes.

Subsequent historical materialism, especially its Marxist-Leninist version, has dealt with these differences in Marx's inquiry through three proposals. The first is that the differences are due to the level of theoretical abstraction in *Capital* and conjunctural history in *The Eighteenth Brumaire*. The second is that these differences are, moreover, transitory, since as capital develops it will in any case tend to become polarized into the two basic social classes. The third is that the theory in *Capital* implies that it is dealing with a social relationship structured independently of people's wills and consciousnesses, and as a consequence the way people are distributed within that social relationship is necessary and inevitable due to a historical law that is beyond them. In this view, social classes are presented as structures created by the nature of the social relationship; their occupants are the bearers of their determinations, and as such people's behaviors should reflect those structural determinations.

The first proposal finds confirmation in Marx's own words. Thus, in the famous incomplete chapter on classes in the third volume of *Capital*, Marx contends that "the owners merely of labor-power, owners of capital, and land-owners, whose respective sources of income are wages, profit and ground-rent, in other words, wage-laborers, capitalists and land-owners, constitute then three big classes of modern society based upon the capitalist mode of production."[18] "Nevertheless," he continues, not even in England—despite its being the most developed and "classic" of modern capitalist societies—can it be said that "the stratification of classes does not appear in its pure form," given that the middle classes "and intermediate strata even here obliterate lines of demarcation." But he immediately notes that all this will be cleared up by the unfolding of the "law of development of the capitalist mode of production," which continuously leads to polarization between the basic classes.

With *The Eighteenth Brumaire*, however, there is a double displacement—of problematics and of perspective—that cannot be explained solely by the fact that the work is a conjunctural history analysis. The movement of Marx's thought entails, first, the idea that the French society of the time contained not only wage labor but also many other diverse forms of labor exploitation, all articulated with the dominion of capital and to its benefit. This fact somehow heralds the differentiation between capital (the relation between capital and wages) and capitalism (heterogeneous relationships between capital and all other forms of labor), confronting it in advance of the theory of the articulation of modes of production later produced by historical materialism. Second is the idea that classes are formed, fall apart, or are consolidated, whether partially and temporarily or definitely and permanently, according to the course of concrete struggles by concrete groups of people struggling for the control of each sphere of power. They are not structures or categories that exist prior to such struggles.

This line of Marx's thought is also present in *Capital*, despite all its well-known ambiguities. Therefore, the third proposal establishes a basic difference between Marx's perspective and that of historical materialism. In the latter, social classes occupy a sort of set of structural pigeonholes into which people are sorted and placed according to their production relationships. In Marx, by contrast, we see a concrete historical process of classifying people, that is, a process of struggles in which some people manage to subjugate others as they dispute the control of labor and production resources. In other words, relations of production are neither external to nor prior to people's struggles but instead are the result of struggles among people for the control of labor and production resources, of victories by some and defeats by others, as a result of which people place themselves or are placed and classified. This is undoubtedly the theoretical proposal entailed in the famous chapter on "primitive accumulation."[19] Otherwise, the line of analysis in *The Eighteenth Brumaire of Louis Bonaparte* makes no sense. In Marx's line of thought therefore, social classes are neither structures nor categories but historically rather produced (and in that sense historically determined) relationships even when this view is reduced to just one of the spheres of power: labor. Historical materialism, on the other hand, as E. P. Thompson points out, sticks to the "static" (in other words, ahistorical) view that attributes to social classes the status of structures established by relations of production coming into existence outside of people's subjectivity and actions, that is, prior to any history.

Historical materialism since World War II has acknowledged that there are complicated outstanding problems with its evolutionist, unidirectional view of social classes and class societies. In the first place, because it has repeatedly been seen that there are some "precapitalist" classes even in the "centers," the peasantry in particular, who have not left the historical scene of "capitalism," nor do they appear disposed to leave, while others, the "middle classes," have tended to increase as capitalism has developed. In the second place, the dualistic view of a passage from "precapitalism" to "capitalism" was not broad enough to account for the experiences of the "Third World," where very complex and heterogeneous configurations of power did not correspond to the expected stages in the Eurocentric theory of capitalism. Nevertheless, historical materialism could not find a theoretical solution backed up by historical experience, arriving only at the proposal of an "articulation of the modes of production" without giving up on the idea that those formed a sequence. That is, such "articulations" were still conjunctures in the transition from "precapitalist" modes to "capitalism."[20] In other words, they consist of the coexistence (transitory, of course) of past and present in their historical vision. Historical materialism is hostile to the idea that these might not be "articulated modes of production" but rather capitalism as a world power structure within which and in the service of which every historically known form of labor and of social labor control and exploitation are articulated.

Then again, the idea of "class" was introduced in the natural sciences before being used in the social sciences. The Swedish naturalist Linnaeus, in his famous eighteenth-century botanical classification system, was the first to employ it. He discovered that it was possible to classify plants according to the number and placement of stamens in their flowers, as those tend to remain unchanged over the course of evolution.[21] Basically the same way of knowing seems to have led French historians in the eighteenth century, followed by Saint-Simonians in the early nineteenth, to classify the population of Europe by "classes." For Linnaeus, the plants were already there, in the "plant kingdom," a given of nature, and based on a few of their empirically differentiable characteristics it was possible to "classify" them. The people who studied and debated the society of north-central Europe in the late eighteenth and early nineteenth centuries applied the same perspective to people, finding that it was possible to classify them too based on their most constant characteristics, especially their place in the social structure of wealth and poverty, command and obedience. It was the Saint-Simonians who discovered that the main source of these differences lay in control over labor and its products and the products of nature that were used by labor.

The theorists of historical materialism did not make any decisive ruptures or changes in this knowledge perspective from the late nineteenth century on. Of course, when they transferred the noun "class" from the natural world to the social world, they had to associate it with an adjective to legitimate that shift: class ceased to be botanical and became social. But the shift was basically semantic. The new adjective by itself could not suffice to cut the umbilical cord linking the newborn concept to the naturalist womb or to provide it with an alternative epistemic atmosphere to develop in. In Eurocentric thinking, heir to the continent's Enlightenment, society was an organism, a given closed order, and social classes were thought of as already given categories within "society," much as were the classes of plants within "nature."

Note in relation to these questions that other terms with the same naturalist origins—"structure," "processes," "organism"—in Eurocentrism pass into social knowledge with the same cognitive attachments as the term "class." The obvious linkage between the Eurocentric idea of social classes and the ideas of "structure" as a given order in society and of "process" as something that takes place in a structure casts a bright light on the persistence in them of the cognitive signs of their naturalist origin and thereby of its lasting impact on the Eurocentric perspective within social-historical knowledge. There is no other way to understand or explain the idea of historical materialism or of sociologists of "industrial society" according to which people are "bearers" of class structural determinations and therefore should act in accordance with them. Their desires, preferences, intentions, wills, decisions, and actions are configured according to those determinations and should correspond to them. The problem created by the inevitable distance between this assumption and the subjectivity and external conduct of people so classified found an impossible solution in historical materialism: this was a problem of "consciousness," which could only be brought to the exploited masses by bourgeois intellectuals, much as pollen is carried to the flowers by bees (Kautsky-Lenin) or be elaborated and developed in a state of continual progress toward an impossible "possible consciousness" (Lukács).

The naturalist, positivist, and positivist-Marxist stamp of the Eurocentric theory of social classes also brings up two crucial issues: (1) In its origins, the theory of social classes is conceived exclusively on the basis of the European experience, which in turn is conceived according to the Eurocentric perspective. (2) The only really meaningful differences that can be perceived among Europeans, since aristocratic hierarchies were abolished by the French Revolution, are those relating to wealth/poverty and command/obedience. These differences refer, on one hand, to people's place and roles with respect to control over labor and the natural resources that serve labor (production relations) and, on the other hand, to people's place and roles in the control of authority, ergo the state. The other differences that were linked in eighteenth- and nineteenth-century European populations to power difference, primarily sex and age, are "natural" from this perspective; that is, they form part of the classification in "nature." In other words, the Eurocentric theory on society classes, not just in positivist-Marxist historical materialism or among Weberians but in Marx himself, is reductionist and refers only and exclusively to one of the spheres of power: control over labor and its resources and products. And this is especially striking above all in Marx and his heirs, because even though his formal purpose is to study, understand, and change or destroy power in society, he considers absolutely no other instances or social existence in which power relations among people are formed or considers them merely as derivatives of "relations of production" and determined by those.

This all means that the idea of social classes was elaborated in Eurocentric thought between the late eighteenth and late nineteenth centuries, when the perception of the totality as seen from Europe, by then the "center" of the capitalist world, had already been definitively organized as a historical duality: Europe (for these purposes, mainly western Europe and England) and non-Europe. This duality implied, moreover, that much of what made up non-Europe, though it existed on the same temporal stage, really corresponded to the past in linear time, the end point of which was obviously Europe. In non-Europe, every nonwage form of labor existed in that same nineteenth-century moment. But from Saint-Simon to the present, Eurocentrism has only seen the "precapitalist" or "preindustrial" past in such forms. That is, those classes are either "precapitalist" or nonexistent. Non-European or "nonwhite" identities had been imposed on non-Europe. But like age or gender among Europeans, such identities corresponded to "natural" power differences between Europeans and non-Europeans. The modern institutions of authority were being formed or had already been formed in Europe: modern nation-states and their respective identities. But in non-Europe, only tribes and ethnic groups were perceived as part of the "premodern" past, as they were to be replaced at some future time by nation-states, "like in Europe." Europe is civilized. Non-Europe is primitive. The rational subject is European. Non-Europe is an object of knowledge. Correspondingly, the science for studying Europeans will be called "sociology," while that for studying non-Europeans will be called "ethnography."

At this point in the debate, it is not good enough to stay within the known parameters, because that will not address all the issues or solve all the problems raised for knowing and acting. Sticking to an insistence that the question of social classes has to be historicized—that is, related to the concrete history of concrete people instead of maintaining a "static" or ahistorical view of social classes, replacing Marx with Weber, or exploring their fruitful intersections, as tends to be done in academic sociology—will lead nowhere. All that happens in any of these options, or in all of them together, is that people get classified by some of their given differential characteristics, and there is really nothing fundamental to be gained if one set of characteristics or another are chosen, or should be chosen, to make the classificatory system less "ideological" and more "objective."

The important factor in the classification of the elements of nature, as befit Cartesian rationality, was discovering the "properties" that define and simultaneously create kindred ties among specific "objects" or that distinguish them individually and show their proximate genus and specific differentia. But with the question of social classes, what is really at stake and has been since the idea was first introduced is something radically different: the question of power in society. And the problem is that none of those options, taken either together or separately, are capable of letting us apprehend and probe how power is historically constituted, much less how world and colonial/modern capitalist power is constituted.

For all these reasons, it is appropriate to leave the Eurocentric theory of social classes behind and move on to a historical theory of social classification. The concept of social classification, in this proposal, refers to the long-term processes by which people compete for control over the basic spheres of social existence, from the results of which a matrix is configured for the distribution of power centered on exploitation/domination/conflict relations among the population of a given society and history. It was pointed out above that in this approach, power is a web of exploitation/domination/conflict relations configured among people in the contest over the control of labor, of "nature," of sex, of subjectivity, and of authority. Therefore, power cannot be reduced to "production relations" or to "order and authority" either separately or together. And social classification refers to people's places and roles in the control of labor and its resources (including "natural" resources) and products, of sex and its products, of subjectivity and its products (above all, the imaginary and knowledge), and of authority and its resources and products.

In this specific sense, any possible theory of social classification of people necessarily requires an inquiry into the history, conditions, and determinations of a given distribution of power relations in a specific society. That distribution of power among the people of a society is what classifies them socially, determines their mutual relationships, and generates their social differences, since their empirically observable and differentiable characteristics are the results of those power relations and their signs and traces. One can start with the latter to attain a first moment and a starting level of comprehension of power relations, but it makes no sense to act as if that is where the nature of people's place in society resides, that is, their social class.

The Heterogeneity of Social Classification

Ever since the Americas were introduced into colonial/modern world capitalism, people have been classified according to three lines, each distinct but articulated into a common global structure by the coloniality of power: labor, gender, and race. Age hasn't been introduced into social power relations in the same way, though it has been in particular spheres of power and also around two central axes: control over the production of resources for social survival and control over the biological reproduction and regeneration of the species. The former entails control over the labor force, the resources and products of labor; this includes "natural" resources and is institutionalized as "property." The second entails control over sex and its products (pleasure and descendants), based on property rights. "Race" was incorporated into Eurocentered capitalism based on both axes. And control over authority is organized to guarantee the power relations thus configured. From this perspective, the resulting "social classes" are heterogeneous, discontinuous, and conflict-ridden. The coloniality of power is the axis that articulates them in a common structure, as will be shown below. Insofar as all the elements that enter into the constitution of a matrix of power originate as discontinuous, heterogeneous, contradictory, and conflict-ridden in space and time—that is, they change or could change in each of these instances based on their changing relationships with each of the others—power relations are not and cannot be a sort of preexisting set of structural pigeonholes into which people are sorted and from which they take on this or that set of characteristics and are supposed to behave accordingly.

The way in which people come to occupy a place and a role with respect to the control of the focal instances of power—completely or partially, temporarily or permanently—is a matter of conflict. In other words, it consists of a struggle, violent or not; of defeats and victories; of advances and setbacks. It takes place on individual and collective terms, with acts of loyalty and betrayal, persistence and defection. And given that every relationship structure is an articulation of discontinuous, heterogeneous, and conflict-ridden spheres and dimensions, places and roles do not necessarily have the same positions and relations in every sphere of social existence or at every moment in their respective space/time. That is, people can have, for example, one place and one role with respect to labor control and another very different, even opposite place and role with respect to the control of sex or subjectivity or in the institutions of authority and not always the same ones over the course of time.

From this point of view, the Eurocentric idea that people who occupy certain places and exercise certain roles at a given moment in a matrix of power constitute, on that basis alone, a community or a historical subject points us in a historically unproductive direction. Such a notion would only be plausible if it could also be accepted that such people occupy places and carry out roles that are symmetrically congruent with one another in every one of the focal instances of power. The sorting of people into relationships of power consequently has the character of processes of social classification, declassification, and reclassification of a population, that is, the character of a sorting articulated within a long-term social matrix of power. This is not just about the fact that people change and may change their places and roles in a matrix of power but also the fact that the matrix, as such, is always at stake, given that people are constantly competing and that the resources, reasons, and needs of these conflicts are never the same at every moment of a long history. In other words, power is always in a state of conflict and in processes of sorting and resorting. Its historical periods can be distinguished precisely in terms of such processes.[22]

It consequently cannot be said, based on an alternative to a Eurocentrist approach, that a population affected at one moment and in one form of a social classification process will never gain the characteristics of a real group, a community, and a social subject. But such characteristics only come about as a part and a result of a history of conflicts, of a memory matrix that is associated with that history, that is perceived as an identity, and that produces a will and a resolve to weave together the heterogeneous and discontinuous particular experiences into a subjective collective articulation that will make up an element in real material relationships. The collective struggles of sectors of workers who organized themselves into unions, into political parties, and the struggles of even broader communities that group themselves together as religious identities and that endure over the long term are historical examples of such processes of subjectivization among broad and heterogeneous populations that are even discontinuous in time and space.

Nevertheless, not every process of social subjectivization or of constituting collective subjects can be recognized as a process of social classification. In some cases we are dealing with a problem of forming identities, an identity process that does not put these instances of social power at stake in any way. From our perspective, only those processes of subjectivization whose sense is conflict over exploitation/domination constitute processes of social classification. In world capitalism, the issues of labor, race, and gender are the three focal instances with respect to which these conflict-ridden relationships of exploitation/domination are ordered. Therefore, the processes of social classification consist in any case of processes in which these three instances associate or dissociate with each other in regard to the exploitation/domination/conflict complex. Of the three focal instances, it is labor—that is, exploitation/domination—that stands out as the central, invariable sphere. Domination makes exploitation possible and finds it acting on its own only very rarely. The other focal instances are, foremost, instances of domination, given that sexual exploitation in particular is discontinuous. That is, while the exploitation/domination relationship between capital and labor is continuous, the same type of relationship does not occur between male and female in every case or under every circumstance; thus, it is not continuous. Likewise, in the relationship among "races," we see foremost domination. In short, the articulation between instances of exploitation and domination is heterogeneous and discontinuous. And by the same token, social classification as a process in which the three instances are associated/dissociated also necessarily has the same characteristics.

One idea originally proposed by Marx as a clearly historical matter was later mystified by historical materialism: that of class interest. To the degree that the idea of class became reductionist and was ahistoricized, class interest in capitalism was reduced to the relationship between capital and wage labor. The interests of other workers were always seen as secondary and subject to being subordinated to those of wage workers, especially to those of the so-called industrial working class.

What happens, however, if we assume, as we must today, that capitalism articulates and exploits workers under every form of labor and that the domination mechanisms used to that effect—"race" and "gender"—are used differentially in this heterogeneous universe of workers? First, the concept of class interest also has to be thought through in terms of its structural-historical heterogeneity.

Next, it is necessary to establish, at each moment and in each specific context, the common axis of the exploitation/domination/conflict relationship between all the workers, subject to every form of labor and every form of domination, and capitalism and its functionaries. For these reasons, the key question about social classification of the processes of social subjectivization in the face of exploitation/domination is determining the specific historical conditions with respect to which it is possible to perceive the modes, levels, and limits for association among people involved in these three instances (labor, gender, and race) in a specific period and context.

In any case, no process of social classification, of subjectivizing people in the face of capitalism, could be so certain as to reproduce and sustain itself over the period necessary for leading the victims of capitalist exploitation/ domination to their liberation if, from the immediate perspective of the concrete people involved, these three instances are perceived and handled separately or, worse, in conflict with each other. Not by chance, maintaining, accentuating, and aggravating the perception among the exploited/ dominated of these differential situations in relation to labor, race, and gender has been and is an extremely effective means that capitalists have of maintaining their control of power. The coloniality of power has had the central role in this history.

Coloniality of Power and Social Classification

In known history before world capitalism, it is clear that in power relations, certain attributes of the species have played a key role in the social classification of people: sex, age, and labor status are undoubtedly the most ancient. After the conquest of the Americas, phenotype was added. Sex and age are differentiating biological attributes, though their place in exploitation/domination/conflict relations is associated with their elaboration as social categories. Labor status and phenotype, by contrast, are not differentiating biological attributes. Skin color, the form and color of hair and eyes, the form and size of the nose, etc., have no impact on a person's biological structure and surely even less on their historical capacities. And similarly, being a "manual" or "intellectual" worker is unrelated to biological structure. In other words, the role that each of these elements plays in social classification—that is, in the distribution of power—has nothing to do with biology or "nature." Such a role is the result of disputes over control of the social spheres.

Hence, naturalizing the social categories that account for the place of these elements in power is a naked product of social history. The fact that these categories that identify places and roles in power relations pretend to be nothing more than terms for "natural" phenomena, whether or not they refer to anything real in nature, is a very effective indication that power, all power, requires this subjective mechanism in order to reproduce. And it is interesting to ask yourself why. While the production of the social category of "gender," based on sex, is without a doubt the most ancient in social history, the production of the category "race," based on phenotype, is relatively recent, its full incorporation into the classification of people in power relations being barely five centuries old: it begins with the Americas and the worldwide spread of the capitalist matrix of power.[23]

The phenotypic differences between victors and vanquished have been used to justify the production of the "race" category, though it is above all an elaboration of domination relations as such. The importance and significance of the production of this category in the Eurocentric and colonial/modern world capitalist matrix of power could hardly be exaggerated: the attribution of the resulting new social identities and their distribution in world capitalist power relations was established and reproduced as the basic form of universal social classification in world capitalism and as the foundation of new geocultural identities and their power relations in the world. It likewise became the backdrop to the production of new intersubjective relations of domination and to a perspective on knowledge that was imposed around the world as the only rational one. The racialization of power relations between the new social and geocultural identities was the mainstay and the fundamental legitimizing reference for the Euro-centered character of the matrix of power, both material and intersubjective. That is, for its coloniality. It thus became the most specific element of the Eurocentered and colonial/modern world capitalist matrix of power, and it penetrated every area in the social existence of the Eurocentered, colonial/modern world matrix of power. The implications of the coloniality of power in the capitalist world need to be studied and established in a systematic (not systemic) fashion. Within the limits of this text, I will confine myself to proposing an outline of the major issues.

A. Coloniality of the Universal Social Classification of the Capitalist World

What began with the Americas was imposed all over the world. The whole world's population was classified, above all, into "racial" identities and sorted between the dominant/superior "Europeans" and the dominated/inferior "non-Europeans." Phenotypic differences were used, defined, as the external expression of "racial" differences: at an early period, primarily the "color" of the skin and hair and the form and color of the eyes; later, in the nineteenth and twentieth centuries, other features as well, such as facial form, skull size, and the form and size of the nose. Skin color was defined as the most significant "racial" marker, being the most visible, for differentiating between the dominant/superior people, or "Europeans," on one hand, and the entire set of dominated/inferior "non-Europeans," on the other. In this way, the dominant/superior Europeans were handed the attribute of "white race," and all the dominated/inferior "non-Europeans," that of "races of color."[24] The gradation ladder between the "white person" of the "white race" and each of the other skin "colors" was taken to be a gradation between superior and inferior in the "racial" social classification.

B. Coloniality of the Political and Neocultural Articulation

Territories and territorially based political organizations, whether partially or totally colonized or not colonized, were classified within the Eurocentered matrix of colonial/modern capitalism precisely according to the place that the "races" and their respective "colors" held in each case. In this way, power was articulated between "Europe," "America," "Africa," "Asia," and, much later on, "Oceania." This helped naturalize Eurocentered control over the territories, over the production resources found in "nature." And each of these categories, imposed from the Eurocenter of power, has ultimately been accepted up to the present day by most people as an expression of nature and geography, not of the history of power on this planet. The dominant groups of the nonwhite races were subject to becoming tributaries, that is, intermediaries in the chain of value and wealth transfer from the colonial periphery to the Eurocenter, or dependent associates. The nation-states of the center were established first with the colonial states and later with the dependent nation-states as their counterparts.

As part of this relationship, the processes of creating citizenship, of unequal but real representation of the various social sectors, and of repaying workers' production and taxation in the form of public services (called the "welfare state"), have ultimately remained a privilege of the center, because the cost of all this is to a great extent paid for through the exploitation of labor in the colonial periphery under undemocratic and nonnational conditions, that is, through overexploitation. Due to these findings, none of the countries whose populations are for the most part victims of racist or ethnicist power relations have been able to emerge from the colonial periphery in the struggle for "development."[25] And the countries that have been incorporated into the "center" or that are on that path are the ones whose societies either have no coloniality relations, precisely because they were never European colonies, or that were colonies but only briefly and partially (Japan, Taiwan, China), or ones where the colonized populations were at first small minorities, such as the "Blacks" during the formation of the United States of North America, or where the aboriginal populations were reduced to isolated minorities if not exterminated, as happened in the United States, Canada, Australia, and New Zealand. All this suggests once more that the coloniality of power entails, both in international power relations and in the internal relations within countries, what in Latin America has been termed structural-historical dependency.

C. Coloniality of the World Distribution of Labor

The world distribution of labor as guided by the coloniality of power has been equally decisive for modern/colonial Eurocentered capitalism. Capitalism has organized labor exploitation into a complex worldwide apparatus based on the predominance of the capital-wage relationship. For many theorists, this is all that capitalism consists of. Everything else is "precapitalist" and, as such, outside of capital. We have known since the Americas, however, that capitalist accumulation has never, at any time, gone without the coloniality of power up to the present day.

This is precisely why the diagram of a capitalist world arranged into a dual "center" and "periphery" is not random, though it probably would have been better to think of them as "colonial center" and "colonial periphery" (in the sense of coloniality and not merely, and not so much, of colonialism), to avoid the "naturalist" spillover of physical geography in the imagery. In the center (the Eurocenter), the form of capital-labor relationship that dominated—not only structurally but also, long-term, demographically— was wage labor, which is to say that the wage relationship was primarily "white." In the "colonial periphery," on the other hand, the wage relationship became structurally dominant over time, but it was always in the minority demographically as in every other way, while the most widespread and sectorally dominant were all the other forms of labor exploitation: enslavement, servitude, small-scale market production, reciprocity. But all of these were from the first articulated under the dominion of capital and in its benefit.

Globally, the wage relationship has always been, to this day, the least widespread geographically and demographically. The universe of labor and workers under capital was, by contrast, diverse and heterogeneous. In consequence, the "social classes" among the world's population were not restricted to the place where people were in control of labor and its products, and moreover, even in that narrow sphere they were in fact still ordered primarily based on the coloniality of power. In the Eurocenter—as conceived in isolation, separate from the colonial periphery—social classification inevitably appeared only in relation to labor, since the "Europeans" still did not perceive themselves as racially differentiated, as they do today, however, now that the victims of the coloniality of power have managed to establish themselves in the original seats of the colonizers. Their "social classes" were therefore conceptually separate from and differentiated from "races," and their reciprocal relations were thought of as external. Globally, however, as was always the very condition for the existence of capitalism, "social classes" were differentially distributed among the planet's population on the basis of the coloniality of power: in the Eurocenter, the dominant ones are the capitalists, while the dominated are the wage workers, the middle classes, and the independent peasants; in the colonial periphery, by contrast, the dominant ones are the dependent tributaries and associates of the capitalists, while the dominated are the enslaved, servants, small-scale independent market producers, wage workers, middle classes, and peasants. This social classification, differentiated between the center and the colonial periphery, has been the central mechanism in the apparatus of global accumulation in benefit of the center. Indeed, it is what has made it possible to produce, maintain, and pay for the loyalty of the exploited/dominated "whites" in the face of the "races," above all on the "colonial periphery" but also within the "center," as is still the case, especially in the United States.

D. Coloniality of Gender Relations

Throughout the colonial world, the formal-ideal norms and matrices of sexual behavior for the genders, and consequently the family organization matrices for "Europeans," were based directly on racial classification: sexual freedom for males and faithfulness for women was, throughout the Eurocentered world, the counterpart to "free" (that is, not paid for, as in prostitution) sexual access for white males to Black and Indian women. In Europe, by contrast, prostitution for women was the counterpart to the bourgeois family matrix. Family unity and integration, imposed as axes of the bourgeois family matrix in the Eurocentered world, was the counterpart of the continuing disintegration of kinship units among the non-white races, who were appropriable and distributable not only like pieces of merchandise but also directly, like animals. Especially among enslaved Black people, since this form of domination over them was more explicit, immediate, and long-lasting. The characteristic hypocrisy underlying the formal-ideal norms and values of the bourgeois family has since then never been absent from the coloniality of power.

E. Coloniality of Cultural or Intersubjective Relations

We have already noted many of the major implications of the hegemony of Eurocentrism for cultural relations, intersubjective relations in general, in the world of colonial/modern capitalism. Here it is worth just pointing out the following. In every society where colonization entailed the destruction of the social structure, the colonized population was stripped of its intellectual wisdom and its exteriorizing or objectifying means of expression. They were reduced to the condition of rural, unlettered people. In societies where colonization did not reach complete social destruction, the intellectual and aesthetic-visual legacies could not be destroyed, but the hegemony of the Eurocentric perspective was imposed on intersubjective relations with the dominated. Over the long term, throughout the Euro-centered world the hegemony of the Eurocentric mode of perception and of knowledge production was slowly imposed, and the imaginary itself was colonized among a very broad swath of the world's population. Last but not least, Eurocentric hegemony in capitalist world culture had entailed a mystified way of perceiving reality, whether in the center or in the colonial periphery. But its effects in the latter, on knowledge and on action, have always led to dead ends. The national question, the question of revolution, the question of democracy are the emblematic examples.

F. Domination/Exploitation, Coloniality, and Embeddedness

There is a clear relationship between exploitation and domination: domination does not always entail exploitation, but exploitation is impossible without domination. Domination is therefore the sine qua non of power, of all forms of power. This is an old historical constant. The production of a mythological imaginary is one of its most characteristic mechanisms. The naturalization of the institutions and categories that order the power relations imposed by the victors/dominators has to this day been its specific procedure. In Eurocentered capitalism, it was through naturalizing the coloniality of power that "world culture" was imbued with mythology and mystification in the elaboration of reality phenomena. The racial loyalty of whites against the other races has served as the cornerstone of the loyalty, even the national loyalty, of the exploited and dominated "whites" with respect to their exploiters around the world and first of all in the "Eurocenter."[26]

The mythological "naturalization" of the basic categories of exploitation/domination is an exceptionally powerful tool for power. The best-known example is the production of "gender" as if it were identical to sex. Many people think the same thing is true of "race" with regard to, above all, "color." But that is a radical confusion. After all, sex really is a biological attribute (it entails biological processes) and has something to do with "gender." But "color" is, literally, a Eurocentric invention as a "natural" or "biological" referent of "race," since it has nothing to do with biology. Moreover, "color" in colonial/modern society has not always been the most important element for successful racialization or for racialization projects, as in the case of "Aryans" with respect to other "whites," including "white" "Jews," and more recently in the racialization processes of Arab-Israeli relations. These are effective historical proofs, if any were needed, of the strictly social-mythical character of the relationship between "color" and "race."

"Race" is a category whose intersubjective origin is, in this sense, provable. Why, then, has it come to be so ubiquitous in "modern" society, so profoundly introjected into the world imaginary, as if it really were "natural" and material? I suggest a path of inquiry, because it entails something very material: the human body. Corporality is the decisive level in power relations. Because the "body" names the "person," if the concept of "body" is cleansed of all the mystificatory implications of the ancient Judeo-Christian dualism (soul-body, psyche-body, etc.). And this is what makes the "naturalization" of such social relations possible. In exploitation, it is the body that is used and consumed by labor and, over much of the world, by poverty, by hunger, by malnutrition, by illness. It is the body that is involved in punishment, in repression, in the tortures and massacres through all the struggles against the exploiters.

Pinochet is a name for what happens to the exploited in their "bodies" when they are defeated in these struggles. In gender relations, we are dealing with the body. In "race," the reference is to the body, since "color" presumes the body. Today, the struggle against exploitation/domination unquestionably entails, first of all, the struggle to destroy the coloniality of power, not just to put an end to racism but because it serves as the axis around which the universal matrix of Eurocentered capitalism is articulated. This struggle is part of the destruction of capitalist power, since it now forms the living framework for every historical form of exploitation, domination, and discrimination, both material and subjective. The central place of "embodiedness" at this level leads to the need for thinking, for rethinking, specific pathways to its liberation—that is, to the liberation of people, individually and in society—from power, from every form of power. And historical experience to date shows that the only path that could lead to such a result is the radical socialization of power. This means returning control to the people themselves, directly and immediately, over the basic instances of their social existence: labor, sex, subjectivity, authority.

Notes

First published in the festschrift for Immanuel Wallerstein edited by Giovanni Arrighi and Walter L. Goldfrank in *Journal of World-Systems Research* 6, no. 2 (2000): 342–86.

1   Coloniality is a different concept than that of colonialism, though the two are linked. The latter refers strictly to a structure of domination and exploitation in which control over a given population's public authority, production resources, and labor is held by another population of a different nationality, whose political centers are moreover located in a different territorial jurisdiction. But it does not always necessarily imply racist power relations. "Colonialism" is obviously more ancient, whereas "coloniality" has over the past five hundred years proved to be more profound and long-lasting than colonialism. But it was unquestionably created within colonialism, and what is more, without the latter it couldn't have been imposed on the intersubjectivity of the world in such a deep-rooted and long-lasting way. González Casanova, "Internal Colonialism and National Development," and Stavenhagen, "Classes, Colonialism, and Acculturation," proposed the term "internal colonialism" to denote the racist/ethnicist power that operates within a nation-state. But this would only make sense from a Eurocentric perspective on the nation-state. On my propositions regarding the concept of coloniality of power, see particularly Quijano, "Colonialidad y modernidad/racionalidad"; Quijano, "América Latina en la economía mundial"; and Quijano, "Colonialité du pouvoir et démocratie en Amérique latine." See also Quijano and Wallerstein, "Americanity as a Concept, or the Americas in the Imaginary of the Modern World-System."

2　The appropriation of the name "America" by the United States has given rise to widespread confusion, forcing us to remind readers that the term originally covered only the Iberian domains on this continent, which ranged from Tierra del Fuego to roughly the southeastern half of the current territory of the United States.

3　See Quijano, "Modernity, Capital, and Latin America Were Born the Same Day," in this volume.

4　I have addressed these questions in Quijano, *Modernidad, identidad y utopía en América Latina*; and Quijano, "Colonialidad y modernidad/ racionalidad."

5　"Europe" here names a metaphor, not a geographical region or its population. It refers to all that was established as a racial/ethnic/cultural expression of Europe, as an extension of it, that is, as a distinctive character of identity not subject to the coloniality of power.

6　An explicit critique of the unilinear and unidirectional evolutionism of Eurocentrism can already be found, for instance, in Haya de la Torre, *El antimperialismo y el* APRA, written according to its author in 1924 but first published in 1928. The perception of Peru's economic power relations implied in the first essay of Mariátegui, *Seven Interpretive Essays on Peruvian Reality*, may be considered the embryo of the concept of historical-structural heterogeneity that was elaborated in the 1960s. See Quijano, *Notas sobre el concepto de marginalidad social*.

7　See Prebisch, *Hacia una dinámica del desarrollo latinoamericano*; Prebisch, "Crítica al capitalismo periférico"; and Prebisch, *Capitalismo periférico*. See also Wallerstein, *The Modern World-System*.

8　The term "social-philosophical" is meant to draw attention to the fact that the intense process of rethinking the philosophical debate has a distinctive hallmark. This isn't just an extension of the old debate on old questions of Eurocentric philosophy; instead, it deals with questions raised in the social-historical debate of the past two hundred years, especially during the second half of the twentieth century. Recognizing this feature is important to us, not so much because it proves the influence of the social sciences on philosophy as because, first and foremost, this debate is vital for creating a rationality to serve as an alternative to Eurocentric rationality and for rethinking the basis of social-historical knowledge.

9　See Anrup, "Totalidad social."

10　The debate on the problem of social classes has been around for a long time, though it grew more intense after World War II. An incisive review is Tomich, "World of Capital/Worlds of Labor." However, it was probably the well-known polemic Wood, *The Retreat from Class*, together with Laclau and Mouffe, *Hegemony and Socialist Strategy*, that reported on the biggest climate shift in the intellectual atmosphere of so-called

Western Marxism with respect to the question of social classes. Since then the concept has quickly fallen into disuse, as has almost every major theoretical issue from the earlier debate. They were simply removed from the debate, and the ideas and concept at play fell into disuse. Their return began rather rapidly with the crisis of global hegemony, which was driven by the predatory appetites of financial capital and the worldwide discredit of neoliberalism.

11 "The only way to think" is the phrase coined and repeatedly used by Ignacio Ramonet in the pages of *Le Monde Diplomatique*, of which he is the editor in chief.

12 Thompson, *The Making of the English Working Class*, 10; and Parkin, *Marxism and Class Theory*, ix.

13 See especially Poulantzas, *Political Power and Social Classes*; and Wright, *Class, Crisis and the State*.

14 See Thompson, *The Making of the English Working Class*; and Thompson, *The Poverty of Theory and Other Essays*.

15 On positivism-Marxism, see Shanin, *Late Marx and the Russian Road*. The work of Althusser and the Althusserians is a convincing and well-known demonstration of the sweeping influence of French structuralism on historical materialism since World War II. One notorious example of how devastating it became for some of them is the book by Hindess and Hirst, *Pre-Capitalist Modes of Production*.

16 Marx and Engels, "Letter to Joseph Weydemeyer, March 5, 1852."

17 We should not overlook the intriguing absence of almost any mention of Saint-Simonian thought in Marx, particularly the *Exposition de la Doctrine de Saint-Simon*, even more so because it employed all the basic concepts and terminology of Marx's works: the full list of antagonistic social classes in the first section of *The Communist Manifesto* is already there in the *Exposition* (freemen and slaves, patricians and plebeians, lords and serfs), as well as the working class, wage laborers, and proletarians. Moreover, it doesn't take a strained reading of the *Exposition* to find that the whole perspective on the relationships between social classes and history and between the exploitation of the working class or proletariat and the revolution that will bring an end to all forms of exploitation are already formulated there, well before they reappeared for posterity as the keys to the revolutionary theory of historical materialism. In this sense, Engels's recognition in *Socialism: Utopian and Scientific* of Saint-Simon's "comprehensive breadth of view," while placing him among the "utopian socialists," is belated and self-serving.

18 Marx, *Capital*, 3:984.

19 Marx, *Capital*, 1:873–76.

20 This line characterized the social science research and debates among French structuralist Marxists, especially in the 1970s (Pierre-Philippe

Rey and Claude Meillassoux, among others). In English, see Wolpe, *The Articulation of Modes of Production*. In Latin America, some researchers opted for a different perspective, according to which capitalism is a structure of domination/exploitation in which every historically known form of labor exploitation is articulated around a common axis: the capital-wage relationship. This is the line followed in my own works, such as "Lo cholo y el conflicto cultural en el Perú"; *Imperialismo, clases sociales y estado en el Perú*; and *Naturaleza, situación y tendencias de la sociedad peruana contemporánea*. Termed the "structural-historical" approach, this perspective appears as far back as my *Notas sobre el concepto de marginalidad social*.

21 Carl von Linné (1707–1778), better known as Linnaeus, was the first to elaborate a system for classifying plants, beginning in 1730. See Larson, *Reason and Experience*.

22 I will leave a more detailed discussion of the question of the "historical subject," as raised by postmodernism, for another work. For the moment I think it only necessary to indicate my skepticism with respect to the notion of the "historical subject," given that it refers, perhaps inevitably, back to the Hegelian legacy, which was not entirely "turned on its head" by historical materialism. That is, it implies a certain teleological take on history as well as an organic or systemic "subject" as the bearer of the respective movement, oriented in a predetermined direction. Such a "subject" can only exist, in any case, in a metaphysical and not a historical sense. At the same time, however, simply denying any possibility that a group of people might become a subject, that they might come to constitute a collective subject under certain conditions and for a certain period of time, goes directly against historical experience if it does not accept that what can be called a "subject," not only in the collective but even the individual sense, is always constituted by heterogeneous and discontinuous elements and that it can only become a single entity when those elements are articulated around a specific axis under concrete conditions, with respect to concrete necessities, and in a transitory way.

23 An extended and specific discussion of the racial question would take us in other directions. See Quijano, "Raza, etnia y nación en José Carlos Mariátegui." The literature on this debate continues to grow. Perhaps the most useful recent publication is Marks, *Human Biodiversity*. Among older works, see Mack, *Race, Class, and Power*. Some pious souls would like to see equality among the races, yet they swear that races really exist. Thus, there are professors of "race and ethnicity" in virtually every university in the United States, and the US Citizenship and Immigration Services has a complex racist/ethnicist classification system based on phenotype features (color above all), even though the

federal government has been forced to accept "racial equality." Almost all the people indigenous to other countries who study at these universities and who pass through that immigration service return to their own countries converted to the religion of "color consciousness" and proclaim the reality of "race."

24 The process of the social production of color, as the main sign of a universal social classification of the colonial/modern Eurocentered world of capitalism, is a question that has yet to be researched in a systematic historical way. It is necessary to note here that before the Americas came into being, "color" was never recorded as a way to classify people in power relations. The Eurocentering of the new matrix of power was unquestionably not inevitable. But its establishment was what gave rise to, explained, and made sense of the imposition of the "race" category and of "color" as its external marker from the sixteenth century to the present.

25 On the relationship between coloniality and development, see Quijano, "América Latina en la economía mundial."

26 This is a very well-known phenomenon, as witnessed by the continued segregation of "Blacks" in the major unions led by "whites" in the United States. But it affects not only the workers themselves; worse, it affects their political ideologues and leaders, who claim to be socialist. The most instructive examples are the divisions among all the socialists, first, and communists, later, in the face of racism and colonialism in Africa and Asia in the nineteenth and twentieth centuries. See the scholarly study by Davis, *Nationalism and Socialism*.

6

THE RETURN OF THE FUTURE AND QUESTIONS ABOUT KNOWLEDGE

This article addresses some issues of the relationships between the imaginary and knowledge and, more specifically, between the historical-critical imaginary and historical-critical knowledge. In view of recent trends in world conflicts and in the debate on capitalism and globalization, the relationship between imaginary and knowledge implies the return of the future in the production of knowledge.

Many, if not all, observers may agree that everyone in the world opposed to capitalism or who resisted or rivaled imperialism had been defeated by the late 1980s. The specificity of that defeat consists, in my opinion, of the extinction of a particular horizon of the future. Allow me to explain.

During the last five hundred years, that is, since America came into being, there has always been a brilliant horizon visible to everyone around the world, shining with promises at certain times: modernity, rationality, progress, liberalism, nationalism, socialism. The time that this horizon announced or promised was far more than a mere continuation of the present and the past. It was something new, it involved change, and it announced or promised what was desired or hoped for, perhaps even dreamt about. In any event, it created a different meaning for each history in each space/time.

For that reason, the numerous defeats of the countless struggles and the many peoples who strove to achieve some of those goals were always understood as transitory and often as being of limited scope or historical duration; never were they accepted as final or definitive. The horizon was still there before us, and the long-sought future was still there undefeated, its brilliance increasing with the passage of time after each defeat. What is more, a great many victories were won in the last three centuries. The worst forms of exploitation were circumscribed. In some parts of the world, the dominant powers were forced to admit—or at least negotiate—the limits, conditions, and forms of domination and exploitation. That was how what we now call bourgeois democracy came into being, with the modern nation-state as its institutional structure. Nearly all the great colonial empires were destroyed. And at one time it even seemed that domination and exploitation had really begun, in certain parts of the world, to be overcome. These victories only confirmed the powerful certainty that the struggles were focused on a real future horizon, not a deceptive dream. In light of that hope, every defeat was a mere momentary incident in the fight. That is why millions of people were able to bear everything: exile, imprisonment, torture, death, and even the most personal and painful of all oppressions, the sacrifice or death of loved ones.

I feel sure that many of you have personal knowledge of this, country by country. Or you may have wondered how the defeated of the Spanish Civil War felt: an entire generation of revolutionaries from all over the world fearing or knowing that the time of defeat would be very long. But there is no testimony from those years implying a renunciation of the path lighted by the horizon. "If mother Spain falls—I mean, you hear that said—go forth, children of the world; go out to seek her!" said César Vallejo.[1] But he was sure that the children of the world would go out to look for it. Latin America's analogous collective experience was probably the fall of Allende in Chile in 1973, preceded by the defeat of the Popular Congress in Bolivia in 1972.

It is not my aim, on this occasion, to inquire into the causes of these defeats. What I propose to do, in the first place, is to point out that the brightest horizon of the age began to lose its radiance—and no longer just for a small and isolated minority as at times in the past—from the late 1960s (Shanghai 1967, Paris 1968, Tlatelolco 1968, Prague 1969), and that between the mid-1970s when the world crisis of capitalism broke out and the late 1980s, when "the wall came down" and the "socialist camp" collapsed, the light went out completely throughout the world. And in the second place, I want to inquire into the implications of that development for the questions of knowledge.

On the first point, I think few will deny that all the political movements, organizations, and regimes seeking a significant deconcentration of power or a radical redistribution thereof had been defeated throughout the world by the end of the 1980s. All of them were extinguished. And with them was also extinguished—not only dimmed—through the 1990s the specific horizon of future unless someone was seriously to posit that neoliberalism was that horizon. For some of the neoliberal thinkers, indeed, history had come to an end.[2] For the first time in five hundred years, the most admirable dreams of the human species appeared to be dead and buried. With hope lost, fear darkened the horizon once again.[3]

Such an extinction of any horizon of future implied for many, perhaps for most, the disquieting sensation that the ideas, proposals, promises, and reasons for radical redistribution of power and radical historical changes in social existence suddenly appeared to belong to some remote past. Then, all the intellectual perspectives and theoretical categories associated with those proposals and promises were also abruptly abandoned. In short, everything that was recognized as "critical thought" or "critical theory" was left without, or almost without, debate. In Latin America in particular, the only debate, if any, took place around the "crisis of paradigms" in social knowledge.

The issues suggested by all of this are many and very important. On this occasion I would like to focus on only two: first, on the relations between the historical perspectives of the imaginary and knowledge, and second, on something more complex, the relations between the imaginary dimension, social action, and the forms of knowledge making.

The Imaginary and Knowledge Dimensions

The idea of a future horizon as a new time for social existence, and hence as the bearer of a new understanding of history, whether total or partial, radical or superficial, clearly points to a specific perspective on the imaginary dimension: that of a historical imaginary, which is far different from a mystical or magical imaginary that might transcend history.

The historic imaginary perspective that has been dominant throughout the world until very recently was born in the Americas, though its core expression was elaborated in Europe. This perspective implied a genuine mutation of intersubjective relations among the populations of the world: acceptance of continuous change not only as a normal historical behavior but also as something at once necessary and desirable. That in turn meant, for Europe in particular, the abandonment of the past as a golden age of humanity in favor of an embrace of the future as the continent of hope.[4]

I want to stress two points about this specific perspective on the imaginary dimension: (1) the idea of modernity/ rationality, associated with the ideas of progress and the market, and (2) the idea of democracy as a concrete social interest, as the highest expression of modernity.[5]

This time I do not go very far in this inquiry. My interest lies in observing that in the absence of these ideas/images and of certain questions posed to social "reality," that is, to social experience, and first of all to power, no elaboration of the respective questions, no search for the components of "reality" in which to find parts of the answer, no fields of relationships that are established or discovered in that search, and no explanations and meanings elaborated for those answers will be possible. Or, it would be possible to do so in a very different way from the one that has led to the establishment of "critical" thought, the perspective on knowledge that made the power of capital the chief object of scientific research, debate, and theory for nearly two centuries. In other words, I suggest that the perspective on knowledge implied in "critical thought" and "critical theory of society" was a companion and a partner to an equally "critical" imaginary, which took root together with modernity.

The Imaginary and History Dimensions

What made these perspectives on the imaginary dimension and knowledge develop together and then collapse and die out together? If the questions asked by the perspective of knowledge stemmed from those about the imaginary dimension, could it be said that the extinction of this specific future horizon was what dragged down the perspective on knowledge that was tied to it? Or was it just the reverse? Was the defeat of the social action inspired by this perspective on knowledge what led to the extinction of the perspective on imagination with which it was so closely associated?

The extinction of an entire horizon on the future, or a perspective on the historical imagination, cannot be explained exclusively by far-reaching changes in the intersubjective sources from which it sprang. But the same unquestionably holds true for what happens or may happen to a given perspective on social historical knowledge. In other words, what I am suggesting is that the intersubjective sources that fed the currents of the specific historical imaginary—which might be called "critical"—and those of the "critical" social knowledge with which it was associated have been drying up or undergoing profound change. On both sides, this is without doubt a major victory for capitalism.

Does it follow from this that capitalism has simply won out because it is invincible? And does it follow that, as is asserted in "postmodernist" thought, that this critique and its proposals and projects were never more than a chimerical "grand narrative" and that it must be accepted that power is either a theoretically irrelevant abstraction or an unchanging datum of life as it is and in regard to which it is therefore senseless to search for the most appropriate crevices in which to play with individual freedom, as is stated today in a postmodernist reading of Michel Foucault?

In society, power is a social relationship composed of an uninterrupted weave of three components, domination/exploitation/conflict over the control of key areas of human social existence: (1) work and its resources and products, (2) sex and its resources and products, (3) collective authority and its resources and products, and (4) subjectivity/intersubjectivity, especially the imaginary and the mode of producing knowledge.[6] These three components of all power relations are there in differing degrees and forms depending on the concrete situations and space/times, configuring a given pattern of power in each case. The one that is articulated around capitalism has turned out to be stronger than its adversaries to date. But that is not necessarily a demonstration of its invincibility; it is, rather, an indication of a relationship of forces that leads to the following question on its adversaries' power pattern: Where does its weakness lie?

I suggest beginning the search for an answer by asking another, indispensable, question: Can a historical imaginary, and particularly a "critical" one, live and develop over a long period of time without being able to boast victories in concrete experience? Probably not. Better put, undoubtedly not, because a historical imaginary is not the same as a mystical or magical one, which posits a universe that transcends concrete reality. As regards the latter, concrete experience either does not serve as the needed point of reference, because the imaginary dimension transcends it, or is always a continuous demonstration of the imaginary's truth. To illustrate, for a person who believes that the universe was "created" by God, experience is a continuous demonstration of that belief. However, for one who believes in the "immaculate conception," experience is wholly irrelevant. But both beliefs are proper to a single mystical imaginary.

From this point of view, it is neither arbitrary nor irrelevant to suggest that the originally close ties between the historical-critical imaginary and concrete historical experience, ties that could almost be described as symmetrical from the eighteenth- and nineteenth-century European perspective and especially in regard to the ideas/images of modernity, rationality, and progress, tended to break apart over the course of the twentieth century, especially in relation to the ideas/images of revolution and socialism. And that separation has led to a steady frustration and an ultimate subordination of the subjectivity linked to that imaginary. That is, a part of the concrete experience of the twentieth century—precisely the part linked to the hegemonic force and therefore the one responsible for the defeats or victories—tended to orient itself and develop in a direction distinct from that of the critical imaginary. And consequently, the actions taken to make that imaginary real were defeated or, far worse, were in fact victories that led elsewhere than imagined.[7]

A brief historical anecdote may be useful here. Since very early in the twentieth century, there has been a progressive reduction of opportunity for debate and activity by those social movements for which the struggle to control the nation-state is not the path leading to the future horizon where domination and exploitation will cease to be the core of social organization. In their place came "historical materialism" as the hegemonic model worldwide, and since the so-called socialist revolution in Russia in October 1917 even the current that conserved the original political name "social democracy" gave way in terms of worldwide hegemony to the one that adopted the name "Marxism-Leninism." This was the current that came to dominate the movement throughout the world from its base in the new Russian state beginning in 1924. For this ideological current, the state is the core of the revolution in society, and its capture and control are therefore the revolution's key task. Especially since the defeat of the Spanish Republic, the opportunity available to opposing currents has been reduced to such an extent that for the great majority of the world's population, they simply do not exist.

It is well known that from 1917 some important minorities expressed radical critiques of the nature and future of the new power installed in Russia, which claimed to be revolutionary and socialist. In the 1917–1920 period, Rosa Luxemburg denounced the new power's despotism; Anton Pannekoek, Hermann Gorter, Paul Mattick, and others exposed the bureaucratic counterrevolution; and Rodolfo Mondolfo described the system of state capitalism that had usurped socialism's place.[8] And from 1927, Trotsky and his followers more than any others denounced, first, the "bureaucratic deformations" and then the crimes committed in the "trials," though they nevertheless acknowledged the presence of a "workers" state.[9]

But in spite of all the critiques, Leon Trotsky's assassination, the experience of the Moscow "trials" and the forced labor camps, Russia and the Bolsheviks were able to establish an authentic prestige among revolutionaries worldwide. In particular, its support for the anticolonial and anti-imperialist struggles throughout the world made the Soviet Union a worldwide pole of attraction and political guidance, and its prestige and influence only increased after World War II and the formation of the "socialist camp," including all the countries of Eastern Europe, China after the revolution of 1949, and Cuba from 1962.

But not long after World War II, a sequence of events occurred in the "socialist camp" that began to reintroduce doubt as to the true nature of that "camp" regarding the horizon of future: the anticapitalist "critical imaginary." And since, the doubts have only grown and deepened. First came Josip Broz Tito's (and Yugoslavia's) break with Iósif Stalin and the Soviet Union, and within Yugoslavia itself the dissidence that described the dominant bureaucracy as a "new class."[10] Then came the workers' revolt in East Berlin in 1953, so brutally repressed that Brecht did not hesitate to make public his ferocious irony: if the state was so unhappy with its citizens, it should choose others. Not long thereafter, in 1956 a revolution broke out in Hungary, and "Soviet" tanks were called upon to crush it in a bloody repression. And to all these events were soon added the repeated worker revolts in Poland during the 1950s and 1960s.

Following each of these events, many intellectuals associated with the communist parties in many places (but especially in Europe) broke with those parties. After the Hungarian uprising, it was estimated that about six thousand European intellectuals abandoned them (I recall the terribly sad balance sheet drawn up in *La somme et le reste* by Henri Lefevre). The great majority, however, did not cease to be Marxists and socialists or to conserve their sympathy toward the so-called Soviet Union. Doubt was consolidated when, following Stalin's death, confirmation of the accusations of despotism, criminality, and abuses by the Stalinist regime began to emerge from within the dominant *nomenklatura* itself. The famous Khrushchev Report to the 20th Congress of the Communist Party of the Soviet Union had a devastating impact, even though the Stalinist parties sought to explain it all away with the ineffable "personality cult" formula. After the Sino-Soviet split came an expansion of Maoist influence as a substitute for Stalinism. But the massacre of the Shanghai Commune in 1967, ordered by Mao Zedong himself, revealed the orientation and future course of the Chinese regime. The final sequence of events leading from the repression and occupation of Prague by the same Soviet tanks in 1969, liquidating what had promised to be a democratic liberalization of the bureaucratic despotism, through the ultimately successful revolt of the Solidarity workers in Poland in 1976 despite General Wojciech Witold Jaruzelski's Stalinist coup d'état, to the fall of the Berlin Wall in 1989 and the disintegration of the "socialist camp" is doubtless still fresh in the memory of all and requires no further commentary.

This sequence lasted long enough to show the world the true nature of the power imposed in Russia and the entire "socialist camp" since October 1917. Its governing minority—as is clear from what it has done everywhere after the "fall"—during that period was more and more interested in the privatization of power, not in its destruction.[11] And due to the dissidents, as the critical revolutionary currents in the countries of the "socialist camp" were called, the conflicts between the holders of power and its victims rapidly grew and became explicit.

However, outside those countries the millions of workers and socialist revolutionaries throughout the world continued to fight for the promises of the brilliant horizon of future associated with the idea of socialism. And the revolutionary critique of power began to confront both capitalism and the bureaucratic despotism of the "socialist camp." As Rudy Dutschke said at a rally in Berlin shortly before becoming the victim of an assassination attempt, a despotic power was visible that had begun to stretch from Washington to Vladivostok, and it was urgently necessary to confront it before it became even stronger.

It was, then, both alongside and separately from the hegemony of "historical materialism" or "Marxism-Leninism" that a new social movement took shape from the 1960s, aiming to subvert not only the capitalist-imperialist power but also that of the bureaucratic despotism of the "socialist camp." The aim was no longer just liberation of the workers from exploited labor but rather liberation of people—all people—from domination and discrimination in all aspects of human life in society: work, sex, subjectivity, authority, that is, for workers, women, homosexuals, youths, and victims of racial or ethnic discrimination and for knowledge and the imaginary. The goal was not the full liberation of subjectivity, knowledge production's break with its ties to power, liberation of the imagination and of all fields of culture (especially art), and defense of nature against human depredation (capitalist depredation in particular). The objective was the liberation of peoples from authority embodied in "raison d'état."

The struggle for the expansion and deepening of democracy in society, and not only in the nation-state, not just as a negotiation of the limits and conditions of exploitation and domination, and not just as a liberation from exploited labor, but above all as a materialization of the idea of social equality of peoples and as a legitimation of their diversity as a form of day-to-day relations among peoples in every sphere of social existence throughout the world, emerged as the brightest core of the new horizon of future. These were the proposals and images put forward by all the youth movements in places as diverse as Shanghai in 1967, Paris in May 1968, Tlatelolco that same year, the streets of Prague in 1969, and the most active part of the youth movement in the United States, including the half million people who attended the festival of subversion at Woodstock.

A still brighter horizon began to take shape, in other words, a more radical and more global critical imaginary that confronted both capitalism and the bureaucratic despotism of "real socialism" at the same time.

After nearly a century, the debate on the state's place in the articulation of power was revived, and the aim of every revolution now was liberation from the state, not its strengthening. What emerged was an imaginary dimension linked to liberating people from power, from all power. And as normally happens in history, music, the visual arts, poetry, and literature were the forms of expression that most faithfully reflected this new imaginary dimension.

It is by no means surprising, from this point of view, that the two powers—private capitalism and bureaucratic despotism—have joined forces to defeat this new assault on heaven. And when they did, they were fully successful. But the outcome was this genuine historical disaster that I am now trying to make perceptible: the defeat of all the movements, organizations, and regimes opposed to or rivaling capital and bureaucracy throughout the world, driving them to the brink of their extinction and, hence, the extinction of a horizon that came to be totally and exclusively occupied by the predatory needs of financial capital.

The defeat of the worldwide revolutionary movement was also the defeat of the "critical imaginary." It did not last long enough to generate its own "critical theory" of society. A decade or a decade and a half is undoubtedly not enough to move from a new imaginary dimension to the production of a new form of knowledge.

It is therefore also relevant to ask what happened to the previous so-called critical thought and its product, the so-called critical theory of society, first because that perspective on knowledge was the one that oriented and conducted in practice the social actions undertaken to achieve the horizon of future and second because it was also the court that judged and evaluated the orientation and efficacy of actions.

Hegemony and the Crisis of Eurocentrism

I do not want to go any further on this subject. For the time being I merely reiterate what I have tried to demonstrate in other texts. First, this "critical thought" and "critical theory" of society were created in the context of the Eurocentric perspective of knowledge and in reference to the specific form of social power prevailing in Europe. Though already troubled by the principal epistemological difficulties of that perspective, the questions it asked about reality, and its basic conceptual categories were developed in and for the European experience. Second, worldwide hegemony was achieved by the most definitely Eurocentric of the versions of this "critical thought" and its respective "critical theory": "historical materialism" or "Marxism-Leninism." And that was the version that dominated the conduct of actions and the evaluation of their orientation and efficacy since the early twentieth century. Third, that current of thought and social theory was fed from the beginning by the cognitive perspective of Eurocentrism, and its development has therefore been closely tied to the growing technocratization proper to that specific form of rationality.[12]

Over time this specific process of the globally dominant form of thought and social theory, which conducted and evaluated actions vis-à-vis the dominant power, generated a growing divide between the critical imaginary, concrete social experience, and social theory. That divide became more and more perceptible—that is, perceptible by more and more people—after the end of World War II.

The most profound trends in capitalism (not just in capital), which have led to the current situation, were already visible from the mid-1960s: growing limitations on the commodification of individual labor power, therefore "structural unemployment"; overaccumulation in some areas and underaccumulation in others; fragmentation of labor, technocratization of knowledge; reduction of opportunity to practice democracy. Because all of these trends were in conflict with an important process that began after World War II of deconcentrating the control of power in most cases and of effective redistribution of power in a few others, they finally conflicted with a worldwide wave of questioning of the very foundations of capitalism's power from the mid-1960s through the mid-1970s.

That is why when the worldwide crisis of capital broke out in the mid-1970s, for the great majority of the "Left" throughout the world it must have seemed that victories over capitalism were imminent. But it was not to be, and that was not because people had begun to turn their backs on the critical imaginary but because the globally hegemonic intellectual and political leadership had deepened and intensified its Eurocentric belonging and perspective. I therefore suggest posing this new question in the labyrinth: the worldwide defeat in the material dimension had previously occurred in the intellectual-political dimension. That defeat left most of the victims of capitalism in a vacuum. This allowed a minority to traverse the conformist paths of the imaginary dimension. But for the overwhelming majority of the professionals of knowledge, it led them to reinforce their Eurocentric propensities and turn their backs—with no psychological difficulties—on the cognitive components of the critical perspective on knowledge.

In the Time of Worldwide Resistance: A Return of the Future?

As the 1990s came to an end, the time of defeat was also approaching its end. Resistance against the most perverse trends of capitalism, subsumed under the term "globalization," is already rising throughout the world. In Latin America and in South America in particular, not one country is a stranger to the growing resistance of workers and the political instability generated by it.

This new period of social action in confrontation with world capitalist power has begun to develop in an almost totally transformed scenario in its structure and its specific components, both material and intersubjective (social relations). In particular, this is happening at a time of nearly total reconcentration of the control of power in the hands of the dominant elites and of fragmentation and social deconcentration among the workers.

It is by no means inevitable that the conventional Eurocentric versions ("historical materialism") will prevail in leading the resistance. But it almost always happens that people begin to act not only in response to their problems and needs but also by appealing to their memory to define the new situations and orient themselves in relation to them.

In any event, the worldwide resistance that has gotten underway implies—or may imply—the reconstruction of a critical imaginary and the rebuilding of a new horizon of future quite different from the one that has been extinguished. That new horizon is not yet visible. But if the resistance is not crushed quickly and totally, it will indicate that there is a new anticapitalist imaginary, a new horizon in the process of formulation. What historical images will it contain? For the time being they can only be guessed at, though their virtuality may already be recognizable: the one that was defeated and seemed to be dead and buried, the brightest hope of the 1960s, democracy as social equality and not just individual citizenship in the nation-state, as a legitimation of the diversity of peoples and the heterogeneity of their creations; as a liberation of life in society from all the forms and mechanisms of exploitation, domination, and discrimination; as a decolonization and liberation of thought and imagination; as the copresence of social equality, social solidarity, and the individual freedom of all people in all societies, tending to seek and produce another institutional universe in which it can really be expressed and defended. The disputes and combinations between the modern nation-state and the new community may be the field of expression for the search for new institutional forms of authority in which power is not present or is reduced and kept under control.

What is truly of interest in connection with this debate is the exploration—barely incipient but nonetheless necessary—of a parallel horizon of knowledge, a non-Eurocentric rationality that can also be part of the horizon of the future. In any event, it is a task to be addressed now.

Notes

First published in *Current Sociology* 50, no. 1 (January 2002): 75–87.

This is a slightly revised version of a communication to the International Seminar on Geopolitics of Knowledge, Duke University, October 2000. —Aníbal Quijano

1   Vallejo, "Spain, Take This Cup from Me."

2   See Fukuyama, *The End of History and the Last Man*. The article bearing that title, which preceded the book, was published in *World Affairs* in 1989. For my debate on the problem, see Quijano, "Colonialidad del poder, cultura y conocimiento en América Latina."

3   Everyone will doubtless recall Aeschylus's Prometheus. I have no copy available as I write these notes, but I cite from memory his dialogue with the Oceanides who go to visit him after he has been chained:

    "What have you done to deserve such a punishment?"
    "I have freed men from fear of death."

"And how have you achieved this miracle?"

"I have made blind Hope take root among them."

4   An extended discussion of this historical change can be found in Quijano, "The Paradoxes of Modernity."

5   In the power of capital, the market is the floor for equality but is also
its ceiling, that is, its limit. Hence, in this system of power, equality
cannot be practiced other than as an ongoing conflict that, on the one
hand, has led to an institutionalization of the negotiation of the limits,
conditions, and forms of domination/exploitation/conflict, expressed
in the legal-political equality of social unequals and in the institutional
universe of the modern nation-state. But on the other hand, this system generates continuous conflict due to the steady reduction of those
limits and the progressive expansion and intensification of inequality
in society, which naturally breaks through the limits of the power held
by capital and the modern nation-state. This relationship is contradictory and conflictual, but it is not avoidable. It is a historical necessity.
In this specific and precise sense, it is a concrete social interest that
defines modernity. See Quijano, "Colonialidad del poder, eurocentrismo y América Latina."

6   Quijano, "The Question of Power and the Question of Democracy."

7   It may have been in Italian cinema, and clearly by no means coincidentally, that the images of that break began to be produced for the first
time and as early as the 1960s. I remember especially the devastated
consciousness, trapped between cynicism and anguish, in *We Loved
Each Other So Much* (1974), directed by Ettore Scola.

8   See Luxemburg, *Crítica de la Revolución Rusa*; and Luxemburg, *Selected
Political Writings*. See also Luxemburg's chapter on the Russian Revo-
lution in Pannekoek, *Lenin as Philosopher*. The articles of Pannekoek,
Gorter, and others are compiled in *La contrarevolution bureaucratique*.
For Rodolfo Mondolfo, see Mondolfo, *State Capitalism and the Russian
Revolution*.

9   It is interesting and intriguing to see that at the end of his principal
book in this debate, *The Revolution Betrayed*, Trotsky appears to suspect
that something more than a "bureaucratic deformation" may have
been underway in Russia (see Trotsky, *La revolución traicionada*). There
can be no other explanation for his suggestion that if the situation
were to last much longer, say for fifty years, it would become necessary
to characterize it as another system of domination and exploitation. But
there is no basis on which to infer an alternative theoretical position
or the perspective on knowledge with which he suspects this evolution
might be associated. His followers, the so-called Trotskyites, never
took up that suggestion even after the passage of those fifty years, not
even when the notable book *Die Alternative* was published by Rudolf

Bahro in 1977. Its core thesis is precisely that the power created in Russia and in the "socialist camp" as a whole was not socialist but instead was a historically new pattern of domination and exploitation. See also Bahro, *El socialismo realmente existente*.

10 Milovan Djilas, *La nueva clase*, Biblioteca del Congreso Nacional de Chile, n.d., https://obtienearchivo.bcn.cl/obtienearchivo?id =documentos/10221.1/35593/2/197782.pdf.

11 "The Dangers of Democracy" is the title of an article by Moscow mayor Gavril Popov, the first elected mayor in Russia's history, after the collapse of the Soviet Union. The ominous argument put forward by Popov, a professor of Marxism and dialectics until the eve of the Soviet system's collapse, is that the destruction of "real socialism" in Russia was the outcome of an alliance between the working masses and the intelligentsia, though the two sectors pursued opposing interests: the masses wanted democracy to achieve social equality and control of power, while the intellectuals sought to create a new hierarchy in society. That is, the broader a democracy is, the more the masses will advance in the direction of social equality and against the interests of the intelligentsia. Hence, for Popov, democracy is a danger that must be controlled.

12 I have put forward certain proposals for debate on these issues in several writings. See, for example, Anibal Quijano, "Coloniality of Power, Eurocentrism, and Latin America" (2000), in this volume.

7

COLONIALITY OF POWER, GLOBALIZATION, AND DEMOCRACY

Introduction

I take this occasion to propose looking into a few issues that I feel have not been sufficiently explored in the debate about the process called "globalization" and about its relationships with current trends in institutional forms of domination, particularly those of the modern nation-state. Any discussion of such matters, however, even a limited one such as this, calls for a theoretical and historical perspective on the question of power, and it is clearly important to note here some of the main lines of thought behind the present analysis.

From this perspective, the phenomenon of power is characterized as a type of social relationship constituted by the permanent copresence of three elements: domination, exploitation, and conflict. Their copresence affects the four basic areas of social existence and both results from and is the expression of disputes over their control: (1) labor and its resources and products, (2) sex and its resources and products, (3) collective (or public) authority and resources and products, and (4) subjectivity/intersubjectivity and its resources and products. The forms of social existence in each of these four areas do not derive from one another, but neither they do exist or operate separately or independently from each other. For this reason, the power relations established in disputes over the control of these areas of social existence likewise do not derive from one another, yet none can exist in any but an inadvertent and precarious way without all the others. That is, they form a structural complex whose character is always historical and specific. In other words, we are dealing with a specific historical matrix of power.[1]

The current matrix of world power consists of the articulation among (1) the coloniality of power, that is, the notion of "race" as the foundation of the universal matrix of basic social classification and social domination; (2) capitalism as the universal matrix of social exploitation; (3) the state as the central, universal form of control for collective authority and the modern nation-state as its hegemonic variant; and (4) Eurocentrism as the hegemonic form of control over subjectivity/intersubjectivity, particularly with regard to the means of producing knowledge.

Coloniality of power is a concept that recognizes one of the foundational elements in the current matrix of power: the basic worldwide classification of Earth's population through the notion of "race."[2] This notion and the social classification based on it ("racism") were created five hundred years ago, along with America, Europe, and capitalism. Together they form the most profound and enduring expression of colonial domination, having been imposed on the planet's entire population over the course of European colonial expansion. Since then, in the current matrix of world power they permeate each and every corner of social existence, forming the deepest and most effective form of social, material, and intersubjective domination and being by the same token the most widespread intersubjective basis of political domination within the current matrix of power.[3]

The category of capitalism refers to the structurally articulated combination of all historically known forms of labor control or exploitation: slavery, servitude, independent small-scale market production, reciprocity, and wage labor. Such forms of labor control are articulated as a combined structure surrounding the preeminence of the wage form, called capital, for producing goods for the world market. Capital is a specific form of labor control that entails the marketization of the labor force that is to be exploited. By its dominance in this structural whole, it confers on the latter its centrality—which is to say, makes it capitalist—but historically it does not exist, never has existed, and probably never will exist in the future separately or independently of the other forms of exploitation.[4]

The state, as a collective authority structure and a collective form of domination, is ancient. It has not been firmly established exactly how old the state is and in association with which historical conditions it was imposed as the central worldwide form of control for collective authority and political domination, much less when, where, and how it became the nation-state. However, we do know that the modern nation-state is, on the one hand, relatively recent and, on the other, has only been consolidated in a few spaces of state domination or countries. Its specific signs are, first, citizenship or the formal presumption of legal and political equality for all who live in its space of domination, regardless of their inequality in all other spheres of power, and second, the political representativity attributed to the state with regard to all of its citizens based on their formal equality and not merely, as with other variants of the state, to the social interests of some individual or sector. The modern nation-state gradually came together during the period known as modernity, which begins with the Americas and in connection with the process of Eurocentering capitalism and modernity. The state attained its current defining features toward the end of the eighteenth century and was recognized during the twentieth century as the globally hegemonic model, which is not the same thing, to be sure, as being practiced globally. In the current stage of colonial/capitalist power, its "globalization," especially since the mid-1970s, works to undo those specific features, even to reverse their various processes, particularly regarding the social conflict over the expansion of social equality, individual freedom, and social solidarity.[5]

Finally, Eurocentrism is the knowledge perspective that has been systematically produced in Europe since the seventeenth century as an expression of and part of the process of Eurocentering the colonial/modern/capitalist matrix of power, in other words, as an expression of the experiences of colonialism and coloniality of power, of the needs and experiences of capitalism and of the Eurocentering of that matrix of power. Eurocentrism was imposed around the world and acknowledged in the centuries that followed as the only legitimate form of rationality, in any case as the hegemonic form of rationality, the dominant means of knowledge production. One of the main elements of Eurocentrism that is particularly worth pointing out for our purposes here is the radical dualisms between "reason" and "body" and between "subject" and "object." These radical dualisms are associated with the reductionist, homogenizing propensity of Eurocentrism's mode of defining and identifying, especially in perceptions of social experience whether in its ahistorical version, which perceives phenomena or objects in isolation, separately, and therefore requires no notion of wholeness or in the version that allows for an idea of evolutionary, organicist, or systemicist whole, even the one that presupposes a historical macrosubject. This knowledge perspective is currently undergoing one of its most open periods of crisis, as is the entire Eurocentric version of modernity.[6]

Because of its characteristics, Eurocentrism was the first domain of the matrix of power in recorded history to be global in nature and vocation. In this sense, what today is called "globalization" is doubtless a moment in the historical development process of this matrix of power, perhaps its moment of peak and transition, as several people have already suggested.[7]

These concepts and categories are obviously all open questions. We should consequently not lose sight of the fact that their systematic exploration and debate has barely begun. This does not mean that my proposals here are made arbitrarily but rather that I will return to them as research and debate continue.

The Central Questions of "Globalization"

What is now termed "globalization" is, obviously, an issue that elicits many questions that have given rise to much debate and a vast and growing literature. The most widely circulated idea in this regard is likely that globalization refers to a continual and growing economic, political, and cultural integration of the world. In practice, this implies that there are phenomena and processes that affect everyone immediately, even simultaneously, or you might say globally. And the primary historical determinant of this putative process is ascribed to the "scientific-technological revolution" in communications media and transportation systems.

Originally, "globality" referred to a drastic change in the relationships between space and time in our subjectivity as a consequence of the speed at which information circulates through the new scientific-technological media so that things that happen anywhere in the world could be perceived simultaneously. In our subjectivity, in our intersubjective relations, not only had the world grown smaller, but this happened because the world had become integrated in time; it was now simultaneous. The famous image of the "global village" was undoubtedly the first mental construction to successfully take notice of this subjective relationship with space and with time.[8]

Though these may still be the first images some associate with the notion of "globalization," it must be admitted that they are getting buried under other more recent images that, for many others, have apparently taken on the consistency of genuine conceptual categories even though they resist leaving the media habitat: "virtual reality," "virtual society," and "the new economy" (which from the same perspective could also be termed "the virtual economy"). The first of these has decisive implications in the debate over knowledge making. It highlights that, above all, current technology not only reproduces, combines, or uses images and sounds that are present in "nature" or "reality" but also produces, manipulates, and disseminates new visual and sound elements, new images produced with those new elements, which taken together constitute a whole "virtual" world that in many ways overwhelms and even displaces and replaces the "real" world to the point that in many diverse areas it is no easy task to distinguish between the two, with all that this signifies for the question of perception, knowledge, and the means of producing knowledge. The notion of "virtual society" extends this image, proposing that social relationships now increasingly take place within and are imbricated with this "virtual reality" and that they somehow have the same consistency. The "new economy," the most recent of these notions, has its origins in the media, like the others, and refers to the idea that the current world economy has been or is in the process of being turned into a single network for the exchange of goods and values. This would be the ultimate expression of the world economy's global integration and is of course based on and imbricated with the notions of "virtual reality" and "virtual society."

The debate does not always manage to avoid a tendency toward mystification. Indeed, in the language of the media the term "globalization" has become virtually synonymous with a vast, systemic, impersonal machinery that exists and evolves independently of any human decisions, that is, in a somehow natural and thus inevitable way, which is seen as encompassing and explaining all human actions today.

But the "world"—if that term is taken to imply a social human existence articulated in a specific historical whole—cannot be understood, whether or not it is "globalized," apart from the fact that a specific matrix of power is what has given it the character of being a "world" or a specific historical whole, without which condition any notion of "globalization" would be simply useless. Otherwise, it would mean that communication networks, information networks, exchange networks, and so on exist and operate in a kind of historical vacuum. It is therefore not merely relevant but also theoretically necessary to investigate each and every area of current control over social life in order to bring to light the possible meaning that this "globalization" might have in actual experience. Within the limits of this text, I will only go so far as to raise the issues that I find central to two primary areas: labor control and the control of public authority.

Capitalism and Globalization

Carefully examining current trends in capitalism, we find that the data are unquestionably impressive, whether we are talking about the political geography of the distribution of income, goods, and basic services or capital flows, whether about relations among forms of capital or relations between capital and labor. As these data are generally accessible to everyone, it is useful for the purposes of this study to point out a few major trends:

1   In 1800, 74 percent of the world's population (then totaling 944 million) generated 44 percent of global gross domestic product (GDP), which then totaled the equivalent of $229,095 million in 1980 US dollars, whereas 26 percent of the world's population generated the remaining 56 percent of GDP. But by 1995, 80 percent of the world's population (of 5,716 million) had only 20 percent of global GDP (which totaled $17,091,479 million in 1980 US dollars), while the remaining 20 percent took in 80 percent of GDP.[9]

2   "The ratio of average income of the richest country in the world to that of the poorest has risen from about 9 to 1 at the end of the nineteenth century to at least 60 to 1 today. . . . Since 1950, the portion of the world's population living in poor countries grew by about 250 percent, while in rich countries the population increased by less than 50 percent."[10]

3   According to the World Bank Report for the year 2000, in 1999 the countries that make up the Group of Seven (G7), which together account for less than 12 percent of the world's population and 16 percent of its land surface, produced 65 percent of global GDP, 3 percent more than in 1980.

4   And in the same historic shift, the gulf between rich and poor within each country in the world has also widened. Thus, in the richest country in the world, the United States, in 1970 there were 24.7 million people living in extreme poverty (11.5% of the population); by 1997 that figure had jumped to 35.6 million (13.3% of the population), a growth of 43 percent in less than twenty years. A recent study shows that from 1977 to 1989, the top 1 percent of families took in 70 percent of total gains in family wealth, seeing a 100 percent increase in their income. In Latin America, income differences have gotten worse since 1973: the

average income of the top 20 percent of income earners is sixteen times higher today than that of the remaining 80 percent. In Brazil, this ratio is now twenty-five to one, as compared to a ratio of ten to one in Western Europe and five to one in the United States. The same is true for the income ratio of "skilled" salary earners compared to all others. For example, this differential grew by more than 30 percent in the 1990s in Peru and by more than 20 percent in Colombia.[11]

5   Given all this, the three richest people on Earth have more wealth than the GDP of the forty-eight poorest countries, that is, one quarter of all the countries in the world. Likewise, regarding Latin America, in 1996 the General Motors Corporation had sales of $168 billion, whereas the combined GDP of Guatemala, El Salvador, Honduras, Costa Rica, Nicaragua, Panama, Ecuador, Peru, Bolivia, Paraguay, and Uruguay came to only $159 billion.

6   At the same time, according to United Nations statistics, the basic needs of Earth's entire population could be met using just 4 percent of the world's 225 largest fortunes.[12] And meeting their health needs (in 1998, 4 billion people living in the Third World did not have access to safe drinking water or electricity) and nutritional needs (50% of all children suffer from malnutrition) would take $13 billion, that is, 13 percent of what the United States and Europe spend on perfume every year.

7   Considering the direction of capital investment flows, statistics show that in the years 1990–1995, for example, 65 percent of total foreign direct investment went toward the "center" and that the remainder went to a handful of so-called emerging countries. Between 1989 and 1993, just ten of these countries received 72 percent of that remaining foreign direct investment (China, Mexico, Malaysia, Argentina, Thailand, Indonesia, Brazil, Nigeria, Venezuela, and South Korea).[13] One critical problem in world capital flows is that Third World debt has risen over less than two decades from $615 billion to some $2,500 billion. And this is, as everyone knows, a never-ending story because it is inextinguishable. But above all, it is a tragic story.[14]

8   In addition, of the 6 billion people who make up the world's population at the outset of this new century, some 800 million do not have paid employment. And this is surely a conservative estimate, since statistics record only those who are seeking jobs,

and the figure should be multiplied by at least a factor of five to account for family and household members who depend on the nonexistent wages. And the total population of unemployed and underemployed amounts to more or less half the people in the world, given that 3 billion people live on less than two dollars a day. Economists have coined the concept of "structural unemployment" to refer to the trend of growing world unemployment. And more than a few have proposed the idea of the "end of work" to refer to the implications of this trend.[15]

9 Additionally, though research on the topic is not yet far enough advanced and therefore the data are still preliminary, it is estimated that more than 200 million people around the world are being held under conditions of slavery.[16]

10 All of these trends in the distribution of capital, jobs, production, earnings, and goods and services in today's world are related to the changing relationships among the diverse forms of capitalist accumulation that favor the absolute hegemony of speculative accumulation. Thus, worldwide currency-exchange transactions amounted to roughly $20 billion in 1970, growing by 1999 to some $1.3 trillion. In the United States alone, in 1980 pension funds, mutual funds, and insurance companies including life insurance companies held financial assets totaling $1.6 trillion, equivalent to roughly 60 percent of the country's GDP. But by 1990 these funds held $5.2 trillion in assets—equal to 95 percent of GDP—and in 1993 more than $8 trillion, or 125 percent of GDP. This predominance of finance is also shown in the so-called financialization of industries, as their productive investments continually decline in favor of financial investments, and also in the swelling size of financial profits on the "periphery" and in "emerging countries." In 1983, stock market profits in the global periphery reached $100 billion; by 1993, that figure had grown to $1,500 billion.[17]

Based on the figures and data listed above, we can draw a few inferences, tentative perhaps yet nonetheless relevant:

1 A process of reconcentration of control over resources, wealth, and income into the hands of a small minority of humans (currently no more than 20%) is underway.

2   This implies that a process of increasing social polarization of
       the world's people is underway, dividing a wealthy minority—
       proportionally shrinking while growing richer and richer—from
       the vast majority, growing proportionally more numerous while
       becoming poorer and poorer.

3   The overexploitation of the great mass of workers around the
       world is on the rise, since along with the reconcentration of in-
       come and wealth, the wage differential among wage earners is
       growing while the proportion of the unemployed, marginalized
       from the key fields of the accumulation structure, is expanding,
       resulting in a continual reduction in average wages.

4   The interest in and the ability of capital to turn labor into com-
       modities is on the decline, especially at the technologically most
       advanced levels of the world's accumulation structure.[18]

5   Unpaid forms of labor control are consequently expanding. Slav-
       ery, personal servitude, independent small-scale market produc-
       tion, and reciprocity are again expanding. Wage labor is still the
       form of labor control that is expanding the most but—to use a
       familiar image—like a clock that is running down.

6   There is an ongoing crisis in one of the basic dimensions incor-
       porated into the capitalist matrix of labor control, the relations
       among the specific forms of exploitation: the mechanisms that
       allocated the world's population from unpaid to wage labor,
       in general from noncapital to capital, over the course of the
       historical development of capitalist accumulation are on the
       decline and perhaps on the way out altogether, while mecha-
       nisms have been set in motion that seemingly indicate, though
       to what degree we cannot yet tell, the beginnings of an inverse
       trend.

7   The configuration of global capitalism—that is, the structure of
       the relationships between capital and every form of labor control
       as well as the relationships of all these with each other—is un-
       dergoing a drastic change, which implies that a transition in the
       system itself is underway.

8   In this specific sense and in this dimension, in the structure of
       the exploitation of labor, a process of social reclassification of the
       world's population must be underway on a global scale.

9   In any case, a process of reconcentrating and reconfiguring labor
       control and control over resources and their products—in sum,

changing the relations between capitalism and labor—is taking place on a worldwide scale.

10 These processes are associated with drastic changes in the global structure of capitalist accumulation, associated with the new position of and the predominant function played by speculation and financial accumulation within that structure, especially since the mid-1970s.[19]

None of these trends are new or unexpected, not even the last ones. They point to a moment, a degree, or a level of maturity and development of trends inherent in the character of capitalism as a major domain of the control of labor in the global matrix of power, trends that have been exhaustively theorized since at least Marx.[20] It thus makes little sense to discuss these processes and the problems that arise from them as if they were exactly new or, worse, as if they were due to a new phenomenon called "globalization," different or separate from capitalism, the result only or mainly of technological innovation and of its capacity to modify all our relations with space/time rather than of the capitalist character of the dominant structure of labor control and the development of its tendencies.

There is no doubt, however, that such basic tendencies in capitalism have deepened and, moreover, have speeded up and are on track for faster acceleration. The question therefore is this: What has prompted the acceleration and the deepening of these tendencies in capitalism? In other words, why has capitalist exploitation grown deeper and somehow easier? No one can exploit another person without dominating that person, much less in a stable and lasting manner. It is therefore necessary to open the question here of the relationship between domination and exploitation in the current matrix of power.

Force and violence are requisites for any form of domination, but in modern society they are not exercised explicitly and directly, at least not on a continual basis; instead, they are veiled by institutionalized structures of collective or public authority and "legitimized" by ideologies constitutive of the intersubjective relationships among the various interest and identity sectors of society. As was pointed out at the beginning of this essay, such structures are what we know as the state. And the coloniality of power is its deepest legitimizing mortar. In consequence, it is necessary to probe what has happened in the relations between the matrix of capitalist exploitation and the two levels of the matrix of domination: the state and the coloniality of power.

Capitalism and State

The relationship between capitalism as a global structure of labor control and its organization in particular spaces of domination as well as the organization of particular structures of collective authority in those spaces remains an open question. In general, the relationship between domination and exploitation is not always clear, much less systematic or organic, in any matrix of power.

While historians and theorists have analyzed the way in which modern colonialism, as created in the Americas, shaped a suitable environment for the formation of capitalism, the question of why capitalism became associated, in the same movement and at the same time, with diverse types of states in diverse spaces of domination, has not been breached or apparently studied. These types include, for example, the modern absolutist/imperial state (all the states of Western Europe except Switzerland between 1500 and 1789), the modern imperial/colonial nation-state (for example, France and England from the late eighteenth century until after World War II), the modern colonial state (North America before 1776 and South America before 1824 as well as the countries of Southeast Asia and of Africa until the mid-twentieth century), the modern despotic/bureaucratic state (the former Soviet Union and the countries of Eastern Europe until the late 1980s; their Nazi and fascist rivals in Germany, Japan, and Italy from the late 1930s to 1945; and China today), the modern democratic nation-state (those of Western Europe, North America, and Oceania today), the modern oligarchic-dependent states (those of Latin America before the late 1960s, with the exception of Mexico, Uruguay, and Chile from the late 1920s), the modern national-dependent states (to various degrees all those of Latin America today as well as most of those in Asia and some in Africa, particularly South Africa), and the modern neocolonial states (many, perhaps most, of those in Africa).

This classification is a working hypothesis, as is the list of respective examples. But it should not be considered arbitrary. To this extent, it allows us to question the Eurocentric historical and sociological perspective according to which the type of state corresponding to capitalism is the modern nation-state, while all others are somehow "exceptions" or "precapitalist" or "in transition" (virtually all the writers who follow "historical materialism").[21]

We will lack, in my view, a truly trustworthy historical theory of the relationship between capitalism and the state until the matter of the coloniality of power is integrated into the respective historical and theoretical research. But this is not the occasion for delving more deeply into this crucial question.

In any case, the recent debate on the relationship between "globalization" and the state, in the dominant (Eurocentric) perspective, is exclusively confined to the alleged crisis of the modern nation-state under the impacts of "globalization."[22]

Capitalism, Globalization, and the Modern Nation-State

What the current trends of capitalism—and particularly the hegemony of finance capital and the predatory actions of the speculative mechanisms of accumulation—have nevertheless made suddenly visible is the fact that modern capitalism, as one of the central aspects of the current globally dominant matrix of power, has been associated with the modern nation-state in only a few spaces of domination, while it has been associated throughout most of the world with other forms of the state and of political authority in general.

It is therefore more useful and more productive to try to elucidate the most dynamic trends underway in the relationships between current changes in the configuration of capitalism and those taking place in structures of collective authority and political domination.

In this respect, the following main trends can be distinguished:

1   The formation of a worldwide imperial bloc, made up of the modern nation-states in the "center" of the world system;

2   The struggle for regional hegemony among the national-dependent states associated with or in conflict with the imperial bloc in the most conflict-affected regions, such as the Middle East (Israel on one side, Syria and Iraq on the other), South America (Brazil, Chile, Argentina), Asia (India and Pakistan at one end, China and South Korea at the other), and Africa in a fluid manner, insofar as regions there do not yet appear to be differentiated in an analogous way to the former with the exception of South Africa;

3   The continual erosion of the national-democratic space, in other words, the continual de-democratization and denationalization of all the national-dependent states where the modern nation-state has not attained consolidation; and

4   The gradual conversion of the least national and democratic states into the local administration and control centers of world finance capital and the imperial bloc.

My aim here is not to explore each of these processes and their interactions systematically and exhaustively. At this time for our purposes, it is above all necessary to insist that the worldwide imperial bloc exists and to stress the de-democratizing and denationalizing of the dependent states and their incremental conversion into little more than political-administrative agencies for world finance capital and the worldwide imperial bloc, because these two trends are the clearest expressions of the reconcentration of world control over public authority, the local reprivatization of the same, and the virtual shadow of a global space of domination.

The Worldwide Imperial Bloc and Local States

It can no longer be denied that a handful of the most powerful modern nation-states—the members of the G7 (or the G8, with the late and subordinate admission of Russia), several of them being capitals of modern colonial empires and all of them seats of twentieth-century capitalist imperialism[23]—now together form a true worldwide imperial bloc. First, they impose the decisions they make on all other countries and on the nerve centers of the world's economic, political, and cultural relations. Second, they do this without having been elected or even appointed by the world's other states, which they thus do not represent and consequently do not need to consult in making their decisions. They are virtually a world public authority, though not a genuine world state.

This worldwide imperial bloc is not constituted solely by the globally hegemonic nation-states. It is, rather, a configuration of a sort of institutional network formed by these nation-states: the intergovernmental organizations for control and the exercise of violence, such as the North Atlantic Treaty Organization; the intergovernmental and private agencies for controlling world capital flows, especially for finance capital (the International Monetary Fund, the World Bank, the Paris Club, and the Inter-American Development Bank being some of the major ones); and the great global corporations. This institutional network already constitutes a sort of de facto invisible world government.[24] In other words, this amounts to a worldwide reconcentration of control over public authority on a global scale. And this, from my perspective, is the most important phenomenon in the so-called globalization of the current world matrix of power.

The emergence of the worldwide imperial bloc—should we just call it the global bloc?—obviously implies that all other states are subject to a steady reduction in their autonomy. This is particularly true of states and societies that have not completed and are not moving forward with the process of forming a modern nation-state. If we furthermore look at what happens to society, to the social, cultural, and political differences produced by the worldwide imposition of neoliberalism as the template for political economy, both within each country and between countries, we soon see that the continual erosion of autonomy (or sovereignty) in these states entails above all the de-democratization of society's political representation within the state and therefore the denationalization of society and the state. This is clearly demonstrated by the structural association between the needs of finance capital—the speculative mechanisms of accumulation—and the worldwide trend toward the reconcentration of control over public authority, whose major expression today is the worldwide imperial bloc.

These linked and interdependent processes do not imply, however, that the public authority of the worldwide imperial bloc might be exerted directly and explicitly on all the "spaces" or countries that they dominate (except as exceptional and transitory measures, as in the case of the Panama invasion and the arrest of Noriega), though they are clearly trending in that direction, as shown by the recent actions in Kosovo, in Chechnya, in Africa, and now in Colombia and potentially throughout the Andean-Amazonian region of South America ("Plan Colombia").[25]

For the moment at least, the worldwide imperial bloc requires the local states to impose their policies on each country. In this way, some of these local states are being turned into institutional structures for the local administration of the bloc's world interests, while the rest are making it more obvious that this is the role they've been playing all along. This process implies a local and global reprivatization of such states insofar as they are becoming less and less politically representative of every social sector in each country.[26] In this way, they form part of the worldwide network of state and private institutions of public authority that together have begun to form a kind of invisible world government.[27]

The Reprivatization of the Control of Collective Authority

This reconcentration of world control over public authority on a global scale implies at the most basic level a reprivatization of control over a central arena of social life and the institutional sphere linked to it. The control over collective authority had only been recognized as public in the modern period, in particular from the eighteenth century on. The modern nation-state emerged precisely as the embodiment of the public character of collective authority, public in the specific and explicit sense that it allowed for the equal participation of all "citizens" and that this fact was what most of all gave it legitimacy.[28] Now, however, though a part—an ever more secondary part, even a basically symbolic part—of this institutional universe remains admittedly public, the fact is that the dominant cores of these institutions are private, as in the case of global corporations, or else private, as with the administrative technocracies of the financial organizations and the political economies of states, even when we are dealing with supposedly public organizations such as the intergovernmental institutions of finance capital, the International Monetary Fund, and what is known as the World Bank.

In the ongoing worldwide debate over this trend toward the continual and growing erosion of the weakest states/societies due to their failure to sufficiently complete and consolidate their processes of democratization/nationalization, the most widely shared theory presents these facts as tending toward the decline of the modern nation-state itself.[29]

This is a clear example of the dominance of the perspective of knowledge. It is true that the modern nation-state, along with the bourgeois family, the capitalist enterprise, and Eurocentrism,[30] is one of the basic institutions of every area in the world matrix of power associated with the modern period, which begins with the Americas. It is likewise true that the modern nation-state is the globally hegemonic institution within the universe of institutions acting in the world in the struggle for control over public authority and its resources, violence in particular. What is not true, however, is that the modern nation-state actually exists in every space of domination that is called a "country." Nor is it true that all the current states of all countries—or spaces of domination—have the character of modern nation-states, much as they may represent themselves as such or even be accepted as such in the imaginary or symbolic universe of each country.

Coloniality of Power and Nation-State

The defining difference between the processes that completed and consolidated modern nation-states and those that did not resides in the manner and degree of their respective relationships with the coloniality of power is the issue. For the former, the coloniality of power was not immediately present in the spaces of domination where the processes of democratizing social relations, which produce and redefine the character of the processes of nationalizing society and its state, were carried out. This is how things took place in Western Europe from the last third of the eighteenth century to the end of World War II.

The coloniality of power, however, was and remains active in any case, for it forms part of the global context within which the processes that affect all concrete spaces of domination take place. This is because the concentration of the processes of democratizing and nationalizing the modern states in Western Europe up to the twentieth century is testimony precisely to the worldwide imposition of the coloniality of power. The Eurocentering of the colonial/capitalist matrix of power was not due solely or even principally to the dominant position of the world market in the new geography but instead was due above all to the basic social classification of the world's population around the idea of race. The concentration of the process of forming and consolidating the modern nation-state in Western Europe cannot be explained or understood outside of this historical context.[31]

The other side of the same process of constituting and consolidating the modern nation-state was the colonized world, Africa and Asia, and the dependent world, such as Latin America.[32] In these parts of the world, the coloniality of power has not only been always present in the global context of the world matrix of power but has also acted directly and immediately within the respective spaces of domination, impeding the processes geared toward the democratization of social relations and their national expression in society and the state.

If anyone thinks the difference is that some spaces were colonized and others were not, all they have to do is compare the processes in Western Europe and Latin America, the two most representative settings for each of the different sides in these processes, which moreover took place during the same period, from the late eighteenth century through the nineteenth and twentieth centuries.[33] In contrast to Europe—a contrast due specifically to the differing distribution of the coloniality of power in the two spaces—in Latin America the most infamous historical paradox experience came about precisely at the end of the so-called Wars of Independence: the association between the independent states and the colonial societies in each and every one of our countries. This association, though doubtlessly strained and continuously yet erratically contested, has nevertheless continued to dominate social and state relations throughout Latin America.

Looking at Latin America, one could not strictly accept the states/societies of the so-called Andean area or of Brazil, for example, as fully formed and consolidated modern nation-states unless they were accepted as national societies and states explicitly founded on the coloniality of power relations. Uruguay and Chile got a bit further along in being constituted as modern nation-states but at the cost of the genocidal extermination of their aboriginal populations and therefore with unsurmountable limitations unless a radical decolonization were to take place with the populations descending from the surviving aboriginal peoples who, as everyone knows, are already forming movements in both countries.

In Mexico, a social revolution from 1910 to 1930 began this process of decolonizing power relations, but its radical tendencies were defeated early on, and the process was unable to be deep and comprehensive enough to allow for the full affirmation of a democratic and national society and state. This defeat soon produced its consequences, visible in the steady choking off of the decolonization of society and in the current tendencies oriented toward reconstituting the association between capitalism and the coloniality of power. Yet for all that, it is the only place in Latin America where society and the state moved forward during an important period in the process of decolonizing power and democratizing/nationalizing. In the other countries, all the revolutions pointing in that direction from 1925 to 1935 were defeated without exception. And since then, the processes everywhere have been erratic, partial, and ultimately precarious. The Central American civil wars from the 1950s until recently, which obviously expressed the same conflicts and interests, demonstrated the illegitimacy and discord inherent in the coloniality of power in these countries as in all others, but the social forces struggling for decolonization were defeated.

Realistically speaking, only in the countries of the "center," first of all, and in those where profound social revolutions were able to win, as in China, or where wars and defeats made relatively important social democratizing processes possible, as in Japan, South Korea, Taiwan, Australia, and New Zealand, can the processes of nation-state development be said to have taken place, though to various degrees of consolidation and maturation in the direction of becoming modern nation-states. China, for example, has been a strong central state since 1949. What is not yet clear is where it has become an entirely national society yet, given that it exists in the same space as a colonial empire, and it definitely has not ceased to be a bureaucratic dictatorship.

Significantly, it is not in these countries, and especially not those in the "center" (the United States, Western Europe, Japan), where the erosion or decline of the institutions of the modern nation-state can be seen. The process now underway of politically unifying the countries of Western Europe signifies not the erosion of the modern nation-state but rather the constitution of a new and broader space of domination in which it may be effective. Or has anyone suggested that the size of the space of domination is the determining factor for deciding whether it has the character of a state? Or that the European Union will once more become an absolutist or dictatorial state merely because it has broadened its sphere of domination?

It is only in all the countries where the processes of democratizing/nationalizing societies and states—or of modern nation-state formation—could not be completed or consolidated that one can observe the erosion of whatever had been gained in that direction.

Here we are talking about processes of de-democratizing society and the state and in that sense denationalizing both, as part of a worldwide trend of reconcentrating world control over institutions of public authority—that is, over the state, in the first instance—and of gradually building a worldwide network of state and private institutions of public authority that may seem to operate like a world government, invisible but real.

Capitalist Globalization: A Global Counterrevolution

Rarely in the history of the modern period has such a remarkable degree of reconcentration of the control of power been seen, specifically in the realms of labor and public authority. This extreme level is almost comparable to what took place with European colonialism from the sixteenth century to the nineteenth century.[34]

This process can be dated to the 1970s, when the world crisis of capitalism erupted. It began to accelerate in the late 1980s at the time of the famous fall of the Berlin Wall in 1989. Notably, it implies a truly dramatic change with respect to the period that immediately preceded it, which in turn may be roughly dated to the years from the end of World War II to the mid-1970s.

Comparing the two periods, the decisive historical significance of this drastic change becomes apparent. For the sake of brevity since this history is well known, I will limit myself here to simply mentioning the most salient trends and facts of the period from 1945 to 1973:

1   The political decolonization of Southeast Asia (India, Indonesia, Indochina, Ceylon, etc.), East Asia (China, Korea), the greater part of Africa and the Middle East, as well as the Antilles, Australia, New Zealand.

2   The victory of profound social revolutions in China, Vietnam, Bolivia, and Cuba and the spread of revolutionary movements oriented toward "socialism" and "national liberation," including those aimed at "African socialisms." In some cases, these entailed the military defeat of hegemonic states, as in Korea, Vietnam, and Algeria, and the fall of authoritarian and colonialist regimes, such as that of Portugal.

3   The spread of welfare state regimes in Europe and the United States.

4   The national-democratic movements and regimes in Latin America that produced social and political reforms aimed at democratizing social and political relations, including the nationalization of productive resources: Peronismo in Argentina, Velasquismo in Peru, and Allendismo in Chile.

5   The development of radically democratic, anticapitalist, antiauthoritarian, and antibureaucratic social movements in Europe, the United States, and some parts of Asia and Latin America, which especially in the second half of the 1960s produced revolutionary waves in France, Germany, the United States, China, and Mexico.

6   The spread of radically democratizing social movements, phrased as "liberation," in sexual relations, gender relations, "racial" and "ethnic" relations, and age relations.

7   The beginnings of the systematic critique of Eurocentrism as a knowledge perspective, especially in Latin America at first, but soon in Europe, Asia, and Africa.

All these processes entailed (a) a broad deconcentration of control over public authority, seizing this control from European colonialism and from European and US imperialism; (b) a limited but important redistribution of labor control among groups of imperialist and local capitalists; (c) a similarly limited but equally important redistribution of profit and income, whether by means of welfare state mechanisms in the countries of the "center" or by means of extending employment and public services (especially public education, health care, and social security) in Latin America, India, etc.; (d) to a much smaller extent, a limited redistribution of control over labor resources, especially by means of "agrarian reform," in diverse countries (Japan, South Korea, Latin America); and (e) last but not least, the spread of anticapitalist criticism and anticapitalistic political movements and other movements that radicalized the anti-imperialist struggles so as to produce a virtual threat to the world matrix of power as a whole.

All of these processes, movements, and conflicts, taken together, produced an unmistakably revolutionary landscape in the sense that although in different ways and to different degrees depending on the region or the issue, they truly placed the world matrix of power as such, whether in its systems of exploitation or of domination or in both dimensions together, at stake and ultimately by the late 1960s at risk.

It was the defeat of this entire framework by the combined means of reconcentrating labor control during the world crisis of capitalism and the defeat of what some call the "antisystem" movements—first by an alliance among rival regimes within the system, then by the defeat and subsequent disintegration of the most influential rival regimes (the former Soviet Union, the European "socialist camp")—that has allowed the most powerful nation-states in the world matrix of power to reconcentrate control over public authority with relative ease and, thus far, without any appreciable resistance and in many cases to clearly reprivatize the state, as in the case of Peru via the Fujimori regime.

What's All This about "Globalization"?

Given all the above, we can lay out a few necessary propositions:

1   "Globalization" is, first and foremost, a reconcentrating of world public authority—strictly speaking, a reprivatizing of the control of collective authority—leading to a deepening and acceleration of the basic tendencies of capitalism.

2   It is, thus, a reconfiguring of the system of political domination, associated with the most recent tendencies in the capitalist exploitation or control of labor.

3   The corresponding institutional expression in the "center" is, on one hand, the establishment of a worldwide imperial bloc made up of the nation-states that were already hegemonic around the world under the dominance of the main one among them, the United States, and on the other hand, the bloc of world finance capital corporations.

4   The worldwide imperial bloc is structurally networked with the institutions for controlling and administering world finance capital, such as the International Monetary Fund, the World Bank, and the Paris Club, and for controlling and administering world violence, such as the North Atlantic Treaty Organization and the Inter-American Defense Board.

5   Taken as a whole, this institutional, state, and quasi-state network tends to operate as an invisible world government.

6   On the "periphery," the most striking expression of this process is the denationalization and de-democratization of states with nationalist tendencies, which in this specific sense demonstrates a continual erosion of the tendencies of the modern nation-state in areas not central to capitalism.

7   To the degree that the sum of these processes is the result of the worldwide defeat of the regimes, organizations, and movements that were rivals or opponents of colonial/modern, Eurocentered world capitalist power, the current "globalization" of this matrix of power has the character of a counterrevolutionary process on a global scale.

This essentially political character of so-called globalization means that unlike its mythical image, it is not some sort of "natural," inevitable, and consequently inescapable phenomenon. Quite the contrary: it is the result of a vast and protracted conflict for the control of power from which the forces representing coloniality and capitalism emerged victorious. As a result, "globalization" is an inevitable arena for conflict both between winners and losers and among the winners themselves, and as such it is subject to other outcomes.

Only in passing, for now, it should be pointed out that the reconcentration of control over labor and over public authority has not brought about a parallel reconcentration of global control over all other areas of power, particularly in the intersubjective relations of social domination such as "race," "gender," and the mode of knowledge production. The coloniality of power, the bourgeois family, and Eurocentrism certainly remain hegemonic around the world. But in these dimensions of the current matrix of power and in its respective institutions, so far the crisis has only grown more profound and more explicit.

From the National to the Global Perspective?

There is also something in this field that, if not exactly new, will nevertheless probably seem novel to many who have not studied the issue. This is the change in perspective entailed in the idea and the image linked to the term "globalization." Now it is at long last possible, almost common sense even, to confront power and most of all capitalism on its genuine, permanent scale: global.

Not only Marx, in fact, but also virtually everyone after him who debated these issues, all the way up to World War I, had world capitalism on their minds. But from World War I until after the world crisis that began in the mid-1970s, the global perspective on capitalism as a world matrix for the control of labor was neglected in favor of the so-called national perspective, referring to the nation-state, that is.

This shift in perspective necessarily entailed a shift in the problems under study as well, that is, a shift in the main questions considered important to ask about experience (or "reality") and in the significance attributed to observations, discoveries, and verifications.

These shifts in perspective and in which problems were addressed took place under the hegemonic imprint of Eurocentrism as the basic knowledge perspective. The privileged reference to the European-style nation-state would otherwise make no sense, given that the nation-state was not then and has not since then become the real structure of public authority on the "periphery."

These shifts affected every side in the debate, though in different ways and to different degrees, touching not only the defenders of capitalism and its associated forms of power but also those who wielded or attempted to wield theoretical and political critiques against it. While the former found a smooth path to defending their system with theory, for the latter both the theory and the politics went disastrously wrong. First, they remain mired in the ahistorical dualist/evolutionist view dividing so-called precapital and capital. Second, they lost sight of the global character of the fundamental relations between processes of domination and of exploitation, of the processes of social classification and their relationships with the particular spaces of domination that, rightly or wrongly, were called "national."

Under these conditions it was impossible to recognize, because it was impossible to see, the tendencies in capitalism that are now clear to everyone, which is the main reason they now seem to be new. These trends include, in particular, the global social polarization of the world's population between a rich minority and a vast and ever more impoverished majority, the continual revolution of the means of production, and the tendency toward depleting interest and the need to turn labor force into commodity goods.

The perspective of that time took a nation-state, real or imagined, not only as its unit of study but also as its theoretical and methodological perspective for research into general trends and processes in capitalism. Such a knowledge perspective was necessarily reductive. And of course, from such a perspective it was not hard at all to show that in modern nation-states—those of the "center"—the global trends that are now so obvious to everyone were simply not taking place or were not yet as visible as they are today. Thus, the difficulties for capitalist development faced by other countries was a matter of "modernization," that is, in the terms of this perspective, of putting them on the same road as the more "advanced" countries or a matter of time and of getting the political economy right, in the case of those who were already embarked on this route. In any case, it was a "national" problem, to be resolved by the nation-state. In other words, it wasn't a problem of world power or of world capitalism.

Coloniality and the Nation-State in Latin America

Latin American nationalism was conceived and enacted from a European perspective on nationalism and the nation-state, in loyalty to an identity established or assumed by the beneficiaries of the coloniality of power, apart from and at times in opposition to the interests of those exploited/ dominated by colonialism and capitalism. For this reason, Latin American liberalism became bogged down in the pipe dream of a modernity without social revolution. "Historical materialism" got stuck in another quagmire, similarly Eurocentric in character: the idea that those who dominated these countries were and are, by definition, "national and progressive bourgeoisies." In this way, the victims were confused and their struggles for democratizing/nationalizing their societies were diverted when social, material, and intersubjective decolonization is the sine qua non for any possible process of democratization and nationalization. Decolonization is the necessary first step for any profound social revolution. Even a vigorous development of capitalism in these countries would first require such a revolution/decolonization, as demonstrated by the fate of this region in the world economy and the current futile and pointless projects and discourses about market "integration," whether in the Andean community (Pacto Andino) or in Mercosur.[35]

Until these conditions are removed, national sovereignty cannot mean defending the interests of the masters of a colonial society state who control its labor, its resources, and its products, the erstwhile junior partners of the imperial interests who today are but their administrative agents in the space of domination that they call national. All this runs completely counter to the interests of the vast majority of workers. Fujimorism is the consummate expression of this perverse experience.[36]

Under the conditions of the world's counterrevolutionary "globalization," the development of European-style nation-states is a dead end. The discourse about our societies being multiethnic, multicultural, and so forth does not and cannot mean that society or the state has been decolonized; in several instances—Fujimorism in Peru is the prime example—this discourse only serves to paper over the pressures for relegitimizing racism/ethnicism and to undo the social struggles against such forms of domination.[37]

For countries in which the coloniality of power is the true foundation of power relations, full citizen participation, democratization, and nationalization cannot be real but can only be precariously modeled after the Eurocentric version of the nation-state. We Latin American peoples will have to find an alternative way. The community and associations of communities as the institutional structure for local and regional public authority have already appeared on the horizon, with the potential of becoming not only more suitable for democratizing daily relations among ordinary people in the institutional framework but also as stronger and more effective stronger institutional structures than the state for the purposes of promoting debate, making decisions, planning, and carrying out and defending the interests, needs, works, and deeds of vast encouragement for the world's population.

The Question of Democracy

What the term "democracy" means in today's world, in the colonial/modern/capitalist/Eurocentric matrix of power, is a concrete and specific system of institutionalized negotiation of the limits, conditions, and modalities of exploitation and domination, whose emblematic institution is citizenship and whose institutional framework is the modern nation-state.[38]

The touchstone of this system is the idea of legal and political equality among people who are not equals in any other areas of social life. It is not hard to see what this implies historically, the convergence and networking of three processes: (1) bourgeois secularization and its expression in the new Eurocentric rationalism; (2) the struggles between the new version of the matrix of power and the "old order" for the distribution of control over collective authority; and (3) the struggles over the distribution of the control of labor and its resources and products, in the period of competitive capital, mainly among the bourgeois groups themselves, and after the monopoly period began, mainly between capital and labor.

Without this historical confluence, it would be impossible to explain or understand how the ideas of social equality, individual liberty, and social solidarity became established as the central issues in social relations, as an expression of rationality, in the modern period. The desacralization of authority in the configuration of subjectivity, so that individual conscience should be autonomous, is part of the secularization of subjectivity, the new way of subjectivizing people, and forms the basis of individual liberty. But on the other hand, the needs of the capitalist market as well as the struggles for control of labor and its resources and products prompted the recognition of social equality and solidarity among all its participants. This confluence of the ideas of social equality, individual liberty, and social solidarity lies at the very foundation of the admission that everyone in society has an equal chance to participate in the control of labor as well as in the control of collective authority, which in this way is made public for the first time. Democracy is thus established as the sum and summary of modernity.

Two aspects decisively shaped these processes, however. To take the first of these, the new version of the matrix of power was not only modern in character but capitalist. Therefore, it was built on the basis not only of rationality and modernity but also of social inequality, exploitation, and domination. The market consequently served as the floor for equality but also as its ceiling, its outer limitation. That is, the market places agents of unequal social conditions in a formal position of equality. Likewise, the individual conscience could not have the same unrestricted freedom for every individual in every realm of social life where power was engaged, sex and its resources and products in the first place. Thus, women were not allowed this freedom of conscience: they could not participate in the public sphere but only in the private one, to which the family, sexual activity, and its products, pleasure and progeny, were consigned. The same was true of labor and its resources and products, in the second place. Those who had been or who would be totally defeated in the struggle over labor control, and who thus could count only on their own labor power to participate in the market, could not be equal, except within the limits imposed by the market, or individually free beyond the limits of their subalternity.

In any case, social relations from then on would take on a new character, their intersubjectivity marked by the dominance of the new rationality and their materiality marked by the capitalist market. Thereafter, social conflict would primarily consist of the struggle to materialize the idea of social equality, individual liberty, and social solidarity. The first of these poses a challenge to exploitation, the others to domination. Democracy would thus become the central area for the conflict of interests within the new version of the matrix of power. The entire historical process of this specific matrix of power has consisted of the long, drawn-out unfolding of this contradiction: on one hand, the social interests always fighting for the continuing materialization and universalization of social equality, individual liberty, and social solidarity; on the other hand, the interests fighting to limit these and in fact to reduce or, even better, cancel them insofar as possible except for the dominant groups. The result so far has been the institutionalization of the negotiation of limits and of the modes of domination, and citizenship is its precise expression. The limits on citizenship determine the negotiations over the limits and modes of exploitation. The institutional realm that has resulted from these negotiations is the so-called modern nation-state. This is what is known, in the current matrix of power, as democracy.

To take the second aspect, the new version of the matrix of power was colonial/Eurocentric. That is, it was based on the coloniality of racial classification as the basic and universal social classification, and because of this specific definition it was Eurocentered. These features gave rise to the fact that over the course of nearly two centuries, from the late 1700s to the mid-1900s, this specific foundational contradiction could not be established anywhere but in Western Europe. First, because the coloniality of the social classification was not present there, thanks precisely to the coloniality imposed between "Europeans" and all other members of the species.

Second, because the commodification of the labor force had been centered in these countries so that capital had become the universal social relationship. Third, because the feudal mode of domination had been eradicated there. In all other places around the world, by contrast, as European colonialism expanded, coloniality was imposed as the basic classification; as a result, the dominant form of exploitation tended to exclude wage labor until the end of the nineteenth century, and the forms of control over authority had a state/colonial/feudal character.

In any case, the negotiation over the limits and modes of domination and exploitation appears to have been fully institutionalized in "European" societies (Western Europe, the United States, Canada, Australia, New Zealand), though under "globalization" this institution is being put on the defensive. It was institutionalized late and in a clearly limited way in those societies that did not result from European colonialism and the coloniality of power, such as Japan, Taiwan, and South Korea. In all other societies, this institutionalization has either not even begun, in many cases, or has not concluded, as in Latin America in particular.

Globalization and Democracy

One of the biggest commonplaces in the current political debate is the idea that democracy is on the upswing everywhere. This idea refers to the fact that most governments in the world today are the result of elections. The vote is consequently taken as the single defining institution of democracy.[39]

This notion of democracy is an expression of the increasingly technocratic character of bourgeois, Eurocentric rationality, and it rests on two problems. First, the fact that the governments of all states, especially the governments of nonnational or not fully national states, are run more and more by unelected technobureaucrats who act completely apart from the will of the voters or, worse, completely in opposition to them.[40] This blatant trend is, however, papered over by a crude intellectual bait-and-switch, an argument that despite being almost ludicrously absurd has been imposed everywhere as virtually a matter of common sense: that governmental management of economic matters, and matters of state government in general are not political problems but merely technical! Second, the fact that this relationship between state politics and votes cannot be explained independently of "globalization," that is, of the current process of reconcentrating power over public authority, which reduces or aims to reduce all political participation by citizens other than the vote, in order to make it possible for a sort of worldwide technocratic government or "transgovernance" to intervene locally and not always in a very hidden way.

As vitally important as the vote is, unless democratic conditions hold sway in basic social relations, elections will inevitably not only be subject to fraud and manipulation but, even when carried out honestly and legally, will provide voters with no guarantee of their ability to control the institutions of public authority.

Under such conditions, it cannot be said that democracy is exactly expanding and emerging victorious all over the world. Quite the contrary. Finance capital and unrestrained speculative accumulation have taken command of world capitalism, the whole world structure of accumulation. And they are exercising it, using all the most advanced technological resources and placing rationality and knowledge production in service of their own ends and interests. This is one current structural tendency of colonial/capitalist power in the world. Its development requires the democratic spaces in society to be reduced, because those spaces necessarily entail an equally democratic distribution of access to and control over labor, resources, and products; over sex and its resources and products; over subjectivity; and above all, over knowledge. For all this, a democratic distribution of control over public authority—that is, over the state—is indispensable. The modern nation-state tends to be constituted in this way and on these bases. But the current needs of speculative accumulation means—also necessarily—that these spaces must be reduced and that their institutions, such as citizenship and the vote, must be undone wherever possible.

The capitalist character of power that is being "globalized" and the predominance of speculative capital within the current stage of capitalism run counter to the democratization of society and in this sense to its nationalization, since any modern nation-state is national only insofar as it represents a democratic society. This specific "globalization" is being unhidden more and more as it goes against the processes of nationalization/democratization in every society and state, most immediately and dramatically against the consolidation of nation-states on the "periphery," particularly wherever the coloniality of power governs social relations, such as in the countries of Latin America.

Moreover, notwithstanding its well-known capacity for bias, Eurocentric rationality could be made to accept the critiques and debates over its biased elements and, more recently, over its coloniality. To this degree and under these conditions, it was one of the central foundations of the worldwide legitimation of the ideas of social equality, individual liberty, and social solidarity, which legitimated the struggles of the exploited, of the subjugated, of the discriminated, not only against their oppressors and not simply to take their turn in power but against oppression itself, against power, against all power. But since the world crisis of the mid-1970s, the needs and interests of exploitation have pressed against such rationality.

The predatory tendencies of today's capital and the reconcentration of world control of power with the worldwide imperial bloc have opened up a space for fundamentalisms, for all the prejudices and myths on which the sacralization of social hierarchies are built; they press for the exclusively technocratic use of knowledge, of science, of technology, with the explicit and exclusive aim of reinforcing exploitation and domination, now even including technological intervention in human biology to perpetuate racist/ethnicist discrimination, in service to privileges imposed by colonialism and imperialism against the vast majority of humankind.

Pressure is actively being applied around the world for de-modernizing people's lives, not in the sense of critiquing and eliminating the colonial character of the Eurocentric version of modernity but for relegitimizing the most oppressive forms of power. Power has been all but eliminated as a topic for research, for debate, and especially for critique except in a technocratic and administrative sense. This lends legitimacy to a cynical posture as an approach to everyday behavior, since power as an element in social relations, in all social relations, cannot be excluded in real life.[41] Finance capital presses for the radical commodification of all knowledge, and the worldwide imperial bloc is set on militarizing control over scientific research and technology.[42] The speculative capitalism that has marked this stage in "globalization" exacerbates each and every one of these trends.

In this specific sense, "globalization" involves the most profound and pivotal threats of the past two centuries. This time it is not only a matter of authoritarian tendencies such as Nazism, fascism, Stalinism, emerging to counter the strong democratic tendencies that still formed part of the historical context of modernity, including not just the exploited and the dominating but also a major portion of the world's bourgeoisie, given that the tendencies of capitalism had not yet been able to attain their present extremes because of world resistance, the conflicts between rival powers, and the world struggles against the current version of the matrix of power. But those struggles were defeated and the conflicts and rivalries over world hegemony have been brought under control, giving rise to the worldwide imperial bloc. The unfortunate result of all this are tendencies that today seem to be taking shape on the very floor of society and culture in this matrix of power, aimed at forming and reproducing a new universal common sense in which power, social hierarchies, the unequal control of labor and its resources and products, the unequal and concentrated control of authority and violence, the repressive and commercialized control of sex, of subjectivity, and of knowledge are all accepted as legitimate and, especially, as natural.

The latest processes of capitalism require the complete instrumentalization of Eurocentric rationality. In this way they lead to the relegitimation of inequality entailed in the present extreme polarization of society, the reduction of the scope of democratic access to control over labor and its resources and products, as well as the scope of access to control over the generation and operation of the institutions of public authority and their resources, violence in particular.

Insofar as capitalism is one of the basic factors at the center of the current matrix of world power and since its processes will necessarily continue to sharpen its current needs or interests, its need for domination will be pushed in the same direction, political and cultural domination in particular. The political and technological efforts of the world "transgovernment" to concentrate all control over communication and information—which is exactly what fascinates its intellectuals and propagandists as a sign of world "integration"—lie on this path.

Perspectives: Discord and Violence

According to the mythical image of "globalization" put out by the publicists for capitalism and the worldwide imperial bloc, we are immersed in a process bigger than any intentions and decisions of ordinary people. If true, that would make it a natural phenomenon in the face of which intentional intervention would be, must be, futile. According to the image circulating everywhere, resisting "globalization" would be like trying to stop a train by standing in front of it. Since it has to do with the economic, political, and cultural integration of the entire world, you would have to admit that it adds up to a systemic whole from which there can be no escape or defense.

Yet, the preceding inquiry makes it worth observing, first of all, that globalization cannot be a singular thing, for there is no way that any given matrix of power can be entirely homogeneous, systemic, mechanical, organic, or described in general as a historical whole. The historical-structural heterogeneity of all power matrices means that the various arenas of social life and the varied forms of control articulated therein cannot have systemically or organically corresponding rhythms. What goes on between "economics," "politics," and "culture"—or, from another perspective, between labor, sex, subjectivity, and collective authority—is a historically and structurally discontinuous relationship, and the same is true within each of these areas. So, it seems worthwhile to look now and see whether there are gaps and contradictions in "the economy," especially between the speculative "bubble" and the production of new material value. Or, in "politics," in the relations between the worldwide imperial bloc and the processes linked to the current struggle for autonomous spaces for national and ethnic identities, etc. And, obviously, between such "economics" and "politics," or between the crisis of Eurocentric rationality and the trends toward recolonizing intersubjectivity; or, in a word, between the crisis in the matrices of social classification and the trend toward reclassifying the world's population on a global scale. On these grounds, some scholars have proposed thinking instead in terms of "globalizations," plural, in every region and in various periods.[43]

Second, the basically political character of what is commonly called "globalization," which has been revealed especially in regard to the sequence of events during a period of revolutionary changes and risks, the defeat of which enabled the imposition of the worldwide imperial bloc, dispels the odd notion that it is some sort of natural phenomenon and not an avatar of disputes over power and therefore undoubtedly subject to individual intentions and decisions, whatever the terms of the conflict or its results might be.

And third, one of the inherent problems displayed by the power structure that is processed in "globalization," in relations both of exploitation and of domination, is an extreme level of discord: between capital and a more heterogeneous and thus less controllable realm of labor, between finance capital and a mass of workers caught between a dearth of paid labor and income and an inescapable need to survive in a market economy, between the rich who grow ever richer and the poor who grow ever poorer and more numerous, between the worldwide imperial bloc and the local states with their national and regional tendencies, among states vying for regional hegemony, between those struggling to narrow or simply eradicate democracy and those fighting to broaden and consolidate society politically, and, in a word, between the growing tendencies of technocratic reductionism in the mode of knowledge production and the worldwide tendencies toward a different, non-Eurocentric rationality.[44]

This list, by no means exhaustive, is enough to reveal some of the sources and tendencies for insurmountable conflict that have already begun to surface and turn into active struggles. The extreme discord inherent in the current moment of the world matrix of power also signals that this situation cannot be stabilized. These conditions indicate that this situation contains an equally extreme potential for violence, which is exploding with a ferocity visible to all: in the Persian Gulf; in the Horn of Africa; in Rwanda, Burundi, and Congo; in the Balkans; in the Middle East; in the former Soviet Union and now Czechoslovakia; and, within Latin America, in Colombia and the entire Andean and Amazonian region. This violence is very likely just the beginning.

And we haven't even touched yet on the possibly more violent conflicts that seem to be gearing up in the dimly foreseeable future: disputes between the imperial bloc and China (and eventually China-India-Russia); within the bloc, between the United States and the European Union; between each of these or both together and Japan or Russia. In view of such prospects, it is hard to accept the mystified images that circulate in the realm of communications and information under the control of global finance capital.

In brief, the "globalization" of the world matrix of power threatens to take social polarization to extremes, reconcentrating control over world power in the hands of a tiny minority of people, with the recolonization of the world within an imperial structure of domination in service to the worst forms of exploitation and domination. It threatens to de-democratize the world, and thus to de-modernize social, material, and intersubjective relations, and to technocratize knowledge in the extreme. It reveals, for the first time explicitly, the old Eurocentric menace of techno-barbarism.

The Alternatives

The first thing that must be established as clearly as possible is that these trends and perspectives on the growth of exploitation and domination around the world—and as a result of permanent discord and extreme violence—have nothing at all to do with the worldwide integration of trade in goods, services, information, and transportation; with the shrinking of the world; with our changing relationships with time and space. What is at issue, then, is not the integration of the world but rather the capitalist, counterrevolutionary, and predatory character of the world power that is "globalizing." The democratic integration of the world is, on the contrary, one of humanity's most illustrious dreams.

The issue, then, is not about trying to keep the world from integrating but instead about allowing it to develop more completely, freeing it as far as possible from systemic discord and extreme violence, so that the diversity of humankind will cease to be an argument in favor of social inequality, so that social relations among the various identities across the world's population may become socially equal and individually free among all humans.

From this perspective, what it is about is, first of all, liberating the process of world integration from the tendencies of capitalism and the worldwide imperial bloc. This necessarily entails redistributing power around the world, that is, control over labor and its resources and products, control over sex and its resources and products, control over collective authority and its resources and products, and control over subjectivity and, most importantly of all, over the mode of knowledge production. This redistribution means returning control over each of the vital spheres of social existence to the daily lives of all the men and women on Earth.

It is true that over the course of more than two decades, the breakup of the "socialist bloc" in Europe, the worldwide defeat of "antiestablishment" movements, the eclipse of "historical materialism" as a legitimizing discourse for "socialism," among the main events set off during the world crisis that began in the mid-1970s, allowed for the "globalization" of imperialist dominance. This political defeat was accompanied by the social and political breakup of the world of labor and its allies. It led to the demoralization and political disengagement of the defeated forces, if not to their open disintegration. It produced a deep, worldwide crisis of social identity, once more subalternizing the social discourse of the dominated and exploited, even reconfiguring their memory matrix. Financial capital, meanwhile, met with almost no resistance to carrying out its predatory actions against the dependent societies and states and against the overwhelming majority of workers. That time is, however, drawing to a close. The resistance is beginning, all over the world. All Latin Americans have to do is look around: the social struggles have already created political crises and instability all across South America.

As long as the exploited and dominated remain defeated, those who control power will be able to carry out profound changes, many of them deep and irreversible, in the social relations of power. It would be pointless or, worse, an admission of defeat beforehand to struggle simply for the restoration of what has been destroyed or changed. Nostalgia does not have the same face as or look in the same direction as hope. But in the absence of a trusted and widely accepted program for reknowing reality and the real options for changing things to benefit the victims of power, in such periods resistance struggles almost always start off with the memory of what has been lost, because they are about winning back the few concessions that had been wrested from the exploiters and dominators.

And the losses in these years have been immense and powerful: stable employment, adequate incomes, public freedoms, and in most countries around the world, the spaces for participating democratically in the creation and running of public authority. In other words, exploitation has grown stronger and domination has grown more direct. Resistance struggles are aimed everywhere precisely at recovering employment, good wages, democratic spaces, and participation in running the state. The problem, however, is that the conditions do not exist within the current tendencies of capitalism for expanding paid employment, only for continuing to shrink it.[45] That being the case, the social, ethnic, and cultural identities of the world population of workers will only continue to grow more fragmented, dispersed, and heterogeneous. Under such conditions, the erosion of the spaces won for democratizing and nationalizing the local states of the "periphery" is probably not reversible either in most cases.[46]

The current needs of capitalism are now applying pressure, even in the countries of the "center," to reduce the democratic spaces where limits to exploitation and domination can be negotiated and to undo their goals, with democracy now identified with nothing more than the vote. In the vast "periphery," the coloniality of power blocked the full democratization and nationalization of societies and states, and today the pressures applied by the worldwide imperial bloc constantly reduce the spaces won and in many cases have almost managed to nullify them. And without control over public authority, without even the ability to participate fully and assuredly in how it is created and run, there is no way to control the limits of exploitation and today's social polarization.

The struggle to democratize and nationalize societies and states is still undoubtedly important all over the world in order to defend or to win again the rights already won. But it is essential to accept that this path is a limited one so long as the Eurocentric perspective on the modern nation-state is retained. And in any case, it is now obvious that in the most modern, democratic, and national of all states, democracy can be nothing more than a space for institutionalized negotiation over the conditions, limits, and modes of exploitation and domination.

At the same time, given the trends of increased limitations on the commodification of the workforce, of creating and broadening paid employment, the heterogenization, fragmentation, dispersion, and multiplication of local interests and identities increasingly conspire against organizing and mobilizing workers in ways that had been established in the nineteenth and twentieth centuries. Under these conditions, the struggle for control over the state is a limited path and may ultimately turn out to be a dead end. That is to say, the more or less democratic control of the state, citizenship as legal equality among power unequals, never has and never will lead to a continuous expansion of social equality, individual liberty, and social solidarity, in sum, to democracy. The spaces that have been won are now under threat in the "center" and are constantly being chipped away on the "periphery." And under current social and political conditions, as the trends that have been noted probably or definitely continue to play out, the struggles of the dominated to gain control over the state will only exceptionally and precariously find success.

Long experience has demonstrated that there is no point in trying to impose our desires and aspirations on reality, no matter how attractive and plausible they may be or appear to be. Instead, it is essential to study the current landscape of the world and identify tendencies and possible tendencies that would call for other forms of organization, of identifying workers and organizing society.

From this perspective, it is clear today that the processes of capitalism and the tendencies of imperial domination themselves are what drive alternative tendencies. So, on one hand, in the area of control over labor and its resources and products, due to the limitations on the commodification of the labor force and the consequent crisis in the production of paid employment, slavery and personal servitude are back, and independent small-scale market production is more pervasive than ever, becoming the heart of what has been dubbed the "informal economy." In the area of control over authority, the formation of the worldwide imperial bloc and the erosion of local nation-state processes on the "periphery" are associated with the reproduction of local premodern forms of authoritarianism, the creation of social hierarchies, and limitations on individualization, as seen in fundamentalist trends everywhere around the world. Yet, countering these trends, we find reciprocity expanding once more in the organization of labor and community as the structure of public authority.

These trends must be studied and debated with regard to their potential for amplifying and consolidating social equality, individual liberty, and social solidarity on a global scale. As everyone knows, slavery and servitude leave not even a glimmer of democracy except for the masters, a tiny minority. What wage labor and capital allow for in terms of democracy we know all too well, just as now we see their growing limitations and, soon enough, their likely dead ends. Reciprocity, on the other hand, consists precisely of the socialized exchange of labor and of the labor force and its resources and products. And community as authority structure is undoubtedly the fullest form of socialization or democratization for controlling the creation and running of public authority. And both trends are taking place right now in the new urban world, in the world produced as the central setting for the society and culture of capitalism and modernity, as free relations between free individuals.[47]

The Eurocentric theory of democracy puts the authority arrangements made among slavers in the Athenian polis of the fifth century BC at the point of origin for the Western European lineage of democracy and puts the institutionalization of the power arrangements among thirteenth-century feudal lords and the English Crown, the famous Magna Carta, and later in Parliament at the modern restart point of that history. This is not by accident but instead because it permits the perpetuation of the myth of the isolated individual, self-contained and counterpoised to society, and of the myth behind this myth, which in reality creates the Eurocentric version of modernity, the myth of the state of nature as the starting point for the development of civilization that reaches its culmination in (what else?) "the West."

This theory, however, blocks our view of a different historical lineage of democracy, an undoubtedly more universal and deeper one: the community as authority structure, that is, direct and immediate control over collective authority by the inhabitants of a given social space. Not to venture too far afield, this lineage can be found in the history of Western Europe itself. In the same thirteenth century as the Magna Carta, peasant communities in the Swiss region got together and agreed to unite, as communities, as the Swiss Confederation in order to defend themselves jointly against feudal despotism and imperial despotism. The current Swiss Republic is the adaptation of this trajectory to the conditions of capitalism and the modern nation-state while maintaining two key institutions of direct democracy: the referendum, a way of consulting citizens on any decision that would significantly affect collective life, and the absence of a professional military beyond the citizens' control. External defense and interior security are realized directly, institutionalized, by the community. No wonder Switzerland has been recognized as a particular model for advanced democracy under conditions of capitalism.

These are, of course, ideas for research and debate. But if they aren't arbitrary, if the tendencies pointed out here are active and vital in the real world today, with the formation of communities and regional associations of communities as genuinely democratic public authority structures, as popular self-governments in many urban and semiurban parts of the world, especially on the "periphery," with reciprocity as the form of organizing labor and democratically distributing its resources and products, today associated in part with the so-called informal economy all over the world, then a new horizon is perhaps emerging for the worldwide struggles for a new society in which democracy will be more than the institutionalized negotiation over the continual conflict between victors and vanquished but rather the everyday way of life for ordinary people.

Notes

First published in Aníbal Quijano, "Colonialidad del poder, globalización y democracia," *Utopías, nuestra bandera: Revista de debate político*, no. 188 (2001): 97–123.

1   See Quijano, "Poder y derechos humanos."
2   Discrimination on the basis of "gender" is perhaps the most ancient type in the history of our species. But in the current world matrix of power, it has been subordinated to the coloniality of power. And insofar as there is a lengthy debate and an immense literature about it, here I find it necessary to emphasize the specific coloniality of the current matrix of power.
3   See Quijano, "Coloniality of Power, Eurocentrism and Latin America." It is worth noting here that the terms "coloniality" and "colonialism" refer to different phenomena and distinct issues. "Colonialism" refers not to the universally basic social classification that has existed for the past five hundred years but rather to the political and economic domination of one people over others, which arose thousands of years before coloniality. The two terms are obviously related, given that the coloniality of power would not have been possible historically without the specific form of colonialism imposed on the world since the late fifteenth century.
4   See Quijano, "Coloniality of Power, Eurocentrism and Latin America."
5   Discussed in Quijano, "Estado-Nación ciudadanía y democracia"; and Quijano, "El fantasma del desarrollo en América Latina."

6   See Quijano, "Coloniality of Power, Eurocentrism and Latin America"; Quijano, "Towards a Non-Eurocentric Rationality"; and Quijano, "Colonialidad del poder y clasificación social."

7   In a sense, the Hegelian concept, developed by Kojève and later taken up by Fukuyama, *The End of History*, implies this idea of the climax of this matrix of power. See Quijano, "¿El fin de cual historia?"

8   On the implications of the "scientific-technological revolution," it is very instructive to follow the thread that runs from the studies by Radovan Richta's group in Prague, before the Russian tanks invaded in 1968, to McLuhan's "global village." See, for example, Quijano, "Tecnología del transporte y desarrollo urbano."

9   Birdsall, "Life Is Unfair," 79.

10   Birdsall, "Life is Unfair," 76.

11   See Krugman, "The Right, the Rich and the Facts," and Bruno, Ravallion, and Squire, *Equity and Growth in Developing Countries*, both cited in Birdsall, "Life Is Unfair," 93. For Brazil, here are the most recent figures: "The Brazilian Institute of Geography and Statistics (IBGE), a federal agency, has just released some terrifying figures that serve as a balance sheet for the past five years and four months of the FHC [Fernando Henrique Cardoso] presidency: the richest 1% control more wealth than the poorest 50% of Brazilians. In other words, roughly 1.6 million people have more wealth than what 83 million Brazilians own altogether. Some 19.6% of families take in a monthly income that comes to the equivalent of half the minimum wage or less." Christo, "Los rumbos de la oposición." And in Venezuela, according to CEPAL, *Panorama social de América Latina*, the income of the poorest 40 percent of city dwellers fell from a 16.8 percent share of national income to 14.7 percent from 1990 to 1997, while that of the richest 10 percent of city dwellers rose from 28.4 percent to 32.8 percent over the same period.

12   CEPAL, *Panorama social de América Latina*.

13   Griffiths, *Annual Editions*, 46.

14   "This past year [1996] the government of Uganda spent only $3 per person on health care, but it spent $17 per person on repaying its foreign debt. Meanwhile, one in five Ugandan children will not reach their fifth birthday as a result of diseases that could be prevented through investment in primary health care." Griesgraber, "Forgive Us Our Debts."

15   For example, Rifkin, *The End of Work*. See also Méda, *Le travail, une valeur en voie de disparition*. Research on trends in the relations between labor and capital refer exclusively to paid work. The findings have produced a large family of categories: "labor flexibilization," "insecurity," "subcontracting," the return of the "putting-out system," and "informaliza-

tion," among the most important in the abundant literature. On Latin America, see, for example, Tokman and Martínez, *Flexibilización en el Margen*; and Tokman and Martínez, *Inseguridad laboral y competitividad*. See also the studies in Santiago, *Revista de Administración Pública*, Vol. 28, *Primer encuentro Latinoamericano de estudios del trabajo*.

16   In 1991, the International Labor Organization recognized the existence of some 6 million people being held in slavery conditions worldwide. The United Nations established a commission to study the problem. The commission's 1993 report indicated the existence of more than 200 million enslaved people around the world. See Martins, "Sociologia e militância," 168.

17   Judging from these figures, the character of finance capital today is almost the direct opposite of what it was in the precrisis period. Previously, finance capital served to foster productive investment. Currently, it is almost entirely parasitic and thus predatory.

18   These trends have been studied and debated in Latin America beginning in the 1960s as part of the debate over the question of marginalization. On this perspective, see especially Nun, "Sobrepoblación relativa, ejército industrial de reserva y masa marginal." See also Quijano, *Imperialismo y "marginalidad" en América Latina*; and Quijano, *Crisis imperialista y clase obrera en América Latina*.

19   In Latin America, though the general debate on the capitalist crisis had been in the air since the mid-1970s, the Brazilian economist Celso Furtado was probably one of the first to call attention to the hegemony of finance capital and its implications. See Quijano, "Transnacionalización y crisis de la economía en América Latina." On the recent debate, from the perspective of capitalism's dependent and peripheral areas, see Singh, *The Globalisation of Finance* and *Taming Financial Flows*.

20   In *Capital* and in his now equally well-known *Grundrisse*, Marx got remarkably far in this formulation, as far as he could get without breaking the ceiling of a Eurocentric perspective of knowledge. In any case, he established the foundations and the major questions of the debate. Thus, the tendency to exhaust the conversion of labor into commodities when greater productivity allows for the automation of production is the central open question as early as 1858, in the section of "The Chapter on Capital" titled "Contradiction between the Foundation of Bourgeois Production (Value as Measure) and Its Development." Marx, *Grundrisse*, 704. It is undoubtedly no accident that the economists of the bourgeoisie and the functionaries of the leading international administrative bodies for capitalism are themselves discovering, to their surprise, how closely Marx's theoretical predictions match the broadest tendencies of "globalized" capitalism, in particular the concentration of capital and global social polarization, which for

so long was simply denied by bourgeois economists. See, for example, Cassidy, "The Return of Karl Marx." Nancy Birdsall, executive vice president of the Inter-American Development Bank, does not hesitate to open her text by saying, "Exactly 150 years after the publication of the Communist Manifesto, inequality looms large on the global agenda." Birdsall, "Life Is Unfair," 76. See also Quijano, *Crisis imperialista y clase obrera en América Latina*.

21 Miliband, *The State in Capitalist Society*, was specifically presented as a study of the state in so-called Western countries. See also Poulantzas, *Poder político y clases sociales en el estado capitalista*. A useful review of the literature prior to the eclipse of "historical materialism" in the worldwide debate is Evers, *El estado en la periferia capitalista*.

22 There is a large and growing literature on this topic. On one part of the debate in Latin America, see, for example, García Delgado, *Estado-Nación y globalización*; and Capuano Scarlato et al., *Globalização e espaço latino-americano*. Regarding the link between political and cultural processes, see Sánchez Parga, *Globalización, gobernabilidad y cultura*; Mato, *Crítica de la moderna globalización y construcción de identidades*; and García Canclini, *Culturas en globalización*.

23 In the sense of Hobson and Lenin.

24 Thomas M. Callaghy has coined the term "transgovernance" to talk about the fact that the institutions of the state are indispensable for imposing or applying the norms and behaviors corresponding to the interests of capital and the market on every country, yet at the same time these state institutions are networked with the specific institutions of capital. Callaghy, "Globalization and Marginalization."

25 For the US version of the successful Plan Colombia in contrast with its detrimental consequences, see Robert Gates, "Plan Colombia: A Development Success Story," U.S. Global Leadership Coalition, April 15, 2010, https://www.usglc.org/media/2017/04/USGLC-Plan-Columbia.pdf.

26 On the issue of the relationship between public and private in the configuration and actions of collective authorities and of state authorities in particular, I have put forward some ideas in Quijano, "Lo público y lo privado."

27 After revising this text of my conference talk, I read Hardt and Negri, *Empire*. Their central thesis is that we already find ourselves within a global empire, with historical and structural characteristics analogous to those of the Roman Empire, that has brought an end to the era of imperialism and of the nation-state, which from their perspective are mutually corresponding institutions. This idea was already expressed in the book by Soros, *The Crisis of Global Capitalism*. Readers will notice where I disagree with their views.

28   See Quijano, "Lo público y lo privado."

29   The literature on this topic is extensive and growing daily. See, for example, the references in García Delgado, *Estado-Nación y globalización*.

30   On this issue, see Quijano, "Coloniality of Power and Its Institutions."

31   See Quijano, "Coloniality of Power, Eurocentrism and Latin America."

32   On the concept of "dependency," see Quijano, "Coloniality of Power, Eurocentrism and Latin America"; and Quijano, "Colonialidad del poder, cultura y conocimiento en América Latina."

33   I have discussed these issues before in a number of texts, principally Quijano, "Coloniality of Power, Eurocentrism and Latin America"; Quijano, "Estado-Nación, ciudadanía y democracia"; Quijano, "El fantasma del desarrollo en América Latina"; Quijano, "Colonialité du pouvoir et démocratie en Amérique latine"; and Quijano, "América Latina en la economía mundial."

34   A panoramic overview of the process of colonialism and anticolonialism over the past five hundred years can be found in the monumental book Stavrianos, *Global Rift*.

35   See Quijano, "América Latina en la economía mundial"; and Quijano, "El fantasma del desarrollo en América Latina."

36   I have discussed this in several places, primarily Quijano, *El fujimorismo y el Perú*; Quijano, "Populismo y fujimorismo"; and Quijano, "El fujimorismo, la OEA y el Perú."

37   Peru's Supreme Court of Justice, controlled and manipulated by the National Intelligence Service and at the service of the country's corrupt speculators and businessmen, declared that the discrimination imposed by big business on Lima's nightlife and dance halls was legal. See Quijano, "¡Qué tal raza!," which has been republished widely in Latin America.

38   For my historical and theoretical statements on this question see, primarily, Quijano, "Coloniality of Power, Eurocentrism and Latin America"; Quijano, "Estado-Nación, ciudadanía y democracia"; and Quijano, "El fantasma del desarrollo en América Latina."

39   On this debate, see the references in Quijano, "Estado-Nación, ciudadanía y democracia."

40   The most outrageous case in Latin America is obviously that of Alberto Fujimori, who won Peru's 1990 presidential election due to the massive opposition of Peruvian voters to the neoliberal economic program of his opponent, Mario Vargas Llosa, but who then immediately imposed the most extreme and twisted version of neoliberalism, against the express will of those who had elected him. Fujimori has kept himself in power ever since through a series of coups and electoral frauds that have been condemned around the world, in other words, once more against the will of the voters. [Translator's note: Following a series of

electoral and corruption scandals that led to massive street protests, Fujimori fled Peru for exile in Japan in November 2000, shortly after this text was written. He was subsequently arrested, tried, and imprisoned in Peru.]

41 On these hard edges in the so-called postmodernist debate, see, for example, Best and Kellner, *Postmodern Theory*.

42 There is a provocative discussion of these topics in Virilio, *La bombe informatique*, translated as *The Information Bomb*.

43 Though his special focus is the cultural arena, Therborn, "The Atlantic Diagonal in the Labyrinths of Modernities and Globalizations," makes useful observations on these issues.

44 There is extensive literature on the limits of the process of globalization for the capitalist economy. Among the most important texts, see Alvater and Mahnkopf, *Grenzen der Globalisierung*; and Boyer and Drache, *States against Markets*.

45 See Quijano, "El trabajo en el umbral del siglo XXI."

46 I have proposed some issues for discussion in Quijano, "Globalización y exclusión desde el futuro."

47 For early contributions to the debate, see Quijano, "*La 'economía popular' y sus caminos en América Latina*; and Quijano, *Modernidad, identidad y utopía en América Latina*.

8

THE NEW ANTICAPITALIST IMAGINARY

In the period from the mid-1970s to the late 1980s, the competition for world hegemony ended with the total defeat of all rivals to Euro-Yankee imperialism. This defeat also swept away the radical opponents of the current world matrix of power. And so, a new historical period began. First, all humanity seemed to be, for the first time in history, boxed into one single matrix of power. Second, the legitimacy of this power seemed virtually all-encompassing: not only had all alternatives to it been defeated, but all criticisms of it and even the basis for such critiques had been driven from public debate as well. As a consequence, for quite some time power ceased to be a topic of study and debate except in the most technocratic sense, taken as an irreducible fact of human social existence. The dominant groups and beneficiaries of this new phase of humanity appropriately dubbed it "globalization," for the whole "globe" was, at last, their exclusive domain. Their victory seemed so complete and definitive that they did not hesitate to proclaim the "end of history."

The matrix of power thus "globalized" is the result of a long process. It was established with the Americas at the end of the fifteenth century, fusing the coloniality of power as the basic system of domination and capitalism as the system of exploitation. All of its fundamentals continued to be shaped and fine-tuned to the end of the eighteenth century, culminating in its Eurocentrism. Shifts and changes in the matrix of power since then have mainly consisted of the unfolding of structural tendencies that by then had already been defined but in an ever more heterogeneous and disconnected way among the central areas of social life that it articulates. Thus, while the crisis of control over relations between the sexes and over intersubjective relations has only intensified since the late nineteenth century, the crises of control over labor and over public authority had been resolved one way or another until precisely the period of their final "globalization." From that point on, history may be different.

For the winners, "globalizing" their matrix of power has allowed them, first, to intensify their domination by reconcentrating their world control over public authority and by blocking—even reversing, wherever possible—the deconcentration or nationalization of that domination. To that end, a worldwide imperial bloc was formed under the hegemony of the United States, a hegemony that was abruptly bolstered after September 11, 2001. In short, imperialism has been reconfigured and intensified. Second, this "globalization" has allowed them to accelerate and deepen—in the face of almost no resistance, for the time being—the reconcentration of their world control over labor and its resources and products. That is, the exploitation of workers and the social polarization of the world's population have intensified.

The results of both dimensions of "globalizing" the current matrix of power have been catastrophic for the vast majority of humanity. On one side, this means that in a growing number of countries the majority of the population is being separated from any real control over the state, which is coming to function almost exclusively as the administrator and guardian for the interests of "global" capitalists. This process of denationalizing the state and de-democratizing political relations in society has mainly affected those countries where the democratization and nationalization of society and its relations with the state had not been fully carried out or where such accomplishments were still very precarious.

On the other side, the reconcentration of control over labor and its resources and products and the social polarization of the world's population have already reached such an extreme that a mere 20 percent of the world's people control 80 percent of world production and vice versa, with 80 percent of the people having access to only 20 percent of production. The gulf between the planet's rich and poor is not only greater than it has ever been in history but also continues to widen daily between countries, between enterprises and countries, and, to be sure, between the inhabitants of each country. Thus, the gulf between rich countries and poor ones has now reached a ratio of sixty to one, whereas less than two centuries ago it stood at barely nine to one. General Motors had revenues of $168 billion in 1996, while the combined gross domestic products of Bolivia, Costa Rica, Ecuador, El Salvador, Guatemala, Honduras, Nicaragua, Panama, Paraguay, Peru, and Uruguay came to merely $159 billion. In Latin America, the income of the richest 20 percent is sixteen times that of the remaining 80 percent. In the United States, the number of people living in poverty has jumped from not quite 25 million to more than 35 million over the past twenty years. Currently, the three richest people in the world have a combined wealth greater than that of the forty-eight poorest countries.

In Latin America, the Peruvian case is undoubtedly one of the most extreme examples of this tendency. Fujimorism (the presidency and political movement of Alberto Fujimori, who ruled Peru from 1990 to 2000) used the "dirty war" against Sendero Luminoso and the Tupac Amaru Revolutionary Movement as a channel for imposing a "state reform" that removed the state from almost any interference on the part of the dominated/exploited except for the vote, which was fraudulently manipulated. Fujimorism repressed protests, including by assassinating opposition leaders and organizers. And Fujimorism controlled, perverted, and corrupted any public institutions that were the expressions of democratic and national achievements: justice tribunals, parliament, and the press. Public administration was emptied of anything that could be used to produce or manage public services, especially education, health, and social security. All such services were privatized or, if not privatized, were commercialized so that medical attention in public hospitals and education in the state school system ceased to be free. All of the country's essential resources and services were handed over to the control of globalized capital. An effective system for extracting taxes from the people was organized, but the major international enterprises in Peru were made exempt from taxation. Tax revenues were dedicated to service payments on foreign debt and, secondarily, to illicitly enriching the civil servants and military officers in control of public administration.

In the course of ten years, Fujimorism thus succeeded in denationalizing and de-democratizing the state and society. In the process, the production and marketing structure that proved inconvenient to the interests of global capital, especially financial capital, was being dismantled. All this has meant that the social relations, social groupings, and social and political identities associated with the prior situation have been fragmented, dispersed, or dismantled. Because of this last fact most of all, Fujimori's recent defeat, though it stemmed from a massive popular outcry that was expressed on the streets and through the vote in reaction to the endless deterioration (four consecutive years of recession) of an already unbearable situation, could only end in agreements between the imperial and local agents of global capital. The Organization of American States returned to monitoring Peruvian elections after preapproval by the US assistant secretary of state for inter-American affairs, the head of the Southern Command of the US armed forces, and their respective assistants.

It is no surprise, then, that the political economy of Fujimorism has been maintained and deepened in the new administration formally headed by Alejandro Toledo, which is to say that the consequences have gotten even worse for the majority of the population. Tax exemption has been upheld for the great globalized enterprises (at a cost of nearly 400 million dollars), at a time when no funding can allegedly be found for education or health services. Creatively, new taxes have been levied on workers' salaries, with the argument that fiscal resources must be found in order to raise those salaries. A few democratic spaces might initially be regained (for example, under pressure from workers protesting in the streets, the government was forced to accept the relegalization of the eight-hour day). But popular street protests against neoliberal economic policies have recently grown all over the country like a tidal wave, while Toledo's and his administration's favorability ratings have fallen below 30 percent in public opinion polls. After the terrorist act of March 20, 2002, even these democratic spaces have been abruptly shut down.[1]

It can easily be seen that the growing reconcentration of world control over political authority, with all that it implies about the denationalizing and de-democratizing of states and societies, is the basis and the means for speeding up and deepening labor exploitation and the control over its resources and products. As a result, the world's people have become polarized between a handful of capitalists, rich and armed to the teeth, be they individuals or enterprises, and the overwhelming majority, who have been robbed of their democratic freedoms and the resources they need to survive.

The "globalization" of the current matrix of power leads above all to this result. It is of course true that "globalization" also means instantaneous communication, simultaneous access to information, and greater visibility for the diversity of human lifeways, in sum a profound change in our relations with each other and with space and time. In other words, globalization leads to profound modifications in intersubjective relations within the world's population, which will perhaps prove to be preludes under historically different conditions to the worldwide integration of humankind in all the richness of our diversity and the heterogeneity of our experiences and historical accomplishments.

No one would deny that these accomplishments in scientific-technological innovation are clearly real, important, and pivotal for the growing cultural and communication integration of humanity. But presumably no one would argue—at least not if they were being honest—that we should not wonder whether, given the "globalization" of the current matrix of power, these transformations of human life have proved to be incompatible with the brutal squeeze that is crushing the majority of people between, on one side, a world structure of exploitation and distribution that is ceaselessly increasing the extreme concentration of control over world production, the loss of jobs and income for workers and the middle classes, the absolute poverty of the majority, and the daily deaths of hundreds of thousands of people for this specific reason and, on the other side, a world political order that globalizes imperialism and undermines autonomy, identity, and democracy for the majority of countries around the "globe" and therefore is inherently rife with an extreme level of discord, as expressed in the growing tidal wave of wars and exchanges between state terrorism and private terrorism. The obvious answer to this question is no. Quite the contrary. This means, then, that these technological achievements of the current civilization take place not in a historical vacuum but rather within a matrix of power. And there can be no doubt that within this matrix of power, they serve not only to further the cultural integration of humankind but also as supports, as instruments, and as vehicles for furthering the domination and exploitation of the majority of people around the world.

The Conditions of the Resistance

For roughly two decades, this imperial "globalization" of the current matrix of power could be imposed to little or, in some areas, almost no resistance. But beginning in the early 1990s, workers returned to open struggle first in the countries dubbed the "Asian tigers," such as South Korea and Indonesia, and subsequently in some of the countries of the "center," such as the United States, France, Germany, and Italy particularly in 1994–2001, the period of economic recovery that followed a worldwide recession.

The resistance is currently spreading across virtually the entire "globe," especially among young people in the central countries. In the case of Latin

America, no country has been exempt from the political and economic crises precipitated in large measure by the massive resistance struggles on the part of the exploited, the dominated, and the discriminated. Without the mass popularization and "globalization" of resistance against globalized imperialism, the first two annual World Social Forum (WSF) meetings in Porto Alegre, in 2001 and 2002, would have been impossible to put on or insignificant in their size and resonance.

Two questions must be raised about the conditions and characteristics of the resistance to imperialist "globalization," because they lead to further questions about the conditions and possibilities of this new period of social conflict. First, there is a need to examine the fact that it was over a rather long period—nearly thirty years—that imperialist "globalization" could be imposed with little or no resistance all over the world, beginning with an abrupt reconfiguration of the accumulation structure and capital-labor relations in the "central" countries, most pronouncedly first in England under Thatcher, then in the United States under Reagan, during the 1980s. The explanation for this must be sought in the convergence, not merely the simultaneity, of two processes: on one side, the erosion and ultimate collapse of the so-called socialist camp, and, on the other side, the decision of the bourgeoisies of the "center," especially the century-long US-British alliance, to take advantage of the weakening of their rivals to go on a worldwide offensive against labor and against the dependent bourgeoisies as a way to reconfigure both the structure of world political power under the explicit hegemony of their alliance and, at the same time, the world accumulation structure under the hegemony of their finance capital.

With the weakening of the "socialist camp" and the final implosion of the Soviet Union, some of the regimes that had until then resisted or even defied imperialist pressures were left unsupported, and all of them were left disoriented, as were the political organizations and movements all over the world that participated on their side of the conflict during this period. This allowed the imperialist interests to promote or simply impose regimes favorable to them in most countries. The demands that had come from "nationalist," "developing," and "reformist" regimes, several of them linked in various ways and to various degrees to the "socialist camp," for a "New Economic World Order" in the late 1960s and early 1970s were quickly dashed in the 1980s as the world switched course toward what President George H. W. Bush, after the Persian Gulf War, unabashedly dubbed the "New World Order."

At the same time and along the same lines, the capitalist crisis that began in the mid-1970s—with its recession, inflation, and unemployment harming workers all over the world—hastened the debilitation and even the disintegration of labor unions in the "central" countries, preventing them from resisting and defending their considerable earlier accomplishments. On the "periphery," this crisis sped the disintegration of social identities and groups and the unstoppable erosion of workers' social organizations. "Structural adjustment" was the result of this convergence between, on one side, the political defeat of the "socialist camp," the "nationalists," and other opponents to the same matrix of power and, on the other side, the crisis of capitalism. Thus, on the "periphery" it blocked the development of earlier trends toward deconcentration or redistribution of power while facilitating the imposition of a reconcentrated worldwide imperialist political power as well as the world reconcentration of capitalist control over labor and world production. The relevant question consequently is this: What explains the reemergence of the world's workers and, in general, of the world's peoples in the absence of the "socialist camp," a great many "nationalist" and "reformist" regimes, and the plans and discourses and movements and political organizations they would have fostered? I suggest looking for two sets of answers corresponding to two different situations, regions, and populations previously mentioned.

In the "center," the first momentum probably came from the economic revival that began in the late 1980s and continued through the 1990s, especially the second half of the 1990s, because it gave significant sectors of workers more security for demanding better wages and working conditions while also giving significant segments of youths the consciousness and the spare time that are indispensable for questioning, critiquing, organizing, and mobilizing. But from Seattle on, it was the new consciousness acquired with respect to the current-day ravages and the dismal future of imperialist "globalization"— the consciousness that can only be confronted as such, globally—that has mobilized these sectors across Europe and the United States.

On the "periphery," the first workers to mobilize for resistance were those of the so-called Asian Tiger countries at a moment when they had experienced an abrupt fall from a long period of social stability into unemployment and poverty, as in South Korea, and, as in Indonesia, when there was an abrupt economic crisis associated with the political crisis of the bloodiest, most corrupt, but also longest-lived and most stable of the satrapies imposed by imperialism. In Latin America, the momentum behind mobilizations for resistance came from basically the same sources. Thinking especially about the uprisings in Brazil and Argentina, the Peruvian uprising that ended Fujimorism, the Mexican uprising from Chiapas on, and what has happened in Venezuela since the "Caracazo" as well as the struggles in Bolivia and Ecuador, all of these, in different ways according to their local particularities, took place after periods of economic stability, even moments of relative prosperity, and political stability.

In any case, the experience of the two meetings of the WSF in Porto Alegre shows that once resistance becomes a mass phenomenon and spreads across the globe, a new consciousness is quickly formed among workers and young people from a destabilizing and disintegrating middle class. This new consciousness is currently the new and most significant element motivating and giving momentum to the mobilization and organization of resistance against imperialist "globalization."

When the first WSF was convened in Porto Alegre in 2001, the resistance movement against imperialist "globalization" was itself rapidly globalizing. Even so, the presence of some twenty thousand people, most of them young, clearly surpassed all expectations. But the presence of more than fifty thousand people from 150 countries all over the world in the WSF of 2002 showed everyone that the struggle against the "globalization" of the current matrix of power really had gone global. There is no better sign of the recognition of this fact than the World Economic Forum in New York, which, while avoiding a direct confrontation with the WSF of Porto Alegre, as had occurred with Davos, did devote a large portion of its formal debates to the problems of poverty and unemployment.

What explains this rapid globalizing of mobilizations against imperialist "globalization"? I suggest that it was the "demonstration effect" of the earlier mobilizations themselves that made the effects of this imperialist "globalization" unbearable, and in this sense the WSF of Porto Alegre undoubtedly played a decisive role. In other words, it was the newly acquired consciousness, the spreading awareness that a world resistance exists, that we are a growing population that is mobilizing, that mobilizing is not only possible but also produces a new "historical subject" (to use the old jargon) whose existence forces the dominators to recognize that there is a real problem for the reproduction of the "globalization" of their power, as the debates of the World Economic Forum in New York confirm. It is true that the situation of the growing majority of peoples in the world is deteriorating day by day and becoming unsustainable. But as always, poverty and the deterioration of the material living conditions for people cannot become a political problem, a problem for society, until the victims organize and mobilize.

From the Resistance to the Alternative? The Experience of the World Social Forum in Porto Alegre

Paying close attention to the formal discourses that were centered at the WSF in 2001 and 2002, the struggle against "globalization" seems to prioritize problems in a few areas:

1 Defending the autonomy of states and national control over natural resources and capital, particularly financial capital;
2 Demanding the recovery of full employment, wages, and basic public services in each country;
3 Calling for a global struggle against the spread and the deepening of poverty, using the resources of finance capital itself;
4 Resisting the growing degradation of "nature" and the ecological environment in society today; and
5 Struggling against discrimination based on "gender" and "race."

The specific proposals made in these discourses, especially during the second WSF in 2002, are strikingly heterogeneous. Not to belabor the point, they can be said to range from "humanizing" and "democratizing" the "globalization" and the basic institutions of the current world order—the International Monetary Fund, the World Bank, the United Nations—as a way of confronting poverty and unemployment to recapturing countries' political autonomy, putting production resources and public services back under state control, and ending neoliberalism so as to make it possible once more for the state to provide employment, salaries, and public services. In short, this would primarily be a matter of anti-imperialist resistance, "antiglobalism" in this specific sense, against neoliberalism as the universal matrix for political economy, rejecting the predatory nature of today's financial capital, rejecting discrimination in these forms and the destruction of the environment. This discourse includes the "anti-imperialists," the "nationalists," many of the "feminists" and "ecologists," and many of those who identify as "socialists" whose place here corresponds to the well-known alliance between anti-imperialism, nationalism, and socialism around a central hub—control of the state, each group for their own purposes—or is a tacit admission that the current tendencies of power are irreversible and that what makes sense and may be achievable is their "humanization" and "democratization." That discourse includes primarily the social liberals and the social democrats who do not align with the "Third Way" of Blair and Schroeder.

As can be seen, the memory of previously achieved, or nearly achieved, gains that have been destroyed by imperialist "globalization" and neoliberalism—autonomy, nationalization and democratization of states and societies, public services, employment, income—are at the forefront of some of the formal discourses that predominated at the WSF, that is, the memory of achievements in terms of the deconcentration and redistribution of this same matrix of power, along with hopes for winning them back. Other discourses instead critique the undesirable aspects of the current matrix of power, such as poverty, violence, discrimination, and ecological degradation but with a tacit admission that the "globalization" of that power is irreversible so that the critiques come bathed in a benevolent hope that it can be "humanized" and "democratized." There is no way to peg most of the participants in the WSF regarding these discourses and proposals in any rigorous way. At most we can guess that there were more people with the first group than with the second but also that a significant number are always moving back and forth between the two.

At the same time, however, both meetings of the WSF, especially the more recent one in 2002, featured an impressive number of mainly young people brandishing slogans that were also very heterogeneous but more radical by far at conference sessions, at workshops, at round tables, at informal meetings, at the encampments, in the streets, and in the corridors of the Catholic University of Port Alegre campus where both WSF meetings took place. The discourse of these young people, who came from all over the planet, targeted the capitalist and not just imperialist character of "globalization," and they were ready for a struggle against the matrix of power itself in each of the basic realms of social life: work, sex, subjectivity, and public authority. The intellectual atmosphere of these young people permeated the entire WSF. This was undoubtedly what gave these meetings, despite the spirit of many of the hundreds of nongovernmental organizations present there, their powerful and vital potential for spreading far and wide, their utopian feeling, their contagious hope that, truly, "another world is possible."

What "Other World Is Possible"?

The deep and protracted defeat of every rival to Euro-Yankee imperialism and every opponent to capitalism has all the historical significance of a counterrevolution. Imperialist "globalization" has that character. That is why it is irreversible in one strict sense: the previous social way of life cannot be restored.

Consequently, any possible changes that the current victims of this imperial "globalization" might achieve cannot be thought of or, by the same token, planned out ahead of time as reversing the current trends in capitalism, much less its effects on and implications for our history, our current social way of life. It is true, after all, that for five hundred years, particularly over the past two hundred, up until "globalization," the struggles of the dominated/exploited allowed them, though not always or everywhere, to moderate, slow down, and negotiate the limits, conditions, and methods of domination/exploitation. Therefore, not only is it necessary and urgent to try once more to impose conditions that will improve workers' situations and prospects within the current matrix of power; it is, in principle, also possible to achieve such changes without necessarily destroying that matrix of power as such.

The question to be investigated and decided, however, is whether such changes are actually feasible, given the level and the scale already attained by the tendencies of capitalism and the whole matrix of power that it employs. Competitive capitalism permitted and in a sense even required a specific sort of democracy, albeit one that was achieved or allowed mainly in the "center." Monopolist capitalism produced tendencies toward reducing that horizon, but the universal spread of a production structure associated with the capital-wage relationship allowed the struggles for the type of democracy specific to that power to be feasible even on the "periphery," while the overexploitation of labor over there yielded enough resources for the bourgeoisie of the "center" to concede a "welfare state" to the struggles of their local workers.

But "globalized" imperialist capitalism is developing tendencies that block and pervert that horizon more and more. The technocratization and instrumentalization of its rationality, the predatory nature of speculative accumulation, and the loss of capacity and of interest in the commodification of the living, individual labor force, which brings about a reduction in stable wage employment, are all tendencies that are structurally associated with the concentration of wealth and income, the correlated polarization of society and between states, and thus with the need for a growing concentration of control over public authority. Under such conditions, how broad or deep must the margin be for the stable deconcentration of power and the relatively significant redistribution of power that any form of democracy necessarily entails? The world that this matrix of power dominates "globally" is, of course, structurally and historically heterogeneous, which means that the matrix of power itself is heterogeneous and discontinuous. It is always possible that this power will be forced, in one or more of its spaces, to accept a bit of its specific form of democracy. What is unlikely, however, is that the matrix of power itself as such could be changed in a generalized or universal way; that it could be turned into a democratic power, even one confined within the specific limits of its own democracy; and that it could be "democratized" and "humanized" without losing its own nature, that is, without being destroyed.

From this perspective, nostalgia for what has been lost by "globalization," with all the mystification such nostalgia entails, cannot be the hoped-for goal of the struggles that have once more begun. On the other hand, the defeat that allowed everything, or almost everything, that had been achieved to be snatched away from us cannot be explained without reference to the nature of those achievements and the struggles behind them. That is undoubtedly what the young people of the world have begun to see, precisely because they are the product of this "globalization." The people who have been educated under this "globalization"—and in the poor countries they make up the majority—need and demand, as do all victims of this power, equal access to all the kinds of goods and services produced in the world today. This is a matter of not merely things or services but also forms of equal social relations in every realm of social life: labor and its products, sex and its products, subjectivity and its products, public authority and its products. And they will attain their goal, one way or the other. If they do so through the means that neoliberalism continues to promise, fine. If that way is closed off, they will take it by force. They have already begun.

The Coloniality of Power and the Question of Democracy Today

The current "globalized" matrix of power is founded on two central hubs. One is a basic system of domination that articulates all earlier forms around the basic universal classification of people according to the criterion called "race." The other is a basic system of exploitation that articulates all forms of labor control around capital. These two hubs are mutually dependent. The conjoining of the pair to form a specific matrix of power is the result of the colonial experience that began with the Americas. Coloniality is thus the foundational and inherent condition for this matrix of power. Coloniality does not solely refer to the "racial" classification of the world's population. Without coloniality, from the global perspective none of the realms of power—the control of labor and its resources and products, the control of sex and its resources and products, the control of subjectivity and its resources and products, or the control of public or collective authority and its resources and products—would have their current specific features. A concise term for this matrix of power would be "colonial-capitalist." Due to this fundamental aspect of its nature, the current matrix of power is, among all known matrices, the one that undoubtedly is most incompatible with democracy. Indeed, on one side, it entails a condition that is radically opposed to democracy: the coloniality of power. But on the other side, because of the historical conditions of the process of capital as a social relationship and its centrality in the system of exploitation, it required a mode and measure of democratic relations, especially in some of the institutions of power, public authority, and subjectivity. The complex historical dialectic between the two poles of this contradiction has been present in the heterogeneous and discontinuous geocultural distribution of the experience of democracy in the world over the past five hundred years, especially in view of the relations between Europe and non-Europe with regard to the nation-state and the secularization of intersubjective relations.

In any case, one of the values that came to be exceptionally prized in this matrix of power, ultimately to the point of being incorporated into the universal imaginary as a vital necessity, is democracy. That is why this matrix of power is now facing a double problem with respect to democracy. In the first place, it is precisely the "globalization" of this matrix that has universalized this value in the world's imaginary, yet at the same time "globalization" has placed democracy at its greatest historical danger of developing or even surviving. In the second place, for accessing all the other goods and services that the world produces, democracy is now literally indispensable. In both cases, all this is the more true the more the "globalized" tendencies of capitalism develop. Democracy has always been a scarce good; gaining access to the use and exercise of democracy has always been very costly, subjectively and materially. But the current power is not only keeping it scarce but also putting it in certain danger. What had been one of the achievements of the modernity that began with the Americas is now beset, in the subjective dimension of our social life, by fundamentalisms of every stripe, some of the most influential of which were produced and cultivated in the very "center" of capitalism and whose aggressiveness and violence are nurtured precisely by the crisis of that power and its "globalization." And in the material dimension, it is under violent siege by the most predatory social interests of today's capitalism.

All this is occurring precisely when it is more distinctly palpable than ever to everyone, and most of all to young people, that democracy today is the basic requirement for equitable access to the main goods and services produced by humanity. And that is certainly the central lesson learned by the youths educated under imperialist "globalization." To begin with, this is because the simultaneity of information and communication implies imaginary access to all goods, to all services, to the multiplicity of options from the diverse and heterogeneous experience of humankind that circulate on the superhighways of the "virtual society." And in contrast to that spread, the "globalization" of the current tendencies of capitalism utterly polarizes all social and even geocultural possibilities of access to the most desired or needed goods and services displayed to people's (and particularly young people's) yearning. The matrix of power that produces and imposes so much polarization has become more and more unbearable. It must be changed. And if recurring experience shows that it cannot be moderated and "humanized," it must be destroyed. Since the late nineteenth century, most importantly, active currents of thought and political organizations have maintained that democracy is the precondition for developing human society.

But the critical takes on capitalism that became the majority view opted for concentrating control over the nation-state and state control over ownership of the means of production and of products, because—especially for the current called "historical materialism" and later on "Marxism-Leninism," which became hegemonic worldwide in the revolutionary movement— that was the most realistic, "nonutopian" way to get out of capitalism. The experience of more than seventy years of "actually existing socialism" and the defeat and ultimate disintegration of "actually existing socialism" unequivocally demonstrated, however, that this is not a feasible way to build an alternative society to capitalism, precisely because it is incompatible with the continual deepening of democratic relations in people's daily lives. Therefore, only the destruction of power, of all power, rather than its concentration, is the true way out.

The subsequent imperialist "globalization" of monopoly finance capital has only confirmed this experience. It is probably true that as Jürgen

Habermas sorrowfully and lucidly points out, there is no guarantee that the experiences and lessons learned during the history of one specific society and matrix of power will form new starting points and will keep people from repeating the same mistakes when they enter a new history, that is, a new society. This is one of the historical tragedies of our species, the only one that stumbles twice over the same stone. But it is also a defining feature of our freedom, our aptitude and willingness to rethink things, to choose again and decide again as many times as might be possible or necessary.

In any case, the experience of the twentieth century has left four clear lessons for the people who have been educated under this "globalization" since the mid-1970s:

1 Democracy, as a continual broadening and deepening of social equality among diverse and heterogeneous people, and of individual freedom and collective solidarity among them, is now the essential precondition both for equal access to the resources, goods, and services that the species produces and for developing the potentials inherent in current scientific-technological resources and thereby for seeking and developing new historical meanings for the life of humanity, for new historical horizons of meaning.

2 The experience of the "socialist camp" proved unconducive to the goals of producing an alternative social existence to the current matrix of power. Its driving goal was the bureaucratic despotism that took over from the start by expropriating the socialization of power that the workers had undertaken.

3 The development of scientific and technological resources produced within the current matrix of power has magnified the productive capacity of humanity and thereby our capacity for our own development and has amplified and constantly continues to amplify the circulation and world exchange of the diversity and heterogeneity of our species' experiences and therefore also the margins of individual freedom and social equality.

4 The development of the tendencies of "globalization" by colonial-capitalist power favors the most antidemocratic elements of that power and therefore constantly narrows and perverts all earlier democratic achievements and blocks the democratic potential of the powerful technological resources in terms of both their productive capacity and their widening of the margins of equality and individual and social freedom.

Consequently, the new imaginary now coming into being, especially among young people, has two main components. First is the need and the search for a new horizon of meaning for humanity's social existence as the founding element for any alternative social existence. This is the imaginary that emerges as the content of the idea of revolutionary utopia. Second is democracy as precondition, point of departure, and focus of any pathway to producing an alternative society, an alternative social existence, to the one imposed by the colonial-capitalist matrix of power. This new perspective could perhaps, going forward, give meaning to debates on the questions surrounding power and the revolution.

Notes

This text was published on the occasion of the 2003 WSF in Porto Alegre, January 23–28, 2003.

1   [Translator's note: On March 20, 2002, two days before the visit of President George W. Bush to Peru, a car bomb attack on the US embassy killed nine people, wounded forty others, and damaged or destroyed dozens of buildings. This was the first major attack attributed to Sendero Luminoso since 1995.]

9

DON QUIXOTE AND THE WINDMILLS IN LATIN AMERICA

What we now call Latin America was formed alongside and as part of the matrix of power currently dominant worldwide. It was here that coloniality and globality were shaped and established as foundations and constitutive modes for the new matrix of power.[1] It was here that the historical process was born that defined the historical-structural dependence of Latin America and gave rise, in the same movement, to the establishment of Western Europe as the world control center of this power. The same movement also defined the new material and subjective elements that founded the mode of social existence that was given the name "modernity."

In other words, Latin America was both the original space and the inaugural moment for the historical and world period in which we are still living. In this specific sense, it was the first historical entity/identity of the current colonial/modern world-system and of the entire period of modernity. Nevertheless, the original home and moment of this historical period, the fount and source of the basal elements of the new world society, was stripped of its central place and of the attributes and the fruits of modernity. This meant that none of the new historical potentials ever developed fully in Latin America, neither its historical period nor its new social existence in the world. Both were instead defined and are reproduced today as colonial/modern.[2] Why?

Don Quixote and the Windmills in Latin America

Jun'ichirō Tanizaki, comparing the histories of Europe and Japan, says that Europeans had the good fortune of having their history develop in stages, each derived by internal transformations from the preceding one, whereas the history of Japan—which is to say, the meaning of its history, especially since World War II—was disrupted from the outside by Western military and technological superiority.[3] This reflection accepts the Eurocentric perspective and its characteristic evolutionist view as valid, thus testifying to the world hegemony of Eurocentrism as a mode of production and of control over subjectivity and especially over knowledge. But in Western Europe itself, this perspective is rather a sign of the belated intellectual hegemony of the center-north regions and is thus foreign and contrary to the heritage of Don Quixote. On the four hundredth anniversary of this foundational book, it is time to look back at that heritage.

The fabulous scene where Don Quixote tilts at a giant and is knocked down by a windmill is surely the most powerful historical image from the entire period of early modernity: the mis/match between, on one side, a feudal ideology of chivalry, the realm where Don Quixote's perceptions dwell, which corresponds to social practice in only the most fragmentary and inconsistent way, and on the other side, the new social practices represented by the windmill, which are on their way to becoming generalized but do not yet have a consistent, hegemonic legitimizing ideology that corresponds to them.

As the old image has it, the new is not yet born, and the old has not finished dying.[4]

The truth is, this mis/match runs through the whole book: the new common sense that was emerging with the new matrix of power produced in the Americas, with its commercial pragmatism and its respect for the "mighty gentleman, Mister Money" (*poderoso caballero es Don Dinero*, in the words of the poet Francisco de Quevedo), is not yet hegemonic, not yet consistently formed, yet even so it already occupies a growing space in people's mentality. In other words, it is already contesting the hegemony of the chivalrous, feudal sense of social existence. And the latter, while giving way in different manners and degrees depending on the people and places involved, is still active, has not yet ceased to dwell in everyone's subjectivity, and resists letting go of its protracted hegemony.

The essential factor to note is that in the specific context of the future Spain of that moment, neither of these sense perspectives can exist or take shape separately and free from the other. This intersubjectivity cannot be, cannot cease to be, anything but a fusion—impossible in principle but inevitable in practice—of commercial pragmatism with chivalrous visions.

This is a historical moment in which the various times and histories are not shaped in any sort of dualist order or any unilineal and unidirectional evolutionary sequence, such as those that Eurocentrism has taught us to think in since the late seventeenth century. These are, to the contrary, complex, contradictory, disconnected associations among fragmentary and changing structures of relationships, senses and meanings, multiple geohistorical origins, and simultaneous interwoven actions, all of which, however, form part of one and the same new world that is in the process of being built. Not by accident, that windmill was a technology that had come from Baghdad and had been integrated into the Muslim-Jewish world of the southern Iberian peninsula when it was still part of the Arab hegemony in the Mediterranean, a productive, rich, urban, cultivated society, sophisticated in its development, the center of world trade in commodities, ideas, and philosophical, scientific, and technological knowledge. Chivalry, meanwhile, was the model of society that the militarily victorious but socially and culturally backward lords of the peninsula's north were attempting to impose, without complete success, on the rubble of the defeated Muslim-Jewish society as they subjugated and colonized the autonomous communities of the peninsula.

This feudal regime, itself dominated by the Counter-Reformation and its Inquisition, did not hesitate to decree the expulsion of the Moors and Jews and to impose the infamous certification of *limpieza de sangre*, purity (literally "cleanliness") of blood, in the first ethnic cleansing of the whole colonial/modern period. The same archaic, feudal model of social existence would likewise move the Crown to centralize its political rule, not exactly by endeavoring to produce a common (national, that is) identity for all other populations but instead by imposing a regime of internal colonialism on the other identities and nationalities of the peninsula, a regime that remains in effect today. The feudal regime thus impeded the process of nationalization that later developed in north-central Europe, in the same channel and the same movement toward bourgeois domination of society.

After the Americas, at a time of rapid expansion for capitalism when a growing segment of the new Iberian society was already immersed in the new matrix of power, such seigneurial lordship could no longer help but keep its feet on the commercial ground even as its head still lived in the archaic, though in its imaginary no less mighty, clouds of its chivalry.

Without this mis/match, which merged with the disastrous effects of the expulsion of the Moors and Jews on material and cultural creativity, it would be impossible to explain why it was that despite the massive profits obtained from the precious metals and plants produced in the Americas by the unpaid labor of Indian serfs and Black slaves, the future Spain was entering, contrary to all appearances, into a prolonged historical trajectory that knocked it down from the center of the greatest imperial power to the enduring backwardness of a periphery in the new colonial/modern world-system.

This trajectory revealed that this chivalrous seigneurial class, which had dominated and benefited directly from the first period of the coloniality of power and modernity, was already too archaic to ride this new unbroken horse and lead it in benefit of its country and the world. The seigneurial class was unable to transform, fully and coherently, into a bourgeoisie, ride the impulses and the democratizing conflicts of the new matrix of power, and guide the nationalization of the heterogeneous population, unlike its rivals and successors in north-central Western Europe who were capable of doing so. To the contrary, the archaic seigneurial class had been decaying for centuries in the ambiguous merchant-lord labyrinth in a dead-end effort to preserve seigneury on the basis of the internal colonialism imposed on the diverse identities in the population, precisely at a time of world capitalism and despite the truly exceptional resources of the coloniality of power.

What made the difference? The difference was, undoubtedly, the Americas. The Crown, which is to say the Hapsburgs, colonial masters of the colossal wealth that the Americas produced and the never-ending unpaid labor of Black slaves and Indian serfs, were convinced that given their control over that wealth, they could expel the Moors and Jews without major losses while gaining effective control over power. This led them to de-democratize, through violence, the social life of the independent communities and to impose on the other national identities (Catalans, Basques, Andalusians, Galicians, Navarrese, Valencians) a system of internal colonialism and seigneurial rule taken from the feudal model of Central Europe. The well-known result was, on one side, the destruction of internal production and the internal market based on it and, on the other, the long-term decline and stagnation of the processes of democratization and enlightenment that colonial/modernity had been opening up, which had created none other than Don Quixote.

What impoverished the future Spain, loaded it up with lordlings, and on top of that turned it into central headquarters for cultural and political obscurantism in the West for the next four centuries was exactly the same phenomenon that allowed the emerging center-north of Western Europe to grow rich and secularize and later fostered the development of the conflict matrix that led to the democratization of the regions and countries of the center-north in Western Europe. And it was precisely the historical hegemony that had thus been made possible that allowed these countries to elaborate their own versions of modernity and rationality and to appropriate, as something exclusive to the historical-cultural identity of the West, the historical legacy of Greece and Rome, which had nonetheless been preserved and elaborated much earlier and over a much longer time as part of the Muslim-Jewish Mediterranean world.

All of this took place—a fact that should never be forgotten, lest we lose the very meaning of this history—during a period in which coloniality was still exclusively a matrix of power connecting the Americas with the emerging Western Europe, in other words, a time when that Western Europe was being invented on a foundation of the Americas. It is impossible not to recognize the historical implications of the establishment of this new matrix of power and of the mutual historical production of the Americas and Western Europe as the headquarters of historical-structural dependency and the control center within the new power.

It is true that the norms of capitalism have finally consolidated in Spain now, with resources and support from the new European Community, which itself is now dominated by the new finance capital regime. Even so, the remnants of the lord let system (*señoritaje*) linger on in its social existence. And the conflict with the current autonomous regions, together with Basque terrorism aimed at national independence, show that this labyrinth has not yet been destroyed, despite all the changes. No one has written about this historical mis/match with greater clarity and perspicuity than Miguel de Cervantes and, of course, Cide Hamete Benengeli.

For us, the Latin Americans of today, this is the greatest lesson in theory and epistemology that we can learn from Don Quixote: structural-historical heterogeneity, the copresence of historical times and structural fragments of forms of social existence from varied historical and geocultural sources, is the primary mode of existence and of movement in any society, any history, not, as in the Eurocentric vision, the radical dualism that is paradoxically associated with homogeneity, continuity, unilineal and unidirectional evolution, and "progress." This is because it is power, hence struggles for power and the mercurial results of such struggles, that articulates heterogeneous forms of social existence produced at distinct historical times and in distant spaces, that joins them and structures them into a single world, into a concrete society, and, in brief, into historically specific and particular matrices of power.

This is also exactly the issue with the history of the specific space/time that we now call Latin America. Because of its historic–structurally dependent formation within the current matrix of power, it has been constrained all this time to be the privileged space for exercising the coloniality of power. And given that in this matrix of power the hegemonic mode of making and control of knowledge is Eurocentrism, we will find fusions, contradictions, and mis/matches analogous to those that Cide Hamete Benengeli was able to perceive in his own space/time.

By its nature, the Eurocentrist perspective distorts or even blocks the perception of our historical-social experience while at the same time leading us to accept it as true.[5] That is, it works in today's world, particularly in Latin America, in the same way that "chivalry" did in Don Quixote's vision. Consequently, our problems can likewise be perceived only in the same distorted way, and they cannot be confronted and resolved except in a similarly partial and distorted manner. Thus, the coloniality of power turns Latin America into a stage for mis/matches between our experience, our knowledge, and our historical memory.

It is therefore unsurprising that our history has not been able to move forward in an autonomous and coherent way but instead has been formed like a long, tortuous labyrinth in which our unsolved problems haunt us like historical specters. And it would be impossible to recognize and understand this labyrinth—that is, to debate our history and identify our problems—without first managing to identify our specters, summon them, and contend with them. Historical specters, however, such as the ghost dwelling in the shadows of Elsinore and the specter summoned in 1848 by Marx and Engels in the *Manifesto*, possess a thick, dark, complex density. And when they make their entry onto history's stage, they always occasion violent turmoil and sometimes transformations from which there is no return. In Elsinore, the hesitant Hamlet is transformed in the end into the exasperated hero whose sword no longer wavers as he mows down the lives of many characters, the direct way of resolving his conflicts. The furtive specter of the *Manifesto* that roamed Europe in the mid-nineteenth century emerged with a leading role in the mid-twentieth century with one of two world wars, violent revolutions and counterrevolutions, powerful though at times ill-fated and frustrated hopes, frustrations and defeats, and the lives and deaths of millions of people, and even now it has not yet disappeared. Today, it besieges the world.

So, the specters produced by history cannot be summoned with impunity. Those of Latin America have already shown many signs of their capacity for conflict and violence, precisely because they were produced by violent crises and by seismic historical transformations, bringing problems in their wake that we have not yet been able to resolve. These are the specters that haunt our social existence, lay siege to our memory, unsettle every historical project, and frequently irrupt into our lives, leaving dead and wounded in their wake, but the historical transformations that would at last set them at rest have so far remained beyond our grasp. That said, it is not merely important to do this, but is also urgent, because while this matrix of power completes its developmental trajectory, at the very moment that its worst tendencies are exacerbated with the planetarization of its rule, Latin America remains imprisoned by the coloniality of power and by its dependency and for precisely that reason risks never reaching the new world that is being formed in the current crisis, the deepest and most global crisis in the entire period of colonial/modernity.

To deal with such specters and perhaps get them to give us some enlightenment before they vanish, we first have to free our historical retina from the Eurocentrist prison and relearn our historical experience.

It is good, then, it is necessary for Don Quixote to ride again in search of wrongs to right, for him to help us right the original wrong of our whole history: the epistemic trap of Eurocentrism, which for five hundred years has obscured the great wrong of the coloniality of power, letting us see only giants, while the dominators have had control and exclusive use of our windmills.

The Historical Invention of Latin America and the Destruction and Re-creation of the Past

The historical invention of Latin America began with the destruction of an entire historical world, probably the worst case of sociocultural and demographic destruction in history that we are aware of. This is a fact that everyone knows, obviously. But it rarely if ever figures as an active factor in formulating the perspectives that compete or concur with each other in the Latin American debate over the production of our own sense of history. And I suspect that even now this is an argument we would not be grappling with if it were not present in today's "Indigenous" movement and beginning to emerge in the new "Afro–Latin American" movements.[6]

As this is not the occasion to dwell at great length or depth on this particular issue, I will just note, first, that it relates to the breakup of the matrices of power and civilizational matrices of some of the most advanced historical experiences of humanity.

Second, the issue relates to the physical extermination—in little more than the first three decades of the sixteenth century—of over half the population of those societies, whose total immediately before their destruction is estimated at more than 100 million people.

Third, the issue relates to the deliberate elimination of many of the most important creators—not merely the bearers—of those experiences: their leaders, their intellectuals, their engineers, their scientists, their artists.

Fourth, the issue relates to the continued material and subjective repression of the survivors over the next several centuries to the point of subjugating them to the condition of unlettered peasants, exploited, culturally colonized, and dependent, that is, to the point of eliminating any free and autonomous matrix for objectifying ideas, images, symbols, in other words, alphabets, writing, visual arts, sound arts, and audiovisual arts.

Not only was one of humanity's richest intellectual and artistic legacies destroyed, but the best crafted, most highly advanced portion of that legacy in particular was made inaccessible to the survivors of that world. From that point on until only recently, they could not possess or produce signs and symbols of their own apart from distortions created in hiding or in that curious dialect that falls between imitation and subversion, characteristic of culture conflict, primarily in the Andean-Amazonian, Mesoamerican, and North American regions.[7]

The Making of the Colonial Matrix of Power: Race and Global Social Domination

That labyrinth, however, had barely begun to be built. Amid the rubble of the marvelous world that was being destroyed and among its survivors, a new system of social domination and a new system of social exploitation were built in a single historical movement. And with those came a new matrix of conflict, in sum, a new and historically specific power matrix.

The new system of social domination had as a basic building block the idea of race. This is the first social category of modernity.[8] Given that it had not previously existed—there are no effective traces of its earlier existence—it did not then have and, indeed, does not now have any point in common with the materiality of the known universe. It was a social and mental byproduct specific to that process of destroying a historical world and establishing a new order, a new matrix of power, and it emerged as a way of naturalizing the new power relations that were imposed on the survivors of the world that was being destroyed: the idea that the dominated are what they are, not as victims of a power conflict but rather as inferior by their material nature and therefore inferior in their capacity for historical-cultural production. This idea of race was so deeply and continually imposed over the next several centuries and on humankind as a whole that for many—too many, unfortunately—it has become associated with the materiality of social relations as well as with the materiality of people themselves. The vast and diverse history of identities and memories in the conquered world (the most famous names among them are known to everyone: Mayas, Aztecs, and Incas) was deliberately destroyed, and a single racial, colonial, and derogatory identity was imposed on the entire surviving population: "Indians." Thus, in addition to the destruction of their previous historical-cultural world, these peoples had the idea of race and a racial identity imposed on them in token of their new place in the universe of power. Worse still, for the next five hundred years they were taught to look at themselves through their dominators' eyes.

In a distinct but equally effective and enduring way, historical-cultural destruction and the making of racialized identities likewise had among its victims the inhabitants of what we now call Africa who were kidnapped, brought over as slaves, and immediately racialized as "Black." They too came from complex and sophisticated experiences of power and civilization (Ashantis, Bakongos, Kongos, Yorubas, Zulus, and many more). And though the destruction of these societies began much later and never reached the scope and depth that was suffered in "Latin" America, for the kidnapped people who were hauled to the Americas it is evident that their violent and traumatic uprooting and the experience and violence of their racialization and enslavement entailed an equally massive and radical destruction of their previous subjectivity, their previous experience of society, of power, of the universe, their earlier experience of the networks of primary and societal relationships. And for individuals and specific groups, the experience of being uprooted, racialized, and enslaved may very likely have been even more perverse and appalling than for the survivors of "Indigenous communities."

Even though the ideas of "color" and "race" are now virtually inter-changeable, the relation between the two came about very late, beginning only in the eighteenth century as witnessed today by the social, material, and subjective struggle over them. Originally, from the initial moment of the conquest the idea of race was created in order to make sense of the new power relations between "Indians" and Iberians. The original, primal vic-tims of those relations and of this idea are thus the "Indians." "Blacks"— as the future "Africans" were called—were a "color" already familiar to "Europeans" for thousands of years, since the time of the Romans, with-out the idea of race ever coming into play. "Blacks" would not be crammed into the idea of race until much later, in the colonial Americas, particularly after the civil wars between encomenderos and royal forces in the mid-sixteenth century.[9]

But "color" as the emblematic sign of race would only be imposed on them well into the eighteenth century and in the British-American colo-nial area. That was where the idea of being "white" was fabricated and es-tablished, because there the primary racialized and colonially embedded population—which is to say, the most dominated, discriminated, and ex-ploited people within British-American colonial society—were the "Blacks." By contrast, the "Indians" of the region did not form part of that society and were not racialized and colonized there until much later. As is well known, in the nineteenth century after the massive extermination of their population, the destruction of their societies, and the conquest of their territories, the surviving "Indians" would be rounded up into "res-ervations" within the new independent country, the United States, as a colonized, racialized, and segregated sector.[10]

With the new idea of race, all earlier forms and instances of domination began to be redefined and reconfigured, beginning with relations between the sexes. Thus, in the vertical and authoritarian model of patriarchal so-cial order carried by the Iberians conquistadors, any male was by definition superior to any female. After the imposition and legitimation of the idea of race, however, any female of a superior race became, by definition, supe-rior to any male of an inferior race. In this way, the coloniality of relations between the sexes was reconfigured to depend on the coloniality of rela-tions between the races. And this was associated with the production of new historical and geocultural identities originating from the new matrix of power: "whites," "Indians," "Blacks," and "mestizos."

Thus, the first basic and universal social classification system for in-dividuals entered into human history, in current jargon terms the first global social classification in history. Produced in the Americas, it was imposed on the population of the entire Earth during the same expansion of European colonialism over the rest of the world. From that point, the idea of race, the original and specific mental offshoot of the conquest and colonization of the Americas, was imposed as the primary criterion and social mechanism of basic universal social classification for every member of our species.

Indeed, as European colonialism expanded, new historical, social, and geocultural identities were fabricated on the same bases. On one hand, "Indian," "Black," and "mestizo" would be joined by "yellow," "olive-skinned," and "brown." On the other hand, a new geography of power was set to emerge, with a new nomenclature: Europe, Western Europe, the Americas, Asia, Africa, Oceania, and, in a different vein, the West, the East, the Near East, the Far East, and their respective "cultures," "nationalities," and "ethnicities."

Racial classification, being based on a bare mental byproduct that has nothing in common with the material universe, could not even be imagined apart from the violence of colonial domination. Colonialism is a very old experience. However, it was only with the Ibero-Christian conquest and colonization of the societies and populations of the Americas in the late fifteenth and sixteenth centuries that the mental construct of "race" was set up. This tells us that it was not a matter of any old colonialism but rather a very specific and particular kind: it took place in the context of the military, political, and religious-cultural victory of Counter-Reformation Christians over the Muslims and Jews in the south of Iberia and of Europe. That was the context that engendered the idea of "race."

Indeed, at the same time the Americas were being conquered and colonized, the Crown of Castile and Aragon—already the nucleus of the future central state of the future Spain—had begun to demand that the Muslims and Jews of the Iberian Peninsula provide a "certificate of purity of blood" in order to be accepted as "Christians" and authorized to live in the peninsula or travel to the Americas. Such a "certificate," apart from bearing witness to the first "ethnic cleansing" of the colonial/modern period, may be considered the most immediate antecedent of the idea of race, since it involves the ideology that religious ideas, or culture more generally, are transmitted through the "blood."[11]

The unremittingly manufactured experience of these new relations and of their assumptions and meanings as well as of their institutions of control and conflict necessarily entailed a genuine reconstitution of the universe of subjectivity, of the intersubjective relations of all humanity, as an essential dimension of the new matrix of power, the new world, and the world-system that was thus being configured and developed. In this way, an entire new system of social domination was born.

Specifically, the control of sex, of subjectivity, of authority, and of their respective resources and outcomes would henceforth not merely be associated with but also would primarily depend on racial classification, because the place, roles, and behavior in social relations as well as the images, stereotypes, and symbols concerning each group in each of those realms of social existence would be linked or attached to each person's place in the racial classification.

The New System of Social Exploitation

A new system of social exploitation—more specifically, a new system of control over labor and its resources and outcomes—arose at exactly the same time as and in close articulation with this new system of social domination: every historically known mode of labor control or exploitation—enslavement, serfdom, independent small-scale market production, reciprocity, and capital—came to be linked, articulated, in a combined structure of commodity production for the world market. Because of the dominant place of capital in the basic tendencies of this new system, it had a capitalist character from the outset, as it still does today.

In this new structure for exploiting labor and distributing its products, each component element was redefined and reconfigured. As a consequence, each of them is sociologically and historically new, not merely a geographical extension of its earlier forms transplanted to another land. The unitary system of commodity production for the world market was a clearly unprecedented historical experience: a new system of labor control or of social exploitation.

These historically novel systems of social domination and exploitation mutually depended on each other. Neither of them could have been consolidated and reproduced everywhere over such a long time frame without the other. In America for that very reason—that is, given the enormity of the violence and destruction of the prior world—the relations between the new systems of domination and exploitation came to be virtually symmetrical, and the social division of labor was for quite a while an expression of the racial classification of the population. By the mid-sixteenth century, this association between the two systems was already neatly structured in a way that would be reproduced for nearly five centuries: "Blacks" were, by definition, enslaved; "Indians" were serfs. Non-Indians and non-Blacks were the masters, the bosses, the administrators of the public authority, the owners of commercial profits, the lords in control of power. And of course, especially from the mid-eighteenth century on, among "mestizos" it was precisely "color," the particular hue of one's "color," that defined each individual's and each group's place in the social division of labor.

Coloniality and Globality in the New Matrix of Power

Given that the category of race had become the basic, universal criterion for social classification of the population and that earlier forms of domination had been redefined around it, particularly those between the sexes, "ethnicities," "nationalities," and "cultures," this social classification system by definition affected each and every member of the human species. It was at the center of the distribution of roles and the relations associated with them in work, sexual relations, authority, production, and the control of subjectivity. It was according to this classifying criterion of the people in power that all social-historical identities were ascribed throughout humankind. Finally, geocultural identities were also established according to this criterion. In this way, the first global system of social domination known to history emerged; no one anywhere in the world could remain outside it. In the same sense, since the social division of labor—that is, the control and exploitation of labor—consisted of the combined association of all historically knowns forms in a unitary system of commodity production for the world market, to the exclusive benefit of those who controlled power, nobody, not one individual person anywhere in the world could stand apart from this system.

People could change their place within the system, but they could not remain outside it. The first global system of exploitation in history thus appeared as well: world capitalism.

Furthermore, this new matrix of power based on the articulation of the new systems of social domination and labor exploitation was established and shaped as a core product of the colonial relations imposed on the Americas. Without it, without colonial violence, it would have been impossible to integrate these new systems, much less their reproduction, over time. So coloniality was—is—the inherent, inescapable core feature of the new matrix of power made in the Americas. Its globality was and is based on this fact.

Eurocentering the New Matrix of Power:
Capital and Modernity

Colonial rule over the Americas, exercised through physical and subjective violence, allowed the conquistadors/colonizers to control the production of precious metals (above all, gold and silver) and precious plants (at first principally tobacco, cacao, and potatoes) by means of the unpaid labor of "Black" slaves, "Indian" serfs or peons, and their respective "mestizos." There is no need to insist here on the historic process that handed to the dominant groups among the colonizers the production of a monetized and regionally articulated market throughout the Atlantic basin as a new center of commercial traffic. But it might be useful to insist on the fact that until the so-called Industrial Revolution of the eighteenth century, those same regions (Western Europe, that is) produced nothing of importance for the world market. And it was therefore the exclusive control of the Americas, and of the unpaid labor of "Blacks" and "Indians" producing precious minerals and plants, that allowed the dominant groups among the colonizers to not only begin to gain a relevant position in the world market but also in particular concentrate enormous commercial profits, thus giving them the ability to concentrate on converting to wage labor and commodifying the local labor forces in their own countries.

All this meant a rapid expansion of capitalist accumulation in these regions; it even allowed the technological innovations produced by the "Black" slaves of the Antilles to be used in support of the Industrial Revolution in the north of the future Western Europe.[12] Only by building on that base could the emerging Western Europe later embark on colonizing the rest of the world and dominating the world market.

In this way, capital as a social relation of production and exploitation could be concentrated in these regions, becoming their almost exclusive brand for many years, while the Americas and later the rest of the colonized world got unpaid relations of exploitation—slavery, serfdom, and reciprocity/tribute payments—that were kept in place through colonial violence. So, despite Eurocentric theories to the contrary, it cannot be denied that capital was developed in Europe not only in association with but also, first and foremost, based on the other forms of labor exploitation, above all "Black" enslavement, which produced the precious plants, and "Indian" serfdom, which produced the precious metals.

In Europe these processes were associated, as is well known, with the making of a new local power structure; the social reclassification of the people of those regions; power conflicts among the dominant groups over spaces of domination, including the church; conflicts over hegemony among them; religious/cultural struggles; the reign of religious/cultural obscurantism in Iberia; and the secularization of intersubjective relations in north-central Europe. In the latter regions, this led to everything that has been presented to the world since the eighteenth century as modernity and as the exclusive brand of a new historical entity/identity that would take itself to be Western Europe.

With roots that can be traced back to the Utopias of the sixteenth century but especially to the philosophical and social theory debate of the seventeenth century and even more clearly the eighteenth century, the new entity/identity established as Western Europe, by now under the increasing dominance of its north-central zones, identified as and took itself to be modern, in other words, the latest, most advanced stage in human history. And the distinctive sign of the modernity of this emerging Western European identity was its specific form of rationality.

Without the coloniality of power built in the Americas, which is to say without the Americas, none of this could be explained. Nevertheless, the Eurocentric version of modernity obscures or distorts this history, because it was the historical experience leading to the production of the Americas that brought to Europe, on the one hand, the idea and the experience of change as a normal, necessary, and desirable mode of history and, on the other hand, the jettisoning of the imaginary of a golden age in a mythic past in favor of the imaginary of the future and "progress." Without the Americas, without contact with or knowledge of the forms of social existence based on social equality, reciprocity, community, and social solidarity found among certain precolonial Indigenous societies, particularly in the Andean region, it would be impossible to explain the European utopias of the sixteenth, seventeenth, and eighteenth centuries that, reimagining, magnifying, and idealizing those Indigenous experiences in contrast to the inequalities of feudalism in north-central Europe, created the imaginary of a society formed around social equality, individual freedom, and social solidarity as the central project of modernity and as the sum and summary of their specific rationality.[13]

In other words, in the same way as for the centralization of the development of capital, the centrality of Western Europe in the production of modernity was an expression of the coloniality of power. This is as much as to say that coloniality and modernity/rationality were from the outset and still are today two sides of the same coin, two inseparable dimensions of a single historical process.[14]

For the Americas and especially for Latin America today in the context of the coloniality of power, this process meant that on top of colonial domination, racialization, and geocultural reidentification, on top of the exploitation of unpaid labor, there was superimposed the rise of Western Europe as the center of power control, as the center of development for capital and modernity/rationality, as the headquarters for the advanced historical model of civilization. This was and is an entire privileged world that imagined itself and still imagines itself as self-produced and self-designed by beings from the superior "race" par excellence, by definition the only ones truly endowed with the capability to achieve these advancements. Thus, from then on the structural-historical dependency of Latin America would be a mark not merely of the materiality of social relations but above all of their new subjective and intersubjective relations with the new entity/identity called Western Europe and that of its descendants and bearers, wherever they happen to be.

The Specters of Latin America

At this point in the debate, it should not be hard to perceive why and in what ways the coloniality of power has generated the mis/match between our historical experience and our primary perspective of knowledge and has consequently frustrated all attempts at effective solutions to our fundamental problems.

Latin America, because of the unresolved nature of its fundamental problems, is being haunted by some very peculiar historical specters. My aim here is not to identify them, much less analyze them all, but instead to try to make the densest of them visible. However, specters have their own place in history and likewise their own history.

From independence to the end of the nineteenth century, the densest and most persistent of the specters haunting us were undoubtedly those of identity and modernity. Beginning in the late nineteenth century, many Latin Americans began to perceive that it was impossible to dislodge those specters from our world without democracy and thus without the modern nation-state. And even though the separation and protracted hostility among the various countries had almost buried the Bolivarian ideal of unity and integration throughout the nineteenth century, today that ideal seems to be making a comeback with renewed force. First with the conquest and colonization by the United States of the northern half of Mexico but especially after the defeat of Spain, when the United States conquered and colonized Cuba, Puerto Rico, Philippines, and Guam, its imperialist and expansionist politics placed the issue of unity and integration once more in the Latin American imaginary. Following World War II, the issue of development was added to all these other unresolved issues; despite seemingly having fallen out of the discussion, development remains present in the imaginary, and implicitly it is even one of the pretended justifications for neo-liberalization in these countries.

So, it can be said that identity, modernity, democracy, unity, and development are the specters that haunt the Latin American imaginary today. Since the end of the last millennium—strictly speaking, since our five hundredth birthday—a new, bleaker, and ultimately more dreadful specter has joined them: that of the continuity or survival of the very process of producing a Latin American identity.[15]

As is implicit in this debate, the solution to the problems that are inseparable from any of these entails, requires the solution to each of the others. This situation has made them invulnerable so far to all attempts to uproot them from our everyday social life as long as the hegemony of the Eurocentrist perspective of knowledge has led the majority, on one hand, to think of such problems as separate from each other and, on the other, to try to resolve them gradually and one by one and therefore to perceive alternative approaches and attempts as mere "utopias"—in the debased meaning of the term—and not as proposals for transforming or producing new historical meanings.

For all these reasons, the specters that haunt us are inextricably intertwined with one another. And they seem to have become permanent. Hence, in the end they have become familiar, indeed intimately so, forming a constituent part of our experience and our images. One could say therefore that now they are virtually inseparable from the materiality and the imaginary of our historical existence. In this sense, they form Latin America's particular set of knotty historical problems.[16]

Coloniality, Modernity, Identity

It is not surprising that the Americas would accept the Eurocentric ideology about modernity as a universal truth especially at the turn of the twentieth century, bearing in mind that the people who claimed the exclusive right to think of and portray themselves as representative of the Americas were precisely the colonial dominators, in other words, the "Europeans."[17] And since the eighteenth century, they were also "whites" and identified with "the West," which is to say with a broader image of "Europe," even after assuming their postindependence "national" identities, as they continue to do today.[18]

In other words, the coloniality of power implied back then and basically still implies today the sociological invisibility of non-Europeans—"Indians," "Blacks," and their "mestizos"—that is, the overwhelming majority of the population of the Americas and especially of Latin America with regard to the production of subjectivity, of historical memory, of the imaginary, and of "rational" knowledge and hence of identity.

And indeed, how could non-Europeans be made visible apart from their place as workers and subjugated peoples if, given their status as inferior and "culturally" primitive races, they were not, by definition could not be, and even today are not entirely considered persons, much less rational?[19]

After the revolution headed by Túpac Amaru in 1780 in the Viceroyalty of Peru was defeated, and after the initially victorious Haitian Revolution in 1803 was isolated, mutilated, and ultimately defeated as well, though in a different way, the non-Europeans of Latin America became even more mentally and intellectually invisible to the world of the dominators and the beneficiaries of the coloniality of power.[20]

Nevertheless, in the world of power, what gets tossed out the front door will climb back in through the window. Indeed, those made invisible were the overwhelming majority of Latin Americans taken as a whole, and their subjective universe, their ways of relating with the universe, were too dense and lively to simply be ignored. Moreover, at the same time that the promiscuity and sexual permissiveness of the Catholic Christians ceaselessly generated and regenerated a growing population of "mestizos"—a very significant portion of whom formed, especially beginning in the late eighteenth century, the ranks of the dominators—the intersubjective ("cultural") relations between dominators and subjugated had been producing a new intersubjective universe considered equally "mestizo" and thus ambiguous and indeterminate except, of course, at the extremes of both sides of power.

Latin American identity has since then become the terrain for a conflict between the European and non-European that has not ceased to widen and grow rockier. But even in these terms, its history is not simple or linear, for it expresses the most persistent elements in the coloniality of power.

First is "racial" relations, enwrapped in or disguised as "color." This is obviously a social hierarchy relationship of "superiority"/"inferiority" between "white," "Black," "Indian," "mestizo" and since the second half of the nineteenth century "Asian" or "yellow" and "brown" or "olive-skinned." Since the eighteenth century, the rise of "mestizos" forced the creation of a difficult and complicated pyramid of "color" hues and discrimination among the "castas" marked by such hues. This social gradation remained in effect well into the nineteenth century.[21] The subsequent growth of "mestizos" has further complicated the social classification system underpinned by "race," particularly because "color" has been superimposed on structural-biological factors mainly due to the struggles against racial discrimination and racism. Moreover, this same effect stems from the formal modern ideology of equality among people of all "colors" on which antiracist struggles are based.

Second is the relations between "European/Western" and thus modernity or, more strictly speaking, the Eurocentric version of modernity, and non-European. This is a crucial relationship given that from the Eurocentric version, which is widely hegemonic in Latin America and not only among the dominators, the place and the status of the original historical-cultural experiences of the precolonial world and thus also the pre–"Western European" world would be characterized as "premodernity," which is as much as to say "prerational" or "primitive," just like those corresponding to the populations kidnapped from Africa, enslaved, and racialized as "Blacks" in the Americas.

Few today would deny that in the dominant discourse, hence the discourse of the dominators, the notion of modernization is still, despite the whole post–World War II debate, equivalent to "Westernization."[22]

Third is the results of resistance by the victims of the coloniality of power, which has been a constant throughout these past five centuries. During the first period of modernity under Iberian rule, the first "mestizo" intellectuals (the names that most will be familiar with from the vast Viceroyalty of Peru, which covered most of modern South America, are Inca Garcilaso de la Vega, Guaman Poma de Ayala, Santa Cruz Pachacuti Salcamayhua, and Blas Valera) initiated the defense of the aboriginal heritage.

Two broad strands can be roughly distinguished. One, arising from the famous *Comentarios reales* by Inca Garcilaso de la Vega, insists on the peaceful, civilizing, and supportive character of everything Incan; the other more critical, originating with Guaman Poma's *La nueva corónica y buen gobierno*, insists on power and its implications. Today the two streams are converging in a way to demand, in opposition to the increasingly predatory nature of current-day capitalism, the restoration of a "Tawantisuyan" society.[23]

Fourth is the changing story of relations among the diverse versions of European in these countries. The most interesting feature about this history began early in the nineteenth century with the political conflict between Hispanophile conservatives and modernist liberals in the face of the hegemonist expansionism of the United States in alliance with England.

The "white" liberals of these countries were encouraged by France, under Napoleon III, to suggest that their European identity went beyond their being Iberian (Spanish or Portuguese) and instead hailed back to a much broader cultural kinship: *latinidad*. Toward the end of the nineteenth century and facing the openly colonialist and imperialist expansionism of the United States after its victory over Spain in 1898, the opposition between the Anglo-Saxon "pragmatism" and "materialism" of North Americans and the Latin "spiritualism" of South Americans, codified chiefly by the Uruguayan writer José Enrique Rodó in his book *Ariel*, acquired a widespread following and support among "white" and "mestizo" intellectuals.[24] This history is not over yet. While the hegemony of the United States has only broadened and solidified especially since World War II, it is certainly no accident that the name "Latin America" has become the option preferred over all others that have been proposed at different moments, also precisely since World War II.

Fifth and last, the recent political-cultural movements of "Indigenous" and "Afro-Latin American" peoples have definitively challenged the European version of modernity/rationality, proposing their own rationality as an alternative. They deny the theoretical and social legitimacy of "racial" and "ethnic" classification, once more proposing the idea of social equality. They deny the relevance and legitimacy of the nation-state founded on the coloniality of power. Finally, though less clearly and explicitly, they propose the affirmation and reproduction of reciprocity and its ethic of social solidarity and an alternative to the predatory tendencies of current-day capitalism.

It is relevant to point out, against this whole historical and current-day background, that the question of identity in Latin America is, more than ever before, an open and heterogeneous historical project and perhaps not so much a matter of loyalty to memory and the past. This history has allowed us to see that there are actually many memories and many pasts that still do not share a channel in common. From this perspective and in this sense, the production of Latin American identity implies, from the outset, a trajectory toward the inevitable destruction of the coloniality of power, a very particular manner of decolonization and liberation: the de/coloniality of power.

Notes

First published in *Revista de Cultura de la Biblioteca Nacional del Perú*, no. 10 (April 2005): 14–16.

The original title of this text was "The Phantoms of Latin America." I decided, however, that it would be better to give it the same title under which the first section of the text was published in *Libros y arte.*— Aníbal Quijano

1   On the definition of these categories, I refer to Quijano, "Coloniality of Power, Eurocentrism and Latin America"; Quijano, "Colonialidad del poder, globalización y democracia"; and Quijano, "Colonialidad y modernidad/racionalidad" (see "Coloniality and Modernity/Rationality" in this volume).

2   Immanuel Wallerstein coined the "modern world-system" concept in his 1974 book *The Modern World-System* as a system of states and regions associated with the expansion of European capitalism. In 1991, Aníbal Quijano introduced the concept of coloniality of power in "Colonialidad y modernidad/racionalidad." The two were brought together in a joint article, Quijano and Wallerstein, "Americanity as a Concept, or the Americas in the Imaginary of the Modern World-System," in 1992. Since then, use of the colonial/modern world-system concept has continued to grow. See, among others, Walter Mignolo, *Local Histories, Global Designs*.

3   Tanizaki, *In Praise of Shadows*. [Translator's note: Though first published in English translation in 1977, this short book was written in 1933, so Tanizaki's reflections on "Western superiority" refer to the period before World War II.]

4   [Translator's note: See Antonio Gramsci's statement "The crisis consists precisely in the fact that the old is dying and the new cannot be born; in this interregnum a great variety of morbid symptoms appear." Gramsci, *Selections from the Prison Notebooks*, 275–76.]

5   I have discussed this topic in Quijano, "Coloniality of Power, Eurocentrism and Latin America"; and Quijano, "Colonialidad del poder y clasificación social" (see "Coloniality of Power and Social Classification" in this volume).

6   I have discussed the implications of the current cultural and political movement of Latin American "Indigenous" peoples in Quijano, "El 'movimiento indígena' y las cuestiones pendientes en América Latina" (see "The 'Indigenous Movement' and Unresolved Questions in Latin America" in this volume).

7   For this theoretical proposition, see Quijano, "Colonialidad del poder, cultura y conocimiento en América Latina."

8   On this issue, see Quijano and Wallerstein, "Americanity as a Concept, or the Americas in the Imaginary of the Modern World-System."

9   During these wars in the Viceroyalty of Peru, many enslaved "Blacks" rose to become military officers, attaining the rank of captain that normally corresponded to "hidalgos," members of the peninsular provincial nobility, and were even liberated from enslavement in rebel encomendero armies. After the defeat of the rebels, the so-called Peacemaker, Pedro de la Gasca, issued the most draconian of all colonial legislation against the "Blacks" to set a definitive racial example by their harsh punishment. [For De la Gasca's role in pacifying Peru in the middle of the sixteenth century, see Manfredi Merluzi, "Mediación política, redes clientelares y pacificación del reuno en el Perú del siglo XVI" Observaciones a partir de los papeles "Pizarro-La Gasca," *Revista de Indias* 66, no. 236 (2006): 87–106. See also Noel Gray, "The Negro in the Civil Wars of Peru," *Primitive Man* 24, no. 4 (October 1951): 55–66.]

10 On the production of the ideas of "white" and "Black" as a "racial" nomenclature in the British American colonial area, see principally Allen, *The Invention of the White Race*; and Jacobson, *Whiteness of a Different Color*. On the complexities and contradictions of the process of racializing "Blacks" in the British-American colonial world, see the suggestive study Martinot, *The Rule of Racialization*.

11 On this issue, see Quijano, "Raza, etnia y nación en José Carlos Mariátegui."

12 See Tomich, *Through the Prism of Slavery*.

13 On this debate, see Quijano, *Modernidad, identidad y utopía en América Latina*.

14 On this issue, see Quijano, "Colonialidad y modernidad/racionalidad."

15 An active debate has—finally—begun in Latin America on the meaning of the expansion of US bases and other military establishments on Latin American territory, in addition to the old and normalized articulations between the armed forces of the United States and those of countries in the region, most especially in the context of the obvious tendencies toward reneocolonializing the world, which began with the invasion and the later occupation of Afghanistan and Iraq. I put forward some predictions—which unfortunately came true all too soon—in a public talk at the University of Florida at Gainesville in late 1992

titled "Will Latin America Survive," published in Portuguese in 1993 under the title "América Latina Sobreviverá?" I have since returned to this topic in Quijano, "El laberinto de América Latina."

16   Because no Alexander the Great has yet appeared to cut through this knot and because it is likely that no eminent Latin American has experienced it with more intensity than the Peruvian José María Arguedas, I think it is only appropriate to call it the "Arguedian knot."

17   I will limit myself here to the issue of identity and its relation to the issues of modernity/rationality. My ideas on those of democracy and the modern nation-state and those of development and integration can be found, respectively, in Quijano, "Colonialité du pouvoir et démocratie en Amérique latine"; Quijano, "Estado-Nación, ciudadanía y democracia"; Quijano, "Colonialidad del poder, globalización y democracia"; Quijano, "Populismo y fujimorismo"; Quijano, "América Latina en la economía mundial"; and Quijano, "El fantasma del desarrollo en América Latina."

18   Not only did some of the intelligentsia—such as, for example, the important Argentine writer and intellectual Héctor Murena (1923–1975)—despair of being one of the "Europeans exiled to these savage pampas" even well into the twentieth century, but their most powerful rulers, from the brutal Argentine military dictatorship of the 1970s to the no less brutal Bush dictatorship of the twenty-first century, also have never hesitated to identify themselves as defenders of "Western and Christian civilization."

19   This way of perceiving non-Europeans is constant and explicit even as late as Hegel, *Lectures on the Philosophy of History*, whose opinions on the inevitable destruction of primitive societies—referring to the Aztecs and Incas, no less—in contact with the spirit, which of course is European, are well known and repeatedly cited and, in more recent times, in Heidegger, for example, for whom philosophizing can only be done in German.

20   The Túpac Amaru revolution was the first attempt in the Viceroyalty of Peru to build a new nation—in other words, a new power structure and perhaps a new nationality, which is to say a new identity—that would include elements that are Hispanic in origin and character but historically redefined by and in the Americas, within a matrix of power with "Indigenous" hegemony. Its defeat paved the way for the future independence in this region to be carried out under the total control of the colonial dominators and for the coloniality of power to be kept firmly in place. The Haitian Revolution, for its part, was the first great decolonizing revolution to achieve victory in the entire colonial/modern period; in it, the "Blacks" defeated the "whites," slaves defeated masters, the colonized beat the colonizers, the Haitians beat

the French, and the non-Europeans beat the Europeans. It was the entire colonial/modern power matrix that was subverted and destroyed. Both revolutions undoubtedly caused tremendous shock and widespread panic among the holders of colonial/modern power. That is why the Túpac Amaru revolutionaries were so cruelly repressed, to serve as an example to others. The same can be said about the repeated and continuing colonial interventions of first the French and later the US forces (or the "Usonians," as José Buscaglia-Salgado calls them in *Undoing Empire*, 4) over the course of two centuries in order to crush the revolution and keep Haiti trapped in the horrifying history that they will not allow to come to an end.

21 In the colonial archives of South America, more than thirty "castas" can be identified, some of which have names that have still not fallen out of use. In Peru, for example, there are *zambo*, originally referring to a "part-Black" "mestizo," born of an "Indian" and a "Black," and *sacalagua*, originally one of the levels of "mulatto." Today, *moreno* (meaning "brown"; the Spanish word derives from the word *moro*, "Moor") is a term used in an attempt to reduce the effect of "Black," or *zambo*, in witness to the fact that the colonial production of the idea of "race" was rooted from the beginning in the social hierarchies imposed in Iberia on the defeated "Moors" and their descendants under the rule of the lords of the North. The arrival of "Asian" populations since the mid-nineteenth century, especially from China, gave rise to new hues and new discriminatory terms.

22 In the days following the recent lynching (on April 26, 2004) of the mayor of Ilave (Puno, Peru) by an angry population identified as majority Aymara, the Peruvian press and certain television programs in particular attributed the event to the "non-Western"—and thus nonmodern, nonrational—status of the "Indigenous" Aymaras. An influential television newsman did not hesitate to proclaim that "the West" had to be imposed on these populations by force. The striking thing about this is that the lynching was only one of several that have taken place in recent months in Peru, albeit in very disparate and distant regions and populations. The others, however, occurred in "mestizo" towns and so did not call forth the same "racist/ethnicist" (to use the currently favored term) impulses. In Ilave, however, Aymaras were involved, and therefore that had to be the particular reason for the event. The pathetic thing about the Lima journalists' opinions is that they could not even imagine that such acts could be due precisely to the "Westernization" of the "Aymaras": extensive trade, both legal and black market; drug trafficking; disputes over the control of municipal revenue; disputes over their political relations with urban political parties based in Lima fighting over control of their power bases and

their resources, and so on. All this, of course, happened in the context of the most serious social, political, and psychosocial crisis in Peru in over a century.

23   Carlos Araníbar has published in Lima a version of Inca Garcilaso de la Vega's *Comentarios reales* in modernized Spanish, with copious erudite notes that are extremely useful for following the historical trail of this remarkable book. The same historian has also published the text by Juan de Santa Cruz Pachacuti Yamqui Salcamayhua. Franklin Pease, another Peruvian historian, published the most recent edition of Guaman Poma de Ayala's *La nueva corónica y buen gobierno*. In the twentieth century, Luis Eduardo Valcárcel was unquestionably the most influential promoter of the Garcilacist version of Tawantinsuyu (the Quechua term for the "Inca Empire"), beginning with *Tempestad en los Andes*. His many publications include, most notably, *Historia del Perú antiguo* and *Ruta cultural del Perú*. More recently, Alberto Flores Galindo, with *Buscando un Inca*, has become a widely influential author in a variant of the same theme.

24   In 1853, the Colombian writer José María Torres Caicedo published an article outlining these ideas, "La colonization de deux Ameriques," in the *Revue des Deux Mondes* in Paris. It was reprinted in Paris in 1868 as an eighteen-page booklet by Vive Bouchard-Huzard.

Napoleon III, with his expansionist ambitions, soon used these ideas to justify the French invasion of Mexico and the imposition of Archduke Maximilian of Hapsburg as emperor. As is well known, the invaders were defeated and expelled and their emperor was executed under the leadership of the Liberal leader Benito Juárez. With *Ariel*, José Enrique Rodó (1871–1917) gave birth to a whole school of intellectual and political thought called *arielista*, which began to fade early in the twentieth century as democratic and nationalist revolts broke out in the wake of the victorious Mexican Revolution (1910–1927), spreading through every country south of the Rio Bravo between 1925 and 1935 and ending with the defeat of the revolutions and the imposition of bloody dictatorships except in Uruguay and Chile.

10

THE "INDIGENOUS MOVEMENT" AND UNRESOLVED QUESTIONS IN LATIN AMERICA

Much ink has been spilled in Latin America and beyond about the "Indigenous movement," especially since the Chiapas uprising in January 1994 and more recently in regard to the political events in Bolivia and Ecuador. This probably demonstrates, above all, a worried recognition of the immediate political impact of Indigenous people's actions and of the conflicts their actions have unleashed and are threatening to unleash among the rest of the population, jeopardizing the stability of the current self-described "democratic" regimes in an ever-growing number of countries as well as the governability of an increasingly disgruntled populace who find their needs harder and harder to meet and are learning to organize themselves by new means and to make demands that their dominators had obviously not anticipated. Most of this literature, however, refers to the theme of identity, though it does so as a demonstration of the endlessness of the discourse on culture, multiculturality, cultural hybridity, and so on, in short, of the always growing family of terms that shroud the issue of identity in order to keep it far from the issue of power. By contrast, we are only beginning to see the first few reflections on the more complex and longer-term implications of the actions of modern-day Latin American Indigenous people, particularly in regard to the conditions of other forms of labor control and control over collective authority on the path toward other forms of social existence.

Here, my primary aim is to raise two issues relating to the Indigenous movement that have not yet been sufficiently discussed but that, in my judgment, may prove to be the most pivotal in the future of Latin America's history: the relationship between the movement and the nation-state and between the nation-state and democracy within the current matrix of power.

A Note on the Indigenous and the Coloniality of Power

To this end, the question of the meaning of "Indigenous" must once more be broached. But given space limitations, I will restrict myself here to raising the most significant points for research and debate.

First, it must be noted that both those who today self-identify as "Indigenous" instead of "Indians" as well as those others who now agree to identify the first group as "Indigenous," "Native," or "Aboriginal," are exactly the same in regard to where they were born or, for the vast majority, even regarding the antiquity—the aboriginality if you will—of all or part of their family lines. That is, from this perspective each and every person on either side fits exactly the same set of identifiers. However, the two groups are not by any means the same in regard to their relationship with the whites and with being European.[1]

And that is precisely the question: any such categories in the Americas only have meaning in reference to the matrix of power that came into being in the colonial experience and that has never since then ceased to reproduce itself and develop, maintaining its same original foundations, which are colonial in character. In other words, this is a matrix of power that has not abandoned, that cannot abandon, its coloniality.

The Coloniality of the Current Matrix of Power

For our specific focus here, the primary products of the colonial experience are as follows:

1   The racialization of the relations between colonizers and colonized. From then on, "race"—a modern mental construct that has no connection to anything in the former reality, generated in order to naturalize the social relations of domination brought

about by the conquest—became the cornerstone of the new system of domination, since earlier forms of domination, such as between the sexes or age groups, were redefined around the hegemony of "race."[2] The original extremes of this new system of domination were, on one side, the "Indians," a colonial term into which were crammed the many historical identities that inhabited this continent before the Iberian conquest, and, on the other side, the colonizers, who since the eighteenth century have self-identified, vis-à-vis the "Indians," "Blacks," and "mestizos," as "whites" and "Europeans."

2   The configuration of a new system of exploitation that articulates in one unitary structure every historically known mode of labor control or exploitation—enslavement, serfdom, independent small-scale market production, reciprocity, and capital—to produce commodities for the world market, based around the hegemony of capital, giving the new system of exploitation as a whole its capitalistic character.

3   Eurocentrism as the new mode of fashioning and controlling subjectivity, the imaginary, knowledge, and memory but knowledge most of all. Eurocentrism expresses the new subjectivity, the intersubjective relations, that are processed in the colonial matrix of power, in other words, the emerging social interests and social needs generated and developed within the experience of the coloniality of power, especially relations between the inchoate system of social domination organized around the idea of "race" and the nascent system of capitalist exploitation. This is the context that moderates the novelty of the experience of radical historical-cultural changes, of pioneering relations with time and space, and the replacement of the past by the future as the promising golden age for realizing humanity's aspirations, in short, the process that would soon be called modernity. The Eurocentering of control over the coming into being of the colonial matrix of power meant that the systematic intellectual elaboration of the mode of modeling and controlling knowledge would take place precisely in Western Europe, which began to come into existence during that same time and in the same historical movement. And the worldwide spread of European colonialism brought with it the worldwide hegemony of Eurocentrism.

4   Finally, the establishment of the emerging system for control-
    ling collective authority, based on the hegemony of the state—
    the nation-state, since the eighteenth century—and on a system
    of states, from the creation and control of which the populations
    "racially" classified as "inferior" were excluded. In other words,
    this is a private system of control over collective authority as an
    exclusive attribute of the colonizers and thus of Europeans, or
    whites.[3]

This matrix of power, which began to be set up five centuries ago, has
been hegemonic worldwide since the eighteenth century. Though anticolo-
nialist struggles have been able to decentralize the control of power relatively
speaking, seizing local control over collective authority from the colonizers,
and in much of the world have even done so formally, accepting the generally pro forma participation of the members of the "inferior races," central
and worldwide control has remained Eurocentered. Moreover, a process
of reconcentrating world or global control over collective authority is underway for the benefit of Europeans.[4] And in much of today's former colonial world, especially the Americas and Oceania, the whites and Europeans
have managed to keep local control of power in all its basic dimensions. In
the Americas therefore, the issues surrounding the debate on the Indigenous can only be investigated and discussed in relation to and from the
perspective of the coloniality of the power matrix that haunts us, because
outside of that perspective such issues make no sense. That is, the question of the Indigenous in the Americas and particularly in Latin America is
a question of the coloniality of the reigning matrix of power, just like the
categories "Indian," "Black," "mestizo," "white."

Consequently, it is not hard to grasp that in every context where whites
or Europeans do not have immediate control over local power, the term "Indigenous" does not have the same significance and therefore does not have
the same implications. Thus, in Southeast Asia, in India, Indonesia, Philippines, the countries of the former Indochina, the people who are identified
as "Indigenous" and have accepted that identification as well as those who
identify them as such never talk about "Europeans," "whites," or European
colonialism at all. The Indigenous groups or populations in those countries
are the people living in the poorest, most isolated zones, generally the forest or the tundra, whose main and sometimes only sources of livelihood
are the trees, the land, the rivers, and the plants and animals that dwell in

them. These populations are oppressed, discriminated against, and plundered of their resources, especially now in times of "globalization," by other "nonwhite," "non-European" groups (who by the same token are just as "Native" or "Aboriginal" as the others), who in these countries now have immediate control over power, though they are doubtlessly associated with the global bourgeoisie whose hegemony corresponds to the Europeans and whites. In countries such as India, the classification of the population in terms of castes aggravates this situation for the Adivasi (Indigenous), tying them and equating them to the Dalit (Untouchables) by imposing an institutionalized, age-old system of discrimination and oppression on them.[5] And under the restored rule of the Brahmins and their "communalist" fundamentalism, this situation is even worse and more violent today. The demands of the Indigenous people of Southeast Asia are thus different in every fundamental way from those of the Indigenous people of Latin America. Their resistance movements are becoming broader and better organized all the time, and the regional conflicts that they already produce will move in the same direction. The current virulence of the fundamentalist chauvinism of communalism is one of the clearest signals of this.[6]

The Coloniality of Power and the National Question in the Americas

With the defeat of first British and then Iberian colonialism, a particular historical paradox arose in the Americas: independent states tied to colonial societies.

Certainly in the case of the United States, the nationality of the new state corresponded to that of the majority of the population of the new country who, despite their European and white origins and affiliation, granted themselves a new nationality with their anticolonial victory. The Black population, at first the only group subjected to the coloniality of the new power within the British American colonial societies and completely prevented from taking part in the creation and control of the new state, were a minority despite their economic importance, like the Indian population who survived their near-extermination, the conquest of their territories, and their colonization following the establishment of the new country, the new nation, and its new state would soon be as well.

In the case of the countries established in the Americas that came from Iberian colonialism, whether in the Spanish area or the later Portuguese one, the process was radically different: those who ultimately managed to assume control of the forming state processes were a small minority of European or white origin, confronted by an overwhelming majority of Indians, Blacks, and their respective mestizos. On the other side, the Indians were serfs for the most part, and the Blacks—except in Haiti, as a result of the first great social and national American revolution of the period of modernity—were slaves. That is, these populations were not only legally and socially prevented from participating in any way in the creation and running of the state process, given their status as serfs and slaves, but they also had never ceased to be populations colonized as "Indians," "Blacks," and "mestizos," and participating in the state process was consequently never an option for them. Society continued to be organized largely according to the matrix of power shaped under colonialism. It still remained a colonial society, during the same time and in the same historical movement in which the new state was becoming independent, forming, and defining itself. This new state was independent of the colonial power, but in its capacity as an autonomous power was limited, it was a concise expression of the larger coloniality of power in society.

Which "nation" did the newly established states belong to? To the "Europeans" or "whites" who now called themselves "Mexicans," "Peruvians," or "Brazilians," that is, who were also giving themselves a new national identity and were actually a very small minority everywhere though relatively less so in Chile? Or to the majority of the "Indian" population that had not yet been colonized and still occupied all the territory south of the Biobío River, resisting for another century before being nearly exterminated and colonized as they had been earlier in Argentina and Uruguay under other conditions and with other results? The nationality of the forming states had nothing to do with the colonized populations of "Indians," "Blacks," and "mestizos." Nevertheless, the latter were the overwhelming majorities living within the boundaries of the states in formation. The nationality of these embryonic states did not represent the identities of the majority population. Strictly speaking, the invented nationality was in opposition to the majority.

In both basic dimensions, the incipient independent state in this (Latin) America did not emerge as a modern nation-state: it was not national with respect to the vast majority of the population, and it was not democratic, not based on or representing any effective majority of the citizenry. It was, precisely, a concise expression of the coloniality of power.

The Question of Democracy and the "Indigenous Problem"

This peculiar situation for the ex-colonial society displaced by the forming nation was no secret to some of the emergent power holders. Immediately after the anticolonial victory was consolidated, by the mid-1820s the question of the character of the state and the problems of citizenship was already under discussion. For the liberals in particular, the gap between their political models, which at the time came mainly from the discourse of liberal revolution in Western Europe, and the concrete conditions of their implementation in their America was too vast and too visible. And the "Indian" population would soon be perceived as a problem for the implementation of the modern nation-state, for the modernization of their society, their culture. Thus, what would be called for nearly two centuries the "Indigenous problem" became part of the political discussion in Latin America right from the beginning. It could truly be said that this "Indigenous problem" was born together with the newly founded Ibero-American republics.

Why were "Indians" a problem in the debate over the implementation of the modern nation-state in these new republics? Aside from the coloniality of power in the new republics, such a problem would make no sense. However, from this point of view, "Indians" were only serfs, just as "Blacks" were only slaves, but were, first and foremost, "inferior races." And the idea of "race" had been imposed as part of not only the materiality of social relations—as was the case with slavery and serfdom, which consequently could change—but also the people themselves, as was precisely the case with "Indians," "Blacks," and "whites." And therefore on that level, no changes would be possible. And that was exactly the "Indigenous problem": it was not enough to relieve the "Indians" of the weight on unpaid forms of the division of labor, such as serfdom, in order to make them the equals of everyone else, as had happened in Europe in the course of the liberal revolutions, or to remove the marks of traditional colonialism, such as "Indigenous tribute," in order to decolonize the relations of domination, as had happened when earlier colonialisms had been defeated or had fallen apart. On top of that, the hegemonic sectors within the dominant group opposed the elimination of tribute and even more so the elimination of serfdom with all their might. If such a thing happened, who would work for the power holders? And the "racial" argument was precisely the tool that the dominators used, explicitly or tacitly, to defend their social interests.

The "Indigenous problem" thus became a genuine political and theoretical sticking point in Latin America. To resolve it would take simultaneously, given that by their nature any change in one dimension entailed changes in each of the others, the decolonization of political relations within the state, the radical subversion of the conditions of exploitation and the end of serfdom, and, as a preliminary condition and a point of departure, the decolonization of relations of social domination, the expunging of "race" as the basic universal form of social classification.

In other words, effectively solving the "Indigenous problem" necessarily meant subverting and breaking up the entire colonial matrix of power. Given the relations of social and political forces in that period, it was consequently not feasible to solve the problem in a real and definitive way, not even partially. This is why the "Indigenous problem" became the specific historical knot, still untied today, that has bound historical movement in Latin America hand and foot: the mis/match between nation, identity, and democracy.

Conversely, political independence from Spain and Portugal under the direction and control of the "whites" or "Europeans" did not mean that these societies had become independent from the hegemony of Eurocentrism. In many respects, to the contrary, it led to a deepening of that hegemony, precisely because the Eurocentering of the matrix of power meant that while modernity was permeating not only thought but also social practices in Western Europe, in this America modernity was cordoned off into the ideological realms of subjectivity, especially into the ideology of "progress," and even then only among the minority groups of the dominant sectors and small groups of middle-class intellectuals.[7]

Democracy and Modernity without Revolution?

This is the context that allows us to explain and make sense of a political phenomenon that is perhaps peculiar to Latin America: the idea that it is possible to attain or establish modernity and democracy in these countries without having to undergo a revolution of power or at least of radical changes in the key fields of power. Thus, modernity and democracy have always played the role here of a political mirage: since they exist in other spaces, the liberal retina can copy their images onto the ideological horizon of the political and social desert of Latin America. This political mirage still fascinates a major share of the Latin American political spectrum, and those who imagine the Latin American revolution as a reproduction of the Eurocentric experience are not free of it either. Here, Eurocentrism reveals all its consequences.

In the Latin American political debate through the nearly two centuries since the defeat of Spanish colonialism, this ideology has meant adopting the paradigm of liberal democracy regarding the state and the relations between state and society but separately from, even indeed in opposition to, the paradigm of bourgeois society. In the latter, which produced liberal democracy, the relations of social power have been not only an expression of capital and the centrality of Europe in the heterogeneous capitalist universe but also—and mainly for the ends of liberal democracy—an expression of a relatively broad if not quite democratic distribution of production resources, income, the internal market, and organizational and representational institutions. In the "central" countries governed by liberal democracy, this is the result of a century of liberal-bourgeois revolutions or equivalent processes. But such processes never took place and could not take place in Latin America, for this is obviously not merely a matter of the persistence here of slavery, serfdom, limited industrial production, and so on and so forth, produced by the distribution of power in the capitalist universe and the process of Eurocentering its control. It results, above all, from the fact that liberal citizenship was and, strictly speaking, still is an impossible aspiration for the vast majority of the population formed by the "lesser races," that is, by nonequals.

In this sense, liberalism in Latin America has always set forth an image of a "rule-of-law state" composed of a universe of political and administrative institutions, almost always designed in precise conformity with the highest hopes of liberalism but supported almost exclusively by constitutional discourse, which not by chance has such a copious history in our countries but a history without correlatives or prior changes in social power relations. Rephrasing liberal discourse, it could be said that in practice, this idea has entailed, almost always, a "rule-of-law state" articulated with a "society of the right." This is why when it functions it cannot last, never has been able to last, or simply has not managed to function.[8]

With respect to the place of the "Indian" population in the potential democratic future, the only important change that could be accepted in the late nineteenth century and be somewhat erratically put into practice in the twentieth century was "Europeanizing" the subjectivity of the "Indians," as one mode of "modernizing" them. The intellectual movement called "Indigenista" in Latin America, with ramifications in the visual arts and in literary writing, was undoubtedly the most accomplished embodiment of this idea.[9] The coloniality of such an idea is blatant, however, for it is based on the inability to accept, even to imagine, the possibility of decolonizing the relations between "Indian" and "European," since by definition to be "Indian" is to be not only "inferior" but also "primitive" ("archaic," they call it now), that is, doubly "inferior" because it is "prior" to "European" on a supposed line of historical human evolution, conceptualized according to the time shift that became inherent to the Eurocentric knowledge perspective. Since it was not possible to "whiten" them all in "racial" terms, despite the intensive practice of *mestizaje* that fills the history of the "races" in Latin America, it was concluded that it was feasible and made sense, in any case, to "Europeanize" them subjectively, that is, culturally if you prefer.[10]

No need to waste time on the obvious. The dominant groups had two main policies for addressing this problem in the Americas, though they were put into practice with many variations among countries and historical moments. One was the virtual extermination of the "Indians" and the conquest of their territories in every country where the dominators, liberals and conservatives alike, quickly concluded that no de-Indianization such as "Europeanization" was feasible. This was done in the United States, Argentina, Uruguay, and Chile. The other was cultural and political assimilationism in Mexico, Central America and in the Andes.[11]

Why the difference? Mainly, no doubt, because "Indian" populations form the majority in the latter countries but above all, unlike in the other countries, are socially disciplined in organized labor within a system of domination and exploitation. These countries, such as Mexico and Peru, were precisely the headquarters of the Spanish colonial empire, whereas Argentina, Chile, and Uruguay were marginal before the mid-eighteenth century. Given these conditions, the policy of the "whites" toward the "Indians" extended, with modifications and adaptations, the colonial-era policy of simultaneous cultural discrimination and assimilation. With the formation of republics, assimilationism was the approach increasingly emphasized, especially from the end of the nineteenth century and throughout the twentieth century.

Cultural assimilationism is the policy that the dominators sought to uphold with the backing of the state through the institutionalized system of public education. The strategy has thus consisted and still consists of "assimilating" the "Indians" to the culture of the dominators, usually spoken of as the "national culture," primarily through formal school education but also through the work of religious and military institutions. Therefore, in all these countries the education system came to be central to relations between "Indian" and "non-Indian" and was even mystified and mythologized by both sides. And there is no doubt that in countries such as Mexico and Peru—more so in the former after the Mexican Revolution but in any case more so in both of these than in other countries—this was a mechanism for the subjective (or cultural, if you prefer) de-Indianization of a not inconsiderable portion of the "Indian" population. An important element in this strategy has also been the appropriation of cultural achievements from the societies that were conquered and destroyed, their populations colonized. These appropriations are passed on as pride in the "Inca," the "Aztec," the "Maya," and so on, in short, pride in everything "Indian" that preceded colonization.

This strategy, however, has always continued to alternate and combine with the policy of discriminating against "Indians" and alienating everything "Indian." In this way, de-Indianization could not encompass the majority of the "Indian" population, who could no more than partially, precariously, and formally incorporate themselves or be incorporated into the process of nationalizing society, culture, and the state. The coloniality of power continues to mean that all or part of the "nonwhite" populations cannot consolidate their citizenship without generating deep and serious social conflicts.

In some countries such as Brazil, Ecuador, and Guatemala and in certain zones of Bolivia, Mexico, and Peru, exactly this is at the root of what perhaps still appears to the dominant group to be nothing more than a new "Indigenous problem" but actually, as we will see shortly, has inaugurated a distinctive and foregrounded historical period for the colonial matrix of power in which it is implicated.

The Trajectory of Today's "Indigenous Movement"

It is worth noting at the outset that today's "Indigenous movement" is the most definite signal that the coloniality of power has entered its worst crisis since it was established five centuries ago.[12]

Of course, the surviving populations of the defeated societies and previous historical identities did not immediately agree to call themselves "Indians."[13] Some of them, such as some of the Incas in Peru, resisted accepting their defeat and the disintegration of their societies and historical identities for a full half century. Today, many groups still claim or reclaim the particular names of their old historical identities (now colonialistically accepted, but only barely, as "ethnicities"). And it is likely that in the future several more names will return to the nomenclature of these populations, and even that today's widespread "identity mania" will lead some identities to be reinvented in order to be covered by those names.

However, the consolidation, development, and worldwide expansion of the coloniality of power proved to be processes of extraordinary historical vitality. Though some of the old names and shreds of historical memories may survive, all those societies and identities, or "peoplehood," ended up being broken, and their surviving populations and their descendants ended up accepting their defeat and the new common colonial identity, which obviously no longer implied any sort of "peoplehood." Three centuries after the conquest as the republican period began, they were all "Indians." And for the next two centuries, that colonial identity remained. One could say, with little risk, that for a majority of these populations, that identity had ended up being accepted as "normal."

Why, then, has the rejection of that term and the reclaiming of the name "Indigenous" now spread and been imposed among these populations throughout virtually all Latin America over the relatively short period of two or three decades? Furthermore, why have "non-Indians"—"mestizos" foremost but "whites" and "Europeans" as well—ended up accepting that claim?

Between Two Crises

I suggest, first, that today's "Indigenous movement" was fermenting during the period of exhaustion that Latin American social researchers have termed the "crisis of the oligarchic state" and that it coalesced and emerged during the process of neoliberalizing-globalizing Latin American society.[14]

In this regard, it is important to bear in mind that under the oligarchic state the overwhelming majority of the population called "Indian" in Latin America was rural, although in both city and countryside alike the domination regime of which they were victims was seigneurial. That is, the social status of the majority of "Indians" was serfdom: domestic servitude in the cities and agro-domestic servitude in the countryside.

The nearly universal serfdom of "Indians" resulted from the continual plunder of their lands in favor of non-Indians from the very beginnings of the republican era. During the colonial period, in order to control the "Indian" populations after formally doing away with the encomienda system, the Crown decreed that "Indians" be granted land to live on and farm as their exclusive property. There was a wide range in the size of the land grants, depending on the region. But they were always substantial. They were quite extensive in Peru and even larger in Bolivia. After the Spanish defeat, Bolívar decreed that throughout the former Viceroyalty of Peru, Indigenous community land was to be privatized and commercialized. Nonetheless, through most of the nineteenth century the Indigenous communities in the Andean republics kept control of most of the land they had been allotted under the viceroyalty. The plunder started up again at the end of the century as one of the consequences of the appropriation of mines, plantations, and haciendas by North American capital and then escalated and spread in the first three decades of the twentieth century after the bloody repression and defeat of Indigenous peasant resistance forced most "Indian" populations to submit to serfdom. What has been called the oligarchic state, based on the relations of domination that are inherent to the coloniality of power, was strengthened by this process. In Mexico, the resistance of the Indigenous peasantry converged with the dispute over the control of power in the heart of the bourgeoisie and middle classes themselves, giving rise to the so-called Mexican Revolution.

This is the historical context that helps us understand why the crisis and the withdrawal of the oligarchic state in majority "Indian" countries would have such decisive implications for the social and political situation of those people and be at the origin of their crisis and change of identity.

Indeed, the crisis of the oligarchic state came to an end together with the predominance of serf-like and semiserf relations and the breakdown of local and state authority structures linked to the power of the seigneurial bourgeoisie and seigneurial landowners. This occurred through social revolutions, as in Mexico (1910–1927) and Bolivia (1952), in which the organized participation of the majority-"Indian" peasantry was decisive; because the massive organized pressure of majority-"Indian" peasants led to the adoption of agricultural land redistribution measures known as agrarian reform, as in Peru between 1957 and 1969; or because the seigneurial landowners themselves were forced, as in Ecuador (1969–1970), to switch from a serf-like labor regime to wage labor. The result everywhere was an expansion of paid labor and commercial activity.

These processes were associated, as is known, with the sudden urbanization of Latin American society as a whole, the relative expansion of industrial production and its internal market, and changes in the urban social structure, with the formation of new industrial-urban bourgeois groups, new professional and intellectual middle classes, and a new population of industrial and commercial wage laborers. And, of course, a part of these changes was the massive migration from the countryside to the cities.

All this was soon expressed in the relative modernization of the state: not only were its social bases expanded, but, most importantly, they were

profoundly changed by the partial and precarious yet no less real and decisive incorporation of new contingents from peasant and "Indian" back-
grounds into the realm of citizenship, though they were still enmeshed
in webs of clientage and forms of political brokering rather than direct
representation.

These processes were more extensive, massive, and, in a word, global
in some countries than in others. For those with majority Indian populations, these differences have proved decisive. It was in Peru that the
process was undoubtedly earlier, swifter, and more sweeping. For a huge
share of the "Indian" population, this meant de-Indianizing their identity
and self-identification, relocating to cities, and shifting toward wage labor
and the market activities (even in the rural world) rather than toward the
peasant activities of the preceding period. This particular process of de-
Indianization was termed "cholification."[15]

The new "cholo" population was undoubtedly the main protagonist and
agent for the process of changes in Peru after World War II. They were, first,
the ones who formed what was until the late 1960s the broadest and most
powerful peasant movement in Latin America,[16] leading to the collapse of
seigneurial power in the countryside and culminating in the agrarian reform under the military dictatorship of Velasco Alvarado in 1969, which was
actually carried out in order to block the development of the peasant movement among the "cholos," with all the negative consequences that had for
rural society and agricultural production. They were the ones who formed
the new contingent of urban industrial and commercial wage laborers,
established a nascent union movement that was a powerful player in the
national political debate until the crisis of the mid-1970s, and achieved
legislative victories that allowed them to negotiate the sale of their labor
with some advantages. They were the ones who filled the state educa-
tional system at all levels, forcing the state to expand it rapidly. They filled
the state universities, forming a different and broader university student
movement, with profound consequences for the country, beginning with
the sudden expansion of the ascending middle classes, who were recruited
precisely from this population. They, more than anyone, filled the shantytowns (*barriadas*) of Peru, which have come to house more than 70 percent
of Peru's urban population and signify its central social, cultural, and symbolic experience in the second half of the twentieth century.

The militarization of the state after its experiences with guerrilla fight-
ers in 1965–1967 and its confrontations with the youngest strata of the
"cholo" population, especially at universities and among young intellectu-

als, obstructed and distorted the social, cultural, and political development of these populations, in particular during the "second phase" of the military dictatorship (1968–1980). This militarization helped exacerbate the serious distortions that the Stalinist and Maoist versions of the already Eurocentered theory of "historical materialism" was introducing in universities and among the young "cholo" intelligentsia in the debate on the Peruvian process (according to them, Peru was a feudal or semifeudal society, like China in the early 1930s, and thus the revolutionary war, from the countryside to the cities, and so on and so forth). Finally, the militarization of the state combined with the young "cholo" intelligentsia until it led, unfortunately for all, to the messy and bloody terrorist exchange between the state and the Maoist Sendero Luminoso group, whose main victims were "Indigenous" or not entirely "cholified" peasant populations themselves (victims numbering, according to Peru's Truth and Reconciliation Commission, more than sixty thousand).[17]

For half a century, the population who de-Indianized, appropriating derogatory labels such as "cholo" and "mestizo" and giving them a positive value, has only increased in numbers, presence, and influence in every sphere of Peruvian society, including of course in the rural world those who are still labeled "Indians" and live as a minority, though it is not certain that they accept that label any more. And it is unlikely that the "cholo" population would go back to identifying themselves as "Indian."

This is surely the answer to the question that now haunts the debate in Peru and Latin America over today's "Indigenous movement." If Peru is the country with the largest "Indian" population of all the Andean countries, why is there no significant "Indigenous movement" there, whereas there are very active and influential movements in Ecuador in particular and in Bolivia?

Neoliberalization-Globalization and Its Implications for the "Indigenous Movement"

For convenience but not at random, I link neoliberalization-globalization together here to refer to the process that Latin America, like the rest of the world, has undergone from the crisis of the mid-1970s to now. There is relative consensus in the current debate, an ocean of writing aside, on the weakening and denationalizing of the state, social polarization, and the de-democratizing of society. I do not need to dwell on these issues.[18] But what these processes mean or have meant for the question of the

"Indigenous movement" has barely begun to register in the Latin American debate. Consequently, it is useful here to broach some of the more important questions.

First, I suggest that the rapid, even sudden, disintegration of the production structure that had been developing in these countries resulted in not only unemployment, rising underemployment, and rapid social polarization but also a process that can be recognized as one of social reclassification affecting all social sectors, workers most of all. This process was associated with a social identity crisis in every sector but most of all among those whose identity had long been or was becoming ambiguous and uncertain, driving them to seek newer identities. In my judgment, this is what explains the fact that, for example, social identities expressed in terms of "social classes" have given way in all these countries to so-called ethnic, regional, or residential identities and those of "informal workers" and "the poor."

This identity crisis and these shifts in identity have taken place explicitly among rural "Indian" workers in the less urbanized Andean and Mesoamerican countries who had been identified in terms of class (as "peasants") and had accepted that identification and have now ended up reidentifying as "Indigenous." Meanwhile in Peru, by contrast, retracting the "peasant" identity is not on the table or, rather, is being addressed slowly and indecisively. Even today, the most important community organization confronting the mining corporations is called the National Coordinator of Communities Affected by Mining, not invoking the idea of the "Indigenous community" in the very country where that notion originated.

Second, alongside these problems so-called globalization has also introduced a new communication universe with a broadening spectrum of resources, media, and technologies ranging from the classic transistor radio—the first tool to break the localized isolation of "peasants" and "Indians"—to email, which has spread to unexpected places, and the portable telephone, the famous cell phone, which is now ubiquitous even in otherwise isolated localities. In this sense, the rural and rural/urban populations in the process of social identity crises and ethnic reidentification in particular have found in the virtual network a way to relearn who they are and identify with those closest to them by place and by name in the "racial" system of discrimination and domination, just as in the immediately preceding period it was important for them to identify with all those affected by the same exploitation mechanism: capital.

Nevertheless, the suggestions that the new virtual realities produced by these digital communication networks should be recognized as "deterritorialization" or "delocalization" must be considered with great caution in the case of "Indigenous" people, because geography, the local, the community, the neighborhood, and the home weigh very differently than they do in the case of the scattered and sometimes temporary or shifting urban populations in industrial societies.

Third, the weakening of the state, its overt denationalization and even its reprivatization in many countries in the region, processes that have all diminished the achievements of the populations of "Indian" identity or origin—public education, public health, urban services, the creation and protection of paid employment—has not only left broad sectors of the subjugated and the exploited in Latin America with no course of appeal for their complaints and needs, which are now greater and more pressing than at any time in the past two hundred years. In several of these countries, the state has been acting, especially in the 1990s, contrary to the interests of the majority of the population in a way analogous to what it did immediately after the defeat of the colonial Iberian empires. That is why after more than three decades of such processes, growing sectors of the working-class population of Latin America, including the "Indians," have learned or are quickly learning that they have to find ways to not just not live from the State but also live without or against the state.

And this specific realm is probably where the core determining factors behind the current reidentification of "peasants" and "Indians" into "Indigenous" will be found. I am referring above all to the direction in managing questions of collective or public authority that have been taken since the early 1980s by the "Indian" populations who first began organizing and mobilizing in the Andean-Amazonian countries and who have gained international celebrity since Chiapas.

One of the most significant aspects that emerged in the course of organizing the Coordinator of Indigenous Organizations of the Amazon River Basin (Coordinadora de las Organizaciones Indígenas de la Cuenca Amazónica, COICA), established in 1984 by the most important Amazonian Basin community organizations from Peru, Bolivia, Brazil, Ecuador, Colombia, and Venezuela), and then later that same decade the National Union of Aymara Communities (Unión Nacional de Comunidades Aymaras, UNCA), founded in Puno in the Peruvian altiplano bordering Lake Titicaca) was the reorganization and revitalization of the community as the structure of collective and public authority specific to these populations. At the conferences that led to the creation of COICA and UNCA, the problem of the state's absence and hostility was explicitly debated, which is why community authority was deemed necessary and urgent.[19] The question of territorial and political autonomy, an empty slogan of followers of the Stalinist International in the late 1920s and early 1930s, now reappeared, autonomously placed in a list of items for discussion by the "Indigenous communities."

The period of tension and pressure between these populations and the state then began, and it has only spread and intensified to the present. That was probably also the moment when "Indian" identity began to be replaced by "Indigenous." It is doubtful and in any case unclear whether a systematic, collective debate took place among "Indians" about the coloniality of the terms "Indian," "Black," "white," and "mestizo," though some social scientists in Mexico and Peru were already discussing these issues.[20] Most likely it was after decisions to reorganize and revitalize the "Indigenous community" as it confronted the state that the "Indian" identification began to be abandoned and that of "Indigenous" taken up.

The "Indigenous community" was a creation of the colonial authorities in the sixteenth century. Under colonial rule, it was the home and refuge for "Indian" populations who had not been immediately reduced to serfdom. So, when the land plunder and subjugation of "Indians" to serfdom began in the republican era, the "Indigenous community" was reclaimed and proclaimed as the emblematic institution of the struggle against serfdom and abuses by haciendas, mines, and the state. Moreover, for many years it became the virtually exclusive home of political democracy for the "Indian" peasant population under the oligarchic state, because all the adult members of "Indigenous communities," men and women from the age of fourteen up, had the right to participate in debates and collective decisions affecting community members. This is no doubt the main reason why the "Indigenous community," despite its colonial origin, now provides peasants, unemployed people, and informal workers of "Indian" origin as well as professionals and intellectuals of the same origin with anticolonial ideological rallying points with respect to both the national problem and democracy.

There is now a prominent well-known active group of "Indigenous" intellectuals in Ecuador, Bolivia, Mexico, and Guatemala and also in Peru, but those who identify as such are mainly among the Aymaras and the inhabitants of the Andean-Amazonian basin. In the recent debate on these issues, they have certainly come to be actively and decisively involved. The creation of the Intercultural Indigenous University (Universidad Indígena Intercultural Amawtay Wasi) and the Institute of Indigenous Research (Instituto de Investigaciones Indígenas) in Quito under the directorship of Luis Macas, one of the founders of the Confederation of Indigenous Nationalities of Ecuador (Confederación de Nacionalidades Indígenas del Ecuador, CONAIE) and, more recently, the minister of agriculture in the Lucio Gutiérrez administration, with whom he has finally broken ties, is one of the most effective demonstrations of this phenomenon.

Today's "Indigenous movement" developed first among the main groups in the Amazonian basin, whose principle organization before COICA was *Ecuarunari* (Peoples of Ecuador), founded in 1972. Though organizations of "Indians," influenced and backed by the Communist Party of Ecuador, were active earlier, seeking political autonomy from the Ecuadorian state, it is unlikely that those predecessors had any weight in the creation of the current Indigenous movement in that country. On the other hand, some religious organizations—Salesian and Jesuit—have been important influences. In 1980, the National Council of Coordination of Ecuadorian Indigenous Nationalities (Consejo Nacional de Coordinación de Nacionalidades Indígenas de Ecuador, CONACNIE) was formed, and finally in 1986 CONAIE was created as the central organization for all organized Ecuadorian Indigenous groups. CONAIE won political legitimacy in the famous national uprising and takeover of Quito in 1990. And CONAIE entered the international stage with its participation in the fall of the Abdala Bucaram administration in 1997 and its leadership in the fall of the Jamil Mahuad administration in January 2000, on which occasion the top leader of CONAIE, Antonio Vargas, briefly occupied the presidency with the support of Colonel Lucio Gutiérrez, who would later be elected president of Ecuador thanks mainly to the backing of the Indigenous movement.[21]

The case of Bolivia is much more complicated. Bolivian peasants had been organized in unions since the 1940s, side by side with the miners' movement. Miners and peasants participated together in the Bolivian National Revolution of April 1952; while the miners took the mines and expropriated them, the peasants took the land and expelled the seigneurial landowners.[22] Together they formed the famous worker-peasant militias that consolidated the revolution, and in alliance with the Bolivian Workers' Confederation (Confederación Obrera Boliviana), they forced the Paz Estenssoro government to legalize and extend their land redistribution. They have been present at every turn in Bolivian politics since then, though they have not always followed the same line. They were even used by General Barrientos, who blocked the revolutionary process with the military coup of 1964 and was responsible for the brutal massacre of mine workers in June of that year.

With the collapse of tin mining and the closure of the state-owned mines, many mine workers, including some of their most respected leaders, decided to go work with the coca farmers in Chapare Province. But they also used their miners' union experience to help the coca farmers organize. This allowed those peasants—"Indians" if you use the "race" criterion—to escape being victimized or used as tools by the mafia-like networks of coca and cocaine traffickers. But it also let them resist the Bolivian state and the United States, which were set on simply eradicating coca cultivation without offering the peasants any profitable alternatives. In that struggle, they have gained strength as a movement of workers and peasants; they have won the support of other social forces that they have supported in their own struggles; they have emerged as a socialist-affiliated political movement, the Movement toward Socialism (Movimiento al Socialismo); and they have produced political leaders of national stature such as Evo Morales, running for president in the recent elections and coming in second in the final results against all predictions by the urban press.

In addition, the Aymaras who live in the altiplano surrounding Lake Titicaca, maintaining their connections with the experiences of the Katarista movement (named after Túpac Katari, an Aymara leader in the Túpac Amaru revolution of 1780) that had been active in the peasant and guerrilla struggles of the 1970s, have been forming and changing other movements. The most important of these today is the Unified Syndical Confederation of Rural Workers of Bolivia (Confederación Sindical Única de Trabajadores Campesinos de Bolivia) headed by Felipe Quispe, nicknamed El Mallku, who has gained considerable authority among the peasantry and become a prominent national figure.

The Movement toward Socialism and the Unified Syndical Confederation of Rural Workers of Bolivia have participated not only in elections but also, most notably, in broad social and political movements to defend national control over production in the country, such as the March for Territory and Dignity in 1991 and, more recently, the well-known series of events that led Gonzalo Sánchez de Losada to resign as president of Bolivia following bloody confrontations with the popular movement.

So, in the Bolivian case these are not strictly "Indigenous movements" in every case as they are in Ecuador; in the Amazon region with COICA; in Chiapas, Guatemala; and, more recently, in the cases of the "Mapuches" of Chile and other smaller groups in Argentina.

With regard to Chiapas and Guatemala, the international press has brought worldwide fame to the movement of the "Indigenous" people of Chiapas and their media spokesperson, Subcomandante Marcos, to a great extent thanks to him. The same has happened in Guatemala through the bloody and protracted civil war and the presence of Nobel laureate Rigoberta Menchú.[23]

Meaning and Perspectives of the Current "Indigenous Movement"

There really is no "Indigenous movement" except in a nominal, abstract sense. And it would be misleading to think that the term "Indigenous" describes anything homogeneous, continuous, and consistent. Just as the word "Indian" served under colonial rule as a common identifier for many diverse and heterogeneous historical identities in order to impose the idea of "race" and as a mechanism for control and domination that could facilitate the division of exploited labor, the word "Indigenous," despite bearing witness to the rejection of the colonial classification and a reclaiming of autonomous identity, is not only no liberation from coloniality but also does not signal any process of homogenization even though now that the old identities have dissolved, homogeneity is undoubtedly greater today than it was yesterday. There is no doubt that the term covers a diverse, heterogeneous reality, nor is there doubt that several specific identities will reappear or already are reappearing apart from the fact that several never did disband, as in the case of the Aymaras, the Amazonian groups, and among the diverse groups in Chiapas and the altiplano of Guatemala.[24]

There is no assurance, then, that all the groups of "Indigenous" people today or those who will emerge in the future have the same orientation, the same perspectives, or are facing the same horizons.

That said, their current presence on the Latin American stage has a few shared implications. First, it is true that there is a shared claim to identity, though largely in response to the discrimination that prevents their full assimilation into the national identity or the dominant culture. But this is an almost traditional assertion of the sort that Indians and Indigenistas have long been committed to as well as anthropologists who wish that what they call "cultures" could be preserved in museums of a sort, regardless of whether the people themselves would like it or benefit from it.

The most organized, however, as in Ecuador first and then in Chiapas, have moved on to proposing the need for a plurinational state. And they are not just talking about filling the constitution with the ritual phrases about pluriethnicity, pluriculturality, plurietcetera that are now typical of all such texts. They want the institutional structure of the State to be fundamentally modified so it can effectively represent more than one nation. That is, their demand is for a multiple citizenship, given that in the current model, "Indigenous" people are not and cannot be fully included.[25] It is also true, however, that this is still not on the horizon for most of the people who have reidentified as "Indigenous" in Latin America. But this demand nevertheless means an end to political and cultural assimilationism in the Americas, since it was, after all, never fully and consistently practiced by the non-Indian or "white" dominant group. And if this really does come to pass, instead of simply being repressed and defeated, it also means an end to the Eurocentric mirage of a nation-state in which some nationalities continue to dominate and colonize others, which moreover constitutes majorities.

A variation on this demand is political and territorial autonomy. And in some cases, in Venezuela and Canada, the dominant groups have preferred not to risk their nation-states by ceding relatively vast, politically autonomous territories to specific Indigenous groups. But in countries such as Argentina, Chile, Uruguay, and Brazil, the "Indigenous" populations are minorities and may well gain access to relatively autonomous spaces someday. Another very distinct case is that of countries with large "Indigenous" populations: Mexico, Guatemala, Ecuador, Bolivia, and even Peru if identity processes there ever move in a different direction. The Aymaras have already explicitly imagined the possibility of an autonomous territory. But they live in five countries, and their situation may someday seem like that of the Kurds in the Middle East. In these countries, the prospects of conflict between the nation-state and the plurinational state is truly serious.

When it comes to globalization, however, with its processes of weakening and denationalizing the state, the demand for plurinational citizenships and states seems much more confused and complicated. Because this demand poses a serious problem regarding democratic control over collective and public authority, most of all for peoples subjected to states created within the coloniality of power but also for other peoples, even those who identify with their own nation-states. And here again, the strongest and most organized Latin American Indigenous movements have already raised the demand for communal authority, or, better, for the community as an authority suitable for democratic control by its base, as they confront states that belong to other nations or, worse, that are under global, distant, imperial, repressive, bureaucratic, corporate, and vertical management of the sort that seems to be emerging from the global imperial bloc under the hegemony of the United States.[26]

Here, the UNCA's initiative, on the Peruvian side, attempted a remarkable project. The communities of each local, base-level jurisdiction (the district, in the case of Peru) create associations with one another in a district-wide multicommunity. The various organizations at that level join to form a provincial multicommunity. Those then come together to form the UNCA. Leaders at every level are elected by their base community and can be removed by them. The design is very similar to the well-known idea of the state that is no longer a state because it has the coherence and coverage of a state, but its bases are different, and the way it is created and controlled is even more so. It amounts to a means of direct self-government for the folks associated in a network of communities but with the force and authority of a real state.

These last demands and exercises did not fall from the sky, nor are they up in the clouds. They resulted from and redefine the age-old experience of local democracy in Indigenous communities. If majority-Indigenous populations in certain countries decide to put these forms of political authority into practice, they could join up with more recent tendencies as well as with incipient tendencies from other social sectors, such as those that emerged from the recent social explosion in Argentina (2001). In a way, then, these movements rise from the emerging horizon shared in common by the reworked imaginaries of social and political change: the democratic creation of a democratic society.

In any case, the redefinition of the national question and of political democracy now seems to be of profound consequences and enormous scope and to be bringing the greatest potential for conflict in this part of Latin America. In this sense, it is the most important challenge that has ever arisen for the matrix of power marked by its coloniality. The latter originated here in the Americas, and it is also here that it is entering its most perilous crisis.

Notes

First published in Aníbal Quijano, "El 'movimiento indígena' y las cuestiones pendientes en América Latina," *Argumentos* 19, no. 50 (2006): 51–77.

1   Any statistic on the "Indians" or "Indigenous people" in the Americas will be messy and dubious. It will obviously depend on the identification

criteria, on who identifies whom and who they identify as. In Mexico, numbers range from 25 million to 50 million, in the Andean countries they range from 10 million to over 20 million. The numbers can only be used as reference guides, not as exact statistics.

2   Quijano and Wallerstein, "Americanity as a Concept, or the Americas in the Imaginary of the Modern World-System"; Quijano, "Raza, etnia y nación en José Carlos Mariátegui"; and Quijano, "¡Qué tal raza!"

3   I have begun to discuss the questions concerning this new matrix of power and its foundations and implications in Quijano, "Coloniality of Power, Eurocentrism and Latin America." See also "Colonialidad del poder, globalización y democracia"; and Quijano, "Colonialidad del poder y clasificación social."

4   The term "European" is used here not in its physical-geographical sense but rather in relation to the coloniality of the reigning power matrix. That is, in reference to the "white" or "European" social groups that have control of world power wherever their respective countries are located now, for this geography continues to be a product of the coloniality of power.

5   There is extensive literature on this debate. See, for instance, Munda and Mullick, *Jharkhand Movement*. The "castification" of power relations in India further complicates the "indigenization" of part of the population. See, among others, Mendelsohn and Vicziany, *The Untouchables*.

6   The fourth World Social Forum held recently (January 15–21, 2004) in Mumbai was unquestionably broader and more popular than earlier forums precisely because of the massive presence of Adivasi/Indigenous people from throughout the southeast of Asia and especially from every region in India, filling alongside the Dalit ("Untouchables") every space at the forum with their marches, their slogans, their demands, and their protest against oppression, discrimination, dispossession, against the violence of "communalist" fundamentalism. For all of them, the forum was also an unprecedented occasion to meet one another. The importance of these facts, whose implications will soon become evident, cannot be minimized.

7   Quijano, *Modernidad, identidad y utopía en América Latina*.

8   For a more thorough discussion of the implications of "race" for citizenship, representation, and participation in the liberal state, see Quijano, "Colonialité du pouvoir et démocratie en Amérique latine"; and Quijano, "Estado-Nación, ciudadanía y democracia."

9   In Peru, the most important debate was that between José Carlos Mariátegui and Luis Alberto Sánchez. See Mariátegui, *Siete ensayos de interpretación de la realidad peruana*, prologue by Aníbal Quijano; Deustua and Renique, *Intelectuales, indigenismo y descentralismo en el*

Perú, 1897/1931; and Ibarra, "Intelectuales indígena, neoindigenismo e indianismo en el Ecuador."

10   Quijano, "Coloniality of Power, Eurocentrism and Latin America."

11   There is a phenomenon in this debate that has not really been studied yet. There is no doubt that the "Indian" population was a demographic majority in the most important republics, in any case the largest, in the Hispanic area and that it was culturally predominant among the colonized in Mexico, Central America, and the Andes. The "Black" population, however, although obviously smaller, was significant in the Pacific north coast of South America and especially, unquestionably, in the Caribbean, not to mention the Portuguese area where it was the overwhelming majority. And curiously, the "white" population was smaller in all these republics. Consequently, demography is surely not the explanation for why the "Black" population does not appear in the political debate over the state, apart from the problem of abolishing or maintaining slavery. I suggest that after the Haitian Revolution, the dominant groups throughout the Americas and those of Europe as well—the latter were then in the process of busily colonizing the "Blacks" of Africa—endeavored and succeeded in making "Blacks" sociologically and politically invisible and so included them only in the debate on slavery. The fact is, in any case, that in the debate over what to do politically with "nonwhite" or "non-European" populations, "Blacks" were virtually invisible in the Hispanic area throughout the nineteenth century. This is why the "Black problem" was not placed on an equal footing with the "Indigenous problem."

12   Its first two great moments of crisis were, first, the Túpac Amaru revolution in the Viceroyalty of Peru in 1780, which was defeated but had serious consequences for the future of the colonial power. The second was the revolution in Haiti in 1804 led by Toussaint Louverture, unquestionably the first great modern revolution, which in a single historical movement produced a victorious social subversion (slaves against masters), an anticolonial and national subversion (the defeat of French colonialism and the formation of the Haitian nationality), and one of global import, the first moment in the disintegration of the coloniality of power ("Blacks" against "whites"). The well-known later vicissitudes of the Haitian process put a dent in the revolution's potential but did not diminish the historical significance of that extraordinary feat.

13   There is not a satisfactory Spanish translation of the English term "peoplehood."

14   Obviously, this hypothesis should not be taken to mean that "Indians" as such began to mobilize only in the past thirty years. The list of their rebellions and attempts to create more permanent organizations, in

the Andean countries for example, is long and amply documented. But my aim here is not to write the history of "Indian" rebellions since colonial times but instead to probe into the specifics and the meaning of today's "Indigenous movement." On the earlier struggles by "Indians," see among others; Bonfil-Batalla, *Utopía y revolución*; and Montoya, *Al borde del naufragio*. It should also be remembered that most Indigenous struggles were subsumed as peasant struggles between 1930 and 1980. On agrarian and peasant struggles, see Quijano, "Contemporary Peasant Movements in Latin America."

15   A number of Peruvian and foreign social researchers took part in the debate on this subject in the 1950s and 1960s. See especially Bourricaud, "Algunas características originales de la cultura mestiza del Perú contemporáneo"; Arguedas, "Evolución de las comunidades indígenas del Valle del Mataro y de la ciudad de Huancayo"; and Quijano, *Dominación y cultura*. *Cholificación* (cholification) refers to the emergence of a new cultural identification of people in Peru provoked by the massive migrations from the mountains to the urban centers on the Pacific coast). "Cholo" is a term used in Latin American Spanish to classify the Indigenous people as well as *métis* with indigenous physiognomy.

16   Quijano, "Contemporary Peasant Movements in Latin America"; and Quijano, "The Crisis of the Colonial/Modern/Eurocentered Horizon of Meaning," in this volume.

17   Comisión de la Verdad y Reconciliación, *Informe Final*.

18   For my own perspectives, see Quijano, "Estado-Nación, ciudadanía y democracia." For the consequences of neoliberalization-globalization on Latin American society, especially on social structure and the structure of power, see my suggestions for discussion in Quijano, "El laberinto de America Latina."

19   I was invited to the UNCA organizing conference and allowed to attend these debates.

20   Bonfil-Batalla, *México profundo: Una civilización negada.* The translation into English provides a meaningful version of the subtitle. See Bonfil-Batalla, *México profundo: Reclaiming a Civilization*, trans. Phillip A. Dennis (Austin: Texas University Press, 1996). While the Spanish subtitle points toward colonial destitution, the English translation points toward decolonial reconstitution. See Quijano, "Coloniality and Modernity/Rationality," in this volume; and Quijano, "Raza, etnia y nación en José Carlos Mariátegui."

21   See Burbano de Lara, "Ecuador, cuando los equilibrios crujen"; and Bustamante Ponce, "¿Y después de la insurrección qué?"

22   Quijano, "Contemporary Peasant Movements in Latin America."

23   Collier and Lowery-Quaratiello, *Basta!*; and Warren, "Indigenous Movements as a Challenge to the Unified Social Movements Paradigm for Guatemala."

24   Not long ago, an Aymara leader on the Peruvian side of the border bitterly confronted a journalist who was interviewing him and who insisted on calling him Indigenous. "Señorita, I am not Indian, nor Indigenous; I am Aymara."

25   On Ecuador, see especially CONAIE, *Proyecto político*. Several documents have been circulated about Peru. See mainly the document presented by the leaders of CONACAMI (Confederación Nacional de Comunidades del Perú Afectadas por la Minería), AIDESEP (Asociación Interétnica de Desarrollo de la Selva Peruana), and CONAP (Comisión Nacional de Áreas Protegidas), among others, in April 2003: Palacín, Quisque, Sebastián, and Sarasara, "Propuesta concertada para incorporar los derechos de los pueblos indígenas y comunidades en la constitución política del Perú."

26   Quijano, "Estado-Nación, ciudadanía y democracia."

COLONIALITY OF POWER, EUROCENTRISM, AND LATIN AMERICA

What is termed "globalization" is the culmination of a process that began with the constitution of America and colonial/modern Eurocentered capitalism as a new global power. One of the fundamental axes of this model of power is the social classification of the world's population around the idea of race, a mental construction that expresses the basic experience of colonial domination and pervades the more important dimensions of global power, including its specific rationality: Eurocentrism. The racial axis has a colonial origin and character, but it has proven to be more durable and stable than the colonialism in whose matrix it was established. Therefore, the model of power that is globally hegemonic today presupposes an element of coloniality. In what follows, my primary aim is to open some of the theoretically necessary questions about the implications of coloniality of power regarding the history of Latin America.[1]

America and the New Model of Global Power

America was constituted as the first space/time of a new model of power of global vocation, and both in this way and by it became the first identity of modernity.[2] Two historical processes associated in the production of that space/time converged and established the two fundamental axes of the new model of power. One was the codification of the differences between conquerors and conquered in the idea of "race," a supposedly different biological structure that placed some in a natural situation of inferiority to the others. The conquistadors assumed this idea as the constitutive, founding element of the relations of domination that the conquest imposed. On this basis, the population of America and later the world was classified within the new model of power. The other process was the constitution of a new structure of control of labor and its resources and products. This new structure was an articulation of all historically known previous structures of control of labor, slavery, serfdom, small independent commodity production, and reciprocity, together around and upon the basis of capital and the world market.[3]

RACE: A MENTAL CATEGORY OF MODERNITY

The idea of race, in its modern meaning, does not have a known history before the colonization of America. Perhaps it originated in reference to the phenotypic differences between conquerors and conquered.[4] However, what matters is that soon it was constructed to refer to the supposed differential biological structures between those groups.

Social relations founded on the category of race produced new historical social identities in America—Indians, Blacks, and mestizos— and redefined others. Terms such as "Spanish" and "Portuguese" and, much later, "European," which until then indicated only geographic origin or country of origin, acquired from then on a racial connotation in reference to the new identities. Insofar as the social relations that were being configured were relations of domination, such identities were considered constitutive of the hierarchies, places, and corresponding social roles and consequently of the model of colonial domination that was being imposed. In other words, race and racial identity were established as instruments of basic social classification.

As time went by, the colonizers codified the phenotypic trait of the colonized as color, and they assumed it as the emblematic characteristic of racial category. That category was probably initially established in the area of Anglo-America. There, so-called Blacks were not only the most important exploited group, since the principal part of the economy rested on their labor; they were, above all, the most important colonized race, since Indians were not part of that colonial society. Why the dominant group calls itself "white" is a story related to racial classification.[5]

In America, the idea of race was a way of granting legitimacy to the relations of domination imposed by the conquest. After the colonization of

America and the expansion of European colonialism to the rest of the world, the subsequent constitution of Europe as a new *id*-entity needed the elaboration of a Eurocentric perspective of knowledge, a theoretical perspective on the idea of race as a naturalization of colonial relations between Europeans and non-Europeans. Historically, this meant a new way of legitimizing the already old ideas and practices of relations of superiority/inferiority between dominant and dominated. From the sixteenth century on, this principle has proven to be the most effective and long-lasting instrument of universal social domination, since the much older principle—gender or intersexual domination—was encroached upon by the inferior/superior racial classifications. So, the conquered and dominated peoples were situated in a natural position of inferiority, and as a result, their phenotypic traits as well as their cultural features were considered inferior.[6] In this way, race became the fundamental criterion for the distribution of the world population into ranks, places, and roles in the new society's structure of power.

CAPITALISM, THE NEW STRUCTURE
FOR THE CONTROL OF LABOR

In the historical process of the constitution of America, all forms of control and exploitation of labor and production as well as the control of appropriation and distribution of products revolved around the capital-salary relation and the world market. These forms of labor control included slavery, serfdom, petty-commodity production, reciprocity, and wages. In such an assemblage, each form of labor control was no mere extension of its historical antecedents. All of these forms of labor were historically and sociologically new: in the first place because they were deliberately established and organized to produce commodities for the world market, and in the second place because they did not merely exist simultaneously in the same space/time, but each one of them was also articulated to capital and its market. Thus, they configured a new global model of labor control and in turn a fundamental element of a new model of power to which they were historically structurally dependent. That is to say, the place and function and therefore the historical movement of all forms of labor as subordinated points of a totality belonged to the new model of power, despite their heterogeneous specific traits and their discontinuous relations with that totality. In the third place and consequently, each form of labor developed into new traits and historical-structural configurations.

Insofar as that structure of control of labor, resources, and products consisted of the joint articulation of all the respective historically known forms, a global model of control of work was established for the first time in known history. And while it was constituted around and in the service of capital, its configuration as a whole was established with a capitalist character as well. Thus emerged a new, original, and singular structure of relations of production in the historical experience of the world: world capitalism.

COLONIALITY OF POWER AND GLOBAL CAPITALISM

The new historical identities produced around the foundation of the idea of race in the new global structure of the control of labor were associated with social roles and geohistorical places. In this way, both race and the division of labor remained structurally linked and mutually reinforcing although neither of them were necessarily dependent on the other in order to exist or change.

In this way, a systematic racial division of labor was imposed. In the Hispanic region, the Crown of Castilla decided early on to end the enslavement of the Indians to prevent their total extermination. They were instead confined to serfdom. For those who lived in communities, the ancient practice of reciprocity—the exchange of labor force and labor without a market—was allowed as a way of reproducing its labor force as serfs. In some cases, the Indian nobility, a reduced minority, was exempted from serfdom and received special treatment owing to their roles as intermediaries with the dominant race. They were also permitted to participate in some of the activities of the nonnoble Spanish. However, Blacks were reduced to slavery. As the dominant race, Spanish and Portuguese whites could receive wages and be independent merchants, independent artisans, or independent farmers, in short, independent producers of commodities. Nevertheless, only nobles could participate in the high to midrange positions in the military and civil colonial administration.

Beginning in the eighteenth century, in Hispanic America an extensive and important social stratum of mestizos (born of Spanish men and Indian women) began to participate in the same offices and activities as nonnoble Iberians. To a lesser extent and above all in activities of service or those that required a specialized talent (music, for example), the more "whitened" among the mestizos of Black women and Spanish and Portuguese men had an opportunity to work. But they were late in legitimizing their new roles, since their mothers were slaves. This racist distribution of labor in the interior of colonial/modern capitalism was maintained throughout the colonial period.

In the course of the worldwide expansion of colonial domination on the part of the same dominant race (or, from the eighteenth century onward, Europeans), the same criteria of social classification were imposed on all of the world population. As a result, new historical and social identities were fabricated: yellows and olives were added to whites, Indians, Blacks, and mestizos. The racist distribution of new social identities was combined, as had been done so successfully in Anglo-America, with a racist distribution of labor and the forms of exploitation of colonial capitalism. This was, above all, through a quasi-exclusive association of whiteness with wages and, of course, with the high-order positions in the colonial administration. Thus, each form of labor control was associated with a particular race. Consequently, the control of a specific form of labor could be, at the same time, the control of a specific group of dominated people. A new technology of domination/exploitation, in this case race/labor, was articulated in such a way that the two elements appeared naturally associated. Until now, this strategy has been exceptionally successful.

COLONIALITY AND THE EUROCENTRIFICATION OF WORLD CAPITALISM

The privileged positions conquered by the dominant whites for the control of gold, silver, and other commodities produced by the unpaid labor of Indians, Blacks, and mestizos (coupled with an advantageous location in the slope of the Atlantic through which, necessarily, the traffic of these commodities for the world market had to pass) granted whites a decisive advantage to compete for the control of worldwide commercial traffic. The progressive monetization of the world market that the precious metals from America stimulated and allowed as well as the control of such large resources made possible the control of the vast preexisting web of commercial exchange that included, above all, China, India, Ceylon, Egypt, and Syria, the future Far and Middle East. The monetization of labor also made it possible to concentrate the control of commercial capital, labor, and means of production in the whole world market.

The control of global commercial traffic by dominant groups headquartered in the Atlantic zones propelled in those places a new process of urbanization based on the expansion of commercial traffic between them, and consequently, the formation of regional markets increasingly integrated and monetarized due to the flow of precious metals originating in America. A historically new region was constituted as a new geocultural *id*-entity: Europe, more specifically Western Europe.[7] A new geocultural identity emerged as the central site for the control of the world market. The hegemony of the coasts of the Mediterranean and the Iberian Peninsula was displaced toward the northwest Atlantic coast in the same historical moment.

The condition Europe found itself in as the central site of the new world market cannot explain by itself alone why Europe also became, until the nineteenth century and virtually until the worldwide crisis of 1870, the central site of the process of the commodification of the labor force, while all the rest of the regions and populations colonized and incorporated into the new world market under European dominion basically remained under nonwaged relations of labor. And in non-European regions, wage labor was concentrated almost exclusively among whites. Of course, the entire production of such a division of labor was articulated in a chain of transference of value and profits whose control corresponded to Western Europe.

There is nothing in the social relation of capital itself or in the mechanisms of the world market in general that implies the historical necessity of European concentration first (either in Europe or elsewhere) of waged labor and later (over precisely the same base) of the concentration of industrial production for more than two centuries. As events after 1870 demonstrated, Western European control of wage labor in any sector of the world's population would have been perfectly feasible and probably more profitable for Western Europe. The explanation ought to lie, then, in some other aspect of history itself.

The fact is that from the very beginning of the colonization of America, Europeans associated nonpaid or nonwaged labor with the dominated races because they were "inferior" races. The vast genocide of the Indians in the first decades of colonization was not caused principally by the violence of the conquest or by the plagues the conquistadors brought but instead took place because so many American Indians were used as disposable manual labor and forced to work until death. The elimination of this colonial practice did not end until the defeat of the *encomenderos* in the middle of the sixteenth century. The subsequent Iberian colonialism involved a new politics of population reorganization, a reorganization of the Indians and their relations with the colonizers. But this did not advance American Indians as free and waged laborers. From then on, they were assigned the status of unpaid serfs. The serfdom of the American Indians could not, however, be compared with feudal serfdom in Europe, since it included neither the supposed protection of a feudal lord nor, necessarily, the possession of a piece of land to cultivate instead of wages. Before independence, the Indian labor force of serfs reproduced itself in the communities, but more than one hundred years after independence, a large number of Indian serfs were still obliged to reproduce the labor force on its own.[8] The other form of unwaged or, simply put, unpaid labor, slavery, was assigned exclusively to the "Black" population brought from Africa.

The racial classification of the population and the early association of the new racial identities of the colonized with the forms of control of unpaid, unwaged labor developed among the Europeans the singular perception that paid labor was the whites' privilege. The racial inferiority of the colonized implied that they were not worthy of wages. They were naturally obliged to work for the profit of their owners. It is not difficult to find, to this very day, this attitude spread out among the white property owners of any place in the world. Furthermore, the lower wages that "inferior races" receive in the present capitalist centers for the same work as done by whites cannot be explained as detached from the racist social classification of the world's population, in other words, as detached from the global capitalist coloniality of power.

The control of labor in the new model of global power was constituted thus, articulating all historical forms of labor control around the capitalist wage-labor relation. This articulation was constitutively colonial, based on first the assignment of all forms of unpaid labor to colonial races (originally American Indians, Blacks, and, in a more complex way, mestizos) in America and, later on, to the remaining colonized races in the rest of the world, olives and yellows. Second, labor was controlled through the assignment of salaried labor to the colonizing whites.

Coloniality determined the geographic distribution of each one of the integrated forms of labor control in global capitalism. In other words, the control of labor determined the social geography of capitalism: capital, as a social formation for control of wage labor, was the axis around which all remaining forms of labor control, resources, and products were articulated. But at the same time, capital's specific social configuration was geographically and socially concentrated in Europe and, above all, among Europeans in the whole world of capitalism. Through these measures, Europe and the European constituted themselves as the center of the capitalist world economy.

When Raúl Prebisch coined the celebrated image of center and periphery to describe the configuration of global capitalism since the end of World War II, he underscored, with or without being aware of it, the nucleus of the historical model for the control of labor, resources, and products that shaped the central part of the new global model of power, starting with America as a player in the new world economy.[9] Global capitalism was from then on colonial/modern and Eurocentered. Without a clear understanding of those specific historical characteristics of capitalism, the concept of a "modern world-system" itself, developed principally by Immanuel Wallerstein but based on Prebisch and on the Marxian concept of world capitalism,[10] cannot be properly or completely understood.

THE NEW MODEL OF WORLD POWER AND
THE NEW WORLD INTERSUBJECTIVITY

As the center of global capitalism, Europe not only had control of the world market but was also able to impose its colonial dominance on all the regions and populations of the planet, incorporating them into its world-system and its specific model of power. For such regions and populations, this model of power involved a process of historical reidentification; from Europe such regions and populations were attributed new geocultural identities. In that way, after America and Europe were established, Africa, Asia, and eventually Oceania followed suit. In the making of these new identities, the coloniality of the new model of power was, without a doubt, one of the most active determinations. But the forms and levels of political and cultural development and, more specifically, intellectual development played a role of utmost importance in each case. Without these factors, the category "Orient" would not have been elaborated as the only one with sufficient dignity to be the other to the "Occident," although by definition inferior, without some equivalent to "Indians" or "Blacks" being coined.[11] But this omission itself puts in the open the fact that those other factors also acted within the racist model of universal social classification of the world population.

The incorporation of such diverse and heterogeneous cultural histories into a single world dominated by Europe signified a cultural and intellectual intersubjective configuration equivalent to the articulation of all forms of labor control around capital, a configuration that established world capitalism. In effect, all of the experiences, histories, resources, and cultural products ended up in one global cultural order revolving around European or Western hegemony. Europe's hegemony over the new model of global power concentrated all forms of the control of subjectivity, culture, and especially knowledge and the production of knowledge under its hegemony.

During that process, the colonizers exercised diverse operations that brought about the configuration of a new universe of intersubjective relations of domination between Europe and the Europeans and the rest of the regions and peoples of the world, to whom new geocultural identities were being attributed in that process. In the first place, they expropriated the cultural discoveries of the colonized peoples most apt for the development of capitalism to the profit of the European center. Second, they repressed as much as possible the colonized forms of knowledge production, the models of the production of meaning, their symbolic universe, the model of expression and of objectification and subjectivity. As is well known, repression in this field was most violent, profound, and long-lasting among the Indians of Ibero-America, who were condemned to be an illiterate peasant subculture stripped of their objectified intellectual legacy. Something equivalent happened in Africa. Doubtless, the repression was much less intense in Asia, where an important part of the history of the intellectual written legacy has been preserved. And it was precisely such epistemic suppression that gave origin to the category "Orient." Third, in different ways in each case, they forced the colonized to learn the dominant culture in any way that would be useful to the reproduction of domination, whether in the field of technology and material activity or subjectivity, especially Judeo-Christian religiosity. All of those turbulent processes involved a long period of the colonization of cognitive perspectives, modes of producing and giving meaning, the results of material existence, the imaginary, the universe of intersubjective relations with the world: in short, the culture.[12]

The success of Western Europe in becoming the center of the modern world-system, according to Wallerstein's suitable formulation, developed within the Europeans a trait common to all colonial dominators and imperialists: ethnocentrism. But in the case of Western Europe, that trait had a peculiar formulation and justification: the racial classification of the world population after the colonization of America. The association of colonial ethnocentrism and universal racial classification helps to explain why Europeans came to feel not only superior to all the other peoples of the world but also, in particular, naturally superior. This historical instance is expressed through a mental operation of fundamental importance for the entire model of global power but above all with respect to the intersubjective relations that were hegemonic and especially for its perspective on knowledge: the Europeans generated a new temporal perspective of history and relocated the colonized population, along with their respective histories and cultures, in the past of a historical trajectory whose culmination was Europe.[13] Notably, however, they were not in the same line of continuity as the Europeans but instead were in another naturally different category. The colonized peoples were inferior races and in that manner were the past vis-à-vis the Europeans.

That perspective imagined modernity and rationality as exclusively European products and experiences. From this point of view, intersubjective and cultural relations between Western Europe and the rest of the world were codified in a strong play of new categories: East-West, primitive-civilized, magic/mythic-scientific, irrational-rational, and traditional-modern, in other words, Europe and not Europe. Even so, the only category with the honor of being recognized as the Other of Europe and the West was "Orient," not the Indians of America and not the Blacks of Africa, who were simply "primitive." Underneath that codification of relations between Europeans and non-Europeans, race is, without doubt, the basic category.[14] This binary, dualist perspective on knowledge, particular to Eurocentrism, was imposed as globally hegemonic in the same course as the expansion of European colonial dominance over the world.

It would not be possible to explain the elaboration of Eurocentrism as the hegemonic perspective of knowledge otherwise. The Eurocentric version is based on two principal founding myths: first, the idea of the history of human civilization as a trajectory that departed from a state of nature and culminated in Europe, and second, a view of the differences between Europe and non-Europe as natural (racial) differences and not consequences of a history of power. Both myths can be unequivocally recognized in the foundations of evolutionism and dualism, two of the nuclear elements of Eurocentrism.

THE QUESTION OF MODERNITY

I do not propose to enter here into a thorough discussion of the question of modernity and its Eurocentric version. In particular, I will not lengthen this piece with a discussion of the modernity-postmodernity debate and its vast bibliography. But it is pertinent for the goals of this essay, especially for the following section, to raise some questions.[15]

The fact that Western Europeans will imagine themselves to be the culmination of a civilizing trajectory from a state of nature leads them also to think of themselves as the moderns of humanity and its history, that is, as the new and, at the same time, most advanced of the species. But since they attribute the rest of the species to a category by nature inferior and consequently anterior, belonging to the past in the progress of the species, the Europeans imagine themselves as the exclusive bearers, creators, and protagonists of that modernity. What is notable about this is not that the Europeans imagined and thought of themselves and the rest of the species in that way—something not exclusive to Europeans—but the fact that they were capable of spreading and establishing that historical perspective as hegemonic within the new intersubjective universe of the global model of power.

Of course, the intellectual resistance to that historical perspective was not long in emerging. In Latin America, from the end of the nineteenth century and above all in the twentieth century especially after World War II, it happened in connection with the development-underdevelopment debate. That debate was dominated for a long time by the so-called theory of modernization.[16] One of the arguments most frequently used, from opposing angles, was to affirm that modernization does not necessarily imply the Westernization of non-European societies and cultures but that modernity is a phenomenon of all cultures, not just of Europe or the West.

If the concept of modernity only, or fundamentally, refers to the ideas of newness, the advanced, the rational-scientific, the secular (which are the ideas normally associated with it), then there is no doubt that one must admit that it is a phenomenon possible in all cultures and historical epochs. With all their respective particularities and differences, all the so-called high cultures (China, India, Egypt, Greece, Maya-Aztec, Tawantinsuyu) prior to the current world-system unequivocally exhibit signs of that modernity, including rational science and the secularization of thought. In truth, it would be almost ridiculous at these levels of historical research to attribute to non-European cultures a mythic-magical mentality, for example, as a defining trait in opposition to rationality and science as characteristics of Europe. Therefore, apart from their symbolic contents, cities, temples, palaces, pyramids and monumental cities (such as Machu Picchu and Borobudur), irrigation, large thoroughfares, technologies, metallurgy, mathematics, calendars, writing, philosophy, histories, armies, and wars clearly demonstrate the scientific development in each one of the high cultures that took place long before the formation of Europe as a new *id*-entity. The most that one can really say is that the present period has gone further in scientific and technological developments and has made major discoveries and achievements under Europe's hegemonic role and, more generally, under Western hegemony.

The defenders of the European patent on modernity are accustomed to appealing to the cultural history of the ancient Greco-Roman world and to the world of the Mediterranean prior to the colonization of America in order to legitimize their claim on the exclusivity of its patent. What is curious about this argument is, first, that it obscures the fact that the truly advanced part of the Mediterranean world was Islamo-Judaic. Second, it was that world that maintained the Greco-Roman cultural heritage, cities, commerce, agricultural trade, mining, textile industry, philosophy, and history, while the future Western Europe was being dominated by feudalism and cultural obscurantism. Third, very probably, the commodification of the labor force—the capital-wage relation—emerged precisely in that area, and its development expanded north toward the future Europe. Fourth, it was only with the defeat of Islam and the later displacement by America of Islam's hegemony over the world market north to Europe that the center of cultural activity also began to be displaced to that new region. Because of this, the new geographic perspective of history and culture, elaborated and imposed as globally hegemonic, implies a new geography of power. The idea of Occident-Orient itself is belated and starts with British hegemony. Or is it still necessary to recall that the prime meridian crosses London and not Seville or Venice?[17]

In this sense, the Eurocentric pretension to be the exclusive producer and protagonist of modernity—because of which all modernization of non-European populations is therefore a Europeanization—is an ethnocentric pretension and, in the long run, provincial. However, if it is accepted that the concept of modernity refers solely to rationality, science, technology, and so on, the question that we would be posing to historical experience would not be different than the one proposed by European ethnocentrism. The debate would consist just in the dispute for the originality and exclusivity of the ownership of the phenomenon thus called modernity, and consequently everything would remain in the same terrain and according to the same perspective of Eurocentrism.

There is, however, a set of elements that point to a different concept of modernity that gives an account of a historical process specific to the current world-system. The previous references and traits of the concept of modernity are not absent, obviously. But they belong to a universe of social relations, both in its material and intersubjective dimensions, whose central question and consequently its central field conflict, is human social liberation as a historical interest of society. In this article, I will limit myself to advancing, in a brief and schematic manner, some propositions to clarify these issues.[18]

In the first place, the current model of global power is the first effectively global one in world history in several specific senses. First, it is the first where in each sphere of social existence all historically known forms of control of respective social relations are articulated, configuring in each area only one structure with systematic relations between its components and, by the same means, its whole. Second, it is the first model where each structure of each sphere of social existence is under the hegemony of an institution produced within the process of formation and development of that same model of power. Thus, in the control of labor and its resources and products, it is the capitalist enterprise; in the control of sex and its resources and products, it is the bourgeois family; in the control of authority and its resources and products, it is the nation-state; and in the control of intersubjectivity, it is Eurocentrism.[19] Third, each one of those institutions exists in a relation of interdependence with each one of the others. Therefore, the model of power is configured as a system.[20] Fourth and finally, this model of global power is the first that covers the entire planet's population.

In this specific sense, humanity in its totality constitutes today the first historically known global world-system, not only a world, as were the Chinese, Hindu, Egyptian, Hellenic-Roman, Aztec-Mayan, and Tawantinsuyan worlds. None of those worlds had in common but one colonial/imperial dominant. And though it is sort of common sense in the Eurocentric vision, it is by no means certain that all the peoples incorporated into one of those worlds would have had in common a basic perspective on the relation between that which is human and the rest of the universe. The colonial dominators of each one of those worlds did not have the conditions or, probably, the interest for homogenizing the basic forms of social existence for all the populations under their dominion. On the other hand, the modern world-system that began to form with the colonization of America has in common three central elements that affect the quotidian life of the totality of the global population: the coloniality of power, capitalism, and Eurocentrism. Of course, this model of power or any other can mean that historical-structural heterogeneity has been eradicated within its dominions. Its globality means that there is a basic level of common social practices and a central sphere of common value orientation for the entire world. Consequently, the hegemonic institutions of each province of social existence are universal to the population of the world as intersubjective models, as illustrated by the nation-state, the bourgeois family, the capitalist corporation, and the Eurocentric rationality.

Therefore, whatever it may be that the term "modernity" names today, it involves the totality of the global population and all the history of the last five hundred years, all the worlds or former worlds articulated in the global model of power, each differentiated or differentiable segment constituted together with (as part of) the historical redefinition or reconstitution of each segment for its incorporation to the new and common model of global power. Therefore, it is also an articulation of many rationalities. However, since the model depicts a new and different history with specific experiences, the questions that this history raises cannot be investigated, much less contested, within the Eurocentric concept of modernity. For this reason, to say that modernity is a purely European phenomenon or one that occurs in all cultures would now have an impossible meaning. Modernity is about something new and different, something specific to this model of global power. If one must preserve the name, one must also mean another modernity.

The central question that interests us here is the following: What is really new with respect to modernity? And by this I mean not only what develops and redefines experiences, tendencies, and processes of other worlds but also what was produced in the present model of global power's own history. Enrique Dussel has proposed the category "transmodernity" as an alternative to the Eurocentric pretension that Europe is the original producer of modernity.[21] According to this proposal, the constitution of the individual differentiated ego is what began with American colonization and is the mark of modernity, but it has a place in not only Europe but also the entire world that American settlement configured. Dussel hits the mark in refusing one of the favorite myths of Eurocentrism. But it is not certain that the individual differentiated ego is a phenomenon belonging exclusively to the period initiated with America. There is, of course, an umbilical relation between the historical processes that were generated and that began with America and the changes in subjectivity or, better said, the intersubjectivity of all the peoples who were integrated into the new model of global power. And those changes brought the constitution of a new intersubjectivity not only individually but collectively as well. This is therefore a new phenomenon that entered in history with America and in that sense is part of modernity. But whatever they might have been, those changes were not constituted from the individual (nor from the collective) subjectivity of a preexisting world. Or, to use an old image, those changes are born not like Pallas Athena from the head of Zeus but instead are the subjective or intersubjective expression of what the peoples of the world are doing at that moment.

From this perspective, it is necessary to admit that the colonization of America, its immediate consequences in the global market, and the formation of a new model of global power are a truly tremendous historical change and that they affect not only Europe but also the entire globe. This is not a change in a known world that merely altered some of its traits. It is a change in the world as such. This is, without doubt, the founding element of the new subjectivity: the perception of historical change. It is this element that unleashed the process of the constitution of a new perspective about time and about history. The perception of change brings about a new idea of the future, since it is the only territory of time where the changes can occur. The future is an open temporal territory. Time can be new and so not merely the extension of the past. And in this way history can be perceived now not only as something that happens, something natural or produced by divine decisions or mysteries as destiny, but also as something that can be produced by the action of people, by their calculations, their intention, their decisions, and therefore as something that can be designed and, consequently, can have meaning.[22]

With America, an entire universe of new material relations and intersubjectivities was initiated. It is pertinent to admit that the concept of modernity does not refer only to what happens with subjectivity (despite all the tremendous importance of that process), to the individual ego, and to a new universe of intersubjective relations between individuals and the peoples integrated into the new world-system and its specific model of global power. The concept of modernity accounts equally for the changes in the material dimensions of social relations (i.e., world capitalism, coloniality of power). That is to say, the changes that occur on all levels of social existence and therefore happen to their individual members are the same in their material and intersubjective dimensions. And since "modernity" is about processes that were initiated with the emergence of America, of a new model of global power (the first world-system), and of the integration of all the peoples of the globe in that process, it is also essential to admit that it is about an entire historical period. In other words, starting with America, a new space/time was constituted materially and subjectively: this is what the concept of modernity names.

Nevertheless, it was decisive for the process of modernity that the hegemonic center of the world would be localized in the north-central zones of Western Europe. That process helps to explain why the center of intellectual conceptualization will be localized in Western Europe as well and why that version acquired global hegemony. The same process helps, equally, to explain the coloniality of power that will play a part of the first order in the Eurocentric elaboration of modernity. This last point is not very difficult to perceive if we bear in mind what has been shown just above: the way in which the coloniality of power is tied to the concentration in Europe of capital, wages, the market of capital, and, finally, the society and culture associated with those determinations. In this sense, modernity was also colonial from its point of departure. This helps explain why the global process of modernization had a much more direct and immediate impact in Europe.

In fact, as experience and as idea, the new social practices involved in the model of global, capitalist power, the concentration of capital and wages, the new market for capital associated with the new perspective on time and on history, and the centrality of the question of historical change in that perspective require on one hand the desacralization of hierarchies and authorities, both in the material dimension of social relations and in its intersubjectivity, and on the other hand the desacralization, change, or dismantlement of the corresponding structures and institutions. The new individuation of subjectivity only acquires its meaning in this context, because from it stems the necessity for an individual inner forum in order to think, doubt, and choose, in short, the individual liberty against fixed social ascriptions and, consequently, the necessity for social equality among individuals.

Capitalist determinations, however, required also (and in the same historical movement) that material and intersubjective social processes could not have a place except within social relations of exploitation and domination. For the controllers of power, the control of capital and the market were and are what decides the ends, the means, and the limits of the process. The market is the foundation but also the limit of possible social equality among people. For those exploited by capital and in general those dominated by the model of power, modernity generates a horizon of liberation for people of every relation, structure, and institution linked to domination and exploitation but also the social conditions in order to advance toward the direction of that horizon. Modernity is, then, also a question of conflicting social interests. One of these interests is the continued democratization of social existence. In this sense, every concept of modernity is necessarily ambiguous and contradictory.[23]

It is precisely in the contradictions and ambiguities of modernity that the history of these processes so clearly differentiates Western Europe from the rest of the world, as it is clear in Latin America. In Western Europe, the concentration of the wage-capital relation is the principal axis of the tendencies for social classification and the correspondent structure of power. Economic structures and social classification underlay the confrontations with the old order, with empire, with the papacy during the period of so-called competitive capital. These conflicts made it possible for nondominant sectors of capital as well as the exploited to find better conditions to negotiate their place in the structure of power and in selling their labor power. It also opens the conditions for a specifically bourgeois secularization of culture and subjectivity. Liberalism is one of the clear expressions of this material and subjective context of Western European society. However, in the rest of the world and in Latin America in particular, the most extended forms of labor control are nonwaged (although for the benefit of global capital), which implies that the relations of exploitation and domination have a colonial character. Political independence at the beginning of the nineteenth century was accompanied in the majority of the new countries by the stagnation and recession of the most advanced sectors of the capitalist economy and therefore by the strengthening of the colonial character of social and political domination under formally independent states. The Eurocentrification of colonial/modern capitalism was in this sense decisive for the different destinies of the process of modernity between Europe and the rest of the world.[24]

Coloniality of Power and Eurocentrism

The intellectual conceptualization of the process of modernity put together a perspective of knowledge and a mode of knowledge making that gives a very tight account of the character of the global model of power: colonial/modern, capitalist, and Eurocentered. This perspective and concrete mode of knowledge making is Eurocentrism.[25]

Eurocentrism is, as used here, the name of a perspective of knowledge whose systematic formation began in Western Europe before the middle of the seventeenth century, although some of its roots are, without doubt, much older. In the following centuries this perspective was made globally hegemonic, traveling the same course as the dominion of the European bourgeois class. Its constitution was associated with the specific bourgeois secularization of European thought and with the experiences and necessities of the global model of capitalist (colonial/modern) and Eurocentered power established since the colonization of America.

This category of Eurocentrism does not involve all of the knowledge of history of all of Europe or Western Europe in particular. It does not refer to all the modes of knowledge of all Europeans and all epochs. It is instead a specific rationality or perspective of knowledge that was made globally hegemonic, colonizing and overcoming other previous or different conceptual formations and their respective concrete knowledges, as much in Europe as in the rest of the world. In the framework of this essay I propose to discuss some of these issues more directly related to the experience of Latin America, but obviously, they do not refer only to Latin America.

CAPITAL AND CAPITALISM

First, the theory of history as a linear sequence of universally valid events needs to be reopened in relation to America as a major question in the social-scientific debate, more so when such a concept of history is applied to labor, and the control of labor conceptualized as modes of production in the sequence precapitalism-capitalism. From the Eurocentric point of view, reciprocity, slavery, serfdom, and independent commodity production are all perceived as a historical sequence prior to commodification of the labor force. They are precapital. And they are considered not only different but also radically incompatible with capital. The fact is, however, that in America they did not emerge in a linear historical sequence; none of them was a mere extension of the old precapitalist form, nor were they incompatible with capital.

Slavery, in America, was deliberately established and organized as a commodity in order to produce goods for the world market and to serve the purposes and needs of capitalism. Likewise, the serfdom imposed on Indians, including the redefinition of the institutions of reciprocity, was organized to serve the same ends: to produce merchandise for the global market. Independent commodity production was established and expanded for the same purposes. This means that all the forms of labor and control of labor were not only simultaneously performed in America but were also articulated around the axis of capital and the global market. Consequently, all of these forms of labor were part of a new model of organization and labor control. Together these forms of labor configured a new economic system: capitalism.

Capital, as a social relation based on the commodification of the labor force, was probably born in some moment around the eleventh or twelfth century in some place in the southern regions of the Iberian or Italian penin-sulas or both and, for known reasons, in the Islamic world.[26] Capital is thus much older than America. But before the emergence of America, it was no-where structurally articulated with all the other forms of organization and control of the labor force and labor, nor was it predominant over any of them. Only with America could capital consolidate and obtain global predomi-nance, becoming precisely the axis around which all forms of labor were ar-ticulated to satisfy the ends of the world market, configuring a new pattern of global control on labor and its resources and products: world capitalism. Therefore, capitalism as a system of relations of production, that is, as the heterogeneous linking of all forms of control on labor and its products under the dominance of capital, was constituted in history only with the emer-gence of America. Beginning with that historical moment, capital has always existed and continues to exist to this day as the central axis of capitalism. Never has capitalism been predominant in some other way on a global and worldwide scale, and in all probability it would not have been able to develop otherwise.

EVOLUTIONISM AND DUALISM

Parallel to the historical relations between capital and precapital, a simi-lar set of ideas was elaborated around the spatial relations between Europe and non-Europe. As I have already mentioned, the foundational myth of the Eurocentric version of modernity is the idea of the state of nature as the point of departure for the civilized course of history whose culmina-tion is European or Western civilization. From this myth originated the specifically Eurocentric evolutionist perspective of linear and unidirec-tional movement and changes in human history. Interestingly enough, this myth was associated with the racial and spatial classification of the world's population. This association produced the paradoxical amalgam of evolution and dualism, a vision that becomes meaningful only as an ex-pression of the exacerbated ethnocentrism of the recently constituted Europe; by its central and dominant place in global, colonial/modern cap-italism; by the new validity of the mystified ideas of humanity and pro-gress, dear products of the Enlightenment; and by the validity of the idea of race as the basic criterion for a universal social classification of the world's population.

The historical process is, however, very different. To start with, in the moment that the Iberians conquered, named, and colonized America (whose northern region, North America, would be colonized by the British a century later), they found a great number of different peoples, each with their own history, language, discoveries and cultural products, memory and identity. The most mature and sophisticated of them were the Aztecs, Mayas, Chimus, Aymaras, Incas, Chibchas, and so on. Three hundred years later, all of them had become merged into a single identity: Indians. This new identity was racial, colonial, and negative. The same happened with the peoples forcefully brought from Africa as slaves: Ashantis, Yorubas, Zulus, Congos, Bacongos, and others. In the span of three hundred years, all of them were Negroes or Blacks.

This resultant from the history of colonial power had, in terms of the colonial perception, two decisive implications. The first is obvious: peoples were dispossessed of their own and singular historical identities. The second is perhaps less obvious but no less decisive: their new racial identity, colonial and negative, involved the plundering of their place in the history of the cultural making of humanity. From then on there were inferior races, capable only of producing inferior cultures. The new identity also involved their relocation in the historical time constituted with America first and with Europe later: from then on they were the past. In other words, the model of power based on coloniality also involved a cognitive model, a new perspective of knowledge within which non-Europe was the past and because of that inferior if not always primitive.

On the other hand, America was the first modern and global geocultural identity. Europe was the second and was constituted because of America, not the inverse. The constitution of Europe as a new historic entity/identity was made possible in the first place through the free labor of the American Indians, Blacks, and mestizos, with their advanced technology in mining and agriculture and with their products such as gold, silver, potatoes, tomatoes, and tobacco.[27] It was on this foundation that a region was configured as the site of control of the Atlantic routes, which became in turn and for this very reason the decisive routes of the world market. This region did not delay in emerging as Europe. So, Europe and America mutually created themselves as the historical and the first two new geocultural identities of the modern world.

However, the Europeans persuaded themselves, from the middle of the seventeenth century but above all during the eighteenth century, that in some way they had auto-fashioned themselves as a civilization, at the margin of history initiated with America, culminating in an independent line that began with Greece as the only original source. Furthermore, they concluded that they were naturally (i.e., racially) superior to the rest of the world, since they had conquered everyone and had imposed their dominance on them.

The confrontation between the historical experience and the Eurocentric perspective on knowledge makes it possible to underline some of the more important elements of Eurocentrism: (a) a peculiar articulation between dualism (capital-precapital, Europe–non-Europe, primitive-civilized, traditional-modern, etc.) and a linear, one-directional evolutionism from some state of nature to modern European society; (b) the naturalization of the cultural differences between human groups by means of their codification with the idea of race; and (c) the distorted-temporal relocation of all those differences by relocating non-Europeans in the past. All these intellectual operations are clearly interdependent, and they could not have been cultivated and developed without the coloniality of power.

HOMOGENEITY/CONTINUITY AND HETEROGENEITY/DISCONTINUITY

As it is visible now, the radical crisis that the Eurocentric perspective of knowledge is undergoing opens up a field full of questions. I will discuss two of them. First is the idea of historical change as a process or moment in which an entity or unity is transformed in a continuous, homogenous, and complete way into something else and absolutely abandons the scene of history. This process allows for another equivalent entity to occupy the space and in such a way that everything continues in a sequential chain. Otherwise, the idea of history as a linear and one-directional evolution would not have meaning or place. Second is that such an idea implies that each differentiated unity (for example, "economy/society," or "mode of production" in the case of labor control of capital or slavery or "race/civilization" in the case of human groups) subjected to the historical change is a homogeneous entity/identity. Even more, they are each perceived as structures of homogeneous elements related in a continuous and systemic (which is distinct from systematic) manner.

Historical experience shows, however, that global capitalism is far from being an homogeneous and continuous totality. On the contrary, as the historical experience of America demonstrates, the pattern of global power that is known as capitalism is, fundamentally, a structure of heterogeneous elements as much in terms of forms of control of labor-resources-products (or relations of production) as in terms of the peoples and histories articulated in it. Consequently, such elements are connected between themselves and with the totality by means that are heterogeneous and discontinuous, including conflict. And each of these elements is configured in the same way.

So, any relation of production (as any other entity or unity) is in itself a heterogeneous structure, especially capital, since all the stages and historic forms of the production of value and the appropriation of surplus value are simultaneously active and work together in a complex network for transferring value and surplus value. Take, for example, primitive accumulation, absolute and relative surplus value, extensive or intensive (or, in other nomenclature, competitive) capital, monopoly capital, transnational or global capital (or pre-Fordist capital), Fordist capital, manual or labor-intensive capital, capital-intensive value, information-intensive value, and so on. The same logic was at work with respect to race, since so many diverse and heterogeneous peoples, with heterogeneous histories and historic tendencies of movement and change, were united under only one racial heading, such as American "Indians" or "Blacks."

The heterogeneity that I am talking about is not simply structural, based in the relations between contemporaneous elements. Since diverse and heterogeneous histories of this type were articulated in a single structure of power, it is pertinent to acknowledge the historical-structural character of this heterogeneity. Consequently, the process of change of capitalist totality cannot, in any way, be a homogeneous and continuous transformation of either the entire system or each one of its constituent parts. Nor could that totality completely and homogeneously disappear from the scene of history and be replaced by any equivalent. Historical change cannot be linear, one-directional, sequential, or total. The system, or the specific pattern of structural articulation, could be dismantled; however, each one or some of its elements can and will have to be rearticulated in some other structural model, as happened with some components of the precolonial model of power in, for instance, Tawantinsuyu.[28]

THE NEW DUALISM

Finally, for the sake of my argument, it is pertinent to revisit the conceptual relations between the body and the nonbody in the Eurocentric perspective because of its importance both in the Eurocentric mode of knowledge making and to the fact that modern dualism has close relations with race and gender. My aim here is to connect a well-known problematic with the coloniality of power.

The differentiation between body and nonbody in human experience is virtually universal in the history of humanity. It is also common to all historically known "cultures" or "civilizations," part of the copresence of both as inseparable dimensions of humanness. The process of the separation of these two elements (body and nonbody) of the human being is part of the long history of the Christian world founded on the idea of the primacy of the soul above the body. But the history of this point in particular shows a long and unresolved ambivalence of Christian theology. The soul is the privileged object of salvation, but in the end the body is resurrected as the culmination of salvation. The primacy of the soul was emphasized, perhaps exasperated, during the culture of the repression of Christianity, as resulted from the conflicts with Muslims and Jews in the fifteenth and sixteenth centuries during the peak of the Inquisition. And because the body was the basic object of repression, the soul could appear almost separated from the intersubjective relations at the interior of the Christian world. But this issue was not systematically theorized, discussed, and elaborated until Descartes's writing (1963–1967) culminated in the process of bourgeois secularization of Christian thought.[29]

With Descartes, the mutation of the ancient dualist approach to the body and the nonbody took place.[30] What in each stage of the human being was a permanent copresence of both elements, with Descartes came a radical separation between reason/subject and body. Reason was not only a secularization of the idea of the soul in the theological sense but also a mutation into a new entity, the reason/subject, the only entity capable of rational knowledge. The body was and could be nothing but an object of knowledge. From this point of view, the human being is, par excellence, a being gifted with reason, and this gift was conceived as localized exclusively in the soul. Thus, the body, by definition incapable of reason, does not have anything that meets reason/subject. The radical separation produced between reason/subject and body and their relations should be seen only as relations between the human subject/reason and the human body/nature, or between spirit and nature. In this way, in Eurocentric rationality the body was fixed as object of knowledge, outside of the environment of subject/reason.

Without this objectification of the body as nature, its expulsion from the sphere of the spirit (and this is my strong thesis), the "scientific" theorization of the problem of race (as in the case of the Comte de Gobineau [1853–57] during the nineteenth century) would have hardly been possible. From the Eurocentric perspective, certain races are condemned as inferior for not being rational subjects. They are objects of study, consequently bodies closer to nature. In a sense, they became domitable and exploitable. According to the myth of the state of nature and the chain of the civilizing process that culminates in European civilization, some races—Blacks, American Indians, and yellows—are closer to nature than whites.[31] It was only within this peculiar perspective that non-European peoples were considered as an object of knowledge and domination/exploitation by Europeans virtually to the end of World War II.

This new and radical dualism affected not only the racial relations of domination but also the older sexual relations of domination. Women, especially the women of inferior races ("women of color"), remained stereotyped together with the rest of the bodies, and their place was all the more inferior for their race so that they were considered much closer to nature or (as was the case with Black slaves) directly within nature. It is probable (although the question remains to be investigated) that the new idea of gender has been elaborated after the new and radical dualism of the Eurocentric cognitive perspective in the articulation of the coloniality of power.

Furthermore, the new radical dualism was amalgamated in the eighteenth century with the new mystified ideas of "progress" and of the state of nature in the human trajectory: the foundational myths of the Eurocentric version of modernity. The peculiar dualist/evolutionist historical perspective was linked to the foundational myths. Thus, all non-Europeans could be considered as pre-European and at the same time displaced on a certain historical chain from the primitive to the civilized, from the rational to the irrational, from the traditional to the modern, from the magic-mythic to the scientific, in other words, from the non-European/pre-European to something that in time will be Europeanized or modernized. Without considering the entire experience of colonialism and coloniality, this intellectual trademark as well as the long-lasting global hegemony of Eurocentrism would hardly be explicable. The necessities of capital as such alone do not exhaust, could not exhaust, the explanation of the character and trajectory of this perspective of knowledge.

Eurocentrism and Historical Experience in Latin America

The Eurocentric perspective of knowledge operates as a mirror that distorts what it reflects, as we can see in the Latin American historical experience. That is to say, what we Latin Americans find in that mirror is not completely chimerical, since we possess so many and such important historically European traits in many material and intersubjective aspects. But at the same time, we are profoundly different. Consequently, when we look in our Eurocentric mirror, the image that we see is not just composite but also necessarily partial and distorted. Here the tragedy is that we have all been led, knowingly or not, wanting it or not, to see and accept that image as our own and as belonging to us alone. In this way, we continue being what we are not. And as a result, we can never identify our true problems, much less resolve them, except in a partial and distorted way.

EUROCENTRISM AND THE "NATIONAL QUESTION":
THE NATION-STATE

One of the clearest examples of this tragedy of equivocations in Latin America is the history of the so-called national question: the problem of the modern nation-state in Latin America. I will attempt here to review some basic issues of the national question in relation to Eurocentrism and the coloniality of power, which, as far as I know, is a perspective that has not been fully explored.[32] State formations in Europe and in the Americas are linked and distinguished by coloniality of power.

Nations and states are an old phenomenon. However, what is currently called the "modern" nation-state is a very specific experience. It is a society where, within a space of domination, power is organized with some important degree of democratic relations (as democratic as possible in a power structure), basically in the control of labor, resources, products, and public authority. The society is nationalized because democratized, and therefore the character of the state is as national and as democratic as the power existing within such a space of domination. Thus, a modern nation-state involves the modern institutions of citizenship and political democracy but only in the way in which citizenship can function as legal, civil, and political equality for socially unequal people.[33]

A nation-state is a sort of individualized society between others. Therefore, its members can feel it as an identity. However, societies are power structures. Power articulates forms of dispersed and diverse social existence into one totality, one society. Every power structure always involves, partially or totally, the imposition by some (usually a particular small group) over the rest. Therefore, every possible nation-state is a structure of power in the same way in which it is a product of power. It is a structure of power by the ways in which the following elements have been articulated: (a) the disputes over the control of labor and its resources and products, (b) sex and its resources and products, (c) authority and its specific violence, and (d) intersubjectivity and knowledge.

Nevertheless, if a modern nation-state can be expressed by its members as an identity, it is not only because it can be imagined as a community.[34] The members need to have something real in common. And this, in all modern nation-states, is a more or less democratic participation in the distribution of the control of power. This is the specific manner of homogenizing people in the modern nation-state. Every homogenization in the modern nation-state is, of course, partial and temporary and consists of the common democratic participation in the generation and management of the institutions of public authority and its specific mechanisms of violence. This authority is exercised in every sphere of social existence linked to the state and thus is accepted as explicitly political. But such a sphere could not be democratic (involving people placed in unequal relations of power as legally and civilly equal citizens) if the social relations in all of the other spheres of social existence are radically undemocratic or antidemocratic.[35]

Since every nation-state is a structure of power, this implies that the power has been configured along a very specific process. The process always begins with centralized political power over a territory and its population (or a space of domination), because the process of possible nationalization can occur only in a given space, along a prolonged period of time, with the precise space being more or less stable for a long period. As a result, nationalization requires a stable and centralized political power. This space is, in this sense, necessarily a space of domination disputed and victoriously guarded against rivals.

In Europe, the process that brought the formation of structures of power later configured as the modern nation-state began, on one hand, with the emergence of some small political nuclei that conquered their space of domination and imposed themselves over the diverse and heterogeneous peoples, identities, and states that inhabited it. In this way the nation-state began as a process of colonization of some peoples over others who were, in this sense, foreigners, and therefore the nation-state depended on the organization of one centralized state over a conquered space of domination. In some particular cases as in Spain, which owes much to the "conquest" of America and its enormous and free resources, the process included the expulsion of some groups, such as the Muslims and Jews, considered to be undesirable foreigners. This was the first experience of ethnic cleansing exercising the coloniality of power in the modern period and was followed by the imposition of the "certificate of purity of blood."[36] On the other hand, that process of state centralization was parallel to the imposition of imperial colonial domination that began with the colonization of America, which means that the first European centralized states emerged simultaneously with the formation of the colonial empires.

The process has a twofold historical movement, then. It began as an internal colonization of peoples with different identities who inhabited the same territories as the colonizers. Those territories were converted into spaces of internal domination located in the same spaces of the future nation-states. The process continued, simultaneously carrying on an imperial or external colonization of peoples who not only had different identities than those of the colonizers but also inhabited territories that were not considered spaces of internal domination of the colonizers. That is to say, the external colonized peoples were not inhabiting the same territories of the future nation-state of the colonizers.

If we look back from our present historical perspective to what happened with the first centralized European states, to their spaces of domination of peoples and territories and their respective processes of nationalization, we will see that the differences are very visible. The existence of a strong central state was not sufficient to produce a process of relative homogenization of a previously diverse and heterogeneous population in order to create a common identity and a strong and long-lasting loyalty to that identity. Among these cases, France was probably the most successful, just as Spain was the least successful.

Why France and not Spain? In its beginnings, Spain was much richer and more powerful than its peers. However, after the expulsion of the Muslims and Jews, Spain stopped being productive and prosperous and became a conveyor belt for moving the resources of America to the emergent centers of financial and commercial capital. At the same time, after the violent and successful attack against the autonomy of the rural communities and cities and villages, Spain remained trapped in a feudal-like seignorial structure of power under the authority of a repressive and corrupt monarchy and church. The Spanish monarchy chose, moreover, a bellicose politics in search of an expansion of its royal power in Europe instead of hegemony over the world market and commercial and finance capital, as England and France would later do. All of the fights to force the controllers of power to allow or negotiate some democratization of society and the state were defeated, notably the liberal revolution of 1810–1812. In this way the combined internal colonization and aristocratic patterns of political and social power proved to be fatal for the nationalization of Spanish society and state, insofar as this type of power proved to be incapable of sustaining any resulting advantage of its rich and vast imperial colonialism. It proved, equally, that it was a very powerful obstacle to every democratizing process, and not only within the space of its own domination.

On the contrary, in France, through the French Revolution's radical democratization of social and political relations, the previous internal colonization evolved toward an effective, although not complete, "frenchification" of the peoples who inhabited French territory, originally so diverse and historical-structurally heterogeneous, just as those under Spanish domination. The French Basques, for example, are in the first place French, just like the Navarrese. Not so in Spain.

In each one of the cases of successful nationalization of societies and states in Europe, the experience was the same: a considerable process of democratization of society was the basic condition for the nationalization of that society and of the political organization of a modern nation-state. In fact, there is no known exception to this historical trajectory of the process that drives the formation of the nation-state.

THE NATION-STATE IN AMERICA: THE UNITED STATES

If we examine the experience of America in its Spanish and Anglo areas, equivalent factors can be recognized. In the Anglo-American area, the colonial occupation of territory was violent from the start. But before independence, known in the United States as the American Revolution, the occupied territory was very small. The Indians did not inhabit occupied territory; they were not colonized. Therefore, the diverse Indigenous peoples were formally recognized as nations, and international commercial relations were practiced with them, including the formation of military alliances in the wars between English and French colonists. Indians were not incorporated into the space of Anglo-American colonial domination. Thus, when the history of the new nation-state called the United States of America began, Indians were excluded from that new society and were considered foreigners. Later, they were dispossessed of their lands and were almost exterminated. Only then were the survivors imprisoned in North American society as a colonized race. In the beginning, then, colonial/racial relations existed only between whites and Blacks. This last group was fundamental for the economy of the colonial society, just as during the first long moment of the new nation. However, Blacks were a relatively limited demographic minority, while whites composed the large majority.

At the foundation of the United States as an independent country, the process of the constitution of a new model of power went together with the configuration of the nation-state. Despite the colonial relation of domination between whites and Blacks and the colonial extermination of the Indigenous population, we must admit, given the overwhelming majority of whites, that the new nation-state was genuinely representative of the greater part of the population. The social whiteness of North American society included the millions of European immigrants arriving in the second half of the nineteenth century. Furthermore, the conquest of Indigenous territories resulted in the abundance of the offer of a basic resource of production: land. Therefore, the appropriation of land could be concentrated in a few large states while, at the same time, distributed in a vast proportion of middling and small properties. Through these mechanisms of land distribution, the whites found themselves in a position to exercise a notably democratic participation in the generation and management of public authority. The coloniality of the new model of power was not cancelled, however, since American Indians and Blacks could not have a place at all in the control of the resources of production or in the institutions and mechanisms of public authority.

About halfway through the nineteenth century, Tocqueville observed that in the United States, people of such diverse cultural, ethnic, and national origins were all incorporated into something that seemed like a machine for national reidentification; they rapidly became US citizens and acquired a new national identity while preserving for some time their original identities.[37] Tocqueville found that the basic mechanism for this process of nationalization was the opening of democratic participation in political life for all recently arrived immigrants. They were brought toward an intense political participation, although with the choice to participate or not. But Tocqueville also saw that two specific groups were not allowed participation in political life: Blacks and Indians. This discrimination was the limit of the impressive and massive process of modern nation-state formation in the young republic of the United States of America. Tocqueville did not neglect to advise that unless social and political discrimination were to be eliminated, the process of national construction would be limited. A century later another European, Gunnar Myrdall, saw these same limitations in the national process of the United States when the source of immigration changed and immigrants were no longer white Europeans but, for the most part, nonwhites from Latin America and Asia.[38] The colonial relations of the whites with the new immigrants introduced a new risk for the reproduction of the nation. Without doubt, those risks are increasing this very day insofar as the old myth of the melting pot has been forcefully abandoned and racism tends to be newly sharpened and violent.

In sum, the coloniality of the relations of domination/exploitation/conflict between whites and nonwhites was not, at the moment of the constitution of a new independent state, sufficiently powerful to impede the relative, although real and important, democratization of the control of the means of production and of the state. At the beginning control rested only among the whites, true, but with enough vigor so that nonwhites could claim it later as well. The entire power structure could be configured in the trajectory and orientation of reproducing and broadening the democratic foundations of the nation-state. It is this trajectory to which, undoubtedly, the idea of the American Revolution refers.

LATIN AMERICA: THE SOUTHERN CONE AND THE WHITE MAJORITY

At first glance, the situation in the countries of the so-called Southern Cone of Latin America (Argentina, Chile, and Uruguay) was similar to what happened in the United States. Indians, for the most part, were not integrated into colonial society insofar as they had more or less the same social and cultural structure of the North American Indians. Socially, both groups were not available to become exploited workers, not condemnable to forced labor for the colonists. In these three countries, the Black slaves were also a minority during the colonial period, in contrast with other regions dominated by the Spanish or the Portuguese. After independence, the dominants in the countries of the Southern Cone, as was the case in the United States, considered the conquest of the territories that the Indigenous peoples populated as well as the extermination of these inhabitants necessary as an expeditious form of homogenizing the national population and facilitating the process of constituting a modern nation-state *a la europea*. In Argentina and Uruguay this was done in the nineteenth century and in Chile during the first three decades of the twentieth century. These countries also attracted millions of European immigrants, consolidating, in appearance, the whiteness of the societies of Argentina, Uruguay, and Chile and the process of homogenization.

Land distribution was a basic difference in those countries, especially in Argentina, in comparison with the case of North America. While in the United States the distribution of land happened in a less concentrated way over a long period, in Argentina the extreme concentration of land possession, particularly in lands taken from Indigenous peoples, made impossible any type of democratic social relations among the whites themselves. Instead of a democratic society capable of representing and politically organizing into a democratic state, what was constituted was an oligarchic society and state, only partially dismantled after World War II. In the Argentinean case, these determinations were undoubtedly associated with the fact that colonial society, above all on the Atlantic coast (which became hegemonic over the rest), was lightly developed, and therefore its recognition as seat of a viceroyalty came only in the second half of the eighteenth century. Its rapid transformation in the last quarter of the eighteenth century as one of the more prosperous areas in the world market was one of the main forces that drove a massive migration from southern, eastern, and central Europe in the following century. But this migratory population did not find in Argentina a society with a sufficiently dense and stable structure, history, and identity to incorporate and identify themselves with it, as occurred in the United States. At the end of the nineteenth century, immigrants from Europe comprised more than 80 percent of Buenos Aires's population. They did not immediately enforce the national identity, instead preferring their own European cultural differences, while at the same time explicitly rejecting the identity associated with Latin America's heritage and, in particular, any relationship with the Indigenous population.[39]

The concentration of land was somewhat less strong in Chile and in Uruguay. In these two countries, especially in Chile, the number of European immigrants was fewer. But overall, they found a society, a state, and an identity already sufficiently densely constituted, to which they incorporated and identified themselves much sooner and more completely than in Argentina. In the case of Chile, territorial expansion at the expense of Bolivia's and Peru's national frontiers allowed the Chilean bourgeoisie the control of resources whose importance has defined, from then on, the country's history: saltpeter, first, and copper a little later. From the middle of the nineteenth century, the pampas saltpeter miners formed the first major contingent of salaried workers in Latin America; later, in copper mines, the backbone of the old republic's workers' social and political organizations was formed. The profits distributed between the British and Chilean bourgeoisie allowed the push toward commercial agriculture and urban commercial economy. New classes of salaried urbanites and a relatively large middle class came together with the modernization of an important part of the landed and commercial bourgeoisie. These conditions made it possible for the workers and the middle class to negotiate the conditions of domination, exploitation, and conflict with some success and to struggle for democracy in the conditions of capitalism between 1930 and 1935. In this way, the power could be configured as a modern nation-state, of whites, of course. The Indians, a scanty minority of survivors inhabiting the poorest and most inhospitable lands in the country, were excluded from such nation-states. Until recently they were sociologically invisible; they are not so much today as they begin to mobilize in defense of these same lands that are at risk of being lost in the face of global capital.

The process of the racial homogenization of a society's members, imagined from a Eurocentric perspective as one characteristic and condition of modern nation-states, was carried out in the countries of the Southern Cone not by means of the decolonization of social and political relations among the diverse sectors of the population but instead through a massive elimination of some of them (Indians) and the exclusion of others (Blacks and mestizos). Homogenization was achieved not by means of the fundamental democratization of social and political relations but instead by the exclusion of a significant part of the population, one that since the sixteenth century had been racially classified and marginalized from citizenship and democracy. Given these original conditions, democracy and the nation-state could not be stable and firmly constituted. The political history of these countries, especially from the end of the 1960s until today, cannot be explained at the margins of these determinations.[40]

INDIAN, BLACK, AND MESTIZO MAJORITY: THE IMPOSSIBLE "MODERN NATION-STATE"

After the defeat of Túpac Amaru and of the Haitian Revolution, only Mexico (since 1910) and Bolivia (since 1952) came along the road of social decolonization through a revolutionary process, during which the decolonization of power was able to gain substantial ground before being contained and defeated. At the beginning of independence, principally in those countries that were demographically and territorially extensive at the beginning of the nineteenth century, approximately 90 percent of the total population was composed of American Indians, Blacks, and mestizos. However, in all those countries, those people were denied all possible participation in decisions about social and political organization during the process of organizing the new state. The small white minority that assumed control of those states sought the advantage of being free from the legislation of the Spanish Crown, which formally ordered the protection of colonized peoples or races. From then on the white minority included the imposition of new colonial tributes on the Indians, even while maintaining the slavery of Blacks for many decades. Of course, this dominant minority was now at liberty to expand its ownership of the land at the expense of the territories reserved for Indians by the Spanish Crown's regulations. In the case of Brazil, Blacks were slaves, and Indians from the Amazon were foreigners to the new state.

Haiti was an exceptional case in that it produced a national, social, and racial revolution—a real and global decolonization of power—in the same historical movement. Repeated military interventions by the United States brought about its defeat. The other potentially national process in Latin America took place in the Viceroyalty of Peru in 1780, under the leadership of Túpac Amaru II, but was defeated quickly. From then on, the dominant group in all the rest of the Iberian colonies successfully avoided social decolonization while fighting to gain independent status.

Such new states could not be considered nations unless it could be admitted that the small minority of colonizers in control were genuinely nationally representative of the entire colonized population. The societies founded in colonial domination of American Blacks, Indians, and mestizos could not be considered nations, much less democratic. This situation presents an apparent paradox: independent states of colonial societies.[41] The paradox is only partial and superficial, however, when we observe more carefully the social interests of the dominant groups in those colonial societies and their independent states.

In Anglo-American colonial society, since Indians were a foreign people living outside the confines of colonial society, Indian serfdom was not as extensive as in Ibero-America. Indentured servants brought from Great Britain were not legally serfs, and after independence they were not indentured for very long. Black slaves were very important to the economy, but they were a demographic minority. And from the beginning of independence, economic productivity was achieved in great part by waged laborers and independent producers. During the colonial period in Chile, Indian serfdom was restricted, since local American Indian servants were a small minority. Black slaves, despite being more important for the economy, were also a small minority. For these reasons, colonized racial groups were not as large a source of free labor as in the rest of the Iberian countries. Consequently, from the beginning of independence an increasing proportion of local production would have to be based on wages, a reason why the internal market was vital for the premonopoly bourgeoisie. Thus, for the dominant classes in both the United States and Chile, the local waged labor and the internal production and market were preserved and protected by external competition as the only and most important source of capitalist profits. Furthermore, the internal market had to be expanded and protected. In this sense, there were some areas of common national interest of waged laborers, independent producers, and the local bourgeois. With the limitations derived from the exclusion of Blacks and mestizos, this was a national interest for the large majority of the population of the new nation-state.

Independent States and Colonial Society: Historical-Structural Dependence

The preceding summary of nation-state formation and colonial relations in America allows us to underline that in certain Ibero-American societies, the small white minority in control of the independent states and the colonial societies could have had neither consciousness nor national interests in common with the American Indians, Blacks, and mestizos. On the contrary, their social interests were explicitly antagonistic to American Indian serfs and Black slaves, given that their privileges were made from precisely the dominance and exploitation of those peoples in such a way that there was no area of common interest between whites and nonwhites and, consequently, no common national interest for all of them. Therefore, from the point of view of the dominators, their social interests were much closer to the interests of their European peers, and consequently they were always inclined to follow the interests of the European bourgeoisie. They were, then, dependent.

They were dependent in this specific way not because they were subordinated by a greater economic or political power. By whom could they have been subordinated? Spain and Portugal were by the nineteenth century too weak and underdeveloped, unable to exercise any kind of neocolonialism like the English and French were able to do in certain African countries after the political independence of those countries. In the nineteenth century, the United States was absorbed in the conquest of Indian territory and the extermination of the Indian population, initiating its imperial expansion on parts of the Caribbean, without the capacity yet for further expanding its political or economic dominance. England tried to occupy Buenos Aires in 1806 and was defeated.

The Latin American white seigneurs, owners of political power and serfs and slaves, did not have common interests with those workers who were the overwhelming majority of the populations of those new states. Actually, they were exactly antagonistic. And while the white bourgeoisie expanded the capitalist social relation as the axis of articulation of the economy and society in Europe and the United States, the Latin American seigneurs could not accumulate abundant commercial profits to pay for a salaried labor force precisely because that went against the reproduction of their dominion. The white seigneurs' commercial profits were allotted for the ostentatious consumption of commodities produced in Europe.

The dependence of the seigneurial capitalists of the new Ibero-American nation-states had an inescapable source: the coloniality of their power led to the perception of their social interests as the same as other dominant whites in Europe and the United States. That coloniality of power itself, however, prevented them from really developing their social interests in the same direction as those of their European peers, that is, converting commercial capital (profits produced either by slavery, serfdom, or reciprocity) into industrial capital, since that involved liberating American Indian serfs and Black slaves and making them waged laborers. For obvious reasons, the colonial dominators of the new independent states, especially in South America after the crisis at the end of the eighteenth century, could not be in that configuration except as minor partners of the European bourgeoisie. When much later it was necessary to free the slaves, freedom was not a transformation of labor relations but rather a reason to substitute slaves with immigrant workers from other countries, European and Asiatic. The elimination of American Indian serfdom is very recent. There were no common social interests with colonized and exploited workers, nor was there an internal market that would have included the wage laborer, since no such internal market was in the interest of the dominators. Simply put, there was no national interest regarding seigneurial bourgeoisie.

The dependence of the seigneurial capitalists did not come from national subordination. On the contrary, this was the consequence of the community of racialized social interests with their European peers. We are addressing here the concept of historical-structural dependence, which is very different from the nationalist proposals conceptualized as external or structural dependence.[42] Subordination came much later, as a consequence of dependence and not the inverse. During the global economic crisis of the

1930s, the bourgeoisie, holding most of Latin America's commercial capital (that of Argentina, Brazil, Mexico, Chile, Uruguay, and, to a certain extent, Colombia), was forced to produce locally its conspicuous consumption of imported products. This period was the beginning of the peculiar system followed by Latin American dependent industrialization: the substitution of imported goods for ostentatious consumption (by the seigneur class and their small groups of middle-class associates) taking the place of local products intended for that same consumption. For that reason, it was not necessary to globally reorganize the local economies, to massively liberate and pay wages to serfs and slaves, to produce its own technology. Industrialization through the substitution of imports is, in Latin America, a defining case of the implications of the coloniality of power.[43]

In this sense, the process of independence for Latin American states without decolonizing society could not have been and was not a process toward the development of modern nation-states but was instead a rearticulation of the coloniality of power over new institutional bases. From then on, for almost two hundred years workers and critical intellectuals have been concerned with the attempt to advance along the road of nationalization, democratizing our societies and our states. In no Latin American country today is it possible to find a fully nationalized society or even a genuine nation-state. The national homogenization of the population could only have been achieved through a radical and global process of the democratization of society and the state. That democratization would have implied and should imply before anything else the process of decolonizing social, political, and cultural relations that maintain and reproduce racial social classification. The structure of power was and even continues to be organized on and around the colonial axis. Consequently, from the point of view of the dominant groups, the construction of the nation and above all the central state has been conceptualized and deployed against American Indians, Blacks, and mestizos. The coloniality of power still exercises its dominance in the greater part of Latin America against democracy, citizenship, the nation, and the modern nation-state.

From this perspective, four historical trajectories and ideological lines can be distinguished today in the problem of the nation-state:

1   A limited but real process of decolonization/democratization through radical revolutions, such as in Mexico and Bolivia. In Mexico, the process of the decolonization of power was slowly limited from the 1960s, until finally entering a period of crisis

at the end of the 1970s. In Bolivia the revolution was defeated in 1965.

2　A limited but real process of colonial (racial) homogenization, as in the Southern Cone (Chile, Uruguay, Argentina), by means of a massive genocide of the aboriginal population. A variant of this line is Colombia, where the original population was almost exterminated and replaced with Blacks during the colonial period.

3　An always frustrated attempt at cultural homogenization through the cultural genocide of American Indians, Blacks, and mestizos, as in Mexico, Peru, Ecuador, Guatemala, Central America, and Bolivia.

4　The imposition of an ideology of "racial democracy" that masks the true discrimination and colonial domination of Blacks, as in Brazil, Colombia, and Venezuela. It is with difficulty that someone can recognize with seriousness a true citizen of the population of African origin in those countries, although the racial tensions and conflicts are not as violent and explicit as those in South Africa and the southern United States.

These trajectories show that there is, without doubt, an element that radically impedes the development and culmination of the nationalization of society and state, insofar as it impedes their democratization, since one cannot find any historical examples where modern nation-states are not the result of a social and political democratization. What is, or could be, that element?

In the European world and therefore in the Eurocentric perspective, the formation of nation-states has been theorized—imagined, in truth—as the expression of the homogenization of the population in terms of common historic subjective experiences. "Nation" is an identity and a loyalty, especially for liberalism. At first sight, the successful cases of nationalization of societies and states in Europe seem to side with that focus. The homogenizing seemingly consists basically of the formation of a common space for identity and meaning for the population. However, this in all cases is the result of the democratization of society that can be organized and expressed in a democratic state. The pertinent question at this stage of the argument is why that has been possible in Western Europe and, with some well-known limitations, in all the world of European identity (Canada, the United States, Australia, and New Zealand, for example). Why has it not been possible in Latin America until today, even in a partial and precarious way?

To begin with, would social and political democratization have been possible, for instance in France, the classic example of the modern nation-state, if the racial factor had been included? It is very unlikely. To this very day it is easy to observe in France the national problem and the debate produced by the presence of nonwhite populations originating from France's former colonies. Obviously, it is not a matter of ethnicity, culture, or religious beliefs. It is sufficient to remember that a century earlier the Dreyfus affair showed the French capacity for discrimination, but its conclusions also demonstrated that for many French people, the identity of origin was not a requisite determinant to be a member of the French nation as long as your "color" was French. The French Jews today are more French than the children of Africans, Arabs, and Latin Americans born in France, not to mention what happened with Russian and Spanish immigrants whose children, having been born in France, are French.

This means that the coloniality of power based on the imposition of the idea of race as an instrument of domination has always been a limiting factor for constructing a nation-state based on a Eurocentric model. Whether to a lesser extent, as is the case in North America, or in a decisive way, as in Latin America, the limiting factor is visible in both cases. As I have shown, the degree of limitation depends on the proportion of colonized races within the total population and on the density of their social and cultural institutions. Because of all of this, the coloniality of power established on the idea of race should be accepted as a basic factor in the national question and the nation-state. The problem is, however, that in Latin America the Eurocentric perspective was adopted by the dominant groups as their own, leading them to impose the European model of nation-state formation for structures of power organized around colonial relations. All the same, we now find ourselves in a labyrinth where the Minotaur is always visible but with no Ariadne to show us the exit we long for.

Eurocentrism and Revolution in Latin America

A final note of this tragic disjuncture between our experience and our Eurocentric perspective of knowledge is the debate about and practice of revolutionary projects. In the twentieth century, the vast majority of the Latin American Left, adhering to historical materialism, has debated two types of revolution: bourgeois-democratic and socialist. Competing with that Left, between 1925 and 1935 the movement called "aprista" proposed an anti-imperialist revolution.[44] It was conceived as a process of purification of the character of the economy and society, eliminating feudal adherences and developing its capitalist side as well as encouraging the modernization and development of society by means of the national-state control of the principal means of production as a transition toward a socialist revolution. The major theorist of the Revolutionary Antiimperialist Popular Alliance, which made such proposals, was the Peruvian Haya de la Torre. From the end of World War II, that project has become a sort of social liberalism and has been exhausted.[45]

In a brief and schematic but not arbitrary way, the Latin American debate about the democratic-bourgeois revolution can be presented as a project in which the bourgeoisie organized the working class, peasants, and other dominated groups in order to uproot the feudal aristocrats' control of the state and organize society and the state in terms of their own interests. The central assumption of that project was that in Latin America, society is fundamentally feudal or, at the most, semifeudal, since capitalism is still incipient, marginal, and subordinate. The socialist revolution, on the other hand, is conceived as the eradication of bourgeois control of the state by the industrial working class heading a coalition of the exploited and the dominated classes in order to impose state control on the means of production and to construct a new society through the state. The assumption of that proposition is, obviously, that the economy and therefore society and the state in Latin America are basically capitalist. In its language, this implies that capital as a social relation of production is already dominant and that consequently the bourgeoisie is also dominant in society and state. It admits that there are feudal remnants and democratic-bourgeois tasks in the trajectory of the socialist revolution. In fact, the political debate of the past half century in Latin America has been anchored in whether the economy, society, and the state were feudal/semifeudal or capitalist. The majority of the Latin American Left until recently adhered to the democratic-bourgeois proposition, following all the central tenets of "real socialism," with its head in Moscow and Peking.

In order to believe that in Latin America a democratic-bourgeois revolution based on the European model is not only possible but also necessary, it is essential to recognize in America and more precisely in Latin America: (1) the sequential relation between feudalism and capitalism; (2) the historical existence of feudalism and consequently the historically antagonistic conflict between feudal aristocracy and the bourgeois; (3) a bourgeoisie interested in carrying out similar revolutionary business. We know that in China at the beginning of the 1930s, Mao proposed the idea of a new type of democratic revolution because the bourgeoisie was neither interested in nor capable of carrying out that historical mission. In this case, a coalition of exploited/dominated classes under the leadership of the working class should substitute for the bourgeoisie and undertake the new democratic revolution.

In America, however, for five hundred years capital has existed as the dominant axis of the total articulation of all historically known forms of control and exploitation of labor, thus configuring a historically structured heterogeneous model of power with discontinuous relations and conflicts among its components. In colonial America, there was not an evolutionist sequence between modes of production, there was no previous feudalism detached from and antagonistic to capital, and there was no feudal seigneur in control of the state whom a bourgeoisie urgently in need of power would have to evict by revolutionary means. If a sequence existed, it is without doubt surprising that the followers of historical materialism did not fight for an antislavery revolution prior to the antifeudal revolution, prior in turn to the anticapitalist revolution. In the greater part of this hemisphere (including the United States, Venezuela, Columbia, Brazil, the coasts of Ecuador and Peru, and all of the Caribbean), slavery has been more extensive and more powerful. But, clearly, slavery ended before the twentieth century, and the feudal seigneurs had inherited power. Isn't that true?

Therefore, an antifeudal, democratic-bourgeois revolution in the Eurocentric sense has always been a historical impossibility. The only democratic revolutions that really occurred in America (apart from the American Revolution) have been the Mexican and Bolivian popular revolutions—nationalist, anti-imperialist, anticolonial—that is, against the coloniality of power and oligarchies, against the control of the state by the seigneurial bourgeois under the protection of the imperial bourgeoisie. In most of the other countries, the process has been one of gradual and uneven purification of the social character, society, and state. Consequently, the process has always been very slow, irregular, and partial. Could it have been any other way?

All possible democratization of society in Latin America should occur in many of these countries at the same time and in the same historical movement as decolonization and as a radical redistribution of power. The reason underlying these statements is that social classes in Latin America are marked by color, any color that can be found in any country at any time. This means that the classification of people is realized in not only one sphere of power—the economy, for example—but also each and every sphere. Domination is the requisite for exploitation, and race is the most effective instrument for domination that, associated with exploitation, serves as the universal classifier in the current global model of power. In terms of the national question, only through the process of the democratization of society can the construction of a modern nation-state, with all of its implications, including citizenship and political representation, be possible and successful. But under the ongoing process of reconcentration of power at a global scale, that perspective may well not be feasible any longer, and a process of democratization of society and public authority may require some quite different institutional structure.

With respect to the Eurocentric mirage about "socialist" revolutions (as control of the state and as state control of labor/resources/product), it should be emphasized that such a perspective is founded in two radically false theoretical assumptions. The first assumption is the idea of a homogeneous capitalist society, in the sense that capital exists only as social relation and therefore that the waged industrial working class is most of the population. But we have just seen that this has never been so in either Latin America or the rest of the world and that it will most assuredly never occur. The second assumption is that socialism consists in the state control of each and every sphere of power and social existence beginning with the control of labor, because from the state a new society can be constructed. This assumption puts history, again, on its head, since even in the crude terms of historical materialism, the state, a superstructure, becomes the base of construction of society. By the same token, this assumption hides the reconcentration of the control of power, which necessarily brings total despotism of the controllers, making it appear to be radical redistribution of the control of power. But socialism, if the word still has some effective meaning, cannot be something other than the trajectory of a radical return of the control over labor/resources/product, over sex/resources/products, over authorities/institutions/violence, and over intersubjectivity/knowledge/communication to the daily lives of the people. This is what I have proposed since 1972 as the socialization of power.[46]

In 1928 José Carlos Mariátegui was, without a doubt, the first to begin to see (and not just in Latin America) that in his space/time, the social relations of power, whatever their previous character, existed and acted simultaneously and together in a single and whole structure of power. He perceived that there could not be a homogeneous unity, with continuous relations among its elements, moving itself in a continuous and systematic history. Therefore, the idea of a socialist revolution by historical necessity had to be directed against the whole of that power. Far from consisting of a new bureaucratic reconcentration of power, it could have meaning only as a redistribution among the people, in their daily lives, of the control over their conditions of social existence.[47] After Mariátegui, the debate was not taken up again in Latin America until the 1960s, and in the rest of the world it began with the worldwide defeat of the socialist camp.

In reality, each category used to characterize the Latin American political process has always been a partial and distorted way to look at this reality. That is an inevitable consequence of the Eurocentric perspective, in which a linear and one-directional evolutionism is amalgamated contradictorily with the dualist vision of history, a new and radical dualism that separates nature from society, the body from reason, that does not know what to do with the question of totality (simply denying it like the old empiricism or the new post-modernism) or understands it only in an organic or systemic way, making it thus into a distorted perspective, impossible to be used, except in error.

It is not, then, an accident that we have been defeated, for the moment, in both revolutionary projects, in America and in the entire world. What we could advance and conquer in terms of political and civil rights in a necessary redistribution of power (of which the decolonization of power is the presupposition and point of departure) is now being torn down in the process of the reconcentration of the control of power in global capitalism and of its management of the coloniality of power by the same functionaries. Consequently, it is time to learn to free ourselves from the Eurocentric mirror where our image is always, necessarily, distorted. It is time, finally, to cease being what we are not.

Translated by Michael Ennis

Notes

First published in *Nepantla: Views from South* 1, no. 3.

I want to thank Edgardo Lander and Walter Mignolo for their help in the revision of this article. Thanks also to an anonymous reviewer for useful criticisms of a previous version. Responsibility for the errors and limitations of the text is mine alone.—Aníbal Quijano

1   On the concept of the coloniality of power, see Quijano, "Colonialidad y modernidad/racionalidad."

2   Even though for the imperialist vision of the United States of America the term "America" is just another name for that country, today it is the

name of the territory that extends from Alaska in the Global North to Cape Horn in the Global South, including the Caribbean archipelago. But from 1492 until 1610, America was exclusively the time/space under Iberian (Hispanic Portuguese) colonial domination. This included, in the northern border, California, Texas, New Mexico, Florida (conquered in the nineteenth century by the United States), and the Spanish-speaking Caribbean area up to Cape Horn in the Global South, roughly the time/space of today's Latin America. The Eurocentered, capitalist, colonial/modern power emerged then and there. So, though today America is a very heterogeneous world in terms of power and culture and for descriptive purposes could be better referred to as the Americas, in regard to the history of the specific pattern of world power that is discussed here, "America" still is the proper denomination.

3   See Quijano and Wallerstein, "Americanity as a Concept, or the Americas in the Imaginary of the Modern World-System."

4   On this question and the possible antecedents to race before America, see Quijano, "Raza, etnia y nación en José Carlos Mariátegui."

5   The invention of the category of "color"—first as the most visible indication of race and later simply as its equivalent—as much as the invention of the particular category of "white" still requires a more exhaustive historical investigation. In every case, they were most probably Anglo-American inventions, since there are no traces of these categories in the chronicles and other documents from the first one hundred years of Iberian colonialism in America. For the case of Anglo-America, an extensive bibliography exists. Allen, *The Invention of the White Race*, and Jacobson, *Whiteness of a Different Color*, are among the most important works on this topic. The problem is that this explanation ignores what happened in Iberian America. Due to this elision, we still lack sufficient information on this specific problem for that region. Therefore, this is still an open question. It is very interesting that despite the fact that those who would be "Europeans" in the future, from the time of the Roman Empire, recognized the future "Africans," as did the Iberians who were more or less familiar with Africans much earlier than the conquest but never thought of them in racial terms before the colonization of America. In fact, race as a category was applied for the first time to the Indians, not to Blacks. In this way, race appears much earlier than color in the history of the social classification of the global population.

6   The idea of race is literally an invention. It has nothing to do with the biological structure of the human species. Regarding phenotypic traits, those that are obviously found in the genetic code of individuals and groups are in that specific sense biological. However, they have no relation to the subsystems and biological processes of the human

organism, including those involved in the neurological and mental subsystems and their functions. See Marks, *Human Biodiversity, Genes, Race, and History*; and Quijano, "¡Qué tal raza!"

7   Western Europe is the location on the Atlantic coast to the west of the large peninsula protruding from the continental mass that Europeans named Asia. Coronil, "Beyond Occidentalism," has discussed the construction of the category "Occident" as part of the formation of a global power.

8   This is precisely what Alfred Métraux, the well-known French anthropologist, found at the end of the 1950s in southern Peru. I found the same phenomenon in 1963 in Cuzco: an Indian peon was obliged to travel from his village, in La Convención, to the city in order to fulfill his turn of service to his patrons. But they did not furnish him lodging, food, or, of course, a salary. Métraux proposed that that situation was closer to the Roman *colonato* of the fourth century BC than to European feudalism.

9   See Prebisch, "Commercial Policy in the Underdeveloped Countries"; and Prebisch, *The Economic Development of Latin America and Its Principal Problems*. On Prebisch, see Baer, "The Economics of Prebisch and ECLA."

10 See Wallerstein, *The Modern World-System*; and Hopkins and Wallerstein, *World-Systems Analysis*.

11 On the process of the production of new historical geocultural identities, see O'Gorman, *La invención de América*; Rabasa, *Inventing America*; Dussel, *The Invention of the Americas*; Mudimbe, *The Invention of Africa*; Tilly, *Coercion, Capital, and European States, A.D. 990–1992*; Said, *Orientalism*; and Coronil, "Beyond Occidentalism."

12 On these questions, see Stocking, *Race, Culture, Evolution*; Young, *Colonial Desire*; Tocqueville, *Democracy in America*; Quijano, "Réflexions sur l' interdisciplinarité, le développement et les relations interculturelles"; Quijano, "Colonialidad del poder, cultura y conocimiento en América Latina"; and Gruzinski, *La colonisation de l'imaginaire*.

13 See Mignolo, *The Darker Side of the Renaissance*; Blaut, *The Colonial Model of the World*; and Lander, "Colonialidad, modernidad, postmodernidad."

14 Around the categories produced during European colonial dominance of the world, there exist a good many lines of debate; subaltern studies, postcolonial studies, cultural studies, and multiculturalism are among the current ones. There is also a flourishing bibliography, too long to be cited here, lined with famous names such as Ranajit Guha, Gayatri Spivak, Edward Said, Homi Bhabha, and Stuart Hall.

15 Of my previous studies, see principally Quijano's prologue in Mariátegui, *Textos básicos*; and Quijano, "Estado-Nacion, ciudadanía y democracia."

16 A summary of the vast literature on this debate can be found in Quijano, "El fantasma del desarrollo en América Latina."

17 See Young, *Colonial Desire*.

18 For a more extended debate, see Quijano, "Modernidad y democracia."

19 On the theoretical propositions of this conception of power, see Quijano, "Coloniality of Power and Its Institutions."

20 I mean "system" in the sense that the relations between parts and the totality are not arbitrary and that the latter has hegemony over the parts in the orientation of the movement of the whole, but not in a systematic sense, as the relations of the parts among themselves and with the whole are not logically functional. This happens only in machines and organisms, never in social relations.

21 See Dussel, *The Invention of the Americas*.

22 Quijano, "La nueva heterogeneidad estructural de América Latina.".

23 Quijano "La nueva heterogeneidad estructural de América Latina"; and Quijano, "Modernidad y democracia."

24 Quijano, "Colonialité du pouvoir et démocratie en Amérique latine."

25 The literature on the debate about Eurocentrism is growing rapidly. For a different (although somewhat related) position than the one that orients this article, see Amin, *Eurocentrism*.

26 See Wallerstein, *Historical Capitalism*; and Arrighi, *The Long Twentieth Century*.

27 Viola and Margolis, *Seeds of Change*.

28 On the origin of the category of historical-structural heterogeneity, see Quijano, *Notas sobre el concepto de marginalidad social*; Quijano, *Imperialismo y "marginalidad" en América Latina*; and Quijano, "La nueva heterogeneidad estructural de América Latina."

29 I have always wondered about the origin of one of liberalism's most precious propositions: ideas should be respected, but the body can be tortured, crushed, and killed. Latin Americans repeatedly cite with admiration the defiant phrase spoken while a martyr of the anticolonial battles was being beheaded: "Barbarians, ideas cannot be beheaded!" I am now sure that the origin of the idea can be found in the new Cartesian dualism that made the body into mere "nature."

30 Bousquie, *Le corps, cet inconnu*, asserts that Cartesianism is a new radical dualism.

31 The fact that the only alternative category to the Occident was and still is the Orient, while Blacks (Africa) and Indians (America before the United States) did not have the honor of being the Other to Europe, speaks volumes about the processes of Eurocentered subjectivity.

32 For a more detailed discussion on these issues, see Quijano, "Colonialité du pouvoir et démocratie en Amérique latine"; and

Quijano, "Colonialidad de poder, cultura y conocimiento en América Latina."

33 Quijano, "Estado-Nacion, ciudadanía y democracia."

34 For an extended discussion of this point, see Anderson, *Imagined Communities*.

35 See Quijano, "Estado-Nacion, ciudadanía y democracia"; and Quijano, "Modernidad y democracia."

36 "Purity of blood" is probably the closest antecedent to the idea of "race" produced by Spaniards in America. See Quijano, "Raza, etnia y nación en José Carlos Mariátegui."

37 Tocqueville, *Democracy in America*, chs. 16–17.

38 See Myrdall, *American Dilemma*.

39 Even in the 1920s, as in the whole twentieth century, Héctor Murena, an important member of the Argentinean intelligentsia, proclaimed, "We are Europeans exiled in these savage pampas." See Imaz, *Nosotros mañana*. During Argentina's social, political, and cultural battles in the 1960s, *cabecita negra* was the nickname for racial discrimination.

40 Homogenization is a basic element of the Eurocentric perspective of nationalization. If it were not, the national conflicts that emerge in European nations every time the problem of racial or ethnic differences arises could not be explained or understood, nor could we understand the Eurocentric politics of settlement favored in the Southern Cone or the origin and meaning of the so-called Indigenous problem in all of Latin America. If nineteenth-century Peruvian landowners imported Chinese workers, it was because the national question was not in play for them except as naked social interests. From the Eurocentrist perspective, the seigneurial bourgeoisie, based in the coloniality of power, has been an enemy of social and political democratization as a condition of nationalization for the society and the state.

41 In the 1960s and 1970s, many social scientists within and outside of Latin America, including myself, used the concept of "internal colonialism" to characterize the apparently paradoxical relationship of independent states with respect to their colonized populations. In Latin America, Casanova, "Internal Colonialism and National Development," and Stavenhagen, "Classes, Colonialism, and Acculturation," were surely the most important among those who dealt with the problem systematically. Now, we know that these problems concerning the coloniality of power go further than the institutional development of the nation-state.

42 Quijano, "Urbanización, cambio social y dependencia."

43 I have advanced some propositions on this debate in Quijano, "América Latina en la economía mundial."

44   Some of the movements include the Revolutionary Antiimperialist
      Popular Alliance in Peru, Democratic Action in Venezuela, the Nation-
      alist Revolutionary Movement in Bolivia, the Movement for National
      Liberation in Costa Rica, and the Authentic Revolutionary Movement
      and the orthodoxy in Cuba.

45   Eurocentric myopia (not only in European and American studies but
      in Latin America as well) has spread and nearly imposed the term
      "populism" on movements and projects that have little in common with
      the movement of the Russian Narodniks of the nineteenth century or
      the later North American populism. See Quijano, "Estado-Nacion, ciu-
      dadanía y democracia."

46   Quijano, *Qué es y qué no es socialismo*; and Quijano, "Poder y
      democracia."

47   It is this idea that gives Mariátegui his major value and continued
      validity as a critic of socialisms and their historical materialism. See,
      above all, the final chapter in Mariátegui, *Siete ensayos de interpretación
      de la realidad peruana*, as well as Mariátegui, "Aniversario y balance,"
      and Mariátegui, "Punto de vista antimperialista."

12

COLONIALITY OF POWER AND DE/COLONIALITY OF POWER

I come before you with fear and trembling, words I've had to borrow from the famous title of a famous book to express my unease at having to present mainly my perplexities and raise questions instead of presenting or propounding some verity to you.

We have come here to question ourselves about Latin America. In order to question Latin America, we have to question ourselves about Latin America. For me, this is an extremely risky undertaking, first because Latin America has always been a question mark and second because we inevitably have to stop and think what it might mean today to question ourselves about Latin America in particular.

This is a place, a space, and an exceptionally important time not only for Latin America itself but also for all of humanity, for the current social existence of humanity. How can this be, how can we question ourselves, from what perspective, from what horizon of meaning, when these perspectives and horizons of meaning—already in crisis, yet still hegemonic—are nevertheless breaking down everywhere, in upheaval everywhere? From what perspective, from what horizon of meaning, can we ask questions of ourselves? Such questions involving knowing what to ask and how to ask, because asking means trying to understand, trying to locate what we must understand, and trying to make sense of what we identify, trying to make it intelligible to us all. This necessarily implies a perspective that allows for such a thing.

What I'm calling a "horizon of meaning" is what could make it possible. But today we have no stable or legitimate horizon of meaning. The hegemonic one we have is in crisis, and the one that seems about to emerge is, to my mind, still not perceptible enough for us all. If it were, we'd be living very differently in a different social existence.

Hence my fear and trembling. Hence also my caution with each and every question and with each and every word used to formulate these questions.

All of us here during this week of committee meetings and roundtables and questions have obviously debated many things. It is far riskier still to try to propose theories, of which there is no shortage in this debate.

This, let me say once and for all, is an exceptional situation not only for Latin America but also for the entire animal species that we call Homo sapiens. We are now faced with a genuine conjunction, not a confluence, not a coincidence, but a genuine conjunction, between what we are calling climate change—the crisis, the risk that the conditions for the existence of life on planet Earth have taken on—and, at the same time and for the same reason, the conditions for our own species' survival.

That's why this is such a special moment. I don't think this has happened before—not in the same way in any case—to this animal species that we call Homo sapiens. This species appears to be very young; the most ancient specimen is a female fossil, found of course in Kenya, which is more or less 200,000 years old. And though we know that climate catastrophes occurred many millions of years ago and even nearly eradicated the conditions for life on the planet for our young species of barely 200,000 years, it is unlikely that we have encountered a situation like today's before.

Why do I call this a conjunction? I do so because with what is happening to planet Earth, the scientific community that is now concerned with this always insists that if we don't deal with it right away, the timeline offers no way back. If so, and if, as we have been talking about here, there is a profound global crisis in our current means of social existence, which everyone refers to as a "crisis of capitalism," then this is a conjunction of trends that have arisen from the same origin. What's happening with the climate—if the scientific community working on it is right—arises from factors that didn't exist in earlier geological eras. It arises from what our species has been doing and above all what it currently is doing to planet Earth. In the same way, what is obviously happening to us all, what is happening to the thing we call "capitalism" and the capitalist crisis, also arises precisely from what our species itself is doing.

This is the conjunction. For this reason, it is absolutely essential—not just essential, but inevitable—that we turn back to the central issue. This means that what our species is doing to our common home, the planet, and what it is increasingly doing to us—killing us, which is to say being predatory to the extreme in one case and extremely, increasingly violent in the other—all corresponds to something that is typical of our species. And that is what I want to get to.

What is typical of our species? Why do we behave like this? This is what's called power. In some strange way, I suspect, the animal species we call Homo sapiens is the only one whose historical sense of existence, whose journey through time and therefore whose central motivation as well is power. Therefore, too, our species' peculiar form of violence today is not, as is commonly thought, testimony to our animality. Quite the opposite. It is an expression of and testimony to the specific historicity of Homo sapiens.

So, we have to question ourselves about this thing we call power. Given that power is what orients, what articulates, what produces the historical prehistory of our species, it is by the same token, moreover, what articulates the very scattered and heterogeneous forms of social existence across vast social warps and wefts in very different spaces and times, capable of reproducing themselves for a very long time, as now.

The one we now dwell in and that dwells in us is also something very specific. This is what we have been proposing for several years to discuss with the theory of the coloniality of power, with the theory of the coloniality and decoloniality of power. This is why Latin America has such an exceptionally important place in what is happening with our species today and with what is happening today with the relations between our species and the planet, because Latin America was the original space and the inaugural time for a new historically specific matrix of power, characterized by its coloniality, which has been its inextricable, foundational, and inherent feature from just over five centuries ago to the present.

Since it would take a long seminar to discuss all this comprehensively, let me just present a couple of ideas.

The first is that this is an effectively new matrix of power that had no precedent in history that we know of—excuse me, that I know of—because it has been building and developing itself around two historical axes. The first axis is the one that gives rise to it, that fashions a mode of classification and of creating inequality among the members of the species. The term we use today is "race."

Race is a mental construct produced in the same moment in which the violence of the conquest begins, the destruction of one of the most extraordinary historical experiences of Homo sapiens, which took place in this territory that we call Latin America. In the moment when the destruction of this exceptionally rich and sophisticated historical world began, at that precise moment this idea that we now know by the term "race" was fashioned. It was thus a product of subjectivity that was very quickly transformed, under the violence of the conquest, into a form of social relations.

We are therefore in the presence of a new mode of social domination that has no precedents in history, because this construct had no place in any prior period. I know that there are others in this debate who propose that this is not true, that the Chinese were already using the same idea and the same form of social relations. But I think there is a central mistake there: they are confusing it with ethnocentrism, the idea of the superiority of some people over others, as happens in other social hierarchies, especially those that entail colonial states or empires. But that idea of superiority/inferiority disappears when those structures of domination disappear. A king thinks he's superior to his subjects until the day he's overthrown and guillotined; then he's no longer the hierarchical superior. Aristotle even says that the slave is a slave by nature, but everyone knows that once a slave stopped being a slave, he went back to being like any other citizen's son. And in Rome, a freedman could become rich and a senator.

Not so from 1492 on, because many changes have taken place over the little more than five centuries since. There have indeed been very profound changes, some of them apparently very radical. The only one that has to this day not gone away from the materiality of social relations is the idea that we now recognize as race, an integral part of the materiality of social relations but one that, I think, the majority of the population still confuses for a constituent element of the materiality of not only social relations but also the individuals who participate in those social relations. This form of social relations—that is, the racialization of hierarchical relations, the racialization of relations in every sphere of power—imbues and pervades each of those instances, each of those spheres. And it modifies and reconfigures all the mechanisms that came before it.

Just one example before moving on quickly: the male/female discrimination, the original distinction of our species, discussed today as a problem of gender and associated as well with a problem of sexuality. I am not sure, forgive me, whether patriarchal domination was always so universal in the history of the species; it seems to be universal today, but we know of experiences in which it seems not to have been so. In any case, today it is imaged as universal up until the moment when hierarchies are racialized. The people who went about destroying the historical world of what is now called the Americas and producing on its rubble, particularly in Latin America, were, as you all remember, Christians of the Counter-Reformation. They were the bearers of the Inquisition, and therefore, as in all the religions produced in that same historical horizon and that same space, they were hierarchical, vertical, repressive, and patriarchal. As such, every male seemed to be by definition superior to every woman until the day when race became part of the materiality of social relations. From that moment, every woman from the "superior" race became by definition superior to every male from an "inferior" race. This reconfiguration demonstrates the exceptional power to penetrate and resignify, to reconfigure previous mechanisms of social domination. We are thus faced with a new unprecedented system of social domination. This is the first axis.

The second axis, equally unprecedented, is a new system of social exploitation. I want to insist on this point, because the crisis that we have been discussing every day is associated with it. We have discussed and the press has discussed books, and the "analysts"—that new suddenly ubiquitous profession—have commented on the crisis of capital and of capitalism. But from this perspective, the word "capitalism" cannot be reduced and does not refer solely to the specific social relation of exploitation called "capital," which is based on the buying and selling of the living labor force of individuals, the commercialization of the labor force. No.

We do not know, I do not know, exactly where and when this particular social relation that we call capital, the commercialization of the labor force, entered into history. It was probably between the ninth and eleventh centuries in the south of what is today the Italian-Iberian Peninsula region under Muslim hegemony in the part of the Mediterranean that was the central basin of all world commercial traffic. But it was emergent, it coexisted with all the others and was not hegemonic over them until the Americas. From then on, from the late fifteenth century to now, with all its crises, transformations, even mutations, what we've had is a configuration in which all known forms of the exploitation of labor have become linked: slavery, serfdom, small commercial production, reciprocity, and capital. All of them, not just together in time, not just simultaneously, and not just coexisting in the same territory at the same time, were linked in order to produce all of them together, merchandise for the world market, for the new world market that has emerged since precisely then.

As the trending hegemony has been tied to capital from the beginning and has accentuated it over the following centuries, world capitalism isn't just capital as a social relation; it is a complex in which every form of social exploitation produced merchandise for the new world market under the hegemony of capital. This hegemony consequently imparts its capitalist character to the whole. Therefore, when we say "world capitalism," we are speaking first and foremost about the hegemonic place that capital as a social relation has in a configuration in which all other forms that we know from history are present. And this only emerges with the Americas, and it has never ended, though all of us, I think, or at least the greater part of us here in Latin America, thought that it was exiting the stage; it probably reduced its space in the historical scene, but not only did it not ever leave, now it is probably even less likely to exit.

The main point for us, the most important thing regarding what I want to ask here, is that this isn't just about a new matrix of power with two axes, one a new system of social domination based on race and the other a new system of social exploitation under the hegemony of capital. This emerges, comes together, and develops over the course of two whole centuries solely on the basis of what is now Latin America. This seems decisive and important to me for what I want to look at next, because this America is in effect the first historical identity/entity of this period, which we later took to calling the period of modernity. And as such, race is the first mental category of the period of modernity, and what we now call Western Europe is a product of that existence, not prior to it, I always insist.

We need to be as cautious as we can with language, especially at a moment such as today when, with all the horizons of meaning bursting, symbols are conspiring against what they seemed to stand for. We've gotten used to saying that Western Europe came to America, but as you know, there was no America and no Western Europe either. We've gotten used to saying that the Spanish came to conquer America: every word of that sentence is false. As we all know, there was no America and no Spain either. What we now call Western Europe and Spain are the historical consequences of this new matrix of power that began to emerge with the Americas, from America on. I won't tell you what you all know already, why the axis of the basin of world traffic shifted to the Atlantic, supplanting the Mediterranean, and why a new historic region then emerged that would come to be called Western Europe. But this whole process had an extremely important consequence, which is that a new matrix of power emerged from this process and was its most integral part. To call this matrix of power its instrument is too instrumental, if you will, or as they say on Peruvian television, "even though I repeat myself." What we have here is that every matrix of power that reproduces itself through time, and this one in particular, also produces its own meaning, produces its own way of understanding, of making others understand, of explaining, of seeing, of distorting, of concealing, like any other horizon of meaning; that is why this is part of this matrix of power. And this matrix produces a very special, very important one, the one that was ultimately called modernity and still is to the present.

Speaking of modernity, I also want to quickly say two necessary words about this. If by "modernity" we mean what many people still accept— what is referred to as its need for measuring, need for observing, for experimenting, for quantifying, for engineering, for mathematics, for the sciences, for technology—then yes, we can admit without a doubt that this matrix of power under the central control of the new specificity and identity that we call Western Europe has gone very far. But in every one of what we've known since the Spengler-Toynbee debate as high cultures *or* high civilizations, each of them had the ability to develop every one of these forms of knowledge and technology in the most advanced way possible. The measurement of time by the Maya calendar is barely a thousandth of a fraction of a second off today from the time measurements of the most advanced instruments of today, but the people who came here called the Mayas barbarians. Yes, there were barbarians, but they weren't the Mayas, and we've lost five hundred years of astronomy, as with many other such things. As in medicine, as in mathematics, as in astronomy, as in many forms of technology, the hydraulic engineering of the ancient Egyptians and the ancient Incas still attract attention and calls for explanations from the most advanced technologies of today. If this part is called scientific, technological, then all high cultures have had great ones. Yes, we should and can admit that in this matrix of power, under Eurocentric control, in each and every field they have gone very far. I remember that on one occasion in Germany I was told that without radical Cartesian dualism and experimentation on the human body none of this would have been possible and that it of course allowed medicine to make great leaps forward. But, I told them, you don't remember that a couple thousand years ago they were doing successful cranial trepanations among the Incas; there is archaeological evidence to prove it.

There was another specific product, and this one is indeed important for us because it was an exceptionally important product specifically of this matrix of power, which is what we will call a Eurocentered coloniality/

modernity. In the process of Eurocentering this new matrix of power, two important processes take place. One is what we call the Industrial Revolution. Tomic and other historians are correct: producing machines is a development, a perfecting, of the technological and mechanical innovations created by enslaved Black coffee and sugar growers on the islands of the Caribbean, and historians have the evidence to prove it.

But at the same time, this process came about because Europe—the new Western Europe—was the control center for this new matrix of power. Western Europe, then, finally had something that the world market was interested in, because before it had absolutely nothing of interest to offer the world market. What it sold was what the Americas produced: precious metals and precious plants, whose massive profits allowed progress to be centralized in the social relations called capital and later industrial capitalism.

As part of this process, particularly from the eighteenth century on, something very important came about, and this is new, this is specific, and this is also a problem for us today. Why is it that this modernity, to which I will now turn, cannot be anything other than a Eurocentered coloniality/modernity? Why? Because this was the first time in history that we know of in which the idea of social equality comes to be common sense among humans. It isn't a new idea. In the four thousand year-old Egyptian papyrus, the famous document "Lament of a Soul," there is a call for social equality. But the idea of social equality has always been attacked, persecuted, repressed. The period since the eighteenth century is the first time when this idea becomes legitimated, especially in Western Europe, and thus when the ideas of freedom and individual autonomy become legitimated. The idea of citizenship therefore becomes legitimated as it never had been before anywhere in the world, because it isn't the same thing that had existed in Athens a few thousand years earlier; this is different.

But remember, the idea of social equality becomes common sense, it is legitimated, but alongside it, the idea of race—the basic, supreme form of social inequality—is legitimated, for it is no longer about poverty or wealth, power, and managing resources but instead is about people's very constitution, in the very image they have of themselves. The worst thing about the idea of race isn't just that it was used to let some people dominate others but that victims were taught to see themselves through their dominator's eyes. So yes, social equality, but alongside it the most profound form of social inequality: race. Yes, citizenship, but alongside it, colonial domination. Yes, autonomy and individual freedom, but alongside them, colonial subjugation. Yes, modernity, therefore, but also a colonial modernity. Coloniality and modernity, absolutely, not just side by side but also giving rise to each other.

I am not saying anything arbitrary, because no sooner had they barely begun to produce their Industrial Revolution, and thus their "modernity," than they began invading the rest of the world over the next two hundred years in order to impose European colonial domination, thereby racializing their populations, making them unequal in those terms, subjugating them to forms of colonial domination and designation. This is how we get to what is most characteristic, most necessary to coloniality/modernity: its incurable ambiguity. You really can't accept social equality so long as the idea of race is in your head. Our colleagues of what is now called African origin and other victims everywhere of the same level of racial discrimination continue to struggle for what they call "racial equality." This is obviously a dead end, because it makes no sense; it is impossible. In order to accept racial equality, you would have to accept that race really is a component part of the person, not of the materiality of social relations between people, which is something else entirely. This is the incurable ambiguity of Eurocentered coloniality/modernity.

Over the course of those two hundred years of expanding colonial dominion over Asia, Africa, and Australia—words and entities that hadn't existed before either—we have European colonialism and a power that has become worldwide, but at the same time the hegemony of this new historical sense is being imposed on all the people who live—heterogeneously, to be sure, and discontinuously, to be sure, but nonetheless subjugated on the whole—under the basic matrices of the new matrix of power, because that's what this is all about. And this is the horizon of meaning that becomes hegemonic; this is the horizon of meaning that we all, all of us in one way or another, had or still have and against which we are finally beginning to face difficulties. And here, this is why I am speaking of this incurable ambiguity of what I'm calling colonial modernity, or the Eurocentered coloniality/modernity: it's impossible to have one without the other; it's impossible to be both things at once, yet nevertheless it is possible.

That's how we have lived. What does this mean? It means that in such a matrix of power—especially after the great worldwide defeat of the rivals to the central empire at the end of the twentieth century—after that defeat, when the entire species finally lived all under one single matrix of power, despite all the heterogeneity of specific experience, we then find something very peculiar, which also comes up only with this matrix of power: we cannot stand outside of it, there's no way to be outside of it, and there's nowhere else to go.

Or is there? Sure, of course, if you shoot yourself or somebody shoots you and you're not there anymore, but otherwise there's nowhere else to go. I remember a rally in West Berlin just one month after Pinochet's coup against Allende in 1973, the largest postwar rally in West Berlin, some fifty thousand people. The people on the sidewalks said to us, "Why don't you go over to the other side, please." They meant the other side of the wall, East Berlin. But now there isn't even that, not even that wall of shame exists. There's nowhere else to go; we have to be here, inside it. But some of us are also against it.

I ask you to think about this specific combination that we're inside of, because there's nowhere to go. But I don't just want it to be me; I am claiming that if you really aren't in agreement, you're also against it. And this isn't a claim about ethics; maybe it started out that way, but it's a mode of social existence. As such, it entails everything, its own epistemology, aesthetics, theory, politics, and life area by area in social existence: sex, work, subjectivity, and authority, its relations with what's called nature. So, that's why now, after the major defeat of 1973 when it began to emerge, what must by now be clear to everyone is that the world we live in today, though the matrix of power is the same, isn't what it was for anyone just thirty, thirty-five years ago; it is profoundly different. The historical period we're in now is a new historical period that has the same significance, the same historical import, as what we call the Industrial Revolution but in a very peculiar way. That is where I want to go now, to free you from being against while being, if you will, on the inside.

Many of us thought that it was somewhat likely, if not certain, that since the end of the Second World War, capital would increasingly be filling the stage while the other noncapital forms appeared to be exiting, that the planet's population was all forced into a single matrix of social classification, and that the defeat was so thorough that its most mediocre philosophers had the audacity to say that "history has ended," as you will all recall. But in the meantime, something has happened that has gone by without our noticing, maybe not for all of us but for many.

Allow me to bring up the history of the debate in Latin America since the end of World War II. In the mid-1960s, some of us began to discover that something was happening in the capital-labor relationship, capital-wage labor, I should specify. When the business cycle contracted and threw people out, in the next expansion phase of the cycle a growing portion of dismissed workers were no longer reincorporated into the structure of accumulation, and this began to grow rapidly. This was a profound change in the capital-wage labor relationship.

Many of you here perhaps remember (others won't; it would be very interesting if you could watch it now) the debate over what was called "marginalization" in Latin America. Beginning in the mid-1950s, Miguel Murmis, to whom we paid tribute at the inauguration of this congress, was one of the main participants in this debate. This was just beginning to trend back then; now it is a major trend but also a fait accompli. If you go to the higher levels, the more technologized and informaticized forms of the structure of the capital-labor relation, the presence of the living, individual labor force has been on the decline, and at the highest levels it is obviously no longer present or literally insignificant. This means that new value isn't being produced, and consequently, the profit rate is also trending in the same way.

This isn't an unforeseen phenomenon. I had occasion to remember this at our first meeting with the Latin American Council of Social Sciences (Consejo Latinoamericano de Ciencias Sociales) and Emir Sader, as I have been insisting since the 1960s. Oddly, this doesn't arise from theory, because it isn't part of the theoretical debate (about capital). But somehow Marx was the first to intuit this strange possibility that there might come a moment when production no longer required the labor force of living individuals but all production would be done by totally mechanized means. He thought—it's in the *Grundrisse*—about something like a force of nature, his words, that would be active there, allowing for production without the need for the participation of a living, active, individual labor force. Also in the 1960s, the United Nations was discussing the need to reduce the level of technology in order to develop undeveloped countries, because technology reduces the workforce.

My reply, then as now, remains the same: But why? Wouldn't it be fantastic if machines could make all we need? Wouldn't it? Then we could devote ourselves to the things we really like doing: studying, imagining, hiking, walking, exploring, discovering, making music, or gardening, as I like to do.

Sure, but that can't be done. Why not?

At this point, the level of capital (I'm talking about capital as a specific social relationship) has changed its relationship with paid work so profoundly that it's not producing jobs, and it obviously will never produce jobs again. To the contrary, paid employment is only produced from the middle down, hence the need to invent the empirical category called "structural unemployment," accompanying the reforms of all the empirical names for labor that have been discussed, such as labor flexibilization and job insecurity.

And what are people supposed to do? Commit collective suicide? Whales do it.

No. Here, our Brazilian colleague knows that on the *fazendas*, the Brazilian plantations that make up a huge share of Brazilian farmland, the *fazendeiros* use tens and hundreds of thousands of enslaved workers to produce commodities for the world market with slaves. Lula passed a law three years ago outlawing slavery.[1] Hurray! But how can it be eliminated? Movimento sem Terra, the landless farmworker movement, discovers slaves on every plantation every day, just as there are in Southwest Asia, as there are in some regions of the United States, as there are along the border between Mexico and the United States, as there doubtless are along other borders everywhere. Slavery is booming again and personal servitude is booming again, as is the system of small dependent industrial production that was the heart of what we used to cynically call the "informal economy," the sort of jargon term we stick on things to keep them from being understood. But reciprocity is also making a return, these forms of producing and exchanging labor without going through the market but without being able to live outside the market and, naturally, capital.

This part of capital is totally hegemonic now over not only capital as such but also world capitalism as such and therefore over all its other relationships with every other form of labor exploitation. So, a phenomenon has happened that is now creating a scandal. A great debate is brewing, but I don't see a debate, and I haven't seen this debate set forth like this, except for here and now, in any text I've seen. How can you make money when producing an object could have a cost, as we know, of less than zero? Producing a mobile telephone costs less than zero at this level, and in some parts you can walk into a store and they'll give you one of the little devices for free, but you'll get signed up for a list of services that you'll have to pay for monthly.

So, what is money, then? Money used to be the payment for the at-cost price plus the profits for an object. No longer. Merchandise has dematerialized. It's our lifestyle; it's our subjectivity, our heads, our forms. That's why they give us the object but not the service, not control over our way of living, our lifestyle. Jeremy Rifkin showed that numbers equivalent to total world gross domestic product can flow in a single week through the twisting pathways of the electronic finance transmissions from New York, just

New York. So, what is money? At this point in 2008 when the New York finance scandal was breaking, everyone was wondering where the money had gone. Bush handed out nearly $800 billion dollars. Obama did the same shortly afterward. Where did the money go? That is why, at last, from inside the core of the dominant group themselves, exactly this problem is beginning to be talked about. They said it was a loss of confidence, precisely. So, I'll go to my question: If you don't believe in the Catholic Church or don't believe in Christianity and the Pope excommunicates you, do you really care? Probably not. But if you absolutely don't believe that race is anything material about a person, that it actually is material about social relations instead, if you were "racially" attacked, would you really care? If the attack is physical, of course; otherwise, the problem is something else.

The same goes for finance capitalism. That's why the structural financialization of the system and the hyperfetishizing of merchandise requires maximum control over people's subjectivity and maximum control over our lifestyle, and that is what this part of production is aimed at. So, as you can see, there are lots of issues, lots of questions. Why? Because now there's finally another horizon of meaning that's emerging, and this is also a confluence. It is also because this power has been taken to predatory extremes across the planet, what has been called "nature" since Descartes, since that radical dualism declared that with the exception of all those who have the divine gift of reason, everything else is nature. There's a basic epistemic kinship between racism in social relations and the predatory relationship with nature, because those who are deemed racially inferior by nature are the ones who are exploited. This is pure nature, so there is an absolutely foundational and intrinsic relationship between racism and nature. You see, power must be decolonized so that its predatory relations with the rest of the planet can also be decolonized.

And that is what will soon happen with the emergence of the peoples called Indigenous, beginning in Latin America but continuing all over the rest of the world where there was colonial European domination and everyone else became indigenized. The Indigenous emerge because it's not just about defending themselves, recovering their identity, or decolonizing; it's about something else, something bigger, because for these people, for a growing number of these people, their physical survival is in question. They therefore cannot accept the foundations of capitalism, not just the exploitation of the living labor force but also the idea of profit and money.

What does the Indigenous population say today? The air can't be merchandise, the water can't be merchandise, and the forests can't be merchandise.

Part of so-called nature can't be merchandise. Why can't it be merchandise? Because then we wouldn't exist. These ideas are beginning to pervade other social groups; there is a confluence with the academic world that is fighting for an end to the depredation of the planet, of so-called nature. This relationship must be denaturalized, decolonized. So, there is a horizon of meaning that's beginning to emerge and therefore new forms of social existence.

And I'll end with this: Why?

It is because in the contemporary world there are two traps that these changes have been producing. Nobody today can live without the market, not anywhere in the world. But if United Nations data is correct, if 80 percent of the six billion humans on Earth, which is more or less what we number, only have access to less than 18 percent of what the world has and produces, then you can't live with the market alone. The first trap: you can't live without the market, but you can't live with the market alone, so you have to learn how to live with the market and without the market.

The same thing happens with the state: you can't live without the state, there's nowhere else, but if the state behaves the way it behaves in most countries, as an agent, a conveyor belt, for corporate interests, when the state is corporatized, then you can't live with the state alone.

You can't live with the market, and you can't live without the market; you can't live with the state, and you can't live without the state. A growing world population, billions of people, are caught in this trap. Another form of social existence is emerging, a very heterogeneous one, and thus another meaning, another historical horizon of meaning, because another horizon of historical meaning is emerging there.

So, this is the situation, this is the moment, these are the options, and so the decoloniality of power is the main option.

Thank you.

Notes

Paper presented at the 27th Congress of the Asociación Latinoamericana de Sociología, September 4, 2009.

1   [Apparently referring to Lei 10.803, passed on December 11, 2003, which specified that the abolition of slavery applied to all conditions "analogous to slavery" and mandated stiff penalties for violations. It was estimated that up to fifty thousand Brazilians were working under forced labor conditions.]

13

THIRTY YEARS LATER: ANOTHER REUNION
NOTES FOR ANOTHER DEBATE

"Reencuentro y debate" first raised the major issues that discussions of José Carlos Mariátegui's works has centered on in recent decades. These issues arose in confronting two of the deepest instances of the historical crisis in which we are still mired.

First, there is the crisis of "historical materialism," as the Eurocentrist version of Marx's intellectual and political legacy has been called since the late nineteenth century. This version began to be assembled when the most Eurocentric elements of Marx's legacy were hybridized with Spencerian Positivism, which was hegemonic in "progressive" liberal thought at the turn of the twentieth century during the boom of social democracy in the social-ist movement.[1] In the debate over this positivism in social democracy, the most critical factions tended to favor a return to the Hegelian movement, as the historical-teleological perspective of Hegelianism, engaged in the idea of a historical macrosubject, legitimated the perspective of unilineal and unidirectional evolutionism in the sequence of "modes of production." After bureaucratic despotism was imposed on Russia under Stalinism in the mid-twentieth century, these hybrids were codified in a systemic corpus, distorting Marx's theoretical ideas—that is, ideas drawn from a perspec-tive of knowledge and understanding, or issues for research and debate—and turning them into a doctrine, that is, a corpus of formulations systemati-cally organized as definitive and beyond dispute. This was then disseminated as "Marxism" or, more precisely, "Marxism-Leninism." After World War II, this doctrine was subjected to a structuralist reading and was administered as such, complete with political procedure manuals and canons, a sort of "Marxist Vulgate,"[2] as it was termed by critics of the ruling power and radical scholars of Marx's legacy and the history of social movements.

As the twentieth century entered its final stretch, the Eurocentric limits of "historical materialism" and "Marxism-Leninism" were becoming more visible, and the understanding of associated political practices that it provided grew more and more distorted the more those practices became instrumental to meeting the technocratic and political needs of the bureaucratic despotism ruling over the so-called socialist camp. Thus, "historical materialism" became linked more closely and deeply with the tendencies of Eurocentrism as a whole toward instrumental technocratization during precisely the same period when, in its capacity as the hegemonic mode of producing subjectivity (social imaginary, historical memory, knowledge) within the colonial/modern matrix of power and world capitalism in particular, it linked its tendencies with the new needs for computerization, finance accumulation, and reduction of the space for democracy within the current power structure.

In this context, "historical materialism" was not just rapidly losing space in the new intellectual and political debate between defenders and critics of the reigning matrix of world power that arose under the world crisis. Most importantly, it was losing attractiveness and legitimacy among the new social movements that were springing up, especially beginning in the 1960s and early 1970s, and trying to subvert that power (from "the center," as in May 1968 in France and the Hot Autumn of 1969 in Italy) and seeking to contain imperial/colonial aggression in Vietnam, Algeria, Africa, and Latin America in the midst of the maelstrom of what would soon prove to be the deepest and longest historical crisis in the five centuries of the ruling world matrix of power.[3]

Second, there was the crisis of bureaucratic despotism itself, which was expressed in two main dimensions. On one side was the swift erosion of the "socialist camp" that had been organized after World War II around the hegemony of the Soviet Union, particularly by the countries of Eastern Europe. On the other side was the growing delegitimization and discord of bureaucratic despotism, despite being rebranded as "actually existing socialism" in view of the criticism it got from the new generations and new revolutionary movements. Indeed, reiterating the redundancy of such titles only made it more obvious that the term "socialism" was illegitimate—especially after the 1930s—for talking about this specific configuration of power, which grew to have less and less relationship to our aspirations and struggles for freedom from every form of control imposed on the core dimensions of our social existence.[4] In other words, instead of covering up the deepening crisis in the "socialist camp," such a term finally allowed a wide majority to see that the aspirations of the dominated/exploited/repressed people of the world for social liberation and their struggles had, under this configuration of power, been genuinely alienated in the name of socialism, a name under which they had originally found shelter.

Indeed, it was no longer just a matter of bitter disputes between political tendencies linked to rival "socialist" regimes, such as the old conflicts between Stalinists and Titoists and the later ones between pro-Chinese and Muscovites. Instead, much more deeply and decisively, there were successive, growing revolts within each of the "socialist camp" countries by movements of workers, students, and intellectuals, called "dissenters," fighting against bureaucratic despotism. Some were oriented toward a radical democratization of power, organizing institutions for social control over public authority; others turned toward a liberalization, at least, of "actually existing socialism." All were victims of bloody repression carried out by the Soviet Union in the so-called Democratic Republic of Germany, Hungary, Poland, Czechoslovakia, and Romania as well as in the Soviet Union itself and in China. As is well known, this was the course that led to the breakup of the "socialist camp" and ultimately to the sudden implosion of the so-called Union of Soviet Socialist Republics (the Soviet Union).

In this context, when dealing with the works of José Carlos Mariátegui, it was therefore imperative not only to try to escape the prison of the "Marxist Vulgate," which exalted the figure of Mariátegui both in Peru and abroad while defending "actually existing socialism" in its discourse and its political practice, but also and more importantly begin a debate on an alternative perspective on knowledge, which in a way was already involved in Mariátegui's legacy and would precisely make its elements and its most fertile examples visible, helping us work once more on a radical critique of the established power.

Given all this, "Reencuentro y debate" raised the following main issues. The first issue was the need to demystify Mariátegui's intellectual legacy and to demystify his political stature, first in view of the diverse range of intellectual and political thought associated with "historical materialism," whether they defended or criticized "actually existing socialism": the "Muscovites," the various denominations of "pro-Chinese," and the "Rumanians"; the even more numerous rival groups in the "Trotskyite" lineage; and social democrats (including the Apristas of that era), social liberals, and social Christians. The second issue was heterogeneity of the place and trajectory of Mariátegui's writing in the Marxist debate, particularly regarding the relations between the materiality and the intersubjectivity of social relations and also regarding the historical relations among "modes of production," especially with respect to the specific case of Peruvian reality. The third issue was Mariátegui's key theoretical subversion, which entailed, at the very moment he tried to use the perspective and categories of the unilineal, unidirectional evolutionary sequence of "modes of production" that lie at the heart of "historical materialism" to interpret Peruvian reality, his conclusion that those "modes of production" were structurally linked to each other in the Peru of his time, thus forming a complex and specific configuration of power in a single historical moment and historical space. The fourth issue was Mariátegui's concept of "Indo-American socialism" as something historically specific, whose meaning could only be grasped in relationship to this theoretical discovery. Finally, the fifth issue was his consequent and parallel conflicts with the American Popular Revolutionary Alliance (Alianza Popular Revolucionaria Americana) and with the hegemonic Stalinism of the Third Communist International.

My preface, given the limits of the genre, merely raised these issues. Much ink has flowed since then in Mariátegui territory. On one hand, more of Mariátegui's written work besides his widely known *Seven Essays* began to appear in print.[5] Soon his entire body of work was being systematically published. Virtually all of his writings have been published in recent decades. With these new resources, the list of publications on his life and work has steadily grown, especially in 1980 following the fiftieth anniversary of his death and in 1994, the first centennial of his birth. Though most of these publications still aim principally to enrich the historical documentation of Mariátegui's personal, intellectual, and political trajectory, specific areas of his thought are beginning to be explored more systematically as they relate to the current debates on matters that they entail, among others the issues of "gender," "Indigenous" identity, "race," and "nation"; on aesthetic "vanguards"; on life stories of his break with the oligarchic world; on Latin America; and on the idea of "Indo-American socialism."[6] A good number of these studies have been presented at the many international meetings devoted to debating Mariátegui's legacy and have been gathered in collective volumes.[7] And, of course, the research on the place of his legacy within "Marxism" continues.[8]

Thirty Years Later

The last three decades have undeniably been characterized by the deepest and most significant historical change in the world matrix of power since the so-called Industrial Revolution. This is, in other words, nothing less than the beginning of a distinct historical period. The change amounts to a complete reconfiguring of the current matrix of power, a complex process, still underway, that began with the outbreak of the world capitalist crisis in mid-1973.

This reconfiguring of the current matrix of power consists above all in the deepening and acceleration of its core tendencies in the conflict over the control of social existence. It is worth noting here, first, that control over public authority (primarily the state) is being reconcentrated all over the world and, second, that control over labor is also being reconcentrated all over the world.[9]

The first of these dimensions of the process has to do with the formation of a worldwide imperial bloc and the continual erosion of the autonomy of those states in which the nationalization and democratization processes could not be consolidated or were precarious or incipient due to the current coloniality of power. This entails a continual erosion of public political space and of liberal democracy in both the center and the periphery. Taken together, it is a process of de-democratizing and denationalizing the state and society within the matrix of power on a planetary scale, in other words, a global imperialism at the extreme of which, if this trend is not contained or defeated, we are at risk of a global recolonization. Iraq, Afghanistan, more recently Somalia, and earlier the former Yugoslavia as well as the gradual expansion of US military bases in Latin America are all clear examples of these dangers.

The second dimension has to do, on one hand, with the utter dominance of the hypertechnologized levels of capital, the levels at which the need and interest of paying the labor force is reduced, whereas at the lower levels there is a demand for the reexpansion of absolute surplus value in relations with paid labor (for "job flexibilization" and "job insecurity," in the empiricist language of the sociology of labor). All of this leads to the expansion of unemployment among paid workers and the reduction of pay scales around the world and thus to the reexpansion of unpaid forms of labor: enslavement, servitude, and reciprocity. Taken altogether, this is world capitalism today. It is linked to the hegemony of financial accumulation, the prolonged duration of which, unlike in previous moments of capitalist crisis, derives from the novelty of its sources in the current world structure of accumulation and labor control. The most visible implication of these processes is continual and extreme social polarization on a planetary and global scale.

These trends have brought about the imperialist reconcentration of control over political authority and labor on a geographically planetary scale, affecting the entirety of the population in a combined process of crisis and change, that is, subjecting them as a whole to a single matrix of power, which is now known as the "colonial/modern world-system."[10] This is how the greatest concentration of world control of power known in history to date has been produced. And this is what is entailed in what is termed "globalization."[11] The new matrix of power produced during the conquest and destruction of the precolonial historical world in what we now call the Americas has entered a period and a process of crisis and transition that is probably the deepest and most decisive in its five hundred–year history.

However, what its publicity agents present as a sort of "natural" phenomenon—one that does not depend on people's interests, will, or opinions, so that it would make no sense to criticize, much less oppose it—is obviously a product of the struggles within the matrix of power between its dominators and its dominated and the struggles for world control among its dominators. The problem is that these struggles led, first, to the worst historical defeat of workers and to all the dominated/exploited/repressed people of the world.[12] And, likewise, the struggles led to the defeat and disintegration of the main rivals to the imperialist bloc through the final disintegration of the "socialist camp," the incorporation of China into the realm of capitalism, or what Boris Kagarlitsky has termed "market Stalinism,"[13] and the disintegration of virtually every regime, organization, and political movement associated with the "socialist camp" throughout the world, with the solitary exception of Cuba.

That defeat also swept away practically all the tendencies, organized or not, of radical critics of the world matrix of power, from both the imperialist bloc and the "socialist camp," since they had lost their place in the worldwide debate, to the extent that for more than two decades power ceased to be a major issue in scientific research and in the related debate except as a reality-based empirical fact. Taken together, the defeat of the exploited/dominated/repressed and also of the rivals and opponents to the current matrix of power produced a virtual worldwide eclipse of the historical horizon that, since the eighteenth century and in particular since the emergence of the idea of socialism as a radical and global democratization of social relations in all their decisive realms and dimension, had begun to illuminate the sometimes winding and labyrinthine path toward liberation from power, from all power.[14]

This total victory of the imperialist bloc does not in any way imply that the bloc is invincible or that it will reproduce itself indefinitely. Far from it. The crisis of the entire matrix of power has only deepened more rapidly during this period. On the other hand, the crisis made the limits and distortions of the knowledge perspective entailed in "Marxism-Leninism" more visible than ever, as that perspective paid ever greater tribute to the technocratizing tendencies of Eurocentrism in the already lengthy period of domination by financial accumulation in the transition of capital and of the modern/colonial matrix of power as a whole, which it dominates and on which it depends, in other words, of its growing inability to facilitate an effective, radical, and global understanding of reality and, to that same degree, of its inability to guide the struggles of victims of the current matrix of power accurately and effectively. Thus, it operated as a decisive element in determining the defeat of revolutionary struggles around the world in this period. The victory of worldwide capitalism was so complete that its intellectuals and politicians felt it was final and absolute, that this was "the end of history."[15]

For some time, the crisis of "historical materialism," the disintegration of the "socialist camp," and the worldwide imposition of what is known as the "globalization of neoliberalism" led to the rejection of research and debate of the critique of the existing power structure virtually all over the world. Thus, the ideology of the dominant power was established as a kind of global common sense. So-called postmodernism became one of the most prevalent versions of this new subalternization of world social thought, because it was an effective way to express, on one hand, the growing discomfort of the world intelligentsia, particularly its socialist-leaning part, with the Eurocentric distortions of "historical materialism." This was also why it became the vehicle for harboring a widespread demoralization among precisely those who had practiced it most orthodoxly, since they could find arguments in it for proclaiming their rejection of that perspective and feeling at last legitimized in abandoning the struggles of the dominated/exploited/repressed against power.

The time of that defeat is coming to an end. In the early 1990s the resistance against the most brutal tendencies of that "globalization" emerged, with worker revolts in countries known earlier as the "Asian tigers" and the successful rebellion against one of the bloodiest and longest dictatorships imposed by US imperialism, that of Indonesia. This resistance began its "globalization" with the massive youth protests in the United States, France, Germany, and Switzerland at the beginning of the current century and started developing with the establishment of the World Social Forum, which has met annually since 2001, precisely as the first "global" agora of this new movement, in which tendencies and theories are already active in guiding the transition from resistance to alternatives against the whole globalized matrix of power. A new horizon, in short, is being established on the path to new struggles against power. It thus signals a new historical period of struggles for power and struggles against power.[16] And today, Latin America is undoubtedly both the central space for this movement and one of its basic, specific modes and moments.[17]

On the Threshold of a New Horizon

This is thus a profoundly and systematically different world from the one we knew just thirty years ago. And now is the time to state unequivocally that in Latin America and beyond, the movement of reflection on Mariátegui's work is precisely the point of departure for the emerging perspectives on knowledge making, research on which is now at the center of the current debate.[18]

Just as there's no such thing as "Marxism," but rather a debate based on and surrounding the heterogeneous theoretical legacy of Marx, exactly the same is true of the debate on Mariátegui. It has taken us a long time, bogged down as we have been in the debates over "Marxism," "actually existing socialism," and Mariátegui's respective place, to admit the full ramifications of the crucial movements of rupture with Eurocentrism in Mariátegui's thought, to resolve—as the historian Jean Ellenstein demanded of his comrades in the French Communist Party in 1985—"to examine our earlier suspicions thoroughly."

In his most recent book *El marxismo de José Carlos Mariátegui y su aplicación a los 7 ensayos*, David Sobrevilla rejects my idea that many central elements of an alternative rationality are implicit in Mariátegui.[19] In his preface to the book, Antonio Melis nevertheless insists that my hypothesis is "fruitful and not arbitrary." Sobrevilla is correct if he is referring to the fact that these terms are not to be found in Mariátegui, nor are there any formal signals that he was proposing to find or produce an alternative rationality. And perhaps it is also true that these are not the most effective terms with which to give an account of the moments and zones of rupture in Mariátegui's reflections on the Eurocentrism that dominates "historical materialism" or of the current lively debate against Eurocentrism and in favor of reconstituting different ways of producing subjectivity or, more generally, a new universe of subjectivities, the imaginary, historical memory, and knowledge and understanding, because it is not about finding one alternative rationality to replace Eurocentrism.

The process that is probably at work in today's history is complex and heterogeneous. First, the process involved the demystification of Eurocentrism by unhiding its most distorting cognitive and intellectual processes and its nature as an intellectual provincialism that imposed its hegemony on the world as a tool of domination in the world coloniality/modernity of power. Second was the reconstitution of other rationalities that had been repressed, even partly or totally buried, under the dominion of Eurocentrism and the whole colonial/modern matrix of power. Last, as I have long insisted, was the creation of a universe of intersubjectivity with a common base of meanings for everyone that, without prejudice to the specific rationalities proper to each historical group or identity, will permit communication around the world, the transmission of elements, even conflicts or, for each of them, the potential options of plural and heterogeneous cognitive orientations.[20]

However, without the strained ruptures that bear witness to Mariátegui's exceptional insight, it would undoubtedly have taken us much longer.[21] Here are just a few signs. The decisive first rupture takes place in his *Seven Essays*, no less, and assumes the character of a real epistemic and theoretical subversion,[22] given that it is produced within the perspective that Mariátegui himself formally accepts, that of "historical materialism," with its evolutionary sequence of modes of production, and in the process of his trying to use that perspective: "I shall make a final observation: the elements of three different economies coexist in Peru today. Underneath the feudal economy inherited from the colonial period, vestiges of the Indigenous communal economy can still be found in the *sierra* (mountain or highlands). On the coast, a bourgeois economy is growing in feudal soil; it gives every indication of being backward, at least in its mental outlook."[23]

This perspective breaks, first, with Eurocentric ideas of an all-inclusive whole and evolutionism, which presuppose a continuous and homogeneous, albeit contradictory, unity moving through time in an equally continuous and homogeneous way until it transforms into another analogous unity. This idea of an all-inclusive whole has been part of every strain of Eurocentrism, whether "organic," as in "historical materialism"; "systemic," as in "structural-functionalism"; metaphysical-philosophical, as in the Hegelian idea of the Absolute; or metaphysical-theological, as in the three religions derived from the Middle East in which everything is related to everything else because it was all created by one omnipotent being. At the same time, it allows us to dispose of a general rejection of any notion of a whole, as in the old British empiricism and the new postmodernism, which would exclude the issue of power. And finally, it opens up a debate on the whole as a field of relationships or a unity of heterogeneous, discontinuous, and contradictory elements in a single historical-structural configuration.[24]

This idea of the whole is epistemically and theoretically indispensable for delivering explanation and meaning to what Mariátegui observes and discovers in his essay on the economic evolution of Peru. Without that epistemic subversion, his treatment of the relations between the intersubjective dimension and the material dimension of social existence could not be fully understood: "In Peru, the meaning of republican emancipation has been violated by entrusting the creation of a capitalist economy to the spirit of the fief—the antithesis and negation of the spirit of the town."[25]

This original epistemic and theoretical subversion can be recognized as the source of the innovation of the Latin American idea of historical-structural heterogeneity as a historically constitutive mode of all social existence, thus breaking with the radical Cartesian's dualism, which lay at the very origins of Eurocentrism, and with the positivist propensity for reductionism and evolutionism. And without this new point of departure, we could not explain the innovative theoretical and political debate, within and beyond Latin America, over the character and history of the current world power, especially the lively debate about the theoretical proposal of the coloniality and de/coloniality of power.

Similarly, without Mariátegui's rupture regarding the place of "race" and the "class factor" in the process of "nationalizing" the state and democratizing society, we could not understand or explain or even make sense of the current "Indigenous movements" in the Americas, especially Latin America, and their significance for the issues of the modern nation-state, democracy, and identity.[26]

And finally, without Mariátegui's insistence on the essential place of the "Indigenous community" in the trajectory of any socialist revolution in these lands, on the specific nature of "Indo-American socialism," as against the positivist evolutionism embedded in "historical materialism," the new revolutionary imaginary that is being built in the new historical horizon would take much longer to reach maturity, to become perceptible as a process of democratically producing a democratic society, of learning to live simultaneously with the state and without the state, with the market and without the market, in the face of the market hyperfetishization tendencies, linked to the remedievalization of subjectivity, which world capitalism is already trying to impose in order to perpetuate the globalization of the entire world population under a single matrix of power.

So, it is time now to recognize that without these moments of theoretical subversion against Eurocentrism in the movement of Mariátegui's thought, current research could not have come to perceive during the current crisis that the whole world matrix of power is, precisely, a specific historical configuration woven around two constitutive axes. One is the idea of "race" as the basis of an entire new system of social domination, for which Eurocentrism is one of the most effective tools. The other axis is the articulation of all "modes of production" into a single structure for producing commodities for the world market, precisely as Mariátegui managed to perceive in the economy of Peru in his time, as a moment of epistemic and theoretical subversion within the framework of "historical materialism" itself. This specific, historically structurally heterogeneous configuration is the nucleus of what is being discussed today about the coloniality/modernity of power.

It is in this specific sense that the debate on Mariátegui must be reassessed in its perspectives and its aims, confronting the current tendencies of world power and the alternative options of the dominated/ exploited/repressed people of the world, because it is precisely in the movement of Mariátegui's reflections that some of the key elements of the ongoing reappraisal of the epistemic, theoretical, and political debate are to be found. This does not mean, obviously, that it is no longer relevant and important to continue, as we have, exploring Mariátegui territory, especially in relation to the history of and earlier perspectives on knowledge and understanding.

Notes

Aníbal Quijano, "Prólogo: José Carlos Mariátegui; Reencuentro y debate," written in 1978 at the request of Ángel Rama and published as "Treinta años después: Otro reencuentro—Notas para otro debate," preface to José Carlos Mariátegui, *7 ensayos de interpretación de la realidad peruana* (Caracas, Venezuela: Biblioteca Ayucho, 1979).

1   See Shanin, *Late Marx and the Russian Road*.
2   In Latin America, it may have first been given this name by the well-known Brazilian social scientist Francisco de Oliveira during a debate organized by the Latin American Council of Social Sciences (Consejo Latinoamericano de Ciencias Sociales) in Montevideo in 1986.

3　The generally intersubjective intellectual atmosphere during the crisis was expressed keenly in the debate resulting from the publication of Laclau and Mouffe, *Hegemony and Socialist Strategy*, in 1985, followed almost immediately by Wood, *The Retreat from Class*.

4　On the debate on these issues within the worldwide revolutionary movement, two studies are particularly worth mentioning: Bahro, "The Alternative in Eastern Europe," and Bettelheim, *Class Struggles in the USSR*.

5　Nearly coinciding with the final collapse of the "socialist camp," two compilations of texts by Mariátegui were published with very different aims, contents, and organization. One, an anthology edited by Alberto Flores Galindo and Ricardo Portocarrero, came out in 1989 under the title *Invitación a la vida heroica*. The other, compiled by Aníbal Quijano in 1991 under the title *Textos básicos*, was divided into sections designed to show basic instances of the movement of Mariátegui's reflections, his implicit perspective on the production of knowledge, and the major areas of philosophical and sociological-political issues. The prologues to each section and to the volume as a whole allowed me to explicate my ideas on the moments of Mariátegui's subversion against the dominant Eurocentrism in "historical materialism," which show that his works are worth studying for more than their historical value, as they are exceptionally fruitful for the new worldwide debate over the production of knowledge and the radical critique of the current world power.

6　See, among others, Guardia, *José Carlos Mariátegui*; Beigel, *El itinerario y la brújula*; Tarcus, *Mariátegui en la Argentina o las políticas culturales de Samuel Glusberg*; Leibner, *El mito del socialismo indígena*; Stein, *Dance in the Cemetery*; Germaná, *El Socialismo indoamericano de José Carlos Mariátegui*; Castrillón Vizcarra, "José Carlos Mariátegui, crítico de arte"; and Aricó, *Marx y América Latina*.

7　Among the collective books worth citing are Aricó, *Mariátegui y los orígenes del marxismo latinoamericano*; Forgues, *Mariátegui y Europa*; Forgues, *Mariátegui*; Monereo, *Mariátegui (1884–1994)*; Adrianzén, Portocarrero, Cáceres, and Tapia, *La aventura de Mariátegui*; Sobrevilla, *El marxismo de José Carlos Mariátegui*; and, of course, the works published in *Anuario Mariateguiano* from 1989 to 1999 whose editorial board I joined, together with Antonio Melis, after the death of one of its founders, the historian Alberto Tauro del Pino, who did much of the work that led to the recovery, research, and publication of Mariátegui's writings.

8　Among the most influential studies, see Flores Galindo, "La Agonía de Mariátegui"; Franco, *Del marxismo eurocéntrico al marxismo latinoamericano*; Fernández Díaz, *Mariátegui, o la experiencia del Otro*; Guibal, *Vigencia de Mariátegui*; Löwy, "Marxisme et romantisme chez José Carlos Mariátegui"; Melis, *Leyendo Mariátegui*; and Sobrevilla, *El marxismo de José Carlos Mariátegui*.

9   On this issue, see Quijano, "Coloniality of Power, Globalization, and Democracy," in this volume. See also Quijano, "¿Entre la Guerra Santa y la Cruzada?"

10   On this, see Quijano and Wallerstein, "Americanity as a Concept, or the Americas in the Imaginary of the Modern World-System"; Quijano, "Colonialidad y modernidad/racionalidad"; Quijano, "Coloniality of Power, Eurocentrism and Latin America"; and Quijano, "Don Quixote and the Windmills in Latin America," in this volume.

11   My expressed views in this debate can be found, first and foremost, in Quijano, "Coloniality of Power, Globalization, and Democracy," and Quijano, "The New Anticapitalist Imaginary."

12   I have proposed a few issues for this debate in Quijano, "El trabajo en el umbral del siglo XXI."

13   [Translator's note: For example, in Kagarlitsky, "The Importance of Being Marxist," 33.]

14   On the implications of this process for the new debate, see my thoughts in Quijano,"El regreso del futuro y las cuestiones del conocimiento," and Quijano, "The New Anticapitalist Imaginary."

15   Much has been written on this since the publication of Fukuyama's well-known text. My thoughts in this debate can be found in Quijano, "¿El fin de cual historia?"

16   For this perspective, see Quijano, "The New Anticapitalist Imaginary."

17   I have discussed these issues in Quijano, "El laberinto de América Latina." See also Quijano, "The 'Indigenous Movement' and Unresolved Questions in Latin America"; and Quijano, "Estamos comenzando a producir otro horizonte histórico."

18   I am speaking primarily of the debate about the coloniality of power, transmodernity and the modern/colonial world-system, and the production of a different kind of democracy, on all of which there is a large and growing literature by such figures as Immanuel Wallerstein, Enrique Dussel, Aníbal Quijano, Walter Mignolo, Boaventura de Sousa Santos, Ramón Grosfoguel, Edgardo Lander, Agustín Lao-Montes, Catherine Walsh, Fernando Coronil, Santiago Castro-Gómez, Kelvin Santiago, Sylvia Winter, Ifi Amadiume, and Fernando Buscaglia, among many others.

19   I have suggested this idea in various texts: the "Prólogo" in Mariátegui, Textos básicos; the "Prólogo" to Díaz, Mariátegui, o la experiencia del Otro; and Quijano, "El precio de la racionalidad."

20   There is a vast literature now on this new debate. For my own unfinished proposals, see Quijano, "Dominación y cultura"; Quijano, Modernidad, identidad y utopía en América Latina and Quijano, "Coloniality of Power, Eurocentrism, and Latin America."

21   In a few brief notes for a new edition of Mariátegui, Seven Interpretative Essays on Peruvian Reality, it would be out of place to begin a debate on

the implications of all these movements of rupture with Eurocentrism in Mariátegui's writings. The main moments in this rupture can be found in Mariátegui, *Textos básicos*.

22 On the notion of epistemic and cultural subversion, see Quijano, "Colonialidad del poder, cultura y conocimiento en América Latina."

23 Mariátegui, *Seven Interpretive Essays on Peruvian Reality*, 16.

24 I have discussed these issues in Quijano, "Coloniality of Power, Eurocentrism, and Latin America."

25 Mariátegui, *Seven Interpretive Essays on Peruvian Reality*, 20.

26 See Quijano, "The 'Indigenous Movement' and Unresolved Questions in Latin America."

14

THE CRISIS OF THE COLONIAL/MODERN/ EUROCENTERED HORIZON OF MEANING

It is with some trepidation that I accept this honor and Professor Julio Mejía Navarrete's cordial and generous words of introduction. A person who has devoted his works and days to trying to understand and explain this world and this time, above all in order to help those who have been humiliated and wronged, the victims of power, to subvert it and free themselves from it, cannot help wondering about the meaning of this recognition, whether it might perhaps be a sign that something is indeed moving in the direction of such changes. In any case, I want to say that I accept it with hope and that I am grateful for the distinction that this university has seen fit to bestow upon me.

And something is moving, without a doubt. The world has come to the very brink of a narrow path from a matrix of power that is now showing the violence at its core to a new historical horizon striving to come fully into being.

Nevertheless, since the collapse of the towers of finance in the United States in the middle of the Northern Hemisphere's Fall of 2009, a torrent of numbers and disclosures revealing spectacular financial scandals has filled virtually the entire channel of immediate world subjectivity with something that everyone has termed a crisis of "capitalism" or, put differently, of "the system." And though some are proposing mechanisms for its recovery while others don't hesitate to proclaim its final, definitive collapse, both sides in the debate seem to me to be coming from a single shared perspective. In it, the thing which they are naming by that term isn't an issue to be researched; it is presented, rather, as a given in the nature of the world and in the very nature of this society. In other words, this all seems to be taking place as a natural phenomenon.

If we don't protect ourselves from drowning in this deluge, for a large number of us it will get harder to find the fissure in this world, the window through which we might see or catch a glimpse of how and whether what I'm calling a hope for change might emerge. And this is what I want to reflect on here: raising a few of the issues that might let us explore this perspective again, trying to locate the other elements that undoubtedly exist there, even perhaps the other horizon that is emerging.

It is unlikely that our species, Homo sapiens, has often been in a situation as peculiar and historically exceptional as the one we are living through now, because now we are faced with a conjunction, not just a convergence, between the global climate crisis—global warming is the most immediate form it has taken—and at the same time the crisis of an entire matrix of power, one whose most visible and salient face at this juncture is unquestionably world capitalism, that historically exceptional configuration in which every form of social exploitation is linked through the hegemony of capital and that was formed and exists as one of the two foundational major axes of that matrix of power.

In this sense, what's at stake today isn't just the survival of world capitalism and especially that of its victims but rather the survival of our species and perhaps of all forms of life on the planet. It is hard to find any equivalent circumstance in the history of humanity. Indeed, as far as we understand our own history, we have never come to a crossroads of this nature.

That is why it seems to me not only necessary but also inevitable to think that this conjunction is no accident. What's happening to the climate isn't happening merely to something called "nature." It isn't a "natural" phenomenon, and in the same way what's happening to world capitalism today isn't just another parallel natural phenomenon. In both cases—in very different ways, of course, but on both sides—we find, first of all, the history of power, and in addition we find the history of a specific matrix of power that we can now recognize, as Professor Mejía Navarrete has just reminded us, as the coloniality of power, established with the Americas and

Western Europe as its two original historical identities beginning in the late fifteenth century.

Thus, it is not just capital and not just capitalism that are in crisis at this moment; it's a whole matrix of power. And that matrix of power has, moreover, brought the crisis of so-called nature into play on our planet. It's a very specific kind of power, one whose current prospects and whose processes for the immediate future, as we can now easily glimpse, run an increasing risk, unless we can find some way to stop them, of not only destroying our common home, the planet, but also destroying us, not only because of the planetary crisis but also because we are killing each other today in favor of and as a function of what that matrix of power needs.

This means that to explore this set of issues, it isn't sufficient or relevant to keep on using the current hegemonic means of knowledge making and meaning making. That is, it isn't enough to accept that the only thing in crisis is something called "capitalism." It's true that world capitalism, including its current crisis, is the main element in the system of social exploitation, which is one of the central axes of the current matrix of power. But in the perspective of the coloniality of power, world capitalism is, first, a historically specific category, as a joint configuration of every historical form of labor exploitation—enslavement, servitude, reciprocity, simple small-scale market production, and capital—for producing commodities for the world market, centered on the hegemony of capital. But this structure is also a historical category, that is, always dynamic and changing, its nature different in each particular historical period. It is therefore not enough for us to name the category, because it is always an historical issue to be researched and understood.

Additionally, world capitalism is not the only historically particular aspect of the current matrix of power, because that matrix is also inextricably linked to the colonial/modern system of social domination founded on the idea/image of "race" as a basic form of social classification. Both axes were formed in the same process, in the same historical movement, jointly constituting the emergent matrix of power in a single configuration that now dwells in us and within which we dwell. Both depend on each other, and both produce the intersubjectivity within which we move, that is, in my terminology, the horizon of meaning that is still hegemonic today even though it is in crisis.

What do I mean by the problem of the horizon of meaning and its crisis? Allow me to suggest something that may sound trite. At school, I don't know if this is still true of most children, but certainly all of us became accustomed to saying "The Spanish came over to conquer America." That sentence is false, word by word. There was no such thing as Spain, and obviously there was no America. Therefore, the idea that Spain came over to conquer America is false. But we became used to saying that sentence and to thinking spontaneously in those terms, in other words, to understanding in this way the historical facts and processes of the destruction of a precolonial historical world and the emergence of a new matrix of power.

Similarly, we are familiar with the idea that in terms of wealth and power, the world is divided into a rich and powerful "North" and a dominated, poor, or underdeveloped "South." That division actually seems like it's strictly a matter of geography. To counter that idea, at the last World Social Forum in Nairobi, Kenya, a group of us decided to organize something we called the Global Commons Foundation in order to raise once more the question of whether there is a Global South, because if the term "the South" speaks to poverty and dependency, we can find those things everywhere, including in the North. Still, even though saying "there is also a South in the North" sounds subversive when we situate ourselves in the Eurocentric perspective that gives meaning to such terms, if we rethink it we find that the idea that there really is a North and a South in the distribution of power around the world entails accepting that geography is what distributes power instead of perceiving that this is all about the history of the geography of power.

Allow me to remind you, with that in mind, of a legendary anecdote that every Peruvian surely knows and perhaps some who are not Peruvian do too. Francisco Pizarro and his troops left Panama in search of a legendary place rich with gold, but they were fought and harassed every step of the way. We are talking about the early 1530s, when the populations along the Pacific coast south of Panama had already learned what these unfamiliar, strange, violent folks meant for them. So, they started harassing, wounding, and killing them. This prevented Pizarro's troops from obtaining enough food and healing their sick and wounded; in fact, they were beginning to die off. Pizarro decided to pull in at the little island called the Isla del Gallo off the coast and belonging to Colombia, and send an emissary to the governor of Panama, Pedrarias Dávila, to ask him to send aid. But some of Pizarro's soldiers had secretly decided to send a message to the governor so that instead of aid, he would send a military force to make Pizarro and his dwindling troops return to Panama. Undoubtedly you recall the famous verse they sent: "*Mírelo bien, Señor Gobernador / mírelo bien por entero / que allá va el recogedor / pero aquí queda el carnicero*" (Look it over, Governor

/ examine it completely, / there goes the one who gives shelter / and here stays the butcher"). Pedrarias Dávila obviously understood the message, and instead of backing up Pizarro's enterprise by sending aid and allowing it to continue, he sent a force to make Pizarro come back. And indeed, the armed force reached the Isla del Gallo and tried to make Pizarro return to Panama with what was left of his troops. But Pizarro then showed what he was made of. He refused to return, took out his sword, drew a line in the sand on the island, and let loose with his famous tirade "That way, North, for those who want to be poor. This way, South, for those who want to be rich." As you all recall, this was Captain Francisco Pizarro, the conqueror of Tawantinsuyu, the Inca Empire.

This historical scene played out just over five centuries ago. It allows us to show the birth of a novel geography of power, North and South, and, at the same time, the birth of an unprecedented horizon of meaning, a pioneering intersubjective perspective that has become hegemonic worldwide over the long period since to the point of making us accept this division of power as part of the natural configuration of our planet. I once heard during a political argument in Lima that the dominance of the dollar in Latin America was a function of geography.

But what was there in the North in the early sixteenth century? If you place it on its geohistorical, geopolitical, geocultural map, you are quite certainly going to find that in the first third of the sixteenth century, what we now call the North, though not devoid of population, was hardly the center of power and wealth. To the contrary, everything that had power, everything that had wealth, everything that had high productivity, the seat of everything that we have since learned to call the "high cultures" was, before this moment, the South. What happened after the Isla del Gallo? A swift, radical, and violent redistribution of power occurred, not merely of the resources for producing wealth but more so, in the first place, for configuring social relations and, as a powerful form of controlling social relations, a novel intersubjectivity, a groundbreaking historical horizon of meaning.

During the period that we call the colonial era, here in Peru and in the Americas there was no professional army or professional police force in the early days. The colonized populations frequently rose in revolt, but in the end they were always subjugated and controlled. What controlled them if there was no professional police force, no professional army? The conquerors and colonizers had brought something more powerful than any of that: a set of ideas of images and myths, of forms of knowing, of explaining, which not only repressed the previous imaginary, the previous matrix of remembering and forgetting, but also repressed it by superimposing on it its own atmosphere, its own mentality, its own means of understanding the world, its own way of seeing, and its own way of keeping things from being seen, that is, by colonizing the subjectivity, the intersubjectivity, of the dominated.

If you go to Cuzco during the fiesta for the Señor de los Temblores (Lord of Earthquakes, an image of Christ on the cross in the cathedral) and listen to the singing of the people, who remain Indigenous, who remain "Indian" in colonial terms, singing in Quechua the dire hymn to the Señor de los Temblores, you can recognize how they were interjected with a foreign element called guilt, which obviously had not existed in these lands before Pizarro drew his famous line in the sand of the Isla del Gallo. That's what I'm talking about here, and here is where I want to leave this issue raised. I mean that the destruction of the prior historical world, the colonization of the surviving population, entailed not only the redistribution of wealth but also the construction of a distinctive matrix of power from the late fifteenth century on. That matrix of power is what we have now learned to recognize as the coloniality of power.

Let me insist. This was a groundbreaking, historically specific matrix of power constructed on two foundational axes: (1) an unknown system of social exploitation that consists and has consisted in a joint configuration of every historical form of exploitation, built around and under the hegemony of capital, and (2) an unknown system of social domination configured on the basis of and around the idea-image of "race," a mental construct without historical precedent. Within the limits of this occasion, I'd like to explore most of all the significance of this second axis.

There are debates about this, obviously. Some think that the idea of "race" had already existed in the Chinese empire. But that's a basic confusion with the idea of superiority-inferiority among persons and groups that are positioned unequally in hierarchies of social domination. That idea has always existed, alongside domination and social inequality. Our species, Homo sapiens, is some 200,000 years old, and domination, exploitation, social inequality, and conflict have been around in our species for, well, many thousands of years.

The point is this: Beyond any doubt, control of some people over others, control over the exchanges of behavior that we call social relations, is ancient, and colonialism in particular has been around for thousands of years. There have been many colonial empires before the Americas, but nowhere do we find this history, this mental construct that we recognize today as race, because it doesn't refer to the superiority-inferiority position in social hierarchies. Normally, especially in countries such as Peru, for example, government ministers think they're superior or act like they're superior to their secretaries. And the ancient Chinese undoubtedly thought themselves "superior" to all the world's other inhabitants. That's a form of "ethnocentrism," to use anthropologist jargon. But that's not what this is. Rather, it is about what was debated early on, in the mid-sixteenth century, in Valladolid regarding the "Indians": What are these? Are they animals? Humans? Half animal, half human? Do they have souls? In other words, do they belong to our species or not? In our current jargon, we'd say that this is an issue regarding a basic inequality in the structure of people's biology and therefore a "natural" difference. Some aren't human or aren't entirely human.

Finally, after the debate in Valladolid, the king of Castile-Aragon, of the future Spain, decreed as the pope had already done that "Indians" are humans but pagans who need to be Christianized. But for half a century, the idea that Indians aren't human or are at most semihuman had been penetrating deeply into social practice for not only the dominators but also their administrators and victims and producing a process of "naturalization" of that idea-image, turning it into a central element in the social relations between the colonizers and their victims. Though the humanity of the newly colonized was legally accepted, that condition was accepted in social practice at a very low level, very close to what would later be called "nature." A new historical meaning was consequently being imposed, a new way to understand relations between not only people and experiences but also between our species and the rest of the universe.

The production of the idea of "race" and the "racialization" of social relations gave rise to a new intersubjective perspective that pervaded each and every realm of social existence while orienting, defining, and legitimating the new colonial relations in their materiality and in their intersubjectivity at the same historical moment when Western Europe began to emerge as the central control headquarters for the nascent matrix of power, that is, in the same process of Eurocentering the new matrix of power, whose foundational base was the racialization of relations in the social existence under colonial Iberian dominion.

In the process of the emergence of the identity that would later be called Western Europe, as the control headquarters of the rising matrix of power and of the expansion of capital based on the other forms of exploitation in the Americas, we also see a Eurocentering of the intellectual, philosophical, and theoretical elaboration of the historical experiences within this matrix of power. In this sense, it is undeniable that without the "racialization" of social relations and of the basic social classification of people, without the dualization of the population into humans and semihumans, into "racially" (i.e., "naturally") "superior" and "inferior" people, the secularization of medieval Christian theology in the new Eurocentric philosophy would hardly have gone so far as to propose the new radical Cartesian dualism (between "reason" and "nature") and to get it accepted as the very basis of "modern rationality," destined to become hegemonic not only across the Americas and Western Europe but also throughout the world of the Eurocentered coloniality of power, after the "industrial/bourgeois revolution" and the worldwide spread of Western European colonialism.

The new radical Cartesian dualism, victorious over Spinozian monism, became the very foundation of the new mental, intellectual perspective that emerged together with the Eurocentering of the coloniality of power. In this context and in this way, this sort of "modern rationality" could be nothing other than a "colonial/modern rationality."

This radical dualism had no historical precedents much like the idea of "race," which is one of its most obvious foundational experiences. Perhaps the oldest recognizable antecedent is in Plato's *Phaedo*, which sets up a profound differentiation between two dimensions in each individual: that which is tangible and that which is not. But in Plato, both dimensions continue to act as linked together within each of us; they are different, differentiable, but inseparable.

Obviously, if we review what took place in what we now call the "high cultures," in all of them everywhere over thousands of years, people learned that we can differentiate between dimensions that aren't the same thing, but nobody ever proposed that they could be separated as different in nature. This proposal appeared for the first time in Descartes. Reason is divine; we are the bearers of reason; therefore, we have something of the divine in us. But the rest of us—the body—is thus not divine, nor is the rest of what exists outside of us divine. This is, as we can see, a new and radical dualism, which became the basis of the Eurocentric means of meaning making and not only differentiates but also separates reason and nature as two worlds foreign to each other.

There were other proposals introduced in the same era. Spinoza was working at the same moment, in the same city, but he was a Sephardic Jew, rejected by his own community, isolated, alone. So, the one who was ultimately established from then on as the manager and producer of the theory of rationality was Descartes.

There is a division, a dualization, that predates that of "race," a much older one: the division between the sex differences in our species. I'm not convinced that patriarchal dominance is as universal and permanent as is now asserted, especially in the so-called Western and Christian world; I think not, I think experiences were much more varied, complex, and multiple. But ultimately, even the earlier distinction proposing that there is an inferior sex—what is discussed today as the gender issue—has been completely redefined since the production and imposition of the idea of race and the racialization of social relations.

As for the conquerors who came over, remember who they were. They were Counter-Reformation Christians and were the bearers of the Inquisition, ready to burn anyone who didn't accept their beliefs, especially the women, since a large majority of those who were burnt were women and not by mistake, obviously. The conquerors were authoritarian, hierarchical, repressive, and patriarchal; that is, from their perspective of meaning, the woman was inferior to man. But beginning in the sixteenth century, every woman from the superior race became, by definition, superior to any male from an inferior race. The so-called inferior races were also hierarchized among themselves, some of them being closer to "nature," especially, of course, the women of those inferior races. Above all, after the conquest and colonization of Africa, Blacks were considered very close to nature, and Black women were considered virtually as nature itself. A bit higher on the scale were the so-called Indians. After the Industrial Revolution, the new historical entity that would later be called Western Europe set off on the conquest and colonization of the rest of the world. Then, the new "Western Europeans" redefined the historical identities of the peoples they conquered and colonized, imposing on them new designations, new hierarchies. Thus, the so-called Orient was formulated as the "Other," though still inferior, to everything that was Western European. Indians and Black Africans never had a chance of being the Other, the West's Orient; they were too inferior from the outset.

As you can see, a new and distinctive historical meaning was being established, and it continued to unfold over the course of the worldwide expansion of this matrix of power, especially with the process we call the Industrial Revolution in the center-north of the new historical identity we recognize as Western Europe. Their colonizing experience in the rest of the world would contribute to producing what they would later call "modernity." "Modernity" is consequently a Eurocentered outcome but made within the global coloniality of power. It is therefore a colonial/modernity.

I'd like to explore this quickly too, given that we don't have much time. Western Europe's experience of colonial domination over the rest of the world entailed the expansion and deepening of the colonial matrix of power that had been built in and from the Americas. Together with the "racialization" of the basic social classification of the world population that had been colonized, the novel system of social exploitation configured around the hegemony of capital also expanded and matured.

We still don't know precisely enough when capital emerged as a specific social relationship. The question has been raised only recently, and research is in progress, but we don't have conclusive answers yet. From what we know so far, capital as a social relationship of control over labor, over the production and distribution of labor through the commodification of the labor force, probably began somewhere in the south of what we now call the Iberian Peninsula or the Italian peninsula or both between the ninth and eleventh centuries, hence under Muslim hegemony. Organized society in the Mediterranean basin under Arab Muslim hegemony was a cultured, urban world, a center of medical, philosophical, technological, scientific, and mathematical research and an exceptionally rich and productive axis of the commercial traffic in the pre-America, pre–Western Europe world, the lively commercial exchange from what we now call India, from what we now call China, from Persia, from Baghdad, Cairo, and so on. So, in the Mediterranean basin there was an urgent need to produce more faster and cheaper. How, when, and who produced this new social technology and turned the living labor force of individuals, willingly or by violence, into a commodity? That's still an open question. But that was where a new division of labor was established, what we call capital today. But capital in the Mediterranean wasn't hegemonic over all other forms of exploitation, over enslavement, over servitude, over reciprocity, over simple small-scale market production. Though mercantile capital began to expand to the north of the Italian peninsula from the thirteenth century, particularly along the riverways, it coexisted with all the other forms without any sort of joint configuration, something that would only be produced with the Americas and based on the Americas, even though its expansion would result from the Eurocentering of the new matrix of power.

With the Americas, not only was the idea of race imposed as the central criterion of social classification for the world's population, but additionally an added commercial basin began to be established, gaining prominence in place of the Mediterranean, in order to carry the massive production coming out of the Americas across the new route, the Atlantic: precious metals such as gold, silver, and copper and precious plants such as cocoa, tobacco, and potatoes that were produced as merchandise for the new world market through enslavement, through servitude, through small-scale market production, through reciprocity, and through capital. All these forms of exploitation or labor control work together, all in a single structure for producing merchandise for the new world market. This is what began to generate what we now call Western Europe and Spain itself. So, the Americas and Western Europe created each other mutually in the same period, the same historical moment, in a matrix of power whose central axes are, on one hand, subjectivity and intersubjectivity built on the idea of race and of racist and sexist ranking, which invades and pervades every sphere of social existence—the imaginary, memory, the feelings, explanations, knowledge, understanding—and, on the other hand, every form of exploitation, of labor control, built around the hegemony of capital, which are consequently capitalist in character, taken as a whole. This is what we recognize as world capitalism. It did not become hegemonic or spread around the world by itself, separately from all other forms of social exploitation. And since the sixteenth century it has never existed or acted as anything other than predominant in this global configuration for producing commodities for the world market then as now, at the beginning of the twenty-first century.

The Industrial Revolution itself, as we have now learned through detailed research, came from the development of technological innovations made by enslaved Blacks in Martinique, Jamaica, and Cuba for the production of tobacco, coffee, and sugarcane. This is because before the Industrial Revolution, what we now call Western Europe had nothing to offer the world market unless someone can remember what it was. All it could offer was what was produced by the unpaid labor of people in slavery and servitude in the Americas: precious metals that allowed Western Europe to metalize money and monetize the market, to have at last a stable and continuous monetary market, and actually make a new world market with new precious minerals and plants.

So, there is a whole new and distinctive horizon of meaning, but the central epistemic axis of all this remains the strange combination of, on one hand, radical dualism and racism-sexism and, on the other hand, the expanded systems and techniques of observation, measurement, and experimentation, which were not invented then but were an enlargement coming from earlier times, particularly from the Mediterranean under Muslim domination. That was the origin of what is now discussed as the issue of modernity and rationality. It's a new and distinctive horizon of meaning. But in the framework of this distinctive matrix of power, in the context and in the process of the coloniality of power, this distinctive horizon of meaning, modernity, can't help but be colonial as well not only because of its origins but also because of its constitutive elements, which have been intrinsic to it from then to now.

Every horizon of meaning, even a dominant one, is always heterogeneous in history. Its hegemony doesn't imply that everyone in every corner of the world thinks exactly alike, feels exactly alike, understands alike, explains alike. The hegemony of a horizon of meaning implies a common axis of orientation, and in a colonial power it implies that the axis invades and even colonizes what doesn't belong to it, represses it, humiliates it, or belittles it.

This colonial/modern/Eurocentered horizon of meaning was dominant up to World War II. It was always resisted and contested. Even during the colonial period, resistance came out of the Americas, especially in what we now call Latin America, not only because it was the first region where the coloniality of power was established but also because of Iberian failure with respect to the first colonial/modern period. After independence in the nineteenth century, movement in the Americas was already resisting the Eurocentric way of seeing the world.

If you carefully compare the whole trend called "subaltern studies," fashioned above all by Indian historians from Ranajit Guha on, with the intellectual output of Latin America from the late nineteenth century, above all from José Martí on, including José Vasconcelos, Victor Raúl Haya de la Torre, José Carlos Mariátegui, and others, you will find that they are dealing with the same issues and that the basic answers are the same, though Guha and his followers are professionals at social history research. But you will probably also find that the debate has, most of all, a rather identitarian, even nationalist origin and meaning such that its epistemic suppositions aren't always necessarily anti-Eurocentric, even when its historical theory is formulated as antihegemonic response, and that it's no accident that the Gramscian categories of subalternity and hegemony play such a central role in it.

Thus, with the lone exception of Mariátegui, none of the others find, discover, or stumble across a way to break or subvert the epistemic roots of the existing horizon of meaning. Mariátegui remains very isolated, politically condemned from the time of the 1929 conference of Latin American communist parties, and was intellectually buried for a long period. Though mystified and glorified for his name, his main theoretical discoveries would not reappear in the Latin American debate until decades later.

Following World War II, after the experiences of Nazism and faced with the experiences of bureaucratic despotism, the predominance of Eurocentrism, of the colonial/modern/Eurocentered horizon of meaning, could not remain untouched. Every historical horizon of meaning is an epistemic/theoretical/historical/ethical/aesthetic/political combination. The currently hegemonic one is openly in crisis. But the crisis of Eurocentrism came about in a very curious way: we went down the narrow alleyway of the "posts," first posthumanism, then poststructuralism, next postcolonial studies, and later postmodernism and postmodernity. This alleyway of posts entails a stammering difficulty, a critique from within Eurocentrism, that cannot, however, manage to produce any real, basic rupture in the racist/sexist episteme that began with "America" and developed to become dominant worldwide in the course and current of the worldwide spread of Western European colonialism. But it is an effective indication that the horizon is in crisis.

And once again—speaking from the Global South, from Latin America and the Caribbean in the first place, but also from Africa and Asia—a whole social movement is emerging right now and gaining rapidly, and there's an emergent debate that not only calls into question the epistemic assumptions of this horizon of meaning and therefore its imaginary, the way it shapes up matrices of memory and forgetting, the way it generates explanations, knowledge, and meaning, but is also generating, moreover, in practice, another possible horizon that is now being set up, because in this period the social protests of those most subjugated under the coloniality of power, the "Indigenous" peoples, are coming together with the crisis of nature, that is, of the planet itself. In this conjunction, the struggle of Indigenous peoples for survival also becomes a struggle for the survival of the entire species and indeed for the livability of the planet. In this context, this is the first time in the past five hundred years that a perspective and discourse have emerged, both of them necessarily anticapitalist and anticoloniality in regard to power, whose origins are not intellectual or ethical-philosophical but instead lie in the most direct needs of survival, because during the same period the most deeply contentious and violent tendencies of the current matrix of power and the most technocratic avenues and lines of coloniality/modernity have come to dominate. It is the crisis of the matrix of power as such that has produced the crisis of its hegemonic horizon of meaning.

Capitalism today—I'm going to close on this note—is still capitalism, but when we look at the debate on the financial catastrophe now taking place, we can see that there's something that still hasn't reached the debate: the fact that it's been thirty-five years, roughly, since capital entered a crisis of transition or a crisis of disruption to its deepest roots and foundations. What do I mean? This is part of the history of social debate in Latin America. We in Latin America were the ones who began to discover, in the mid-1960s, that a very profound change was beginning to take place in the capital-labor relation. The studies that talked about "marginalization" took note of this. A growing portion of workers fired during moments of contracting production were not being rehired in moments of expansion, and that portion has been growing constantly. Why?

The studies of the famous Group of Prague,[1] disbanded with the invasion of Russian tanks in 1968, helped us understand what the "scientific technological revolution," as it had already been named at that time, meant or might mean—a decisive change, a mutation, in the relations between space and time and between them and us—because this scientific-technological revolution made it possible to get along with less and less of the living labor force of individuals. But at that moment—we're talking about the 1960s—this was still an incipient trend though a perceptible one. Today it isn't a trend; it's an established situation. There is an ultratechnologized, computerized level of production at which an individual, living labor force is virtually inexistent; there isn't one. As a consequence, at such places there are no jobs added in the conventional sense; they produce unemployment. The rest of the workers can find jobs only at the middle and low end. Hence the talk of structural unemployment, and not of the conjuncture; hence job flexibilization and insecurity. Hence also the reexpansion of enslavement, of servitude, of the small-scale market production that was once at the very heart of the informal economy and also of reciprocity.

I'm sure that many of you know, perhaps even have experienced yourselves, that the most recent electronic gadgets tend to get smaller and cheaper all the time, and some of them can be and indeed are given away for free. Why? Because the individual production cost for these goods is constantly dropping, at times to less than zero. But when they are given away, you are also asked to register for a service that has to be paid for monthly. This means that the production cost is no longer the axis of the market but rather financial speculation. Therefore, the finance capital that exists today isn't the old finance capital that has always showed up with every crisis but always for a short time, ten or fifteen years on average; the kind we have now has been hanging around for forty years already, and it doesn't look like it plans to leave unless we throw it out. The more inventive, the more "creative," the mechanisms of speculation are, the greater the profits they promise. Thus, financial speculation tends to become more deregulated and consequently more fraudulent all the time. This is a necessary part of any explanation of the current great financial crisis: it's a gigantic financial fraud, painstakingly assembled, but we're talking about trillions of dollars.

Jeremy Rifkin has shown that the entire world's annual gross domestic product can flow in just one week through all the interstices of electronic communications and transmission in New York City. And as we might imagine, that amounts to millions of millions of dollars. Is any of that money real? People ask what's happened to all the money from the recent financial crisis. That was trillions of dollars. Where did it go? But the money didn't go anywhere, and it didn't die either. It was fictional money; it had no meaning. So, it's no longer the same old money that was a symbol of equivalences between products in the marketplace. Today's finance capital doesn't work with that sort of money. Therefore, even though George W. Bush and Barack Obama have now invested billions more dollars in the great finance corporations, they continue to collapse. Recently the American International Group, the largest insurance underwriter, failed because it needed more money, and consequently the stock market fell 13 percent the next day in New York and then around the world. Why? Crisis of confidence, exactly. As many people are starting to understand, money is the shadow of power. If you don't believe, it doesn't exist or doesn't work. It's like the idea of "race." Our comrades who are victims of racism have fought to democratize race relations. But that's not possible in reality. If you fight to democratize "race" relations, then you're accepting that race is a phenomenon of nature, not of power. Consequently, the demand makes no sense, as progressive as it may sound. "Race" doesn't exist if you don't believe in it. It's the same with finance capital and the crisis today. It isn't about whether the state is nationalist or socialist or something else.

There is an emerging horizon of meaning that is beginning not to believe all this, even to refuse it, because now everybody's survival is at stake at every level. So, the market and profit are beginning to be called into question, as is the idea of exploiting nature, which arose in association with the idea of "race," because that idea supposes precisely that "the inferior races" were so "by nature" and that it's "natural" for them to be exploited. That idea has been carried out, exacerbated, and perverted especially over the three hundred years since the Americas, together with the Americas.

There is thus one horizon of meaning that is bankrupt and another horizon of meaning that is emergent, and we're somehow in the middle of this; if we're incapable of making it visible, active, truly visible in the "other possible world" that is being sought and debated at the World Social Forums, central stage for the debate on resistance and alternatives, maybe there will be another possible world, but it might be much worse, and in a way that's starting to happen. So, we all have a choice to make here: one possibility or the other.

Thank you.

Notes

This is a lightly revised transcript of a talk that I gave at the Universidad Ricardo Palma on March 15, 2009, when I was awarded an *honoris causa* degree by that university.—Aníbal Quijano

1   [Translator's note: Referring to the study group headed by Radovan Richta.]

15

LATIN AMERICA
TOWARD A NEW HISTORICAL MEANING

We are in the midst of a furious crisis that brings global climate change together, at the same time, with a ferocious financial capitalist crisis virtually indistinguishable from the global crisis of the capitalist system itself. These two major crises—one of the climate, in other words, the things happening to what we call "nature," and the other of the world finance system, which drags the whole machinery of capital accumulation in with it—are not separate, nor are they "natural." What is happening to nature, so-called global climate change, is the product of what our species has been doing to Earth, a process destroying the very conditions that make life on the planet possible.

This is no accident. It reflects the matrix of power in which we dwell, reflects the way in which capital and world capitalism have developed, a trend that becomes ever more perverse, ever more technocratic, in which the one and only thing that matters is how to use everything, absolutely everything, as commodities, consequently making profit the one exclusive aim: the whole meaning of history focused on commodities and the profits they generate.

This was how over a relatively lengthy cycle a model was consolidated that entails the use and exploitation of nature, which is now intensifying rapidly, daily. So, what is happening to nature is not natural. It is historical. It is what is happening with power among us. It is a type of power that is not only destroying our common home, the planet, reducing or eliminating living conditions on it, but also making us kill each other, as has happened in Iraq, in Afghanistan, in Gaza, as happened earlier in the Horn of Africa—Sudan, Rwanda, Burundi, and Nigeria—and as happened in the Balkans and will soon be getting started in Latin America if we let it.

This really is an exceptionally critical circumstance for our species. It is not just a moment like any other; it is not just a cyclical crisis. It is true that capitalism has been marked by cyclical crises, but this is not just one more cycle. It is something else.

Why isn't it another cyclical crisis? Very briefly and schematically, a major change in relations between capital and labor began in roughly the mid-1960s, when not only was part of the labor force fired during the contraction cycle but also, importantly, new entering workers were not absorbed by capital. This is what we conceptualized in Latin America as the marginalization of the new workforce: the live individual labor force began increasingly to be left outside the production apparatus and thus left jobless. This development took place at top speed so that by the middle of 1973, an explosive moment arrived.

That year, the process of changing relations between capital and labor culminated in a growing exclusion of labor. The crisis, the combination of stagnation and inflation, was called "stagflation" in North America, because the virtually total, worldwide stagnation of production was accompanied by rising inflation, a phenomenon that had never occurred at any previous moment in history. Stagnation always means deflation, falling prices; for the first time in five hundred years of history, we had worldwide productive stagnation together with rising inflation. That was the moment when what is called "structural unemployment" began to form, causing a breakdown in the workers' movement worldwide, a virtual breakdown of their social tools, the dispersion of the great manufacturing conglomerates. This moment marked the transition to a new stage.

Capital as such appears divided into two extremely precise parts, one of which, growing, has practically no need for a live individual labor force, because the whole computerizing and technologizing process allows it to produce anything at any time in any quantity without having to turn to a live labor force. This means that anything the process produces can at this moment be virtually (if you will) distributed for free, because it doesn't use live labor. Instead, the process uses accumulated and socially accumulated labor. It uses knowledge accumulated from all of us, but it does not use the live individual labor of most of us so that its profit rate trends at some moments reach zero.

An example of this is the way the big stores can give away cell phones, but if you get one of them you end up subscribed to a service network for which you will have to pay a monthly fee. This happens because the cost of producing that gadget is zero or less than zero. The commodity, which is the mainstay of accumulation, is the brain of whoever acquires the product, their subjectivity, their mentality. In this situation, workers who are excluded from these dynamics have to accept impossible conditions—job instability, job flexibility—or exit the apparatus of capital as capital and accept or be forced into other forms. Enslavement is rapidly reexpanding around the world, not just in Brazil, not just in the Amazon basin, but all over the world. Personal servitude is back, small-scale market production is back, and, of course, reciprocity is back in much of the world.

This situation entails three things that must be understood in order to visualize not only what might happen but also what is already beginning to happen:

1   The relation between capital and labor has changed drastically to the point that the portion that dominates capital is not only unable but also uninterested in creating jobs; to the contrary, the push is to eliminate labor. So, we can no longer expect capital to produce more jobs ever again.

2   For the same reason, we cannot expect capital to contribute to the minimal public freedoms associated with the market, as was the case in previous processes. Therefore, political democracy is being reconcentrated, and the public sphere is being steadily reprivatized from the center to the periphery.

3   Hence, the very basis for capital is no longer buying and selling the labor force but rather controlling our subjectivity, controlling our mentalities. The main dispute of the moment is over that control.

The reason this last is happening is not just because capitalists are bad people or because the journalists informing us lack expertise. No, it comes from the structure of the moment, which increasingly requires control over mentalities, control over information, and control over thought, because otherwise it could not exist.

We were witnesses and protagonists only a very short while ago in what is being called the great financial crisis of capital. But this is no financial crisis; it is, rather, the largest and most scandalous financial fraud in all of contemporary history, carried out in a well-planned and absolutely pre-meditated fashion. Does anyone in their right mind think that a banker, especially in the United States, would lend money to someone that they know perfectly well cannot pay them back? Obviously not. But in this case, the bankers were not just lending to people that they knew could not pay; bankers were prodding them to ask for credit, knowing full well that they were not going to pay. The mechanism was this: a bank that had thousands of these credits would sell them to the next insurance company, and with that it made money; that insurance company would sell them to the largest insurance company and make more money; and that next insurance com-pany—the largest one, let's say the American International Group—would negotiate with the state, because the banks were starting to get in on the scam.

Banks were in a condition to organize all this, to make the state—before US president George W. Bush left office, by the way, not at any old time—give them as much money as possible. Money from where? From the tax-payers, from the people of the United Sates, and from us, who in one way or another pay taxes to the empire's capital.

This is a scandalous financial fraud, systematically organized and pro-moted. Once the Bush administration managed to give the bankers $700 billion to begin with, they celebrated with a huge feast at a San Francisco restaurant. The bill came to several hundred thousand dollars.

What were they celebrating? Exactly the same thing that happened in England. When Gordon Brown gave banks almost the same amount in pounds sterling, the bankers went out to celebrate in a very expensive res-taurant, and once more, the bill came to several thousand pounds. Obvi-ously they were celebrating not the crisis but rather the way they managed to pull off a gigantic financial fraud to benefit themselves. And every mem-ber of every one of the bankrupt companies brought home tens of thou-sands of millions of dollars in compensation.

We are not talking about a natural financial crisis, a cyclical crisis, because there is a portion of capital that has almost no use for a live indi-vidual workforce. So, financializing is the only way to realize such yields in the market; without financial capital—that is, without the constant, active speculation favored by the fabulous media—none of this would have been possible.

The world's entire annual gross domestic product flows in one week through the channels and mechanisms of financial communications of New York City alone. This amounts to trillions upon trillions of dollars.

Who really believes that such a quantity of money exists? Who believes that they are producing that physical quantity of money, that it is real? If the United States did not have the military and war-making powers that give it the ability to print money and send it into circulation around the world, the country would be bankrupt.

We are thus in something new, a new financial capital system that has little to do with the previous one, because the new one does not respond to business cycles; it responds exclusively to its own speculative needs, and in order to guarantee that the downward trend in profits can be compensated for by every possible means, it requires control over people's consciences, the commercialization of our consciences, and not a live labor force.

We Are Going through a Major Historical Change

I want to insist not on the notion but instead on the real historical fact that we are living in a very different world from the one we had just thirty or thirty-five years ago, that there is a major historical change, and that this is a new historical period in actual fact, not in a rhetorical sense.

Between roughly the middle of 1973 and the late 1980s, a set of processes took place that blew up what had come before. That year, 1973, brought a combination that had never been seen before in economic history of stagnation in productive activity and increasing inflation. It was always the opposite. In every great crisis, especially those since 1870—in 1912, 1914, 1929, 1940, in other words, every important crisis—productivity stagnation was accompanied by a drop in prices. This was the first time that stagnating production came with rising inflation. That led, at the same time, to the creation of the Organization of Petroleum Exporting Countries and the creation of so-called petrodollars, another thing that had never been seen before: a new pile of financial capital whose size made it virtually independent of every central bank, even the banks of the most powerful countries, beginning with the United States. We are witnessing the collapse of a very central part of the structure that existed at that moment.

But the 1960s also closed with a great defeat of what had seemed to be opening a new horizon that would soon give us its fruits: the disestablishment in 1967 by Mao Zedong of the Shanghai People's Commune, the end of May 68 in France, the Tlatelolco massacre of October 1968, and Italy's Hot Autumn of 1969–1970.

How did so-called neoliberalism begin? How did the combination of stagnating productivity, high inflation, and the growth of the novel financial system get its start? It started with Augusto Pinochet. What we call neoliberalism began precisely with Chile and its "Chicago boys." It was then picked up by Margaret Thatcher in Great Britain and then by Ronald Reagan in the United States.

This too began in Latin America and not by accident, because here was where a new and equally unheard-of form of change was also emerging. There was, unfortunately, despite our songs about international solidarity, no link between the Bolivian process of 1971–1972, the most radical and deepest historical change in Latin America at the time, and the other important parallel change, that taking place in Chile. The two had nothing in common. The defeat of one was a prelude to the defeat of the other, but the other did not understand it, never tried to understand it.

But let's get back to the economic moment: how to manage this gigantic new financial mushroom and accumulate speculative profits in the center of everything else. The "stop inflation" campaign produced an enormous process of deindustrialization and worldwide unemployment, that is, a defeat for labor and the breakup of the gigantic labor union world in the United States, Europe, and other parts.

It was a defeat for labor, in the first place, but one that was also linked to the incredibly rapid breakup of the so-called socialist camp, which fell apart in just a few years, ending with an implosion in a single week—not even a year—without war, without bombs, without earthquakes, without major catastrophes. The powerful, seemingly solid, immutable object called the Soviet Union evaporated in one week. So, we had two parallel processes of worldwide defeat, that of the "stop inflation" campaign and its crisis and the defeat of the other camp. It was an entire historical horizon that was being eclipsed.

For the past five hundred years we have had an historical horizon that emerged gradually from the new and distinct matrix of power and its center. The historical identity that we now call Western Europe came after the Americas; moreover, it was the Americas that gave Western Europe its first source of identity as a center, and it was from the Americas that it extracted the power of defining so-called modernity, which is almost purely Eurocentric. Subsequently, there came anticolonialism, nationalism, and socialism.

But the defeat of that historical horizon appeared to be so complete that Francis Fukuyama, a bleak official in some obscure bureaucratic office, could perform a crude interpretation of one wing of Hegelian and post-Hegelian thought, especially that presented by Alexandre Kojève in his famous workshops in France, and attain worldwide celebrity by declaring "the end of history."

We come out of that defeat, which also entailed the defeat of labor, the defeat of all the rivals of imperialist power, but also the defeat of its opponents and all its critics.

This allowed the owners of the new form of capital to proceed, full-speed ahead; the acceleration and deepening of the trends in the existing power matrix were brutal. Control over the public authority of the state was reconcentrated around the world. Bookstores filled up with publications on the crisis of the nation-state; there was even one book that became famous, *Empire* by Michael Hardt and Antonio Negri, with the central thesis that the nation-state no longer exists, that what we have now is an empire like that described by Polybius. In other words, not only was the structure of the previous social existence coming to an end, but the so-called industrial working class was also ending, the old bourgeoisie was being knocked out, and a totally new bourgeoisie was being created, with its own peculiarities and tendencies.

This proceeded with almost no resistance for the first thirty years, but then the first signs of resistance began in Southeast Asia; the European or Eurocentric press says it began in Seattle, of course, but that is not the case. It began in South Korea and Indonesia; these were the great popular revolts that not only brought down the government in South Korea but also generated a restructuring of the bloody dictatorship that had imposed North American imperialism on Indonesia, producing half a million deaths in three months in 1965. A US Central Intelligence Agency report had stated that the rivers were running red with blood.

There is much more resistance in Latin America now and not only through the processes taking place in Ecuador, Bolivia, and Venezuela. Latin America is new for several reasons; it is at the very center of worldwide resistance. In the first place, because the deepening and the acceleration of the basic trends—control over labor—has produced not only a lot of polarization but also two irreversible limits, and that is where we are: first, the new approaches take into consideration the limits relating to the living conditions on the planet, and second, they address the limits on relations regarding social existence based on the perverse combination of two mental constructs, race and gender. The thing called race is being subverted. The victims of the coloniality of power are creating true subversion; without that, it is impossible to understand what is happening in Ecuador, Bolivia, and Peru. On other horizons, the Adivasi, the so-called Indigenous peoples of India, and the Dalit, the untouchables of India, had a strong presence at the World So-cial Forum in Mumbai (2006), indicating similar concerns.

In the second place, here in Latin America is where the unfeasibility of theses such as that of the end of history have begun to become evident. The "end of history" meant that everything you people were thinking is pointless, a bunch of tall tales. The so-called postmodernists maintained that moder-nity had ended and, with it, the ideas of liberation, which were considered tall tales, were just talk; power is nothing but a question, and it's a "fact of life" whether we like it or not, they said.

The Radical Critique of Eurocentrism

In Latin America today we are producing the most profound and effective critique of Eurocentrism, which is a means of creating and generating sub-jectivity, imaginary, historical memory, a means of knowledge making that allows one to see certain things and not to see others.

What we call European capitalism was formed not alongside of but in-stead on the basis of enslavement, on the basis of servitude, because to-gether they constituted a scheme to produce commodities for the new world market. Hence, the precious metals and precious plants of the Amer-icas brought to the world market. The Atlantic became the preferred basin for the world market instead of the Mediterranean.

If we review the history of the map, what we call Western Europe is a peninsula of Asia, but if we are asked how many continents there are, then we ourselves will say five, and we will start off by naming Europe. That did not exist before 1500. The central Global North appropriated the legacy of the southern Mediterranean and subsequently of the Americas, and it was based on the latter that region came together as such.

This is why the most radical and effective critique of Eurocentrism is emerging in Latin America today—as a means of creating and generating subjectivity, imaginary, memory, knowledge—in the theory of coloniality and the coloniality of power, which operates on the basis of rediscovering and rejecting the racist episteme that secularizes, together with Eurocen-trism, the medieval Christian theology that generated the radical dualism to which, with its positivist evolutionism, we have been captive since the late nineteenth century.

We are not simply proposing to replace this with something new. What is going on is that other rationalities are reappearing out of those that were colonized; they are even constructing new other-ones. What we will probably have in the future is not so much a rationality shared by all, decreed by some God, but rather several rationalities—that is, several means of producing meaning and explanations—that nevertheless must have common ground so as to be able to communicate. We are speaking of something different where people can communicate, learn from each other, and even choose to leave one identity for another or have many diverse identities. Many of us have several diverse identities, not just one.

This is what we are talking about when we say "radical critique of Eurocentrism," and this is happening in and from the perspective of Latin America. There is a profound critique of authority that is emerging all over the world, but Latin America is at the center because the perverse combination that assembled the system of social domination over the course of five hundred years is being subverted there, the combination, that is, of race and gender, two mental constructs that have teamed up and have been imposed to such a degree that they almost seem real, almost natural. It is an episteme, an acceptance that this is implicitly natural and has to be thought of in this way: that is what is being subverted, and this subversion brings with it a subversion of authority.

Contrary to Hardt and Negri's argument—that there is an empire now like the one Polybius described—I argue that there is no such thing; instead, there is an imperial bloc. When not only the most powerful states meet in Davos but also their great financial corporations, their professionals, politicians, and their presidents, they make decisions that affect us all. That is imperial. So, it is a global imperial bloc made of states and nonstate entities, some of which are intergovernmental and others of which are simply private but powerful. This allows them to exercise control over authority.

In Latin America, we never managed to democratize society to the point of making us all appear to be socially, legally, and politically equal despite our being unequal, as is the case in a bourgeois absolute democracy. I take as the most advanced example Switzerland, which does not come from the Magna Carta tradition but instead comes from the tradition of the Helvetic communities that rose up against the empire in the thirteenth century and founded the Helvetic Republic—this fact explains why it has no professional army or police force and why it has the referendum and popular consultation as permanent mechanisms—but even there, where the law recognizes the most profound legal and political equality, it is impossible to hide the real inequalities in other terms among the population. The kind of democracy that we call liberal-bourgeois is a democracy of legal-political equality under law among people who themselves are unequal in every realm of power. But in Latin America and elsewhere, it is not that inequality alone but rather a greater one: the race-gender inequality, which became the very basis for the social classification of people and the way their place in power was distributed. Therefore, it is only by subverting the control of authority, hence subverting the state that was imposed and not produced by that society, that a different political authority can be had.

If we forget the word "state" for a moment and talk instead about political authority, which may or may not include the state, other forms appear that are in fact emerging and competing with the state. Gangs are a political authority in today's world as, for example, in Brazil, where they can occupy the favelas of Rio de Janeiro and São Paulo whenever they want. The president of one, called the First Commando of São Paulo, did an interview with the newspaper *Folha da São Paulo*. He was illiterate when he was first sent to prison; now he reads five languages, cites all the same sources we do at our meetings—all the structuralists—cites Gilles Deleuze, Jacques Derrida, Félix Guattari, even Hardt and Negri of course, citing them with a lot of realism but from the flip side. And he tells them you are our agents, and it's true—the police, many members of parliament, the military—and as such we exercise authority jointly. And he is right.

The idea that the state has the monopoly on violence ended a long time ago. Therefore, when we talk about the state we cannot continue to do so from the perspective of the last historical period; when we say "social classification," we are not talking about the social classification from the last period; when we talk about capitalism, we are not speaking of the capitalism of the last period. Now, there is capital, servitude, enslavement, and small-scale market productions, all operating in the same marketplace. And when we say "capital," we have to remember that as the technologically more sophisticated portion of it increases, the presence of the live individual labor force declines until at last it becomes virtually insignificant.

How is it possible, though, that it is not only the dominant portion of the whole combination but also can continue gaining all the profits it gains? There is no diminishing rate of returns; you can still make much more profit than before not because you cannot produce and distribute for free—today you can, as a large portion of things are distributed for free—but because it has control over authority and because it has control over subjectivity. If a different imaginary is impossible for all of us, if our imaginary is captive to what existed in the last historical period, then it really is impossible. But this is a different period; we have entered other processes, and so in Latin

America we are producing not only a critical new subjectivity but also a new political imaginary.

The subversion of race/gender and the subversion of Eurocentrism are linked to the assembling of a different form of social existence in which diversity exists in all things, reciprocity, for one: the exchange of labor and the labor force without necessarily going through the market except that it is impossible to produce anything today without the market or to disassociate yourself from it. This is a new thing; self-subsistence no longer exists anywhere on the planet, much less in Latin America. So, you cannot live without the market, but how can you live with only the market? That's impossible. Nobody can live without the state, but it is equally impossible to live with it. So, a new form of social existence is emerging.

Reciprocity and the community are two things that are being linked together, creating a new social ethics. It does not matter if the people in that community were fascists, leftists, or "caviars," as ex-leftists are called in Peru, and rightly so. This new social relationship creates a new subjectivity, creates a new social ethics, which is why Latin America is different now, because the world we are living in is now different.

The Facets of Power

What we call power, the word "power," generally evokes one's place in the state and one's place in what is called the economy, but it is not just that. When we ask ourselves what other model of economic development, what other model of the economy might be created, the implicit assumption is that everything else can come out of a so-called model of the economy. That never has been the case, and it certainly is not so today. Power is much more complicated. Domination probably existed in our species before any kind of exploitation did; the first mechanism of domination—if archaeology and paleoanthropology are good for anything—probably took place between the sexes; before anyone exploited anyone else's labor, before anyone made anyone else produce anything, they were already making others regenerate the species, because that is what controlling sex is about: it allows the species to reproduce.

Today, technology makes it possible to regenerate in other ways. Cloning is possible; it really is possible to manufacture "real races," with this or that characteristic according to the client's tastes, and perhaps someday this will be done. But control over every sphere of social existence, control over sex, over its resources and products, over nature, is the logic that was thus established. In the control over labor, its products and resources, control over subjectivity, over the imaginary, over historical memory, knowledge, control over collective authority, the biggest one today, the strongest authority, is the state.

We can scarcely imagine now that it is possible to live without the state, but the state was imposed from above. The state runs on financing by taxpayer contributions; the society as a whole pays to run the state with their taxes, with the things they consume, with exploitation at work, at home and away from home; we all pay for public services. The notion that public services are free is an intellectual and political sham. It would not be possible without having control over subjectivity, the imaginary, the ways to make sense of experience.

It is time to get rid of these forms of control, especially those associated with nature: the body itself, the bodies of the dominated. We are told that the body is not divine reason, but it is the body that is exploited, tortured, that feels pain, fatigue, hunger, desire. There is a liberal slogan from the nineteenth century that goes "Barbarians, ideas cannot be killed." Of course ideas cannot be killed; the one who gets killed is the person who thinks them.

Power is a structure for disputes about control over each of its spheres; that is the matrix for its practice. But the power that is colonial in origin and character is the one that has become explosive, and the center for that combustion today is Latin America. This is something new, because at every turn of power we are now doing something different.

At every turn of power, control over sex is there, trying to reimpose itself. Every variety of fundamentalism—from Christianity, from Islam, from Judaism—insists that its codes prohibit having a sex life, banning sexuality. It is very curious, for example, that in so-called constitutional debates these problems go almost deliberately unmentioned; it is only those on the other side who insist that there must be no abortion, there must be no homosexuals, love is only between a man and a woman, between male and female, and so on, all of these being things that, obviously, never were so, are not so, and will simply never be so. The aim is to produce control over sex again, because that is the very basis for control over so-called nature, not over reason but instead over the body. The body, however, is precisely the organism that thinks, dreams, feels, desires, makes love, becomes hungry, and so on.

The dispute today is about the thing called capitalism, which is now less and less about paid work; its paid portion is more and more depressed, and as a consequence the precapitalist forms that were always contemporaneous with and a part of capitalism are returning. This is bringing about a brutal social polarization that puts a growing portion of the species at risk of extinction. In Africa south of the Sahel, 150,000 children die of hunger each day, while the amount spent on perfume in the United States and Europe would be enough to pay for safe drinking water for the population of the entire planet.

Control over labor, like control over sex, over subjectivity, and over authority, has reached the combustion point. So, this is a matter of more than mere resistance; we are coming up with alternative practices and proposals. For the first time in the five hundred–year history of this matrix of power, we have begun to not only hope for a future but also work for that future. We are, in a way, living with the future we need, because we are shaping it right now. This idea is not merely an image, not only an expression of hope and perspective; in this classic sense it is not a mere utopia, something that has no place in the universe. This does have its place in the universe: it is here, so this can make sense not simply as an image but also as a phenomenon, as a real and necessary tendency for this reality.

For the first time after five hundred years of defeat—the defeat of everyone, not only some—it is not a discourse but rather a new historical meaning that is emerging, a new horizon of historical meaning in which commodities and profits are no longer at the very center of the proposal. When the enormous movement called the Indigenous movement—which is not at all homogeneous but totally heterogeneous and has even begun to use and appropriate a colonial-origin term—emerges not just to make speeches but also to organize, to act, to say that our forests, our fields, our water cannot be commodities, cannot be sold, then what they are referring to is the defense of the last conditions for the survival of their way of life in the world. They cannot continue to live without that forest, without the oxygen, without the water, without the materials that allow them to produce cultural goods for their existence. This is the first time that a different proposal for historical meaning has emerged.

This is, moreover, linking up with the fact that a large segment of the contemporary intelligentsia, especially the contemporary scientific community, insists on destroying the conditions for life on the planet. So, both the movement of the most subjugated people in this world, those who would not be able to exist if they sold their means of subsistence, and those who realize that if all this comes to an end no one will be able to survive, come together in a shared analysis.

At last, another horizon of historical meaning is here already, is beginning already, and it's not just about discourses and assemblies. Communities are reorganizing and joining forces; they are generating a new form of political authority that is going to have to compete with the state so long as the state still exists. Not only is this a utopia, but we are also starting to live with the future. We might even be overthrown. Even the whole world may come to an end, but for this there is no turning back.

Note

First published as "América Latina: Hacia un nuevo sentido histórico," in *Sumak Kawsay/buen vivir y cambios civilizatorios*, ed. Irene León (Quito: FEDAEPS, 2010), 55–71.

16

COLONIALITY OF POWER AND SUBJECTIVITY IN LATIN AMERICA

Whenever a new era arrives, one that doesn't merely prolong the past but ushers in a new world or brings massive, radical changes to the current world, nothing signifies the same anymore. Symbols and signs conspire against their signifiers or are avoided in order to leave room for other signs being built for the new way of life. No one, no person, no act, no relationship will ever be the same again. All references, all horizons, change. It might be hard even to tell hopes from memories. In this way, a new world emerged five hundred years ago with the Americas for not only the initial vanquished or the victors but also all of history. Nothing since then has been as it was before anywhere in the world. Social experience had a total restart. That world is still with us; we dwell in it, and it dwells in us. But it has changed, massively and profoundly, several times. The most recent change, the entrance into a whole dissimilar historical period, took place in the last third of the twentieth century with the global defeat of social liberation movements, the drastic global reconcentration of control over the power of capitalism, and the beginnings of the exhaustion of the process of commodifying the labor force at the dominant levels of colonial/modern capitalism. Vast and profound areas of experience for all the people of the world have been transformed. Nothing will ever again reproduce their familiar forms, relationships, institutions, aspirations, dreams, or hopes. Acts no longer have the same meanings they did up to the mid-1970s. References have changed. The horizon seems to be gone. This is what a re-originalization of experience and subjectivity is like, because experience is made historically (not ontologically) original. But the world is always very heterogeneous, and the relationships among its diverse elements are very discontinuous. The impact of a new era is therefore also heterogeneous and discontinuous in the world, in space and in time. The effects of the world-wide defeat of workers are still in full swing. But there are new social movements now, and new horizons of historical meaning are being produced in these movements. The era of defeat may be coming to an end.

"Globalization" and the Reoriginalizing of Experience and Subjectivity

Since colonial society was formed, every such crossroad in our cultural history has been produced by a process of reoriginalizing experience, a tempestuous and massive process but one that has never discovered or succeeded in fashioning a reliable perspective and channel to help it define and structure itself as a new matrix of social existence, instead ending up rechanneled within the established power. Thus, for example, the "cholo" phenomenon, specific to the cultural process of Peru, emerged in connection with the process of social urbanization immediately following World War II. This process, with its sudden, magmatic, almost chaotic nature, entailed a drastic, rapid, and profound reoriginalizing of the social experience of the population as a whole, particularly due to the massive turbulent irruption of the cultural experience of the dominated, together with their demands and pressures, into every realm of society.

Analogous phenomena are taking place right now. Since the worldwide crisis began in the mid-1970s, a process has come into view that affects every single aspect of social existence for people in every country on Earth. The world that was formed five hundred years ago is culminating with the formation of a productive, financial, and commercial structure perceived as more integrated than before, because control over it has been reconcentrated under fewer and smaller groups. Along with this has been a drastic reconcentration of control over the state, labor, and production resources in the hands of the functionaries of capital, especially finance capital; the final universalization of the core of capitalist civilization, the commodification of every element, means, and sphere of social existence; and the formation of a central power bloc that appears as the final authority for the entire world order. All of this is called "globalization," a term that is undeniably apt for signaling and describing such trends but also serves to gloss over the social nature of the process in the eyes of the dominated, since the drastic reconcentration of control over power in the hands of the functionaries of capital testifies to the fact that the process is being carried out as a capitalist counterrevolution at, well, a global scale. This is why it should be easy to accept that it has produced a profound and massive modification in the lives of all people in every society. This is a genuine transformation, not merely changes within continuity.

These changes do not affect every country or every group, every phenomenon, every aspect, every institution of contemporary social existence in any organic, systemic, coherent way. Quite the contrary. It is all happening in a patchy, discontinuous, heterogeneous, contradictory, conflict-ridden way. Thus, the brutal reconcentration of political power, military might, and production resources is the flip side of the fragmentation, disintegration, and de-structuring, above all in the world of labor, of the major areas of social clustering, classification, identification, and organization of interests and social conflict. The formation of the imperial bloc by the Great Seven (now formally the G8, with the addition of Russia, though that country's situation allows it to participate only in a subordinate role) is the flip side of the denationalization of the societies in which the coloniality of power was not, or was not fully, voided. But it also entails the globalization of the struggles by the exploited and dominated of the world, of the arrival of a new period of social conflicts marked precisely by their globalization. And this whole jumble of contradictions makes this moment of profound and radical reoriginalization of experience all the more intense. And as always under such conditions, impulses and tendencies are unleashed for creating new perspectives and new cultural channels in the subjective dimension of social relations and of our relations with the rest of the universe. This is why the universalization of capitalist civilization is the flip side of the irruption of diversity and heterogeneity into the cultural experiences that exist in the world and flow through the same highways of global communication. Some of these lead or can lead to processes of cultural reoriginalization. The open crisis of Eurocentrism as a perspective for knowledge is one example of this. In Latin America, given its foundational place in the history of colonial/modern power, these are key questions that must be investigated, debated, and decided.

Coloniality of Power, Historical-Structural Dependence, and Eurocentrism

It might be easier to see these questions clearly if we return briefly to the historical experience of the formation of the coloniality of power in the Americas, unquestionably one of the key examples of these moments of sudden and drastic transformations of historical experience in the world. As is known, the destruction of the aboriginal societies and cultures meant that the dominated populations were condemned to being integrated into a matrix of power basically configured along the following lines:

1   The matrix of domination between the colonizers and the others was organized and established on the basis of the idea of "race," with all that it implied for the historical perspective on relations among the diverse types of the human species.[1] That is, the factors of classification and social identification figured not as tools in the immediate conflict or as necessities for controlling and exploiting labor but instead as matrices of historically necessary and permanent relationships, regardless of the needs and conflicts originated in the exploitation of labor.[2]

2   The matrix was based on the perspective that the colonizers defined the new identity of the colonized aboriginal populations: "Indians." For these populations, colonial domination consequently entailed having their original identities (Mayas, Aztecs, Incas, Aymaras, and so on) stripped from them and repressed and over the long haul losing them and accepting a negative shared identity. The population of African origin, also coming from heterogeneous experiences and historical identities (Congos, Bacongos, Yorubas, Ashantis, and so on), was subjected to an analogous situation in every fundamental way and to an equally negative shared colonial identity: "Blacks." The colonizers identified themselves at first as "Spaniards," "Portuguese," "Iberians," "Britons," and so on. By the end of the eighteenth century and even more so after the so-called wars of emancipation, they would identify as "Europeans" or, more generically, as "whites" (a late category, produced in the eighteenth century in the British American colonial area). And the descendants of genetic relationships among all these new identities would be known as mestizos.

3   This distribution of social identities would henceforth be the basis for all social classification of the population, first in the Americas and, beginning in the eighteenth century, in the rest of the world. The various forms of exploitation and control of labor and gender relations would gradually be built with and on top of it in changing ways depending on the needs of power in each period.

4   A matrix of power was thus imposed with these specific linchpins: (a) the existence and continual reproduction of these new "racialized" historical identities; (b) the hierarchized and unequal relationship between these "European" and "non-European" identities and the domination of the former over the latter in every instance of power—economic, social, cultural, intersubjective, political; (c) and due to this, the redesign of the institutions and mechanisms of societal domination—the subjective and political ones, first and foremost—that were destined above all for preserving this new historical basis for social classification, the birthmark of the American historical experience, later reproduced and imposed across the world in the course of the expansion of Eurocentric colonial/modern capitalism.

5   The colonized populations were reduced to being illiterate peasants. Before the coloniality of power, the more developed original societies had a sophisticated urban culture, and some had writing. Writing was, to be sure, the exclusive patrimony and instrument of the dominant and urban groups. But that urban culture and their writing were an original product all their own, autonomous in other words; they were the means and vehicles for expressing a subjectivity of a rich, ancient history, of an exceptionally lively and creative imaginary. That was undoubtedly a dominant cultural matrix, in other words, one of the instances of the existing domination in those societies. Nevertheless, as in every domination society with its own autonomous culture, this matrix was also the expression of the historical experience of the population as a whole. When those who had them were stripped of their urban culture and of their writing, the subjugated populations were confined to subcultures that were not only those of illiterate peasants but, worse, were continuously repressed and interfered with by foreign hostile matrices and elements. And in colonial society, only some among the colonized could manage

to gain access to letters, to writing, exclusively in the language of the dominators and to serve their ends.

6   They would be prevented from objectifying their own images, symbols, and subjective experiences in an autonomous way—that is, with their own matrices of visual and artistic expression. Without such freedom of formal objectification, no cultural experience can develop.

7   They couldn't exercise their needs and skills for visual and artistic objectification but instead could only express themselves exclusively through the dominators' matrices of visual and artistic expression.

8   They were compelled, through repression, to abandon their practices relating to what they originally considered sacred or to realize them solely through clandestine means, with all the distortions that implied.

9   They were led to accept or to pretend to accept in the presence of the dominators the dishonorable condition of their own imaginary and of their own previous universe of subjectivity.[3]

10   It was only in what could be preserved of their own world, though their institutional forms were modified according to the matrices of their dominators—especially in their "communities," in the family setting, and in networks of kinship and ritual relationships—that their own values of reciprocity, social equality, and control over public authority could be practiced, albeit continually readapted to the changing imperatives of the global matrix of coloniality.

11   Together with these elements and processes of the new system of social domination, the new system of social exploitation was organized by configuring every historically known form—enslavement, servitude, reciprocity, simple small-scale market production, and capital—into a single structure for producing commodities for the new world market under the hegemony of capital. This was how the system that we now call colonial/modern capitalism emerged.

12   The matrix of power fashioned from these foundations, traits, and trends of historical movement or development and its long-term implications are encompassed in the concept of "coloniality of power."[4] Given this configuration of power, conflict explicitly became a necessary and permanent feature. Thus, although

the initial military resistance of the aboriginal populations was defeated in a few decades in the sixteenth century (Inca resistance endured for forty years, the longest of any), rebellions by "Indians," "Blacks," and "mestizos"—that is, already under their new identities and living in a new intersubjective and cultural universe—erupted frequently throughout the eighteenth century, while political and cultural resistance became massive and widespread. The wars of emancipation had their origins in these rebellions, though for well-known historical causes they ended up under the control and in benefit of the dominators.[5]

13   After emancipation, the dominant "white" minorities controlled independent states, but their societies remained colonial, for they long retained the colonial link between the racial classification of the dominated and colonial/capitalist control over labor and production. For this coloniality of power and the conflicts that were intrinsic and inevitable in it, the central historical antagonism was established between "Europeans" or "whites" and "Indian" servants, enslaved "Blacks," and "mestizos" in one situation or another. Given this power structure, the dominant social groups in postcolonial Iberian America had social interests at odds with the enslaved "Blacks" and the "Indian" servants and, as a result, no shared, nationalizable interests. The dominant social groups thus were always more readily disposed to identify their interests with those of the dominators of Eurocentric capitalism, despite their mutual differences and sectoral conflicts. And given their situation, they could only associate with people from the position of being junior partners, personally subjecting themselves and subjecting their societies to the control of the owners of world capital and to the imperatives of the historical "logics" of development, or the historical movement of the global matrix of power. Thus, the coloniality of power necessarily has, then and ever since, entailed structural-historical dependency.[6]

14   For these reasons, the dominators tended to perceive relations between the "centers" of the colonial capitalist world and the colonial societies exclusively at the level of their own social interests, that is, as if those relations took place between historically homogeneous groups, despite the radical structural-historical heterogeneity between the societies on either side of the world of capitalism and within each of those sides. The coloniality of

power and structural-historical dependency both entail the hegemony of Eurocentrism as the perspective on knowledge.[7]

15   In the context of the coloniality of power, the dominated populations of every new identity were also subjected to the hegemony of Eurocentrism as a way to produce and control intersubjective relations, the imaginary, social memory, and knowledge, especially to the degree that some of their sectors could learn the dominators' writing system. Thus, over the long time frame of coloniality, which has not yet come to an end, these populations ("Indian" and "Black") were trapped between the aboriginal epistemological matrix and the Eurocentric matrix, which in addition was being channeled as instrumental or technocratic rationality particularly in regard to the social relations of power and in relationship to the surrounding world.

Between Imitation and Cultural Subversion

In this way, the colonized populations were subjected to an extremely perverse experience of historical alienation. However, a history that is cruel to the vanquished also tends to be vengeful toward the victors. The consequences of this cultural colonization were not only terrible for "Indians" and "Blacks." They were, it is true, forced to imitate or simulate what was not theirs and to feel shame for what was their own. But no one could keep them from soon learning to subvert everything they had to imitate, simulate, or venerate. The artistic expression of the colonized peoples of the Americas bears clear witness to this continuous subversion of the visual and artistic matrices, of the themes, motifs, and images coming from elsewhere, in order to express their own subjective experience, if not their earlier then instead that of their new experience, dominated, yes, colonized, yes, but always subverted and thus also converted into a space and means of resistance. We only have to look once more at the paintings of the schools of Cusco and Quito, the sculptures of Aleijadinho, the marvelous portal of the Iglesia de San Lorenzo de Carangas in Potosí, the baroque altars and baroque facades of the churches in Juli (Puno, Peru) with ears of corn instead of grape clusters, the tiles and fabric in the Mexican–Central American and Andean-Amazonian regions, the fiestas and dances of Antilleans and Brazilians and among the populations of the Peruvian-Bolivian altiplano. And everyone, even in the most recalcitrant corners of the Christian churches, now knows that their religious rites and practices were likewise subverted everywhere.

In short, the dominated learned, first, to give another sense and meaning to the outsiders' symbols and images and then to transform and subvert them by including their own in regard to images, rites, or expressive matrices of outsider origin. Finally, it wasn't possible to practice the imposed matrices without subverting them or to make them their own without reoriginalizing them. That is what they did.

By contrast, the heirs and followers of the colonizers had only two paths open to them. One was servile, imitative repetitions of European models. Given that this had to be done in the absence of any of the material or subjective resources of the European sociocultural experience,[8] the inevitable result was the continued mediocrity, even banality, of every attempt they made on their own in this direction. The other was to express their own experiences—non-European, to their dismay—and to develop their own talents, resources, and creative abilities, but in order to be able to do this they would have had to learn from and imitate the work of the dominated or, better, to identify with them, because it was only in them that they might find the sources and perspectives of something distinct, original, or entirely their own vis-à-vis Eurocentric models.

This second path could only be followed in actuality by the new middle strata between the "European" and the "Indian" or "Black," which had been forming socially and culturally while the space won by struggles against the coloniality of power gradually expanded. In most parts of Latin America, this only clearly began to take place in the early twentieth century, which, no doubt not coincidentally, was also when the first great social revolution of that century erupted: the Mexican Revolution. It is probably also no coincidence that in the plastic arts as in music and literature, the great Latin American cultural renewal that joined in this perspective beginning in the 1920s took place at the same time as the discovery of African plastic and visual arts by the European artistic avant-garde and the irruption of "Black" music in the Caribbean and the United States, all this in the context of the first great worldwide social and political conflicts.[9]

Cultural Subversion/Reoriginalization and Social Revolution/Counterrevolution

Subversion, whether of a global matrix of power or only of its expressive matrices of images and symbols or of matrices of knowledge and knowledge production, never produces other alternative matrices by itself unless it is successful and unremitting and endures over the long run. It is only a step in that direction. It is true that without subversion it would be impossible to produce any alternative, much less for that alternative to succeed and consolidate as a new hegemony. But it is also true that with subversion alone, unless it wins out, it is more likely that its products, proposals, and potentials will be or could be co-opted and assimilated within the dominant matrix to the degree that they are useful and compatible with the changes and adjustments it requires and, of course, at the cost of adapting those elements to the ends and imperatives of such a matrix, in other words, procrusteanized, distorted, even twisted against their own nature or degraded.

If the global matrix of power is what's immediately at stake in this subversion, the subversion cannot endure, cannot be kept going for long. The level and intensity of the conflict entailed will always bring it to a swift and drastic resolution. If the subversion is radical, massive, and leads to a revolution—that is, to a democratic redistribution of authority and not to a reconcentration of power—then all relations among the various sides, institutions, and cultural elements will be able to develop in the same direction and profundity. But if the subversion is defeated, the most likely sequence is a counterrevolution, not merely the preservation of the order that had previously prevailed. In that case, if any of the elements produced by the dominated and by the subversion appear useful to the restructuring of power, they will be totally expropriated from those who produced them and then returned to them as the original products of their dominators, that is, transformed into instruments of domination.

This is exactly what seems to have happened to the elements being constructed around *lo cholo* (the cholo complex) in Peru's cultural process, after the defeat of the subversion entailed in the popular movement that developed there from the end of World War II to the late 1970s. In its origins, *lo cholo* emerged as a complex that linked together more than the traits praised by the dominant group: the tremendous energy, the persistence, the sobriety, the discipline, the capacity for organized work, and certainly the facility with learning the work techniques and market rules of capital with all that might imply for the behavior and subjectivity of the bearers of this new cultural orientation. However, this complex also contained reciprocity, solidarity, and the complex density of subjectivity derived from the mis/match between aboriginal perspectives on knowledge and, on the other side, the growing pressure for technocratic rationality in capital. In short, the sense of social equality was forged by a long-shared history, to be sure, but also by a prolonged subjection to a single "Indian" identity imposed on heterogeneous and unequal identities, which had already been virtually disbanded in most cases. All of this was the product of a long history of relations between coloniality and resistance, between state and community, of resistance struggles and subversion against the domination of both colonial and republican-era capitalism.

In this sense, *lo cholo* could be considered the first great product of the development of this cultural imitation/subversion/reoriginalization dialectic among a portion of the dominated population, under the new conditions of the urbanizing process in Peruvian society. Together, these components were already producing a new social, cultural, and political identity among an important portion of Peru's population. A proposal arose among them for democratization, that is, for the de/colonization and nationalization of Peruvian society and its institutions of authority, the state first of all. This particular association of heterogeneous elements in a specific linkage was what gave *lo cholo* its potential for cultural autonomy and originality and that set it against both the "criollo-oligarchic" image of the coastal region and the "Andean-*gamonal*" image of the Sierra region, the two main forms, now in ruins, of the matrix of cultural domination that reigned in Peru before its society was urbanized.[10]

Thus, *lo cholo* entailed a first perspective on cultural reoriginalization in Peru and perhaps throughout the so-called Andean world, because it was the first time that a restructuring of cultural elements was produced not merely as "acculturation" or "transculturation" or "*mestizaje*" or "hybridity"—that is, as something that remained dependent on another structuring matrix—but rather as a process that was being constructed with new elements by innovating with those previously acquired regardless of provenance and using new matrices of linkage, development, and change. It was, most of all, an alternative for the de/coloniality of the imaginary, the practices, values, and institutions of cultural relations among the country's inhabitants. In this sense, it was a genuine proposal for reconstituting identity for the vast majority of the people of Peru.

Under these conditions, for its development this process entailed de/coloniality, a profound restructuring of Peruvian society as a whole, changing its central matrices of articulation. First of all are the relations between "European" and "Indian," "Black," and "mestizo," making the difference and the heterogeneity between them cease to be a means of or an argument for social inequality and thus bringing the material and intersubjective relationships of power around to decolonization. In other words, bringing these relationships to the democratization of society, of the social relations among all the inhabitants of the country, and to the democratic creation and running of its authority structures and, in this specific sense, to the granting of full citizenship to all the members of this society.

This democratic redistribution of control over the country's resources and over political authority would have meant, in this period, not only the nationalization of its society and state. Given that such a democratic redistribution of power was not actually possible except in the course of a global social and cultural revolution, which at that moment would have entailed a decisive presence of the potentials of *lo cholo*, that same process would also have included tendencies for the consolidation and expansion of reciprocity relationships, with their values of social equality, social solidarity, and authority structures with communal natures or tendencies. But that is not how the process took place. Other social tendencies and interests turned out to be stronger in Peruvian society, and the process as a whole was rechanneled into a substitute, "Velasquismo."[11]

Velasquismo was a political regime with very particular features. On one side, it was an expression of and a vehicle for the interests and aspirations of the emerging middle-strata groups, their interests, that is, in being political intermediaries between the bourgeoisie and the exploited and dominated people of the country and in gaining space of their own in the state and a place of their own in the administration of capital and, in order to do this, pressing for the "modernization" of power.[12] On the other side, it brought together the two groups that best represented the middle-strata interests in that period, both of them deep into "modernization theory": one, the military technocracy in command and control of the regime, with their own needs for authoritarianism and efficiency, and the other, an "intelligentsia" that included, not without conflict, both professionals of a markedly technocratic slant and intellectuals raised politically on a vague discourse about a possible "humanist utopia." The latter were quickly subdued or, for many of them, won over to the technocratic necessities of a regime led by the armed forces. And before long, the regime developed in an alliance with the most "modern" sectors of the local and international bourgeoisie.[13] Given these characteristics, Velasquismo in practice ended up boosting the elements of pragmatism, social-climbing careerism, and imitation in intersubjective relationships and authoritarianism and corporatism in political and social relations. In this way, the potentials and possibilities of *lo cholo*, especially the democratic redistribution of power, the legitimizing of diversity and relationships of autonomy and equality among all the historical strands that take part in our society, were ultimately butchered.

The collapse of Velasquismo, caught between the internal conflicts among its agents and the storms of the world crisis in the mid-1970s, led to worker resistance movements, but those were contained and defeated on the brink of the 1980s. That defeat allowed the capitalist counterrevolution currently underway around the world whose ideology is called "neoliberalism" and whose first completely representative political regime in Peru was Fujimorism, to be carried out in its most extreme version in this country.[14] This counterrevolution has brought massive pressure for channeling the intersubjective relations of Peruvian society as a whole into a conduit that only accepts and promotes the linkage of individualistic opportunism, the pursuit of profit at any cost, and social pragmatism and careerism on one side, with the celebrated qualities that emerged with *lo cholo*—energy, sobriety, hard work, and discipline—on the other. Thus, from the "criollo-oligarchic" image they co-opted the "lively spirit" without the "grace," and from the "Andean-*gamonal*" they co-opted the "strength" without the "gentility."[15] "Fujimorism" is the expression and the vehicle for this cultural matrix, which was imposed on society and suits the interests of capitalism on today's periphery to a tee. The results are plain to see. At the moment, the strongest trend in the social subjectivity of Peruvians in the association between private opportunism, pragmatism, and rudeness, the "colts of barbarous Attilas" (*potros de bárbaros atilas*, a line I am stealing from César Vallejo's poem "Los heraldos negros") on which capital gallops over the backs of most Peruvians with a saddlebag in which a lack of scruples is piled high with cynicism.

Nonetheless, recognizing the dominance of a matrix in the intersubjective and material relationships of a society at a given time is not the same thing as refusing to recognize the existence, or rather the coexistence, in the same history and in the same sociocultural space of other matrices, even of elements that cannot be clearly placed in a discernible matrix, and are or might be not only subaltern and integrated into the dominant matrix but also different, discordant, and alternative in the same way that *lo cholo* emerged in Peru in its time. But that's another story.

That other story is beginning. The populations now called "Indigenous" instead of "Indian" are emerging with a new subjectivity produced over more than five hundred years of racialization/domination/discrimination and exploitation but also of resistance movements, struggles, learning from other rationalities, subversion/imitation, and the reoriginalization of historical experiences. This is the new movement of society that has plunged the very foundations of the coloniality of power into crisis. This movement is taking place not in Latin America alone but all over the colonial/modern world, because the Eurocentric control over this matrix of power turned all racialized/ dominated/discriminated populations into "Indigenous" people, especially those exploited by colonial/modern capitalism.[16]

The frustration of the liberal Eurocentric project of the modern nation-state for all the victims of the coloniality of power has been made blatantly clear to them all. In Latin America, all racialized/dominated people are now pushing for plurinational states in not only the texts of rewritten constitutions but also a new universe of political institutions in which their new plurinational, pluricultural citizenship can actually be exercised, especially communal forms of collective authority. On the other hand, in the same movement growing sectors of these populations are refocusing on expanding and developing forms of reciprocity in the organization of labor, production, and distribution of products, whether tangible or not. They are increasingly aware of being the producers and bearers of a new social imaginary, of new forms of knowledge production, of establishing nonexploitative forms of relating with the universe.

In this way a social movement is growing all over the world, though currently centered in Latin America, for producing a new horizon of historical meaning whose development is strictly necessary for achieving the other possible world, liberated from the coloniality of power and capable, by the same token, of defending the ability of our planet to sustain life.

Notes

This is a revised version of a text originally published under the title "Colonialidad del poder, cultura y conocimiento en América Latina," in "Crítica Cultural en Latinoamérica: Paradigmas globales y enunciaciones locales," special issue, *Dispositio* 24, no. 51 (1999): 137–48. Published by the Center for Latin American and Caribbean Studies, University of Michigan, Ann Arbor.

1   The idea of "race" probably began to form during the wars of the so-called Reconquest in the Iberian Peninsula. In these wars, the Christians of the Counter-Reformation and the Inquisition amalgamated their perceptions of religious differences with supposed biological differences that were transmitted by the blood. It is difficult to understand any other explanation for the urgent need the victors felt to establish "purity of blood" (*limpieza de sangre*) certificates for Muslims and Jews. But as the core and source of concrete social and cultural

relations founded on supposed biological differences, the idea of "race" was established alongside the Americas as part of and in the same historical movement as the world of colonial capitalism, together with Europe as the center of this new world and with modernity. On this issue, see my 1993 text "Raza, etnia y nación en José Carlos Mariátegui" and also my 1999 text "¡Qué tal raza!"

2   "Race" has ever since been the basic and universal criterion for social classification for the entire population of the planet, in other words, the basic form of power relations, their coloniality.

3   On the issues of the imaginary and the colonization of the imaginary, it is useful to see Serge Gruzinsky's book *La colonisation de l'imaginaire*.

4   The current international debate on the epistemic/theoretical/historical/aesthetic/ethical/political perspective entailed in the proposed theory on the coloniality of power began with Quijano, "Colonialidad y modernidad/racionalidad," written in 1991 and first published in 1992. See also Quijano and Wallerstein, "Americanity as a Concept, or the Americas in the Imaginary of the Modern World-System"; Quijano, "Coloniality of Power, Eurocentrism and Latin America"; Quijano, "Colonialidad del poder y clasificación social"; Quijano, "Colonialité du pouvoir et démocratie en Amérique latine"; and Quijano, "América Latina en la economía mundial." You may also look at Quijano, *Modernidad, identidad y utopía en América Latina*.

5   For a general discussion of this point, see Quijano and Wallerstein, "Americanity as a Concept, or the Americas in the Imaginary of the Modern World-System."

6   This is the basic idea of my proposals regarding "structural-historical dependency" in Latin America. As should be noted, they are only partly and tangentially related to the theories that gained greater influence and good editorial fortune in the debate over "dependency." I first suggested it in 1964, following Balandier, *Sociologie actuelle de l'Afrique noire*, in Quijano, "La emergencia del Grupo Cholo y sus implicaciones en la sociedad peruana," reprinted in *Dominación y cultura: Lo cholo y el conflicto cultural en el Perú*. I returned to the topic in the summer of 1966 in "El proceso de urbanización en América Latina." I presented my basic idea in a general form in August 1967 in "Dependencia, cambio social y urbanización en Latinoamérica." An extended discussion of the concept of structural-historical dependency can be found in Quijano, "Coloniality of Power, Eurocentrism and Latin America."

7   There is an ongoing worldwide debate about Eurocentrism that partially develops the issues raised in Latin American social science research, first in the 1920s and again following World War II, in particular on the structural-historical heterogeneity of the entire complex of social relations, perceived as a whole. In addition to my previously

cited texts, I have addressed these questions principally in Quijano, "Coloniality of Power, Eurocentrism and Latin America." See also Quijano, "Prólogo: El sueño dogmático"; Quijano, "Prólogo" to Mariátegui, *Textos básicos*; Quijano, "La nueva heterogeneidad estructural de América Latina"; and Quijano, "El precio de la racionalidad." Beyond Latin America, see the related approach by Amin, *Eurocentrism*.

8   On this relationship between Latin America and Europe, see Quijano, *Modernidad, identidad y utopía en América Latina*.

9   The revolutions in Mexico in 1910, China in 1911, Russia in 1917, and Turkey in 1919; the anticolonial struggles in India during those same years; the maelstrom of revolution and counterrevolution in Europe from 1917 to 1936; and the two world wars in 1914–1918 and 1939–1945.

10   On this point, see Quijano, *Dominación y cultura*. The "Andean-*gamonal*" concept, as a cultural variant distinct from the "criollo-oligarchic" side in pre-1970s Peru, refers to the intersubjective or cultural dimension of the domination/exploitation/conflict relationships between landlord rule and the "Indians" and "mestizos" in the Andean mountain zone. The "criollo-oligarchic" side had its stronghold in the coastal zone and was originally established in the context of domination between ruling landlord-merchants and enslaved "Blacks" and "mestizos."

11   "Velasquismo" is the term given to the self-styled Revolutionary Government of the Armed Forces that seized control of the state after a coup toppled President Fernando Belaunde Terry on October 3, 1968, under the command of General Juan Velasco Alvarado. This was a military dictatorship that combined nationalist, "populist" discourse with corporatist politics in reforming the state and carried out partial reforms, especially those it called the Agrarian Reform and the Workers' Community. Velasco Alvarado was replaced by General Morales Bermúdez through another military coup in August 1975. This inaugurated the so-called second phase of the Revolutionary Government of the Armed Forces, which, confronted by the increasing mobilization of the masses and some of the bourgeoisie, ultimately convened a Constitutional Assembly and called a general election that was won by Fernando Belaunde Terry in 1980.

12   The discourse on "modernization" at that time was nearly the opposite of what dominates today. It was directed at the need to give more flexibility to the power structure, in each of its aspects, in order to expand the space for the middle strata and expand the social representativeness of the state and its respective institutions, accommodating the more organized worker groups. In some countries such changes were and, more to the point, appeared radical; they came to have para-revolutionary discourses, though from a long-term perspective their meaning was instead counterrevolutionary, since they aimed at block-

ing trends that were certainly underway toward a genuine subversion and a profound and massive democratic redistribution of power, that is, toward a revolution. "Velasquismo" was one of the most concise examples of this type of "modernization" politics.

13 The bibliography on "Velasquismo" is extensive. My own participation in the debate can be found primarily in Quijano, *Nacionalismo, neoimperialismo y capitalismo en el Perú*; Quijano, "Imperialismo y capitalismo de estado"; and Quijano, "La 'segunda fase' de la 'revolución peruana' y la lucha de clases."

14 Fujimorism is a sui generis political regime in Latin America that combines a dictatorial character, based on the armed forces and articulated around a quasi-fascist core of military-civilian control, with paraphernalia of liberal institutions directly controlled by the National Intelligence Service and employed to control the population politically. It is based on a project drawn up by the Joint Command of the Armed Forces between 1987 and 1990 in order to impose a dictatorial government on Peru that was to last fifteen to twenty years, with the aim of installing radically neoliberal economic policies and reorganizing the state along the same lines. The regime began with a coup in April, 1992, with Fujimori, winner of the 1990 presidential election against Mario Vargas Llosa, as the leading figure. After the national and international reaction, the dictatorship felt forced to simulate the institutions of the liberal state. The dictatorship fraudulently imposed Fujimori's reelection in 1995 and once more in 2000. The second time, the fraud was so scandalous that it produced national and international protests. The Organization of American States was forced to discuss the situation, but Fujimorism avoided sanctions thanks to support from the governments of Brazil and Mexico. The consequent illegitimacy and instability of the regime have now resulted in the documented uncovering of corruption scandals involving politics, finances, drug trafficking, and arms trafficking under the direction of Vladimiro Montesinos, the strong man at National Intelligence Service and Fujimori's main partner in the administration, also accused of being the brains behind the state terrorism established in 1990. The crisis led to the collapse of Fujimorism. See Quijano, *El fujimorismo y el Perú*; and Quijano, "El fujimorismo, la oea y el Perú."

15 "Grace" (*gracia*) is a term that connotes, in this context, a personal manner that brings together a certain levity and extroversion of character with an elegance of gesture that is highly appreciated in the "criollo-oligarchic" sector of the cultural matrix that used to be dominant in the coastal region, supposedly the product of the harmonious coexistence of "Spaniards" and "Blacks." The term "gentility" (*delicadeza*) connotes the association between courtesy, modesty, and discretion, an

"Andean-*gamonal*" code of expected social behavior produced by the mis/match between "Indians" and *gamonales* (large landowners and political bosses in southern highland Peru from the mid-1800s to the 1960s).

16 My discussion of these issues can be found in Quijano, "The 'Indigenous Movement' and Unresolved Questions in Latin America" (in this volume). See also Quijano, "Estado-Nación y movimientos indígenas en la región andina"; Quijano, "'Solidaridad' y capitalismo colonial/moderno"; and Quijano, "Des/colonialidad: El horizonte alternativo."

17

"BIEN VIVIR"
BETWEEN "DEVELOPMENT" AND
THE DE/COLONIALITY OF POWER

The whole extensive historical formational process of the global coloniality of power has entered a deep crisis. "Bien Vivir," an expression of the Indigenous populations of Latin America, is shaping an alternative for social life that can only be realized as a de/coloniality of power.

What I am proposing here opens a crucial question of our crucial moment in history: Bien Vivir,[1] in order to be an effective historical realization, cannot be but a complex of social practices oriented toward the democratic production and reproduction of a democratic society, another mode of social existence with its own and specific historical horizon of meanings, radically alternative to the global coloniality of power and the Eurocentered coloniality/modernity.[2] This model of power is still globally hegemonic today but is also in its deepest and most existential crisis since its constitution not much more than five hundred years ago. In these conditions today, Bien Vivir might make sense as an alternative form for social existence, as a de/coloniality of power.

"Development," a Eurocentric Paradox: Modernity without De/Coloniality

Development was, most of all as debated in Latin America, a key term of a political discourse associated with an elusive project of deconcentration and relative redistribution of the control of industrial capital as part of a new geography within the configuration of global colonial/modern capitalism at the end of World War II.

At the first moment it was a virtually official discourse. Nevertheless, it gave space to complex and contradictory questions, which derived in a rich and intense debate with worldwide resonance as a clear expression of the magnitude and the deepness of the sociopolitical conflicts of interest that were part of this whole new geography of power, particularly in Latin America. In this way, a wide range of categories became produced (mainly development, underdevelopment, modernization, marginality, participation on the one hand and on the other imperialism, dependency, marginalization, and revolution), which was deployed in close contact with conflictive and violent movements of and in society that led to dead-end processes or relatively important but unfinished changes in the distribution of power.[3]

In short, one could say that in Latin America the main result was the destitution of the "oligarchic state" and of some of its expressions in the social existence of those countries' populations. But neither its historical-structural dependency in the global coloniality of power nor the modes of exploitation and domination inherent to this power model have been eradicated or sufficiently altered in order to make space for a democratic production and management of the state, its resources of production, or the distribution and appropriation of the product. Despite its intensity, this debate never managed to liberate itself from the hegemony of Eurocentrism. In other words, these changes did not lead to "development." Otherwise, it would not be possible to understand why the term always manages to reappear, for instance now, as the ghost of an unfinished past.[4]

The Global Coloniality of Power and the Ghost of the Nation-State

In this debate, the hegemony of Eurocentrism led to perceiving "development" in Latin America only in relation to the nation-state. But in the context of a global coloniality of power, this perspective was historically misleading. What is more, precisely after World War II, this power model entered a long period of decisive changes on a global scale. It is pertinent to summarize those:

1   Industrial capital began to be structurally connected with what was known at that time as the "technological-scientific revolution." This relationship implied, on the one hand, a reduction of

the need for a living and individual workforce and consequently for paid labor as structurally inherent to capital in that new period. Unemployment ceased to be a temporary or cyclical problem. "Structural unemployment" was the term that later was employed by more conservative economists to make sense of that process.

2   These transformative tendencies of the relationships between capital and labor implied an amplification of the range of speculative accumulation—not only cyclically but also as a structural tendency—that was understood as a progressive "structural financialization." In that way a new industrial-financial capital was formed, which soon experienced a relatively fast global expansion.

3   A process of technocratization/instrumentalization of subjectivities, imaginaries, and all historical horizons of meanings specific to the Eurocentered colonial modernity are, strictly, about the growing withdrawal of the original promises of the so-called modern rationality and, in that sense, a deep change in the ethical-political perspective of the original Eurocentric version of "coloniality/modernity." Despite its new character, it did not cease to be attractive and persuasive, although it turned out to be more and more paradoxical, ambivalent, and ultimately historically impossible.

4   Development and the expansion of the new industrial-financial capital, together with the defeat of national-socialist/fascist sectors of the global bourgeoisie, in a struggle over the hegemony of capitalism during World War II, facilitated the disintegration of European colonialism in Asia and Africa and, at the same time, the prosperity of bourgeois groups, the middle classes, and even considerable sectors of the exploited Euro-American working classes.

5   The consolidation of the bureaucratic despotism (renamed "really existing socialism") and its sudden expansion inside and outside of Europe happened inside the same historical process. This mode of domination became affected more profoundly and irremediably by this technocratic and instrumental flow of colonial/modern "rationality."

6   In this context, the hegemony of that version of "modernity" had the function of the most powerful domination mechanism of subjectivity, as much through the global bourgeoisie as through the despotic bureaucracy of the so-called socialist bloc. In that way and despite their rivalry, both modes of domination, exploitation, and

conflict converged in a repressive antagonism of the new movements of and in society, particularly regarding the social ethic of labor, gender, subjectivity, and collective authority. Contrarily, it would be much harder to explain the successful alliance of both modes of domination to overthrow most youth movements (be they in Paris, New York, Berlin, Rome, Jakarta, Tlatelolco, Shanghai, or Prague). At the end of the 1960s and the beginning of the 1970s, they fought as a minority in the whole world against not only labor exploitation, colonialism, and imperialism but also colonial-imperial wars (for that period Vietnam is the emblematic case), the social ethic of productivism and consumerism, pragmatic bourgeois and bureaucratic authoritarianism, domination through "race" and "gender," the repression of all nonconventional forms of sexuality, and the technocratic reductionism of instrumental rationality and for new aesthetical-ethical political frameworks. They were fighting, consequently, for a radically different historical horizon of meanings than that of the Eurocentered coloniality/modernity.

7   At the same time, a new model of conflicts came up. First was the delegitimation of the whole domination system assembled through the axis of "race"/"gender"/"ethnicity." This tendency had already begun by the end of World War II as a result of the global repudiation regarding the atrocities of national socialism and Japanese military authoritarianism. The racism/sexism/ethnicism of those despotic regimes was consequently not only defeated in war but also to no lesser extent and as a part of the delegitimizing references of racialization, patriarchy, ethnicism, and militarist authoritarianism converted within the power relations. But it was mostly during the decade of the 1960s in the twentieth century that a great debate on "race" and "gender" could gain a new and definitive prominence, announcing the enormous contemporary global conflict regarding the control over these areas of social behavior and praxis.

8   Despite the defeat of those antiauthoritarian and antibureaucratic movements and the following imposition of "globalization" as the new global colonial capitalism, the seed of a new historical horizon was able to survive among the new historical-structural heterogeneity of global imaginaries and momentarily germinate as one of the most visible signs in the proposition for a Bien Vivir.

The New Historical Period: The Existential Crisis of the Global Coloniality of Power

The evolvement of these new historical tendencies of industrial-financial capital led to a prolonged booming and changing period, culminating in an explosion of an existential crisis in the power model as such, the global coloniality of power and its ensemble and crucial elements, since the second half of 1973.

Together with that crisis, the world entered a new historical period whose specific processes have a similar deepness, magnitude, and implication with the period that we call the "industrial-bourgeois revolution" although with opposing signs. The terms "neoliberalism," "globalization," and "postmodernity," which cannot be discussed here at length,[5] present with reasonable efficacy and despite all their ambivalences and complexities the character and the main tendencies of this new period.

The first of these processes consists basically in the ultimate imposition of the new financial capital in the control of global colonial/modern capitalism. Precisely, it is about the worldwide imposition of a "structural unemployment" woven by the "structural financialization." The second process is about the imposition of that definitive framework on all countries and the whole human population, initially in Latin America through the bloody dictatorship of General Augusto Pinochet in Chile and later through the governments of Margaret Thatcher in Britain and Ronald Reagan in the United States together with the support or subjugation or both of all other countries.

This imposition produced a social dispersion of the exploited workers and the disintegration of their main social and political institutions (mainly trade unions) and the defeat and disintegration of the so-called socialist bloc and virtually of all regimes, movements, and political organizations involved. China and later Vietnam chose to be on the side of the new industrial-financial and globalized "really existing capitalism" under a reconfigured bureaucratic despotism as a partner of the major global financial corporations and of the global imperial bloc.[6]

Finally, "postmodernity" denominates, in a rather unsatisfactory way, the ultimate imposition of technocratization/instrumentalization of what was known as "modern rationality," that is the Eurocentered colonialiy/modernity.

We are then deep within a historical process of a complete reconfiguration of the global coloniality of power, the hegemonic power model of the planet. It is about, in a first stance, the acceleration and deepening of a re-concentration tendency regarding the control of power.

The central tendencies of that process consist, in a brief overview, in

1   The reprivatization of public spaces, mainly the state;
2   The reconcentration of control over labor, the resources of pro-duction and of production redistribution;
3   The extreme and increasing social polarization of the world population;
4   The aggravation of the "exploitation of nature";
5   The hyperfetishization of the market, even more than of the product;
6   The manipulation and control of technological resources of com-munication and of transportation in order to impose the techno-cratization/instrumentalization of coloniality/modernity;
7   The mercantilization of subjectivity and life experiences of indi-viduals, mainly of women;
8   The universal aggravation of individualist dispersion of people and of egoistic conduct, cross-dressed as individual liberty, which is the equivalent of the universalization of the "American dream" in social praxis, perverted as the nightmare of brutal in-dividual quest for wealth and power against others;
9   The "fundamentalization" of religious ideologies and their cor-responding social ethics, which ultimately relegitimizes the con-trol over the main areas of social existence; and
10 The growing use of the so-called cultural industries (most of all images, cinema, TV, video, etc.) in the industrial production of terror and mystification of experiences, leading to a legitima-tion of the "fundamentalization" of ideologies and repressive violence.

The "Exploitation of Nature" and the Crisis of the Global Coloniality of Power

Although only in an allusive way, it is pertinent to point out that one of the foundational elements of Eurocentered coloniality/modernity is the new and radical Cartesian dualism that separates "reason" from "nature."[7] Hence, one of the most characteristic ideas/images of Eurocentrism in any of its expressions is the "exploitation of nature" as something that does not require any further justification, expressed properly in the productivist ethic originated in the Industrial Revolution. It is not difficult at all to perceive the inherent presence of the idea of "race" as part of "nature," as an explanation and justification for the exploitation of "inferior races."

Under the protection of this metaphysical mystification of human relations with the rest of the universe, the dominant groups of Homo sapiens, within the global coloniality of power and especially since the Industrial Revolution, lead the species to impose its exploitative hegemony on all other species of animals as well as a predatory conduct over all other existing elements of the planet. Based on that, global/colonial capitalism performs an increasingly fierce and predatory conduct that leads to jeopardizing not only the survival of the whole species on the planet but also the continuity and reproduction of the conditions of life, the whole life on the planet. With its imposition, today we are killing each other and destroying our common home.

From that perspective, the so-called global warming of the global climate, or the climate crisis, far from being a natural phenomenon that happens within something we call "nature" and supposedly separated from us as members of that animal species Homo sapiens, is the result of the aggravation of that global disorientation of our species on Earth, which has been imposed by the predatory tendencies of the new industrial-financial capitalism within the global coloniality of power. In other terms, it is one of the most central expressions of this existential crisis of this specific power model.

The New Resistance: Toward the De/Coloniality of Power

Since the end of the twentieth century, a growing proportion of the victims of that power model began to resist these tendencies in virtually the whole world. The oppressors, the "servants of capital," whether as owners of big financial corporations or rulers of despotic-bureaucratic regimes, answer with violent repression not only inside the conventional borders of their own countries but also passing through and by them, developing a tendency of global recolonization using the most sophisticated technological resources, which allow them to kill more people quicker and with less cost.

Based on these conditions, the crisis of the global coloniality of power and especially of Eurocentered coloniality/modernity, the aggravation of conflictivity and violence has been set up as a globalized structural tendency.

Such aggravation of conflictivity, fundamtentalism, and violence, coupled with the growing and extreme social polarization of the world population, causes the resistance itself to produce a new conflict model.

Resistance tends to evolve as the production of a new sense of social existence, life itself, precisely because the vast concerned population perceives with a growing intensity that what is at stake here and now is not only poverty as their never-ending way of existence but also and nothing less than their own survival. Such a discovery implies necessarily that one cannot defend human life on Earth without defending at the same time and in the same movement the conditions of the very life on Earth.

In that way, the defense of human life and its conditions on the planet becomes the new sense for resistance struggles for an enormous majority of the world population. And without subverting and disintegrating the global coloniality of power and its colonial-global capitalism in its most predatory period today, these struggles may not advance toward the production of a historical meaning alternative to Eurocentered modernity/coloniality.

De/Coloniality of Power as a Continuous Democratic Production of Social Existence

This new historical horizon of meanings, the defense of the conditions of one's own and others' life on this planet, is already under consideration in the struggles and alternative social practices of the species, consequently against all forms of domination/exploitation within social existence, that is, a de/coloniality of power as a point of departure and the democratic self-production and reproduction of social existence as a continuous orientational axis of social practices.

It is this historical context where it is necessary to locate the whole debate and elaboration of the proposition of Bien Vivir. Following, it is most of all about admitting this open question not only in debate but also in the everyday social praxis of populations who decide to warp and inhabit historically this new possibility of social existence.

In order to evolve and consolidate itself, the de/coloniality of power would imply social practices configured by

a   The social equality of heterogeneous and diverse individuals, against the de-equalizing racial and sexual social classification and identification of the world population;

b   The movement away from identities and difference as the source of argument for the social equality of individuals;

c   The groups, belongings, and identities might be the product of free and autonomous decisions of free and autonomous individuals;

d   The reciprocity between socially equal groups and individuals in the organization of labor and in the distribution of products;

e   The egalitarian redistribution of resources and products, tangible and intangible, of the world between the world population;

f   The tendency of communal association of the world population on a local, regional, or global scale as a way of producing and managing collective authority directly and, with that precise meaning, as the most efficient mechanism to distribute and redistribute rights, obligations, responsibilities, resources, and products, between groups and their individuals, in every area of social existence (sex, labor, subjectivity, collective authority) and a coresponsibility regarding the relationship with all other living beings and entities on the planet or the whole universe.

The "Indigenous" of the "Global South" and the Proposition of Bien Vivir: Open Questions

It is not an historical accident that the debate about the coloniality of power and Eurocentered coloniality/modernity has been produced, foremost, in Latin America and that the proposition of *Bien Vivir* comes from, basically, the new movement of Latin America's "Indigenous" peoples.

Latin America is the place constituted through the "Accidental Indies" (ironic reference to the common idea of the "West Indies").[8] And by that, as the kickoff time and space of a new historical world and a new power model, is the global coloniality of power. At the same time, it is the original time/space of the first "indigenization" of the survivors of the colonizing genocide, as the first population of the world suppressed through the "racialization" of their new identity and their subjugated place inside the new power model.

Latin America and the "Indigenous" population, then, have an elemental, foundational role in the constitution and history of the coloniality of power. From there derives their actual place and role in the political-ethic-aesthetic-historic-theoretic-epistemic subversion of this power model in crisis, implied in the proposition of a de/coloniality of power and Bien Vivir as an alternative social existence.

But still, if America, particularly Latin America, was the first new historical identity of the coloniality of power and the colonized populations were the first "Indigenous" of the world, since the eighteenth century all the rest of the planet and its populations have been conquered by Western Europe. And those populations, the vast majority of the world, have been colonized, racialized, and consequently "indigenized." Their contemporary emergence does not constitute, then, just another "social movement." It is about a whole new movement of and in society whose development could lead to a global de/coloniality of power, meaning to another social existence liberated from domination/exploitation/violence.

The crisis of the global coloniality of power and the debate and struggle for the de/coloniality prove at plain sight that the social relation of domination/exploitation grounded upon the idea of "race" is a product of the history of power relations and not of any Cartesian "nature." But it also shows the extreme historical heterogeneity of the "indigenized" population, first in their precolonial history and second in their history produced through the experiences under the coloniality of power for almost half a millennium. During the latter, a new historical movement of and in society is now producing the de/coloniality of power.

It would make no sense, though, to wait for this historically heterogeneous population, which is the overwhelmingly vast majority of the world, to produce or take over a universal, homogenous historical imaginary as an alternative to the global coloniality of power. This would not even be conceivable taking into account only the population of Latin America or the Americas as a whole.

In fact, all these populations, without any exception, come from historical experiences of power relationships. Until now, power seems to have been, in all known history, not only a phenomenon of all long-term social forms of existence but also particularly the main motivation of the historical collective conduct of the species. Such experiences of power relations are without any doubt different from each other and regarding the coloniality of power but are nevertheless possible common experiences of colonization.

However, the "indigenized" population under colonial rule, first in Iberian "America" and later in the whole world under the rule of "Western Europe," not only shared universally the perverted forms of domination/exploitation imposed by the global coloniality of power. Also, paradoxically but effectively, the resistance against those forms made it possible to share common historical aspirations against domination, exploitation, and discrimination: the social equality of heterogeneous individuals, the freedom of thought and expression of all those individuals, and the equal redistribution of resources as well as the egalitarian control over all of the central areas of social existence.

It is because of this that within the historical "indigeneity" of those victimized populations under the global coloniality of power lies not only the heritage of the past but also the lessons for a historical resistance on such a long time span. We are therefore walking toward the emergence of a new historically-structurally heterogeneous identity whose development might produce a new social existence liberated from domination/exploitation/violence, which is one central demand of the World Social Forum: another world is possible!

In other words, the new historical horizon of meanings is emerging in all its historical-structural heterogeneity.

In that perspective, the proposition of Bien Vivir is necessarily a historically open question,[9] one that requires continuous inquiry, debate, and praxis.

Notes

This text was originally published in *Ecuador Debate* (Quito), no. 84 (December 2011): 77–87; as well as in Aníbal Quijano, *Cuestiones y horizontes* (Buenos Aires: CLACSO, 2014), 847–59. The English translation by Sebastián Garbe was published in *Alternautas*, January 20, 2016, http://www.alternautas.net/blog/2016/1/20/bien-vivir-between-development-and-the-decoloniality-of-power.

1   "Bien Vivir" and "Buen Vivir" are the most common terms in a debate of and in the new movement of society, most of all of the indigenized populations in Latin America toward a different social existence than that imposed by the coloniality of power. "Bien Vivir" is probably the oldest formulation within "Indigenous" resistance against the coloniality of power. Interestingly, it was adopted in the Viceroyalty of Peru by no one else but Guamán Poma de Ayala approximately in 1615 in his *Nueva Crónicas y buen gobierno*. Carolina Ortiz Fernández is the first who paid attention to this historical fact. See Fernández, "Felipe Guamán Poma de Ayala, Clorinda Matto, Trinidad Henríquez y la teoría crítica." The differences cannot be merely linguistical but rather conceptual. It will be necessary to demarcate the alternatives in Latin American Spanish as well as in the most common South American

variants of Quechua and Aymara. In Quechua of northern Peru and in Ecuador, one says "Allin Kghaway" or "Alli Kawsay" (Well Living) or "Allin Kghawana" (Good Way of Living), and in Quechua of southern Peru and in Bolivia one says "Sumac Kawsay," which is translated into Spanish as "Buen Vivir" (Good Living). But "Sumac" or "Sumak" in the north of Peru and in Ecuador means pretty, nice, beautiful. So, for example, "Imma Sumac" (How Beautiful!) is the artistic name of a Peruvian singer. "Sumac Kawsay" would be translated as "Living Nicely." What is more, there are uninformed Eurocentrists who want to make "Sumac" or "Sumak" the same as "Suma" and propose to say Suma Kawsay.

2   The theory of the coloniality of power or global coloniality of power and of Eurocentrism or Eurocentered modernity/coloniality as its specific historical horizon of meanings has been originally proposed in my writings since the beginnings of the last decade of the twentieth century. For the purpose of the present debate, it might be useful to cite only the most important ones. "Colonialidad y modernidad/racionalidad," originally published in *Peru Indigena* 13, no. 29 (Lima 1991); "Americanity as a Concept, or the Americas in the Imaginary of the Modern World-System," published jointly with Immanuel Wallerstein in *International Journal of Social Science*, no. 134 (November 1992, UNESCO/Blackwell): 549–59, Paris, France; "América Latina en la economía mundial," published in *Problemas del desarrollo: Revista Latinoamericana de Economia* 24, no. 95 (October–December 1993), Mexico; "Raza, etnia y nación en José Carlos Mariátegui: Cuestiones abiertas," in *Jose Carlos Mariategui y Europa* (Amauta, 1993), 167–88, Lima, Peru; "Colonialité du pouvoir et democratie en Amérique latine," in *Futur anterieur: Amérique latine, democratie et exclusion* (Paris: L'Harmattan, 1994); "Colonialidad, poder, cultura y conocimiento en América Latina," in *Anuario Mariateguia* 9, no. 9 (1998): 113–22; "¡Qué tal raza!," in *Familia y cambio social* (Lima: Cecosam, 1999); "Colonialidad del poder, eurocentrismo y América Latina," in *La colonialidad del saber, Eurocentrismo y ciencias sociales: Perspectivas latinoamericanas*, ed. Edgardo Lander (Buenos Aires: CLACSO, 2000), 201–46; "Colonialidad del poder y clasificación social," originally published in "Festschrift for Immanuel Wallerstein," ed. Giovanni Arrighi and Walter L. Goldfrank, special issue, *Journal of World-Systems Research* 6, no. 2 (2000): 342–86; and "Colonialidad del poder, globalización y democracia," *San Marcos* 2, no. 25 (July 2006): 51–104. At the moment, this theory is being debated on a worldwide scale.

3   The names Raúl Prebisch, Celso Furtado, Aníbal Pinto, Fernando Henrique Cardoso, Enzo Faletto, Andrew Gunder Frank, Rui Mauro Marini, Theotonio Dos Santos, and José Nun among those who took part in that debate are probably known to most of the readers. And there is, of course, a huge body of literature available in that regard.

4   See Quijano, "El fantasma del desarrollo en América Latina." See also Quijano, "Os fantasmas da America Latina."

5   My contributions to that debate are principally in Quijano, *Modernidad, identidad y Utopía en América Latina, sociedad y politica* (Lima, 1988); and Quijano, "Colonialidad del poder, globalización y democracia," originally in *Tendencias basicas de nuestra era*, Instituto de Estudios Internacionales Pedro Gual (Caracas, Venezuela, 2001). An updated version appeared in *San Marcos*, no. 25, July 2006, Universidad de San Marcos, Lima, Peru; "¿Entre la Guerra Santa y la Cruzada?," originally in *America Latina en Movimiento*, no. 341, October 2001, Quito, Ecuador; "El trabajo en el umbral del siglo XXI, in *Pensée sociale critique pour le XXIe siècle: Mélanges en l'honneur de Samir Amin*, ed. Bernard Founou-Tchuigoua, Sams Dine Sy, and Amady A. Dieng (París: L'Harmattan, 2003), 131–49; and "Paradojas de la colonialidad/modernidad/Eurocentrada," in *Hueso Humero*, no. 53, April 2009, 30–59, Lima, Peru.

6   On the global imperial bloc concept, see Quijano, "Colonialidad del poder, globalización y democracia."

7   A more detailed debate can be found in Quijano, "Colonialidad del poder y clasificación social."

8   Finley, *Las Indias accidentales*.

9   In that regard, for example, the recent interviews by Aymaran leaders in Bolivia, made and diffused by email of the Coordinadora Andina de Organizaciones Indigenas. The journal *América Latina en Movimiento* of the Latin American Information Agency dedicated its issue 452, February 2010, under the general title "Recuperar el sentido de la vida," entirely to this debate. Regarding the social praxis itself, there is a very important movement of specific research. See "Agencia Latinoamericana de Informacion (ALAI)," Ritimo, https://www.ritimo.org/Agencia -Latinoamericana-de-Informacion.

18

LABOR

The vast majority of observers of late twentieth-century processes and perspectives agree that globalization is the fundamental hallmark of this period. Almost all of us use the term "globalization," although there's little point in trying to find a clear consensus on what it means. Probably the most familiar notion, or at any rate the most widespread, is that it refers to the way the population of the entire globe has been integrated into a single web of economic and communication relationships, with this integration coming as a result of the high level of technology that is available and, indeed, continually innovating today.

This is not the occasion to discuss these issues in depth. Still, just to clarify the perspective from which I mean to debate the question of labor, it is worthwhile pointing out a few major signposts to a different option.

What Gets "Globalized" and Why?

First and foremost, I feel that I should point out that what is called "globalization" is, first of all, the mode in which the world matrix of power is processed today, the coloniality of power, that got its start when the Americas and Europe were established in 1492. Its mainsprings are

1   A new system of social domination founded on the basic, universal social classification of the world's population based on and in the context of the idea of "race." This idea and its effects on power relations produced a racist episteme in the process of the

worldwide spread of European colonialism from the eighteenth century on. Imposed on the entire world's population, this system constitutes the first global form of social domination.

2   In conjunction with this idea, the formation of a structure of control over labor and its resources and products that joined together every historically known form of labor control structure (slavery, servitude, independent small-scale market production, reciprocity, and capital) around and under the domination of the capital-wage relationship (henceforth capital) and the world market. Given the central and dominant place of capital within it, this structure took on a fundamentally capitalist character and was imposed over the entire world. In this way the structure of control over labor constituted a new pattern of exploitation: worldwide capitalism. And given that it was a structure of control over every form of labor and thus one that affects the whole world's population, it also became the first global form of social exploitation.

3   The division of the globe between regions that were identified, first, in terms of their place in the coloniality of power, with "whites"/Europeans being dominant and people "of color" the dominated; second, in terms of their place in the world structure of capitalism, between imperial centers and dependent regions; and third, in terms of Eurocentering, that is, the formation of Western Europe as the central control headquarters for the entirety of this world power structure.

4   Eurocentrism as the dominant perspective on intersubjectivity—the social-historical imaginary, memory, and knowledge—as a means of producing and controlling subjectivity and intersubjective relationships, an instrument of the coloniality of power.

In short, this matrix of power was worldwide, capitalist, Eurocentered, and colonial/modern from the outset.[1] This specific configuration of power entailed the establishment of a new world order, one all its own. Given the nature of its fundamental mainsprings, its central tendencies involved the entirety of the world's population from the beginning. In this precise sense, it was "global" all along. That is, historically it has always and necessarily moved as a single complex, although given its structural-historical heterogeneity, its specific processes have affected the daily lives of the world's people, especially those in its immediate proximity, in discontinuous and diverse ways. Therefore, the relationships between the global nature of the configuration of power and its historical movement, on the one hand, and the perception of those involved in it, on the other, have necessarily been discontinuous. Not all people have always been in a position to perceive the global nature of the matrix of power or their places or relationships within it. Now as we approach the end of the century, things have changed. Virtually everyone talks about globalization. So, what has caused these relationships and particularly people's perceptions of them to change?

There is virtual consensus that the most important factor has been the increasing speed of communications and information and that this growing speed came about through the availability today of new technologies. It is obviously true that the means of communication and transportation, the means of producing and circulating information and knowledge—in short, the means of producing and circulating material and symbolic objects—are now faster and more effective than ever, encompass or could encompass the entire planet, and have transformed the way we perceive time and space as well as our own positions relative to time, space, and each other. The human world thus seems to have not only shrunk but also come together into a single world with a single economy, a single politics, and a single society with a single culture. Though the idea of multiculturalism has already been used to cover that last point, this rubric seems to refer mainly to aspects that are lateral or even external to the others, especially the economy. Thus, these other dimensions of social life and power are not called into question. What is indeed questioned is identity. In other words, it would seem that we are all part of a single systemically integrated worldwide power, which in this sense is globalized. And all this is seen as the natural consequence of existing technology.

This perspective is not altogether false, but neither is it free of risks. Let us look at some of the major ones.

1   This image implies, first, that globalization takes place like natural phenomena, that is, without people being able to intervene in them to control them, and second, that it is in this sense inevitable, that is, as with natural phenomena, normal people's decisions can't make much difference. It's like a given, something about which you can do nothing but ask a few specific, factual questions and that can and will be used to explain almost all the most important facts about what's going on today in the world that we inhabit and that inhabits us.

2   The idea that the matrix of power that emerged with the establishment of capitalism, the Americas, and Europe is virtually entirely integrated has allowed an old Eurocentric idea to come back. Given that the whole world's population is now at last integrated into a single cultural-historical world configured according to the Eurocentric matrix (domination by the market, by liberal political institutions, and by rational thought), humanity must have reached its historical goals. This would mean that history has now been fully realized. From here on out there will be no more reason to desire, seek, or hope for any basic historical change. This globalized world is thus ahistorical in nature. In this sense, we shall have arrived at "the end of history."[2]

3   From this point of view, history is not what people do and decide to do but rather something that operates far above them: a macrosubject, such as destiny, providence, and Hegelian absolute idealism, that is realized by steering the existence and history of our species. It is thus unsurprising that many people accept that globalization cannot possibly be controlled by human intervention and that therefore there is nothing that can be done with regard to globalization other than adapt our individual and collective behaviors, goals, and projects to it or resign ourselves simply to be its victims.

4   Finally, globalization would mean that the world and power are as completely and systemically tied together as a dovetail joint, like a seamless assemblage or piece of machinery from which there can consequently be no escape and from which it would make sense to attempt an escape.

This is, of course, a mystifying view, given that it obscures the fact that history is produced by the actions of people. This prevents us precisely from perceiving people, their actions, their relationships, and the processes in which they take part including, among other things, what has happened and is happening today with regard to power relations. Indeed, the dominant image of globalization makes it impossible to question power.

In short, the globality inherent in the current matrix of power has been imposed on the perceptions of the population under its sway but at the cost of profound distortions regarding the other foundational traits of the power structure. Taken together, the fact that this globalization is now perceived all over the globe has crucial implications.

Beyond what each person thinks about globalization, there is one very important point: the debate over it has forced us all to take a second look at the world as a whole, that is, to elaborate once more a global perspective on this world and its particular matrix of power. This undeniably allows us to see new things. But just as important, it lets us see things we had seen before, but perhaps only partially or poorly, in new ways and, moreover, to observe things that we had not really seen. This is not only important but also truly decisive, because it relates to the perception of knowledge itself, not just to the specific perception of the phenomena with which we are going to work. We should all keep this changed perspective in mind as we set out on our conversation about the question of labor.

The Crisis of Labor Relations in Capitalism

I would like to begin exploring the significance or possible significance of a fact that all of us here are probably familiar with. The most common statistical estimate is that by the end of this century—in other words, very soon—there will be roughly 800 million unemployed people in the world. This is a conservative estimate, since it only counts those currently seeking a paid job but unable to find one, not those who have given up or have never looked for one.

What might this information mean? Economists have coined the term "structural unemployment" as an empirical admission that rising world unemployment is not a temporary situation that can be overcome when the situation is fixed but rather a new trend in the world structure of capital-labor relations, a feature inherent in the conditions of the capitalist system now and in the future. Therefore, the traditional notion of "full employment" under capitalism, whether in the center or on the periphery, should finally be abandoned.

Furthermore, it's no longer as marginal as it was twenty or twenty-five years ago to think that the higher the level of technology in the structure of accumulation and appropriation in contemporary economy, the more likely it will be that individual work will tend to disappear so that at the highest levels of technology, employment will probably be insignificant. If this is the expression not of a temporary conjuncture but instead of a structural tendency that will continue to grow as technology develops, we must necessarily admit that we are dealing with a global trend of continuing declines in paid employment.

As we know, these trends have already given rise to the idea that labor itself is coming to an end. This idea, the end of labor, has been circulated fairly widely though not really debated by writers such as Jeremy Rifkin in the United States and Dominique Méda in France, among the most well known.[3]

Why this idea of the end of labor? In the first place, you must realize that in our minds, in the minds of many of us, the idea of paid labor has come to be taken as equivalent to the idea of work or labor in general. Thus, in our everyday way of talking, we say "I'm out of work" or that someone "isn't working," when what we mean is "I don't have a paid job" or "they don't have a job." This means that we've turned paid employment into a synonym of the idea of work or labor in general.

Why does this happen? The truth is, it's an indication of the presence of the logic of capitalism in our way of thinking and specifically of one of its particular forms, what we call the Eurocentric perspective on knowledge and knowledge making. One of the characteristics of this perspective on knowledge is the tendency to homogenize phenomena that are heterogeneous by nature, such as labor. Saying that all work is equivalent to paid employment obviously makes us perceive something that is naturally heterogeneous as homogeneous, and this is precisely the point at which we have to reopen the doors.

If we recognize that paid labor, as individual work transformed into a commodity, is trending downward, especially as the technological level of the productive apparatus rises, and that this is no longer a temporary crisis situation but rather a secular trend inherent in the capitalist structure from here on out, this means that paid labor is definitely in question, in crisis. Other questions then inevitably arise: What are the workers who can't find jobs supposed to do? What happens to the people most closely associated with them, primarily their family members, that is, to the "social class" of wage laborers? In this regard, we'll have to multiply the number 800 million by at least five, won't we? Well, then, what are all those workers to do, commit collective suicide? If this is an economy where you can't live today without an income and the only possible source of an income for workers comes from having a job, then we're talking about an absolutely crucial problem. This is a question that's undoubtedly on everyone's mind now. As proof, there's now an extensive literature on "poverty."

In 1991, the United Nations recognized the need to name a special commission to study contemporary slavery around the world. Its most recent report, from 1993, indicates that roughly 200 million people worldwide are held in a state of enslavement. Around the same time, the International Labor Organization, for its part, reported that its investigations showed there were between roughly 6 million and 10 million enslaved people in the world. A recent report by a research organization in India even concluded that there were around 3 million enslaved people in that country alone.[4]

What does all this mean? To begin with, enslavement isn't as over as it had seemed or else it is rebounding. In reality, there are plenty of signs that enslavement is growing or reproducing itself again, as are personal servitude, small-scale market production, and reciprocity. But these are obviously not being reproduced as "precapitalist modes of production." Quite the contrary, they are the product of current trends in world capitalism and its tendency toward "structural unemployment." Workers who have to live in the market but are unable to sell their personal labor are also forced to accept any form of exploitation in order to survive, even enslavement. Similarly, enslavement networks are beginning to be reproduced, for instance, along the US-Mexican, in the southern United States, and in the Amazon basin, which means that the corresponding social ethic is also being reproduced. Under these conditions, it isn't gratuitous to point out a connection between these trends and the growing limits to the presence of commodified individual labor at the technologically most advanced levels of the world structure of accumulation.

This contradicts one of the most widespread ideas that virtually all of us have dealt with over the past century, doesn't it? I think all of us can recognize this. We'd gotten used to thinking that capitalism linked the world's entire population, with differences in the rhythm and timing depending on the place, into a single social classification pattern corresponding to capital-wage relations and that we would all tend sooner or later to be turned into wage laborers, the middle sectors, or the bourgeoise. Many have insisted, however, that peasants have not disappeared and that this phenomenon has proved intractable in the theory of capitalism and its social classes, thus "the awkward class."[5]

Nevertheless, if there are 200 million enslaved people, if personal servitude is back, if small-scale market production is ubiquitous around the world, since it is the central element in what is called "the informal economy," if reciprocity—that is, trading labor and work without going through the marketplace—is expanding once more, then we have a theoretical and historical obligation to ask ourselves whether all this means that there's something to the idea that capitalism generates this single classification pattern that we failed to see. And I think the conclusion is inevitable: that idea was basically erroneous, because it didn't happen that way and most likely would never happen that way. And I believe that Latin America is an excellent example for showing that it never did happen that way.

The Americas and the Capitalist Control of Labor

Latin America—allow me to remind us all, Latin Americans and Latin Americanists alike—is a fundamental topic for the history of the past five hundred years. With the historical creation of what we now call the Americas came the creation of world capitalism and the beginning of the period of modernity. To make these facts visible, I'd like to propose the following. Let's imagine that we're in the early sixteenth century in the Americas, which back then was exclusively made up of what today is Latin America. What things will we find in terms of the forms of labor control and exploitation? Probably the following: enslavement, personal servitude, reciprocity, small-scale market production, and wage labor. Not to mention what economists term natural economy, right? Five centuries later, what will we find in Latin America and now all over the world? Once more, the following things, but now in this order: wage labor, small-scale market production, personal servitude, enslavement, reciprocity, and, still, the last spaces of natural economy. This means that over these five hundred years as capitalism and the world market have become dominant, there really has only been a change in the form in which elements that were there all along have been joined together.

We should contrast these facts with a few suppositions that the dominant historical perspective is still based on today. There are two main suppositions. The first is the idea that world history can be divided into two major periods: precapitalism and capitalism. Reciprocity, enslavement, and servitude are undeniably precapitalist in the chronological sense, since capital as a social relationship based on wage labor came later. But this periodization of history also implies that such forms of exploitation ought to be eliminated from the historical scene sooner or later, replaced solely by the capital–wage labor relationship, until they are historically wiped away. The second is the idea that capitalism is therefore a concept referring exclusively to the capital–wage labor relationship.

Yet, enslavement in the Americas wasn't a carryover from classical slavery. Instead, it was a historically and sociologically new phenomenon, deliberately established and developed as a commodity for supplying the world market. The same thing happened with personal servitude. Even reciprocity, probably the polar opposite of market relationships—as in the history of Mesoamerican societies and Andean societies, where the nonmarket exchange of work and labor was the central pattern of labor and production organization—was reconfigured to produce commodities for the world market. The *mita*, the central institution of Andean reciprocity, was used to bring people to work in the mines, in the sweatshops, and on the haciendas in order to produce commodities for the world market. So, all the forms of labor control and exploitation that we know today were reorganized from the beginning of the Americas, no longer as a continuation of earlier modes of production but instead as forms of organizing labor control and exploitation for commodity production. That is, they did not merely exist simultaneously, at the same historical moment and in the same historical space, but they were articulated around the market and the capital–wage labor relationship, which since then has gone on to dominate all other production relations throughout the world.

With the Americas, a new configuration of control over labor and its resources and products was established in which all forms were articulated around the capital–wage labor relationship and the world market. Capitalism is thus a category that refers historically to not only the capital–wage labor relationship but also the totality of the new structure of global labor control, joined together under the dominance of capital. And significantly, what began in the Americas is what exists today all over the world, that is, world capitalism.

From a global perspective, the capital–wage labor relationship has not existed, in its dominant position, separated (much less isolated) from the other forms of labor control and exploitation. And in all likelihood it couldn't have developed in any other way. Consequently, the concept of world capitalism refers to not only the presence of the capital–wage labor relationship around the world but also the totality of the global capitalist structure of control over labor and its resources and products.

By contrast, of course, if one drops the perspective of world capitalism and replaces it with an exclusively local viewpoint, it would be possible to find the virtually exclusive presence of the capital–wage labor relationship. This has led liberal economists, especially since World War I, to postulate, first, the idea of national capitalism and the homogeneity of the capitalist economies in the countries that we now call "central," and second, using this criterion, to pigeonhole the "central" countries as capitalist and all the rest as precapitalist or on the way to becoming capitalist. The economists of so-called historical materialism were also drawn to this view. That is, this curious Eurocentric amalgamation of unilinear, unidirectional evolution-ism and structural dualism won over almost everyone.

It is doubtful, however, that such a thing happened at the scale of an entire nation-state, especially if we are dealing with vast, complex entities, not even among the so-called central countries. In all of them, structural-historical heterogeneity remains an inescapable feature of reality if one thinks, for example, of the differences between Chicago and southern Appalachia or, from World War II on, the extreme heterogeneity in labor relationships between maquiladoras and family work in shoe production in the Mediterranean, not to mention what goes on in Asia, Africa, and Latin America.

The Structural-Historical Heterogeneity of Capital-Wage Labor Relationships

This is one of the theoretical and historical problems facing us today, because we can now see that we have a new, more complex universe of social relations between capital and labor and that we therefore need to reconsider the capital–wage labor relationship within this global perspective as well as the relationship between capital and nonwage labor and the relationship between wage and nonwage labor.

Wage labor has always been a small piece of the totality of labor in the capitalist world, given that all forms of labor have operated within their articulation with capital and in service of capital and thus as part of capitalism. This doesn't negate the fact that the capital–wage labor relationship was the axis around which all forms of labor were articulated from the very beginnings of capitalism.

This assessment raises another important question: it means that wage labor isn't the sole antagonist or alternative to capital, though it was indeed central in the global formation of capitalism. This centrality was undoubtedly more visible up until the crisis of the 1970s. But if wage labor in the most technologically advanced parts of the world structure of accumulation continues in its process of decline, what will happen to the centrality of wage labor in the confrontation between labor and capital? Is that also entering into crisis? And is it therefore necessary to reconsider the relationships between the labor force as a whole and capital?

We are discussing a very delicate point here. The idea that the industrial working class or proletariat was the antagonist par excellence of capital was already running up against the difficulty of turning something heterogeneous, the industrial proletariat, into a homogeneous category; yet, that heterogeneity wasn't visible to everyone, given the dominance of the national perspective in the debate over capitalism. Now, however, the heterogeneity of all workers subject to capital under all forms of exploitation articulated to its dominance has become more visible due precisely to the global perspective. Therefore, the antagonist of capital is no longer a single homogeneous whole but, to the contrary, is a vast heterogeneous plurality with a diverse range of concrete identities and interests. Nevertheless, they all have a single antagonist facing them: capital. Therefore, their conflictual relationships with capital, whether to negotiate with it or to destroy it, constitute a new and different problem that must be reconsidered.

The Coloniality of Capital-Labor Relations

This entails a necessary change in the standard perspective on our experience, and it runs counter to the Eurocentric perspective that hasn't allowed us to perceive these problems or ponder them. Nor has it allowed us to see other problems that affect capital-labor relations in equally important ways. Our colleagues who work on the history of labor unions in the United States are undoubtedly well aware that one of the central issues in that country's union movement was social discrimination based on the idea of "race" or "color," which divides so-called white workers from those of "color" and ranks them hierarchically. This conflict, which for a moment seemed on its way to a solution, has nevertheless not been resolved. Instead, it has returned again, in much cruder fashion, in other areas.

We should spend some time on the questions raised by racial domination with regard to relations between capital and labor. The idea of race doesn't exist in world history before the Americas. But ever since then, since colonial domination relationships first began, this idea was established and imposed as the most effective tool for social domination in the past five hundred years as the foundation of the basic social classification of the world's population and thus is linked to capitalism, which in turn was the first and most effective global matrix for labor control.

The idea of race is completely unsupported by any field dealing with the biological reality of the species. But it was deeply and lastingly imposed on the intersubjectivity of the world's population among its beneficiaries and its victims alike. It is the most deep-rooted and enduring product of the colonial experience, and without the colonialism that originated with the Americas it could not have existed. But colonialism has been left behind; yet, its most enduring product still forms an integral part of the specific current matrix of power. Race is thus an element of coloniality in such power relations.[6] This is not the occasion to explore the implications of this coloniality of power in capital-labor relations in any depth. But there's still something we can note. And it is, indeed, very noteworthy: it can't be a coincidence or a mere historical accident that the vast majority of the lowest-paid workers and unpaid workers—that is, the most exploited, dominated, and discriminated workers, wherever they live, all over the world—are from the so-called lower races or "people of color." And then again, the vast majority of them live precisely in the countries we call the periphery, underdeveloped, and so on, every one of which was curiously a European colony.

Up until the crisis of the 1970s, wage labor was located primarily in what we call "the center." Unpaid labor—enslavement, personal servitude, reciprocity—was mainly on the "periphery." But even though these constituted a single system, we got used to thinking of them as two worlds separated not only in the geography of capitalism but also in time, between capitalist and precapitalist. The view of the transition between the two thus consisted in a process of becoming like Europe or the United States. In other words, every country would someday have a homogeneously capitalist economy, and its population would be arranged in the various social classes according to the roles and ranks of capitalism.

Such a view obviously ignored the close and deep-rooted association between the social domination matrix constructed around the idea of race and the labor exploitation matrix under the domination of capital as well as the resulting fact that the classification of people in power is not based, and really never has been based, simply on their roles and their place in the system of exploitation except in local terms and only in spaces where racial discrimination is absent. And now, looking at it from a global perspective, from a view of the world matrix of power configured around coloniality and capitalism, we can finally see that it was never so, that the classification of people, from the Americas onward, always had the whole globe as its context and its stage, and that the differences between "center" and "periphery," the distribution of geocultural identities, the distribution of labor, and the distribution of sociocultural and political regimes around the world cannot be explained without taking into account this articulation between the two axes of the world matrix of power.

The Social Reclassification of the World's Population

As we've seen, the current world matrix of power consists of not only capitalism but also a racial domination matrix. Therefore, the social classification of people in this matrix of power is the result of the way in which the two axes (social classification and exploitation of labor) of power in the world are joined together. This raises a question we must address. Labor control and exploitation is much more complex today, and it is undergoing profound changes due to the new relations between capital and wage labor, capital and nonwage labor. And the domination matrix is likewise in crisis on a worldwide scale.

Even though the wage earners never ceased to be a minority among the entire population of workers subject to world capitalism, the trend toward commodifying the labor force still predominated up until the crisis of the mid-1970s. In that sense, it could be said that there was some justification for the perception that one of the axes of the social class matrix under capitalism might sooner or later become the only one, not merely the dominant one. Currently, however, even though the commodification of the labor force is perhaps the most universal trend regarding labor under world capitalism, the fact that its limits are now visible and growing at the technologically most advanced levels of the world structure of capitalist accumulation implies that workers around the world will continue to be shifted to wage labor in a one-step-forward, one-step-back fashion.

If enslavement, personal servitude, small-scale market production, and reciprocity tend to be reproduced as the current trends in capital deepen, and if wage labor consequently is merely one of the current trends, all this would imply that those who dominate the capitalist system and its associated middle sectors are not connected in their control over labor only to the wage labor force either in current reality or in the way things are trending.

Furthermore, the modalities of universal social domination based on sexual differences or on so-called racial differences are unquestionably in full-blown crisis. In a world marked by structural-historical heterogeneity and the discontinuity of its historical movements, this crisis has many different moments, forms, and limits. In some areas it's a matter of imposing the relegitimation of the worst forms of this domination, whereas in others the intersubjectivity on which this domination is based is falling apart, though unevenly. In any case, this form of domination is materially and subjectively in crisis globally.

One hypothesis seems inevitably to suggest itself, though it must remain provisional while research on this continues: we are engaged in a process of social reclassification on a global scale. In other words, people are distributed in power relations in a trend that not only restricts capital–wage labor relations but is also now concerned with everything taking place under capitalist exploitation as a whole, including the old forms of social domination that are now stuffed into the mental constructs of modernity known as race and gender.

Capitalist Power and the Crisis of Labor Relations

What might these trends imply for the future of power as a whole, especially for workers? There are many important questions here; I want to address only some of them on this occasion, since we don't have a lot of time. Today we are working on this and thinking it all through in the context of a profound world defeat. And I think it's absolutely necessary to survey what's been defeated. "Actually existing socialism" is what has been defeated; the "national liberation movements," including "African socialism," have been defeated. Efforts at "development"—that is, at becoming like the countries of the "center"—have been defeated in the countries of the "Third World" or the "periphery." Even the rudiments of the "welfare state" that were being created in some "peripheral" countries have been defeated. And in the "center" itself, the "welfare state" is up against the wall. The union movement is on the defensive, ceding one trench after another and being forced to make ever larger concessions. One of the emblematic moments in this defeat of unionism took place not long ago in Germany, the seat of one of the most successful and long-lasting experiments in creating a "welfare state" and explicit pacts between capital and wage labor, when Volkswagen workers were forced to accept drastic wage cuts as a condition of keeping their jobs. This is the end of Weimar, said Oskar Negt, the last radical heir of the Frankfurt School and professor at the University of Hannover.

What we see, what we are able to see, is that a lot of very disparate things have been defeated but things that all have one element in common, as I see it. All of these movements, organizations, and regimes had raised the issue of power in terms of a single structure of public authority: the nation-state even when their political discourse invoked a so-called internationalism.

This left two larger issues unaddressed. The first is that the basic social classification of the world's population in terms of race—that is, in terms of the coloniality of power—has allowed the processes of nationalizing/ democratizing societies and states to develop in the "center" while being constantly blocked on the "periphery." For example, even though Latin America was one of the first regions to eliminate European colonialism, the coloniality of power has never been completely eliminated there, and in some parts it has never even been diminished or seriously questioned. This is why, from my point of view, there isn't a single fully constituted nation-state in Latin America. Mexico launched a process of nationalizing its society early on, given that the revolutionary civil war of 1910–1927 was first and foremost a process of decolonizing social relations, which is to say democratizing society. But that process was soon mangled, and since the end of the 1970s it has been not only "interrupted" (Adolfo Gilly coined the term "the interrupted revolution") but also defeated, with consequences visible for anyone to see. In Latin America's Southern Cone, Chile and Uruguay were countries where nationalizing was the other face of the genocidal extermination of aboriginal populations. But the process has been restrained and put at risk everywhere, precisely because social decolonization—the democratizing of society and the state—is at greater risk now than at any moment in the past two hundred years. I'll speak about my own country, Peru, for example. There, after decades of efforts to democratize Peruvian society and its representation in the state, the process has been brought to a halt and is suffering a profound setback. This might be an extreme example within Latin America, but that is the trend everywhere.

The second issue is that even in those cases that saw seeming success in the project of capturing the nation-state as the crux and starting point for solving the problems of people being dominated and labor being exploited, experience has made it abundantly clear that this was not the best way forward. Indeed, the worldwide defeat to which I have already alluded, the breakup of "actually existing socialism" in particular, was a logical consequence of the adoption of this strategic path.

Both issues relate to a problem in the perspective of knowledge, ultimately in Eurocentrism. We won't have time today to examine such a complicated matter.[7] In any case, I suggest that the propensity to think of social-historical phenomena as if they were homogeneous, dual in structure, and acting historically in a unilinear and unidirectional evolutionary way is one of the key explanations for this defeat.

Indeed, if social classes were homogeneous and acted in a linear, evolutionary way in history, the dominated/exploited would, as a homogeneous unit, be able to capture a homogeneous state. More controversially, it might be suggested that they would also be able to guide the state homogeneously and evolutionarily toward its own destruction. But the working population has always been heterogeneous not only at the scale of the whole world but also in every place, every country. They cannot act historically in a homogeneous, continuous, or evolutionary way. Now they are more heterogeneous and discontinuous than ever. And even though all workers find a common antagonist in capital, every sector does not find it in the same way at every moment. This makes it hard for workers to transform themselves into a single organized force whose sole joint interest is fighting to control a unitary state and from there to "construct" a new society, as they used to say before the defeat.

The state has not disappeared, nor will it disappear in the short term. Capital needs it more than ever but not the so-called modern nation-state, because for the latter to be effective, it requires a process of relative but real and important democratization of control over labor and public authority. This is absolutely incompatible with the current dominant trend in capitalism, which is subject as a whole to the interest of growing reconcentration of control over labor, resources, and products, all of which requires it to reconcentrate state control even more. Neoliberalism insists—this is almost funny—that the market is opposed to the state. In reality this makes no sense. Without the state, the market would simply be impossible. Handing production and distribution of public services over to the corporation-dominated market is a state imposition. But in order to do that, they first had to oust the political representatives of the social interests of the middle sectors and workers from the state. That is, the state had to be reprivatized in order to reprivatize control over the economy.

In other words, capitalism requires that societies and states be de-democratized and denationalized. Therefore, the main thrust of the power conflict seems at first glance to be to maintain or restore the nation-state character of public authority. And indeed, at first and for a considerable time thereafter, the struggle of workers and the impoverished middle sectors against the most harmful effects of neoliberalism will undoubtedly tend toward recapturing what has been taken from them. And to do that, they will also have to recover the level of representation, or at least political intermediation, that they had managed to achieve in the state.

In this struggle, however, it will be discovered sooner or later that these achievements cannot be asserted or stabilized except through the continual, daily expansion of democracy in society and that this entails free, socially equal individuals who therefore all enjoy equal access to taking part in creating and managing society's institutions of public authority, that is, a citizenship that is not restricted to or exhausted in the ritual exercise of voting, because this is the main achievement of modernity: to be free, individuals must be socially equal. Democracy is therefore a material social interest of society, not just an ethical-aesthetic aspiration. Thus, it is also a field of conflict in society, as is any genuine social interest.

To affirm and stabilize democracy in a society requires a constant struggle to expand it in that society. This unquestionably requires that power relations must first of all be decolonized. And given the remarkable and complex structural-historical heterogeneity of the population that is dominated by and subjected to capitalism, in all the forms of control and domination over labor, race, gender, of control over sex, subjectivity, authority, "nature" and their respective resources and products, democracy as a form of daily life in society requires an equally heterogeneous institutional universe, which would undoubtedly surpass the institutionality of the nation-state. Even the most modern—that is, the most democratic—of nation-states is built in accordance with the power of capitalism, in which democracy is now primarily a field of conflict because it has become less and less in the interests of the bourgeoisie because, due precisely to globalization, the interests of the latter lead to a continual reduction in the margins of democracy in society and the state.

It is well known that in enslavement or personal servitude no form of democracy is possible in society or the state. The limits of what can be achieved in wage-capital are known. And "actual socialism" demonstrated those limits even more decisively. This surely suggests instead that full citizenship, individual freedom, cultural diversity, social equality, and social solidarity could best be made feasible over the long run, as daily forms of social existence in the vast universe of diversity and structural-historical heterogeneity, under social relationships of reciprocity and communal forms of authority. It is therefore surely no accident that communal forms of public authority and forms of organizing labor in terms of reciprocity are appearing in many parts of the world. Such forms now serve not only to ensure survival but also as part of an alternative to the historical process of a power based on coloniality as a tool of domination and on capitalism as a mode of exploitation. These experiences of reciprocity and community combine and articulate with the state and the market in many ways. Nothing could exist today apart from the state and the market. But now it is also obvious that nothing could exist with them alone. What we will perhaps see in the future therefore in a heterogeneous world might be heterogeneous combinations of all these processes.

The world really is very diverse. Surely we will see not only combinations but conflicts as well from here on out. Such conflicts will move between the market-state extreme and the community-reciprocity extreme, making many combinations possible.

In Latin America this became relatively visible very early on for one part—a small part, to be sure—of the debate. Our research on the famous debate on marginalization in Latin America back in the 1960s already pointed to the idea that wage labor was shrinking due to the fact that capital was losing its interest in and capacity for commoditizing the entire world workforce. This process is now becoming more and more visible to more people, so much so that one even hears talk of the end of labor.

The Outlook Today

I have endeavored here, first and foremost, to raise some questions that I feel there is an urgent need to debate, especially among workers. I've done it in a very compressed and schematic way, given how little time we have. Allow me to conclude now with a few notes about the new period we are now entering.

Surveying the world scenario, there are two points we can see clearly. First, the neoliberalism imposed by the bourgeoisie after the world crisis that began in the mid-1970s has lost the luster it once enjoyed. The appalling effects of neoliberalism on most of the world's population are not only so obvious but, more importantly, are so likely to drive conflict that the political bosses of the world bourgeoisie have become alarmed. The growing impoverishment of the world's population and the extreme social polarization (20 percent of the population controls 80 percent of the world's products) will not lead to a stabilization and relegitimization of the current world matrix of power but rather to a worsening crisis both in capital-labor relations and in the relations between the "races" and "genders" as well as in the Eurocentric mode of knowledge production. Second, these trends and the unsustainable situations that have been created around the world have already unleashed the resistance of the victims of neoliberalism, heightening the alarm felt by its beneficiaries. Frequent strikes by wage laborers around the world, political struggles against regimes that serve only the ends of financial capital, disputes about hegemony over the markets of Asia and Latin America: these are the signs that we have already entered a period of great social and political upheavals worldwide. The time of defeat is over.

Resistance, however, will not be enough even to recapture what has been lost. Though struggles always resume after a defeat based on what people remember, so that they seek to regain what they've lost, it isn't nostalgia but hope—that is, the future—that must animate us. As we head in this direction, the struggle to continue expanding democracy in everyday social relations and thus beyond the limits of the nation-state is already on the horizon.

Notes

First published in *Pensée sociale critique pour le XXIe siècle: Mélanges en l'honneur de Samir Amin*, ed. Bernard Founou-Tchuigoua, Sams Dine Sy, and Amady A. Dieng (París: Forum du Tiers-Monde, L'Harmattan, 2003), 79–102.

Slightly revised version of a transcribed lecture delivered in October 1998 in the Auditorio de la Universidad de Puerto Rico, Río Piedras, on the occasion of the first centennial of the foundation of the General Confederation of Workers of Puerto Rico and the Caribbean, who generously invited me to speak. It is dedicated to them.—Aníbal Quijano

1   This question is thoroughly discussed in Quijano, "Coloniality of Power, Eurocentrism and Latin America."

2   Hegel originally proposed this in his *Lectures on the Philosophy of History* (1837). It was picked up again by Alexandre Kojève in France after World War II. And it acquired a worldwide audience, together with the imposition of neoliberalism, with the celebrated essay by Fukuyama, *The End of History*. On this debate, see Quijano, "¿El fin de cual historia?"

3   Rifkin, *The End of Work*; and Méda, *Le travail, une valeur en voi de disparition*.

4   On these questions, see Quijano, *La economía popular y sus caminos en América Latina*.

5   Shanin, *The Awkward Class*.

6   The idea of race or color is one of the central products of the specific form of colonial domination that got its start in the Americas. As a basic criterion of social classification for the world's population, it has served the white settler colonists to control world power, and as an element in the social division of labor, it has served for the control of world capitalism. See Quijano, "¡Qué tal raza!" On the relationship between race and biology, see Marks, *Human Biodiversity*.

7   I discuss these questions at somewhat greater length in Quijano, "Coloniality of Power, Eurocentrism and Latin America." See also Quijano, "El fantasma del desarrollo en América Latina."

19

NOTES ON THE DECOLONIALITY OF POWER

First, I'd like to congratulate the organizers of this gathering and thank them for bringing me here to talk about the coloniality and decoloniality of power. When I proposed a debate on the decoloniality of power to the people who invited me, it was an acknowledgment that a new question has arisen in the current debate, especially but not only in the social sciences. This new question is actually a bundle of issues, several of which we will now try to explore.

This time I'd especially like to focus on one of the biggest issues. Every time we think and talk about the contemporary world, the most obvious word that comes into our minds, the first one we say is "crisis." We are living—and this seems to be more or less the general consensus—in a world in crisis. What is it that's in crisis in this world? That's a bit more complicated. At the moment, the word "crisis" is associated in the international debate with the word "capitalism." Therefore, what seems to be in crisis is capitalism, because this world is capitalist.

However, the word "capitalism," the word itself, is rife with questions, many of them open questions, because it refers to not only capital as a social relation of production but also to a complex of social power relations and, furthermore, covers a very extensive and heterogeneous universe of behaviors and subjectivities. This is why when capitalism is said to be in crisis, the word usually doesn't refer to that whole complex universe, though at times that may seem to be implied by what we read and hear.

What I want to do now is reopen one of the questions about this panorama. What's in crisis, in my opinion, isn't just capitalism, regardless of the image or vision we might have regarding that word. The ruling power structure, which surpasses the idea of capitalism, is what we have designated the "coloniality of power." This undoubtedly calls for a brief explanation first, which will allow us to go beyond the question that prompted this exposition.

The matrix of power that now lives within us and within which obviously we now live emerged a bit over five hundred years ago with what's known as the conquest of the Americas. In this period, not only were new historical identities produced (America is the first, Europe the second), but so too was a major product that we know today as race. This idea/social relationship was produced from the first moment of the process called the "discovery and conquest" of the Americas and was the very basis for colonial power. Other modalities of power were later produced, after all, in the subsequent historical trajectory. The oldest of these, the "gender" relationship between male and female (probably the oldest relationship of inequality) was nevertheless recodified, redefined, after the idea of race.

The conquerors came over with the idea that males were, by definition, superior to females until the category of "Indians" and, soon afterward, the category of "Blacks" appeared, both considered to be "inferior races." This completely redefined the oldest relationships of social inequality (male-female). Henceforth it would no longer be true that every male was instantly superior to every female. Henceforth too, every female of the "superior race" would also be, by definition, superior to every male of an "inferior race." So, the idea of race not only serves as the primary anchor on which a new universe of social relationships is set up; it also redefines old forms of inequality. Of course, many other modalities would be produced around the latter. Here I only want to situate one of them, one of the most frequently recurring ones to date. We can see that there has been a fusion regarding the idea of race, the idea of gender, and the idea of ethnicity. Of course, an ethnicity is classified not only as distinct but also in terms of inferiority and superiority. This power matrix, which has only existed since the late fifteenth century but became the central power matrix from the end of that century up to today, is what we designate the coloniality of power.

Why the coloniality of power? Why isn't the word "colonialism" sufficient? Because colonialism is much too ambivalent a word. When regions, peoples, and finally countries achieve their "independence" as legal-political bodies and colonialism is therefore no longer with them, the cluster formed by race, gender, and ethnicity doesn't cease to be active within each of them, without exception. Therefore, there is no colonialism anymore if we are referring to a political body called an independent country or nation-state. But to the degree that "race" is the basic category of social classification for the population in that country, even though it's now independent of European colonialism, the nature of power remains colonial. And that's an example of the coloniality of power.

The word "coloniality" is a neologism, obviously. In this sense, I am establishing a link between two neologisms: a recent one, "coloniality," and the neologism "modernity," coined in the mid-nineteenth century by a French poet named Baudelaire. Just as the word "colonialism" wasn't sufficient to name the social relations of internal power in an independent country, requiring the neologism "coloniality," the same thing happened in the second half of the nineteenth century with the word "modernism," which wasn't up to the task of saying exactly what modernism entailed. What is the nature of the modern? Its modernism? No, naturally, it is its modernity. So, once again we have a new word. A neologism, a century before the term "coloniality."

Why is it important to situate these two words, these two neologisms, in this argument? Because the coloniality of power had full legitimacy even for most if not all of its victims. The so-called inferior races, inferior sexes, and inferior ethnicities were treated in every field of social practice as part of a hierarchy from inferiors to superiors. The dominant ones at the level of race, gender, and ethnicity, especially from the eighteenth century onward, were treated as the most advanced members of the species. Thus, a way of knowing was being established. An episteme was being established, a way of imagining, a way of perceiving, a way of understanding, a way of producing language and knowledge: an epistemology based on this organization of power. The dominant ones, whose center was becoming fixed in the new Western Europe, seemed to be the most advanced in the species. The rest were therefore inferior because they hadn't made progress along the path, which is to say, along the process of historicizing the species. Some were more advanced than others. Others, more backward. The most advanced were called modern.

The word "modernity" is thus an ingredient, a noun within power relations. "You are inferior. You are, moreover, backward, even primitive. We are the modern ones. Modernity is our characteristic. Yours is tradition or primitivism." There's a real way of producing the historical imaginary, a way of perceiving power relations, so that they are totally destined to legitimize these peculiarities of power. This happened for a long time because, I am afraid, even today some of the dominant population and some of the dominated population, the victims of the coloniality of power and probably a far from negligible part, still accepts the legitimacy of these power relations. Each of us knows it in this way, because each one of us has witnessed acts, thoughts, publications, and words telling us that this structure of power founded on race, on ethnicity, and on gender as redefined by those things indeed remains legitimate.

This therefore produces a power structure that we are calling the coloniality of power, which is a matrix of power that did not exist before but still exists to this day, despite its various crises, and for that very reason has been an area of permanent conflict. Since the 1545 debate in Valladolid over the question of whether Indians were human or not and Blacks were human or not (the word "white" had not yet made its entrance, as it comes from the eighteenth century from the British American colonial area and not from Europe), this is what we've been talking about, the organization of social power relations on the basis of the social classification of peoples in the imbricated terms of race, ethnicity, and gender. And that's where they gained full legitimacy for many centuries. All this has been debated since the colonial period began. The Iberian conquerors considered neither the "Indians" nor the "Blacks" to be human. In the famous debate at Valladolid in 1545, Bartolomé de las Casas was a lonely defender of the humanity of the "Indians," though in the end he accepted that they were not at the same advanced level as the dominators; because he did not accept the enslavement of Indians, he ended up accepting the enslavement of Blacks. Therefore, even for one of the most enlightened among those who debated this problem, the problem was not fully clarified.

For most members of the species, this certainly remains a debatable issue. This is the topic now: proving that this is an issue that derives from a long colonial period and that it must be open for debate now. What does it mean to be up for debate? It means that we can't keep accepting the legitimacy of a power structure based on things that power itself created to form and legitimize itself. This is, I think, part of the experience of Latin America.

Why of Latin America? This is the second point I want to make, not only because this was the original universe where this power structure was formed, since it was here that the idea of race was invented: Indians and

Blacks, though the Blacks already came with the conquerors. Significantly, in the capture of Cajamarca, the only one who died among the conquerors was an enslaved Black man who came with them. These are the anecdotes that make history what it is.

The idea of race, like the idea of gender, no longer has the legitimacy it once had. In World War II, part of the population were the Nazis and fascists in Germany, Italy, Spain, and Portugal. The power regimes in these regions were based on the idea of race, on the inferiority of the female gender, and on the inferiority of ethnicity tied to these categories. They were defeated, and therefore the idea of race itself was defeated not merely because its users, its beneficiaries, were defeated but also because the idea itself was debated. Since the nineteenth century, attempts to scientize the idea of race have been dismantled and defeated. But their political defeat, especially in World War II, meant that their intellectual defeat would be associated with the military-political defeat of the users of the idea of race. Therefore, this idea was finally left without legitimate standing. But this hasn't meant that the idea of race and the power relationship based on it have been eliminated. Would anyone say that they have been?

The entire history of the debate in Peru is full of such complications not only explicitly, as in the nineteenth and much of the twentieth century, but also implicitly in the arguments, discourses, and political deals. Ethnicity tied to race continues to reside in people's subjectivity. Power continues to be associated with ethnicity. This happens as much in Peru, for example, as in Chile, though we are independent countries. It is no accident that the Mapuches are in open insurgency against official domination. Nor is it an accident that here, in Peru, both Indians and Black people alike are in open insurgency. It isn't just Peru and Chile where this is happening. It's a worldwide phenomenon. There is an issue here. The coloniality of power remains active. But the power structure based on the idea of race and its association with ethnicity and gender, that power relationship, no longer enjoys the absolute legitimacy it had up to World War II, though it remains active in everyday life and remains active in our subjectivity. The larger dimension determines, in practice, social behavior. This is why the coloniality of power must be called into question, its bases called into question, the very idea of race called into question, the idea of gender and of ethnicity. It isn't an idle question. The answer to it isn't just academic; it is political and vital. That is, it doesn't refer to official politics via the state but instead to the politics of daily life. It is interesting that this should not be an issue for debate among sociologists from Latin America.

This is why I told the organizer of this event that there was an unaddressed issue. This issue is called "decoloniality of power." How can we resolve, or dissolve, the set of issues that have come together in our history and that form part of the coloniality of power, which is the power matrix within which the entire population of the species lives? There is no place on Earth where these categories are not active to one degree or another. There is a global matrix of power, to use the word that is familiar to us: global, in its fullest sense, because there is no country in the world where the coloniality of power isn't the current, active matrix of power.

If that's the case, there's another unaddressed issue. If you think about it, the matrix of power isn't just an issue, it's actually our lives, our behavior, our social relations. It's here, among us. Therefore, there's a whole set of issues here but one of them above all: How do we get out of all this? We have long used the word "revolution," but it was meant for other categories, for changing power but not the fundamental bases that we are talking about today. I'm not saying that power is made of these things alone. As such, the idea of revolution isn't entirely useless, but it has to be filled with new contents or it won't be enough. We are thus at a new horizon.

What I want to propose here for this debate is this. Another and distinctive historical horizon is emerging. And what is the signal coming from that horizon, the most important one? A distinctive episteme is emerging, one that no longer departs from the legitimacy of the idea of race, of gender, or of ethnicity, that doesn't depart from any of the founding materialities of the current power structure that are our daily life and thus produce our thought, our imaginary, our social memory, our way of thinking, perceiving, and looking. In other words, they create and manage our episteme.

So, in the contemporary crisis, I argue that it isn't just what's happening to capital and capitalism that must be examined. That's very important, but there's a crisis around a more important matter, which is the power structure, whose legitimacy is in crisis, whose bases no longer have legitimacy. Though they might still have legitimacy for the majority of the population, in practice or, to put it clearly, in their conscience, there is an important minority for whom, especially since World War II, the legitimacy of the idea of race, the legitimacy of the idea of gender, and the legitimacy of the idea of inequality among ethnicities are no longer acceptable. The number of people who no longer accept these things grows around the world every day. If I were to ask, here in this auditorium, whether you believe that there are inferior or superior races, you would probably all say no even if a significant number still thinks so in their subjectivity. We all know this. What I'm sure of is that there is at least a show that they don't have as much legitimacy as before. Few people would dare to say "Yes, I believe in racial inequality." Few would say "All males are superior." That's over. They act it and they think it, without a doubt, but they no longer dare proclaim it. Its legitimacy is gone. This means that in their minds, subjectivity is generating other ways of knowing, other ways of perceiving. There is a worldwide epistemic subversion, and its center is Latin America.

Why Latin America? Because it was the center where the process leading to the formation of this matrix of power began. It is also the first territory where indigeneity began to emerge, relegitimizing its own place in the universe. We can give the name of indigeneity to all those subjugated by European colonization, by those who ended up calling themselves "white": the so-called Africans, Afro or Black, and the so-called Indians from Alaska to Tierra del Fuego and in Australia. There's a worldwide emergency among these populations that cuts through everything, that's at the base of everything, which is much more important, since it is long-term, than the crisis of capital and will ultimately determine what will happen and what won't happen to capital as the power structure.

So, what is the symbol, the symptom, of what's starting to happen? There's a process of decoloniality of power, an indigenized population around the world that's starting to emerge. Therefore, another distinctive episteme is emerging. There's an epistemic subversion, and it not only has an important field of activity in Latin America; it also forms part of the ideas that are up for debate around the world at this moment, ideas that originated in Latin America. The very notion of the coloniality of power and its epistemic foundations and the idea of decoloniality of power are of Latin America in origin. This is no historical accident, of course; quite the contrary. This is what I wanted to suggest in debate this morning.

Note

First published as "Notas sobre la descolonialidad del poder," *Yuyayku-sun* 8 (2015): 15–30.

20

MODERNITY, CAPITAL, AND LATIN AMERICA WERE BORN THE SAME DAY
INTERVIEW BY NORA VELARDE

Part 1: "The Changing Reality Is Not What Is under Debate Now. It Is the Problem of Identity."

ILLA A debate about modernity is currently brewing around the world. Unfortunately, in Latin America this debate is being approached mainly from the viewpoint of modernization as instrumentalized by capital, due to the general crisis affecting the region. In Peru, the severe economic emergency has practically eliminated this debate, but the tragic severity of the subversion and the corresponding repression have reduced the ability to discuss the historical nature of the crisis in depth, analyzing the limits of capitalism and the problems of "actually existing socialism," among other factors, to a minimum. So, what nearly dominates the world of ideology—and social science—now is perhaps a sort of fundamentalism, with respect to which modernization as instrumentalized by capital is the only valid alternative.

Rightly recognizing that in this case you have become almost the only analyst warning about the need to situate this discussion in a broader dimension—that is, to look at it from the perspective of history, the world, and from within cultural reality—our journal, *Boletín Illa*, wished to interview you. Thank you for cordially accepting. We feel a need to clarify substantively a few short-sighted and biased ideas that are circulating in the media as well as to help bring back confidence in rigorous thinking about all the alternatives and options that the current social process presents.

A. QUIJANO   Thank you and *Boletín Illa* for this opportunity to talk about this topic, which obviously I find important.

ILLA   In your essays, especially those published in your book *Modernidad, identidad y utopía en América Latina* [1988], you grant special weight to Euro–North American modernity in your understanding of the new rationality to which the Latin American process and its crisis contribute. Is this because of our historical ties to that world or because it is, in your judgment, the only benchmark, despite the temporality to which all social rationality is of course subject?

QUIJANO   First, there's a distinction to be drawn here between the two basic trend lines in the historic movement that ultimately culminated in modernity. The marriage between state authority and the idea of reason takes place early on, I think, in the north of Europe, particularly in England, whereas in the south, mainly in France and the area including the Italian and Iberian peninsulas, there's a more protracted conflict between the idea of modernity, the idea of rationality, and state authority for historic reasons that would frankly take too long to review here.

The fact is, the relationship between the idea of modernity and state authority is constructed in England before it is elsewhere in Europe, so the implementation of modernity that the intellectual movement in England brings about is less radical, a movement that is, moreover, linked virtually from the outset to the so-called modern state, such as is found in England. In the south of Europe, however, because of the nature of the struggles there, the conflict between modernity and the absolutist state is associated with the struggle for liberation and is therefore much deeper and more protracted. This factor makes the proposals of modernity much more radical in this part of Europe.

ILLA   Another point that needs clarification in this moment is whether the world crisis, which is truly a crisis of modernity, has been exacerbated by the instrumentalization of modernization, especially as compared to the struggle of the new social forces striving for different alternatives. In particular, it seems to us that this exacerbation of the crisis and the intransigence of capital in continuing to aggravate it by imposing modernization, as if the illness could somehow be turned into a cure, are not only radicalizing the conflicts but generating as by-products a number of culturalist responses that are totally or almost totally immersed in expressions of fundamentalism. This point has nothing to do, of course, with the great cultural richness that you recognize that Latin America has for configuring a new social rationality. It is just that this other acknowledgment by you of the Latin American reality is so important that it merits an explanation, if only a brief one.

QUIJANO These points you mention are indeed associated with a really broad, complex set of issues. First, I think we are in a moment in which there's a collapse, a very visible disintegration of what could be called the cognitive paradigms, the epistemological paradigms at the origin of European rationality, especially the one associated with the aims of power. Of the relationship and formation of the subject and object categories as two mutually independent entities, separate from one another. Of the idea, in other words, of the relationship between cause and effect as a sequence and not in a complex that might sometimes even be circular.

Separating what could be called the objective from the subjective, which probably comes from the Judeo-Christian tradition, the expression of which peaks in the formidable image of the separation between the tree of knowledge and the tree of life, is called into question. Yes, not only is all this being questioned, but in my opinion it's starting to draw to an end, because it had always been questioned to some degree. Its cycle of dominance indeed seems to be ending. How much longer its effects will last is another matter, but historically, we are witnessing a truly radical moment of transformation.

Second, this phenomenon is also bound up with the fact that by the same token, what gets produced through this sort of European rationalism is a kind of disenchantment of the world, as the Weberian phrase that you have brought to mind expresses so well. Because, to be sure, its enchanted side is segregated. And so the scientific, the objective, the rational appear like polar opposites and rivals and enemies of whatever might be mythical, magical, and so on, which, in that European rationalism, is placed in association with the primitive and thus as also forming part of the sequence from primitive to civilized, barbarian and civilized, tradition and modernity.

In short, that sequence has not only been called into question, but now it is very clear that this separation was arbitrary and sent knowledge down a dead-end road, one that was certainly fruitful for a long time for many things but that still has no way out today. Hence, the relationship between *logos* and *mythos* can now begin to be rebuilt in a way. And I think the current progress in the natural sciences is leading in that direction to a significant degree, as is research in the social sciences, where debate has been more or less constant, if not everywhere, at least to a certain significant level.

This complex, contradictory way of thinking about the universe and the place of the species—our species—became split in European rationalism. There was a unilinear position in European rationalism, a position that arbitrarily sectioned one dimension of man's relationship to the world off from another, making only one of them true and legitimate, like the split between subject and object, which no doubt couldn't be validly supported today. But that's why the legacy of the cultural history of the non-European world begins to be reclaimed, rediscovered, and rethought, as needed, to raise a lot of perspectives and things again. Latin America has a special place reserved for itself in this regard; a special place, because I think it is the only space in the historical and cultural totality of the contemporary world that was virtually remade by European invasion and domination, beginning in the late fifteenth century. The same thing didn't really happen anywhere else in the world. It didn't happen with European colonization in Asia, or China, or India and the southeastern part of the Hindustani peninsula. Likewise, it didn't happen in the Middle East or Africa, though the European presence in the latter was definitely more powerful.

In Latin America, though, the conquest didn't consist solely of territorial occupation plus deploying pillage and resource extortion at the outset; it also included an enormous process of genocide. Demographic history shows, for example, that for the so-called Aztec area—Mesoamerica—the estimated pre-Hispanic population was between twenty and twenty-five million people; fifty years later, only about two or two and a half million remained. The same is recorded for the area of Tawantinsuyu and its vicinity, where population estimates are uncertain but are calculated to range around twelve to fifteen million people, falling later to one million or, at most, a million and a half.

We aren't just looking at an enormous demographic catastrophe, then, but at the virtual destruction of societies and cultures. I repeat, this isn't only a matter of social structures becoming disorganized but rather the destruction of societies and cultures as such. Might this not be what explains why cultures that were later recognized as high cultures, in the language of anthropologists and historians, for the most part ended up being merely peasant subcultures? That isn't the case in India; that isn't the case in China; that isn't the case in the Mideast, nor is it certainly the case with African cultures. So, this is why the society and culture that emerge after European conquest, specifically after the Iberian conquest, is in fact a different society and not a prolongation of the previous one or simply an extension of the colonizing society. It's something in which extremely divergent elements, historically speaking, are fused in a very conflict-ridden and contradictory way.

This process has given Latin America a very special place among the other non-European parts of the world. It is no accident, for example, that someone recently published a book under the title *Latin America: The Far West*.[1] There is, indeed, a larger presence of the Western in Latin America in this sense. But the elements originating in pre-Hispanic culture were at the same time so strong and dense that not even the tremendous disaster of the demographic catastrophe could finish them off. The elements of pre-Hispanic culture were truly so dense and so strong that, upon entering into contact and into conflict with European culture, they ultimately shaped precisely the moment in which this movement of modernity emerged. Therefore, as you will note, their capacity for again producing original elements is surprisingly large. This is surprising because after such a huge demographic catastrophe and so many centuries of continual Western domination, it would be hard to expect that such a thing might happen.

I'd like to sum all this up in a proposition that obviously is a debate proposition. Look, I'm thinking that in the present moment, Latin America is in a period of cultural reoriginalization. In other words, a period that constitutes something that, to my understanding, is taking place in reality and is simultaneously beginning to arise as a project for a large number of Latin Americans. There's no certainty, of course, that it will materialize. It could happen, though not necessarily, that Latin America will disintegrate and be defeated. But there are its new elements, blooming. What am I referring to as the reoriginalization of culture? It's the capacity to constitute itself as something different from other existing cultures but, at the same time, as something different from what it was before the conquest. It isn't a continuation, in this sense but rather, I insist, something where what existed before remains but is present through other things, not as something independent but rather there through itself, permanently modified by its relationship with the other elements.

It is precisely because of this special situation and this particular relationship that Latin America has with all other cultures, and with Western culture in particular, I think, that its contribution to a new alternative rationality will be very large and very robust. But as the book you mentioned at the beginning noted, there's a very important double legacy here. On one hand, it's a legacy of reciprocity, a legacy of joy in collective labor, which thus constitutes a legacy of social solidarity. But it's also a legacy of individualizing people; it's a legacy of desacralizing authority and concepts of every sort, including concepts of knowledge. This legacy therefore constituted the legacy of desacralizing social or individual hierarchies, which is, accordingly, what we call democracy.

These democratic elements, however, could not really come to fruition even in Europe due to the fact that they never managed to transform or transcend social hierarchies or the means of exploitation and domination. In my view, it's only to the degree that these elements could indeed be based on something else, be linked to something else—in this case, to reciprocity and social solidarity—that we might finally get democracy as an everyday form of life, as a way of being in society and not merely as a relationship between citizen and state, which is the relationship of these entities to which Western-origin liberal democracy was ultimately restricted.

In this sense, that is the scope of the proposition that Latin America is one of the important centers of possibilities for a different rationality.

ILLA When criollo-oligarchic culture loses its hegemony, two problems, among others, arise. The first is figuring out what new social product is going to try to fill that void. The other, just as important as the first, is examining the causes that brought about this process.

Although the historical crisis confronting Latin America is clearly behind all this, there can be no doubt that specifically in Peru, the political and ideological leadership vacuum is aggravated by the lack of alternatives. First, because the traditional dominant class is too discredited to continue justifying itself with the historical liberational rationales it has declaratively turned to in the past. And again, because the other power groups that are its direct heirs share its inability to act as implementers or intermediaries of instrumental reasoning, as this very inability causes such instrumentalization to undermine the group's power and the supremacy of criollo-oligarchic culture. The modality of this instrumentalization, moreover, as you have long studied, has also modernized, even more than what's still being characterized as "the transnationalization of capital." It has thus situated itself at an unreachable distance from the ideology and the practice of these power groups, even though they paradoxically continue to defend it and present it as the only possible alternative.

So, what we are most interested to hear are your reflections on the form that the phenomenon of the demise of criollo-oligarchic culture takes within this modernization process as well as your ideas about whether a new historical rationality—that is, the basis for a modernity of our own—is emerging as a result of this phenomenon or whether we are mainly heading instead toward the formation of a new sector that will implement the current modernization.

QUIJANO Two things about your observations, one of which I'd like to clarify. In the past I've drawn a distinction between the notions of modernity and modernization. Modernity, you see, has two aspects. One is linked to the ends of power, in this case to the ends of the power of capital. This aspect shapes the meaning of instrumental reason, which is precisely what is behind the modernization that runs through the history of Latin America. Such a modernization thus consists in the region's continual readaptation to the needs of capital at every moment in its current process.

The second aspect refers to the fact that in this relationship, what I'm saying is, criollo-oligarchic culture is the special result of this mis/match between modernity in the other sense—that is, as the idea of liberation—with regard to the history of Latin America. From this other perspective, it should be noted that the problem with criollo-oligarchic culture shouldn't be seen so much as its merely going extinct; rather, first, its hegemonic character, what allowed it to superimpose itself on every other culture existing in Latin America, is already finished. That relationship, or the fundamental part of that relationship, is what's finished. Thinking about Peru, for instance, I'd like to start off with a point about music. Until shortly after World War II, the *vals criollo* (criollo waltz) was a whole movement. But how many people are still writing valses criollos? Not too many, right? Seriously, they must not be selling many vals criollo records anymore. Maybe to tourists, but very few Peruvians buy them. Yet, we see that the only new Peruvian musical product of the past fifty years is *chicha*. And what's chicha? It's a magmatic product still, the result of a mash-up between the melody structures of *huayno*, the rhythmic structure of cumbia, plus sounds from international music, including rock. In other words, as I was saying, it's still magmatic. As such, it hasn't been refined, clarified yet. But for all that, it remains the product not only of that mash-up but, socially and culturally speaking, the product of the great migratory waves that have crossed Peru from one end to the other and that have, in particular, converged on Lima. Second, the result of the phenomenon of inequality and social and cultural discrimination that shunted a large portion of that migratory mass into what in Peru are called *barriadas* [shantytowns or slums]. And third, of the fact that these *barriadas*—where the vast majority of the urban population lives all over the country, not just in Lima—are also the broadest social and cultural experience and therefore the experience with the greatest weight for the urban population. Additionally, since this is all taking place at the moment of the world's current transnationalization, not only of the economy but also of contemporary culture, I repeat, all this is going to join together in the creation of what we're calling chicha.

So you see, there's a type of criollo-oligarchic culture expressed in that level of popular culture, for example, that is receding, fragmenting, losing its hegemonic power. By contrast, what used to be culturally and socially discriminated against is now emerging: Indian culture, first; cholo culture and its variants, second. But all this can't be reduced to a mere extension of what came before. Huayno has spread all across Peru, but I suspect that the *barriadas* consume a lot more chicha, especially the younger generations. I therefore maintain that while the formerly dominant criollo-oligarchic culture has lost its dominant place, its elements are falling apart, such as the values of *criollismo* that are still found in people's behavior and everyday relationships but that no longer hold any prestige. They are certainly still there, they endure, like during the crisis when people turn to *facilismo* [taking short-cuts], to *la viveza criolla* [criollo cleverness], paying little attention to others, and all the other tools that were drawn from criollo values. But at the same time, there's the whole aggressive drive, the whole tremendous capacity for work, for organization, for perseverance and constancy that were never a part of the criollo spirit at all. Otherwise there's no way to explain how these things called *barriadas* exist, with all the amazing expenditure of energy signified by life, or rather, by the daily struggle for life in this country. And all this is not just Indian anymore; it's not just criollo. It's something else completely different. . . .

ILLA And the part of the question about the undermining role of the instrumentalization of capital in the process of criollo-oligarchic culture's extinction and also about the social consequences of that phenomenon?

QUIJANO Yes, yes. In any case, there's been a limited process, an unequal, frustrating, deficient process of modernization in the instrumental, capitalist sense of the term, even in the Euro–North American sense of the term, in Latin America. I don't think there can be any doubt about this. From this perspective, the social institutions and behaviors that characterize all the stuff that wasn't part of the relatively "nicer" forms of capital have been losing relevance, losing currency; they haven't disappeared, not in the least. But, in the first place, they aren't systems that span society from one end to the other anymore. In the second place, they don't have the influence they used to. In the third place, the bases for their production have grown tattered, though they haven't disappeared.

If we think, for example, of the place of servitude within the relations of exploitation and domination in Latin America, there's no doubt that all that has receded and fragmented quite a bit, though it hasn't disappeared. Likewise, if we think about the systems of social and cultural discrimination associated with the institution of servitude, the conclusion is the same. The current Peruvian elections, for example, have revealed how much cultural discrimination, how much discrimination based on color or so-called race, still exists in society. But not just that it still exists; in my view, to the degree that the social identities of the middle and dominated sectors of society in Latin America have fallen into crisis, finding refuge and seeking out other identities have risen to the top. Thus, it is readily apparent that ethnic identities now have a much larger and more visible place than they used to in the 1960s or 1950s.

What we have, then, isn't a linear process in which modernization clears away something you might call traditional or in which precapitalism ends and is succeeded by something that's already capitalist. All this, I repeat, is once again a Eurocentrist way of reasoning that belongs to the old European mode of thinking. What we have here is something more complex, which I've been calling, in another work previously published in Caracas that I've just republished here in *Hueso Húmero*, the "New Structural Heterogeneity of Latin America." That basically implies the following things, which I'll list now very schematically. First, every form of labor exists in Latin American society, but none of them make up part of a comprehensive structure in the way it probably once did, such as in the case of servitude. Servitude can't be viewed as a part of a compact structure anywhere in Latin America, I'd say, but nevertheless it exists. We can say the same of reciprocity and even of para-slavery forms of labor in the Amazon basin, in coca plantations, or in the gold deposits in northern Madre de Dios [an Amazonian department of southern Peru with widespread illegal gold mining], or among logging groups that have attracted mountains of documents denouncing para-slave labor. And alongside these forms of labor, there are also the wage-labor forms.

Second, we must point out that all these labor forms are directly linked to capital so that when we refer to labor and capital today, we can't think just about wage labor; we have to think about all the other labor forms as well. But more than that, we also have to think about all the social institutions that form part of this complex universe, which are likewise there, since they haven't disappeared but have only been reconstituted and now mean something different. Third, it has to be kept in mind that processes of class-like social group formation have undergone profound modifications, such as a significant reduction in one part of what used to be, in Latin American terms, the prior working class of the region. Nevertheless, the salaried workforce has probably grown much larger, though without yet producing a new process of social group formation of the same nature, such as might allow for reasonably well-recognized and established social identities. Quite the contrary, there's what I call a social multi-inclusion in the base.

Only in the dominant part of society are the phenomena of social identification much more marked so that the classist nature of the dominant sectors is currently much more visible. By contrast, the relationship between their social interests and their national identity is very tenuous, even almost completely divorced, since what their dominant core seeks is to participate in the formation of the transnational bourgeoisie—and not as an embattled piece of the nation—whereas from the middle sectors on down, this relative crisis in social identity produces a reemergence of the ethnic sort of identities and thus a growing search for identity.

So the debate over identity in Latin America today is largely a result of this whole process. But back in the '70s, we were very busy trying to change this reality. It isn't that we had forgotten that an identity problem existed. No, it was just that social change was positioned as a path toward identity, not toward a fixed, stable identity but toward one permanently open and being constituted. While changing reality isn't what's up for discussion today, the central issue is the problem of identity, that is to say, who we are.

I think that this divorce is unhelpful, a dead end. The claim is that an identity exists that we have to discover or recognize. Identity, it's worth recalling, is a process, a project, a historical movement. And in this sense I consider it simply impossible to define an identity, since no utopia of identity can have a future if it's divorced from the utopia of liberation. I think that this is exactly what I have called, in some texts, the Arguedian knot, that is, this specific intersection between the utopia of identity and the utopia of liberation, which isn't the heritage of the Andean world. It is in fact the heritage of every society that has been constructed somehow in relation to colonial domination.

ILLA Though I feel that concepts not based on categories drawn from social reality can only be considered preliminary, susceptible as they are to being used very generically and in other ways, I find your work on "structural heterogeneity" quite useful: first, for its globalizing scope, a thing that most social researchers seem to have given up on lately, as most of them have turned to specific, sectoral analyses based on theoretical perspectives that are equally specific and limited in scope; second and basically, because it notes that Latin America is much more complex yet quite different from how certain theories common in recent decades have made us see it.

With structural heterogeneity enabling us to perceive the social whole formed by diverse but articulated structural matrices, we might also recognize that among the products of a social reality in crisis, such as Peru's, are ideological and cultural expressions that are not scattered and separated but rather are interlinked, constituting the core structure of the ways this reality is understood and expressed. And if this reality is true, its wealth of manifestations is being revealed to us daily as these manifestations align into a range of tendencies.

Appreciating the importance that these and other tendencies have for understanding reality and valuing their role in the process of social configuration, I'd like to ask you to go on reflecting on at least the major ones and their relations to each other, of course putting it briefly and in general terms, as the interview sadly demands.

QUIJANO Regarding the central portion of your statement and addressing it in the general terms you call for, I think the first part of the question you formulate at the end needs clarification. I see that on one side there is what's been called an antiquarian and sentimental idea of seeking ancient cultures, and on the other side there's this idea of modernization in the sense of, say, the things Fredemo [the center-right party of Mario Vargas Llosa in the 1990 election] has put forward in Peru or Latin American neoliberalism in general. I think that these instances are surely polar opposites, but in my view they're hardly the only ones. It's true that there's a sort of culturalist fundamentalism in many places that runs the risk of throwing out the baby with the bathwater, that is, throwing out everything that's modern. This includes not only its instrumentalist variant but also the other kind, the one associated with the idea of liberation, which is there in the same tub of dirty bathwater, being preserved only in local cultural tradition.

I think this is probably the distinguishing feature of many contemporary currents: part of the Jewish religious establishment in Israel, part of its equivalent in the Muslim world, in particular, that's come to power since the fall of the shah and the rise of Ayatollah Khomeini's followers. Maybe in Latin America too among those who think that if people sing only huaynos, great, but if they listen to other music styles, it means they're alienated, as I've heard many say on the Peruvian Left. That's undoubtedly a fundamentalist position, and in that sense it is indeed antiquarian, though I don't know how sentimental it is.

It seems to me that all this is even worse. It's certainly one instance, just as on the other side there's the betting on the idea of modernization, in the current strictly North American sense. For example, in an interview in Paris, Vargas Llosa said, and I quote from memory, that modernizing is Europeanizing and that societies shouldn't be exotic, indicating by this that whatever is exotic isn't European, and therefore whatever is European constitutes the universal matrix for modernity. He was of course aware that other cultures exist in Latin America, but in his view they are primitive and archaic and therefore have no right to survive.

So, one position is fundamentalist. It takes refuge in something that can be called tradition, which I don't know what it means and don't know how it could exist, because that's an ahistoricizing of the very idea of tradition. But the other position of modernization is equally fundamentalist. It's just as fundamentalist as the first, because it likewise posits a single center of tradition, the North American one, which it takes to be a universal matrix to the degree that other centers have no right to differentiate between themselves. In short, both are fundamentalist. But I think that these two don't make up the full panorama. I think there are many more between them. To begin with, it isn't true that the crisis of modernity has to be the crisis of all modernity. There's no such thing as modernity. There are various aspects and various modes of modernity, such as the ones I've sketched out here. Second, I don't think it's true either that everything European can in this sense be seen only as one of the variants of this modernity. Third, I also don't think it's necessary, by the same token, to simply renounce the whole vast number of elements contained in this concept of modernity.

As I may have said before, I think it's important that in the struggle to transform the world, the idea of social liberation will unavoidably be internalized as rationality: liberation from oppressive and sacralized hierarchies, liberation from despotism and arbitrary rule, liberation from the oppression of just one type of thinking over all others, such as that of European instrumental rationality and its conflict-ridden epistemological apparatus, and so forth. In other words, there's a much more complicated, much richer territory that needs exploring, that needs to be reevaluated, and that moreover needs redefining as alternative historical projects.

We have to break away from both fundamentalisms, obviously. Fundamentalism entails the risk of mystifying conquest. And all this is a way of ahistoricizing categories, ahistoricizing ideas and projects. We have to protect ourselves from all that, in my opinion.

Part 2: "In the Struggle to Transform the World, the Idea of Social Liberation Will Unavoidably Be Internalized as Rationality."

ILLA   In direct connection to these topics, I'd like to bring into this interview another one that has gathered attention over the past year as having some importance at the level of theory. I am referring to the Andean utopia.

In your work cited above, you don't mention it. You do reflect on the Latin American utopia. However, you include two suggestive analytical pieces in it, but I think their relationship needs some additional explanation to know whether they cover the so-called Andean utopia.

The first contains a conclusion of yours that I think I can recite almost word for word, saying that utopia is, after all, a project of reconstituting a society's historical meaning. And the second includes your observation on the current process, in terms of which a large portion of the population has been driven during the crisis to rediscover and reconstitute for a new and complex historical context, one of the deepest veins of a long, rich cultural history, the Andean.

So, could you explain to us whether or not the idea of Andean utopia is there in these two statements?

QUIJANO   Actually, I'm not sure if I agree with you about trying to find the idea of Andean utopia inside those two statements of mine. First, because such a notion of utopia doesn't seem useful to me for the purpose of an alternative rationality. Second, because in my thinking the meaning of alternative rationality is not equivalent to Andean utopia.

I should make clear that I still feel they're handling the idea of Andean in an extremely vague way there. I frankly don't know what each of them means when they talk about it. I think it's imperative, as I've been saying for a while now, that we historicize: infuse this category with history to make it useful. Furthermore, we have to define exactly what Andean means. Being Andean isn't just about geography, which is why it isn't the same thing as being from the mountains. Nor is it just about being pre-Hispanic, as I said at the start of our conversation. The process of reoriginalizing culture shows the presence of something that was there before the Spanish and that continued to be present later but with its presence extending to everything else. It isn't changeless. Quite the contrary.

It's an element that's being reconstituted all the time and reconstituted through its relationship with the other elements, just as those are reconstituted through their relationship with it, so that the quality that could be called Andean is something that can only be characterized historically, not metaphysically or ontologically. There's no original or primal object that travels through history without changing. Therefore, to turn the Andean into a category, it must be rehistoricized. Otherwise, it becomes very vague, the same way the word "utopia" isn't too far behind in terms of vagueness. So, if we stick two very vague things together, we'll end up with a concept that could mean almost anything.

Furthermore, I'm talking about Latin America being the possible center of a new rationality. As you'll note, this idea isn't exclusionary, since it wouldn't make sense to reject the rest of the species all over the planet; reject, for example, their ability to put forward equally valid proposals about rationality or at the least to take part in configuring an alternative rationality. In this sense, I'll repeat, Latin America is a special world for historical reasons, which of course doesn't exclude those from other regions. And those are the reasons why it's capable of becoming the headquarters of an alternative rationality.

An alternative rationality, as I understand it, cannot but be tied to the requirement that any project such as utopia constitutes a project of historical meaning. Hence, it can only result from the convergence of many elements but, first of all, that of reinstating the idea of the Other, the idea of the Other on which reciprocity and social solidarity, for instance, are based. This is why I propose that reciprocity and solidarity must be foundational elements in an alternative rationality. And it's not because those are exclusively Andean concepts, because they aren't, but rather because they contain the idea of a relationship with the Other within a connection of solidarity, since the aim is not at all to dominate or exploit the Other. Precisely here, it seems to me, is where the central idea of alternative rationality can be found.

Such a rationality cannot, in consequence, put itself forward as a homogenization of the culture and the species, of manners and norms. In this sense, reciprocity and solidarity exclude the ideas of exploitation and domination; they thus exclude the sacralization of all that in subjectivity and in material relationships. So, when I refer to these institutions of liberation from hierarchies, from arbitrary rule, from despotism and vertical structures and, on the other hand, to the ideas of reciprocity, solidarity, diversity, and joy in collective work, it isn't to restore the collective in the face of the individual or the individual in the face of the collective, because the collective as a closed thing is simply almost impossible after the experience of the past five hundred years. I think it's important to emphasize that the idea of individuation is as coherent as the idea of working with collective joy. What I mean, what I'm talking about, is the collective as a relationship among free individuals.

And in Latin America we have these two cultural aspects, which are drawing together. That's why it could really be an important center of an alternative rationality project. But it seems to me that this real possibility should exclude the idea of totality in a systemic sense, just as it should exclude the idea of totality in an organic sense, whether in the positivist vein deriving from Saint-Simon or in the Marxist-positivist vein leading from Engels to Lenin and his followers. Because from either of these two perspectives, it would entail a totalizing design that would impose a single axis that would homogenize all that is naturally diverse and particular and original and specific. It would undoubtedly turn into a closed collective what could have been an association of free individuals.

Quite to the contrary, a historical totality is historical in that sense. In other words, because it is the articulation of many diverse things that come from different historical sources, and therefore it can never inform any system or any organism. The idea of alternative rationality is in effect a field still to be explored and constituted but whose foundational elements are, in my view, reasonably clear.

ILLA The revelation of "actually existing socialism" is being followed by an equally bad or worse concealment. That's the concealment of the world capitalist crisis, as it provides a justification to point to now, in order to present the instrumentalization of modernization imposed by capitalism as a sound alternative and private forms as the only ways out, given the failure that informs not only everything to do with the state but also the collective.

Though this process might cause the specter of those who cultivate what you call the deceitful illusion of modernity without revolution to grow larger, given that there's already been the experience of adopting modernity as ideological justification rather than as everyday practice, don't you think that this revelation might likewise clear away the storm clouds so we can see with clarity what indeed is the modernity that is to be designed, constructed, and attained? In any case, I think that it is useful now above all to talk about what this category, revolution, contains, because something must have happened to it throughout this process to problematize and clarify it.

QUIJANO   To begin with, revolution is any process aimed at reducing and ultimately eliminating what's contained in the categories of exploitation and domination in society. The forms that this process adopts may be very varied at each moment, because the elements and conditions that exist at each moment are likewise varied. It's a matter of modifying the conditions in which daily life, everyday relationships, takes place. Revolution is consequently a process that cuts through all of society as a whole. It isn't about pole-vaulting into power, only to fill it with functionaries and bureaucrats, or about designing a coherent alternative society with central planning, which of course is nothing other than authority and the state. Not, then, about transforming what's associated with the ideas of rationality and liberation only to send them in the end in the direction of despotism and arbitrary rule, as has happened.

When I speak of modernity without revolution, what I mean is that modernity can't consist of how to perfect the existing social relationships, which are those of capital. And not only capital in its most developed form but in all its historical instances, such as those that exist today, with all their attachments of various origins so that in a place like Latin America, perfecting only the relationships entailed by capital is, to put it precisely, modernization. But not even that is possible, in my view. Rather, it isn't viable historically, simply because there's no way to turn Latin America into a copy of West Germany or of Sweden, even if that's what the most illustrious intellectual in the world proposes. It's no accident that Latin America,

Asia, and Africa continue to be what they are in the contemporary global world of capital. What they are is the product of capitalist history. And Latin America's like that not because of our incompetence, or our primitivism, or our backwardness, or because they're the bad guys and we're the good guys.

What we are is expressed as a historical product in the contemporary history of capitalism. Therefore, merely perfecting these relationships won't lead us to a place where exploitation and domination are being reduced or eliminated. Thus modernity, in the instrumentalist sense, can obviously go no further. Sure, it can continue to suck the juice out of Latin America. But even that, not for much longer.

Looking inside this context at the trends that the current world structure of accumulation is coming up with, we can find in them four central trends that are already more or less reasonably visible: computing, high tech, biological engineering, and the production of new materials to replace natural ones in manufacturing. These, however, are not the four great trends where everything else has ended up but rather the ones that are reordering the world structure of accumulation. But what will happen to labor? This is a question that is strangely not up for debate and hasn't been for a long time.

In Latin America, we've been debating the problem of marginality since the mid-'60s, just as now we've been debating the problem of informalized labor, though the notion of informalized labor doesn't emerge from Latin America; it emerges from a study on Ghana in the late '70s. But Latin America is the only place where a debate started over what's going to happen to the labor category under capitalist civilization. And that's what has now been thrown into crisis as the world structure of accumulation is being reordered, when there's more and more of a global order, not just in the structure of production but in the structure of trade, in the structure of finance. When, moreover, there's a virtual world hegemony of North American culture at the very same moment that its sources are in crisis, as is the problem of modernity, for example.

So, it's essential at this very moment to explore and start debating what's happening to the labor category, to be sure, but not only in the conventional sense—wage labor versus capital—but in all the many forms of labor that are directly tied to the dominance of capital. Within this panorama, current trends entail or imply two things that are also more or less visible. One is that there isn't really a world power system in which every piece has its place. That's why I've been contending that it isn't systemic but rather, say, more comparable to a large sack, like a shopping bag that a housewife might take to the market to put everything she buys into it. Well, unlike that bag, the current international bag has four dominant things in it, which are those central trends. But their relationship to everything else isn't necessarily either systemic or organic. Nevertheless, these other things aren't rigorously separated. No; they're in the bag, and they can't get out. There is undoubtedly no world system in the systemic sense of the word or an organic structure in the organicist sense. And how does Bolivia, or perhaps Peru or most of Africa, fit in such a structure? The fact is, they're there in that bag, and they can't get out.

The second aspect of these current trends in labor is that there's a growing portion of the labor force that can't be bought or sold. This isn't just a problem of underemployment and unemployment; instead, it seems that it's a moment in which a growing limit to the commercialization of the labor force is beginning to emerge. And this is a serious problem, because the labor force can only exist in the world of capital if it is bought or sold. So, what's going to happen to the labor force that can't be bought or sold? Are they going to commit mass suicide? Leave for another planet? Submit to any other form of labor, even slavery, perhaps, as has already begun to crop up in various places, for the sake of survival? On the southern border of the United States, for example, coyotes lead gangs of illegal migrants to the United States and sell them for forced labor in maquila factories or on large farms. Similar things are taking place in the Amazon basin and of course in certain places in Africa and Asia.

I'm not talking, of course, about imaginary events or exclusive alternatives but of things that are already happening. We see in this sense that part of the labor force feels compelled to restore relationships of reciprocity, relationships that won't decouple them from the market or from capital, since they don't form a self-contained universe but rather exist together alongside capital and are even tending to spread. So, these relationships don't add up to a return to the past; they are a product of the history of capital. Now, what sort of relationships are going to be established between this spreading reciprocity and capital, that remains to be explored. What relationships between solidarity and the market or reciprocity and the market, that too remains to be explored. After all, reciprocity and the market are two of our species' most ancient institutions of labor and exchange; they've been around for thousands of years. Capital, for barely five hundred.

The idea that capital is a totally homogenizing system is absurd in my view, and I think that's been a bad habit for lots of people and definitely a wrong perspective even for several people with tendencies that adopt the name of Marxism. If we think, for example, about Latin America, we find that it's five hundred years old, the same five hundred years as the age of capital. Modernity, capital, and Latin America were born, then, on the same day. So, we have lots to celebrate on this five hundredth anniversary. To start with, it seems extremely important to go beyond the matter of whether the Spanish conquered us and left us their religion, their language, their vices, and their virtues. We have to get past all that, because the substantive fact is that on this five hundredth anniversary we are celebrating modernity and its crisis, capital and its crisis, Latin America and its crisis. But within this, what do we still find? Let's see. What would a Martian researcher find in the sixteenth century as to forms of labor? They would find, in this order, reciprocity, servitude, slavery, wage labor, and so-called predatory relationships; in other words, the latter are not yet productive but rather forms that allow people to live off of what nature offers. Okay, and what would they find five hundred years later? The same things, but in this order: wage labor, reciprocity, servitude, para-slavery relationships, and predatory relationships.

Therefore, the idea, in the sense of precapitalism and capitalism, that it would come to an end and would all exist only as homogenization was always wrong. Here's the evidence: after five hundred years, we have the same thing not only in Latin America but all over the world, considered globally, though of course more in some places and less in others. This process, this phenomenon, this reality, is what's called structural heterogeneity, a category that, incidentally, was formulated and coined in Latin America by Latin Americans, even if it comes back later on from other lands wearing a tie and new clothes. . . .

ILLA Though it's undoubtedly not the case with you, given that you've previously covered this cultural problem, of course from a holistic perspective that we'd call sociological—as in your piece on the cholification process and later in the one on domination and culture, which was read in universities all over the country in rough but widely circulated mimeographs—I'd like for you to address an important and visible trend in current social analysis, that of approaching reality from the angle of culture.[2] The reasons for this trend are surely because we are coming to grips with the fact that reality is more complex than we had assumed and that problems are more interiorized than what we had observed, despite of course the current perspectives and alarms of the great majority of economists.

The issue is that after your subsequent works, especially the one on modernity, identity, and utopia in Latin America that we've cited several times today, I find a certain affinity in you for this trend, an affinity that in any case wouldn't be a major change of direction for your interpretive approach, more of a temporary return. Given the role you've been playing in social research in Latin America, it would be interesting and useful to hear about a few specific questions these new approaches to understanding reality have brought up.

QUIJANO Well, I don't know if we see the problem the same way. I agree that the debate in Latin America has been dominated by problems termed economic, social, and political, but it doesn't seem to me that other problems have been missing from the debate. First, because I've reached the conclusion that when people talk about the social sciences, for some strange reason they only mention sociology—technocratic sociology, shall we say—and economics and perhaps the so-called political scientists. But they forget about anthropology and history. If this set of disciplines was understood in a more global way, one would say that the problem of culture in Latin America has always been on the scene and in the analysis. So, from this perspective it would be hard to say it's been missing.

Now, if you're referring to my own case, I wouldn't say that cultural problems have been missing. On the contrary, I've often been accused of being a "culturalist," for the reason I just pointed out. As you'll remember, one of my works, one of the first, in fact, talks about a process that's global because it's economic, social, cultural, and psychosocial. It refers to the process of the emergence of the cholo phenomenon in the Peruvian culture conflict. I don't treat the process as a cultural phenomenon, to be sure, but the cultural aspect is more prominent there. And why is it more prominent? Because at that moment there are people talking about the cholo class, and in my consideration the cholo phenomenon is divided among several social classes; it doesn't constitute a single class. Therefore, there was a need in the debate to specify that the cholo phenomenon is a part of the culture conflict. Specifying this was, I felt, useful for me because that allowed me to see more clearly why certain things happen that we observe in Peru today. Even to see what came out in the recent elections, which I'd had an inkling of in this direction.

That work was also published later on together with the other article you mention, which had made its way around Latin America, called "Dominación y cultura." Somewhere in there, there's also the first text on urbanization, which was written in the summer of '66 in Santiago de Chile.[3] That work does much more to cover the so-called cultural aspects of the process, as Solari and Franco put it, more or less in those very terms, when they critique it in their volume on theory and social change.[4] Likewise, a friend was talking to me recently about another work of mine, the one about peasant movements and their leaders. It certainly does talk about peasants, without forgetting that they are Indians and cholos and criollos and therefore that they aren't a single social class, that they have other identities, or else you could never understand their movement. Otherwise, you'd be conceptualizing as if they were, say, the German peasantry of the late nineteenth century. And that's not it.

Likewise, if we look at what's happening in the area of the intersubjective universe in works on marginality, we find that it's part of what we've been talking about. The text published in a journal in Paris, on the universe of the marginal urban world in Latin America, speaks much more about this cultural aspect than about the other things.[5] So, I'd say I don't feel that culture has been missing from the movement of my thought, neither as a theme nor as an issue, though it's true that during some periods, because of the nature of the debate in Latin America, I have certainly put more emphasis on the other aspects.

Another point I'd like to add is that although I've been long in arriving at my current conclusions on this subject-object polarity as absolutely impossible and floundering, these conclusions agree with conclusions from a much early moment in my reflections, as you've seen, for example, in the text on the cholo. There's an element in there that I probably didn't succeed in clarifying sufficiently. It's the idea not of a society *in* transition, but a society *of* transition. Why *of*, not *in*? Because it's a rejection of the idea that something is happening from A to B or from A to Z; rather, it's *of* transition because it doesn't have a historical dynamic that leads only in one or two reasonably clear directions, in other words, because it leads instead in several contradictory directions at the same time. As a result, it has a certain plasticity that delays its constitution as something sanitized and ordered within a historical logic and in just one logic, which is normal.

Indeed, the idea is raised there that was formulated in a different way in another unpublished text. That different way was that there were many interlinking modes and relations of production, and therefore, though the logic of one of them, such as capital, was dominant, the others were so strong that when that one pulled to one side, another one would pull to another side, and each of the others would pull to their own sides, which precluded the idea that there might be some unilinear way of perceiving the universe called cause and effect, subject-object, and so on. That's why I'd much sooner talk instead of about being objective, about the material dimension of social relations and the intersubjective dimension of these relations. Those dimensions are essential; they're like two sides of the same coin. Which indeed are different, but you can't separate them, because then the coin wouldn't exist.

ILLA The social science and social philosophy explanation to which you have contributed has certainly helped us to understand Latin America as a heterogeneity in search of an identity with the tense intersubjective universe of an unestablished culture. Given this historical particularity, social sciences are naturally confronted with problems that are difficult, even impossible, to assess, because they are by the same token somewhat metaphysical-ideological problems, and I believe that is how we too must see them in the strict sense of the terms. We find that this understanding matches the conviction you say you got from the debates on dependency, that Euro–North American rationalism was blocking the view that the relationship between history and time is different in Latin America and that the elements fostering this culture present counterpoints that have not yet become new historical meanings.

With these ideas reinforcing the perception of the distance between reality and science, it is logical that you should wonder whether it might take an aesthetic-mythical mode to become aware of this intersection, of the simultaneity of historical times that Latin America presents, as, for example, the writers Gabriel García Márquez, Juan Rulfo, José María Arguedas, and others reveal to some extent through their works.

Knowing that what you glimpsed in this post—which for some is a proposition—does not concord with other ideas that have also been formulated, it would be useful if you could explain this limitation of the social sciences and the possibilities of the aesthetic-mythical direction. Why, for example, some analysts think it's important to turn to art, but not because it can give a true account of this reality, but rather because, being part of reality, art lets us observe it through its manifestations, its heterogeneity, and not the establishment of its historical unity. Other analysts even maintain that as Latin America is not yet an established subject since it does not have a set historical consciousness, the art it inspires is, for lack of original, settled formal codes, confused, stereotyped, and false.

QUIJANO Yes, the problems you raise are huge, and I don't think we'll be able to air them in this conversation, do you? So, I'll just make a few general observations. I think, based on the nature of Latin America's historical configuration, one of its central themes is this special tension in the makeup of its subjective and intersubjective universe. A tension that's expressed in many ways at different moments.

In Latin America, the separation between the tree of knowledge, which is a disenchantment of the world, and the tree of life never totally took hold. So, that phenomenon never came about, but there was always pressure for it to do so. That's why there's so much tension not only among Latin Americans but also, of course, among Africans, Asians, and certain underground parts of the cultures in the so-called modern Europe.

The European conquest was unable to break that essential unity of the tree of life, but it exerts constant pressure in that direction, generating the phenomenon I call the tension in the thought and, in general, in the subjectivity of Latin Americans. This fact has already been seen in Latin America many times and in many ways, regarding a number of things. People refer to it, for example, as the "mestizo soul." They'll say, "I'm Indian *and* white, and therefore I'm not all in one or all in the other. I'm traditional *and* modern." They'll also say, "I'm Indian *and* European," and so on. All these expressions are a way of feeling, each in their own way, that original tension in Latin American subjectivity. That tension, I stress, doesn't stem from the fact there's any sort of duality, though in some text I did phrase it as a duality, but in an inadequate and imperfect way.

The European conquest, then, didn't succeed in completely splitting this idea of the tree of life, which includes *logos* and *mythos* in a cordial relationship where each complements the other. It didn't manage to break it, true, but it has been putting pressure on it all this time, and it continues to put pressure. I think, for example, that when [Vargas Llosa's party coalition] FREDEMO (Frente Democrático) promises us modernization in the literal sense of Europeanization, it's pressuring us in that direction: everything archaic and primitive is worthless. And just like this perception, for certain people this situation entails a duality, and when you put it that way it obviously is a duality. But for most people, I think this is less and less so, because there's a growing awareness that it isn't a duality and that we have to ward off that pressure, that we have to save the wholeness of the tree of life, where *logos* and *mythos* are tightly linked in a real, harmonious way. Naturally, harmonious doesn't mean devoid of contradictions; it just means not in open conflict, not in open polar opposition. For example, a typical Eurocentric such as Louis Althusser put forward this strange idea in Europe that there's no relationship between ideology and theory, which is simply "nonsense," as the gringos say: it lacks any real sense. And indeed, it doesn't refer to anything in reality, only to a mental utopia, in the bad sense of the term. Because all the questions that theory tries to answer are constructed on the other side, aren't they?

There isn't one rationality, of course; there are several rationalities. Let's look at this fact: in German, the word "sun" is feminine and "moon" is masculine. Why should the expressions "la sol" and "el luna" be logical in German, in the strict sense of the discipline of logic, instead of saying [as in Spanish] "el sol" and "la luna"? The answer is that a series of grammatical derivations follow from saying "la sol" or "el sol," and those draw on the logic of the structure: Where does this come from? Why? What is it? And so on.

Well, then. This is a tiny, garden-variety problem, just to show that many of the great questions that science tries to address are not framed in science itself. Of course, theory doesn't self-regenerate. All the questions people ask the universe every day are therefore part of their subjectivity, of their ideology, of their culture, of their philosophy, of their religion, and so on. In other words, *logos* and *mythos* cannot be divorced. They each mutually feed off of and control the other. This is why fundamentalisms, whether the sort that solely seeks myths to counter rationality or the sort that tries to impose modernity in the rationalist sense against myth, each lead in their own way to a splitting of the world, a splitting that could only be imposed by authority and by despotism and by arbitrary rule.

In this I don't think I'd say so much that there's not enough social science to uncover what's going on in the history of Latin America. I'd say instead that if there really isn't enough, it's because social science still pays too much tribute to the ethnocentrist European position, so that's what needs to end.

Now, as for my reference to García Márquez in particular, it could be that whether or not he knew about these problems we've been discussing today, he was able to show this relationship that Latin America is experiencing in the terms I have used. Really, as you pointed out today, those of us who were debating the problems of dependency, of structural heterogeneity, and so on, back in the '70s, were covering the same ground. That is, this specificity of time in Latin America, which is a history with a different time than other places and also a time of a history that is likewise different. Because in Latin America there's a specificity to temporality, by virtue of which its history is also specific. That's why I have held that Latin America can't be studied as if it were Europe. At any rate, it can be studied in relation to, but not modeled on, Europe. Therefore, this specificity of the intersubjective universe in Latin America is a particular achievement of García Márquez and to some degree of other writers, such as Juan Rulfo, José María Arguedas, and undoubtedly Jorge Luis Borges.

ILLA Thank you so much, Aníbal, for this long interview that you've granted to *Boletín Illa*. But I should tell you that your patience is justified, because you have given us some very important contributions precisely at a time when a large portion of the thinking populace has been distracted by whether or not neoliberal policies will succeed, thus losing the independence and depth of analysis that the complexity of the Peruvian and Latin American process demands.

Notes

First published in *Illa, Revista del Centro de Educación y Cultura* (Lima), no. 10 (January 1991): 42–57.

1   [Rouquié, *L'Amérique latine*.]
2   [Quijano, "La emergencia del Grupo Cholo y sus implicaciones en la sociedad peruana," and Quijano, "Dominación y cultura," both reprinted in Quijano, *Dominación y cultura*.]
3   [Quijano, "El proceso de urbanización en América Latina."]
4   [Solari, Franco, and Jutkowitz, *Teoria, acción social y desarrollo en América Latina*.]
5   [Quijano, "La formation d'un univers marginal dans les villes d'Amérique Latine."]

BIBLIOGRAPHY

Achebe, Chinua. *Things Fall Apart*. London: Heinemann, 1958.

Adrianzén, Alberto, Gonzalo Portocarrero, Eduardo Cáceres, and Rafael Tapia, eds. *La aventura de Mariátegui: Nuevas perspectivas*. Lima: Pontificia Universidad Católica del Perú, 1995.

Allen, Theodore. *The Invention of the White Race*. 2 vols. London: Verso, 1994.

Alvater, Elmar, and Birgit Mahnkopf. *Grenzen der Globalisierung: Oekonomie, Oekologie und Politik in der Weltgesellschaft*. Münster: Verlag Westfälisches Dampfboot, 1996.

Amin, Samir. *Eurocentrism: Modernity, Religion, and Democracy; A Critique of Eurocentrism and Culturalism*. New York: Monthly Review Press, 1989.

Anderson, Benedict. *Imagined Communities*. London: Verso, 1991.

Anrup, Roland. "Totalidad social: ¿Unidad conceptual o unicidad real?" *Revista de Extensión Cultural* 20 (1985): 5–23.

Arguedas, José María. *El zorro de arriba y el zorro de abajo*. Buenos Aires: Losada, 1971.

Arguedas, José María. "Evolución de las comunidades indígenas del Valle del Mataro y de la ciudad de Huancayo." *Revista del Museo Nacional* 26 (1957): 78–151.

Aricó, José. *Mariátegui y los orígenes del marxismo latinoamericano*. Mexico City: Pasado y Presente, 1978.

Aricó, José. *Marx y América Latina*. Lima: Centro de Estudios para el Desarrollo y la Participación, 1980. Translated as *Marx and Latin America* (Leiden and Boston: Brill, 2014; Chicago: Haymarket Books, 2015).

Arrighi, Giovanni. *The Long Twentieth Century*. London: Verso, 1994.

Auffret, Dominique. *Alexandre Kojève: La philosophie, l'état, la fin de l'histoire*. Paris: B. Grasset, 1990.

Baer, Werner. "The Economics of Prebisch and ECLA." *Economic Development and Cultural Change* 10 (1962): 169–82.

Bahro, Rudolf. "The Alternative in Eastern Europe." *New Left Review* 1, no. 106 (1977): 3–37. Translation of *Die Alternative: Zur Kritik des realexistierenden Sozialismus* (Köln: Europäische Verlagsanstalt, 1977).

Bahro, R. *El socialismo realmente existente: Seis conferencias críticas.* Prologue by Aníbal Quijano and Mirko Lauer, Serie Debate Socialista No. 3. Lima: Mosca Azul Editores, 1981.

Balandier, Georges. *Sociologie actuelle de l'Afrique noire: Dynamique des changements sociaux en Afrique centrale.* Paris: Presses Universitaires de France, 1955.

Beigel, Fernanda. *El itinerario y la brújula: El vanguardismo estético-político de Mariátegui.* Buenos Aires: Biblos, 2003.

Best, Steven, and Douglas Kellner. *Postmodern Theory: Critical Interrogations.* New York: Guilford, 1991.

Bettelheim, Charles. *Class Struggles in the USSR.* 3 vols. New York: Monthly Review Press, 1976–1996. Translation of *Les luttes de classes en URSS*, 3 vols. (Paris: Maspero/Seuil, 1974–1982).

Birdsall, Nancy. "Life Is Unfair: Inequality in the World." *Foreign Policy* 111 (1998): 76–93.

Blaut, J. M. *The Colonial Model of the World: Geographical Diffusionism and Eurocentric History.* New York: Guilford, 1993.

Bonfil-Batalla, Guillermo. *México profundo: Una civilización negada.* Mexico City: Grijalbo, 1987.

Bonfil-Batalla, Guillermo. *Utopía y revolución: El pensamiento político contemporáneo de los indios en América Latina.* Mexico City: Nueva Imagen, 1981.

Bourricaud, François. "Algunas características originales de la cultura mestiza del Perú contemporáneo." *Revista del Museo Nacional* 28 (1954): 2–48.

Bousquie, Paul. *Le corps, cet inconnu.* Paris: L'Harmattan, 1994.

Boyer, Robert, and Daniel Drache, eds. *States against Markets: The Limits of Globalization.* London: Routledge, 1996.

Bruno, Michael, Martin Ravallion, and Lynn Squire. *Equity and Growth in Developing Countries.* Washington, DC: World Bank, 1996.

Burbano de Lara, Felipe. "Ecuador, cuando los equilibrios crujen." *Anuario Social y Político de América Latina* 3 (2000): 65–79.

Buscaglia-Salgado, José. *Undoing Empire: Race and Nation in the Mulatto Caribbean.* Minneapolis: University of Minnesota Press, 2003.

Bustamante Ponce, Fernando. "¿Y después de la insurrección qué?" *Ecuador Debate* 49 (April 2000): 42–56.

Callaghy, Thomas M. "Globalization and Marginalization: Debt and the International Underclass." *Current History* 96 (1997): 392–96.

Capuano Scarlato, Francisco, et al. *Globalização e espaço latino-americano: O novo mapa do mundo.* São Paulo: Hucitec-Anpur, 1993.

Cassidy, John. "The Return of Karl Marx." *New Yorker*, October 20, 1997.

Castrillón Vizcarra, Alfonso. "José Carlos Mariátegui, crítico de arte." *Cuadernos de Reflexión y Crítica* (Facultad de Letras de la Universidad de San Marcos, Lima) 4, no. 6 (1993): 260–66.

CEPAL (United Nations Economic Commission for Latin America and the Caribbean). *Panorama social de América Latina.* Santiago de Chile: CEPAL, 1998.

Christo, Carlos Alberto (Frei Betto). "Los rumbos de la oposición." *América Latina en Movimiento*, ALAI 314 (2000): 2–3.

Collier, George A., and Elizabeth Lowery-Quaratiello. *Basta! Land and the Zapatista Rebellion in Chiapas*. Oakland, CA: Food First Books, 2005.

Comisión de la Verdad y Reconciliación. *Informe Final: Perú, 1980–2000*. Lima: Universidad Nacional Mayor de San Marcos, 2004. https://www.cverdad .org.pe/ifinal/.

CONAIE. *Proyecto político*. Document No. 4. Quito, 2002. https://conaie.org /proyecto-politico/.

Coronil, Fernando. "Beyond Occidentalism: Toward Nonimperial Geohistorical Categories." *Cultural Anthropology* 11, no. 1 (1996): 51–87.

Davis, Horace. *Nationalism and Socialism: Marxist and Labor Theories of Nationalism to 1917*. New York: Monthly Review Press, 1967.

De la Cadena, Marisol. "El racismo silencioso y la superioridad de los intelectuales en el Perú." *Socialismo y Participación*, no. 83 (September 1998): 54–98.

Deustura, José, and José Luis Renique. *Intelectuales, indigenismo y descentralismo en el Perú, 1897/1931*. Cusco, Peru: Centro Bartolomé de las Casas, 1984.

Djilas, Milovan. *La nueva clase*. Buenos Aires: Ed. Sudamericana, 1957.

Djilas, Milovan. *La nueva clase*. Biblioteca del Congreso Nacional de Chile, n.d. https://obtienearchivo.bcn.cl/obtienearchivo?id=documentos/10221.1/35593 /2/197782.pdf.

Dussel, Enrique. *The Invention of the Americas: Eclipse of the Other and the Myth of Modernity*. New York: Continuum, 1995.

Engels, Frederick. *Socialism: Utopian and Scientific*. Translated by Edward Aveling. New York: Scribner, 1892.

Evers, Tilman. *El estado en la periferia capitalista*. Mexico City: Siglo XXI Editores, 1979.

Fernández, Carolina Ortiz. "Felipe Guamán Poma de Ayala, Clorinda Matto, Trinidad Henríquez y la teoría crítica: Sus legados a la teoría social contemporánea." *Yuyaykusun* (Lima: Universidad Ricardo Palma), no. 2 (December 2009).

Fernández Díaz, Osvaldo. *Mariátegui, o la experiencia del Otro*. Lima: Amauta, 1994.

Finley, Robert. *Las Indias accidentales*. Barcelona: Barataria, 2003.

Flores Galindo, Alberto. *Buscando un Inca: Identidad y utopia en los Andes*. Lima: Editorial Horizonte, 1988.

Flores Galindo, Alberto. "La agonía de Mariátegui." In *Obras completas*, vol. 2. Lima: Fundación Andina/Sur, 1994.

Forgues, Roland, ed. *Mariátegui: Una verdad actual siempre renovada*. Lima: Amauta, 1994.

Forgues, Roland, ed. *Mariátegui y Europa: El otro aspecto del descubrimiento*. Lima: Amauta, 1993.

Franco, Carlos. *Del marxismo eurocéntrico al marxismo latinoamericano*. Lima: CEDEP, 1981.

Fukuyama, Francis. "The End of History." *National Interest* 16 (Summer 1989): 3–18.

Fukuyama, Francis. *The End of History and the Last Man*. New York: Free Press, 1992.

García Canclini, Néstor, ed. *Culturas en globalización: América Latina, Europa, Estados Unidos: Libre comercio e integración*. Caracas: Nueva Sociedad, 1997.

García Delgado, Daniel. *Estado-Nación y globalización: Fortalezas y debilidades en el umbral del tercer milenio*. Buenos Aires: Ariel, 1998.

Gates, Robert. "Plan Colombia: A Development Success Story." U.S. Global Leadership Coalition, April 15, 2010, https://www.usglc.org/media/2017/04/USGLC-Plan-Columbia.pdf.

Germaná, César. 1995. *El "socialismo indoamericano" de José Carlos Mariátegui: Proyecto de reconstitución del sentido histórico de la sociedad peruana*. Lima: Amauta, 1995.

Gobineau, Artur de. *Essais sur l'inegalité des races humaines*. Paris: 1853–1857.

González Casanova, Pablo. "Internal Colonialism and National Development." *Studies in Comparative International Development* 1, no. 4 (1965): 27–37.

Gramsci, Antoni. *Selections from the Prison Notebooks*. New York: International Publishers, 1971.

Griesgraber, Jo Marie. "Forgive Us Our Debts: The Third World's Financial Crisis." *Christian Century*, January 22, 1997, 70–92.

Griffiths, Robert, ed. *Annual Editions: Developing World 99/00*. Guilford, CT: Dushkin/McGraw Hill, 1999.

Gruzinski, Serge. *La colonisation de l'imaginaire: Sociétés indigènes et occidentalisation dans le Mexique espagnol, XVI–XVIII*. Paris: Gallimard, 1988.

Guaman Poma de Ayala, Felipe. *La nueva crónica y buen gobierno* [c. 1613]. Edited by Franklin Pease. Lima: Fondo de Cultura Económica, 1993.

Guardia, Sara Beatriz. *José Carlos Mariátegui: Una visión de género*. Lima: Librería Editorial Minerva, 2006.

Guibal, Francis. *Vigencia de Mariátegui*. Lima: Amauta, 1999.

Hardt, Michael, and Antonio Negri. *Empire*. Cambridge, MA: Harvard University Press, 2000.

Haya de la Torre, Raúl. *El antimperialismo y el APRA*. Santiago de Chile: Ediciones Ercilla, 1928.

Hegel, Georg Wilhelm Friedrich. *Lectures on the Philosophy of History* [1837]. Lincoln: University of Nebraska Press, 1995.

Hindess, Barry, and Paul Q. Hirst. *Pre-Capitalist Modes of Production*. London: Routledge and Kegan Paul, 1975.

Hopkins, Terrence, and Immanuel Wallerstein. *World-Systems Analysis: Theory and Methodology*. Beverly Hills, CA: Sage, 1982.

Ibarra, Hernán. "Intelectuales indígena, neoindigenismo e indianismo en el Ecuador." *Ecuador Debate* 48 (December 1999): 71–74.

Imaz, Eugenio. *Nosotros mañana*. Buenos Aires: Editorial Sudamericana, 1964.

Jacobson, Matthew Frye. *Whiteness of a Different Color: European Immigrants and the Alchemy of Race*. Cambridge, MA: Harvard University Press, 1998.

Kagarlitsky, Boris. "The Importance of Being Marxist." *New Left Review* 1, no. 178 (1989): 29–36.

Krugman, Paul. "The Right, the Rich and the Facts: Deconstructing the Income Distribution Debate." *American Prospect* (Fall 1992): 19–31.

Laclau, Ernesto, and Chantal Mouffe. *Hegemony and Socialist Strategy: Towards a Radical Democratic Politics*. London: Verso, 1985.

La contrarevolution bureaucratique. Paris: Arguments, 1969.

Lander, Edgardo. "Colonialidad, modernidad, postmodernidad." *Anuario Mariáteguiano* 9 (1997): 122–32.

Larson, James L. *Reason and Experience: The Representation of Natural Order in the Work of Carl von Linné*. Berkeley: University of California Press, 1971.

Leibner, Gerardo. *El mito del socialismo indígena: Fuentes y contextos peruanos de Mariátegui*. Lima: Pontificia Universidad Católica del Perú, 1999.

León, Ramón. *El país de los extraños*. Lima: Fondo Editorial de la Universidad Ricardo Palma, 1998.

Löwy, Michael. "Marxisme et romantisme chez José Carlos Mariategui." *Actuel Marx* 25 (1999): 187–201.

Lunn, Eugene. *Marxism and Modernism: An Historical Study of Lukács, Brecht, Benjamin, and Adorno*. Berkeley: University of California Press, 1982.

Luxemburg, R. *Crítica de la Revolución Rusa*. Buenos Aires: Ed. La Rosa Blindada, 1969.

Luxemburg, R. *Selected Political Writings*. Edited by R. Looker. London: Monthly Review Press, 1970.

Mack, Raymond, ed. *Race, Class, and Power*. New York: American Book Co., 1963.

Mariátegui, José Carlos. "Aniversario y balance." Lima: Biblioteca Amauta, September 1928.

Mariátegui, José Carlos. *Invitación a la vida heroica*. Edited by Alberto Flores Galindo and Ricardo Portocarrero. Lima: Instituto de Apoyo Agrario, 1989.

Mariátegui, José Carlos. "Punto de vista antimperialista." In *Obras completas*, vol. 11. Lima: Biblioteca Amauta, 1929.

Mariátegui, José Carlos. *Siete ensayos de interpretación de la realidad peruana*. Caracas; Biblioteca Ayacucho, 2007.

Mariátegui, José Carlos. *Seven Interpretive Essays on Peruvian Reality* [1928]. Translated by Marjory Urquidi. Austin: University of Texas Press, 1971. Translation of *Los siete ensayos de interpretación de la realidad peruana* (Mexico City: Editorial ERA, 1970). Republished as *7 ensayos de interpretación de la realidad peruana* (Caracas: Biblioteca Ayacucho, 1979).

Mariátegui, José Carlos. *Textos básicos*. Edited by Aníbal Quijano. Lima: Fondo de Cultura Económica, 1991.

Marks, Jonathan. *Human Biodiversity: Genes, Race, and History*. New York: Aldine de Gruyter, 1995.

Martinot, Steve. *The Rule of Racialization: Class, Identity, Governance.* Philadelphia: Temple University Press, 2003.

Martins, José de Souza. "Sociologia e militância: Entrevista com José de Souza Martins." *Estudos avançados* (Instituto de Estudos Avançados da Universidade de São Paulo) 31 (1997): 137–87.

Marx, Karl. *Capital: A Critique of Political Economy.* Translated by Ben Fowkes. New York: Vintage Books, 1977.

Marx, Karl. *Grundrisse: Foundations of the Critique of Political Economy (Rough Draft)* [1858]. Translated by Martin Nicolaus. London: Penguin Books and New Left Review, 1973.

Marx, Karl, and Frederick Engels. "Letter to Joseph Weydemeyer, March 5, 1852." In *Marx-Engels Collected Works,* Vol. 29, 58. New York: International Publishers, 1975.

Mato, Daniel. *Crítica de la moderna globalización y construcción de identidades.* Caracas: Universidad Central de Venezuela, 1995.

Méda, Dominique. *Le travail, une valeur en voie de disparition.* Paris: Aubier, 1995.

Melis, Antonio. *Leyendo Mariátegui, 1967–1998.* Lima: Amauta, 1999.

Mendelsohn, Oliver, and Marika Vicziany. *The Untouchables: Subordination, Poverty and the State in Modern India.* New Delhi: Cambridge University Press, 2000.

Michel, Henri. *Philosophie et phenomenologie: Le corps.* Paris: PUF, 1965.

Mignolo, Walter. *The Darker Side of the Renaissance: Literacy, Territoriality, and Colonization.* Ann Arbor: University of Michigan Press, 1995.

Mignolo, Walter. "Diferencia colonial y razón postoccidental." *Anuario Mariateguiano,* no. 10 (1998): 3–28.

Mignolo, Walter. *Local Histories/Global Designs: Coloniality, Subaltern Knowledges, and Border Thinking.* Princeton, NJ: Princeton University Press, 2000.

Miliband, Ralph. *The State in Capitalist Society.* New York: Basic Books, 1969.

Mondolfo, R. *State Capitalism and the Russian Revolution.* New York: Monthly Review Press, 1956.

Monereo, Manuel, ed. *Mariátegui (1884–1994): Encuentro internacional: Un marxismo para el siglo XXI.* Madrid: Talasa, 1995.

Montoya, Rodrigo. *Al borde del naufragio: Democracia, violencia y problema étnico en el Perú.* Madrid: Talasa Ediciones, 1992.

Morrison, Toni. *Song of Solomon.* New York: Knopf, 1977.

Mudimbe, Valentine. *The Invention of Africa: Gnosis, Philosophy, and the Order of Knowledge.* Bloomington: Indiana University Press, 1988.

Munda, Ram Dayal, and S. Bosu Mullick. *Jharkhand Movement: Indigenous People Struggle for Autonomy in India.* Copenhagen: Bindrai Institute for Research Study and Action (BIRSA) & IWGIA, 2003. https://www.iwgia.org/images/publications/0120_jharkhand_movement.pdf.

Myrdall, Gunnar. *American Dilemma.* New York: Harper and Brothers, 1944.

Nun, José. "Sobrepoblación relativa, ejército industrial de reserva y masa marginal." *Revista Latinoamericana de Sociología* 5, no. 2 (1969): 3–25.

O'Gorman, Eduardo. *La invención de América*. Mexico: FCE, 1954.

Palacín, Miguel, Antonio Iviche Quisque, Hildebrando Ruffner Sebastián, and César Sarasara. "Propuesta concertada para incorporar los derechos de los pueblos indígenas y comunidades en la constitución política del Perú." Presented at La Gran Consulta Indígena sobre Reforma Constitucional, Lima, April 14, 2003.

Pannekoek, A. *Lenin as Philosopher*. New York: Breakout, 1948.

Parkin, Frank. *Marxism and Class Theory: A Bourgeois Critique*. New York: Columbia University Press, 1979.

Popov, G. "The Dangers of Democracy." *New York Review of Books*, August 16, 1990. https://www.nybooks.com/articles/2014/03/20/dangers-of-democracy/.

Poulantzas, Nicos. *Poder político y clases sociales en el estado capitalista*. Mexico City: Siglo XXI Editores, 1969.

Poulantzas, Nicos. *Political Power and Social Classes*. London: Verso Editions, 1978.

Prebisch, Raúl. *Capitalismo periférico: Crisis y transformación*. Mexico City: Fondo de Cultura Económica, 1981.

Prebisch, Raúl. "Commercial Policy in the Underdeveloped Countries." *American Economic Review, Papers and Proceedings* 49 (1959): 251–73.

Prebisch, Raúl. "Crítica al capitalismo periférico." *Revista de la CEPAL* (Santiago de Chile: CEPAL) 1 (1976): 7–73.

Prebisch, Raúl. *The Economic Development of Latin America and Its Principal Problems*. New York: ECLA, United Nations, 1950.

Prebisch, Raúl. *Hacia una dinámica del desarrollo latinoamericano*. Mexico City: Fondo de Cultura Económica, 1963.

Quijano, Aníbal. "América Latina Sobreviverá?" *Revista São Paulo em Perspectiva* (SEADE) 7, no. 2 (1993): 60–66.

Quijano, Aníbal. "América Latina en la economía mundial." *Problemas del desarrollo: Revista Latinoamericana de Economia* 24, no. 95 (1993): 43–59.

Quijano, Aníbal. "Colonialidad del poder, cultura y conocimiento en América Latina." *Anuario Mariateguiano* 9, no. 9 (1998): 113–22.

Quijano, Aníbal. "Colonialidad del poder, cultura y conocimiento en América Latina." In "Critica Cutural en Latinoam'erica: Paradigmas globales y enunciaciones locales," special issue, *Dispositio* 24, no. 51 (1999): 137–48.

Quijano, Aníbal. "Colonialidad del poder, eurocentrismo y América Latina." In *La colonialidad del saber: Eurocentrismo y ciencias sociales: Perspectivas latinoamericanas*, ed. Edgardo Lander. Buenos Aires: CLACSO, 2000.

Quijano, Aníbal. "Colonialidad del poder, globalización y democracia." *Utopías, nuestra bandera: Revista de debate político*, no. 188 (2001): 97–123.

Quijano, Aníbal. "Colonialidad del poder y clasificación social." In "Festschrift for Immanuel Wallerstein," ed. Giovanni Arrighi and Walter L. Goldfrank, special issue, *Journal of World-Systems Research* 6, no. 2 (2000): 342–86.

Quijano, Aníbal. "Colonialidad y modernidad/racionalidad." *Perú indígena* 13, no. 29 (1992): 11–20. English versión in *Cultural Studies* 21, nos. 2–3 (2007):

168–78. Also printed in *Los conquistados*, ed. Heraclio Bonilla, 437–49 (Lima: Tercer Mundo Ediciones/flacso, 1992).

Quijano, Aníbal. "Colonialité du pouvoir et démocratie en Amérique latine." In *Futur anterieur: Amérique latine, democratie et exclusion*, by Alejandro Álvarez Béjar et al., 93–101. Paris: L'Harmattan, 1994.

Quijano, Aníbal. "Coloniality of Power, Eurocentrism and Latin America." *Nepantla* 1, no. 3 (2000): 533–81. Translation of "Colonialidad del poder, eurocentrismo y América Latina," in *La colonialidad del saber: Eurocentrismo y ciencias sociales: Perspectivas latinoamericanas*, ed. Edgardo Lander, 201–46 (Buenos Aires: CLACSO 2000.)

Quijano, Aníbal. "Coloniality of Power and Its Institutions." Paper presented at the conference "Coloniality and Its Disciplinary Sites," Binghamton University, April 1999.

Quijano, Aníbal. "Contemporary Peasant Movements in Latin America." In *Elites in Latin America*, ed. S. M. Lipset and A. E. Solari, 39–72. New York: Oxford University Press, 1967. Translation of "Movimientos campesinos contemporáneos en América Latina," in *Elites y desarrollo en América Latina*, ed. S. M. Lipset and A. E. Solari, 58–70 (Buenos Aires: Paidos, 1967).

Quijano, Aníbal. *Crisis imperialista y clase obrera en América Latina*. Lima: Editorial Achawata, 1974.

Quijano, Aníbal. "Dependencia, cambio social y urbanización en Latinoamérica." Santiago de Chile: CEPAL, 1967. Reprinted in *Revista Mexicana de Sociología* 30, no. 3 (1968): 525–70, and in Aníbal Quijano, *Dependencia, cambio social y urbanización en América Latina* (Lima: Mosca Azul, 1977).

Quijano, Aníbal. *Dependencia, cambio social y urbanización en América Latina*. Lima: Mosca Azul, 1977.

Quijano, Aníbal. "Des/colonialidad: El horizonte alternativo." *Boletín del Programa Estudios de Transformación y Democratización* (Lima: Universidad de San Marcos, 2008).

Quijano, Aníbal. *Dominación y cultura: Lo cholo y el conflicto cultural en el Perú*. Lima: Mosca Azul, 1980.

Quijano, Aníbal. "Dominación y cultura (notas sobre el problema de la participación cultural)." *Revista Latinoamericana de Ciencias Sociales* (Santiago, Chile) 1 (1971): 2–17. Reprinted in Aníbal Quijano, *Dominación y cultura: Lo cholo y el conflicto cultural en el Perú*, 17–43 (Lima: Mosca Azul, 1980).

Quijano, Aníbal. "Don Quijote y los molinos de viento en América Latina." *Libros y arte: Revista de Cultura de la Biblioteca Nacional del Perú* 10 (April 2005): 14–16.

Quijano, Aníbal. "El fantasma del desarrollo en América Latina." *Revista Venezolana de Economía y Ciencias Sociales* (Universidad Central de Venezuela) 6, no. 2 (2000): 73–90.

Quijano, Aníbal. "¿El fin de cual historia?" *Análisis político* 32 (1997): 27–34 (Institute of Political and International Studies, National University of Colombia, Bogotá).

Quijano, Aníbal. "El fujimorismo, la OEA y el Perú." *América Latina en movimiento* (Quito) July 25, 2000.

Quijano, Aníbal. *El fujimorismo y el Perú*. Lima: SEDES, 1995.

Quijano, Aníbal. "El laberinto de América Latina: ¿Hay otras salidas?" *Revista Venezolana de Ciencias Económicas y Sociales* 6, no. 2 (2004): 73–90. Also published in *OSAL: Observatorio Social de América Latina* 5, no. 13 (2004): 3–18; and *Journal of Iberian and Latin American Research* 10, no. 2 (2006): 173–96.

Quijano, Aníbal. "El 'movimiento indígena' y las cuestiones pendientes en América Latina." *Argumentos* 19, no. 50 (2006): 51–77.

Quijano, Aníbal. "El precio de la racionalidad." *Gaceta Sanmarquina* (Lima) 22 (1994): 4–5.

Quijano, Aníbal. "El proceso de urbanización en América Latina." Santiago de Chile: CEPAL, 1966. Reprinted in Aníbal Quijano, *Dependencia, cambio social y urbanización en Latinoamérica* (Lima: Mosca Azul, 1977).

Quijano, Aníbal. "El regreso del futuro y las cuestiones del conocimiento." *Hueso Húmero* 38 (2001): 3–17.

Quijano, Aníbal. "El trabajo en el umbral del siglo XXI." In *Pensée sociale critique pour le XXIe siècle: Mélanges en l'honneur de Samir Amin*, ed. Bernard Founou-Tchuigoua, Sams Dine Sy, and Amady A. Dieng, 131–49. Paris: L'Harmattan, 2003.

Quijano, Aníbal. "¿Entre la Guerra Santa y la Cruzada?" *America Latina en Movimiento* (Quito) 341 (2001): 12–22.

Quijano, Aníbal. "Estado-Nación, ciudadanía y democracia: Cuestiones abiertas." In *Democracia para una nueva sociedad: Modelo para armar*, ed. Helena González, Heidulf Schmidt, and Manuel Alcántara Sáez, 139–58. Caracas: Nueva Sociedad, 1997.

Quijano, Aníbal. "Estado-Nación y 'movimientos indígenas' en la región andina: Cuestiones abiertas. *Observatorio Social de América Latina* (Buenos Aires) 7, no. 19 (2006): 3–12.

Quijano, Aníbal. "Estamos comenzando a producir otro horizonte histórico." *Revista de Sociología* (Facultad de Ciencias Sociales, Universidad Mayor de San Marcos, Lima) 14, nos. 16–17 (2006): 13–29.

Quijano, Aníbal. "Globalización y exclusión desde el futuro." *La República* (Lima) 18 (August 1997): 375–82.

Quijano, Aníbal. *Imperialismo, clases sociales y estado en el Perú: 1890–1930*. Lima: Mosca Azul, 1978.

Quijano, Aníbal. "Imperialismo y capitalismo de estado." *Sociedad y Política: Revista de Análisis y Debate Político* (Lima) 1 (1972): 3–18.

Quijano, Aníbal. *Imperialismo y "marginalidad" en América Latina*. Lima: Mosca Azul, 1977.

Quijano, Aníbal. *La 'economía popular' y sus caminos en América Latina*. Working paper. Lima: Mosca Azul, CEIS-CECOSAM, 1998.

Quijano, Aníbal. "La emergencia del Grupo Cholo y sus implicaciones en la sociedad peruana." *Memoria del VII Congreso Latinoamericano de Sociología*. Bogotá:
Asociación Colombiana de Sociología, 1965. Reprinted as "Lo cholo y el conflicto cultural en el Perú" in Aníbal Quijano, *Dominación y cultura: Lo cholo y el
conflicto cultural en el Perú* (Lima: Mosca Azul, 1980).

Quijano, Aníbal. "La formation d'un univers marginal dans les villes d'Amérique
Latine," *Espaces et Sociétés*, July 1971.

Quijano, Aníbal. "La nueva heterogeneidad estructural de América Latina." In
Duda, certeza, crisis: La evolución de las ciencias sociales de América Latina, ed.
Heinz R. Sonntag et al., 9–27. Caracas: UNESCO/Nueva Sociedad, 1988.

Quijano, Aníbal. "La 'segunda fase' de la 'revolución peruana' y la lucha de clases."
Sociedad y política: Revista de Análisis y Debate Político (Lima) 5 (1975): 10–35.

Quijano, Aníbal. "Lo público y lo privado: Un enfoque latinoamericano." In *Modernidad, identidad y utopía en América Latina*, by Aníbal Quijano. Lima: Ediciones Sociedad y Política, 1988.

Quijano, Aníbal. "Lo público y lo privado: Un enfoque latinoamericano." In *Por
la imaginación política: De la socialización a la descolonialidad del poder*, comp.
Danilo Assis Clímaco, 213–36. Lima: Red de Descolonialidad y Autogobierno
Social/Programa Democracia y Transformación Social, 2000.

Quijano, Aníbal. *Modernidad, identidad y utopía en América Latina*. Lima: Ediciones
Sociedad y Política, 1988.

Quijano, Aníbal. "Modernidad y democracia: Intereses y conflictos." *Anuario
Mariáteguiano* 12 (2000): 2–21.

Quijano, Aníbal. *Nacionalismo, neoimperialismo y capitalismo en el Perú*. Buenos
Aires: Periferia, 1971.

Quijano, Aníbal. *Naturaleza, situación y tendencias de la sociedad peruana contemporánea*. Lima: Universidad Nacional Mayor de San Marcos, 1972.

Quijano, Aníbal. *Notas sobre el concepto de marginalidad social*. Santiago de Chile:
CEPAL, 1966.

Quijano, Aníbal. "'O movimiento indígena' e as questôes pendentes na América
Latina." In *Política Externa* (Instituto de Estudos Economicos e Internacio-
nais, Universidade de São Paulo) 12, no. 4 (2004): 77–97.

Quijano, Aníbal. "Os Fantasmas da America Latina." In Adauto Novais, *Oito visoes
da America Latina*, 49–87. Sao Paulo: Senac, 2006.

Quijano, Aníbal. "Otro horizonte de sentido." *América Latina en Movimiento* 441
(July 2, 2014): 2–5.

Quijano, Aníbal. "Paradojas de la colonialidad/modernidad/Eurocentrada."
Hueso Humero, no. 53 (April 2009): 30–59.

Quijano, A. "The Paradoxes of Modernity," *International Journal of Politics, Culture
and Society* 3, no. 2 (1989): 193–214.

Quijano, Aníbal. "Poder y democracia." *Sociedad y Política* 12 (1981): 33–50.

Quijano, Aníbal. "Poder y derechos humanos." In *Poder, salud mental y derechos humanos*, ed. Carmen Pimentel Sevilla, 9–26. Lima: CECOSAM, 2001.

Quijano, Aníbal. "Populismo y fujimorismo." In *El fantasma del populismo: Aproxi-mación a un tema (siempre) actual*, ed. Felipe Burbano de Lara, 171–207. Caracas: Nueva Sociedad, 1998.

Quijano, Aníbal. "Prólogo." In *Mariátegui, Textos básicos*, ed. Aníbal Quijano, vii–xvi. Lima: Fondo de Cultura Económica, 1991. Translated as "Beyond Eurocentrism," Verso, https://www.versobooks.com/blogs/3976-beyond -eurocentrism-on-jose-carlos-mariategui.

Quijano, Aníbal. "Prólogo: El sueño dogmático." In *Mariátegui, o la experiencia del Otro*, by Osvaldo Fernández Díaz, xi–xv. Lima: Amauta, 1994.

Quijano, Aníbal. *Qué es y qué no es socialismo*. Lima: Ediciones Sociedad y Política, 1972.

Quijano, Aníbal. "The Question of Power and the Question of Democracy." *Utopías, nuestra bandera: Revista de Debate Politico*, no. 188 (2001): 97–123.

Quijano, Aníbal. "¡Qué tal raza!" In *Familia, Poder y Cambio Social*, ed. Carmen Pimentel. Lima: CECOSAM, 1999. Reprinted in *Revista venezolana de economía y ciencias sociales* 1 (2000): 141–52.

Quijano, Aníbal. "Raza, etnia y nación en José Carlos Mariátegui: Cuestiones abiertas." In *José Carlos Mariátegui y Europa, el otro descubrimiento*, ed. Roland Forgues, 167–87. Lima: Empresa Editora Amauta, 1993.

Quijano, Aníbal. "Réflexions sur l' interdisciplinarité, le développement et les relations interculturelles." In *Entre savoirs: Interdisciplinarité en acte: Enjeux, obstacles résultants*, 25–41 . Paris: UNESCO-ERES.

Quijano, Aníbal. "'Solidaridad' y capitalismo colonial/moderno." *América latina en movimiento* (Quito), 430 (2008): 4–8.

Quijano, Aníbal. "Tecnología del transporte y desarrollo urbano." In *Aproximación crítica a la tecnología en el Perú*, by Jorge Bravo Bresiani, Manfred Horn, et al. Lima: Mosca Azul, 1982.

Quijano, Aníbal. "Towards a Non-Eurocentric Rationality." Unpublished paper for the Symposium on Subalternity and Coloniality, Duke University, October 1998.

Quijano, Aníbal. "Transnacionalización y crisis de la economía en América Latina." *Cuadernos del CEREP*. San Juan, Puerto Rico, 1984.

Quijano, Aníbal. "Treinta años después: Otro reencuentro—Notas para otro de-bate." Preface to *7 ensayos de interpretación de la realidad peruana*, by José Car-los Mariátegui, ix–cxii. Caracas: Biblioteca Ayacucho, 1979.

Quijano, Aníbal. "Urbanización, cambio social y dependencia." In *América Latina: Ensayos de interpretación sociológica*, ed. Fernando Henrique Cardoso and Francisco Weffort, 87–103. Santiago: Editorial Universita-ria, 1967.

Quijano, Aníbal, and Immanuel Wallerstein. "Americanity as a Concept, or the Americas in the Imaginary of the Modern World-System." *International Jour-nal of Social Science* 134 (1992): 549–59.

Rabasa, José. *Inventing America*. Norman: Oklahoma University Press, 1993.

Rifkin, Jeremy. *The End of Work: The Decline of the Global Labor Force and the Dawn of the Post-Market Era*. New York: Jeremy Tarcher/Putnam, 1995.

Rodó, José Enrique. *Ariel*. Montevideo: Imprenta de Dornaleche y Reyes, 1900.

Rouquié, Alain. *L' Amérique latine: Introduction à l'Extrême-Occident*. Paris: Seuil, 1987.

Rushdie, Salman. *The Satanic Verses*. New York: Viking, 1989.

Said, Edward. *Orientalism*. New York: Vintage, 1979.

Sánchez, Luis Alberto. *Apuntes para una biografía del* APRA: *Los primeros pasos, 1923–1931*. Lima: Mosca Azul, 1978.

Sánchez Parga, José. *Globalización, gobernabilidad y cultura*. Quito: Abya-Yala, 1997.

Santa Cruz Pachacuti Yamqui Salcamayhua, Juan de. *Relación de antigüedades de este reino del Perú* [c. 1613]. Edited by Carlos Araníbar. Lima: Fondo de Cultura Económica, 1995.

Santiago, Carlos, ed. *Revista de Administración Pública*, Vol. 28, *Primer encuentro Latinoamericano de estudios del trabajo*. San Juan: Universidad de Puerto Rico, 1996.

Segato, Rita. "Aníbal Quijano and the Coloniality of Power." In *The Critique of Coloniality: Eight Essays*, trans. Ramsey McGlaze, 21–48. London: Routledge, 2022.

Shanin, Theodore. *The Awkward Class: Political Sociology of Peasantry in a Developing Society; Russia, 1910–1925*. Oxford, UK: Clarendon, 1972.

Shanin, Theodore. *Late Marx and the Russian Road: Marx and "the Peripheries of Capitalism."* New York: Monthly Review Press, 1983.

Singh, Kavaljit. *The Globalisation of Finance: A Citizen's Guide*. London: Zed Books, 1999.

Singh, Kavaljit. *Taming Financial Flows: Challenges and Alternatives in the Era of Globalization; A Citizen's Guide*. London: Zed Books, 2000.

Smart, D. A. *Pannekoek and Gorter's Marxism*. New York: Pluto, 1978.

Sobrevilla, David, ed. *El marxismo de José Carlos Mariátegui*. Lima: Universidad de Lima, 1995.

Sobrevilla, David. *El marxismo de José Carlos Mariátegui y su aplicación a los 7 ensayos*. Preface by Antonio Melis. Lima: Universidad de Lima, 2005.

Solari, Aldo, Rolando Franco, and Joel Jutkowitz. *Teoria, acción social y desarrollo en América Latina*. Mexico City: Siglo Veintiuno, 1976.

Soros, George. *The Crisis of Global Capitalism: Open Society Endangered*. New York: Public Affairs, 1998.

Stavenhagen, Rodolfo. "Classes, Colonialism, and Acculturation: Essay on a System of Inter-ethnic Relations in Mesoamerica." *Studies in Comparative International Development* 1, no. 5 (1965): 53–77.

Stavrianos, L. S. *Global Rift: The Third World Comes of Age*. New York: William Morrow, 1981.

Stein, William W. *Dance in the Cemetery: José Carlos Mariátegui and the Lima Scandal of 1917*. Lanham, MD: University Press of America, 1997.

Stocking, George W. Jr. *Race, Culture, Evolution: Essays in the History of Anthropology*. New York: Free Press, 1968.

Tanizaki, Jun'ichirō. *In Praise of Shadows*. Translated by Thomas J. Harper and Edward G. Seidensticker. New Haven, CT: Leete's Island Books, 1977.

Tarcus, Horacio. *Mariátegui en la Argentina o las políticas culturales de Samuel Glusberg*. Buenos Aires: El Cielo por Asalto, 2002.

Therborn, Göran. "The Atlantic Diagonal in the Labyrinths of Modernities and Globalizations." In *Globalizations and Modernities: Experiences and Perspectives of European and Latin America*, ed. Göran Therborn, 11–40. Stockholm: FRN, 1999.

Thompson, E. P. *The Making of the English Working Class*. New York: Pantheon Books, 1964.

Thompson, E. P. *The Poverty of Theory and Other Essays*. New York: Monthly Review Press, 1979.

Tilly, Charles. *Coercion, Capital, and European States, A.D. 990–1992*. Cambridge, UK: Blackwell, 1990.

Tirkey, Agapit. *Jharkhand Movement: A Study of Its Dynamics*. New Delhi, India: AICFAIP, 2002.

Tocqueville, Alexis de. *Democracy in America*. New York: Vintage Classics, 1835.

Tokman, V. E., and D. Martínez, eds. *Flexibilización en el margen: La reforma del contrato de trabajo*. Lima: OIT, 1999.

Tokman, V. E., and D. Martínez, eds. *Inseguridad laboral y competitividad: Modalidades de contratación*. Lima: OIT, 1999.

Tomich, Dale. *Through the Prism of Slavery: Labor, Capital and World Economy*. Lanham: Rowman and Littlefield, 2004.

Tomich, Dale. "World of Capital/Worlds of Labor: A Global Perspective." In *Reworking Class*, ed. John Hall, 287–313. Ithaca, NY: Cornell University Press, 1997.

Trotsky, L. *La revolución traicionada*. Buenos Aires: Claridad, 1938.

Valcárcel, Luis Eduardo. *Historia del Perú antiguo*. Lima: Editorial J. Mejía Baca, 1964.

Valcárcel, Luis Eduardo. *Ruta cultural del Perú* [1945]. Lima: Siglo Veintiuno Ediciones, 1984.

Valcárcel, Luis Eduardo. *Tempestad en los Andes*. Lima: Populibros Peruanos, 1926.

Vallejo, César. *Spain, Take This Chalice from Me and Other Poems*. London: Penguin, 2008.

Vargas Llosa, Mario. "Entretien," *Le Nouvel Observateur*, no. 89. July 27, 1966.

Vega, Inca Garcilaso de la. *Comentarios reales de los Incas* [1609, 1617]. Edited by Carlos Araníbar, Lima: Fondo de Cultura Económica, 1991.

Viola, H., and C. Margolis. *Seeds of Change: Five Hundred Years since Columbus*. Washington, DC: Smithsonian Institute, 1991.

Virilio, Paul. *The Information Bomb*. Translated by Chris Turner. London: Verso, 2000. Originally published as *La bombe informatique* (Paris: Editions Galilée, 1998).

Wallerstein, Immanuel. *Historical Capitalism*. London: Verso, 1983.

Wallerstein, Immanuel. *The Modern World-System*. 3 vols. San Diego: Academic Press, 1974–1989.

Warren, Kay. "Indigenous Movements as a Challenge to the Unified Social Movements Paradigm for Guatemala." In *Cultures of Politics and Politics of Culture*, ed. S. Alvarez, E. Dagnino, and A. Escobar, 165–96. Boulder, CO: Westview, 1998.

Wolpe, Harold, ed. *The Articulation of Modes of Production: Essays from Economy and Society*. London: Routledge & Kegan Paul, 1980.

Wood, Ellen Meiksins. *The Retreat from Class: A New 'True' Socialism*. London: Verso, 1986.

Wright, Erik Olin. *Class, Crisis and the State*. London: NLB, 1978.

Wynter, Sylvia. "Unsettling the Coloniality of Being/Power/Truth/Freedom: Towards the Human, after Man, Its Overrepresentation; An Argument." *New Centennial Review* 3, no. 3 (2003): 257–337.

Young, Robert. *Colonial Desire: Hybridity in Theory, Culture, and Race*. London: Routledge, 1995.

INDEX

accumulation, 123–24; changing forms of, 87, 102, 141, 153–55, 193, 217, 313, 434; novel sources of, 321–22; primitive (original), 22, 34, 43, 102, 112, 277; trends in restructuring of, 434–35. *See also* financial capital: financial/speculative accumulation

aesthetics: mythical-aesthetic, 43–44, 439; political-ethic-aesthetic frameworks, 343, 387, 408; relationship with utopia, 64–66, 70–71; subversion of, 65–66, 387. *See also* visual and artistic expression

Africa, 53, 69, 76; "Africans," not originally associated with race, 213, 298n5; heterogeneity of civilizations, 212, 275, 364

"Afro–Latin American" movements, 211, 223

agrarian reform, 165, 241–42, 376n11

Allende, Salvador, 133, 312

alternative rationality, 41, 44–45, 66, 67, 70, 128n8, 423; issues and risks of, 54–62; Latin America as opportunity for, 51–54, 431–32; liberationist, 5–6, 51–56, 62; in Mariátegui, 324–25; and modernity, 267–72; multiplicity of, 354–55. *See also* bien vivir ("life in plentitude"); reciprocity; reoriginalization; social-private; subversion

Althusser, Louis, 441

Alvarado, Velasco, 242, 376n11

Amaru II, Túpac, 288

America: Atlantic basin as center of world trade, 90–91, 217, 260, 275, 308, 340–41, 354; capital and capitalism as originating in, 273–74; and capitalist control of labor, 398–401; coloniality of power and the national question in, 233–34; coloniality originated in, 95, 256; creation of modernity in, 34–36, 38, 52, 256, 270; creation of "race" in, 2, 12–13, 16, 89, 120–21, 147, 256–57, 403; *encomenderos*, civil wars with, 213, 225n9, 261; Euro-North American rationalism, 42–44, 170, 420–21, 439; Europe mutually created with, 34–38, 52, 208, 256, 270, 308, 332–33, 352, 365; as first stage of Euro-centered colonialism's defeat, 73; and historical imaginary, 134–35; as name imposed on existing sign systems, 16; as New World, 22, 23; term appropriated by United States, 128n2, 297–98n2; utopia not possible without, 34–35. *See also* Latin America

American International Group, 345, 350

American Popular Revolutionary Alliance (Alianza Popular Revolucionaria Americana), 320

Andes, 7–8, 35, 37; Andean utopia, question of, 430–31; *gamonalismo*, 377–78n15, 48, 63n4, 317; Pacto Andino, 169; racial question in, 11–12, 238, 253n11; reciprocity in social community, 23, 35, 48–49 anthropology/ethnography, 115, 249, 436

anticapitalist imaginary, 138, 143, 164–65; alternatives, possible, 198–99; coloniality of power and the question of democracy today, 199–203; conditions of the resistance, 192–96; and Porto Alegre World Social Forum experience, 193–97; priorities, 196; and survival of planet, 343. *See also* capitalism; imaginary

anti-imperialism, 138, 165, 196, 293–94

"aprista" anti-imperialist movement, 293–94, 320

Argentina, 285–87; Peronismo, 164; social explosion, 2001, 251

Arguedas, José María, 23, 44, 62–63n2, 69, 439

"Arguedian knot," 23, 69, 226n16, 428

Aricó, José María, 29n28

Ariel (Rodó), 223, 228n24

Aristotle, 306

Asia/"Orient," 90, 94n15; high cultures subordinated, 75–76; Japan, 16, 73, 205, 382; as other to the "Occident," 263, 265, 267, 300n31, 339

assimilationism, 238–39, 249–50

Atlantic basin as center of world trade, 90–91, 217, 260, 275, 308, 340–41, 354

atomistic perspective, 57, 79, 80, 104–5

authoritarianism, 39, 164, 174, 372, 382; justification of, 55–56; local premodern forms reproduced, 180; "traditional," 51. *See also* domination

authority: collective/public, 4, 136, 147–48, 156, 157, 245–46; desacralization of, 54, 170, 271, 423, 430, 432; as element in power, 120, 136, 171, 178, 200, 268–69, 281; erosion of in weakest states, 159, 160, 179, 189; invisible world government, 158–59, 163, 166; naturalization of by liberalism, 101; reconcentration of control over, 160, 165, 174, 194, 321, 349, 361, 384, 407; as sphere of contestation, 98, 102, 116; subversion of, 356–57;

worldwide imperial bloc, 157–59, 166, 174, 251. *See also* state; violence

Aymaras, 227n22, 255n24, 391n9; Amazonian basin organizations, 245–48; autonomous territory imagined by, 250; National Union of Aymara Communities, UNCA, 245–46, 251; return of the future, 25, 31n53

barriadas, 49, 60, 63n5, 242, 425

Barrientos, General, 247–48

Basques, 208, 283

Baudelaire, Charles, 413

Benengeli, Cide Hamete, 208, 209

Berlin Wall, fall of, 7, 21, 67, 139, 163

Bermúdez, Morales, 376n11

bien vivir ("life in plentitude"), 4, 18, 389n1; and de/coloniality of power, 379, 386–87; and "Indigenous" population, 387–89; new historical horizon for, 382–84

"Blacks," 90, 253n11, 257, 412; 1920s artistic revival, 369; "Africans" not originally associated with race, 213, 298n5; "color" associated with, 89, 213; heterogeneity of geocultural identities, 212, 275, 364; and Latin American revolutions, 225n9, 226–27n20; as "premodern" and "primitive," 222, 265, 339; as replacement for exterminated populations, 292; slavery imposed on, 216, 259, 262; in United States, 131n26, 283–84. *See also* race; "racism"

body: brain (mind, nonbody)/body dualism, 81–82, 91–92, 94n11, 148, 277–79, 300n29; in Christian theology, 91, 126, 278; and control of sex, 358; as "object," 91, 278; relegated to "nature," 91–92, 114, 227–29, 338; in struggle against domination, 126–27

Boletín Illa, 419

Bolívar, Simón, 240–41

Bolivarian ideal, resurgence of, 219–20

Bolivia, 81, 286, 287; constitution, 18; March for Territory and Dignity (1991),

248; miners' movement, 247–48; Popular Congress, 133; process of 1971–1972, 352; revolution, 240–41

Bolivian National Revolution (April 1952), 247

Bolivian Workers' Confederation (Confederación Obrera Boliviana), 247

bourgeoisie, 9, 207; bourgeois reason, 38–40; and democracy, 170, 237; family matrix, 124–25; historical-structural dependence of, 289–93; national-socialist/fascist sectors defeated, 381, 415; revolutionary, 294–95; transnational, identity of, 427; US-British alliance against, 193

brain (mind, nonbody)/body dualism, 81–82, 91–92, 94n11, 148, 277–79, 300n29; soul, primacy of, 91, 278, 337

Braudel, Fernand, 8

Brazil, 162, 183n11, 288; gangs in, 356; slavery in, 93n9, 314, 316n1

Brecht, Bertolt, 138

Britain, 39, 193, 223, 267; and Chilean production, 286–87. See also England

Brown, Gordon, 350

bureaucracy, 25, 46–47, 137–38

bureaucratic despotism, 25, 107, 109, 139–40, 317–19, 343, 383

Buscaglia-Salgado, José, 227n20

Bush, George H. W., 193, 203n1

Bush, George W., 315, 345, 350

business cycles, 312–13, 351

Cadiz parliament (Cortes de Cadiz), 36

Cajamarca (enslaved Black man), 415

Callaghy, Thomas M., 185n24

capital: capitalism distinguished from, 111, 307–8; coloniality of capital-labor relationships, 402–3; Eurocentering of, 217–19, 260–63; foreign direct investment, 152; "functionaries" of, 110, 119, 184–85n20, 297, 362–63, 433; hegemony of, 307–8; limits on expansion of, 53, 144n5, 404; marketization of labor, 147;

Marx's perspective on, 110; mercantile, 35, 37, 47–48, 57, 340; origin in America, 273–74; phase of inter-or transnational maturity, 33; primitive accumulation phase, 22, 43; stages of as layers in Latin America, 42–43; transnationalization of, 423–25; two basic social classes of, 110–11; as underdeveloped, 48, 53; workers as antagonists to, 401–2. See also capitalism; labor, forms of

Capital (Marx), 110–12, 184n20

capitalism: acceleration of, 155; capital distinguished from, 111, 307–8; class interest in, 119; cognitive needs of, 96; and coloniality of power related to globalism, 2–4, 259–60; competitive capital, period of, 170, 198, 272; conquest and colonization as precondition for, 22; and crisis of labor relations, 396–99, 405–9; de-democratization required by, 407–8; definitions of, 411–12; differing meanings in Wallerstein and Quijano, 9, 11; elements of, 277; and globalization, 151–55; heterogeneity of, 87–88, 276–77; historical, 8, 10–11; homogeneity attributed to, 435–36; Iberian Peninsula as origin of, 273–74, 307, 340; labor, race, and gender as three focal issues, 118–20; mode of production, 111, 231, 276; national, 400–401; and nation-state, 157–58; as new structure for labor control, 258–59; not reduced to "capital," 307; origin of in America, 273–74; Potosi as origin of, 22; private, 46–47, 67, 70, 107, 140; and state, 156–57; subjectivity, control of, 348, 356; and universal social classification, 121–22, 147, 216; world crisis of, 32, 40, 50, 87, 107, 129n11, 142, 163–65, 193–94, 304, 321, 331–33, 411–12. See also accumulation; anticapitalist imaginary; capital; capital-wage relationship; financial capital; "informal economy"; market; "precapitalism"; production capital-wage relationship, 110–11, 198, 272, 405; all labor forms concentrated in, 258, 393, 398–401; among other power axes, 110, 123; coloniality of, 402–3; emergence of, 267; mid-1960s changes, 312–14; structural-historical heterogeneity of, 130n20, 401–2; workforce reductions, 313, 321, 344, 348, 356, 380–81, 409, 427. *See also* employment

Carpentier, Alejo, 44, 63n3

"castas"/castes, 222, 227n21, 233, 252n5

Castile, Crown/Kingdom of, 24, 214, 259, 337. *See also* Spain

Catholic Church, 80–81, 221, 315

center/periphery compound, 3, 8–10, 97; "colonial center" and "colonial periphery," 123–24; denationalization within, 321; and finance capital, 173; forms of labor in, 403; and globalization, 162–63, 166–67, 173, 179–80, 193–94, 263, 321–22; and social classification, 115, 122–23

Central American civil wars, 162

chica music, 424–25

Chile, 59, 133, 162, 285–87; Allendismo, 164; origins of neoliberalism in, 351–52; Pinochet dictatorship, 126, 312, 352, 384

China, 138, 162–63, 376n9; democratic revolution proposed, 294–95; ethnocentrism, 306, 336–37; in global imperial bloc, 383

chivalry, 205–7, 209

citizenship, 122, 143, 148, 170–71, 242, 280; and Indigenous peoples, 235; legitimation of, 310

"civilization," 3, 13, 90, 91, 115, 181

civil society, 50, 55–56

class: formed through struggle, 111–12, 117; "middle classes," 110, 111, 115, 124; "precapitalist," 112–13, 115; as static, 108, 112, 115, 117–18. *See also lo cholo* movement; peasants; social classification

climate change, 304–5, 332–33, 343, 347–48, 385

coca farming, 248

coercion, 98, 101. *See also* domination

Cold War: failures of decolonization during, 17; fall of Berlin Wall, 7, 21, 67, 139, 163

collective organization, 3–4, 27n10, 48, 52–53; reemergence of communal structures, 23, 25–26, 180–81, 387, 408; as relationship among free individuals, 432; reprivatization of the control of, 160

Colombia, 292

colonialism: 1492 as year of establishment, 22, 24, 298n2, 306, 392; ambiguity of term, 412–13; and centralization of European states, 281–82; coloniality of power as longer-lasting than, 85, 412–13; continuance of under Western imperialism, 74–76, 291, 367–68; "criollo-oligarchic" culture, 44–45; defined, 127n1, 182n3; Eurocentered, defeat of, 73, 133; internal, 3, 127n1, 206–7, 282–83, 301n41; neocolonialism, 156, 225n15, 289; oldest territories of, 69; recolonization, 177, 321, 385; universal social classification system imposed by, 2–3, 121–22, 172, 216

coloniality: of capital-labor relationships, 402–3; as cornerstone of globalization, 74, 76, 85; definitions, 95, 127n1; delinking from modernity/rationality, 17; enacted through either/or logic, 13–14; of knowledge, 21, 30n36; lived weight of for Indigenous peoples, 3; as neologism, 413; as part of modernity/rationality, 218–19; as time that remains, 24

"Coloniality and Modernity/Rationality" (Quijano), 11, 17

coloniality of power, 256–302, 390n2; Americas and national question in, 233–34; colonial/modernity, 22, 83, 207, 271–72, 310–11, 340, 342–43; continuity of, 17, 19, 21–22, 73–74, 161, 221, 239, 252n4, 272, 415–16; creation of in Europe and America, 208, 305, 332–33,

387–88, 414–15, 417; crisis of, 373–74, 383–84, 412; and democracy, 146–87, 200; and democracy today, 199–203; and Eurocentrism, 272–79; formation of, 364–68; in former colonized areas, 232; and gender, 5, 30n34, 124–25, 182n2, 213; and ghost of the nation-state, 380–82; and global capitalism, 2–4, 259–60; and globalization, 256–72; and historical-structural dependence, 364–68; introduction of concept, 1–2, 224n2; longer-lasting than colonialism, 85, 412–13; modern world-system distinguished from, 7–8; and nation-state, 161–63; need for debate on, 411–15; neocultural articulation, 122–23; as open structure, 4–5, 14; permanence of, 14, 21–22, 25; poststructuralism approximated by, 26; "race" as central to, 2, 76–77, 121, 147, 171, 413; and social classification, 2–3, 95–131, 120–27, 147; social movements as cause of crisis in, 373–74; state formations linked by, 280; and universal social classification of the capitalist world, 121–22; and world distribution of labor, 123–24. See also de/coloniality of power; globalization; world-system, modern/colonial: (Quijano's) view

"Coloniality of Power, Eurocentrism, and Latin America" (Quijano), 8–9, 28n25

colonial (world) matrix of power, 3–4, 16–17, 318, 327, 392, 403–4; as colonial-capitalist matrix of power, 121, 148, 161, 200, 202, 203; coloniality and globality in, 199–200, 216; coloniality as constitutive feature of, 16, 95; crisis of/struggles against, 165–67, 170–71, 174, 177, 333; current, 159, 182n2, 188, 404, 409; democracy in, 170; Eurocentering of, 76, 85, 131n24, 148, 161, 217–19, 337–38; everyone on inside of, 311–12; expansion of, 340; founded on exploitation and "race," 199–200; as humanity in its to-

tality, 268–69, 300n20; "inferior races" processes, 3–4; making of race and global social domination, 211–15; mutual creation of in Europe and America, 34–38, 52, 208, 256, 270, 275, 307–9, 332–33, 341, 352, 365, 412, 436; as new system of exploitation, 211–12, 215–16, 231; and production of meaning, 309; reconfiguring of post-1973, 321–22; reproduction of, 308–9; and social classification, 95–96, 106–7; untouched during Cold War, 17. See also globalization; world-system, modern/colonial

"color," 6, 87–90, 93, 126, 131n24, 213, 215–16, 222, 257, 298n5

Columbus, Christopher, 101

Comentarios reales (Garcilaso de la Vega), 222, 228n23

commercialization, 69, 307, 351, 435

commodification: centralized in Europe, 172; decline of, 154, 179, 183–84n15; of every sphere of social existence, 361–62; intensification of, 347; of knowledge, 174; of labor, 2, 87, 141, 179–80, 184n20, 198, 267, 271, 273–74, 340, 398–400, 404

"communalist" fundamentalism, 233, 252n6

communal structures, reemergence of, 23, 25–26, 180–81, 387, 408

communications media, 46, 67–68, 84, 149–50, 244, 384, 394

Communist Manifesto, The (Marx), 129n17, 185n20, 209

Communist Party of Ecuador, 247

Communist Party of the Soviet Union, 138

concrete experience: and historical imaginary, 135–37, 141; and social classification, 104, 107, 111–12, 115, 120, 130n22

National Council of Coordination of Ecuadorian Indigenous Nationalities (Consejo Nacional de Coordinación de Nacionalidades Indígenas de Ecuador, CONACNIE), 247 conquest: conquistadors, 2, 213, 217, 257, 261; continuous with colonization, 24; as discovery, 34; mystified by fundamentalism, 430; phenotypic differences between victors and vanquished, 121, 257; as precondition for capitalism, 22; and production/fashioning of "race," 2, 12–13, 305–6, 412, 414; violent concentration of world's resources, 73

"consciousness," 114

co-optation, 60, 75; "America" as term appropriated by United States, 128n2, 297–98n2; cultural, 14, 208, 239, 264, 267, 275; of Greco-Roman culture, 208, 267, 275, 354; of Indigenous knowledge, 74, 239, 264; of Indigenous lands, 284, 286; of subversion, 369–74

Coordinator of Indigenous Organizations of the Amazon River Basin (Coordinadora de las Organizaciones Indígenas de la Cuenca Amazónica, COICA), 245–46

corporations, 152, 160, 166, 244, 269; finance capital, 166, 345, 355, 383, 385; as imperial, 158, 355; verticalism of, 46, 61–62; violent repression by, 385; in worldwide imperial bloc, 158, 355

Counter-Reformation, 206, 214, 307, 339, 374n1

counterrevolution, 163–65, 363, 369–74. See also neoliberalism

"criollo-oligarchic" culture, 44–45, 376n10, 438; decline of, 53, 71, 371, 423–26; gamonalismo, 48, 63n4, 371, 377–78n15; vals criollo (criollo waltz), 424

crises: of 1870, 261, 351; of 1930s, 290–91; 2009, 331; of bureaucratic despotism, 318; climate change, 304–5, 332–33, 343, 347–48, 385; of coloniality of power, 373–74, 383–84, 412; concealment of, 432–33; cyclical, 348, 350; diversity strengthened by, 53; of entire matrix of power, 333; of Eurocentrism, 44–45, 141–42, 148–49, 343, 363; and fictional

money, 345; financial scandals, 315, 331–32, 349–50; and Indigenous movement, 240–43; Indigenous movement as signal of, 239–40; and instrumentalization of modernization, 418–19; of labor relations and capitalism, 396–99, 405–9; of modernity, 33, 40–41, 68, 96, 148–49; of oligarchic state, 240–41; in race and gender relations, 404–5; reconcentration of power as response to, 160, 165, 174, 194, 349, 361–63, 383–84; of representation, 55, 60, 159, 407; of social classification, 87–88, 107–8; social movements as cause of for coloniality of power, 373–74; social reclassification due to, 404–5; workforce reductions, 313, 321, 344, 348; world crisis of capitalism, 32, 40, 50, 87, 107, 129n11, 142, 163–65, 193–94, 304, 321, 331–33, 411–12. See also genocide/extermination

"critical thought"/"critical theory of society," 134–35; critiques of Soviet Union, 137–38; defeat of, 134–37, 140–41, 322, 353; Eurocentrism of, 141–42

Cuéllar, Mario, 31n53

cultural coloniality, 75–78

culturalism, 26, 51–52, 68, 428–29

daily life, politics of, 7, 19, 182, 220, 407–8, 415, 433; democracy in everyday life, 52, 410, 423

Dalits (Untouchables), 233, 252n6, 353–54

Dávila, Pedrarias, 334–35

debt, 152, 183n14, 190

de/coloniality, 4–7, 28n16, 305, 316, 371; epistemic shift, 6–7, 10, 18, 22, 24, 84, 420; globalization and race linked, 15–16; process of, 18–19

de/coloniality of power, 7, 16, 19, 305, 316, 407–8, 411, 416–17; bien vivir as, 379, 386–87. See also coloniality of power

decolonization, 3, 77, 164; and dualism, 91; as epistemological reconstitution, 11, 17, 83–84; as first step in revolution,

169, 407–8; limited, 291–92, 380, 406; Mexico, 162

de-democratization, 157–59, 163, 166, 177, 189–91, 243; of Iberian Peninsula, 207; required by capitalism, 407–8; and worldwide imperial bloc, 321. *See also* democratization

defeat of political movements, 25, 144n7, 361–62; 1960s, 133, 318, 351, 382; 1973 fall of Allende, 133, 312; anticapitalism, defeat of, 132–33, 188; coming to an end, 323–24; "critical thought"/"critical theory of society" abandoned, 134–37, 140–41, 322, 353; effect of Eurocentrism in Latin America, 293–97; and horizon, 25, 132–33; and imaginary, 134–37, 140–42, 144n7; "socialist camp," breakup of, 133, 138–39, 202, 297, 318–19, 322–23, 328n5, 352, 383; "stop inflation" campaign, 352; worldwide, 405–6. *See also* revolution

deindustrialization, 352

delinking/relinking, 10, 17–19

democracy, 145n11; and bourgeoisie, 170, 237; and coloniality of power, 146–87, 200; direct, 59–61, 70, 181; elections seen as defining institution of, 172–73, 408; and equality, 170, 202; in everyday life, 52, 410, 423; expansion of as necessary, 407–8; and globalization, 172–75, 199–203; as highest expression of modernity, 135; and the "Indigenous problem," 235–36; integration of world, possibilities for, 177–78, 191–92; liberal-bourgeois, 355–56, 423; local, in Indigenous communities, 251; private capitalism incompatible with, 47; question of in globalization, 170–72; redistribution of power, 178, 371–73, 377n13; Switzerland as European model for, 181, 255; without revolution, 236–39

democratization, 199, 207–8, 291–96; and coloniality of power, 160–63; community as authority structure for, 187;

decolonization necessary for, 4, 175; limited in Latin America, 291–93, 380, 406, 423; limits on, 160, 167; and modernity, 271; and nationalization, 89, 164, 169, 173, 179, 280, 282–83, 291, 301n40; WSF discussions of, 196–97. *See also* de-democratization

"demonstration effect," 195

denationalization, 157–59, 163, 166, 189, 321, 363; required by capitalism, 407

"dependency theory," 7, 8, 43

Descartes, René, 78, 91, 96, 278, 338–39

"deterritorialization" or "delocalization," 245

development, 14, 30–31n45, 220; called into question, 8, 13, 18; cultural Europeanization as aspiration, 75; development-underdevelopment debate, 266; geocultural distortions of, 334; and "modernization," 33–36; "neodevelopmentalism," 47; without de/coloniality, 379–80

Diderot, Denis, 36

direct democracy, 59–61, 70, 181

discovering, novelty of, 22, 25, 34

disenchantment of the world, 44, 68, 420, 440

dispossession, 3–4, 275, 283

"Dominación y cultura" (Quijano), 436–37

dominated, the: colonization of imagination of, 74–76, 88; "color" categories used to signify, 89, 213; family disintegration, 124–25; guilt imposed on, 336; spatial distribution of, 69; as "white man's burden," 82. *See also* "inferiority"

domination, 16, 357; assimilationism, 238–39, 249–50; body in struggle against, 126–27; coercion, 98, 101; coexistence of with other matrices, 373; coloniality as general form of, 76; exploitation, relationship with, 125–27; force and violence as requisites for, 155; by "functionaries" of capital, 110; and instrumental reason, 51–52; and making domination (*continued*)

of race, 211–15; matrix of, 155–56, 364; mythological imaginary of, 125–27; new system of exploitation, 211–12, 215–16, 231; patriarchal relations of, 88, 90, 213, 306–7, 339; in pre-colonial societies, 57, 365–66, 388; "race" as classification of, 89, 120–21, 364–65; "race" as most efficient instrument of, 85–87, 257, 295–96, 364, 402; reconfiguration of, 165; relegitimation attempts, 88, 175, 404; and sex, 357–58; and social classification, 125–27; "transgovernance," 173, 175, 185n24; utopia as struggle against, 65; visual and artistic expression, stripped from autonomous cultures, 74–76, 125, 211, 366, 368. *See also* instrumental reason; labor control

Don Quixote figure, 205–7

dualism, 94n11, 440–41; association with individualism, 79; brain (mind)/body, 81–82, 91–92, 94n11, 148, 277–79, 300n29; Eurocentric mystification of, 91, 126, 274; and Eurocentrism, 96–97, 276; and evolutionism, 148, 265, 274–76, 279, 401; new/radical, 90–92, 277–79, 297, 309, 315, 326, 338, 341, 354, 384, 401; and "race," 338; "racism" and new "Western," 90–92; of sex differences, 339; "subject"/"object" polarity, 78–80, 91, 148, 438–39. *See also* center/periphery compound

Duárez, Morales, 36

Dussel, Enrique, 269

Dutschke, Rudy, 139

Echevarria, Jose Medina, 33

economy, 10–11; "economic dependency," 8; "informal," 60–61, 180, 182, 183–84n15, 244, 314, 398–99, 434; means of production, 45–46, 168, 201, 285, 294; "new," 150; paralysis of, 46–47; productive forms, 23

Ecuador, 241, 247; constitution, 18

Ecuarunari (Peoples of Ecuador), 247

education system, 238–39; and "cholo" population, 242–43; distortions of history in, 333–34; and "Indigenous" intellectuals, 246–47

Eighteenth Brumaire of Louis Bonaparte, The (Marx), 110–12

Einstein, Albert, 17

elections, 172–73; Bolivia, 248; Peru, 186n40, 191, 377n14, 426, 428, 437

Ellenstein, Jean, 324

El marxismo de José Carlos Mariátegui y su aplicación a los 7 ensayos (Sobrevilla), 324

Empire (Hardt and Negri), 185n27, 353, 355

empiricism, 80, 83, 98–99, 104–5, 297, 321, 324, 326

employment, 152–53; "end of work," 153, 183–84n15; "full employment," abandonment of, 396; paid as synonym for work in general, 397; "structural unemployment," 141, 153, 314, 344, 348, 381, 383, 396, 398; underemployment, 87, 244, 321, 396, 435. *See also* capital-wage relationship

encomenderos, civil wars with, 213, 225n9, 261

end of history, 67–68, 134, 183n7, 188, 312, 323, 353, 354, 395

End of History, The (Fukuyama), 68, 72n3, 143n2

Engels, Friedrich, 129n17, 209

England, 96, 111, 181, 290; 350, 419. *See also* Britain

Enlightenment, 36, 38, 82, 96

epistemology, 10–11; epistemic shift, 6–7, 10, 18, 22, 24, 84, 420; epistemic subversion, 6–7, 18–19, 326, 416–17; epistemological reconstitution, 11, 17, 83–84, 214–15

equality, 407–8; Afro-Latin American perspective, 223; and bien vivir, 386; and democracy, 170, 202; Eurocentric legitimation of, 173–74; formal presumption of, 148; legitimation of citizenship, 310; market as limit on, 170–71, 271; and nation-state, 160; and "race," 130–31n23, 311, 313n24, 345; and reciprocity, 57–59, 170, 387; social inequality alongside of, 310–11, 355–56

"ethnic cleansing," 214

"ethnicities," 16, 130–31n23, 239, 412–16, 426, 427

ethnocentrism, 96, 264, 267, 274, 441; Chinese superiority-inferiority relations, 306, 336–37

ethnoracial pentagon, 13

Eurocentrification: of capital, 217–19, 260–63; of modernity, 2, 34, 217–19, 265–72, 339–40; of world matrix of power, 76, 85, 131n24, 148, 161, 217–19

Eurocentrism, 6, 16, 52, 68, 231; acceptance of in Latin America, 220–21, 226n18; and coloniality of power, 272–79; crisis of, 44–45, 141–42, 148–49, 343, 363; critique of as knowledge perspective, 164; and cultural coloniality in modernity/rationality, 77–78; dualisms of, 96–97, 276; hegemony of, 25, 96, 141–42, 148–49, 367–68; of "historical materialism," 97–99, 141, 142, 317–18, 324–25; homogeneity, ideology of, 69, 82, 99, 102, 105–7, 148, 214, 276–77, 367–68, 403, 406–7, 435–36; intellectual provincialism of, 84, 267, 324; and intersubjective relations, 66, 77, 96, 266, 325, 368, 393; as knowledge perspective, 96–97, 141, 272–76, 279; legitimation of equality, liberty, and solidarity, 173–74; of Marxist orthodoxy, 9–10; mystification of knowledge, 75, 91, 125–26; and nation-state, 280–83; naturalization of, 96, 265, 395; post-Cold War reemergence of, 21; process of, 76; question of power in, 97–99; radical critique of, 354–57; return of, 395; and revolution in Latin America, 293–97. See also domination; dualism; homogeneity; reductionism

Europe: America as prior to, 22; centering new matrix of power in, 217–19, 263–65;

337–38; coloniality of power and nation-state in, 161; creation of nation-state in, 281–82; distinction between northern and southern, 38–39, 205–8, 217–18, 267, 270–71, 419; Enlightenment movement in, 36–37; Euro-North American rationalism, 42–44, 170, 420–21, 439; "European" as social classification, 4, 16–17, 171–72, 252n4, 257, 364; "Europe" as metaphor, 128n5; feudalism, 35, 172, 181; as geocultural identity, 79, 91; Greco-Roman culture, appropriation of, 208, 267, 275; as hegemonic center of world, 2–3, 90–91, 113, 205–7, 218, 270–71; and historical imaginary, 134–35; Ibero-American societies dependent on, 288; as *id*-entity, 257, 261, 266; imagination of stretched by America, 34–35, 52; immigrants from, 284–86; intellectual hegemony of center-north regions, 2–3, 113, 205–7, 218, 270–71; male experience of renaissance, 12; modernity as category of, 2, 34; modernity linked with north-central, 270–71, 339–40, 419; mutually created with America, 34–38, 52, 208, 256, 270, 308, 352, 365; myth of preexistence as power, 96, 117, 264–65, 269–70, 274; non-Europe, relation with, 115, 200, 265, 274–76; nothing of importance produced for centuries, 217, 310, 341; power and modernity in, 38–41; premodern hierarchies, 78–79; social class differences, 114; social reclassification in, 217–18; Western Europe, production of, 208, 218, 308, 337–38. *See also* Spain

European Community, 208

European Union, 14, 15, 163

evolutionism, 82; and dualism, 148, 265, 274–76, 279, 401; transition from "precapitalism" to "capitalism," 82, 112–13, 167, 400–401, 426, 436; unidirectional perception of history, 112, 297, 325, 400–401, 438

exchange of labor, 259, 357, 400, 435

exoticism, 76, 429

exploitation, 16, 51; under capitalism, 23, 51; domination, relationship with, 125–27; under imperialism, 30, 51; of nature, increase in, 384–85; "racism" as basis for, 10, 22

Exposition de la Doctrine de Saint-Simon, 109, 129n17

Faller, Martina, 31n53

family disintegration, 124–25

Fanon, Frantz, 8

fazendas, 314

Fernand Braudel Center, 7

feudalism: in Don Quixote's perceptions, 205; European, 35, 172, 181; Latin American, 12, 205, 294–95, 299n8, 324. *See also* serfdom: imposed on "Indians"

financial capital, 60, 129n11, 318; anti-imperialist resistance against, 196; banks and financial fraud, 349–50; emergence of speculative finance, 351–54, 359; European Community, 208; expansion of, 344–45; financial/speculative accumulation, 153, 155, 157, 159, 173, 198, 321–23, 347, 349, 381; fraudulent, 345, 349–50; industrial-financial capital, 381, 383, 385; intergovernmental and private agencies for controlling, 158, 166; predatory needs of, 129n10, 140, 178, 190, 196; productive investments no longer needed, 153, 184n17; "structural financialization," 315, 381, 383. *See also* capitalism

Foucault, Michel, 136

France, 80, 223, 228n24; Dreyfus affair, 293; French Communist Party, 324; French Revolution, 114, 283; labor exploitation during Marx's time, 111; nation-state consolidation in, 282–83

FREDEMO (Frente Democrático) (center-right party, Peru), 428, 440

French Encyclopedists, 36

French structuralism, 109, 129n15

Fujimori, Alberto, 186–87n40, 190–91, 377n14

Fujimorism (Peru), 88, 165, 169, 186n37, 190–91, 195, 373, 377n14

Fukuyama, Francis, 68, 72n3, 143n2, 352–53

functionalism, 98, 103

fundamentalisms, 180, 384, 420, 441; ahistoricizing of ideas, 429–30; capitalist modernization seen as only alternative to, 418; "communalist," 233, 252n6; and control of sexuality, 358; culturalist, 26, 51–52, 68, 428–29; and reconcentration of world power, 174, 201. *See also* instrumental reason

Furtado, Celso, 184n19

gamonalismo, 48, 63n4, 371, 377–78n15

gangs, 356

García Márquez, Gabriel, 43, 439, 441–42

Garcilaso de la Vega, Inca, 222, 228n23

gender: and coloniality of power, 5, 30n34, 124–25, 182n2, 213; European male experience, 12; as focal issue for capitalism, 118–20; and "inferiority," 92, 213, 279, 307, 339, 412; and Inquisition, 339; limits on secularization of subjectivity, 170–71; as mental construct, 6, 88, 353, 355, 405, 412; mercantilization of women's subjectivity and life experiences, 384; naturalization of, 126; patriarchal relations of domination, 88, 90, 213, 306–7, 339; and race, 17, 87–90, 93n6, 307, 339, 355–56; sex/"gender" and "color"/"race," 87–90, 126, 213; as sphere of contestation, 98, 102, 116. *See also* sex

genocide/extermination, 3, 123, 162, 238, 421; as attempt at homogenization, 292; elimination of intellectual producers, 211; and nation-state, 162; through expendable labor, 75, 261; in United States, 283. *See also* crises

"gentility" (*delicadeza*), 377–78n15

geocultural identities: diversity of destroyed, 212–14; "Europe" as, 79, 91; heterogeneity of Indigenous and "Black," 212, 249, 274–75, 364; and intersubjective relations, 263–65; produced by "race," 76–77, 83, 91, 95–96, 121, 214, 259–61, 393, 403

geography of power, 334–35

Germany, 405; National Socialist (Nazi) project, 86, 382, 415

Ghana, 434

Gilly, Adolfo, 406

Ginés de Sepúlveda, Juan, 90

Global Commons Foundation, 334

globalization: alternatives, 177–82; and America, 256–72; capitalism, and modern nation-state, relation with, 156–58; and capitalism, 151–55; and center/periphery compound, 162–63, 166–67, 173, 179–80, 193–94, 263, 321–22; central questions of, 149–50; changed perception of, 394; coloniality as cornerstone of, 74, 76, 85; and coloniality of power, 256–72; coloniality of power and nation-state, 161–63; as "common sense," 108, 175, 205, 268, 310, 323; and communications media, 46, 67–68, 84, 149–50, 244, 384, 394; counterrevolution, 163–65, 363, 369–74; de-democratization, 157–59, 163, 166, 177, 189, 191, 207, 243, 321; and democracy, 172–75; and denationalization, 157–59, 163, 166, 189; discord and violence, 175–77; of Eurocentrism, 149; "globality" and subjectivity, 149; heterogeneity of, 175–76, 363, 393–94; heterogeneity of workers, 401–2; and Indigenous movements, 243–49; "integration" of world, 175, 177–78, 191–92; intergovernmental and private agencies, 158, 160, 166, 196; and Latin America, 256–72; limits on expansion of capital, 53, 144n5, 404; main ideas of, 392–96; mystification of, 150, 166, 175, 177, 394; naturalization of,

322, 394–95; necessary propositions, 165–67; and networks, 49–50, 150, 158–60, 163, 166; "new economy," 150; as outcome of globalism, 15; and plurinationalism, 250; political character of, 176; and "race," 15–16, 199–200; as reconcentration of world public authority, 160, 165, 174, 194, 321, 349, 361; reoriginalization of experience and subjectivity, 362–63; of resistance, 192–93; resistance to, 142–43; "scientific-technological revolution," 149, 183n8, 192; shift from national to global perspective, 167–68; start of at beginning of European colonialism, 393–94; and state, 148, 156–59; technocratization, 141, 172–73, 198, 202; "transgovernance," 173, 175, 185n24; and utopia, 68–69; and wealth inequality, 151–54, 168, 183n11, 189–90; worldwide imperial bloc, 157, 158–59, 166, 174, 251; young people as product of, 199, 201. *See also* coloniality of power; world matrix of power

Global South and North, myth of, 334–35

"global village" image, 149

Gobineau, Arthur de, 90, 278

Gramsci, Antonio, 8, 224n4, 342

Granada, conquest of, 22

Greco-Roman culture, appropriation of, 267

gross domestic product (GDP), 151–53, 190, 314–15, 350–51

Group of Prague, 344

Group of Seven (G7) (G8), 151, 158, 363

Guamán Poma de Ayala, Felipe, 222–23, 228n23, 389n1

Guha, Ranajit, 342

guilt, 336

Habermas, Jürgen, 201–2

Haitian Revolution, 221, 226–27n20, 234, 253nn11–12, 287, 288

Hamlet (Shakespeare), 209

Hardt, Michael, 185n27, 355

Haya de la Torre, Víctor Raúl, 294

Hegel, G. W. F., 226n19

Hegelianism, 317, 352–53

Helvetic Republic, 355

heritage, cultural, 50–54, 59, 267, 286, 389, 428

heterogeneity: of African civilizations, 212, 275, 364; of capitalism, 87–88, 276–77; of change, 4–5, 276–77; of globalization, 175–76, 363, 393–94; of horizon of meaning, 341–42; of Indigenous identities, 212, 249, 274–75, 370–71; of industrial proletariat, 401–2; of labor, 397, 407; of Latin America, 23, 53–54, 112, 231, 274–75, 432; as primary mode of existence, 208–9; of reality, 83; of social classification, 117–20; of social movements, 196–97; and totality, 106–7. *See also* structural-historical heterogeneity

historical identities, 2–3, 216, 249, 259; of African origin population, 364; America and Europe as two original, 231, 333; "racialized," 231, 339, 365, 412; reclaiming of, 239; redefinition of by "Western Europeans," 87, 222, 231, 339, 412. *See also* subjectivity

historical materialism, 102, 119, 129n17, 130n22; class as static, 108, 112; Eurocentrism of, 97–99, 141, 142, 317–18, 324–25; and Latin American nationalism, 168–69; of Mariátegui, 62n1, 320, 324–25; "Marxism-Leninism," 109, 110–11, 137, 139, 317–18; and question of social classification, 107–15; "Reencuentro y debate," 317, 319–20; relations of production, 98–99, 112, 115; versions of, 108–9, 243, 317–18

historical meaning, 32, 34, 41, 43, 59, 107; alternative, 45, 52, 59, 65–66, 68; defense of conditions of life on Earth, 386; and facets of power, 357–60; major historical change, 351–54; and new social movements, 362, 374; radical critique of Eurocentrism, 354–57; utopia as project of reestablishing, 65. *See also* horizon

historical rationality, 33, 52, 54, 59, 82, 424

historical reason, 33, 38–41, 47, 51, 56

historical-structural dependence, 204, 208–9, 289–93; and coloniality of power, 364–68

"historical subject," 25, 82, 83, 118, 130n22, 195

history: end of, 67–68, 134, 183n7, 188, 312, 323, 353, 354, 395; evolutionist, 82, 265, 274–76, 401; imaginary and dimensions of, 135–41; as macrosubject, 395; reordering of, 22–23; seen from perspective of coloniality of power, 1, 19; specters produced by, 209–10, 219–20; unidirectional perception of, European, 43, 53, 96, 99, 102–3, 106–7, 110, 128n6, 206, 265–66, 274, 320, 400–401, 406

Hobbes, Thomas, 98, 99

Hollinger, David A., 29n33

homogeneity: alternatives to, 325, 359, 388; attempted through genocide, 292; attributed to capitalism, 435–36; attributed to society, 82, 99; as continuity, 276–77; in Eurocentric perspective, 69, 82, 99, 102, 105–7, 148, 214, 276–77, 285, 367–68, 397, 400, 403, 406–7, 435–36; fantasy of in globalization, 69; genocide as attempt at, 292; impossibility of, 4, 82, 102, 208–9, 276–77, 281; and nationalization, 291–92, 296, 301n40; racial, 287, 291–92; and totality, 105–7, 432. *See also* heterogeneity; structural-historical heterogeneity

Homo sapiens, 304–5, 332, 385

hope, 5–6, 410; in 1960s revolutionary wave, 70; in Aeschylus's Prometheus, 143–44n3; horizon for, 332; and nostalgia, 178–79, 199; pragmatism in opposition to, 67–68; and work for future, 359 horizon: and defeat, 25, 132–34; for hope, 332; Mariátegui's contributions to, 324–27; and modernity, 271; "open horizon as destiny," 21, 24–26. *See also* historical meaning; horizon of meaning; return of the future

horizon of meaning, 203, 303–4, 308–11, 315; and belief, 345–46; colonial/modern/Eurocentered, 343; in crises, 343; in education system, 333–34; as epistemic/theoretical/historical/ethical/aesthetic/political combination, 343; as heterogenous, 341–42; produced by colonial matrix of power, 308–9; and work for future, 359–60

Horkheimer, Max, 38

Hueso Húmero, 426

"humanization," 196–97, 199, 201

Hungary, 138

Hurtado de Mendoza, William, 31n53

Iberian Peninsula: Arab hegemony in, 206; Castile, Crown/Kingdom of, 24, 214, 259; Counter-Reformation, 206, 214, 307; Dalits (Untouchables), 233, 252n6, 354; de-democratization, 207; Muslim-Jewish society, defeat and expulsion of, 206, 214, 227n21, 267, 281–82; as origin of capitalism, 273–74, 307, 340; unification of, 22, 24. *See also* "Spain"

identities, 6, 64; "cultures," 249; de-Indianization, 238–39, 243; delinked from power in discussions, 229; eradication of Indigenous, 125, 264, 275, 364–66; "ethnicities," 16, 130–31n23, 239, 412–16, 426, 427; and Euro–North American rationalism, 43; and globalization, 394; *id*-entity, 257, 261, 266; liberation linked with, 427–28; and memory matrix, 118; nation as, 292; and nation-state, 280–81; "nonwhite," 115, 239, 352n11; search for, 41, 220–24, 239, 244, 250, 279–80, 427–28, 439; in United States, 284. *See also* subjectivity

imaginary: and concrete experience, 135–37, 141; and "critical thought"/"critical theory of society," 134–35; defeat of, 134–37, 140–41, 144n7; European, unidirectional, 265–66; hegemony and the crisis of Eurocentrism, 141–42; historical-critical, 132, 135–37, 393, 414; and history dimensions, 135–41; and Indigenous movements, 374; and knowledge dimensions, 134–35; perception of historical change, 270, 276–77; societal, 65–66. *See also* anticapitalist imaginary

imagination, colonization of, 74–76, 88

imitation, 368–69, 371–72

imperial bloc, worldwide, 157–59, 166, 251, 355; after September 11, 2001, 189; crisis of, 323; formation of, 321–23, 362–63

imperialism, Western: 1960s movements against, 318, 351; continuance of colonialism under, 74–76, 291, 367–68

Incas, 239, 309; resistance by, 367; Tawantisuyan society, 223, 228n23, 335

India, 233, 252n6, 342, 398

"Indians": as first racial category, 89, 213, 298n5, 364, 387–88, 412, 414; imposed on heterogenous identities, 212, 231, 370–71; nobility, 259; not associated with skin color, 89; as serfs, 63n4, 207, 216, 217, 234–36, 240–41, 246, 259, –261–262. *See also* Indigenous movement; Indigenous peoples

Indigenous movement, 162, 211, 229–55, 253–54n14; Amazonian basin organizations, 245–49; Chiapas uprising, 195, 229, 248–50; and crises, 240–43; heterogeneity of, 359; "Indigenista" intellectual movement, 237–38, 249; meaning and perspectives of, 249–51; and nation-state, 230; and neoliberalization-globalization, 243–49; trajectory of, 239–40; university student movement, 242; worker-peasant militias, 247–48. See also *lo cholo* movement; Indigenous peoples

Indigenous peoples, 3–4, 251–52n1; in Anglo-American territories, 283; and bien vivir, 387–89; and citizenship, 235; in contexts outside of direct colonialism, 232–33; cultural and political assimilationism of, 238–39, 249–50; Dalits (Untouchables), 233, 252n6, 354; de-Indianization of, 238–39, 243; gamonalismo in Andes, 377–378n15, 48, 63n4, 317; genocide/extermination of, 3, 75, 123, 162, 211, 238, 261, 283, 292; geocultural identities of destroyed, 212–13; heterogeneity of geocultural identities, 212, 249, 274–75, 370–71; "indigenization" of, 387–89; "Indigenous community" as colonial creation, 246; "Indigenous problem," 235–36, 239, 301n40; land, expropriation of, 3, 240–41; and national question, 233–34; as not quite human, 337–38; physical survival of in question, 315–16, 359; as "primitive," 13–14, 82, 90, 221–22, 238, 265, 275–76, 413–14; Pueblos Originarios/First Nations, 17, 30n36; Quechua thought and language, 25, 31n53, 389–90n1; racialization of, 3, 21, 89, 213, 230–31, 298n5, 364, 387–88, 412, 414; Valladolid debate, 90, 337, 414. See also "Indians"; Indigenous movement

individualism: aggravation of, 384; dualism, association with, 79; in European order, 78–79; myth of, 181, 269; of subject, 78, 269–71

individuation, 4, 271, 432

Indonesia, 323, 353

industrial proletariat, as heterogeneous, 401–2

Industrial Revolution, 217, 310, 312, 321, 339–41, 385

"inferiority," 12–14; attributed to "objects" of knowledge, 80; and Eurocentrism, 96–97, 121–22, 278–79; and extermination through expendable labor, 75, 261; and gender, 92, 213, 279, 307, 339, 412;

implanted in subjectivity of dominated population, 14, 212, 220–21, 279–80, 310, 335–36, 364–66; naturalization of, 14, 80, 90, 92, 212, 257, 264–65, 345–46; phenotype used to attribute, 121–22; racialized, 2–4, 12, 121–22, 336–38. See also dominated, the; "race"

"informal economy," 60–61, 180, 182, 183–84n15, 244, 314, 398–99, 434

Inquisition, 36, 206, 278, 307, 339, 374n, 374n1

Institute of Indigenous Research (Instituto de Investigaciones Indígenas), 247

instrumental reason, 5, 28n15, 430; crisis of, 45, 47, 51; and globalization, 175; hegemony of, 33, 40–45, 48, 50–54, 68; and modernization, 418–19, 423–24, 433; rationality linked to in northern countries, 38–39; resistance to, 53–54, 56, 71; technocratic reductionism of, 66, 176, 382. See also fundamentalism

"integration" of world, 175, 177–78, 191–92

intellectual producers, Latin American: elimination of, 211; "Indigenista" movement, 237–38, 249; "Indigenous" intellectuals, 246–47; "intelligentsia," heterogenous, 372; strains of thought, 222–23

Intercultural Indigenous University (Universidad Indígena Intercultural Amawtay Wasi), 246–47

intergovernmental and private agencies, 158, 160, 166, 196; Latin American alternatives to, 169

International Labor Organization, 398

intersubjective relations/universe: chivalry and technology, 205–6; continued effect of coloniality on, 14, 21–22; control of, 10; Eurocentrism of, 66, 77, 96, 266, 325, 368, 393; and historical imaginary, 134–36, 368; knowledge as, 78–79; Latin American, 41–51, 71, 221, 438–42; and marginality, 438; and modernity,

265–72; New World and new model of world power, 263–65; power, 66; tension between intersubjectivity and subjectivity, 439–42. *See also* subjectivity

invisible world government, 158–59, 163, 166

Italian peninsula, and origin of capitalism, 274, 340

Japan, 16, 73, 205, 382

Jaruzelski, Wojciech Witold, 139

Kagarlitsky, Boris, 322

Kant, Immanuel, 15

Katari, Túpac, 248

Khrushchev Report, 138

Kipling, Rudyard, 82

Kirkpatrick, Jeanne, 38–39, 51

knowledge: cognitive needs of capitalism, 96; coloniality of, 21, 30n36; and coloniality of power, 2–3, 21, 270–71; colonization of, 74–76, 88, 264; epistemic shift, 6–7, 10, 18, 22, 24, 420; Eurocentric imposed throughout world, 96, 148; Eurocentric mystification of, 75, 91, 125–26, 199; Eurocentric perspective, 96–97, 141, 272–76, 279; expropriation of Indigenous, 74, 239, 264; externalization of, 78–80, 83, 86, 96, 101; gnoseological reconstitution of, 11, 18; imaginary, relationship with, 132, 134–35; as intersubjective relationship, 78–79; *logos* and *mythos*, relationship between, 420–21, 440–41; regulation of, 9, 10–11, 13; repression of Indigenous, 74–75, 238–39, 264; shift from national to global perspective, 167–68; and "subject-object" relations, 68, 78–80, 82, 148; totality in, 10, 17, 80–83, 104–5; tree of life and tree of knowledge, 17, 44, 53, 68, 440–41. *See also* rationality

Kojève, Alexandre, 352–53

Korea, South, 353

Kristol, Irving, 38

labor: accumulated and socially accumulated, 348; commercialization of, 69, 307, 351, 435; commodification of, 2, 87, 141, 179–80, 184n20, 198, 267, 271, 273–74, 340, 398–400, 404; crisis of relations in capitalism, 396–99; as element in power, 102–3, 120, 136, 200, 268–69, 281; end of, 397, 409; extermination through, 75, 261; heterogeneity of, 397, 407; historical model for control of, 2, 9, 263; overexploitation of, 122, 154, 198; as primary sphere of contestation, 97–98, 102, 116, 119; redistribution of, 164; shift to wage labor, 241–42; and utopia, 69–70. *See also* labor, distribution of; labor, forms of; labor control; reciprocity; serfdom; slavery

labor, distribution of, 85, 164, 340, 403, 410n6; "race" linked with, 2, 77, 91, 109–10, 215–16, 259–60, 410n6; social classification and coloniality of power, 123–24; "whites" as only paid labor, 262. *See also* labor

labor, forms of: configured into single structure, 100, 102, 130n20, 147, 231, 259, 268, 308, 333, 366, 393, 400, 426–27, 436; deliberate establishment of, 258–59, 273, 339–41, 399–400; in Europe, 111, 123; nonwage, 87, 115, 123–24, 154, 172, 258, 262; racial categories, 109–10, 123, 217; totality of, 258–59, 262, 400. *See also* labor

labor control, 393; and Americas, 398–401; capital as specific form of, 147; capitalism as new structure for, 258–59; and democracy, 170–71; "job flexibilization" and "job insecurity," 314, 321; as prime factor for power, 102–3; reconcentration of, 154–55, 321, 349, 361. *See also* capital-wage relationship; domination; labor

"Lament of a Soul" (Egyptian papyrus), 310

land, question of, 3, 9–10

La nueva corónica y buen gobierno (Guamán Poma), 222, 228n23

Las Casas, Bartolomé de, 414

La somme et le reste (Lefevre), 138

Latin America: acceptance of Eurocentrism in, 220–21, 226n18; "Accidental Indies"/"West Indies," 387; another private and another public active in, 47–48; Bolivarian ideal, resurgence of, 219–20; at center of worldwide resistance, 353; civil wars and wars of rebellion, 162, 190, 213, 243, 249, 364, 367, 406; coloniality, modernity, and identity in, 220–24; coloniality and globality in world matrix of power, 216; countries as junior partners of imperial interests, 169, 367; "criollo-oligarchic" culture, 44–45, 53, 71, 371, 376n10, 377n15, 423–26, 438; decolonization limited in, 291–93, 380, 405–6; democratization limited in, 291–93, 355, 406, 423; dependent industrialization, 291; dependent societies, 41; destruction and re-creation of the past, 210–11; Eurocentering new matrix of power in, 217–19; Eurocentrism and historical experience in, 279–89; Eurocentrism and revolution in, 293–97; feudalism in, 12, 205, 294–95, 299n8, 324; headquarters of Spanish colonial empire, 238; heterogeneity of, 23, 53–54, 112, 231, 274–75, 432; high cultures destroyed by colonizers, 75–76, 125, 211, 306, 364, 366, 421–22; historical invention of, 204, 210–11, 433–34; historical-structural dependence of, 204, 208–9, 289–93, 364–68; identities, 219, 220–24; incorporation of into Europe, 34; "Indigenous problem" in, 235–36, 239, 301n40; intellectual producers, elimination of, 211; intersubjective relations/universe, 41–51, 71, 221, 438–42; as "Latin" America, 3, 212; making of race and global social domination in, 211–15, 414–15; marginalization debate, 312–13, 344, 348, 409; market "integration," 169; mis/matches, 205–10,

219, 370, 378n16, 424; modernity and "modernization" in, 33–36; modernity without de/coloniality, 379–80; modernity without revolution, 37–38, 39, 168, 236–39; "modernization" imposed on, 33–36, 39, 44; nation-state in, 161–62, 168–69; as opportunity for alternative rationality, 51–54, 431–32; as origin of utopia, 70–72, 218; paradoxes of modernity in, 37–38; as passive recipient of modernity, 33–34; private and public, relationship between, 32–33; as product of capitalist history, 210–11, 433–34; relationship between history and time in, 42–44; revolutions, 162, 190, 221, 225n9, 226–27n20, 241; Southern Cone and white majority, 285–87; specters of, 209–10, 219–20; stages of capital as layers, 42–43; tension of subjectivity in, 41–51; theories originating in, 7, 19; as victim of world crisis of capital, 32, 40; Wars of Independence, 162; wealth inequality, 151–52, 183n11, 189–90. *See also* America; "Indians"; Indigenous movement; Indigenous peoples; modernization; reoriginalization

Latin America: The Far West (Rouquié), 422

Latin American Council of Social Sciences (Consejo Latinoamericano de Ciencias Sociales), 313, 327n2

latinidad cultural kinship, 223

Lefevre, Henri, 138

legitimation, 155, 213, 384, 414; challenges to, 223; of citizenship and race, 310; of diversity of peoples, 140, 143, 173–74; of nation-state, 160; source of moved from past to future, 22, 35, 275

Lenin, Vladimir, 81, 114

Le Nouvel Observateur (Vargas Llosa), 71

liberalism, 36, 98, 300n29; capitalist state, 25; and competitive capital, 272; instrumental reason as central to, 48; loyalty to nation, 292; modernity without revolution, 37–38, 39, 168; and national identity, 69, 71; naturalization of authority, 101; "rule-of-law state," 237; utopia as alternative for, 65

liberation: as historical interest of society, 267–68; identities linked with, 427–28; of identity, and utopia, 69–71; of intercultural relations from coloniality, 84; internalized as rationality, 430; order, relationship with, 55–56; from rigid social hierarchies, 78–79; theology of, 7, 59

limpieza de sangre ("purity of blood"), 206, 214, 282, 301n36, 374n1

Linnaeus, Carl, 15, 113, 130n21

lo cholo movement, 236, 242–43, 254n15, 362, 425, 436–38; counterrevolution against, 370–73; democratization of heterogeneous relations, 371–72

Locke, John, 96

logos and *mythos*, relationship between, 420–21, 440–41

"Los heraldos negros" (Vallejo), 373

loyalties: decline of, 21, 23, 25; malleability of, 59–60; to national identity, 126, 168, 282, 292; racial, of whites, 126

Lula da Silva, 93n9, 314

Luxemburg, Rosa, 137

Macas, Luis, 247

macrosubject, historical, 83, 148, 317, 395

"magical realism," 45, 62–63n2

Magna Carta, 181, 355

Mao Zedong, 294–95, 351

Marcos, Subcomandante, 249, 319

marginalization debate, 312–13, 344, 348, 409, 434, 438

Mariátegui, José Carlos, 8, 42, 62n1, 296; isolation of, 342–43; "Reencuentro y debate," 317, 319–20; subversion in thought of, 324–25, 328n5, 342; on threshold of a new horizon, 324–27; *Works: Seven Interpretive Essays on Peruvian Reality*, 9–10, 11–12, 320

Mariateguí y los orígenes del Marxismo Latinoamericano (Aricó), 29n28

market, 2, 147, 161; as ancient institution, 435; called into question, 345–46; fragmentation implied by, 57; hyperfetishization of, 315, 326, 384; as impersonal, 57; as limit on equality, 170–71, 271; living with and without, 316, 357; reciprocity side by side with, 60–61, 357; as replacement for reciprocity, 57; said to be opposed to state, 407. *See also* capitalism

Marx, Karl, 98, 102, 109–10; limitations in theory of, 114–15; mechanization, view of, 313; theory of turned into doctrine, 317–18; *Works: Capital*, 110–12, 184n20; *The Communist Manifesto*, 129n17, 185n20, 209; *The Eighteenth Brumaire of Louis Bonaparte*, 110–12; *Grundrisse*, 184n20, 313. *See also* historical materialism

Marxism, 8; as debate, 324; "Marxist Vulgate," 318, 319; race and racism outside of orthodox, 9–10; Western, 128–29n10. *See also* historical materialism; Mariátegui, José Carlos

"Marxism-Leninism," 109, 110–11, 137, 139, 201; limitations of, 317–18, 323

Mayas, 309

meaning. *See* horizon of meaning

means of production, 168, 201, 285, 294; nationalization of, 45–47

Méda, Dominique, 397

Mediterranean, 267; Muslim hegemony in, 206, 307; supplanted by Atlantic, 308

Mejía Navarrete, Julio, 331, 332

Melis, Antonio, 324

Menchú, Rigoberta, 249

mercantilism, 35, 37, 47–48, 57, 340

mestizaje, 25, 238, 371

"mestizos," 93n6, 216, 221–23, 261, 364; in administrative hierarchy, 259–60; reappropriation of label, 243

metals, Latin American, 22, 34, 217, 261, 286

Métraux, Alfred, 299n8

Mexican Revolution, 228n24, 239, 241, 372, 376n9, 406

Mexico, 228n24, 287; decolonization, 291–92; nationalization in, 406; social revolution from 1910 to 1930, 162

"middle classes," 110, 111, 115, 124; and anticapitalist resistance, 195, 241; growth of, 110, 115

militarization of state, 60, 242–43

Modernidad, identidad y utopía en América Latina (Quijano), 419

modernity: alternative rationality, options for, 51–62, 267–72; ambiguities of, 271–72, 311; antimodernist movement of North American neoconservatives, 38–39; basis of in precolonial Indigenous societies, 218; and capital, 217–19; coloniality enacted through either/or logic, 13–14; colonial/modernity, 22, 83, 207, 310–11, 340, 342–43; crisis of, 33, 40–41, 51, 68, 96, 148–49; culturalist rejection of, 51; delinking from coloniality, 17; democracy as highest expression of, 135; differentiated from modernization, 34, 424; England as origin of, 419; Eurocentered, 2, 34, 217–19, 265–72, 339–40; Latin America seen as passive recipient of, 33–34; and "modernization" in Latin America, 33–36; mutual creation of in Europe and America, 34–38, 52, 208, 256, 270, 307–9, 352, 365; as neologism, 413; north-central Europe linked with, 270–71, 339–40, 419; oppositions, rhetoric of, 13–14; "original state of nature" as foundational myth of, 90; paradox of in Latin America, 37–38; as phenomenon of all cultures, 266; and power in Europe, 38–41; production of, 34, 42, 44; public and private debate, 45–51; race as mental category of, 12, 16, 211–12, 257–58, 308; as social hierarchy, 413–14; state linked with, 419; technology present in all societies, 266–67, 309–10; and tension of subjectivity in Latin America,

41–51; and totality of global population, 268–70, 300n20; "transmodernity," 269, 329n18; without de/coloniality, 379–80; without revolution, 37–38, 39, 236–39, 433. *See also* alternative rationality; instrumental reason; modernity/rationality; nation-state; world-system, modern/colonial

modernity/rationality, 10, 96, 104, 223, 226n17; constitution of, 77–78; epistemological reconstitution and decolonization, 83–84; Eurocentering of, 2, 34, 217–19, 265–72, 339–40; Eurocentrism and cultural coloniality, 77–78; extrication from as necessary, 17, 83; and progress, 135; "race" and coloniality of power, 76–77. *See also* modernity; rationality

modernization, 241–42, 294, 372, 376–77n12; capital linked with, 18, 33, 39, 42, 44, 168; by capital seen as only alternative, 418, 432–33; deficient processes of, 425–26; and demise of criollo-oligarchic culture, 53, 424; differentiated from modernity, 34, 424; as Europeanization/Westernization, 71, 222, 237, 266–67, 279, 429, 440; impact of in Europe, 271; instrumentalization of, 418–19, 423–24, 433; of landed and commercial bourgeoisie, 287; and modernity in Latin America, 33–36; "modernization theory," 266, 372; and nation-state, 287, 291; right-wing proposals, 428; Southern Cone, 287; of state apparatus, 60; transition from oligarchic state, 39; as "Westernization," 222

Modern World-System, The (Wallerstein), 224n2

"modes of production," 320, 327, 398. *See also* relations of production

money: and financial fraud, 345, 350–51; petrodollars, 351

Morales, Evo, 248

movement of society, 23, 373–74, 389n1

Movement toward Socialism (Movimiento al Socialismo) (Bolivia), 248
Movimento sem Terra, 314
multicommunity project, 251
multiculturalism, 394
multi-inclusion, social, 427
Murena, Héctor, 226n18, 301n39
Murmis, Miguel, 313
music, 424–25, 429
Muslim-Jewish society, 206, 208, 214, 278, 281–82, 374n1
Muslim societies, 206, 214, 227n21, 267, 281–82; technology arising from, 206, 340, 341–42
Myrdall, Gunnar, 284–85

Napoleon III, 223, 228n24
national capitalism, 400–401
National Coordinator of Communities Affected by Mining, 244
national identity, 233–34, 284, 286, 427; loyalties to, 126, 168, 282, 292; and social liberation, 69, 71
nationalization, 406–7; and democratization, 89, 164, 169, 173, 179, 280, 282–83, 291, 301n40; of means of production, 45–47; and nation-state formation, 281; of productive resources, 164; racialized, 77; Spain, failures of, 206–8; transnationalization of capital, 423–25
National Socialist (Nazi) project, 86, 382, 415
National Union of Aymara Communities (Unión Nacional de Comunidades Aymaras, UNCA), 245–46, 251
nations, 280
nation-state, 3–4, 17, 85, 97, 100, 115, 405–6; in America: United States, 283–85; capitalism and globalization, relation with, 157–58; in center/periphery compound, 162–63, 166–67, 179; citizenship, 122, 143, 148, 170–71, 242, 280; in colonial hierarchy, 122; and coloniality of power, 161–63; coloniality of power

and ghost of, 380–82; "country" differentiated from, 160; developed during modernity, 148; as embodiment of the public character of collective authority, 160; and Eurocentrism, 280–83; and identity, 280–81; and Indigenous movement, 230; Indigenous people excluded from, 283–84, 287; in Latin America, 161–62, 168–69; as "national question," 125, 233–34, 251, 280–83, 293, 296, 301n40; in "periphery," 162–63, 166; political representation as sign of, 148, 280, 296; as power structure, 280–81; Southern Cone, 285–87; territories of, 281. See also state
naturalization: of globalization, 322, 394–95; of "Indian," 240; of "inferiority," 14, 80, 90, 92, 212, 257, 264–65, 345–46; of "race," 89–90, 120, 126, 212, 257, 265, 315, 337
"nature": body relegated to, 91–92, 114, 277–79, 338; climate change not natural, 332, 347–48, 385; increased exploitation of, 384–85; inequalities attributed to, 79–80, 278–79; as merchandise, Indigenous critique of, 315–16, 359; as "object," 78–80, 300n29; "original state of," 90; predatory relationship to, 315–16, 3840385; "race" attributed to, 86–87, 120, 315; as sphere of contestation, 97–98; "state of nature," 90, 279; and "virtual" world, 150; Western concept of, 12
Negri, Antonio, 185n27, 355
Negt, Oskar, 405
neocolonialism, 156, 225n15, 289
neoconservatism, 38–40
neocultural articulation, 122–23
neoliberalism, 5, 28n15, 46–47, 98, 129n10, 134, 384; anti-imperialist resistance against, 196; Fujimorism, 88, 165, 169, 186n37, 190–91, 195, 373, 377n14; and Indigenous movements, 243–49; and "informal" economy, 61; opposition to,

neoliberalism (*continued*)
186, 191, 196, 409; ordering of society as
underpinning of, 98; origins of in Chile,
351–52; resistance to, 409–10; worldwide imposition of, 108, 159, 186–87
networks: and globalization, 150, 158–60,
163, 166; of reciprocity, 49–51, 59
"New Economic World Order," 193
"New Structural Heterogeneity of Latin
America" (Quijano), 426
Newton, Isaac, 96
New Zealand, 15
non-Europe, 115, 200, 265, 274–76
nonnational conditions, 4, 122, 172
nonstate populations/public, 22, 50–51,
54–62
"nonwhite" identities, 115, 239, 352n11
North-South geopolitical border, regulation of, 1, 19
nostalgia, 178–79, 199, 410

Obama, Barack, 315, 345
object, 438
"object": body as, 91, 278; "nature" as,
78–80, 300n29; other cultures as, 80;
"properties" of, 78, 116
Olavide, Pablo de, 36
oligarchic state, 240–41, 286, 380
One Hundred Years of Solitude (García
Márquez), 43
oppositions, rhetoric of, 13–14
organicism, 81–82, 99, 107, 148, 435
Organization of American States, 191
Organization of Petroleum Exporting
Countries, 351
"Other," 26; absence of, 79; "Orient" as
other to the "Occident," 263, 265, 267,
300n31, 339; required for social totality, 83

Panama, 334
Paris, May 1968, 70
patriarchal relations of domination, 88,
90, 213, 306–7, 339

Paz Estenssoro government, 247
Paz Zamora, Jaime, 81
peasants, 59, 115; heterogeneity of, 438;
as identity, 244; Indigenous people reduced to, 125, 264, 365; and revolutions,
241. See also *lo cholo* movement
Pease, Franklin, 228n23
pedagogy of the oppressed, 7
"peoplehood," 240
Peru, 36, 186n37; *barriada* slums and
shanty towns, 49, 60, 63n5, 242, 425;
"cholo" population, 242; elections,
186n40, 191, 377n14, 426, 428, 437; feudalism in, 326; Fujimorism, 88, 165,
169, 186n37, 190–91, 195, 373, 377n14;
ideological leadership vacuum, 423;
Ilave (Puno) incident, 227n22; militarization of state, 242–43; multicommunity project, 251; political, economic,
and subjective transformation of, 9;
propagandistic denominations of institutions, 59–60; racial discrimination disguised in, 86; revolutions, 190,
221, 225n9, 226n20; Sendero Luminoso,
190, 203n1, 243; Spanish defeat, 240–41;
Túpac Amaru Revolutionary Movement, 190, 221, 226–27n20, 248, 253n12,
287; Velasquismo, 60, 63n6, 164, 372–73,
376–77n12, 376n11, 377n13; violence of
economic crisis in, 50. See also *lo cholo*
movement
petrodollars, 351
Phaedo (Plato), 338
phenotype, 120–21, 130–31n23, 257
Pinochet, Augusto, 126, 312, 352, 384
Pizarro, Francisco, 334–36
Plato, 338
plurinational state, calls for, 249–50, 374
Poland, 138, 139
Polybius, 353, 355
Popov, Gavril, 145n11
populism, 46, 376n11; Russian Narodniks,
81, 110, 302n45
positivism, 107, 114, 129n15, 317, 432

postmodernism, 40, 83, 299n14, 343, 354; coexistence with empiricism, 98–99, 104–5, 297, 324, 326; as imposition of technocratization/instrumentalization, 383; social-philosophical, 104, 128n8

"posts," 343

poststructuralism, 26, 105, 343

Potosí, as origin of capitalism, 22

Poulantzas, Nicos, 108

poverty, 151–52n4, 190, 194–96, 334, 386, 397

power: authority as element in, 120, 136, 171, 178, 200, 268–69, 281; de-modernization, 174, 177; distribution of, 110, 116, 120, 134, 141, 194, 237, 297, 334–35, 372–73, 377n13, 380; as domination/exploitation/conflict, 120, 136, 144n5, 285, 366–67, 376n10; elements of, 120, 136, 146, 171, 173, 178, 200, 268–69, 280–81, 300n20; elimination of as subject of study, 174, 188; in Eurocentrism, question of, 97–99; geography of, 334–35; and historical meaning, 357–60; and Homo sapiens as species, 305; intersubjective relationships of, 66; labor as element in, 102–3, 120, 136, 200, 268–69, 281; legitimation and naturalization of under globalization, 174–75; matrix of, 95, 146–47; mesh of relations between domination, exploitation, and conflict, 16, 116, 136; and modernity in Europe, 38–41; money as shadow of, 345; mystification of, 395; reciprocity as part of structure of, 58; reconcentration of world control of, 160, 165, 174, 194, 349, 361–63, 383–84; redistribution of, 178, 194, 296–97, 372–73, 377n13; seduction as main instrument of, 75; sex as element in, 120, 136, 146, 171, 173, 178, 200, 268–69, 281; socialization of, 127, 202, 296; as social relationship, 136; spheres of contestation, 97–98, 100, 102–3, 116, 358; structural-historical heterogeneity of, 100–103, 175–76, 268, 300n20;

subjectivity as element in, 120, 136, 200, 214–15, 268–69, 281. *See also* colonial (world) matrix of power; instrumental reason; world matrix of power

"pragmatism," 223, 372–73, 382; commercial, 205–6; in opposition to hope, 67–68

Prebisch, Raúl, 8–9, 18, 97, 263

"precapitalism," 123, 156, 167, 273–74, 398–401, 403; and class, 112–13, 115; evolutionist view of, 82, 112–13, 167, 400–401, 426, 436; modes of production, 398, 399; return of forms of, 358–59. *See also* capitalism

"premodernity," 115, 222

primitive (original) accumulation, 22, 43, 102, 112, 277; Latin American metals at base of, 34, 217. *See also* accumulation

"primitive," African and Indigenous peoples as, 13–14, 82, 90, 221–22, 238, 265, 275–76, 413–14

private: capitalist sphere of, 45–49; civil society as, 55–56; multiple spheres of, 48; and public, relationship between, 32–33, 45–51; "social-private," 48–50, 54–60

production: capitalist mode of, 111, 231, 276; Latin American, 37; means of, 45–46, 168, 201, 285, 294; relations of, 98–99, 112, 115, 274, 276, 438; and social-private, 56–57; zero cost/free/subscription rates charged, 344, 348, 356. *See also* capitalism; relations of production

"progress," 135, 208, 218, 236, 279

"progressive" liberal thought, 317

Prometheus, 143–44n3

"properties," 78, 116

property, 20, 79, 117; private and state, 45–51, 54

protagonists, 23, 52, 242, 266–67, 349

public services, 122, 190, 196, 197, 358, 407

public sphere, 15, 58, 171, 349; of social-private, 49–50; state-public, 45, 48, 54–55

Pueblos Originarios/First Nations, 17, 30n36

Quechua thought and language, 25, 31n53, 389–90n1

Quevedo, Francisco de, 205

Quijano, Aníbal: academic career, 7, 28n21, 29n31; as activist, militant, and scholar, 1, 7, 26–27n1; conceptual framework of, 6–19, 30n34; English translation, need for, 19–26; foreword to 2007 reprint of *7 ensayos*, 9–10, 320; and modernity/(de)coloniality group, 28n16; theoretical universe of, 20–21; three representations of time in work of, 24; vocabulary of separated from original matrix, 19–20; world relevance/key interventions of, 2–6

Quispe, Felipe (El Mallku), 248

Quito uprising, 247

"race": "Africans" not originally associated with, 213, 298n5; attributed to "nature," 86–87, 120, 315; as basis for social classification, 21–22, 76–77, 85–87, 147, 213–16, 256–57, 336, 340–41, 356, 364–65, 375n2, 410n6, 414; and brain(mind,nonbody)/body dualism, 91–92, 278–79; as classification of domination, 89, 120–21, 364–65; as colonial connector between planetary localities, 11, 13–14; and coloniality of power, 2, 76–77, 121, 147, 171, 412–13; and "color," 87–90, 93n6, 126, 131n24, 213, 215–16, 257; creation of in "America," 2, 12–13, 16, 89, 120–21, 147, 256–57, 403; "criollo-oligarchic" culture, 44–45, 53, 71, 371, 376n10, 377n15, 423–26, 438; as epistemic issue, 7, 15; ethnic relations restructured by, 16; and gender relations, 17, 87–90, 93n6, 307, 339, 355–56; geocultural identities produced by, 76–77, 83, 85, 91, 94–96, 95–96, 121, 214,

259–61, 393, 403; and globalization, 15–16, 199–200; land expropriation justified by, 3, 9–10, 14; legitimation of, 310; linked with division of labor, 2, 77, 91, 109–10, 259–60, 410n6; making of, and global social domination, 211–15; in Mariátegui's writing, 9–10, 11–12; as mental category of modernity, 12, 16, 211–12, 257–58, 308; as mental construct, 3, 88–89, 212–14, 230–31, 256–58, 298–99n6, 306; *mestizaje*, 25, 238, 371; as most efficient instrument of domination, 85–87, 257, 295–96, 364, 402; naturalization of, 89–90, 126, 212, 257, 315, 337; and new system of social exploitation, 215–16; new "Western" dualism and "racism," 90–92; no biological basis for, 2, 13, 76, 87–90, 120, 126, 257, 298–99n6, 375n1, 402; outside Marxist orthodoxy, 9–10; and predatory relationship to "nature," 315, 385; production/fashioning of, 2, 12–13, 305–6; as product of conquest, 2, 12–13, 305–6, 412, 414; and "racism," 86–87, 93n6; sex/"gender" and "color"/"race," 87–90, 126, 213; social hierarchies racialized, 13, 79–80, 87, 222, 227n21, 259, 306–7, 336–39, 365, 393, 402, 413; subversion of, 6, 353–54; as unquestioned, 86–87; "white replacement theory," 14–15; "whites" as constructed identity, 88–89, 122, 213, 216, 231, 257, 364, 414. *See also* "inferiority"

"racial democracy," ideology of, 293

"racial equality," 130–31n23, 311, 313n24, 345

"racism": delegitimation of, 19, 86, 318, 382, 415–17; disguised due to condemnation, 86; and dualism, 90–92; in local histories and historical periods, 10; "purity of blood" (*limpieza de sangre*), 206, 214, 282, 301n36, 374n1; and "race," 86–87; relegitimation attempts, 88, 175, 404; resistance to, 87–88 rationalism: differentiated from rationality, 53; Euro–North American, 42–44, 170, 420–21, 439

rationality: Afro–Latin American, 223; of dominated cultures, rediscovery of, 51, 52; Euro–North American, 43, 51–52, 439; historical, 33, 52, 54, 59, 82, 424; liberation internalized as, 430; liberationist, 5–6, 51–56, 62; loss of faith in, 51–52; of market, 57; multiplicity of, 6, 41; non-Eurocentric, 97, 143, 176; "social-private" as alternative, 48–50, 54–60; utopia, relationship to, 35. *See also* alternative rationality; knowledge; modernity/rationality; reason

Reagan, Ronald, 193, 352, 384

Reaganism, 38, 193

reason: bourgeois, 38–40; historical, 33, 38–41, 47, 51, 56; reason/subject, 278; "subject" as bearer of, 78. *See also* instrumental reason; rationality

reciprocity, 2; in Andean social community, 23, 35, 48–49; and *lo cholo*, 372; community as authority structure, 180–81; and diversity, 57–58; and equality, 57–59, 170, 387; expansion of, 23, 123, 147, 154, 180–82, 321, 349, 357, 435; and labor, 69–70; market as replacement for, 57; *mita* institution, 400; networks of, 49–51, 59; reconfigured by capitalism, 399–400; side by side with capitalist market, 60–61, 357; and social-private, 48–50, 57; solidarity required by, 57–59, 170, 387

reconcentration of world control of power, 160, 165, 174, 194, 349, 361–63, 383–84

reconstitution: epistemological, 11, 17, 83–84, 214–15; of global perspective, 97; of Latin American culture and identity, 32, 41, 48, 70, 324–25; of subjectivity, 214–15, 324–25

redistribution, 178, 194, 296–97, 377n13, 387; and *lo cholo*, 371–73

reductionism, 66, 81, 83, 114, 119, 326; technocratic, 148, 176, 382

"Reencuentro y debate," 317, 319–20

referendum, 181, 355

reformist political regimes, 59–60, 63n6

relations of production, 98–99, 112, 115, 259, 276–77, 411, 438–39; capital as, 217, 294; historically impossible assumptions, 99; labor as primary sphere of, 98, 102. *See also* "modes of production"

reoriginalization, 69, 361–62, 422–23, 431; and cultural subversion, 369–74; of experience and subjectivity, 362–63; and imitation, 371–72; new lexical framework, 22–23, 24–25; and social revolution/counterrevolution, 363, 369–74; of world, 14, 22–25. *See also* alternative rationality; subversion

representation, crisis of, 55, 60, 159, 179, 407

repression, 60, 382; body as object of, 278; systematic, 74, 385

resistance: Andean social organization as, 48; by coca farmers, 248; defense of conditions of life on Earth, 386; to globalization, 142–43; globalization of, 192–93; by Incas, 367; by Mapuches, 248, 415; March for Territory and Dignity (1991), 248; to neoliberalism, 409–10; Quito uprising, 247. *See also* anticapitalist imaginary; revolutions, specific; social movements

return of the future, 23–26, 132; rooted in Aymara thought and language, 25, 31n53; in the time of worldwide resistance, 142–43. *See also* horizon

revolution: "aprista" anti-imperialist movement, 293–94, 320; and "color," 295–96; decolonization as first step in, 169, 407–8; democracy without, 236–39; and Eurocentrism, 293–97; ideas/images of, 137; modernity without, 37–38, 39, 168, 236–39, 433; as redistribution of power, 296–97. *See also* counterrevolution; defeat of political movements

Revolutionary Antiimperialist Popular Alliance, 294

revolutions, specific, 376n9, 415; early rebellions, 253–54n14, 366–67; Haitian Revolution, 221, 226–27n20, 234, 253nn11–12, 287, 288; Latin America, 162, 190, 221, 225n9, 226–27n20, 241, 287; liberal-bourgeois in "central" countries, 237; Túpac Amaru Revolutionary Movement, 190, 221, 226–27n20, 248, 253n12, 287

Ricardo, David, 110

Rifkin, Jeremy, 314, 345

Rodó, José Enrique, 223, 228n24

Romans, 81, 99n8, 213, 267, 298n5, 306; historical legacy of Greece and Rome, 208, 275

Rulfo, Juan, 44, 62–63n2, 439

Russia, so-called socialist revolution in, 137

Russian Populists, 81, 110, 302n45

Saint-Simon, Henri de, 109, 129n17

Saint-Simonian perspective, 80, 109–10, 113, 129n17

saltpeter miners, 286

Sánchez de Losada, Gonzalo, 248

Santa Cruz Pachacuti Salcamayhua, Juan de, 222, 228n23

scientific research: atomistic perspective of, 80; categorization in, 15, 74; natural sciences, 113–14; racialization, 86; "sociology" versus "ethnography," 115; subject-object relation, 78

"scientific-technological revolution," 69, 149, 183n8, 192, 344, 380–81

"Scottish–Anglo–North American" thought, 55

secularization, 91, 99, 338, 354; of European thought, 266, 272, 278; of subjectivity, 170–71, 218

self-government, 182, 251

"self-management" (autogestion) institutions, 59, 60

semiperiphery, 8

Sendero Luminoso, 190, 203n1, 243

Señor de los Temblores (Lord of Earthquakes), 336

sequence versus simultaneity, 42–44

serfdom: in Europe, 262; imposed on "Indians," 63n4, 207, 216, 217, 234–36, 240–41, 246, 259, 261–62. See also feudalism

Seven Interpretive Essays on Peruvian Reality (Mariátegui), 9–10, 11–12, 320

sex: and domination, 357–58, 382; as element in power, 120, 136, 146, 171, 173, 178, 200, 268–69, 281; "race" linked with, 93n7, 124, 213, 215, 279; sex/"gender" and "color"/"race," 87–90, 126. See also gender

sign systems, 16, 30n36

slavery, 14, 262; Brazilian law against, 314, 316n1; "color" first associated with, 89; continuation and expansion of in present, 23, 53, 87, 93n9, 154, 180–81, 184n16, 314, 321, 344, 348, 397–98, 426; current networks of, 314, 398, 435; mothers of mestizos, 259–60; new forms of in Americas, 399–400; para-slave labor, 426–27; United Nations commission to study, 397–98

Sobrevilla, David, 324

social classification: age as, 110, 114, 115, 117, 120, 164; and center/periphery compound, 115, 122–23; and coloniality of power, 120–27, 147, 403; and concrete experience, 104, 107, 111–12, 115, 120, 130n22; crisis in, 87–88, 107–8; diverse civilizations brought together by, 11, 22; domination/exploitation, coloniality, and embeddedness, 125–27; emotional impact of, 14–15; ethnoracial pentagon in United States, 13; Eurocentrism of, 74, 85, 114–15, 117–18; "European," 4, 16–17, 171–72, 252n4, 257, 364; and gender/sex, 98, 102, 116, 124–25; heterogeneity of, 117–20; historical materialism and question of, 107–15; labor, race, and gender as three focal instances in capitalism, 118–20; in Marx's works, 110–11; middle strata between "European" and the "Indian" or "Black," 369, 372; natural sciences as model for, 15, 113–14; neocultural articulation, 122–23; new lexical framework, 22–23, 24–25; nonexistent before 1492, 15; oppositions, Western, 13–14; and permanence of coloniality, 22; and phenotype, 120–21, 130–31n23, 257; as process, 114, 118–20; question of, 107–16; race as basis for, 21–22, 76–77, 85–87, 147, 213–16, 256–57, 336, 340–41, 356, 364–65, 375n2, 410n6, 414; reclassification due to crisis, 404–5; relationships of conflict, 97–98, 116; Saint-Simonian view of, 80, 109–10, 113, 129n17; social-historical debate, 97, 103–7, 114, 128n8, 216, 393, 406; Spanish vocabulary used, 30n36; spheres of contestation, 97–98, 100, 102–3, 116; as structure, 111–12, 117; totality, question of, 82, 97, 103–7; universalism of, 2–3, 121–22, 147, 172, 216; "whites" as constructed identity, 89, 122, 213, 216, 231, 257, 364, 414; and world matrix of power, 95–96, 106–7. *See also* class; "race"; structural-historical heterogeneity; totality

"social democracy," 137, 317

social ethics, creation of, 357, 382, 384

social existence/relations: commodification of every sphere of, 361–62; de/coloniality of power as continuous democratic production of, 386–87; forms of in Americas, 34–35; four basic areas of, 146; historical/structural heterogeneity of in Americas, 23; private and public in, 32–33; and reconfiguring of world matrix of power, 321. *See also* authority; "inferiority"; labor; "race"; sex; subjectivity

socialism: conflicts between regimes, 319–20; defeat of, 66–70, 107–8, 178, 201, 405–6; delegitimization of, 318–19;

demoralization due to defeat of, 178, 323; East Berlin workers' revolt, 138; expansion of, 383; impossibility of revolution in Latin America, 295–96; "Indo-American," 320, 326; left critiques of, 137–38; social democracy, 137, 317; "socialist camp," breakup of, 133, 138–39, 202, 297, 318–19, 322–23, 328n5, 352, 383

social movements, 23, 302n44, 343, 362; 1960s youth movements, 139–40, 164, 318, 382; "Afro–Latin American," 211; "antisystem" movements, 165; arts in, 140; in "Asian tigers" countries, 192, 323; as cause of crisis in coloniality of power, 373–74; defeat of, 25, 67–68, 107–8, 132–37, 165, 166; "demonstration effect," 195; "dirty wars" against, 190; against globalization, 177; "globalization" of resistance, 192–95; heterogeneity of, 196–97; Hot Autumn of 1969 in Italy, 318, 351; of Indigenous peoples, 162, 211; Indonesia, 323, 353; May 1968 in France, 318, 351; and redistribution, 164–65, 178, 296–97, 372–73, 377n13; reduction of opportunity for debate and activity, 137; reemergence of, 194; Seattle, 194, 353; time of defeat coming to an end, 323–24; worker movements, 1970s, 373, 383. *See also* Indigenous movement; resistance; revolution; Velasquismo

social-private, 54–60; *barriada* as, 49; and freedom, 56; nonstate populations/public, 22, 50–51, 54–62; organizations of, 49–50; and production, 56–57; and reciprocity, 48–50, 57

social reality, 41–42, 80, 135, 428; power as most persistent form of structural articulation within, 104–5; whole and parts, relationship between, 103–7

social sciences, 7, 19–20, 97, 113, 115, 128n8, 436–39, 441

Sociedad y política, 26–27n1

Societies of the Friends of the Country (Las Sociedades de Amigos del País), 36 society: in atomistic view, 105; as homogenous, 82, 99; of transition, 438; "virtual," 150, 201. *See also* structural-historical heterogeneity

"society of the right," 237

solidarity, 173–74; in ancient Andean community, 48; networks of, 59; required by reciprocity, 57–59, 170, 387

South Africa, 86

Southern Cone (Argentina, Chile, and Uruguay), 285–87, 292

Soviet Union, 137–39, 144–45n9, 193; breakup of in one week, 352; repressive actions by, 319

"Spain," 282; "America" as prior to, 24; Crown of Castile and Aragon, 214; exploitation of Americas, 208; liberal revolution of 1810–1812, 283; nationalization, failures of, 206–8; ongoing conformation of, 24–25; seigneurial class, 205–7; Spanish Enlightenment, 36. *See also* Castile, Crown/Kingdom of; Iberian Peninsula

Spanish Civil War, 133, 137

speculative accumulation. *See* financial capital: financial/speculative accumulation

Spinoza, Baruch, 91, 96, 338–39

"stagflation," 348

stagnation, 348, 351

Stalin, Iósif, 138

Stalinism, 33, 40, 45, 317; "market," 322; "Marxism-Leninism," 109, 317–18; of Third Communist International, 320

Stalinist International, 246

state: as ancient, 147–48; and capitalism, 156–57; and civil society, 55–56; colonized, in Latin America, 161–62; corporatist reorganization of, 60; denationalization of, 157–59, 163, 166, 189, 321, 363, 407; end of monopoly on violence, 356; formations linked by coloniality of power, 280; forms of, 156; freedom and order, relationship between, 55–56;

and globalization, 148, 156–59; imposed from above, 358; living without or against, 245, 316; local, 158–59; market said to be opposed to, 407; militarization of, 242–43; military and police sectors, 60; modernity linked with, 419; "modernization" of, 39; national-dependent, 156, 157; oligarchic, 240–41, 286, 380; plurinational, calls for, 249–50, 374; reformist political regimes, 59–60, 63n6; representativeness, crisis of, 55, 60, 159, 179; "rule-of-law state," 237; state-public, 45, 48, 54–55; as superstructure, 10, 66, 296; and worldwide imperial bloc, 157, 158–59, 166, 251. *See also* authority; nation-state; violence

"state of nature," 90, 279

"structural adjustment," 194

structural-historical dependency, 123, 208, 219, 367–68, 375–76n7, 375n6; of white colonial society on Europe, 289–93

structural-historical heterogeneity, 326, 382, 389, 404, 408, 426, 428, 436, 441; of capital-wage relationship, 130n20, 401–2; and class interest, 119; determinations not unidirectional, 4–5, 102–3, 106–7, 438–39; and field of relations, 78, 97, 101, 103–7, 326, 375–76n7; lessons from Don Quixote, 208; of power, 100–103, 175–76, 268, 300n20. *See also* heterogeneity; social classification

structuralism, 98, 103, 318; French, 109, 129n15

"structural unemployment," 141, 153, 314, 344, 348, 381, 383, 396, 398

"subalternity," 20, 23, 98, 342. *See also* historical materialism

"subject," 78–80, 91, 438

subjectivity: capitalistic control of, 348, 356; as element in power, 120, 136, 200, 214–15, 268–69, 281; as European, 115; and "globality," 149; "historical subject," 25, 82, 83, 118, 130n22, 195; individuation of, 78, 269–71; intersubjectivity, tension with, 439–42; and knowledge production, 78, 178, 318; mutation of, 24; and perception of historical change, 270; "race" linked with, 93n7, 124, 213, 215, 279; reason/subject, 278; reconstitution of, 214–15, 324–25; secularization of, 170–71; sequence versus simultaneity, 42–44; as sphere of contestation, 98, 102; state as universal form of control over, 147; "subject"/"object" polarity, 78–80, 91, 148, 438–39; tension of in Latin America, 41–51. See also historical identities; identities; intersubjective relations

subversion, 5–7; of aesthetics, 65–66, 387; of authority, 356–57; epistemic, 6–7, 18–19, 326, 416–17; and imitation, 368–69, 371–72; in Mariátegui's thought, 324–25, 328n5; of race, 6, 353–54; and reoriginalization, 369–74. See also alternative rationality; reoriginalization

surplus value, 102, 277, 321

survival: physical survival of Indigenous peoples in question, 315–16, 359; of the planet, and anticapitalist imaginary, 343; reciprocity and solidarity as condition of, 57–59, 170, 387; and resistance, 386

Switzerland, 181, 355

Tanizaki, Jun'ichirō, 204, 224n3

Tawantisuyan society (Inca), 223, 228n23, 335, 421

taxation, 122, 190–91, 350, 358

technocratic reductionism, 66, 176, 382

technocratization, 141, 172–73, 198, 202, 323, 381; "historical materialism" linked with, 318

technology: appropriation of "Black" innovations, 217; present in all societies, 266–67, 309–10; production costs, 344–45; "scientific-technological revolution," 69, 149, 344, 380–81; used for global recolonization, 386; workforce reduced by, 313, 321, 344, 348, 356, 380–81, 396

teleology, historical, 83, 130n22, 317

temporality, 265, 270–71, 276, 419; mythical-aesthetic, 43–44; sequence versus simultaneity, 42–44; space/time, 2, 22–23, 117, 136, 155, 256–58, 270, 296; specificity to in Latin America, 441–42. See also return of the future

territorial autonomy, 250

Thatcher, Margaret, 193, 352, 384

Thompson, E. P., 108, 112

Tito, Josip Broz, 138

Tocqueville, Alexis de, 284

Todas las sangres (All the Bloodlines) (Arguedas), 23

Toledo, Alejandro, 191

Torres Caicedo, José María, 228n24

totality, 34, 44–45; coloniality as open, 4; and decolonization, 83–84; denial of, 79, 104–5, 297; of global population, and modernity, 268–70, 300n20; heterogeneity of, 106–7; and homogeneity, 105–7, 432; and knowledge production, 10, 17, 78–83, 104–5; of labor forms, 258–59, 262, 400; organicist, 81–82, 99, 107, 148, 435; question of, 103–7; reality as, 44; social, 78–83; social-historical, 97, 103–7, 216, 432; and social-private, 49; in structural-functionalism, 81, 325

"transgovernance," 173, 175, 185n24

transition, society of, 438

"transmodernity," 269, 329n18

tree of life and tree of knowledge, split between, 17, 44, 53, 68, 420, 440–41

Trotsky, Leon, 137–38, 144–45n9

Trotskyites, 144n9, 319

Truman, Harry, 18, 30–31n45

Túpac Amaru Revolutionary Movement, 190, 221, 226–27n20, 248, 253n12, 287

unemployment, "structural," 141, 153, 314, 344, 348, 381, 383, 396, 398

Unified Syndical Confederation of Rural Workers of Bolivia (Confederación Sindical Única de Trabajadores Campesinos de Bolivia), 248 unions, 49, 81, 247, 383, 402; and "cholos," 242; defeat of, 194, 405

United Nations, 313; commission to study slavery, 397–98; Economic Commission for Latin America and the Caribbean, 8

United States: "America" appropriated by, 128n2, 297–98n2; American Revolution, 283, 285, 295; "Blacks" in, 69, 123, 131n26, 283–84; "colonial center" and "colonial periphery" in, 124; ethnoracial pentagon, 13; and fraudulent money, 351; immigrants to, 284–85; imperialist expansionism, 220, 223, 225n15, 289–90, 321; "Indians" exterminated, 213; Indigenous people as foreign to, 283, 288; military expansion, 321; as nation-state, 283–85; racial conflict, increase in, 284–85; racialization in union movement, 402; September 11, 2001, 189; social whiteness of, 284; US-British alliance, 193, 223; wealth inequality within, 151; and worldwide imperial bloc, 166, 189, 251

universalism: of colonial social classification system, 2–3, 121–22, 147, 172, 216; provincialism imposed as, 84

urban cultures, pre-colonial, 365–66

urbanization, 77, 79, 241, 260–61; Andean social organization, 49; lo cholo movement, 236, 242–43, 254n15, 362, 370–73, 436–38; impoverished populations, 59; as site of reciprocity, 181

Uruguay, 162, 285–87

utopia, 21, 25, 203; aesthetics, relationship with, 64–66, 70–71; Andean, question of, 430–31; debased meaning of, 220; dominated cultures as inspiration for, 34–35, 51; emergence of, 67–70; and global world, 68; Latin America as origin of, 70–72, 218; liberation of identity interwoven with, 69–71; past replaced with future, 22, 35; of time to come, 70. See also alternative rationality

Valcárcel, Luis Eduardo, 228n23

Valera, Blas, 222

Valladolid debate, 90, 337, 414

Vallejo, César, 133, 373

vals criollo (criollo waltz), 424

Vargas, Antonio, 247

Vargas Llosa, Mario, 71, 186n40, 377n14, 428, 429, 440

Velasco Alvarado, Juan, 63n6

Velasquismo, 60, 63n6, 164, 372–73, 376–77n12, 376n11, 377n13

verticalism, 46, 61–62

violence: coercion, 98, 101; colonial, 216, 217; end of state monopoly on, 356; and globalization, 175–77; of Homo sapiens, 305; as requisite for domination, 155; responses to resistance, 385–86; and specters of history, 209–10, 219–20. See also authority; conquest; state

"virtual" technologies, 149–50, 201, 244–45

visual and artistic expression, 439; imitation and subversion, 368–69, 371–72; stripped from autonomous cultures, 74–75, 74–76, 125, 211, 366, 368. See also aesthetics

Wallerstein, Immanuel, 7, 22, 97, 224n2, 263

wealth inequality, 151–54, 168, 183n11, 189–90, 358–59, 409

"welfare state," 47, 122, 164–65, 198, 405

whales, collective suicide committed by, 314

"whites," 221; as constructed identity, 88–89, 122, 213, 216, 231, 257, 364, 414; lack of common interests with non-white population, 289–90, 367; and latinidad, 223; loyalty of, 126; as only paid labor, 262; "white replacement theory," 14–15; "white superiority," 15

"Who are the Friends of the People" (Lenin), 81

whole and parts, relationship between, 103–7, 324–26

windmill technology, 206

worker-peasant militias, 247–48

World Economic Forum, New York, 195

world matrix of power. *See* colonial (world) matrix of power; globalization

World Social Forum (WSF), 7, 323–24, 346, 389; Mumbai, 252n6, 353–54; Nairobi, 334; Porto Alegre, 193–97

world-system, modern/colonial, 1, 91, 97, 204, 207, 215, 263–70, 322, 329n18; and intersubjectivity, 263–65; Quijano's view, 7–8, 13; Wallerstein's view, 7–8, 13, 97, 224n2, 263–64; white exploitation of, 22. *See also* coloniality of power; colonial (world) matrix of power; modernity

World War I, 40

World War II, 33, 39, 86; delegitimation of racism after, 19, 86, 382, 415–17

Wright, Erik Olin, 108

writing, stripped from autonomous cultures, 365–66, 368

Yugoslavia, 138